Understanding Child Behavior Disorders

DONNA M. GELFAND

University of Utah

WILLIAM R. JENSON

University of Utah

CLIFFORD J. DREW

University of Utah

Second Edition

Understanding Child Behavior Disorders

An Introduction to Child Psychopathology

HOLT, RINEHART AND WINSTON, INC.

FORT WORTH   CHICAGO   SAN FRANCISCO   PHILADELPHIA

MONTREAL   TORONTO   LONDON   SYDNEY   TOKYO

Library of Congress Cataloging-in-Publication Data

Gelfand, Donna M., 1937-
  Understanding child behavior disorders.

  Includes bibliographies and index.
  1. Behavior disorders in children.   I. Jenson, William R.
II. Drew, Clifford J., 1943-

III. Title.   [DNLM: 1. Child Behavior Disorders.
2. Child Psychology.   WS 350.6 G316u]
RJ506.B44G45   1988   618.92'89   87-19753

ISBN 0-03-016618-7

Printed in the United States of America
8 9 0 1   039   9 8 7 6 5 4 3 2

Holt, Rinehart and Winston, Inc.
The Dryden Press
Saunders College Publishing

PREFACE

It is gratifying that classroom use of the first edition of this textbook was sufficient to justify the preparation of a revised version. The second edition offers updated and expanded coverage in a number of areas and presents the most recent theories and research developments. As before, the book is a text for courses on child psychopathology, abnormal child psychology, exceptional and maladjusted children, child adjustment and behavior problems, and educational psychology. Some familiarity with introductory psychology or child psychology provides a helpful background for the use of this text, but is not absolutely essential. Throughout the book, we have attempted to avoid unnecessary technical terms when possible and to concentrate on clear and straightforward explanations. As a further aid to students, unfamiliar key terms are defined at the beginning of each chapter. Students should read these brief definitions before beginning a chapter, and should review them afterward to ensure that they understand the material.

This book's coverage and orientation reflects the varied professional backgrounds of the authors. Donna Gelfand was trained as a clinical psychologist and later specialized in developmental psychology. She first taught psychology at San Jose State University, and for many years has taught at the University of Utah. William (Bill) Jenson earned a master's degree in experimental psychology and a Ph.D. in child psychology. Following postdoctoral training in clinical psychology, he directed a child and family treatment unit of a community mental health program. He is now a faculty member in educational psychology at the University of Utah. Clifford Drew teaches in the special education and the educational psychology departments at the University of Utah, where he

has published 13 textbooks and specializes in research design, mental retardation, and public policy issues. Thus we each contribute somewhat different perspectives on childhood psychological problems. Together, we represent the views of researchers, teachers, and practitioners in diverse fields.

Our shared commitment is to a level-headed, rational approach to the study and treatment of children's problems, based on the best, most definitive research available. This means that we give greater weight to replicated findings from well-controlled research studies of the origin, nature, prognosis, and treatment of behavior disorders than to more subjective clinical case studies, while recognizing that the latter also prove informative. This book reflects our belief that in addition to sensitive clinical observations, probing and objective research is the best means for understanding children's disturbances and ultimately for treating and preventing them. Inevitably, a research orientation favors some theories and treatments over others that are less empirically based. For example, social learning theory and behavior therapy have particularly lent themselves to rigorous research scrutiny. However, no contemporary theory or type of treatment is completely successful or free from flaws, and even the most seemingly misguided have some strengths. We aim for good, impartial scholarship rather than favoritism to any particular orientation. We have tried conscientiously to present all schools of thought accurately and fairly, and to criticize each according to objective criteria.

Users of the first edition will note that this revision covers most of the original topics, but in a modified order. Instructors can assign chapters in any order they prefer, but will find that for users' convenience we now introduce the history and explanations of child psychopathology first and then review the various disorders before presenting material on research methods, classification, assessment, and treatment. Each chapter stands alone, because the book is designed for use by teachers like ourselves who prefer to vary the order of class presentation from time to time. New material in this edition is noted in the following summary:

Chapter 1, the introduction to the book, features new historical material, a further explanation of criteria used to judge deviance, and a new section on comparisons between adult and child psychopathology.

Chapter 2, on theories of psychopathology, reviews the major explanations and presents recent critiques.

Chapter 3, on sociocultural factors in child disturbances, presents new data on the effects of early malnutrition, lead poisoning, poverty, discrimination, parental conflict and divorce, and child physical and sexual abuse and neglect.

Chapter 4 reviews the effects of stress on children's functioning and presents new research on disorders such as school refusal, childhood depression, suicide, and physical illnesses with psychological components.

Chapter 5 describes attention deficit disorder with hyperactivity, conduct disorder, and delinquency, presenting the results of many new studies.

Chapter 6 is a notable feature of our book because it deals exclusively with smoking, drinking, and other illicit drug use—their prevalence according to the latest statistics, their prevention, and their treatment.

Chapter 7 also covers material not typically found in such texts, including sleep, speech, and toileting problems, as well as eating disorders such as anorexia nervosa and bulimia that have gained recent prominence.

Chapter 8 will be of special interest to educational psychologists, for it deals with recent advances in the understanding of learning disabilities.

Chapter 9, on mental retardation, thoroughly covers etiology and treatment in addition to preventive measures.

Chapter 10 has been described by reviewers as one of the best, most informative chapters in the book. Childhood psychosis and pervasive developmental disorders, especially autism, are described by author Jenson, who has done research, clinical care, and teaching on these topics for many years.

Chapter 11 uses clear, understandable language to describe the rationale underlying research methods and the research designs and procedures themselves. Applications to clinical topics are emphasized, such as use of nonexperimental paradigms.

Chapter 12 covers classification of child disorders, especially the widely used DSM-III system. Approaches are compared on various important criteria.

Chapter 13 introduces child assessment methods, ways of evaluating them, and their appropriate use. Contemporary methods are described, such as child interviews, behavior checklists, and self-monitoring techniques.

Chapter 14 considers the child's developmental level as a factor in the choice of treatment interventions. Major approaches to treatment are described in some detail.

Chapter 15 reviews innovations in child assessment and treatment, presenting up-to-date coverage of children's legal and human rights; new treatment approaches featuring children's regulation of their own behavior; the use of developmental psychology theory and research on child diagnosis and therapy; and the latest programs for the prevention of child psychopathology. The effects of alternative child care patterns such as day care are also reviewed.

The preceding summary presents some new aspects of the present revision and emphasizes features such as the descriptions of prevention efforts that set this textbook apart from most others. As an aid to instructors, a manual including test questions is available upon adoption of the text.

We hope to convey a sense of intellectual curiosity and respect for and enjoyment of the ingenuity and rich variety of contributions of many researchers and theorists. Insofar as we have succeeded in this effort, we thank the people who have so generously read portions of the manuscript and offered their very useful revision suggestions. They, of course, are not responsible for any mistakes appearing here. We particularly thank Paul Goddard, Linda James, Nancy Worsham, Eric J. Cooley (Western Oregon State College), Janet R. LeFrancois (Converse College), A. J. Pappanikou (The University of Connecticut), Paul Michael Ramirez (Hunter College), Lee A. Rosén (Colorado State University), Thomas Schevers (Northeastern Illinois University), and Mary Anne Siderits (Marquette University).

A word about writing style is necessary. This edition continues our practice of alternating between "she" and "he" when referring to a hypothetical person. This is our response to the social and grammatical problems posed by the traditional English-language practice of referring to everyone in the masculine gender. That customary form now sounds sexist, but no alternative has as yet received widespread acceptance. We hope that readers will bear with us during this time of grammatical transition.

The advent of personal computers has allowed us to type this manuscript ourselves and largely without the assistance of secretaries. Nevertheless, we wish to thank office staff members who have helped us in many ways at crucial times. Thanks are due to Christine Rydalch, other office staff members, and our helpful and efficient editors, Jane Knetzger, Jean Ford, and Jeanette Ninas Johnson.

Writing a book (or even preparing a new edition) places considerable stress on busy authors with otherwise full schedules, as well as on their families. Spouses are good sports, although they sometimes make unhelpful observations such as "I want you *never* to do this again." But they relent and we take on other writing assignments. We couldn't have completed this project without you, Sid, Kathy, and Linda. Thanks for your support and willingness to let us work on this book when there were other important things to do.

D. M. G.
W. R. J.
C. J. D.

CONTENTS

chapter

1

Introduction

KEY TERMS

Continuity Hypothesis.   The view that, unless successfully treated, childhood problems will persist rather than be overcome.

Delusion.   A false belief, such as that one's thoughts are controlled by microwave transmissions or that one is a holy or historical personage.

Growth Hypothesis.   The view that childhood psychological problems are typically outgrown or overcome without recourse to professional treatment.

Hallucination.   A compelling but false perception, such as that worms are crawling on one's skin or that disembodied voices are belittling one.

Identity Crisis.   Erik Erikson's concept that in adolescence the person undergoes a stressful transition and develops a new adult character.

Psychopathology.   A general term referring to any type of emotional, social, or cognitive disturbance severe enough to require professional attention.

Psychosis.   A serious psychological disorder often involving delusions, hallucinations, thought disturbances, impaired social functioning, and bizarre emotional reactions.

Syndrome.   A constellation of problem behaviors that together constitute a psychological disorder; for example, the delusions, thought disturbances, social impediments, and other symptoms of psychosis.

HISTORY OF CHILD PSYCHOPATHOLOGY

Child Care before the 18th Century

Today, children's rights to proper care are guarded and respected. In previous times, however, the level of care and consideration accorded children was generally low by today's standards. For millennia Europeans tolerated the suffering of abused and neglected babies and the tormenting of the mentally retarded and insane. Our ancestors might not have understood present-day professional attention to children's disturbed behavior, or *psychopathology*. Concern for physical survival and spiritual well-being outweighed niceties such as children's rights to autonomy and humane care.

In the past, interest in studying and treating children's disturbed behavior paled in comparison to protecting them from omnipresent threats to their lives. Although most parents were concerned and responsible, they must have realized that many of their children were doomed to an early death. As one author has observed:

> The statistics available from the eighteenth century in England and on the continent are terrifying in the inevitability of the death of children: The century had almost closed before children born in London had an even break of surviving until their fifth birthday, and before 1750 the odds were three-to-one against a child completing five years of life. (Kessen, 1965, p. 8)

Why did children die in such huge numbers? Threats such as grinding poverty and recurrent famines, wars, and epidemics made life precarious, most especially for the young, who were the weakest and among the most expendable of all. Foolish sentimentality could endanger the whole family, so poor parents were forced to be harshly realistic. Babies were closely confined and tightly wrapped in swaddling bands, ostensibly to ensure that their limbs grew straight. Swaddling kept them quiet and out of harm's way while the older family members worked. Because so many babies died, parents may have resisted forming emotional attachments to them (Tuchman, 1978). Or

perhaps parents grieved over their children's deaths as keenly as they do in our time, but there is no record of it. High infant mortality rates do not necessarily cause parents to avoid bonding with children (Pollock, 1983). Nevertheless, in the unyielding world of pre-18th-century Europe, sentiment seems to have had little place among the less privileged, and relationships within most families were more functional than obviously affectionate (Shorter, 1975). Children were needed to transmit the family name, to help provide family subsistence, and to care for parents in their old age. Spouses were needed to ensure the viability of the family, and love matches were virtually unknown at any level of society.

Two or three centuries ago, European babies were likely to be seriously neglected or abandoned by poor or unmarried mothers. In 18th-century Paris, parents deposited one-third of all babies at foundling homes, and more came from the countryside despite a law prohibiting transporting babies into the city to abandon them. Desperately poor parents may have been trying to save their infants' lives by delivering them to charitable institutions where they might receive adequate food and shelter. Most of the babies died anyway. In Dublin between 1775 and 1800, 10,272 infants were admitted to foundling homes, but of this vast number only 45 survived (Kessen, 1965, p. 8). Starving and ill, they endured unsanitary, crowded conditions, a meager and nutritionally inadequate diet, and deadly contagious diseases.

The babies who remained with their parents also had high mortality rates. Prior to the late 18th century, less than about a third of the babies born survived the first year of life (Borstelmann, 1983). The practice of sending babies away to live in the care of wet nurses took its toll. Families who could afford it hired wet nurses who lived in the country to breast-feed their babies and raise them until they were 4 or 5 years old. These very poor women accepted the babies of richer families long after their own babies had grown and they could no longer breast-feed. They solved the problem by feeding their charges a despicable mixture of gruel made from cereal, water, and a little sugar if possible. They lived in cold, dark huts, and some babies' diapers went unchanged for hours, chilling them. Many died of malnutrition, disease, and neglect (Beckman, 1977). Of course, some of the more capable nurses provided reasonably good care. Nevertheless, it is puzzling why parents would expose their babies to the perils of wet nursing. One reason was their belief that having sexual relations would curdle a mother's milk and sicken her baby, and an alternative was to hire a wet nurse for the baby (Pollock, 1983). Other mothers were unable to nurse their own babies and a wet nurse was necessary. Undoubtedly, most parents were doing what they considered best for their children by placing them with experienced wet nurses in supposedly wholesome country surroundings.

Responsible parents expressed their concern about their children's welfare in the forceful measures they used to ensure their children's conformity to religious and social commandments. Many children were caned or whipped into obedience, immersed in ice water, confined in dark cupboards, and threatened with abandonment or abduction (deMause, 1974). Disobedient children were thought to be in imminent peril of hellfire and damnation, and could endanger their parents' salvation as well, so all the resources of family, church, and community were devoted to their reform. In the 16th century, babies who persistently cried and were unsoothable were thought to be possessed by demons and were sometimes put to death on the advice of Christian church leaders (deMause, 1974). Concerns about social acceptance and salvation were paramount, and they guided disciplinary practices.

It is possible that modern writers have over-emphasized the rigor of the earlier child-rearing practices (Gordon, 1978; Pollock, 1983). Diaries of upper-class parents in the 17th to the 19th centuries showed great love for and enjoyment in their children. Lady Anne Clifford (1590–1676) wrote about her ill 2-year-old: "The Child had a bitter fit of her ague again, insomuch I was fearful of her that I could hardly sleep all night, so I beseeched GOD Allmighty to be merciful to me and spare her life" (Clifford, 1923, p. 54). It must be recalled, though, that the diarists tended to come from more recent historical periods and from the highest social classes. Thus they were not representative of earlier periods or of the bulk of the population.

Stern discipline was the norm and might not have represented parental rejection or indifference. In fact, Kagan (1978) has argued that today's children are more vulnerable to lack of love than in the past, when children were viewed less sentimentally. Now children's behavior problems and emotional disturbances are often attributed to insufficient parental affection (Kagan, 1978). It may be that "sufficient parental affection" is impossible to attain because children always crave more than they receive. Thus modern people may have an insatiable craving for unqualified love and regard from others, and the inevitable frustration of this unrealistic need makes them feel unfairly deprived. Feeling neglected may be characteristic of middle-class children who have less parental supervision now than was the case in their grandparents' time. The present divorce rate of 50 percent, high maternal employment rates, and strict grading by age in educational and recreational settings all decrease children's opportunities for experiencing the instructive and enjoyable aspects of their parents' company. Some psychologists (Bronfenbrenner, 1979; Winn, 1983) have asserted that the rise of peer influences at the expense of parental ones is causing increasing child problems, such as a lack of internalized values and controls, which may result in drug misuse, drinking, smoking, and sexual activity. As a consequence, it is difficult to tell whether modern children are more psychologically advantaged than were the children of the past.

The Beginning of Modern Attitudes toward Children

In the 18th century, attitudes toward children became more positive and humane. Children were increasingly valued for their innocence, charm, and playfulness. The English philosopher John Locke (1632–1704) taught that children are not born perverse, but mentally resemble a blank slate (tabula rasa) to be developed through suitable education and experience. Thus adults need not combat the child's evil nature through cruelty, since the child is not innately corrupt. Later, the French philosopher Jean Jacques Rousseau (1712–1778) promoted the glorification of childhood by writing that children have a natural tendency toward healthy growth in both body and spirit. Accordingly, children were thought to require only developmentally appropriate instruction and a clean, healthful, and nonrestrictive environment in order to develop optimally. Only the malevolent influences of adults' cruelty and teachers' ignorance of their pupils' limited capacities were believed to interfere with healthful, normal development. Accordingly, educated parents began to view their children more positively and affectionately and to perceive them as innocent rather than as depraved.

Ironically, the later growth of industry (1750–1850) threatened the health of impoverished child workers, of whom there were many:

> According to the 1870 [U.S.] census about one out of every eight children were employed. By 1900 approximately 1,750,000 children, or one out of six, were gainfully employed. Sixty percent were agricultural workers; of the 40 percent in industry over half were children of immigrant families. (Bremner, 1971, p. 601)

Poor immigrant and rural children put in 12- to 15-hour days in the mines, mills, farms, and manufacturing plants. The typical 19th-century urban workplace was dangerous and unsanitary. Child workers were found to be useful in factories, where they were paid less than adults and where their small stature enabled them to work in restricted places at dangerous jobs such as cleaning or oiling machinery while it was still in operation.

In the 19th century, poor children labored long hours in hazardous conditions before child labor laws were enacted. Working them hard and paying them little was viewed as "good business" and morally correct.

Children even worked in the dark, cold, damp English mines, where they were harnessed to carts like animals to haul coal. Clad in rags and underfed, the mine children were beaten when their energy flagged. The working conditions of black and Native American slave children in the Americas were as bad or even worse. Profit was king, and the children's welfare was not considered by the businessmen. To their credit, some clergy and concerned citizens spoke out against this inhumane treatment of children, and eventually managed to outlaw the worst abuses; however, reform came slowly.

It is a human tendency to blame others in order to explain their misfortunes, and the peasant immigrants and their scruffy, undersized offspring were natural targets for such prejudice. Many well-educated and wealthy people drew a parallel between evolutionist Charles Darwin's principle of the survival of the fittest in the animal kingdom and their own prosperity, which they attributed to their own genetic superiority. In contrast, they viewed the poor, uneducated, and ill as genetically unfit and unworthy of education, decent employment, or medical treatment. The fact that some of the poor were defenseless children did not inspire the rich to help them. This selfishness was rationalized by the assertion that it was better for them to die young than to grow up to breed additional generations of the socially dangerous and unfit. Such an interpretation is indefensible genetically, historically, and morally, but it prevailed in law and practice. Consequently, children who were impoverished, orphaned, or abandoned were left to live or die by their own devices. Today we realize that some childhood behavior disturbances do have a genetic basis or genetic contribution, but we recognize that no social class or ethnic group is genetically inferior—or superior—to any other.

The Rise of Mental Testing and the Study of Child Psychopathology

Formal education is a relatively recent historical development. No schools existed in Europe before the 15th century. School attendance was considered inappropriate for females until the 18th and 19th centuries, and compulsory school for all children began only in the later 19th century (Aries, 1962). With the advent of compulsory education, it became evident that some children were not progressing normally, but the nature of their incapacity was not understood. In 1909, the French Minister of Education charged the psychologists Binet and Simon with developing standardized tests to identify children who lacked the intellectual ability to cope with the regular school curriculum. Children thus identified were given special education in the schools if their deficiency was minor or were institutionalized if their retardation was more severe. Institutions for the retarded were not viewed as dead-end placements, but aimed to equip the children to return to regular community life (Rie, 1971). The test devised by Binet and Simon was a great success; it was translated into English and eventually revised to become the Stanford-Binet Intelligence Test. A more recent revision of this test remains in use today. These mental status tests were among the first systematic assessments of children's developmental disorders.

Other types of juvenile psychological abnormalities were also recognized by 19th-century writers. Prominent German and English physicians such as Friesinger and Maudsley provided sketchy descriptions of various childhood adjustment disorders. Mental retardation or deficiency was distinguished from *psychosis*, which was defined as a broad category including hyperactivity, antisocial-aggressive behavior, generalized anxiety, suicidal behavior, and schizophrenic reactions (Rie, 1971). In all, just two disorder categories were recognized: mental deficiency and insanity (psychosis).

Perhaps because of the great popularity of Darwin's evolutionary theory, 19th-century psychiatrists believed that most forms of deviance had a hereditary basis. Family heredity was thought to account for desirable as well as undesirable characteristics, and the power of social influences was little appreciated. Francis Galton's discovery of disproportionately large numbers of eminent persons in certain prominent English families was widely considered to prove the hereditary basis of intellectual and personality characteristics. It was recognized in passing that membership in the lower social classes limited opportunities for success, yet heredity was believed to be the prime determinant of character, intelligence, and wealth (Kessen, 1965).

Victorians believed that despite favorable heredity, certain types of environmental events and personal practices could bring on madness. The most dangerous practice was thought to be masturbation, the presumed cause of adolescent "masturbatory insanity," a mysterious malady with ill-specified characteristics. The lack of specificity was understandable, since there was no such disorder. In a good example of faulty reasoning, mental institution staff members observed that many of the insane engaged in frequent masturbation, so they assumed that the masturbation had produced the insanity. Undoubtedly they greatly underestimated masturbation rates among normal adolescents, whom they could not observe, and concluded that the rates were abnormally high among the inmates who were under constant surveillance (Rie, 1971).

The value of objective scientific research is illustrated by other 19th-century medical beliefs, which were based solely on intuition and clinical lore rather than on experimentation. It was believed that psychological disorders could be brought on by any form of excess, such as studying or working too hard, changes in climate, and a sudden fright or shock (Spitzka, 1890). More nearly accurate Victorian beliefs were that high fever, head injuries, and intestinal parasites might lead to "brain irritability" and consequently to deviant behavior. Superstition, morality tales, and popular beliefs formed the basis for medical practice, because there was virtually no systematic and objective study of the development of psychological disturbances.

Most 19th-century medications left something to be desired. Fussy, irritable infants were sometimes soothed with laudanum, a potent mixture of opium and alcohol. Various other medicines containing generous amounts of alcohol or opiates were used to treat children's lassitude, fearfulness, and academic problems. Addictive drugs were prescribed freely and were available over the counter, so dependence was widespread, compounding the sufferers' original problems.

Exploitation and Protection of Children

In the 19th century, many children lacked the necessities of life. A little over 100 years ago, which is practically the present in historical time, children were cruelly treated by employers, and were left without food and shelter if they were orphaned or abandoned. Lone children lived in the streets, surviving by their wits; they could be found patronizing neighborhood saloons when they acquired enough money to buy a drink. Some became thieves, and if caught, they were imprisoned along with adult criminals who exploited them socially and sexually. Attempts to reform or protect delinquent children were primitive, as Box 1-1 describes.

However, reform was in the air. During the early 1900s, reform schools were established to attempt to teach and rehabilitate young offenders. The now-familiar funding problems arose, and increasing demands on limited state revenues forced reform schools to support themselves through contracting child inmates' labor to local manufacturers (Bremner, 1971, p. 439). These arrangements led to the types of abuses described in Box 1-2.

In the late 19th century, reformers in the United States and Great Britain publicized the severe social problems created by rapid industrialization and the urbanization of masses of immigrants and rural poor. Great numbers of people were displaced from their farms and neighborhoods to live in teeming city slums. Their plight and fears about their potential for political unrest stimulated public interest in social reform. Socially concerned clergymen and educated middle-class women set up settlement houses and formed social clubs devoted to furthering the education and welfare of the poor. Ironically, institutions for protecting suffering animals predated those for the protection of children. The first American branch of the Society for the Prevention of Cruelty to Children was formed in 1874 as a part of the Society for the Prevention of Cruelty to Animals. By

---

BOX 1-1 • A New Life: Juvenile Delinquents Sent to the Colonies

When many of the world's continents were still sparsely settled, British criminals were sometimes sent to exile in remote locations rather than being imprisoned at home. This legal practice had the advantages of isolating criminals from potential victims and of providing European labor to uninviting but vital parts of the British Empire. In addition, such relocation in a presumably less squalid environment might provide an opportunity for a fresh start and a new life. *Transportation* (as this type of exile was called) was a common sentence, and some 150,000 convicts were sent to Australia alone between 1787 and 1868.

In addition to the adult criminals shipped to North America, South Africa, Australia, and New Zealand in the 17th to the 19th centuries, there were some consignments of delinquent boys. Like their elders, most of the boys had been convicted of theft; many were repeat offenders; and many wore tattoos signifying their membership in delinquent gangs (Jordan, 1985). Their very poor nutrition was reflected in their stunted growth. Compared to today's London boys at 14 and 15 years, the boy convicts resembled 10-year-olds in height, and they were distinctly shorter than their peers who also were from poor families but became sailors (Gandevia, 1977).

Those who survived the voyage and made homes in a new country may in fact have made better lives for themselves and their families. Records indicate that their children were much taller and better-nourished than their fathers (Gandevia, 1977), and many of their descendants are prosperous and productive citizens today.

Sources: T. E. Jordan. (1985). Transported to Van Diemen's Land: The boys of the *Frances Charlotte* (1832) and *Lord Goderich* (1841). *Child Development, 56*, 1092–1099; B. Gandevia. (1977). A comparison of the heights of boys transported to Australia from England, Scotland, and Ireland c. 1840, with later British and Australian developments. *Australian Paediatric Journal, 13*, 91–97.

1900 there were 250 such societies devoted to rescuing children from neglect, physical abuse, and exploitation as beggars, entertainers, workers, or prostitutes (Bremner, 1971). An unintended effect of child protection efforts was to place the children in large, impersonal, and inadequate institutions. Gradually it became apparent that the care of dependent and neglected children should be handled by appropriate branches of state and local government, rather than through the efforts of well-intended but untrained volunteers from private organizations.

Treatment Services for Children

When social reform was ascendant, special treatment services were initiated for children. Ironically, some American school systems of the 1800s and early 1900s had more extensive mental health service delivery systems than are available in some school districts today. At that time, public school systems hired visiting teachers to coordinate and deliver a wide range of services to children who had special problems that interfered with their academic achievement. Visiting teachers were forerunners of today's school social workers and home teachers. Box 1-3 presents a case study written by a resourceful visiting teacher early in the 20th century.

If there is one date to remember from this chapter, it is 1896, when Lightner Witmer established the first true psychological clinic for children at the University of Pennsylvania. Witmer's clinic specialized in the treatment of children's broadly defined educational problems. The approach used was surprisingly modern, for it emphasized the joint efforts of the clinic, the school, and the family in the solution of the child's problems (Levine & Levine, 1970).

With the emerging agreement that the com-

BOX 1-2 • Nineteenth-Century Exploitation of Institutionalized Juvenile Delinquents

Following is an excerpt from testimony given by William Pryor Letchworth, a commissioner of the New York State Board of Charities in 1882. Letchworth testified before the New York legislature in support of a bill which would forbid refuges and reformatories for children from contracting the children's work, for a fee, to private employers. Although the 1882 bill was vetoed, similar legislation went into effect in New York in 1884 (Bremner, 1971, p. 469).

Children under sixteen years of age, when subjected to long hours of labor, in irksome positions, under a task contract system, are likely to be retarded in their development, and fagged out at the end of their long confinement, are too weary to derive due advantage from the teachings imparted in the evening school.

While flogging has long been abolished in the Navy and the use of the "cat" in the State Prisons, it is still thought necessary, in order to realize a fair pecuniary return from the children's labor, for the contractor to inflict severe corporal punishment for deficiency in imposed tasks. One institution in the State, in order to meet the expectation of contractors, was forced in a single year to inflict on the boys employed, upon the direct complaints of contractors, their superintendent, overseer and employes, corporal punishments *two thousand two hundred and sixty-three times.* This was administered with a strap or rattan on the hand, or on the posterior bare or covered, as the gravity of the case demanded. During the same period the punishments in school, in order as it was said, to "wake up" their already overtaxed attention, was so considerable as to swell up the aggregate punishments for the year to the magnitude of *ten thousand.*

The tendency of the contract system in reformatory institutions for boys, is to retain as long as possible those who are most valuable to the contractor, and as these generally belong to the most dutiful class and consequently entitled to an early discharge, a great injustice is done, which sometimes drives boys to desperation. On the other hand, the intent of the contractor being to rid himself of the unskillful and careless workers, there is danger of a premature discharge of such before the work of reformation is completed.

Source: W. P. Letchworth. (1882). *Labor of children in reform schools* (New York), pp. 3–7. Reprinted in R. H. Bremner (Ed.). (1971). *Children and youth in America: A documentary history. Vol. 2: 1866–1932* (Cambridge, MA: Harvard University Press), pp. 469–471.

---

munity as well as the family was responsible for children's welfare, concern arose for the fate of juveniles who had committed crimes. Imprisonment with adult criminals no longer seemed appropriate for children. Recognizing the special needs of these children, the public-spirited Women's Club of Chicago helped to organize the first juvenile court in the nation. The court's charge included protecting children in addition to rehabilitating and punishing them for their illegal behavior.

It soon became apparent that many of the delinquents were also seriously emotionally disturbed, so in 1909 the psychiatrist William Healy

was chosen to head the new Juvenile Psychopathic Institute for the treatment of children under the jurisdiction of the juvenile court. Together with psychologists Grace Fernold and Augusta F. Bronner, Healy studied the origins of delinquency and attempted to rehabilitate individual juvenile offenders. Their treatment methods were flexible and varied, and included psychoanalytic techniques, residential treatment, consultation with judges and police officers, child guidance advice to parents and short-term child counseling.

In the 1920s, such services to children were offered in urban areas nationwide. A private foundation, the Commonwealth Fund, sponsored the

---

BOX 1-3 • The Visiting Teacher to the Rescue

The following vignette is excerpted from Johnson's 1916 book on the work of the visiting teacher. The visiting teacher's services were many and varied, reaching into many aspects of the child's life in an effort to provide the child a healthful and emotionally supportive environment.

Nine-year-old Sadie had a bad reputation, was neglected, disheveled, and often fell asleep in school. Home visits soon established that her mother lived away from her home at her place of employment. Her father drank heavily, and he and the child slept together in the only bed. The visitor helped Sadie's mother make arrangements to be home more often, and arranged for the child to have lunch money. The visitor taught the child to fix her hair, gave her hair ribbons and dresses, and made it a point to inspect her frequently. She arranged for a tutor at the nearby settlement and helped to program the hours after school. The neighborhood librarian took an interest in Sadie, she joined a club at the settlement house, and was admitted to a gym class after the visitor obtained the proper shoes and costume. A kindly neighbor took the child in when the parents were away. All of this attention resulted in a marked transformation. Sadie's appearance changed and she began to bring perfect papers for the visiting teacher to see. Apparently the family situation also cleared up considerably, but it is not clear why.

Source: H. M. Johnson. (1916). *The visiting teacher in New York City.* (New York: Public Education Association of the City of New York). Reprinted in M. Levine and A. Levine, *A social history of helping services* (New York: Appleton-Century-Crofts, 1970).

---

development of community child guidance clinics as part of an effort to prevent juvenile delinquency. The clinics typically were headed by a psychiatrist and included social workers and psychologists on their staffs. Child guidance workers then believed, as they do today, that prevention is essential because it is impossible to meet all of the existing and future service and treatment needs. Nevertheless, over the years clinics came to neglect the more challenging prevention and consultation services and to concentrate on treating families who presented themselves to the clinic for services (Levine & Levine, 1970). Because poor and ill-educated families seldom sought out such mental health services, many clinics came to serve primarily middle-class, affluent, and well-educated parents and children with minor adjustment problems. The office-based interview and play therapy methods used at the time proved ineffective with the more seriously troubled children—those who were brain-damaged, psychotic, mentally retarded, learning-disabled, or seriously emotionally disturbed. Children with these types

of problems were institutionalized in inadequate state hospitals, treated by the public health services, or officially ignored.

The growth of federally sponsored community mental health services in the 1960s offered help to more children and families than ever before. The services ranged from inpatient care to clinic counseling, family therapy, consultation to schools and other community agencies, psychological services offered in schools, and prevention services. Although the need was always greater than the services available, many community mental health services were exemplary. However, the economic and, more importantly, the political climate turned against the generous provision of treatment services during the late 1970s and 1980s. Helpless psychotic patients were turned out of state and federal hospitals to live on the streets as best they could, and treatment services for children and families were severely curtailed. Legislation opposing drug abuse was toughened, but funding for drug abuse prevention, for treatment of addicts, and for law enforcement was cut during the Reagan administration. Educational services for children have suffered, too; funding for impressive federal compensatory education programs such as Head Start and Follow Through continues to be seriously threatened. It is probable, however, that in the longer term Americans will again recognize the social and moral wisdom in providing good educational and mental health services to all of the nation's children.

MODERN VIEWS OF NORMAL AND ABNORMAL PSYCHOLOGICAL DEVELOPMENT

Sometimes it is difficult to determine whether an individual child is displaying normal or deviant behavior. Growing up is often difficult, and there is scarcely a child who has not had adjustment problems from time to time. A young child may prove extremely resistant to his parents' toilet-training attempts; another may resist separation from her mother when it comes time to go to kindergarten; and a third may be troubled by restless inattentiveness during classroom work periods. Professionals who work with children must determine whether these types of difficulties are a normal part of the child's psychological and social development or whether they represent more serious problems. The variability of children's behavior adds to the diagnostic challenge; a child's pattern of responding may change within weeks, days, or hours. Developmental shifts in the child's companions and circumstances, as when entering a new school, and the child's increasing physical and mental maturity all open new avenues for responding. Most children display a mixture of desirable and undesirable behavior. The playground bully may be responsive to his friends and sweet to his grandmother, or a girl who is painfully shy at school may be outspokenly demanding toward her family. Children may show even more situational variability in their behavior than do adults, making it challenging to diagnose their behavior.

Certain problems are common at particular ages and may even constitute a normal part of growing up. For the most part, children's adjustment disturbances are transitory rather than

long-lasting. Lacking a knowledge of the factors responsible for problem formation and disappearance, most parents say that their children have outgrown their undesirable behavior. As will be seen, child psychopathology consists largely of those childhood problems that are not outgrown. In the remaining sections of this chapter, we first present some examples of child behavior and consider whether each one probably represents a normal reaction or a pathological one. We then describe the criteria used by different groups to judge the normality of children's behavior and compare them to adult standards. Certain types of problems are particularly prevalent at certain periods during development, and the typical progression of adjustment problems will be described. Not all of children's difficult behaviors are truly problematic, but they may represent immature attempts at achieving autonomy from adult direction or may serve other important developmental functions. Both the goal and the type of behavior must be considered in characterizing it as normal or deviant. Some problems are transitory and others may prove permanent, as will be described.

Case Descriptions

Here are descriptions of three children whose behavior concerns their parents and others. From these brief characterizations and from your knowledge of child development, try to decide whether the child's behavior should be classified as normal or disordered, and identify the criteria you used to make your decisions.

Cheryl Cheryl is a 9-year-old girl who was caught stealing other children's lunch money at school. She also took younger children's possessions away from them through threats and force. When confronted with evidence of her thefts, Cheryl denied taking anything and blamed another girl. Her classmates dislike her because she steals and because she quarrels with them and sometimes attacks them physically. In one of her rages at home, she tore apart a sofa. Is Cheryl's behavior pattern permissible in a 9-year-old, or does it require professional attention?

Bobby   Bobby is a cute little 3-year-old boy with big blue eyes, but he hardly speaks a word yet. His mother says that her pregnancy and delivery were normal, and that Bobby was a very good baby who hardly ever fussed or cried. Yet he seems distant and unresponsive, and lacks the affectionate nature of a normal preschool child. And he hasn't learned to talk. His parents ask how worried they should be about their son.

Steve   Steve, aged 17, has led his parents to despair and uncharacteristic outbursts of rage. Formerly an average to good student, Steve has virtually stopped studying and rarely attends school. His closest friends are drug-using truants, and his parents have come across drug paraphernalia in his closet. Their friends console them with descriptions of similar problems with teenaged sons, but Steve's parents continue to worry. To what extent is Steve's behavior characteristic of an adolescent boy or does it represent psychopathology?

As these three cases illustrate, it is not always easy to determine whether a child or adolescent is acting in a developmentally normative fashion or is disturbed. In order to make this determination, child mental health workers use a set of criteria that we now examine. These considerations include the behavior's age- and sex-appropriateness and its social and cultural acceptability. Other criteria are the behavior's frequency, intensity, and pervasiveness or generality. It also is important to consider whether the child's conduct is personally fulfilling and whether it enhances the long-term well-being of the child and others. In addition, we consider the degree of resemblance between adult and child psychopathology and the predictability of future problems from childhood disturbances.

Criteria for Normality

Age-Appropriateness   It is not by accident that each youngster's age receives prominent mention in the preceding case descriptions. A child's age and developmental status are of paramount importance in determining the normality of the

child's behavior. As an example, strong fears of dogs and of being separated from one's parents are quite acceptable in a 3-year-old, but would be suspect if the child were 13 years old. Similarly, adult-like behavior such as drinking and smoking is common among high school students, but would arouse considerable concern in a 9-year-old. These illustrations indicate that certain problem behaviors are more socially acceptable and much more frequent at some age periods than at others. When a high proportion of children in a particular age period engage in certain behavior patterns, then behaving similarly is developmentally normal and does not indicate that a child has some form of psychopathology. That is, if nearly all high school seniors have tried alcohol, it would be unfair to say that any senior is disturbed simply because he or she has had a drink.

Some knowledge of the behavior typical of children of various ages is required in order to determine whether a particular youngster's reactions are normal or not. Many behaviors that concern parents and teachers actually occur in one-third to one-half or more of children at a particular age, and so might be considered statistically normal, even if undesirable. The research literature charts the types of difficulties exhibited by children throughout postnatal development. We now review the problems characteristic of children of different ages.

Preschool years. Children have been described as negativistic at the ages of 1½ to 3 years because of their frequent temper tantrums and contrariness (Goodenough, 1931; Macfarlane, Allen, & Honzik, 1954). According to mothers' reports, at least half of children at these ages throw temper tantrums and often disobey their mothers' commands. In addition, many toddlers demand constant adult attention and protest loudly when they are overlooked. These observations come primarily from older reports such as the Berkeley Guidance Study (Macfarlane et al., 1954), but the original findings seem trustworthy, since they were confirmed again more recently with a day care and a nursery school sample (Crowther, Bond, & Rolf, 1981; Rolf, Hakola, Klemchuk, & Hasazi, 1976). In the Vermont Child Development Project study of the problems of 588 pre-schoolers (Rolf et al., 1976), 35.7 percent of 2-year-old boys and 30 percent of the girls had an overabundance of energy, according to their parents and teachers. In addition, 28.6 percent of the boys (but only 18.2 percent of the girls) had problems in paying attention to an activity, and other types of problems were less frequent. Problems with aggression and shyness became less prevalent in the 3- to 5-year-old group. Table 1-1 summarizes the troublesome behaviors found in normal children of different ages. As the table indicates, the nature of the problems changes somewhat during development.

Children's angry protests and tantrums, and their destructiveness, bullying, and lying, decrease after the age of 5 (Rutter & Yule, 1982, cited in Rutter & Garmezy, 1983; Shepherd, Oppenheim, & Mitchell, 1971), much to the relief of their caretakers. Yet kindergarten children (particularly the boys) continue to engage in tantrums, and also display some new problems. Adults complain that from one-third to one-half of 5-year-old boys lie

and that they have an overabundance of energy that exhausts their parents and teachers. In addition to those who are aggressive and overactive, some kindergarten children are oversensitive to minor slights. At this age, too, children may become very shy and withdrawn and develop specific fears of animals, electrical storms, of being in the dark, or of entering the water (Macfarlane et al., 1954).

Elementary school years. Typical problems among elementary school children continue to include temper tantrums, lying, and oversensitivity. About one-third of 7- to 8-year-old boys are described by parents and teachers as overactive (Rolf et al., 1976), but this problem decreases thereafter. Jealousy of siblings and other children characterizes nearly a third of the children at this time. During the later elementary school years, excessive reserve, oversensitivity, and temper outbursts are common, and a new problem, moodiness, emerges. Their mothers report that a third or more of preadolescents display unaccountable and troublesome mood swings. They are happy,

TABLE 1-1
Problem Behaviors Characteristic of Children and Youth at Various Ages

Age Period	Problem Behaviors
1½–2 years	Temper tantrums, refusal to do things when asked, demanding attention constantly, overactivity, specific fears, inattentiveness
3–5 years	Temper tantrums, refusal to do things when asked, demanding attention constantly, overactivity, specific fears, oversensitivity, lying, negativism
6–10 years	Temper tantrums, overactivity, specific fears, oversensitivity, lying, school achievement problems, jealousy, excessive reserve
11–14 years	Temper tantrums, oversensitivity, jealousy, school achievement problems, excessive reserve, moodiness
15–18 years	School achievement problems, skipping school, cheating on exams, drinking, smoking, drug misuse, sexual misconduct, trespassing, shoplifting, and other minor law violations

excited, and energetic one day and sulky, irritable, and withdrawn the next, leaving their families and friends perplexed and at a loss as to how to treat them. Overactivity is considered a problem for only about one-fourth of 10- to 12-year-old boys, and becomes increasingly rare in the older age groups (Macfarlane et al., 1954).

Many children experience at least fleeting behavior problems during the elementary school years. In a several-year study of over 1500 Minnesota school children, teachers identified 58.6 percent of the children as having had a behavior problem. Fortunately, only 11.3 percent of the boys and just 3.5 percent of the girls were consistently rated as behaviorally disturbed by their teachers. Many more were considered disturbed by a single teacher. Nevertheless, these findings suggest that the majority of elementary school children suffer some social adjustment difficulty in the early to middle grades.

As might be expected, academic achievement problems are common. A study of the children of the Hawaiian island of Kauai revealed that more than half of the 10-year-old boys (51 percent) and more than a third of the girls (37 percent) had serious academic achievement problems (Werner, Bierman, & French, 1971). Many were earning unsatisfactory or failing grades in basic skill subjects such as reading or arithmetic, or were enrolled in remedial classes. Hawaiian children have long had many academic achievement problems, perhaps because their traditional culture conflicts with the more impersonal, directive atmosphere of the schools (Jordan & Tharp, 1979). Consequently, the Hawaiian children studied by Werner and colleagues may not be representative of school children elsewhere. However, similar academic problems are common in all school systems. It appears that large numbers of the nation's elementary school children have academic and social woes that warrant professional attention.

Adolescence. The adolescent years are often considered particularly stormy, emotional, and conflict-ridden. Many adults remember adolescence as the most turbulent, confusing, and troubled period of their lives (Macfarlane, 1964).

This view of troubled adolescents is an ancient one, dating back to the classical period of Greece and the teachings of Plato, who referred to youth as a "drunkenness of the spirit." A similar opinion is found in the doctrine of the 20th-century child psychoanalysts Anna Freud and Erik Erikson. Classical psychoanalysis maintains that middle childhood is a latency period of quiet intellectual and social development, which draws to a close in the emotional upsets and personality turmoil of puberty. Erikson's (1956) influential concept of the *identity crisis* portrays adolescence as a time of stress and strain, during which problem behavior is common but of little permanent consequence. However, some authors have disputed this view and have found evidence indicating very little adolescent turmoil or personality instability among American adolescents (Douvan & Adelson, 1966; Offer & Offer, 1975). Contrary to popular belief, most adolescents report that they respect and admire their parents, want to emulate them, and say they get along well with them and with other adults (Meissner, 1965; Weiner, 1982). Yet, at the same time, most American teenagers also experiment with alcohol, drugs, and illicit drugs (see Chapter 6), and a great number engage in petty crimes. Many boys in a large group of high school sophomores studied by Bachman (1970) reported engaging in various forms of aggressive and antisocial behavior. Forty percent of the boys had skipped school at least once, and 60 percent admitted cheating on exams. More serious transgressions were reported as well. Over one-third had been in trouble with the police at least once, one-half had shoplifted, and 43 percent had been guilty of trespassing. However, most of their illegal behavior was of a one-time, experimental nature. As an illustration, only a small fraction of the boys had shoplifted more than a single time.

Teenage girls also engage in antisocial and rebellious behavior at times. In fact, a careful analysis of a group of Colorado youths (Jessor & Jessor, 1977) found no notable sex differences in antisocial behavior rates. About two-thirds of the teenagers interviewed drank alcohol, and one-third were frequently drunk, which led to conflict with family, teachers, and law enforcement officers. Sexual activity and the use of alcohol and marijuana were so prevalent among the older adolescents that Jessor and Jessor concluded that such activities are typical of the growing-up process for many American young people. Thus, in some groups, adolescents' drug taking and sexual activity might be considered predictable rather than deviant or pathological. Those who were behaviorally more deviant and who had become so earlier in life had a more stormy transition to adulthood, as could be expected. Nevertheless, one-third of the entire group continued to accept conventional parental values, which would suggest that parents are important influences even in the teen years, when peer values seem to predominate.

Research studies have provided examples of adolescent conflict and of adolescent stability. Which reaction is the more representative? There is an apparent disparity between what teenagers tell interviewers about their harmonious relationships with their parents and what they say about their minor law infractions and their use of illicit substances. One might conclude that their responses are affected by considerations of social desirability. That is, teenagers may exaggerate the excellence of their relationships with their parents, which is socially desirable, but they may also boast about their daring, which makes them appear more sophisticated and enhances their reputations among their peers. It seems probable that the teen years are neither as tumultuous as most people believe nor as smoothly adaptive as some interview data indicate. At the very least, we may conclude that emotional upheaval is not a necessary part of normal adolescent development (Weiner, 1982). It is noteworthy, however, that adolescents and young adults who display one type of culturally deviant conduct (such as cocaine use) are likely to engage in others as well, including problem drinking, delinquent acts, and age-inappropriate sexual activity (Donovan & Jessor, 1985).

Fortunately, many adolescent problem behaviors seem to be minor and transitory. About one-half of girls between the ages of 13 and 15 years are reported to be oversensitive, as compared with just 20 percent of the boys. Approximately one-third of teenagers of both sexes have mood swings and display jealousy, while temper tantrums become rare among girls, but continue in about one-quarter of the boys (Macfarlane et al., 1954). Offer and Offer (1975) studied a group of representative adolescent boys and found that only 23 percent of this normal group entered young adulthood uneventfully and without outbursts of antisocial rebellion or backsliding into childish dependence on their parents. The remaining 77 percent experienced periods of anger, anxiety, and self-doubt, as described in Box 1-4. Again, however, these troubled periods tended to be brief.

To return to the cases of the three children described earlier, each can be considered using the information on age-appropriateness just presented. By the standard of behavior typical of 9-year-olds, Cheryl, who was stealing, lying, and fighting, would be highly unusual. Very few girls her age have such serious problems with antisocial and aggressive behavior. Similarly, 3-year-old Bobby's failure to speak and his profound social unresponsivity are highly unusual and suggestive of infantile autism or pervasive developmental disorder. It is unclear whether 17-year-old Steve's school problems and alcohol and drug misuse are transitory and within the range of normal late-adolescent behavior or whether they represent psychopathology. In either case, they cause trouble with his family, his school, and the law.

Ideal or Optimal Adjustment   The case of Steve raises the interesting question of whether a behavior pattern can be pathological in itself, regardless of how many other youngsters engage in it also. Harmful drug use, smoking, and overindulgence in alcohol provide good cases in point. These all can endanger health and personal adjustment, regardless of how many other teenagers engage in the same behavior. This suggests that in addition to a *statistical* definition of abnormality based on a behavior's prevalence, there must be a concept of optimal adjustment, or even ideal adjustment. In the optimal adjustment model, a behavioral reaction would be considered pathologi-

---

BOX 1-4 • Patterns of Adolescent Development

Daniel Offer and Judith Baskin Offer studied a group of adolescent boys from the time the boys were 14 until their 22nd birthdays. Unlike most groups subjected to psychiatric scrutiny, these boys were chosen because of their normality. They scored normal on a personality test and were described as normal by the teachers and their parents, who had never sought psychological help for any of them.

Surprisingly, only about one-quarter of this carefully selected group of adolescents were largely trouble-free. Of the remainder, 35 percent had particular difficulty in coping with stress such as that occasioned by a death in the family, although their overall adjustment was good most of the time. However, 21 percent of the group experienced a stormy adolescence marked by increasing conflicts with their parents, social and academic problems, and recurrent periods of extreme self-doubt. Of this latter "tumultuous growth" group, 46 percent eventually received psychotherapy. (As in most classification systems, one subgroup of 21 percent was impossible to characterize and so proved unclassifiable.)

CASE STUDY

Carl was typical of those with the tumultuous growth profile. His adoptive parents had some marital difficulties. They also disagreed on how severely to judge Carl, although both felt that he was overly sensitive to criticism, didn't study, and had difficulty controlling his temper. Carl, who was above average in intelligence, worked only enough to get average grades, but was discontented with his failure to perform better. He was active in sports, however, and got along well with his friends.

Although Carl had originally wanted to attend law school, his poor grades prevented that and he had to settle for a job as a salesman, which was a disappointment to him. He did not date much in high school, but in college he found companionship and sexual satisfaction with a steady girlfriend.

The investigators predicted that, following his difficult teen years, Carl would probably make a good social and vocational adjustment. They believed that he might never be very happy and contented, however.

Source: D. Offer and J. B. Offer. (1975). *From teenage to young manhood: A psychological study* (New York: Basic Books).

---

cal if it caused a health or an adjustment hazard to a child or to the functioning of the child's family or associates (Coleman, Butcher, & Carson, 1980). Conceivably, some behavioral patterns can be pathological even if engaged in by 90 percent of youngsters if they prove demonstrably harmful. The ideal adjustment definition is yet more demanding, and includes as pathological any factors that interfere with "the actualization of potentialities" (Coleman et al., 1980, p. 14). By this absolute standard of adjustment, Steve's failure to realize his academic potential, his reckless lack of consideration for his own health, and his callousness toward his parents would all be considered maladjusted behaviors; it would not matter how many other teenagers behave similarly. Blind application of a statistical definition is inadvisable, as Steve's case demonstrates. Even very common reactions can be undesirable and psychologically crippling. Consequently, diagnosticians should consider a behavioral pattern's effect on the child's present and future functioning, in addition to taking note of its statistical frequency or prevalence.

Intensity   Steve's heavy use of illicit substances suggests another criterion by which to judge behavior—intensity. A particular reaction may be relatively common, but still may constitute disordered behavior because of its extreme intensity. For example, it is normal for a 5-year-old child to have temper tantrums. But if the tantrums involve destruction of valuable possessions or physical assaults on other people, as in the case of Cheryl, then the behavior is deviant. Behavior that is so intense as to do major damage to oneself, to other people, or to property certainly qualifies as deviant.

Problem Persistence   We have observed previously that many childhood problems are transitory, and should not be defined as behavior disorders. A preschool child who has a temper tantrum *every day* for several weeks probably should not be considered deviant. Nor should the adolescent who has dramatic mood swings from day to day. If these behaviors persist, however, and become more or less permanent aspects of the child's life, then a clinical problem may be diagnosed and professionally treated. Unfortunately for diagnosticians, there are no established standards for use in judging whether a particular problem is persistent enough to be classified as a genuine psychological disorder. The criteria to use in judging the normality of behavioral persistence include (1) comparison with the duration or problems among children of the same age and developmental level; and (2) the type, number, and severity of environmental stressors which the child must contend with—for instance, parental abuse or neglect, parental physical illness or psychological problems, peer rejection, or academic failure. For example, a child may undergo a period of irritability, anxiety, and physical symptoms after a parent becomes seriously ill or abandons the child. When such behavioral and somatic disturbances persist for extended periods of time, however, the child's reaction must be considered clinically significant.

Severity, Number, and Diversity   Additional criteria include the severity of a child's problematic behavior and the number and diversity of the maladaptive behaviors. Some behaviors such as fire setting or extreme cruelty to animals may be very rare, but are severe and quite pathological. Even if it has happened only a few times, an adolescent's *delusion* that the actors on television shows are saying evil things about him probably represents serious adjustment difficulties, possibly of a psychotic nature. There is even more cause for concern if the delusion is combined with other indicators of serious disturbance, such as marked neglect of hygiene and physical appearance, inappropriate emotional reactions, *hallucinations* (such as imagining hearing voices), illogical speech, or outbursts of physical or verbal aggression. Readers who are acquainted with the diagnostic criteria for a schizophrenic disorder will recognize features of that disorder in the preceding list of symptoms. In general, the more persistent the adjustment problem, the more serious it is. But even a brief problem may be highly pathological if it is highly intense, bizarre, or dangerous, and appears as a part of a *syndrome* in which it is accompanied by a characteristic set of other disordered behaviors. The concept of a related group of problems (a psychiatric syndrome) is important in abnormal psychology. Only very rarely does a single problem behavior define a psychiatric diagnostic category. As Chapter 12 reveals, diagnostic classification depends on the occurrence of several characteristic problem behaviors as a group. Consequently, the co-occurrence of several problem behaviors is usually considered to be more serious than is the presence of a single one.

Sex-Appropriate Behavior   All cultures have somewhat different behavior expectations for males and for females. In our own culture, boys are expected to behave more boldly and aggressively than girls, who are expected to be more nurturant and sensitive. These expectations are communicated to children both directly and through the actions of adult men and women. Children who behave in a sex-appropriate fashion fit into society well, and those whose behavior is at variance with sex stereotypes may be considered to be psychologically abnormal. Deviant sex-role behavior is generally more acceptable for girls,

Little boys who tenderly care for baby dolls may be teased and considered sissies. Ironically, when they later become husbands and fathers, such parental behavior will be expected and desired.

who are considered tomboys, than for boys, who may be viewed as effeminate sissies (Fagot, 1977). As a result, a girl as aggressive as 9-year-old Cheryl will certainly be considered aberrant, although girls who simply enjoy athletics and the company of boys rather than girls will probably be classified as unusual rather than deviant. In contrast, boys who have predominantly feminine interests (playing with dolls, interior or fashion design, makeup) are often ridiculed and shunned by other boys, even in the preschool years (Huston, 1983; Lamb & Roopnarine, 1979). Boys who are inactive, noncompetitive, and interested in feminine pursuits may be inappropriately identified as having a gender disorder (Rekers, 1977). Nevertheless, in other social groups these boys' interests may be encouraged and may lead to respected career directions. The definition of sex-role-appropriate behavior depends on a largely unspoken social consensus that may change over time. At present, sex-role definitions for adults are less severe and restrictive than in past decades, and many more occupations are considered to be acceptable for women than has been so in any previous peacetime period. (Women are encouraged to fill male jobs during wartime.) Yet sex-role prescriptions for children, and especially for boys, remain highly traditional. It is only later in life that people feel more free to express their individual interests and that strict sex-stereotyping of attitudes and interests breaks down (Nash & Feldman, 1981). Children who defy cultural sex-role prescriptions may be excluded from play groups.

Teachers' Expectations

Teachers are often the first to notice a child's problem and to label it as deviant. They do so with amazing frequency. In a study of 1366 Minnesota school children rated by at least three different teachers in different years of elementary school, only 53 percent of the girls and 30 percent of the boys were consistently rated as having *no* behavior problems (Rubin & Balow, 1978). This finding suggests that only a very narrow band of behaviors is considered acceptable in the schools. Children who do not fit into this limited range are classified as presenting problems. The idealized expectations teachers sometimes hold regarding children's behavior may lead them to pressure children to meet unrealistic standards. Problems are the predictable result.

The school system and the curriculum pose difficulties for many children. Intelligence test scores are good predictors of children's school grades. The approximately 50 percent of children who have IQ scores lower than 100 will probably have difficulty in acquiring basic academic skills, such as reading, composition, and mathematics. The lower the child's IQ, the less able the child is to deal with the school curriculum. Poor school performance often makes the child anxious and depressed, creates tension with parents, draws negative attention from peers, and may lead to truancy and other types of undesirable behavior. Thus, pressures for adequate academic achievement may cause emotional problems in large numbers of children who lack sufficient ability, who have a limited command of English, or who have specific learning disabilities in such basic areas as reading or mathematics.

In addition to limitations imposed by intellectual capacity, cultural factors may contribute to school problems. Conflict and misunderstanding may result when children from one cultural group enroll in the educational system of another culture. Teachers complain that their traditional instructional methods are ineffective with children from ethnic minority groups and with the children of the poor. Then, rather than developing more appropriate teaching methods and materials, educators too often abandon the effort as futile and blame the children's cultural background or low income status for their school failure. Because of the repeated frustration of school failure, cultur-

ally different children may withdraw from school, or may remain enrolled but cease trying to succeed. Some become resentful and hostile toward their teachers (Rosenfeld, 1971). School becomes a misery for these children, and their achievement levels are dismal.

This depressing scenario is not inevitable, however. Some ethnic groups such as Orientals so prize scholarship that parents demand and get extremely high levels of effort from their children. In contrast to the 6 hours of homework per week completed by black males and 8 hours per week by whites, male Asian-Americans do an average of 12 hours of homework each week ("Asians in College," 1986). In this case, extra effort seems to compensate for cultural and linguistic differ-

---

BOX 1-5 • Learning to Teach Native Hawaiian Children

For many years native Hawaiian children had adapted poorly to schools, and their achievement had been extremely low. However, researchers at the Kamehameha Early Education Program, or KEEP, have devised new teaching methods that have transformed these children into industrious, eager, and successful learners (Jordan & Tharp, 1979). How was this possible? KEEP researchers first studied modern Hawaiian culture very closely, then attempted to incorporate Hawaiian elements into the children's school curriculum. When the children enter the KEEP kindergarten, they are welcomed by an affectionate, demonstrative teacher who hugs, praises, and smiles at them like their familiar "auntie." This behavior builds emotional ties between the children and the teacher and sets the stage for learning.

Since Hawaiian children have a strong peer and sibling orientation, instruction takes place in small groups to allow much interaction. A child moves often from place to place within the classroom, working with a changing group of one to six children at each location. The atmosphere is informal, but the children are busy learning school material.

Finally, the investigators discovered a Hawaiian practice that engaged the children actively in speaking, listening, and problem solving. This is the "talk-story," in which a group of friends joins together to create or recall a story (Watson-Gegeo & Boggs, 1977). In the school setting, about five children join the teacher in reading a text silently. Then the teacher begins asking questions about the characters' motives and feelings, the outcome, other details of the story, and the children's personal experiences related to the theme of the story. The children respond spontaneously, noisily, and enthusiastically to this familiar custom. In contrast to their listlessness and inattentiveness in the traditional classroom with large, teacher-oriented classes, the children are active and happy learners. They are now achieving above national norms, an outcome that few previously thought to be possible.

Sources: C. Jordan and R. G. Tharp. (1979). Culture and education. In A. Marsella, R. Tharp, and T. Ciborowski (Eds.), *Perspectives on cross-cultural psychology* (New York: Academic Press); K. A. Watson-Gegeo and S. T. Boggs. (1977). From verbal play to talk-story: The role of routines in speech events among Hawaiian children. In S. Ervin-Tripp and C. Mitchell-Kernan (Eds.), *Child discourse* (New York: Academic Press).

ences and for lingering social prejudices. Another method for overcoming a mismatch between students' culture and the demands of schooling is to transform the nature of the school. Through a combination of generous funding from private foundation and the creative efforts of a group of educators and social scientists, an effective educational program was devised to significantly enhance the achievement of Hawaiian school children, as described in Box 1-5. White school teachers and Hawaiian children had long misunderstood each other. In fact, the children were acting as good members of their culture; they were not obstinate, nor were they uninterested in learning. When this misunderstanding was corrected, the children's school achievement levels soared. Obviously, cultural factors must be considered in framing definitions of behavior disorder.

Cultural and Temporal Differences in Definitions of Disorder

This question lies at the very heart of the study of psychopathology: Are definitions of psychopathology time-bound and specific to a particular era, or is deviance recognized regardless of temporal factors? As Box 1-6 indicates, the self-starvation of adolescent girls, which is currently considered to be pathological and is diagnosed as anorexia nervosa, once was seen as a sign of extreme and highly admired spirituality and religious zeal. It appears that recognition of some forms of abnormality appears and disappears over the centuries. There are changes in values, religious beliefs, and social practices over time, and we do not live in exactly the same culture as our own ancestors. There is commonality but not identity in concepts of deviance over time.

Definitions of psychopathology vary geographically and culturally as well as temporally. Is there a universal definition of disordered behavior shared by all cultures, or do definitions of abnormality differ across the world? A common factor is that virtually all cultures recognize some types of behavior as abnormal; for example, behaviors generally considered deviant include delusions, hallucinations, sexual deviations, *phobias* (strong,

irrational fears) (Strauss, 1979), and culturally deviant violence. However, some aspects of disorder do vary across cultures, such as which types of behaviors are considered deviant, and the frequency of particular types of deviant behavior.

As to the particular behaviors culturally defined as deviant, Eskimos label as *nuthkavik,* or crazy, people who do bizarre things such as hide in strange places, talk to themselves, drink urine, refuse to eat, and scream at nonexistent listeners. However, the behaviors in themselves do not define abnormality, since across the world somewhat different patterns of behavior are culturally defined as deviant. The highly respected Indian leader Mahatma Gandhi refused food and fasted until near death in protest over British colonial policies, and made a practice of drinking his own urine daily as a health and religious measure (two of the behaviors considered deviant by Eskimos). Yet Gandhi would not have been considered psychologically disordered in his own culture, since his behavior was recognized as principled and highly rational rather than disordered. Here is another example of culturally defined psychopathology: The Yoruba people of tropical Africa recognize as insane *(were)* people who hear voices, babble incoherently or refuse to speak, set fires in inappropriate places, and tear off their clothing (Murphy, 1976). The particular behaviors recognized as insane differ somewhat from the Arctic tundra to the African jungle, but severe psychotic reactions are recognized by both groups. Worldwide, it is the deranged quality of the person's behavior that is recognized as deviant, regardless of the particular acts engaged in that define psychopathology.

Surprisingly, the *prevalence* (frequency) of certain psychiatric disorders is higher in some areas of the world than in others. For example, clinical depression is much more common in Western countries than in non-Western societies in Asia and other parts of the world (Marsella, 1979). Depression rates may vary because of genetic factors, environmental influences, or differing definitions of depression. In contrast, certain childhood disorders such as *school refusal* (fear-motivated avoidance of school) and hyperactivity show very

BOX 1-6 • **Anorexia Nervosa: A New Disorder?**

Imagine the most fanatic dieter possible—someone who eats almost nothing and exercises vigorously and continuously. Someone who carries this regimen to life-threatening extremes while continuing to insist that she is too fat. This is a description of a young woman with *anorexia nervosa*—a condition that affects mostly females and is described more fully in Chapter 7. There are so many anorexics among high school and college students that most readers will know of at least one. Anorexia nervosa may strike as many as 1 in every 100 girls between the ages of 16 and 18 years (Bruch, 1982; Crisp, 1976). In a related eating disorder called *bulimia*, the weight-conscious person will go on eating binges in which thousands of calories may be consumed. Then, to avoid the weight gain associated with the excessive eating, she will self-induce vomiting. These eating disorders are not rare, and so it would seem that they always have been as common and as visible as they are at present. However, historical documents indicate no such disorders prior to the 19th century. Apparently our predecessors failed to recognize these eating syndromes, or such practices did not exist until recently.

Anorexia nervosa appears to have been identified as a psychiatric condition only in the late 19th century. Earlier, extreme fasting was found among female saints who were supposed to subsist exclusively on the Eucharist (the communal wafer and wine symbolizing the body and blood of Christ) (Brumberg, 1986). In addition, a few celebrated "miraculous maids" gained popular attention by seemingly consuming almost nothing for long periods of time. In contrast to modern views, these fasting women were considered to be highly spiritual, and their living without food was seen as a demonstration of divine providence, not as psychopathology. Brumberg (1986) has suggested that *secularization*, a societal transformation in recent times, may be responsible for the rise of the view that voluntary starvation represents a psychiatric disease. In secularization there is a decline in religious explanations of events, of one's own behavior, and of states of health or illness. Piety and psychopathology cannot coexist as explanations of severe fasting, and so the religious explanation may have been replaced by the secular and social one. Nevertheless, it is impossible to determine whether the early "miraculous maids" and present-day anorexics are sufficiently similar in their motivations for self-starvation, their behavioral patterns, and the course of their eating problems to say that they suffered from the same syndrome of psychopathology. Therefore, it is safest to conclude that dangerous and excessive fasting practices have long been known and that the primary sufferers have always been young women. At present these types of disorders are relatively common. Societal interpretations of the young women's fasting have varied dramatically, however, from considering them to be miraculous instruments of the divine will to diagnosing them as psychologically disturbed and in need of force-feeding in severe cases.

Sources: H. Bruch. (1982). Anorexia nervosa: Therapy and theory. *American Journal of Psychiatry, 139,* 1531–1538; J. J. Brumberg. (1986). "Fasting girls": Reflections on writing the history of anorexia nervosa. In A. B. Smuts and J. W. Hagen (Eds.), History and research in child development. *Monographs of the Society for Research in Child Development, 50* (4–5, Serial No. 211); A. H. Crisp. (1976). How common is anorexia nervosa? A prevalence study. *British Journal of Psychiatry, 128,* 349–354.

similar prevalence rates in many countries of Europe and the Americas (Granell de Aldaz, Vivas, Gelfand, & Feldman, 1984; O'Leary, Vivian, & Nisi, 1985). It is probable that regional differences in diagnostic practices account for some cross-national discrepancies in the rates of certain disorders. Psychiatrists in one part of the world and their colleagues elsewhere sometimes label the same syndrome differently, and of course official estimates of psychopathology will be low in countries and regions with very few trained diagnosticians. In most instances, however, similar mental and emotional difficulties are recognized cross-nationally, even though particular syndromes and prevalence rates may vary.

Prevalence of Serious Behavior Disorders

It is natural to wonder how many children are afflicted with psychological disorders, but it is almost impossible to provide a definitive answer to such a question. Comparing the results of different studies is difficult because they vary in their definitions of disorders, in the training of the persons making the assessment (teachers, professionals, parents, or the children themselves), and in the sex, age, and backgrounds of the children studied. Consequently, the studies are not comparable and are unlikely to yield similar results. Nevertheless, well-conducted studies of large groups of children living in the same region can provide some idea of the range of problem rates. Table 1-2 provides information on current U.S. estimates of child psychopathology. Estimates of the prevalence rates of children's problems vary with assessors' training, experience, and familiarity with the children. Those who have the least contact with children, such as school principals, re-

port fairly low rates of disorder; higher rates are reported by teachers who deal with children on a daily basis (see Table 1-2). Estimates from the U.S. Office of Education are based largely on surveys of school principals, and indicate that only 2 percent of school-age children are emotionally disturbed. The principals themselves reported behavioral problems in just 1.5 percent of the children attending their schools (U.S. Office of Education, Bureau of Education for the Handicapped, 1975). Principals probably do not know all that goes on in classrooms and playgrounds in their schools, and so fail to observe a certain amount of disordered student behavior.

In marked contrast, teachers must deal with their students for extended time periods each day and may see problems that they fail to draw to the attention of the principal or others. It is possible that the demands of managing difficult children may lead teachers to be oversensitive to deviance and to overestimate its prevalence. Amazingly high rates are generated when teachers' nominations are used to identify children with behavioral and academic problems (Rubin & Balow, 1978). Teachers judged between 23 percent and 31 percent of a large group of children to have "attitude and/or behavior problems" at some time between kindergarten and third grade.

TABLE 1-2

Estimates of Rates of Behavior Problems Among School-Age Children

Estimators	Estimated Rates (in percent)
1. School principals and U.S. Office of Education	1.5–2.0
2. National Association of Mental Health	10–11
3. President's Committee on Mental Health	15
4. Psychologists, psychiatrists, and other child-helping professionals	17–33
5. School teachers	20–33

Sources: U.S. Office of Education, Bureau of Education for the Handicapped (1975, May 16). *State education agency estimates unserved by type of handicap* (Washington, DC: Author, Aid to State Branch); R. A. Rubin and B. Balow. (1978). Prevalence of teacher identified behavior problems: A longitudinal study. *Exceptional Children, 45,* 102–111; T. J. Kelly, L. M. Bullock, and M. K. Dykes. (1978). Behavioral disorders: Teachers' perceptions. *Exceptional Children, 43,* 316–318; E. E. Werner and R. S. Smith. (1977). *Kauai's children come of age* (Honolulu: University of Hawaii Press); E. E. Werner, J. M. Bierman, and F. E. French. (1971). *The children of Kauai* (Honolulu: University of Hawaii Press); K. J. Snapper and J. S. Ohms. (1977). *The status of children 1977* (Washington, DC: U.S. Government Printing Office).

In another study of kindergartners through high school seniors, teachers perceived 20 percent as having behavior disorders, although only 2.2 percent of the children were considered disturbed enough to require placement in special classes or special schools (Kelly, Bullock, & Dykes, 1978). Highest estimates are obtained when psychologists' judgments are combined with teachers' impressions. A long-term longitudinal study of a group of elementary school children in New York State revealed that such combined judgments yielded a maladjustment rate of one-third of all children (Zax & Cowen, 1967).

The exhaustive study of all children born on the Hawaiian island of Kauai in 1955 (Werner & Smith, 1977) found that by the age of 10 years about one-quarter had behavior problems, and about 17 percent had problems severe enough to interfere with their school achievement (Werner et al., 1971). Ten percent of the children were judged to be in need of short-term mental health services, mostly for excessive shyness, anxiety, and chronic nervous habits; an additional 4 percent were judged to require long-term mental health services, largely because of their antisocial and aggressive behavior. The assessment was carefully performed by a panel composed of a pediatrician, a psychologist, and a public health nurse, who judged 14 percent of the children to have adjustment problems serious enough to warrant professional attention, and another 3 percent to require special education services because of serious reading and communication difficulties.

Official U.S. estimates of the prevalence of childhood psychological disturbance and learning problems are roughly comparable to the rate yielded by the Kauai study. Dismissing the school principals' estimates as probably too low and the teachers' estimates as too high leaves a more generally agreed-on range of 11 to 17 percent. The President's Committee on Mental Health has offered perhaps the best single estimate — 15 percent (Snapper & Ohms, 1977).

Prevalence of Academic Achievement Problems

It is somewhat easier to estimate the number of children who have academic problems than the number of those with adjustment disorders. Widely shared standards of academic performance and the availability of standardized achievement tests make it relatively easy to identify children with school achievement problems. However, many children with academic problems have emotional ones as well, so the two groups are not mutually exclusive. For example, Werner and Smith (1977) found that children with serious academic underachievement problems had *nine times* as much contact with police, mental health, and other social service agencies as did children with no academic problems. Cultural differences, poverty, and language problems contribute to children's school difficulties, so that on the ethnically diverse and impoverished island of Kauai, 51 percent of the boys and 37 percent of the girls had serious academic difficulties. In contrast, a more environmentally favored group of English-speaking Minnesota school children had rates of academic problems averaging 31 percent for the boys and 17.7 percent for the girls (Rubin & Balow, 1971, 1978). These two sets of estimates differ greatly. Selecting the one to use depends upon the similarity between the group used to derive the prevalence rate and the type of group to which one hopes to generalize. In considering impoverished groups composed largely of rural minority children, the Hawaiian statistics would be more useful, while the Minnesota figures more likely represent middle America.

Age Differences in Gender Distribution of Psychopathology

The most prevalent types of problems experienced by boys and girls differ in various age groups. During childhood, many more boys than girls are identified as having psychological problems. This is especially true for antisocial aggression, with between 4 times and 12 times as many boys as girls having this type of problem (Gelfand & Peterson, 1985). As many as 10 times more boys than girls are diagnosed as having attention deficit disorder with hyperactivity, which often accompanies aggression (American Psychiatric Association, 1980; Quay, 1979). Boys also clearly outnumber girls in the prevalence of mental retardation (2:1) and of infantile autism and childhood psychosis (3:1) (American Psychiatric Association, 1980). Boys also predominate as victims of language disorders and learning disabilities (Gelfand & Peterson, 1985). It may be more the type of problems than the number of problems that discriminates between the sexes. Boys have more trouble in controlling their impulses and aggression—the types of problems that cannot easily be ignored, especially in structured school situations. Boys also tend to have more serious problems associated with developmental delays and disruptions that require professional attention. Girls are more likely to suffer from disorders of overcontrol (e.g., phobias, social withdrawal), whereas boys exhibit more problems with undercontrol (antisocial aggression, attentional deficit and hyperactivity) (Achenbach & Edelbrock, 1978).

In adolescence, the pattern of sex differences in psychopathology changes. Girls lose their apparent adjustment superiority over boys, and begin to develop the adult pattern of double the males' rates of affective or emotional disorders, especially those involving depression (Al-Issa, 1982b). In adolescence, too, girls begin to develop high rates of eating disorders such as bulimia (alternate gorging and vomiting) and anorexia nervosa (self-imposed starvation and compulsive overexercise), as noted in Box 1-6. Although some males also develop these eating disorders, it is estimated that 95 percent of the victims are young women (American Psychiatric Association, 1980). The swing to increased female psychopathology during adolescence may stem from heightened cultural demands for female attractiveness and accomplishment at that age, or possibly from hormonal changes associated with puberty (Al-Issa, 1982b), or from some combination of environmental and physiological factors. Certainly, the appearance of adolescent eating disorders and affective disturbances suggests that there are radical age-related changes in the nature of psychopathology (Gelfand & Peterson, 1985). Males continue to predominate in the disorders involving antisocial aggression throughout the life span (Al-Issa, 1982a; Eaton, Sletten, Kitchen, & Smith, 1971; Zigler & Phillips, 1960).

In adulthood, sex patterns of psychology

change. In industrialized Western countries, about twice as many women as men are treated for depression (Lewinsohn & Amenson, 1981), especially in the higher-cost treatment services. In less expensive treatment agencies, the depression rates for men and women are more nearly equivalent (Al-Issa, 1982a). When the entire range of mental disorders is considered, the sexes are approximately equally represented as clients at community mental health centers and outpatient psychiatric services, with the proportion of men being higher than the proportion of women at lower-cost facilities, such as state and county hospitals (Kramer, 1977). The only safe conclusion is that, according to available evidence, neither sex can be described as generally more plagued with psychological problems.

Predicting Future Development

Life would be much simpler, if less interesting, if we could accurately predict what sort of person a child would become. Do a girl's violent temper tantrums at the age of 3 years indicate that she will have a stormy, difficult adolescence? Will her joy in helping her mother predict that she will be a good, diligent student in school? Perhaps a curiosity about how things work will enable her to become a successful scientist, or perhaps it is just a passing phase. The research data indicate that success in long-term prediction depends largely on what one is attempting to predict. Although some aspects of future development can be anticipated, others defy prediction. We now discuss three factors to consider in attempting to predict children's long-range adjustment outcomes: developmental status of the child, changes in the child's environment, and accuracy in measuring the child's behavioral characteristics.

Developmental Status As children mature physically, socially, and cognitively, they encounter new challenges, restrictions, opportunities, and hazards. Many developmentally significant events are shared by most children; these include learning to speak, entering kindergarten, graduating from high school, and other such milestones. The developmental milestones make prediction difficult because they require children to adjust to changed circumstances. New demands are met more adequately or less so by different children, and their ability to cope with one milestone, such as kindergarten, may affect their future adjustment. Prediction is difficult because change is the essence of development. Yet, as Kohlberg, La-Crosse, and Ricks (1972) have observed, some degree of prediction is possible. Favored children who are cognitively and socially advanced can usually be expected to continue their superior adjustment in later years. The direction of development for virtually all children is from less to more advanced—physically, intellectually, socially, and emotionally—and there is relatively little backsliding. Thus, a child who has come to realize that the moon does not actually follow him as he walks, but only appears to do so, will not revert to his earlier incorrect belief.

Kohlberg et al. (1972) distinguish between *general traits,* such as intellectual capacity, ego development (self-control and general psychological maturity), and moral development, on the one hand, and "symptoms" or *discrete problem behaviors* on the other. Kohlberg and his associates view problem behaviors as temporary and relatively useless for prediction. Particular problems such as a child's jealousy of a sibling cannot be used to predict the child's personality characteristics in 10 years' time. In contrast, the more general, adaptive traits do help to predict later status, although the level of accuracy is far from perfect. Kohlberg's group maintains that the general traits of intellectual capacity, ego development and moral development are the best predictors of adult mental illness and maladjustment. The presence or absence of problems and symptoms, however, is believed to have little predictive utility (Kohlberg et al., 1972). In other words, children of superior general competence can be expected to continue their superiority, but those with specific behavior problems may perhaps overcome them. Thus, developmental changes make prediction of later adjustment status difficult but not impossible. The best predictors are broad, general capacities, such as intellectual ability or moral judgment. It should be pointed out that this view is persuasive but not conclusive. Some specific predictors, such as the presence, severity, and persistence of antisocial aggressive behaviors, do in fact correlate with long-term problems with control or hostility and aggression.

Environmental Change It is more difficult to predict long-term child behavior if there are dramatic changes in the environment than it is if life continues as usual. Such dramatic changes might include parental divorce and dissolution of the family, serious illness of a family member or of the child herself, a reverse in the family's financial fortunes, or a move to a very different social and geographical setting. Even commonplace events can prove upsetting. As an example, the birth of a sibling is often accompanied by increases in the older child or children's behavioral problems, particularly among 2- to 3-year-olds (Dunn, Kendrick, & MacNamee, 1981; Gelfand & Peterson, 1985; Moore, 1976). The preschoolers' regressive toileting problems and aggressive outbursts can set the stage for poor parent-child relations that may endure. And, as Chapter 3 indicates, parental combat and divorce can stimulate children's aggression, school problems, and other types of adjustment difficulties. Young children in particular do not take well to change, and their behavior becomes difficult to predict following major life transitions.

Measurement Accuracy Prediction is most possible with measures that are most accurate or error-free. For example, a child's height and weight, which can be very reliably measured, can be used to make useful estimates of her height and weight several years in the future. The child's adult stature can be predicted fairly well from measurements taken as early as age 3, barring major physical problems such as serious malnutrition, injuries, or other conditions that could adversely affect physical development.

One reason why psychological characteristics are difficult to predict is that they are difficult to measure adequately. Intelligence tests are carefully devised, but examiners who vary in experience, motivation, and skill in test administration may report varying IQ scores for the same child. Moreover, child factors such as fatigue, poor motivation, language problems, and illness can all distort IQ test performance. In addition, the tests themselves may vary in adequacy. Thus, there are many more sources of error in psychological measurements than in physical ones, which may simply require reading a scale or meter.

Some characteristics are more difficult to measure than others. The order of difficulty in measuring different types of characteristics proceeds from easiest to most difficult as follows: (1) physical, (2) cognitive or intelligence, and (3) personality and social. As Macfarlane (1963) has observed, physical measures taken on a child at 3 years of age are more accurate predictors of adult status than are mental (intelligence) test measures, which in turn surpass personality measures. Correlations between relative height and weight from early childhood to adulthood range from .70 to .80 (as compared to 1.00, indicating perfect prediction). The same correlations for intelligence test scores are around .40, and for personality characteristics the correlations are usually less than .40, indicating that it is extremely difficult to predict adult personality outcomes for normal children.

Prediction is better for severely deviant children. Adult intellectual status is highly predictable, although discouragingly so, for severely developmentally delayed and mentally retarded youngsters. As he becomes older, the extremely developmentally disabled child will continue to score much below average on intelligence and achievement tests. It is only within the large normal range that prediction is difficult.

Short-term prediction is more accurate than longer-term forecasts, perhaps because fewer dramatic environmental changes that are likely to affect a child's adjustment will occur between two closely spaced occasions than between two distant ones. Children change so much as they develop that different types of tests must be used at different ages. For example, infant intelligence tests assess alertness, coordination, and the following of instructions, while tests for adolescents chiefly evaluate verbal skills. Because the tests measure

different skills at various ages, it is virtually impossible to predict adult intelligence level for any but the most retarded infants. Prediction improves when tests assess very similar skills. There is a correlation of .85 between children's intelligence scores between the ages of 9 and 12 years and those obtained at 18 years, because tests at these ages are highly similar in abilities assessed. This strikingly high correlation across the ages of 9 to 18 years indicates great stability for most youngsters, although individual children may show marked changes in their IQ scores over time. In one study, a third of the children had IQ scores differing by up to 30 points on separate testing occasions when they were between the ages of 2½ and 17 years (McCall, Appelbaum, & Hogarty, 1973). Thus a child who scored at 70, or possibly retarded, on one occasion could have scored at 100, or average, on another. Such dramatic differences in IQ scores are exceptional, however. Obviously prediction becomes problematic if behavior is changeable or unstable. We cannot make long-range predictions from observation of infants, because their behavior changes so much from one observation period to another (Bell, Weller, & Waldrop, 1971). A baby who is fussy and irritable one day may be placid and relaxed the next. If it is impossible to predict the infant's reactions from one day to the next, it is also impossible to predict the future.

Then there is the problem of making a precise individual prediction from averages obtained from a group of children. Sometimes we can predict relatively well for most members of a group, but not for the individual of interest, who may be quite different from the others. Unfortunately, it is predictions about individuals that are needed by parents, teachers, and treatment agencies. At present, only imprecise forecasts about the futures of certain groups of children are possible. That is, data from large numbers of children with particular characteristics can be used to provide a *probability statement* about the development of other children with similar characteristics. For example, if four of each five children from a particular group have serious underachievement problems that fail to improve over time (Werner &

Smith, 1977), then we can expect that about 80 percent of a similar group of children in the same school system will also fail to improve. But it will still be difficult to predict the fate of a single child, which is our eventual goal.

Continuity in Disordered Behavior   The question of whether or not children "grow out of" deviant behavior is an important one for caretakers and researchers alike. If the answer is yes, then a child's disordered behavior should produce less cause for concern, but if it is no, then help is necessary. The child development literature presents two possibilities. One, the *continuity hypothesis* (Lewis, 1965), is that adjustment status is relatively stable. That is, maladjusted children continue to be maladjusted as they grow older. Either their original problems persist or new ones develop, but in either case there is a poor prognosis (expected outcome) for children with problems. The more optimistic *growth hypothesis* is that children have an extraordinary capacity to overcome their problems. With development come increasing experience and greater intellectual and social skills, which may enable people to overcome childhood problems. If the continuity hypothesis holds true, then children's behavior problems

should persist; however, if the growth hypothesis is correct, then children's problems should be transitory and not predictive of adult adjustment difficulties. The following examination of research findings may indicate which viewpoint is the more accurate.

Persistent Characteristics   The type and severity of a problem are related to its persistence. As we have stated earlier, specific problem behaviors tend to be less persistent than are general attributes such as social and intellectual competence. Table 1-3 shows some of the more enduring academic and social characteristics, both desirable and undesirable, and others that tend to change over time. Research data indicate that children who are socially outgoing and self-confident are likely to remain that way into adulthood, and that those who are determined to master skills of any type, whether athletic, academic, artistic, or mechanical, continue to be achievement-oriented as adults. The older studies showed that children who preferred traditionally sex-typed activities remained more strongly sex-typed in adult pursuits. There is insufficient research evidence to determine whether there is continuity in level of sex-typing in today's changing world.

TABLE 1-3
Persistence of Childhood Characteristics

Persistent characteristics
  Self-confidence and sociability
  Intellectual interests, achievement motivation in various activities
  Preference for sex-typed rather than opposite-sex activities
  Obsessional, recurrent thoughts
  Developmental disorders such as autism, psychotic reactions
  Highly aggressive, antisocial, illegal, defiant behavior
  Academic underachievement and other school problems
  Poor relationships with classmates
  Negative self-image, strong inferiority feelings, tension, physical complaints
  Marked mental retardation
  Severe or numerous adjustment problems

Transitory, nonpermanent characteristics
  Shyness and social withdrawal if not severe
  Anxiety, fears, and phobias, except for agoraphobia (terror at leaving the house), which is more persistent
  Chronic nervous habits such as nail biting
  Sleeping disturbances and eating problems, except for obesity or anorexia (self-starvation), which persist

Regrettably, some negative characteristics are as persistent or even more so than the more desirable ones. Both *retrospective studies*, which examine the past histories of disturbed adults, and *prospective studies*, which follow the development of groups of children, have provided information on the persistence of various child characteristics. Sometimes the nature of the problem behaviors changes somewhat over time, although a child continues to have adjustment difficulties. For example, one study (Maziade et al., 1985) found that children who were rated as having difficult temperaments at age 7 had more clinical psychiatric disorders when they were 12 than did children who were easier to manage. The difficult-temperament children came from less well-functioning families, also, so it is impossible to determine whether genetic factors or environmental ones produced their long-term adjustment disadvantage.

Sometimes very subtle childhood differences help in predicting long-term psychiatric adjustment status. Researchers have spent many years attempting to identify the childhood precursors of adult schizophrenia, which accounts for so many psychiatric hospitalizations. No childhood symptom syndrome resembles adult schizophrenia very closely, and prediction of who will become schizophrenic has proven difficult, except that children of schizophrenics are at heightened risk of later developing the disorder. Some risk studies have revealed that children of schizophrenic parents have subtle problems in attention and information processing, but other research has failed to confirm these findings (Watt, 1986). To date, the only variable that clearly places a child at increased psychiatric risk is having a schizophrenic parent, although it is not known why this is so.

Research has revealed that children who are highly disturbed (e.g., psychotic) continue to be very deviant and developmentally delayed throughout their lives. As children they lag behind developmentally, never mastering normal speech, social skills, or even appropriate self-care and toileting skills in severe cases. In addition, psychotic children may exhibit uncontrolled tantrums and assault others or injure themselves, often appear-

Even such profoundly disturbed children as Noah (on the left, see Box 1-7) can enjoy themselves at times. Noah is shown here in a pleasant interaction with his nondisturbed brother. Relatively normal behavior such as this gives parents hope that their very developmentally delayed children will overcome their handicaps.

ing nearly totally unresponsive to other people. The more severely psychotic the child's behavior, the poorer the outlook, especially if the child's IQ is very low (50 or less) (Bartak & Rutter, 1975). If the developmental delay and psychotic reaction appear within the first several years of life, the child may be diagnosed as autistic, and the chances are only one in four that the child will ever improve appreciably (Bartak & Rutter, 1975). Such cases are rare, but each one is tragic; Box 1-7 presents excerpts from the diary of a father of a severely disabled brain-damaged or autistic boy. The diary portrays the agony of parents who realize that, despite all of their hopes and efforts, their son is failing to improve and may not be able to remain at home. Most severely retarded or psychotic children eventually must be institutionalized because their parents cannot pro-

---

BOX 1-7 • **Living with Noah**

December 4, 1971

Foumi [Noah's mother] had a good day with Noah, teaching him to put out his tongue. And touch his nose. The only problem is that as he learns a new thing he proceeds to forget the last thing he learned. Leaky, freaky kid, head moving from side to side as he continually sings the gibberish song of himself.

September 13, 1974

When Noah came home from school yesterday he ran out into the middle of the street to lay down. Foumi tried to drag him back onto the sidewalk. He kicked her in the stomach so hard that she doubled over in pain. She has been in tears all evening, not only from the physical hurt but also from the spiritual one.

Yes, the time has come to separate Noah from us. Oh that we could part from him irrevocably. . . .

September 20, 1974

I've spent my love on Noah. I know it's an existential situation, that I should enjoy him as long as I can, but I've turned the corner. I dread the future more than any pleasures I can possibly derive from the present.

September 22, 1974

Another bloody weekend. On Saturday I tried to go shopping with Noah. He sat himself down in the middle of the street and would not move. On Sunday we took him to the cat show. Again the same thing: he would sit down and not move whenever the whim hit him. He is harder for me to handle physically, impossible for me to deal with any longer spiritually.

July 1, 1975

We never all quite had breakfast together this morning. But a moment came when Noah, draped over the golden love seat in his color-coordinating yellow Charlie Brown pajamas, lis-

---

Source: J. Greenfeld. (1978). *A place for Noah* (New York: Holt, Rinehart and Winston), pp. 32, 180, 183, 232, 294–295.

---

vide the continuous, exhausting, and intensive care they require.

We all remember some child from our past who was the least popular, most despised member of the class. Most children are relieved to find that someone else will play that uninviting role—the butt of the jokes, the one excluded from play groups, the rejected one. Unfortunately, such outcast status is sometimes not shed as the years pass. One study found that children who were nonpreferred by classmates and who were also highly aggressive and immature were likely to remain rejected over periods of a year or more (Bu-

kowski & Newcomb, 1984). Being rejected by other children at one time period was not predictive by itself of future social standing, but the addition of aggression and immaturity added greatly to the stability of peer rejection. That is, being aggressive and acting immaturely increased children's chances of remaining unpopular rather than becoming more acceptable to age-mates over time. Similarly, popularity with peers was found to be more stable over time if the popular children were also seen as cooperative and as leaders than if they were considered to be disruptive and aggressive (Coie & Dodge, 1983). These

Box 1-7 (Continued)

tened to us sing "Happy Birthday" to him. He shyly rose when we reached "Stand up. Stand up. Stand up and show us your face," and ran into Foumi's arms. So it was tear time again at the sentimental Greenfelds'.

November 8, 1976

Noah has taken to moistening the tips of his fingers with his tongue—as if he were about to turn the page of a book—and then touching a wall, a surface, an object, or a person instead. It's a habit he picked up from one of his day-care classmates and it annoys me greatly. Yesterday he did two other things that upset and frightened me:

I was watching television in the den. I thought Noah was in the living room. When suddenly he attacked me from behind, scratching at my face, clawing at my throat, and going off in a painful yowl himself after I beat him off.

Later, at dinner, for no discernible reason he turned to me and pulled my hair. I can only suspect that on both occasions he suddenly had a pain—a toothache, for example—and he was reacting to it, assigning me the cause of it, and hence also the source of possible alleviation.

Both incidents frightened me. Not physically but psychically. I do not look forward to a future in which he could overpower me.

Josh Greenfeld has recently published a book describing life today with an older Noah. The fears of Noah's parents came true, and they eventually found that they were no longer able to care for their son at home. His mother has developed arthritis and his father has heart disease; neither their health nor their marriage could survive Noah's continued failures in toilet training, his extreme moods, and his destructive rages. Now 20 years old, Noah lives in a residential group home and is visited frequently by his parents and brother. It is clear that he never will grow up mentally, socially, or emotionally, despite the best psychological and medical care. His father says "With Noah, you think of the old Pearl Buck line—a continuing sadness that never ends."

Source: J. Greenfeld. (1986). *A client called Noah: A family journey continued.* New York: Henry Holt.

research findings suggest that even the less severe antisocial, aggressive tendencies may portend continuing adjustment problems for children.

Highly antisocial tendencies can be remarkably persistent. When children constantly are in trouble because they start fights, defy teachers, lie, steal, and assault people verbally and physically, they often continue to be troublesome as they become older. Highly aggressive behavior is especially difficult to control if it occurs frequently and in more than one setting, such as at home as well as at school. Also, antisocial behavior tends to continue if the child displays a number of dif-

ferent types of aggression (e.g., fighting, stealing, lying, and cruelty), rather than confining himself to just a few different types of aggressive acts, and if his problematic aggression begins before the age of 15 years (Loeber, 1982). If a boy meets all of the preceding criteria, his chances of continuing his antisocial aggression are very high. However, with increasing age the nature of the aggressive behavior changes, and public confrontations decline while covert activities such as stealing and vandalism become more common (Loeber, 1982).

Children whose academic work is significantly below their capacity (as measured by their IQ scores) are likely to continue to be underachievers as they grow older. Four out of five of the Kauai study children who were underachievers in elementary school continued to show significant academic underachievement throughout secondary school (Werner & Smith, 1977). In adolescence they engaged in increasing absenteeism, sexual misconduct, and problems with the police. Nearly all of those who became deviant in adolescence had earlier academic difficulties or social adjustment problems by the age of 10 years. Other investigators (Robins, 1966) also have found that becoming a delinquent in adolescence is predicted by earlier poor peer relations, work below capacity in school, and conflicts with teachers. In general, poor adjustment to the academic and social demands of school forecasts future problems in establishing and maintaining harmonious relations with others.

The handicap of mental retardation may or may not persist over the years, depending upon its severity. When they become adults, mildly retarded children may score within the dull-normal range rather than the retarded range on intelligence tests. Many of them hold jobs and perform better vocationally than might be expected from their childhood intelligence test scores (Sparks & Younie, 1969). In contrast, the more severely retarded rarely improve significantly and may require continuing supervision in sheltered workshops and institutions. The prognosis is especially poor for children with IQ scores of 50 or lower. Many of the low-scoring group can acquire basic eating, toileting, and self-care skills, and can learn simple, repetitive jobs, but few become capable of independent living.

Some mild and ambiguous childhood problems are significantly but not strongly related to later difficulties during adulthood. Young adults with psychosomatic problems (e.g., peptic ulcers, asthma, migraine headaches, or high blood pressure with no apparent physical basis) were found to have childhood histories of feelings of inferiority, complaints of tension, and numerous vague physical complaints (Stewart, 1962). Further research is necessary to test the stability and strength of these relationships.

To conclude, it appears that future prospects are brightest for children who are bright, work hard, achieve in school, and are popular and cooperative. This is not surprising, of course, but the persistence of meanness and antisocial aggression is a bit less expected. In fact, early, frequent, and varied antisocial aggression is highly predictive of continuing problems in self-control. In general, the outlook is worst for children with two types of problems: (1) severe or intense psychopathology, as in serious autistic or psychotic reactions, uncontrollable aggression, severe retardation, or developmental delay; and (2) a large number of problems, especially after the age of 5 years (Macfarlane et al., 1954).

Shyness is usually a nonpersisting characteristic, and some shy children, like this little girl, grow up to become fearless and assertive adults.

Nonpermanent Characteristics Many childhood problems either diminish or disappear over time. For example, extreme shyness and social withdrawal are certainly a source of concern for parents and teachers, but in most cases these problems neither persist nor precede other types of adjustment difficulties. Approximately 70 percent of such problems disappear as the child becomes older. The same is true for chronic nervous habits such as nail biting and hair twirling, and for food finickiness and sleep disturbances. Strange food preferences and aversions are often overcome, but overeating and resulting obesity are likely to persist (Berg, 1970). Eating finickiness is more socially acceptable in children than in adults, so many people adopt more conventional eating habits as they grow up. In the same vein, most childhood fears dissipate with age, even the severe ones called phobias (Agras, Chaplin, & Oliveau, 1972; Macfarlane et al., 1954), as we describe in Chapter 4.

SUMMARY

In past centuries, children were cruelly treated by today's standards. Many were abandoned, sent into the care of wet nurses as infants, and ruthlessly exploited by employers. However, it is impossible to determine whether they were more disadvantaged psychologically than children are now. Only recently have there been special education classes and psychological treatment services. The 19th-century social reform movement produced juvenile courts, special education services, and treatment programs, first for delinquents and ultimately for children with various types of problems.

Several criteria are used to determine whether a child's problem is truly deviant and worthy of clinical attention: when the behavior is inappropriate for the child's age, gender, or sociocultural group, or when the problems are intense and persistent. Children may be misdiagnosed when they confront unrealistically high adult standards or when they are judged by the standards of a different culture. Approximately 15 percent of school children suffer from behavior disorders serious enough to merit special treatment, and as many as one-half of boys and one-third of girls experience significant academic achievement difficulties.

Some types of problems persist. The severely developmentally disordered, severely mentally retarded, and psychotic all continue to have significant problems as they mature. In addition, academic underachievement is difficult to remedy, and severely antisocial behavior of early onset tends to persist, although the type of aggressive behavior engaged in changes with increasing age. The more enduring positive characteristics include sociability, self-confidence, achievement strivings and a work orientation, and general social and intellectual competence. Many mild social and emotional problems do not persist. For example, fears and phobias, shyness, social withdrawal, and nervous habits all tend to abate with time. The answer to whether a child will "outgrow" a problem depends on many factors, including the age of onset; the type, severity, and persistence of the problem; the presence of additional problems; and, as Chapter 14 describes, the availability of an effective treatment intervention.

chapter

2

Explanations of Child Behavior Disturbance

KEY TERMS

Cognitive Development.   The growth of intellectual functions, such as memory, reasoning, planning, and problem solving.

Diathesis-Stress Hypothesis (or Vulnerability-Stress Hypothesis).   The view that psychopathology arises from a combination of some pre-existing physical or psychological vulnerability and some later physical or psychological stress.

Parsimony.   Simplicity. A criterion for judging theoretical explanations specifying that if theories are otherwise equivalent, the simpler one is better.

Psychoanalytic Theory.   Any theory in basic agreement with Freud's view that psychopathology derives from unconscious psychological conflict.

Reinforcement.   Occurrence of any stimulus that increases or maintains the rate of a preceding behavior. Positive reinforcement serves as a reward and increases the behavior it follows, while negative reinforcement increases behavior by removing an aversive stimulus (avoidance).

OVERVIEW OF THE CHAPTER

The ultimate question in the field of child psychopathology is why one child develops disordered behavior while another does not. This challenging question has no final answer at present, although there are many competing explanations of the etiology of childhood psychological disturbance. This chapter reviews and evaluates some of the most influential explanations of abnormal behavior, including the psychoanalytic approach, learning and cognitive theories, the humanistic model, and some of the basic physiological models of psychopathology. We present criteria for evaluating theories and then describe the major theories of behavioral deviance. Since no single account deals with all disorders equally well, we describe the types of disorders each theory explains best and least well.

Why Do We Need Theories?

The study of theories of human functioning can be a course's high point for students with a lively curiosity and an abstract turn of mind. Such individuals are rare, however, and many readers plod through the pages on theories dutifully while they long to read dramatic accounts of exotic disorders and their treatment. It would be a mistake to dismiss the material on theories of psychopathology prematurely, though, because even misguided or out-of-date theories have a beauty of their own. To develop a theory, someone has thought long and hard about some facet of human experience, and has tried to present a logical, consistent, powerful, convincing, and perhaps even elegant account of the phenomenon. As the descriptions of the major theorists presented in this chapter reveal (see the Boxes), they are a group of very human and highly intelligent visionaries with a fascinating range of interests and some peculiarities.

Since no one knows precisely why most psychopathology develops, many different explanations are possible, ranging from an appeal to witchcraft to molecular activity. When fully elaborated, these guesses are conceptual models or

theories of psychological deviance. A theory provides a general explanation for a variety of related events or behavioral patterns. A theoretical model is based upon a set of stated assumptions and attempts to fit research and clinical observations into a comprehensive and convincing account of psychological processes. In the study of child behavior disorders, for example, a theory might explain why troubled parents so frequently have disturbed children by suggesting a genetic or a learning mechanism for the transmission of problems from one generation to the next. The theory organizes what is known about some aspects of behavior, and goes beyond simple description to offer an explanation of the causes of the behavior.

How to Judge a Theory

Evaluating theories is not easy, because each one is highly complex and has subtle implications. A number of criteria are typically used to determine whether theories meet formal standards of acceptability. Epstein (1973) has offered six criteria for the evaluation of theories of human social behavior: the theory's extensiveness, parsimony, empirical validity, internal consistency, testability, and usefulness. Scientific theories have long been judged by these particular characteristics, which can be used as a guide for assessing the theories to follow.

Extensiveness   The more general and inclusive a theory, the better, if all other characteristics are equally good. However, it is much easier to construct theoretical models of limited types of psychopathology than it is to develop an all-embracing theory covering many types of disorders. Many different theories may be formulated for the different disturbances, each featuring its own causal mechanisms and unique explanations. The resulting hodge-podge of competing, contradictory minitheories will prove confusing and difficult to work with. A better alternative is to devise a more general explanation suggesting a common cause for many problems. A broader theory is preferred when it can explain the same phenomena nearly as well as several more limited ones.

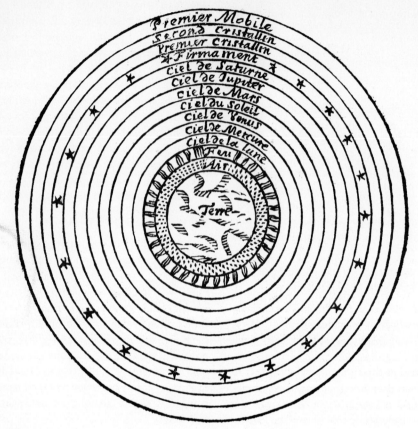

COSMOGRAPHIE.   *161*

Premier Mobile
Second Cristallin
Premier Cristallin
Firmament
Ciel de Saturne
Ciel de Jupiter
ciel de Mars
Ciel du Soleil
Ciel de Venus
Ciel de Mercure
Ciel de la Lune
Feu
Air
Terre

Ptolemy was a Greco-Egyptian astronomer of the 2nd century A.D. who represented the earth as the stationary center of the universe, with the other heavenly bodies revolving around it. In order to account for astronomical observations, this clever but incorrect model was made more and more complex, with planets moving in small circles, called epicycles, whose centers revolved around the earth. The system became unwieldy and was replaced by the much simpler, correct Copernican system.

Parsimony   Simpler, more elegant theories are preferred to unnecessarily complex ones. Simplicity or parsimony makes the theoretical model less cumbersome and easier to apply. Kepler's famous model for the movement of the planets provides a dramatic example of the attractiveness of parsimony. Kepler's explanation of planetary movement was much simpler than Ptolemy's older one. Ptolemy assumed that the planets moved in highly complex concentric circles around the earth. With many adjustments, and assuming the existence of paths of circles within circles, Ptolemy's model could be made to work, but it was cumbersome and unwieldy. Kepler's revolutionary assumption that the planets revolved around the sun in elliptical circuits simplified astronomers' calculations dramatically, reduced calculational errors, and ultimately proved more accurate. The parsimony of Kepler's theory increased its acceptance and led to the rejection of Ptolemy's model. More parsimonious explanations are generally preferred, but only if they account for the observations as well as more complex theories, or nearly so. There are no such striking examples in psychology, because psychological theories usually do not cover precisely the same behavioral domain and so cannot be compared on the criterion of parsimony alone.

Empirical Validity   Scientific theories should be solidly based on established facts. To be valid, a theory must correspond with the facts as revealed in controlled scientific observations. Perhaps it would be wise to recall, however, that there are fashions in types and topics of scientific research; yesterday's "facts" can turn into tomorrow's pseudoscientific fables. For example, some early psychologists firmly believed that their measurements had established that head circumference was highly related to intelligence. Big heads were supposed to indicate powerful minds. This "fact" was based on faulty laboratory procedures, however, and poor science can never legitimately be used to confirm theoretical conjectures.

The most crucial test for a theory is its support from controlled observation and experimentation. A problem in the social sciences is that researchers and theorists sometimes disagree on the nature of acceptable evidence more often than do most chemists, biologists, and physicists. Some psychological theorists accept informal case reports and introspective accounts of one's own thoughts and feelings as evidence on which to base and test a theory. Others insist on evidence in the form of publicly observable and precisely measured occurrences, as is the case in the natural sciences.

Because theories go beyond the available evidence in their explanations of behavior, subsequent research may find a theory's predictions to be incorrect in some respects. Kuhn (1970) has noted that theories account for data for a while, but eventually inexplicable results are reported. When such empirical contradictions arise, theories are typically modified or replaced in a fashion that Kuhn describes as a *scientific revolution*. As Epstein (1973) observed, "No theory, whether a scientific theory or a self theory, is ever completely valid. The most that can be hoped for is that it will be self-correcting" (p. 409). When too many exceptions or corrections are required (e.g., hypothesizing a maze of circular paths for the planets), a theory's popularity will decline in favor of a new and dramatically different approach.

Internal Consistency   A good theory is logically consistent. The conclusions drawn from one set of theoretical assumptions and propositions should not contradict the conclusions drawn from other parts of the theory. This apparently simple axiom can be difficult to achieve in practice when complex human behavior is being explained. The various assumptions and predictions of a model should fit together into a coherent whole. Theorists use research in order to reconcile possible contradictions in their models and to account for discrepant data. Research findings indicate whether theories are internally consistent or not.

Testability   Some psychological theories (such as Freud's psychoanalytic theory) are not amenable to controlled empirical testing. Freud's theory has withstood the test of time, but in general, testable theories are preferred to ones that are not. If we cannot test predictions drawn from a theory, then it cannot be scientifically verified or refuted, which brings its usefulness into question. Although children's misbehavior may be explained by causes such as demonic possession or violating cultural taboos, such explanations are not scientifically useful if they are untestable (see Chapter 11 for a discussion of scientific method). Scientific procedures are exact; favored beliefs and hypotheses must be abandoned if careful observations contradict them.

Usefulness   Theories are developed in order to solve problems. Psychological theories are expected to explain and predict behavior. A theory of child psychopathology should help us understand children's problems and should eventually lead to the prevention and treatment of behavior disorders. The more obviously useful a theory is, the more proponents it will have among clinicians who work with children. Theories that do not prove useful are gradually replaced by those that do. In general, preferred theories stimulate the creation of new research techniques and areas of study, and they promote the discovery of new knowledge (Thomas, 1979).

THEORIES OF NORMAL DEVELOPMENT

Theories of child deviance must also consider the processes of normal growth and development. There is no single view of normal development to serve as a gauge for assessing childhood abnormalities. Rather, theories of human development vary along certain specific dimensions:

1. *Model of development,* varying from the *organismic,* in which the child is viewed as an active, highly complex, organized entity whose properties or components cannot be examined in isolation, to the *mechanistic,* which systematically and painstakingly examines the effects of different stimuli and events on each of the child's subsystems (for example, anxiety level, aggression, beliefs about altruism, learning of algebra, and so on) (Reese & Overton, 1970).

2. *How development takes place.* Is the process presumed to be continuous, by small increments of growth, or discontinuous, as in the stages or periods of Piaget's and Freud's theories? Is change presumed to be qualitative (so the child thinks and reacts quite differently at different points in development) or quantitative (so the child can solve new and more complex problems because of accumulated knowledge, rather than because of a new and more mature form of thinking)?

3. *Influence of early experience.* Do traumatic early experiences doom a child for life, or can they be later overcome? The psychoanalytic theories in particular credit great power to early experiences in determining the course of personality development, whereas the learning theories maintain that present events primarily direct behavior.

4. *Child characteristics versus environmental characteristics as determiners of behavior.* Some theorists such as Freud attribute psychopathology

more to aspects of the child's own nature than to external events. At the other extreme, behaviorists and learning theorists assign major importance to observable precipitating events in the child's home and school. Each of the theories reviewed in this chapter can be viewed as occupying some point on each of the preceding dimensions.

Piaget's Theory of Cognitive Development

To illustrate what is meant by developmental theories, we now review the broad outlines of perhaps the most influential developmental approach, Swiss psychologist Jean Piaget's conceptualization of cognitive development. Then we briefly describe its applicability to some aspects of education and clinical psychology.

Piaget's and other developmental theories (1) trace the transformations that take place in a person over a lifetime, but particularly during childhood and youth; and (2) attempt to explain how people remain identifiably the same but also may change radically in some respects as they grow older (Cairns & Valsiner, 1984; Gelfand & Peterson, 1985). Cognitive developmental theories such as Piaget's deal largely with the intellectual rather than the social or pathological aspects of development. Piaget's theory attempts to explain the general developmental sequence in thinking and problem solving stimulated by children's self-directed explorations. This approach stresses children's initiative in seeking out and analyzing new experiences, rather than passively reacting to them.

In encountering a new phenomenon, children can *assimilate* the novel happening into their pre-existing concepts or *schemas,* or they can adapt and *accommodate* their schemas and learn something new. Good examples of assimilation occur when children play and use one object in place of another—for example, using a playmate's head as a drum or a stick as a sword. In contrast, accommodation is most noticeable when children imitate the actions of others. Many actions contain elements of *both* assimilation and accommodation, which are different but not incompatible processes. Children pass through a sequence of cognitive stages, beginning in the *sensorimotor phase,* in which babies begin to appreciate that objects remain the same even when they are hidden briefly, change speed or direction, or undergo some other change in appearance. In the next phase, *preoperational* thought, the young child begins to use language and other symbolic processes. Then, in the *concrete operational* phase, the older child begins to solve tangible or nonabstract problems, such as whether a clay ball (which is shown to the child) gains or loses mass when it is reshaped to present a different visual appearance. Finally, in the mature *formal operations* phase, the young adult solves abstract problems in a systematic, logical manner.

It now appears that stages are much less general and inclusive than Piaget thought. In fact, as they encounter different quandaries in varying settings, children usually think in a manner representative of several different levels or stages, and not of just one (Flavell, 1963; Gelman & Baillargeon, 1983). Thus, an 8-year-old may recognize that the volume of water remains the same when poured into one type of new container, but be unable to solve the same problem when a differently shaped container is used. Despite these limitations, Piaget's basic approach appeals to many developmental psychologists because of his perceptive observations of children's problem solving and the theory's predictive power. Inspired by Piaget's work, Kohlberg (1969, 1981a) has developed a detailed theory of the development of moral reasoning. This widely accepted approach has led to formulation of educational curricula featuring discussions and group resolutions of moral dilemmas. Such interactions are intended to promote prosocial, mature reasoning about values conflicts (Kohlberg, 1981b), although there is little research support for the effectiveness of such educational programs.

Nevertheless, of all the theories described in this chapter, Piaget's is perhaps the least utilitarian. Piaget himself repeatedly denied any interest in individual differences, child psychopathology, or special education, where his work might be applied. Undeterred, many psychologists and educators have applied Piaget's concepts in practical

work such as the construction of intelligence tests (Elkind, 1976; Phillips, 1975), and in planning the sequence and grade placement of mathematics and science concepts in school curricula (Thomas, 1979). In recent years, the *developmental psychopathology* movement (Cicchetti, 1984; Sroufe & Rutter, 1984) has urged the necessity for incorporating developmental principles such as Piaget's into the study of child psychopathology. Developmental psychopathologists have advocated a wide-ranging, interdisciplinary study of the etiology and course of individual patterns of behavior adaptation, such as mental retardation and hyperactivity. This group is especially sympathetic to the views of Piaget, and also to the ethologists, developmental neurologists, and physiologists. Thus the extent of Piaget's intellectual heritage has not yet been completely traced.

THEORIES OF CHILD PSYCHOPATHOLOGY
Freud's Psychoanalytic Theory

Sigmund Freud's is the single most influential personality theory of the 20th century, affecting such diverse fields as psychiatry, medicine, social science, history, literature, and art. His work has dramatically altered our views of the nature of childhood, parent-child relations, and human nature in general. And yet Freud (1856–1939) began as a fairly unsuccessful Viennese physician who treated people with mysterious illnesses of undetermined origin, including irrational fears, compulsive rituals such as repeated hand washing, and psychologically based paralysis and numbness of the limbs (see Box 2-1). In treating these "neurotics," Freud became convinced that their symptoms derived from unconscious psychological conflicts that were out of their awareness and beyond their control. He concluded that human motivation is basically irrational and that people are driven by powerful and relentless unconscious sexual and aggressive desires. These unconscious forces are expressed indirectly and in symbolic form in dreams, speech, and play. For

A charming photo of Sigmund Freud and his daughter Anna in Bavarian dress. Anna applied her father's psychoanalytic concepts in her writing and clinical work, which was devoted mostly to children.

example, an unconscious need to punish oneself may be responsible for a person's acting so clumsily as to get caught in deceptions, having repeated accidents, or failing in school despite superior ability. In this view, nearly all behavior has a purpose and is not attributable to chance or accident.

The following passages present a brief overview of Freud's influential theory of psychological development and the origins of behavior disorders. More extensive secondary sources can also be consulted, such as Hall (1954), Munroe (1955), and Hall and Lindzey (1978).

The Structure of Personality   In Freud's view, personality is composed of three systems: the id, the ego, and the superego, which interact to produce normal and abnormal behavior. The first system to develop is called the *id,* a primitive component of personality. The id is the primary source of *psychic energy,* which enables the person to think, perceive, dream, remember, and perform other mental work. Psychic energy originates in the two major inborn instincts: the *life instincts,* which include libido or the sex instinct, and the aggressive or *death instincts,* which work toward the individual's destruction. The id seeks immediate gratification of needs, regardless of circumstances or of consequences to the self or others. Because it strives to reduce unpleasant tension, the id is said to operate on the *pleasure principle.* "It [the id] is demanding, impulsive, irrational, asocial, selfish, and pleasure-loving. It is the spoiled child of personality" (Hall, 1954, p. 21).

No one is allowed to act in a purely selfish way, however, and the id has no existence separate from the rest of personality. The realities of our physical and social worlds prevent the immediate fulfillment of sexual and aggressive id impulses. Even the baby's hunger is not always satisfied at once. Planful action is required to satisfy one's needs, so the *ego* develops in response to the need to operate realistically. The ego operates on the *reality principle,* taking existing constraints into account in seeking satisfaction. Rather than impelling a man to snatch away someone else's food or mate or to physically attack him (as the id would urge), the crafty ego postpones action until the time is right or directs him to engage in more socially appropriate behavior, such as requesting the food, asking a woman for the pleasure of a dance, or criticizing instead of physically assaulting the other person. The ego serves as the decision-making or executive branch of personality. It must deal with the demands of the infantile, impulsive id; it must take reality factors into account; and it must simultaneously serve a third, equally demanding system of the personality, the superego.

The *superego* represents the person's harsh, internalized moral code. It derives from the child's idea of the strict, unforgiving parents, and it drives the person to try to meet unattainably high standards in controlling the sex and aggression instincts. The superego is the last structure of per-

---

BOX 2-1 • About Sigmund Freud

His mother's favorite, the young Sigmund Freud was determined to achieve fame and prestige. Only the field of medicine promised such rewards to an Austrian Jew in the late 19th century, so Freud entered medical school hoping to become a noted research neurologist. He was successful in neurology, but exciting discoveries eluded him. When it appeared unlikely that he would become so outstanding that he would obtain a secure academic position in neurology, he entered medical practice and began to treat patients suffering from psychologically based paralyses and other nervous disorders.

With Joseph Breuer, Freud developed a treatment method in which patients achieved relief from symptoms by talking about them. Freud went on to develop the method of free association, requiring patients to say whatever occurred to them, however irrational or embarrassing. From the study of patients' free associations, Freud became convinced there was a sexual basis of emotional disorders. This notion earned him a reputation among his medical colleagues as an irresponsible sensation-seeker, but Freud managed to attract a handful of like-minded associates and the psychoanalytic movement began to grow.

In over 40 years of work, Freud did achieve the fame he hoped for. He attracted and broke with a number of well-known followers; he conducted an extensive self-analysis; he developed a theory of human behavior; and he devised the psychoanalytic treatment technique that is still in use a century later. Today Freud stands with Darwin in his impact on modern concepts of the nature of the human being.

Source: E. Jones. (1953–1957). *The life and work of Sigmund Freud* (3 vols.). (New York: Basic Books).

---

sonality to develop and stems from the child's learning and acceptance of his parents' strictest, idealized standards of conduct. Only morally perfect behavior is acceptable to the superego, which punishes the ego with guilt even for thinking about satisfying the id's demands, whether or not they are carried out. Freud viewed the id, ego, and superego systems as separate but interacting portions of the personality and not as miniature, antagonistic persons. Nonetheless, his vivid descriptions give readers the impression that autonomous personalities are at work. For example, here is what Freud said about the predicament of the ego: "Thus the ego, driven by the id, confined by the superego, repulsed by reality, struggles to master its economic task of bringing about harmony among the forces and influences working in and upon it; and we can understand how it is that so often we cannot suppress a cry: 'Life is not easy!' " (Freud, 1933/1965, p. 78).

Psychoanalysis maintains that great portions of the personality are at work outside of the individual's conscious awareness. Freud devised a diagram similar to that shown in Figure 2-1 to illustrate the relative domains of the ego, id, and superego. As the figure shows, each system is at least partly unconscious in the adult psyche, and an even larger share of the personality of the child is unconscious.

Anxiety and the Defense Mechanisms
Anxiety is painful, so we attempt to reduce it by any means, whether realistic or not. *Defense mechanisms* represent unrealistic methods by which the ego reduces unbearable anxiety. Because they are less powerful and experienced than adults, children tend to rely on *denial*—one of the most primitive, least realistic of the defense mechanisms. Children may simply deny the existence of unpleasant facts such as being displaced in the parents' favor by a new sibling, and may act as though the upsetting event had never happened. Older children cannot so readily ignore reality, so they may use *repression* to defend

relationship of id, ego, and su-
her and to conscious, precon-
cious states.

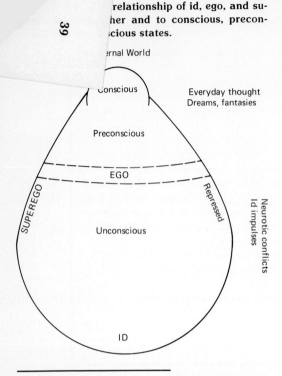

Source: Reprinted from *New introductory lectures on psychoanalysis* by Sigmund Freud, translated and edited by James Strachey, by permission of W. W. Norton & Company, Inc. Copyright © 1965, 1964 by James Strachey. Copyright 1933 by Sigmund Freud. Copyright renewed 1961 by W. J. H. Sprott.

against anxiety. Repression involves the forgetting or pushing from awareness of objectionable impulses or perceptions. The impulses and thoughts still persist, but the child remains unaware of them. For example, a boy may repress his hatred and jealousy of his father, but his hostility continues and is expressed indirectly in the form of abnormal behavior.

The ego's other defense mechanisms include *projection,* which is denying one's own hostile or sexual impulses but attributing them to others, and *reaction formation,* or the concealing of one type of feeling by expressing its more acceptable opposite. In reaction formation, a boy who hates his father may appear to be overly loving and highly dependent on his father instead, or a resentful housewife may smotheringly overprotect her children.

In *fixation,* anxiety is relieved through the failure to progress and grow psychologically or respond flexibly; the child remains "fixed" at a certain level of development without further maturation. Such fixations must be overcome if the child is to progress psychologically. If the threat is too great, the person may *regress* to earlier, less mature states. A child under stress may mentally construct a dream world complete with protective imaginary companions. In these and other ways (discussed by A. Freud, 1946), the person attempts to reduce the threat of utter panic stemming from unacceptable impulses.

The Stages of Psychosexual Personality Development Freud believed that much of adult personality is formed during the first 5 years of life. During early development, pleasant sensations that Freud called "sexual" are focused on different parts of the body or erogenous zones. First, prior to and during weaning, the *oral* area of the mouth and lips is the major source of gratification for the infant. At this time, either overgratification or frustration can produce a *fixation* at the oral stage, which is thought to result in lifelong character traits such as dependency and to lead to later dependence on tobacco, alcohol, and other types of "oral" activity. Freud believed that a baby weaned too harshly or another who is overindulged may develop a characteristic tendency to be acquisitive or greedy, not only for food, but possibly later for possessions and love. Next, the *anal* stage appears in the second year of life, when the anal area supposedly becomes the focus of pleasurable stimulation. Toilet training occurs at this time and can help determine later personality traits, such as overeagerness to please others by producing products such as projects, art, or books. By contrast, frustration in the anal stage may produce a person who is compulsively neat, stingy, and unable to complete projects. Freud metaphorically relates the production of feces in toileting to personality traits of producing or withholding objects and creative products.

At about the age of 4 or 5 years, the *phallic* stage begins, and the child's sex organs and genital area become the primary focus for gratification. The child's experiences at this time are believed to be of extreme importance in psychological development. This is the time of the *Oedipus complex*, when the child is supposed to become sexually attracted to the parent of the opposite sex, much as the ancient Greek mythical hero Oedipus did to his own mother. The little boy feels sexual rivalry toward his father and fears his father's retaliation by castration for having sexual feelings toward his mother. To relieve his anxiety, the boy is presumed to *repress* his incestuous desire for his mother and his hostility toward his father by *identifying* closely with his father and trying to be as much like him as possible. In this way, the boy reduces anxiety, possesses the mother at least vicariously through his bond with the father, and forms a masculine sexual identity. Failure to resolve the Oedipal conflict can result in a wide variety of psychopathologies, such as phobias (irrational fears of objects reminding the child of the father) or psychologically based visual, motor, or speech problems. The resolution of the Oedipus complex results in the formation of the superego, which Freud supposed to be stronger in the boy than in the girl. Consequently, males were presumed to be more moral and more principled than females—a view not held by contemporary psychoanalysts. Freud maintained that a girl believes that she was originally a boy who was punished by castration. As a consequence, the girl suffers from *penis envy* of males and unfulfillable sexual desire for her father. Psychoanalysts attribute many older children's and adults' psychological problems to unresolved Oedipal feelings.

After the drama of the Oedipal crisis, the child enters a time of psychosexual inactivity called the *latency* period. This period lasts from approximately 6 years of age to adolescence, and serves as a psychologically quiet time during which the child's energies can be directed to intellectual and academic development and to peer relations. At puberty, the person enters the *genital* stage. This is the final developmental period, marked by a mature sexual attraction to members of the opposite sex that continues throughout life.

Evaluation of Freud's Psychoanalytic Theory Despite its long history, Freud's is still perhaps the best known of all the psychological explanations of human conduct. Before Freud, most people believed that children lacked sexual interests and that adults generally behaved rationally. Freud changed these fond beliefs with his concepts of childhood sexuality, of psychological causes of disturbed behavior, and of the existence of unconscious motives and conflicts. Moreover, as Chapter 14 and Box 2-1 describe, Freud contrib-

TABLE 2-1
Evaluations of Major Theories of Child Behavior Disturbance

Theory	Criteria					
	Extensiveness	Parsimony	Empirical Validity	Internal Consistency	Testability	Usefulness
Psychoanalytic	High	Low	Debatable (see text)	Low	Low	High, as indicated by the number of clinicians using it
Skinner's learning approach	High	High	Debatable (see text)	High	Moderate to high	High, especially in clinical and educational settings
Bandura's social learning theory	High	High	High	High	High	High, but has been used with limited range of clinical problems thus far
Rogers's theory of the person	High	High	High	High	High	High, especially in counseling and clinical psychology

Note: Because of their number and diversity, physiological explanations of abnormal behavior are not included in this table.

uted a major approach to the study and treatment of emotional disorders.

Yet Freud's work has been criticized on several counts. As Table 2-1 indicates, Freud's and subsequent psychoanalytic theories are extensive, and have been found useful by a number of therapists over the years. Nevertheless, psychoanalytic theories are less internally consistent and less parsimonious than competing theories. There are persistent complaints about the nontestability and lack of rigorous research support of psychoanalytic propositions. Psychoanalysts claim that clinical accounts from case studies and the experience of a personal psychoanalysis sufficiently verify Freud's work, while opponents question the validity of such scientifically uncontrolled and subjective investigation procedures. Other psychoanalysts have regretted the emphasis on sex and aggression in Freud's theory of personality development, and have suggested that it is possible to attend more to the less conflicted and more rational aspects of the psyche.

Erikson's Psychoanalytic Ego Theory

During the second half of the 20th century, psychoanalytic writers have turned to *ego theory*, which has stressed the more social and less irrationally dominated factors in personality (Hartmann, Kris, & Loewenstein, 1947; Rapoport, 1951). This is an optimistic account of human development that features harmony more than conflict and offers the possibility of psychological growth throughout life. Erik Erikson, a German-born American psychoanalyst, developed a stage theory that extends through adulthood and portrays a continuing interaction between social and biological factors in personality development (Erikson, 1963). Freud concentrated on the study of individual psychiatric patients, whereas Erikson wrote about the development of the healthy personality in the broader culture. In addition, Erikson pursued the theme of *ego identity,* or the individual's healthy solution of *identity crises* associated with each psychosocial stage of growth. The individual's interaction with the social environment produces a progression of eight major psychosocial crises, each of which must be worked through in order to achieve psychological health (ego identity). These psychosocial crises are presented in Table 2-2.

Some of Erikson's psychosocial stages correspond to Freud's stages, at least in their ages of occurrence, while others do not. Note, in particular, that Erikson's stages extend to much later age ranges than do Freud's. Although the stages are labeled as though the two alternatives are absolute opposites (for example, trust versus mistrust), this is not what Erikson had in mind. Rather, he believed that most individuals can be placed somewhere between the opposite poles of each scale. Thus we all have some trust of others and some mistrust. The mother's handling of the feeding situation can determine how trusting the infant will be, and her mishandling can lead the baby to be wary and produce some permanent scar. Sim-

Erik Erikson, a contemporary psychoanalyst who maintained that personality development continues through the lifespan. His explanation of identity formation during adolescence has been particularly influential.

TABLE 2-2

Erikson's Psychosocial Stages

Stage Name	Age	Description
Basic trust versus mistrust	Year 1	The infant learns to trust or mistrust the mother and others.
Autonomy versus shame and doubt	Year 2	At the time of toilet training, the child learns independence, self-control, and self-esteem or hostility, compulsivity, and low self-esteem.
Initiative versus guilt	Years 3–5	At the resolution of the Oedipal conflict, the child develops initiative and competency or guilt and inability to function.
Industry versus inferiority	Before puberty	The child realizes his abilities through work or sloth and inferiority.
Identity versus role diffusion	Adolescence	The adolescent's successful resolution of the identity crisis yields comfort and good adjustment or the opposite.
Intimacy versus isolation	Young adulthood	The young adult chooses between love and marriage or loneliness.
Generativity versus stagnation	Maturity	The adult chooses children and interests in others or selfish self-interest.
Integrity versus despair	Old age	The elderly person feels pride in her life or despair.

Source: E. H. Erikson. (1963). *Childhood and society* (2nd ed.). (New York: Norton).

ilarly, a very good, trust-building infancy may dispose a person to rely comfortably on herself and others in later years. Autonomy versus shame and doubt surround toilet training and the child's growing sense of independence. Good experiences lead to self-control and high self-esteem, and bad ones to problems such as compulsivity, stinginess, low self-esteem, and hostility. Next comes the time of the Oedipal conflict, the resolution of which can produce initiative in all areas of competency or guilt and inability to function. During the "latency" years prior to puberty, parents can help the child realize his abilities through industry or can fail to do so and condemn the child to feelings of inferiority.

Erikson believed that early adolescence is a particularly important period during which the child faces an identity crisis (Erikson, 1968). Body changes and changed expectations for the young person can lead to role diffusion, in which the youth is confused about who she is or should be.

Successful resolution of this crisis produces a strong sense of one's own individuality and comfort with one's place in society. The three adult stages are of less concern in a textbook on child psychopathology, so they are described here only very briefly. The first of these is intimacy and distantiation (the ability to stand up for oneself) versus self-absorption and isolation. The choices are the ability to form a mature intimacy with a partner of the opposite sex and defend one's interest as opposed to isolation and weakness. Next comes generativity (having children or otherwise looking beyond oneself to a concern with the future of the world) versus stagnation and absorption in one's own welfare, followed by the final crisis of integrity versus despair and disgust in old age. Integrity is accepting one's own life style as valid, and the opposite is disgust and despair with one's life.

Erikson's view is that the sequence and general timing of these psychosocial stages are genetically determined, but that the way a psychosocial crisis is resolved largely depends on the way the person interacts with cultural social institutions. Unfortunately, although Erikson's theory is more health-oriented and more social in orientation, it is scarcely more verifiable than Freud's (Thomas, 1979). On this vital criterion, all psychoanalytic theories fail.

Learning Theories

During the 1930s and 1940s, American social scientists such as Robert Sears, John Dollard, and Neal Miller attempted to unite psychoanalytic and learning concepts into a more comprehensive account of human development. This approach was fruitfully pursued for a number of years, but psychoanalytic explanations remained extremely difficult to translate into testable propositions, and the research results were often ambiguous or mixed (Chaplin & Krawiec, 1979). Predictably, a scientific revolution ensued, producing dramatically different learning and personality theories. One of these was Skinner's operant conditioning approach.

Skinner's Operant Conditioning Theory   B. F. Skinner's work is as natively American in flavor as Freud's was European. His grounding in empirical research and his interest in solving practical problems equipped Skinner (born in 1904) to attempt to apply the methods of natural science to the study of human behavior. Skinner was as optimistic as Freud was negative about changing human behavior, and he felt that determining the contemporary causes of behavior could lead to its successful modification:

> If we are to use the methods of science in the field of human affairs, we must assume that behavior is lawful and determined. We must expect to discover that what a man does is the result of specifiable conditions and that once these conditions have been discovered, we can anticipate and to some extent determine his actions. (Skinner, 1953, p. 6).

In pursuit of this vision, Skinner and his many followers have engaged in the *experimental analysis of behavior,* or the discovery of the lawful impact of observable environmental events on precisely defined and measured behaviors of both animals and humans.

Skinner is an experimental psychologist (see Box 2-2) who initially conducted extensive, detailed observations of simple forms of behavior, such as the bar-pressing rates of rats and the pecking rates of pigeons, in a small, well-controlled experimental chamber commonly called the "Skinner box." From this laboratory experimentation, and building upon the earlier work of other learning theorists, Skinner formulated a set of behavior principles that he presumed to apply across species. These principles primarily concern the effects of various schedules of *reinforcement* (reward that affects behavior rates) on the frequency of voluntary behavior (such as speaking, performing an action, smiling, or any other non-reflexive act). According to Skinner, such simple procedures as reinforcing a rat's pressing of a bar with food have counterparts in complex human behavior, and principles derived from the animal laboratory can be used to explain human thinking, language, classroom learning, and the development of behavior disorders.

Conditioning procedures. Skinner maintains that operant and respondent conditioning are the two basic types of learning. In most cases respondent conditioning involves purely involuntary behavior, such as salivation, release of gastric juices, or the electrical activity of the skin. However, recent work in biofeedback has shown that some apparently involuntary responses, such as heart rate, can be conditioned as though they were voluntary rather than completely reflexive. Nevertheless, most psychologists distinguish between automatic and voluntary responses and their conditioning. *Respondent conditioning* (also called classical conditioning) was studied by the Russian physiologist Ivan Pavlov (1927) and concerns behaviors elicited automatically by some preceding stimulus. For example, dogs salivate when presented with food, and can be trained to salivate to other stimuli also. Pavlov conditioned dogs to salivate to the sound of a bell by repeatedly sounding the bell just before giving the animals meat. Before the training, the salivation was the *unconditioned response,* or the animal's involuntary reaction to food. The food was the *unconditioned stimulus,* because its effects were auto-

---

BOX 2-2 • About B. F. Skinner

As a boy, B. F. Skinner (b. 1904) was fascinated by mechanical devices. To teach himself to hang up his pajamas, Skinner constructed a string-and-pulley system extending from his pajama hook to a sign reading, "Hang up your pajamas!" When the pajamas were left off the hook, the sign was automatically lowered into the middle of his door frame as a reminder. Later his continuing interest in building things led Skinner to design a light-and-sound-controlled chamber for experiments with small animals, teaching machines for classroom use, and an improved crib (the Aircrib) which maintains a comfortable temperature for a lightly clad baby.

He had initially hoped to become a writer, but when the goal eluded him, Skinner entered Harvard's graduate school in psychology. He was later to combine his interest in literature with his scientific work in writing the novel *Walden Two* (1948), which presents Skinner's vision of an ideal society run on learning principles. Skinner's writing skills are immediately evident in his forceful and persuasive books.

Skinner retired recently after teaching psychology at Harvard for many years. Still professionally active after his retirement, he has recently published a two-volume autobiography (*Particulars of My Life*, 1976, and *The Shaping of a Behaviorist*, 1979) and a highly controversial book, *Beyond Freedom and Dignity* (1971), in which he argues that freedom is an illusion and human behavior is controlled by environmental factors. The achievement of humane goals, he contends, is more likely through the development of planned societies run on behavioral principles than through the absence of planning for fear of loss of freedom. There is no more controversial or better known contemporary psychologist than B. F. Skinner. He has offered a complete, consistent, and unflattering view of human behavior—a view that may be rejected, but cannot be ignored.

Source: B. F. Skinner. (1967) In E. G. Boring and G. Lindzey (Eds.), *A history of psychology in autobiography* (Vol. 5). (New York: Appleton-Century-Crofts).

---

matic and unlearned. Both stimulus and response were called "unconditioned" because they occurred together naturally without training. After many conditioning trials in which the food was presented together with the bell, the animals responded to hearing the bell alone (the *conditioned stimulus*) by salivating (now called the *conditioned response*). Originally the bell did not cause the dogs to salivate, but after it was paired with food, the bell by itself stimulated the conditioned response of salivation.

Conditioned responses can be weakened or eliminated by repeatedly presenting the conditioned stimulus by itself, without the unconditioned stimulus. In the Pavlov example, the bell would be rung many times but never followed by meat. Eventually the dog would cease to salivate upon hearing the bell, although the natural response of salivating when presented with food

(unconditioned stimulus and response) would continue.

Some human responses, such as involuntary eye blinks and fears, may be conditioned in the same way as animal respondent behaviors. Several decades ago, the famous behaviorist John B. Watson set out to condition an infant boy named Albert to fear a white rat (Watson & Rayner, 1920). The rat was presented to the child together with a loud noise made by striking an iron bar with a hammer. Watson and Rayner believed that they had succeeded in conditioning Albert to fear the rat and similar stimuli such as furs, and their study was widely reported in textbooks. However, more recent scrutiny of their evidence has revealed that their study was so flawed as to raise grave doubts about their claimed success in conditioning the boy's fear of rats (Harris, 1979). For example, Watson's description of his procedures varied significantly over time, making it un-clear what he actually did. Other investigators were unable to replicate his work (Bregman, 1934; English, 1929), and Albert actually showed little fear of rats or other animals following training (Harris, 1979). There is little acceptable evidence that humans can acquire fears simply through re-spondent conditioning.

Most human social and intellectual behavior is voluntary or operant rather than reflexive. *Op-erant behavior* alters or operates on the environ-ment in some way. Operant behavior is not an elicited reflex under the control of a preceding stimulus, but is controlled by the events that follow it. Examples of operant behavior include actions such as gesturing, walking, dancing, marching, and reading, as well as speaking, singing, helping, hitting, and a host of other voluntary behaviors. Operant acts that produce reinforcing conse-quences become more likely to be repeated in similar circumstances in the future *(operant con-ditioning)*. What is reinforcing for a person at one time (for instance, food or praise) may not be so at another time, and what one person finds rein-forcing may be ineffective for another or might even be aversive. So the identification of reinforc-ers is a purely empirical, observational search to find something that is effective for each person on each occasion. Some generalized reinforcers, such as money and praise, are widely effective. How-ever, even these stimuli are not invariably rein-forcing, since praise from the wrong people or de-livered at the wrong time can be repugnant. Perversely, a child may find adults' scolding to have reinforcing properties, simply because it ne-cessitates attending to the child. This means that scolding may paradoxically increase the rate of the child's misbehavior. Unusual reinforcer pref-erences can be examples of deviant behavior.

In Skinner's view, much deviant behavior is maintained because of reinforcing consequences, such as the special attention it draws. Even the schizophrenic patient shouting gibberish on the street corner may eventually cease if there is no audience. Operantly conditioned deviant behavior can be eliminated through *extinction,* in which cus-tomary reinforcement is withheld. For example,

parents may stop responding to their 5-year-old daughter's use of baby talk and only reply to her when she speaks in a more age-appropriate fash-ion. Because her parents' attention is reinforcing, the little girl will choose to speak appropriately to maintain it. Preschool teachers make use of rein-forcement and extinction procedures when they praise the behavior of children who are behaving well and ignore aggressive or immature acts.

Attempts at extinction may be unsuccessful if the behavior receives even occasional intermittent reinforcement. Ferster and Skinner's (1957) ex-haustive analysis of the effects of different sched-ules of intermittent reinforcement revealed that under some schedules pigeons would peck thou-sands of times for a single grain of food, and would continue pecking until exhausted when the food was withdrawn during extinction. Similarly, human aggression or bizarre psychotic behavior that has been maintained on very intermittent re-inforcement schedules may be highly resistant to extinction. These intermittent reinforcement ef-fects make some types of abnormal behavior ex-tremely difficult to change.

Superstitious behavior. Operant behavior can be produced by misperceived rather than genuine reinforcement contingencies. Whether its delivery is planned or accidental, reinforcement will increase the rate of preceding behavior. Skin-ner inventively presented some pigeons with reg-ular but unearned food reinforcement, regardless of their behavior. They could have been looking up, turning to the right, or lifting a foot just before the food was automatically delivered. The results were startling. The birds acted as though they had been reinforced for bizarre behavior. Some devel-oped wing-flapping routines; others turned in cir-cles, strutted, or raised their heads, despite the fact that reinforcement was delivered every 15 seconds regardless of what they did.

Skinner termed such behavior *superstitious* because it had no real effect on the delivery of reinforcement. Superstitious behavior does not produce reinforcement, but the illusion of a rein-forcement contingency can significantly affect what an animal, or perhaps a person, does. Su-perstitious rituals abound in human behavior. Children ensure their mothers' health by refraining from stepping on sidewalk cracks. Athletes swear by the power of "lucky" shirts, necklaces, and warm-up rituals, and in a certain number of instances these superstitious acts appear to succeed. A rain-making ritual may be followed by drought relief, particularly if it is carefully timed. Knocking on wood does not produce good luck, but may precede it. There are many more such examples of superstitious behavior in all human cultures. In fact, human superstitions may prove more resistant to extinction than animal ones, because engaging in culturally prescribed rituals will draw the reinforcing approval and support of other people, whether or not it has other beneficial results.

Punishment and negative reinforcement. Two procedures discussed by Skinner are often confused, although they are quite distinct. *Negative reinforcement* increases the rate of the behavior it follows exactly as positive reinforcement does. In negative reinforcement, the reinforced action removes an aversive stimulus and so becomes more likely to be repeated. For example, when Mark's loud stereo (an aversive stimulus for his parents) blares on hour after hour, his father may get angry and begin to shout at Mark to turn it off or have it taken away. If Mark is wise, he will remove the aversive stimulus of his father's threats by turning down the stereo. This is an example of negative reinforcement. Similarly, the father's shouting reduces the unpleasantly loud teenage music, and so is reinforced and is more likely to be repeated in similar situations in the future. In contrast, *punishment* is the delivery of an aversive stimulus following some action. Spanking Mark or depriving him of some privilege for playing loud music would be examples of punishment.

Skinner views negative reinforcement and punishment as less effective in improving a child's behavior than is giving positive reinforcement for good behavior. Negative tactics merely remove some annoyance, but do not teach the child how to behave in a desirable manner. In contrast, positive reinforcement is provided only for appropriate behavior and does indicate how best to behave. Skinner deplores the widespread use of punishment. He considers punishment less useful than reinforcement because its effects can be unpredictable and are little understood. Skinner and many others believe that punishment is used too freely and is often ineffective in deterring people from misbehaving. On the contrary, punishment creates resentment and invites retaliation. Skinner prescribes the use of positive teaching methods wherever possible.

Evaluation of Skinner's psychology. B. F. Skinner is perhaps the most controversial psychologist of our time. Revered by many as a humane, perceptive, and wise thinker, he is reviled by others as cold, unfeeling, mechanistic, and naive. Whatever his ultimate place in the history of psychology may be, Skinner has had tremendous influence in the fields of education, child rearing, and the treatment of disordered behavior. Many of the behavior therapy procedures discussed in Chapter 14 and elsewhere in this book stem directly from the practical application of Skinner's work. His approach ranks very highly on the criterion of usefulness (see Table 2-1), and he has propounded one of the most easily understood and parsimonious explanations of behavior. A limited number of mechanisms are proposed to account for a wide range of abnormal and normal behavior.

The behavioral model is extensive, perhaps excessively so. The Skinnerian explanation for less easily observed and quantified human skills, such as language, memory, and thinking seems labored, clumsy, and unconvincing. Critics such as linguist Noam Chomsky (1959) have contended that in dealing with topics such as language, Skinner has been vague and imprecise, and that one cannot meaningfully speak of simple stimuli and responses in analyzing complex grammatical structures. Skinner may have gone too far beyond laboratory observations and known facts in his attempt to apply conditioning concepts to language acquisition (Marx & Hillix, 1979). Ironically, it has been in the treatment of the complex and ill-understood syndrome of infantile autism that Skinner's work has seen its most impressive application (see Chapters 10 and 14). Skinnerian psychologists have made great strides in the treatment of the mentally retarded, psychotic, conduct-disordered (antisocial), withdrawn, delayed, and physically handicapped. Skinner's work has been highly generative in inspiring others to extend or to attempt to discredit his efforts. Some have viewed his learning principles as of limited utility in explaining complex human abilities. For example, Bandura (1977) has criticized Skinner for failure to deal appropriately with people's impressive cognitive and self-regulation abilities. The next theory we discuss attempts to integrate learning, cognition, and social factors in the explanation of human behavior.

Social Learning Theory To what extent can people control their own behavior and determine the basic course of their lives? Social learning theory holds that humans' impressive mental abilities allow us to exert more control over our own conduct than is the case for animals. An individual's *interpretation* of an event is the chief determinant of her reaction to that happening. For example, being called on to answer a question in class can be a welcome event, a matter of little importance, or a public humiliation, depending on the student's preparation and interpretation of the teacher's reason for singling her out. Thus, it is helpful to know a child's interpretation of a teacher's behavior in order to predict her reaction. The social learning position maintains that taking such cognitive processes into account should improve prediction of people's behavior beyond the level possible from knowledge of external events alone. This emphasis on reasoning and interpretation has led Mischel (1973) to term this approach a *cognitive social learning* conceptualization of human behavior, and Bandura has referred to it as *cognitive social theory.*

The theory is considered to be social because of its focus on interpersonal influences in the development of aggressive and prosocial (helpful) behavior, sex-typing, observational learning, and self-regulation. Unlike psychoanalytic approaches, the social learning formulation shuns the idea of general traits (e.g., generalized stinginess, hostility, dependence, conscientiousness) and of the clash of opposing impulses and constraints within

the personality. Like the Skinnerians, the social learning theorists have emphasized the impact of *current* life events in directing behavior (Mischel, 1976). As people and circumstances change, the person's behavioral responses change. Consequently, most people are not invariably kind or aggressive, but alter their behavior depending upon their companions, resources, current psychological state, and the provocation present. A person's own *skills* and *competencies* also affect what actions he will take (perhaps being helpful in this situation depends upon some acquired skill such as swimming or cooking), but behavior is determined by current factors rather than by childhood experiences, as psychoanalytic theory maintains.

There have been many major contributors to the social learning viewpoint (e.g., Miller & Dollard, 1941; Rotter, 1954; Mischel, 1968), but at present the best-known and most comprehensive account is that of Albert Bandura. Bandura (see Box 2-3) believes that most human learning involves thought rather than simple conditioning. In his early collaborative work (Bandura & Walters, 1963), Bandura pointed out that humans are remarkably adept at *observational learning* (also called *imitation, modeling,* and *vicarious learning*). When we teach a child to speak, we do not go through a laborious process of waiting until the infant happens upon each correct sound and then administering reinforcement; that would take forever. Instead, the child simply listens to people speaking around her and imitates their language as best she can. Some praise may be used to inform the child that her speech is correct, but external reward is largely unnecessary. Many key skills are acquired through imitation alone.

Children imitate only some of the behavioral sequences available to them, and Bandura (1977) has outlined the factors that determine whether observers later imitate the actions of a model. These steps are as follows

1. **Attending to the model's demonstration. Of course, inattention deprives an observer of crucial information on how to act.**
2. **Mentally encoding and remembering the behavior. A faulty memory of what was**

BOX 2-3 • About Albert Bandura

Albert Bandura was born in 1925 in a small town in northern Alberta. After completing his earlier education in the only school in town, and before entering college, Bandura worked on a road crew repairing the Alaska highway. As he described it, "Finding himself in the midst of a curious collection of characters, most of whom had fled creditors, alimony, and probation officers, [Bandura] quickly developed a keen appreciation for the psychopathy of everyday life, which seemed to blossom in the austere tundra" (personal communication).

After graduating from the University of British Columbia, Bandura earned his Ph.D. in clinical psychology from the University of Iowa, where the psychology program was extremely research-oriented. At that time the Iowa psychology department was predominantly influenced by the learning theories of Hull and Spencer, which caused Bandura to become interested in the application of learning concepts to clinical problems.

Both a clinician and a researcher by training, Bandura has taught at Stanford University for many years. Now David Starr Jordan Professor of Social Science, Bandura is a major social learning theorist. He has stressed the importance of observational learning in normal and atypical human development, and has made important contributions to the study of imitation, aggression, human development, behavior problems, behavior therapy, and the application of psychological concepts to the solution of social problems.

Bandura's awards and honors include election to the presidency of the American Psychological Association, and he has received that group's Distinguished Scientific Contribution award. True to his scientific beliefs, Bandura has served as an exemplary model of ethical and scientific excellence. He has influenced contemporary psychology as much as any living person.

Sources: A. Bandura. (1980, September 9). Personal communication; Awards for distinguished scientific contributions: 1980. (1981). *American Psychologist, 36,* 27–34.

---

done would prevent its emulation, so an observer must take care to encode the action vividly and accurately.

3. **Being able to perform the necessary behaviors.** One must have the requisite athletic, musical, educational, or social skills in order to imitate the model.

4. **One must be motivated to imitate the model.** That is, the observer must anticipate positive consequences for repeating the behavior if imitation is to take place.

All steps must be successfully completed, or the observer will fail to pattern his behavior on that of the model.

Causes of deviant behavior. Like Skinner, Bandura believes that both normal and deviant behavior develop from the same learning processes. Bandura has listed a number of ways in

which faulty social learning may result in behavior problems (Bandura, 1968, 1969):

1. *Exposure to socially deviant models* can teach the child inappropriate forms of behavior. Such deviant models could be found in homes with addicted, depressed, schizophrenic, or bizarre and fanatically religious parents, or in delinquent gangs.

2. *Insufficient reinforcement* could lead to extinction of appropriate behaviors, as in the case of hostile or dangerously neglectful parents failing to reinforce a child's appropriate behavior.

3. *Inappropriate reinforcement or reinforcement of undesirable behavior* can promote problem behavior. Delinquent subcultures may differentially reinforce youths' cruel and violent acts as follows:

Here is an example of what one young gang member said about a murder in which he was in-

Albert Bandura. His view that people initiate actions as well as being acted upon by their environment has changed psychology in the United States. He believes that one of the strongest determinants of behavior is a person's self-perception.

volved: "If I would have got the knife, I would have stabbed him. That would have gave me more of a build-up. People would have respected me for what I've done and things like that. They would say, "there goes a cold killer." (Yablonsky, 1962, p. 8)

This is a chilling example of the effects of the search for social reinforcement from a deviant group. Inappropriate reinforcement can also take the form of parental inconsistency. Parents can bewilder a child by violently punishing him for talking back to them on one occasion and then later praising him for sticking up for himself. Such inconsistent handling fails to teach the child to discriminate how to behave in different circumstances in order to obtain reinforcement. The irrationally treated child may come to behave unpredictably and perhaps violently because of his parents' inappropriate reinforcement and deviant modeling.

4. *Faulty respondent conditioning* of negative emotional states can derive from experiencing fear and anxiety, either directly or vicariously from observing another person. The child may develop a persistent fear of doctors through being hurt while at the doctor's office, or may be alarmed by observing a parent terrified at the thought of medical treatment.

5. *Fictional reinforcement contingencies* (Skinner's *superstitious behavior*) can exert great control over some people's behavior. Confused beliefs that household objects are dangerously contaminated by dirt can lead to compulsive cleaning and hand-washing rituals, and many other irrational beliefs may be acquired through the teachings of other people or may be self-generated. These fictional reinforcement contingencies can be even more powerful than real ones.

6. *Faulty self-reinforcement* can occur when people hold themselves to overly strict or too-generous standards. Some people maintain such exalted standards for themselves that success is impossible, so they eventually cease trying (Bandura, 1979). Others are content with nearly anything they do, be it lazy, heartless, dangerous, or illegal. Self-standards are learned from others through modeling and when we are taught by caretakers or teachers. Inappropriately demanding or highly permissive families and schools can instill unrealistic expectations and deviant self-reinforcement practices.

Self-efficacy theory. Bandura's (1979, 1981) self-efficacy theory attempts to explain the mutual interacting influences of people's self-perceptions and their behavior. *Self-efficacy* is belief in oneself—a conviction that positive outcomes of a certain type can be achieved through effort and persistence. People high in self-efficacy are convinced of their own effectiveness; those who are low in self-efficacy believe that their efforts are doomed to failure. Self-efficacy convictions can prove self-fulfilling. People who have failed repeatedly in certain situations begin to believe that they can never succeed at those types of tasks. Their pessimism leads them to avoid such situations and to dread them. Their fear and avoidance further handicaps people when they are forced to act. They do so ineffectually, and a cycle of fear and performance failure is established.

Appropriate psychological treatment can break the sequence of negative emotion and inadequate performance in several ways. The client's self-evaluation can be improved so that he faces formerly avoided situations with new confidence. His confidence leads to vigorous, persistent, and possibly more successful attempts to cope with the problem. Successful resolution of problems increases his perceived self-effectiveness even further, creating a more positive cycle of optimistic beliefs and effective behavior, as shown in Figure 2-2.

A person's faulty self-perceptions can be improved in several different ways, each varying in probable effectiveness. Chief among these is *performance accomplishment,* or actually succeeding at some difficult task. This success heightens expectations for future victories. For example, the snake-phobic person who manages to touch a snake, the shy student who asks several reasonable questions in class, and the fearful toddler who manages to go to sleep without a night-light have all learned that they have the resolve and competence to perform a challenging task. Such success is the most potent and convincing source of increased self-confidence.

Other sources of information also may be helpful at times. Observing others succeed *(vicarious success)* can also boost insecure observers' self-confidence, but not as much as experiencing one's own success does. The other person may be perceived as unusually brave, skillful, or lucky, none of which may be seen applicable to the hapless observer. People who have had problems tend to doubt their own skills until they have actually succeeded in performing a difficult task.

Many forms of instruction and psychotherapy rely on *verbal persuasion,* an even less convincing source of self-efficacy expectations than the preceding one. Readers probably have had the experience of attempting to convince a reluctant friend to engage in some feared activity, or have received such advice themselves. It does not work very well in most cases. If only verbal persuasion

FIGURE 2-2 Bandura's explanation of the mutual influences of self-efficacy beliefs and performance effectiveness before and after successful psychological treatment.

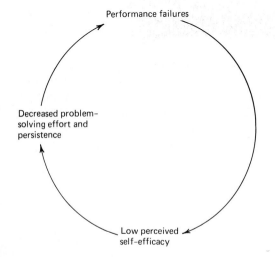

Before Psychological Treatment

Performance failures

Decreased problem-solving effort and persistence

Low perceived self-efficacy

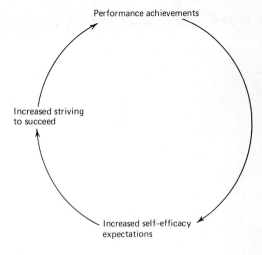

After Successful Psychological Treatment

Performance achievements

Increased striving to succeed

Increased self-efficacy expectations

and enthusiastic encouragement are used, and the recipient ineffectually tries but fails to perform the task, then the situation is worse than ever.

Finally, the person's own *emotional arousal state* can increase or undermine her expectations of success. The child who observes herself tremble at the thought of going to school may be negatively affected by her own nervousness and less able to approach the school than a less shaky student. The junior high school student who begins giving a class report with a dry mouth, quavering voice, and shaking hands does not expect to give a good speech. In observing our own emotional states, we reach conclusions about our own probable effectiveness. Extreme anxiety can interfere with many types of performance, whether in the form of stage fright, social anxieties, writer's block, or inhibited athletic performance. Anxiety reduction through relaxation training, tranquilizing drugs, or social support can bolster self-confidence and increase the chances of success.

Evaluation of social learning theory. Social learning theory ranks very high in utility, making it popular among experimentally oriented clinicians. The social learning approach offers explanations for the source and maintenance of both normal and abnormal behavior and has yielded some effective treatments (see Table 2-1 and Chapter 14). Many research studies have demonstrated the usefulness of social learning formulations. In their influential textbook on theories of learning, Hilgard and Bower (1975) concluded: "In broad outline, social learning theory provides the best integrative summary of what modern learning theory has to contribute to solutions of practical problems" (p. 605). But other critics have pointed out that most of the supportive evidence comes from highly controlled, artificial laboratory studies, rather than from confirming observations of everyday life (Stevenson, 1983). The degree of correspondence between laboratory and naturalistic study findings appears to be high, but it is not perfect, leaving the theory's validity in some doubt. This is a persistent question with all of the theories we consider in this chapter. Many are carefully devised and elaborated and appear intuitively appealing, but they may not be

valid models of human development and psychopathology.

Social learning theory is adequately internally consistent, and it is comprehensive. It draws together cognitive psychology, social-psychological concepts, and learning phenomena in the explanation of normal and deviant behavior. Some Skinnerians have charged that it is too broad, ambitious, vague, and loosely conceptualized. Biglan and Kass (1977) have suggested that it would be safer and more conservative to refer to the specific procedures used (e.g., expectancy ratings or experimental instructions) and to the behaviors they affect (e.g., approaching a feared object), rather than to a less precise concept such as expectancy. In defense of the social learning position, Audi (1976) has asserted that it is logically consistent to maintain that both external and internal variables affect behavior. Perhaps a procedure such as modeling produces a change in a second variable (self-efficacy expectations), which in turn causes a change in a third variable (approaching a feared stimulus). Then *both* the first and the second variables can be said to produce the behavior change. It is logically permissible, then, to speak of self-efficacy (the inferred second variable) as determining the person's behavior.

Both Skinner's and Bandura's theories are useful in predicting and controlling behavior. It is not yet clear which is superior in this respect. If both prove equally effective, then the operant formulation may be more attractive because of its greater simplicity and parsimony. The question of predictive superiority remains unresolved and requires more research. At this time, the Skinnerian conceptual model appears to have reached maturity and is stimulating few new, testable ideas (Stevenson, 1983). In contrast, the social learning approach has proved quite flexible in incorporating concepts from other branches of psychology and in stimulating new ideas and a healthy degree of controversy.

Humanistic Psychology and Rogers' Theory of the Person

Human nature is at worst morally neutral and very probably positively good. This tenet of humanistic psychology contrasts sharply with Freud's pessimistic view of human motivation and the behaviorists' neutrality, which stresses that a person can learn to be either good or bad. According to the humanists, such as Abraham Maslow (1970) and Carl Rogers (1961), we all have powerful *self-actualization* needs for continuing individual growth, greater ability to experience feelings, and accomplishing something in which we believe (Buhler & Allen, 1972). When these needs are blocked by circumstances, psychological growth ceases. The ultimate evil is deviance from the pursuit of one's potential and one's own nature. Carl Rogers is one of the most prominent humanistic psychologists, and this section features his theory of the person.

Rogers (see Box 2-4) firmly believes that people strive toward growth and self-actualization. His theory is called *humanistic* because it is concerned chiefly with human experience and the fulfillment of human potential. It is *phenomenological* because it studies conscious experience, including beliefs, values, feelings, and perceptions. People's perceptions of events (subjective

---

BOX 2-4 • **About Carl Rogers**

Of himself, Carl Rogers has written:

> I am a psychologist; a clinical psychologist, I believe, a humanistically oriented psychologist certainly; a psychotherapist, deeply interested in the dynamics of personality change; a scientist, to the limit of my ability investigating such change; an educator, challenged by the possibility of facilitating learning; a philosopher in a limited way, especially in relation to the philosophy of science and the philosophy and psychology of human values. (1967, p. 343)

A recipient of the American Psychological Association's awards for distinguished scientific contribution and for distinguished clinical contribution, Rogers was one of the first psychotherapists to devise and conduct carefully controlled research investigating the process and outcomes of therapy.

Rogers began his career as a graduate student at Union Theological Seminary because he was interested in going into religious work. However, religious doubts coupled with his lifelong commitment to individual freedom of thought made it impossible for him to profess a required set of beliefs in order to pursue a career in religion. Consequently, he entered the clinical and educational graduate program at Teachers College, Columbia University, where he studied methods of research and applied psychology. He earned the Ph.D. in 1931, then worked with abused and delinquent children several years before commencing his university teaching career. After many years as a professor at various universities, Rogers gave up traditional teaching because he believed that many faculty members held unduly rigid and punitive attitudes concerning graduate education. In contrast, Rogers maintained that courses should be student-centered and largely student-directed.

In recent years Rogers has continued to write his challenging and influential books and has served first as a Visiting Fellow and then as a permanent staff member at the Western Behavioral Sciences Institute, a center for interdisciplinary research in interpersonal relationships. Throughout his professional life Carl Rogers has stressed the importance of warmth, genuineness, and concern for others, a set of values that, if adopted widely, would surely improve our lives.

Source: C. R. Rogers. (1967). In E. G. Boring and G. Lindzey (Eds.), *A history of psychology in autobiography* (Vol. 5) (New York: Appleton-Century-Crofts).

reality), rather than the events themselves (objective reality), are the subject matter for the phenomenologist. The somewhat related *existentialist* view of philosophers such as Kierkegaard, Camus, and Sartre, and of psychological writers such as May and Binswanger, pictures humans as capable of making choices and assuming responsibility for their own destinies, even in the most restrictive environments. These conceptual roots quite naturally lead to reliance on self-report for understanding the person. This emphasis on exploring conscious self-awareness contrasts with the psychoanalysts' focus on unconscious processes and with the behaviorists' concentration on environmental factors as determining behavior.

The Fully Functioning Person Rogers based his person-centered theory on many years of clinical work with troubled people. As his clients improved, Rogers noted that they went from discontent with themselves to self-satisfaction and decreased discrepancy between their self-concepts and the type of person they wished to be. They saw themselves as coming closer to their ideal selves, and in so doing they became less defensive and more accurate in their perceptions of self and others; their relationships with other people also improved. Most important of all, the clients became more open to their own feelings of all types. Rogers described this transformation as follows:

> . . . [the client] becomes acquainted with elements of his experience which have in the past been denied to awareness as too threatening, too damaging, to the structure of the self. He finds himself experiencing these feelings fully, completely, in the relationship, so that for the moment he *is* his fear, or his anger, or his tenderness, or his strength. And as he lives these widely varied feelings in all their degrees of intensity, he discovers that he has experienced *himself*, that he *is* all these feelings. . . . He approaches the realization that he no longer needs to fear what experience may hold, but can welcome it freely as a part of his changing and developing self. (Rogers, 1961, p. 185)

The well-adjusted person accepts others as well as accepting himself, and so social adjustment improves as inner turmoil decreases.

Origin and Management of Children's Problems From Rogers's perspective, when the child's parents find some aspects of her behavior unacceptable, then the child may come to share her parents' disapproval. To ensure her acceptance, the child may deny her own socially dangerous tendencies, such as hostility toward siblings. She may demand irreproachable behavior of herself as a condition of worth, just as her parents did. She denies her hostility and projects it onto others, treating them as though they were threatening, thus creating interpersonal problems.

To improve, the child should experience *unconditional positive regard*, or whole-hearted and complete acceptance just as she is. Parents and therapists must create safe environments in which children can express themselves freely without fear of rejection. As portrayed in Chapter 14, such positive and accepting relationships free the child of the need to be shy or defiant, and behavior problems disappear.

Evaluation of Rogers's Person-Centered Theory Rogers was one of the first counselors to encourage research scrutiny of therapy process and outcome; thus in some respects his approach rates high in testability (see Table 2-1). Research shows that counseling does lead clients to speak more positively of themselves, as the theory predicts. However, it is unclear whether the improved self-description comes about through greater self-acceptance or through undetected subtle influence by the counselor, as the Skinnerians suggest. Also undemonstrated is the positive influence of heightened self-esteem on the client's behavior. Regardless of the therapeutic change mechanisms at work, Rogers's easily taught client-centered counseling methods are extremely popular with clinicians, educators, nurses, and the clergy, so the Rogerian model receives high marks for utility.

Like the other psychological theories, Rogers's explanation of human behavior is incomplete and raises as many questions as it answers. Self-actualization sounds admirable, but precisely what does it mean? Perhaps different people mean different things when they use the same humanistic term, which would be a weakness of the theory (Thomas, 1979). Human conscious experience is supremely important to Rogers's model, but the phenomenon is elusive and difficult to specify, communicate, and quantify. Consequently, one cannot really determine whether tests of the theory are adequate. Like the psychoanalytic approach, the humanistic model must be evaluated largely on the basis of personal experience and conviction, rather than by the tests of science.

Physiological Explanations of Abnormal Behavior

Some types of abnormal behavior appear to be better explained by psychological mechanisms and others by physiological activities, and each type of explanation has staunch advocates. For example, the noted and controversial scientist Linus Pauling (1962) has asserted, "Most mental diseases are molecular diseases, the result of biochemical abnormality in the body" (p. 32); according to Pauling, this abnormality usually stems from heredity, but sometimes from environmental causes. Scientists have not identified physical causes for most forms of deviant behavior, however. As research psychiatrist John Werry has cautioned, "the diagnosis of brain damage or dysfunction in the majority of children is no more than an enlightened guess. . . . even where the diagnosis of brain damage can be firmly established, there is as yet usually no way of proving that it is causally related to the behavior observed" (1979, p. 98). Despite Werry's caution, some progress has been made. For example, in Chapter 9, we describe some striking successes in identifying the genetic basis of some types of severe mental retardation.

Both psychosocial and physical factors are implicated in the etiology of many forms of psychiatric disturbance. The relative contributions of each factor vary from one disorder to another, with physical factors fairly directly causing some types of disturbance and social factors predominating in others. Down's syndrome, for example, is a form of mental retardation that has been conclusively traced to genetic abnormalities. Never-

theless, environment does make a difference in this syndrome. These children develop better in some family environments and treatment centers than in others, and more effective environmental treatments may yet be developed.

Physical causes are suspected but have not been conclusively demonstrated in other types of disturbances, including hyperactivity, autism, childhood schizophrenia, and depressive disorders. In contrast, situational origins are generally proposed for such behavior disorders as mild mental retardation, delinquency, specific fears, and anxiety disorders. It appears that the balance of psychological and physical contributors varies across the different types of disorders.

Biological explanations provide a *medical model* (sometimes called a *disease model*) of abnormal behavior, in which behavioral problems are compared to the symptoms of physical illness or malfunction. Behavioral disturbances supposedly derive from physical disease or defect, much as a fever results from infection, movement constraints from knee injury, or breathing difficulties from bronchial asthma. There is a clear biological basis in alcoholics' delerium tremens, illicit drug users' stimulant-induced euphoria, and the genetically determined forms of dementia (disorder of thought and memory) and mental retardation. In other cases, physiological causes are suspected because the disorder resembles one produced by some type of intoxication, neurotransmitter imbalance, or genetic mechanism. There have been significant breakthroughs and an even greater number of disappointments in the search for physical causes of psychological disorders.

The Diathesis-Stress Hypothesis A person may have a physical predisposition to develop a certain type of problem, but does so only under particular environmental conditions. The physical problem itself is insufficient to cause abnormal behavior, but the physically vulnerable person develops behavioral difficulties when forced to cope with stress. This has been called the *diathesis-stress hypothesis* (or the *vulnerability-stress hypothesis*) because it postulates both a predisposition or diathesis and an immediate cause (stress), which combine to produce a breakdown in psychological functioning. The stress may be emotional, as in the death of a parent, or physical, as in birth injuries or infections (see Box 2-5). In either case, *both* the predisposition and the current factors are necessary to create psychological abnormalities.

In psychological versions of the diathesis-stress hypothesis, the predisposing factors are not physical, but result from inadequate early care and early traumatic experiences. Freud, Rogers, and many learning theorists have maintained that early experiences predispose children to develop later deviant behavior. Some form of the diathesis-stress hypothesis is accepted by most authorities on psychopathology, as is indicated in most of this book.

Our knowledge of physical malfunctions as causes of abnormal behavior is at best highly incomplete. Many key physiological processes are not yet understood, and their relationship to deviant behavior is only speculative. Explanations in this field are very technical and unintelligible to nonscientists. Therefore, we limit the present discussion to a simplified outline of the role of genetics in certain disorders. The following chapters discuss biological factors in etiology and treatment as each type of disorder is considered. The next section describes one type of biological model of the etiology of psychopathology.

The Genetic-Biochemical Model   The genetic-biochemical model traces certain psychological disorders to genetic deviancies. Hereditary char-

---

BOX 2-5 • Selye's General Adaptation Syndrome

Hans Selye is one of the pioneers and leading figures in the study of stress and its effects on mind and body. In Selye's opinion, any severe mental or physical demand on the body can prove stressful. Stressors include but are not limited to high levels of pain, effort, concern, fatigue, concentration, or even sudden great success (Selye, 1982). Selye discovered that many different types of stressors are alike in their physiological impact. The body's initial and subsequent lines of defense against the effects of stress are termed the *general adaptation syndrome.* The first response to stress is the *alarm reaction,* a generalized mobilization of the body's defensive forces through increased activity of the cortex of the adrenal glands, decreased blood pressure, irregular heartbeat, decreased temperature, loss of weight and appetite, diminished muscular strength, and listlessness. There may be a rebound reaction featuring increased activity of the adrenal gland cortex after the initial shock. This leads to the *stage of resistance,* when there is an acquired resistance to the stress and a return to normal weight. But if the extreme stress persists, adaptative resources diminish and a *stage of exhaustion* is reached as "reserves of adaptation" are exhausted. Stress is now thought to be related to the onset and course of various physical and psychological disorders. The most common stress-related problems include peptic ulcers of the stomach and upper intestine, high blood pressure, cardiovascular disease, persistent anxiety, and affective (emotional) disorders such as depression. The role of stress and the general adaptation syndrome in the etiology and course of these disorders is not well understood, although it is agreed that stress alone does not account for disease. Instead, problems may stem from a complex interplay of genetics; environmental factors such as infection or injury; and additional stressors at home, in school, or on the job.

Sources: H. Selye. (1980). The stress concept today. In I. L. Kutash, L. B. Schlesinger, & Associates (Eds.), *Handbook on stress and anxiety.* San Francisco: Jossey-Bass; H. Selye. (1982). History and present status of the stress concept. In L. Goldberger & S. Breznitz (Eds.), *Handbook of stress: Theoretical and clinical aspects.* New York: Free Press.

acteristics are transmitted from parents to their offspring by means of the genes, with one of each gene pair coming from each parent. Genes are chains of molecules occurring in a longer strand of dioxyribonucleic acid (DNA), which forms the chromosome.

X-linked disorders. Each person has 23 pairs of chromosomes, one pair of which are the sex chromosomes. Females have two similar sex chromosomes, XX, with the mother and father each contributing one X chromosome. Males have XY, with the X member coming from the mother and the Y from the father. X chromosomes are large and contain many genes that determine various characteristics in the offspring. The Y chromosome is small and primarily determines the development of the male sex glands. Consequently, males are highly vulnerable to gene defects appearing on their single X chromosome. Having two X chromosomes, females may not display the ill effects of a defective gene if there is a corresponding dominant normal gene on their other X chromosome. In effect, having an extra X chromosome provides an insurance policy protecting against some genetic diseases. The less genetically fortunate males develop a number of *X-linked disorders* that are rare or absent in females, such as color-blindness or the blood coagulation deficit called *hemophilia.* Nevertheless, females can be carriers of X-linked disorders and transmit them to their children.

Box 2-6 describes a fatal X-linked disorder called Lesch-Nyhan syndrome. Figure 2-3 shows the probability of developing or carrying a disorder such as Lesch-Nyhan syndrome among the children of a genetically normal father and a mother who is a carrier. On the average, only a quarter of the children will develop the disorder, although half of the boys will. Half of the daughters will carry genes for the disorder, which they can transmit to their own children.

Genes that are located close together on the same chromosome tend to be transmitted together *(genetic linkage).* Thus since the genes for color-blindness and hemophilia are adjacent, these two abnormalities tend to co-occur (Scarr & Kidd,

---

BOX 2-6 • Lesch-Nyhan Syndrome, a Genetic Abnormality That Produces Abnormal Behavior

Fortunately only about 1 in 50,000 boy babies develops Lesch-Nyhan syndrome, for it follows a tragic course (Reed, 1975). This is an X-linked disorder affecting males only and is produced by a deficiency of an enzyme essential for purine metabolism. Parents notice that something is wrong when their baby is about 6 months old, but cannot crawl or sit unsupported, and develops scissoring movements of the legs. The baby appears quite retarded. When the child is about 3 years old, he develops persistent self-mutilation, he may bang his head repeatedly, bite his hands and lips until the blood flows, and strike out at objects and people. Curiously, such children may appear happy and pleasant when physically restrained, but scream and cry as if frightened when they are released. Their biting is so destructive and persistent that often their teeth are removed to prevent them from mutilating themselves. Nevertheless, most die before adulthood. They live out their brief existence toothless and physically restrained. A further irony is that at least a few of these children are of normal intelligence (Scherzer & Ilson, 1969), but have severe difficulties in speaking, moving, and exerting self-restraint. There is as yet no cure for this condition, but it can be detected before birth, and carriers of the disease can be identified. Thus, prevention, at least, is possible.

Sources: E. Reed. (1975). Genetic anomalies in development. In F. Horowitz (Ed.), *Review of child development research* (Vol. 4) (Chicago: University of Chicago Press) A. L. Scherzer and J. B. Ilson. (1969). Normal intelligence in the Lesch-Nyhan syndrome. *Pediatrics, 44,* 116–119.

FIGURE 2-3. The distribution of affected sons, daughters who are carriers, and normal children of a genetically normal father and a mother who is a carrier of Lesch-Nyhan symdrome, an X-linked disorder.

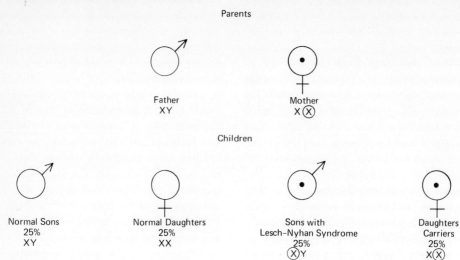

Parents

Father
X Y

Mother
X ⊗

Children

Normal Sons
25%
XY

Normal Daughters
25%
XX

Sons with
Lesch–Nyhan Syndrome
25%
⊗Y

Daughters
Carriers
25%
X⊗

1983). Furthermore, in some families, susceptibility to manic-depressive affective disorder appears to be transmitted on the X chromosome and linked to the chromosomal location for color-blindness (Mendlewicz, Linkowski, Guroff, & van Praag, 1979). Contradictory findings from other studies render this observation inconclusive, however (Scarr & Kidd, 1983).

Autosomal dominant and recessive disorders. In *autosomal* (not sex-chromosome) *dominant disorders*, the presence of a bad gene from one parent is sufficient to cause the appearance of the disorder. There is a 50 percent chance that an afflicted parent will have an afflicted child, since about half of the offspring will inherit the defective dominant gene. Each child born to the couple has a 50 percent chance of inheriting the disorder. An example of an abnormality inherited in this manner is Huntington's chorea, a tragic progressive neurological disorder that produces irrational psychotic behavior and eventually total mental and physical disability.

In *autosomal recessive disorders*, both parents must carry a defective gene, and both must transmit it to the child in order to produce the dis-

order. The children of such parents have a 25 percent chance of developing the condition. Phenylketonuria, or PKU (described in Chapter 9), is an autosomal recessive disorder causing failure to produce the enzyme that breaks down phenylalanine, a protein found in common foods such as milk. This enzyme deficit can result in damage to the central nervous system and mental retardation.

Gross chromosomal damage. Major chromosomal damage results in very serious disorders and many early spontaneous abortions (Reed, 1975; Witschi, 1971). There may be an extra chromosome; or part of a chromosome may be missing, attached to another chromosome, or completely absent. Such problems seem to occur during ovum formation or division, and are more frequent among older mothers. Down's syndrome is caused by gross chromosome abnormalities, most frequently from an extra chromosome (trisomy of chromosome 21) or some other major abnormality of the 21st chromosome pair. As Chapter 9 describes, Down's syndrome produces mental retardation and various physical deformities.

Complexities of behavioral genetics. The

types of genetic disorders described above are easily understood and detected, but others are not so straightforward. Many disorders are produced by the action of several gene pairs, rather than just one or two, and perhaps by certain environmental conditions in addition. Multiple genes are suspected to be responsible for conditions such as multiple sclerosis, cleft lip and palate, some reading disorders, schizophrenia, Tourette's syndrome, and some affective disorders such as manic-depressive syndrome. Furthermore, a person's genotype (genetic makeup) may not be fully realized in his phenotype or physique and behavior. Genes differ in *penetrance,* or the degree to which they produce observable body and behavior characteristics. Some, such as those determining eye color, are difficult to counteract by any known environmental manipulation, while others, such as those determining height, can be radically affected by environmental factors such as nutrition.

The combination of the operation of multiple genes and of differing penetrance levels makes it difficult to verify a possible genetic basis for many types of psychopathology. In addition, whole groups of genes can appear at different locations on chromosomes, making their presence and action elusive. Sometimes genetic researchers derive much of their evidence from family pedigrees revealing heightened prevalence of some disorders within particular families. Family pedigrees provide merely suggestive evidence for a hereditary basis of disorders, since families share environments as well as genes.

The psychotic reaction called schizophrenia seems to run in some families and thus may have some genetic or environmental cause, or both (see Table 2-3). Schizophrenia rates are highest in people most closely related to a person with schizophrenia—for example, among children of schizophrenic parents and those who have both affected parents and affected siblings. Schizophrenia is a serious psychotic disorder characterized by unusual, inappropriate emotional expressiveness and marked defects in logical thinking and problem solving. Researchers have attempted to untangle the effects of genetics and of family environment by examining schizophrenia rates among

TABLE 2-3
Estimated Risk of Developing Schizophrenia Among Relatives of Schizophrenics

Type and Degree[1] of Relationship to Schizophrenic Patient		Percentage of Risk
Identical twin	1.00	20.0–50.0
Fraternal twin	0.50	5.0–15.0
Sibling	0.50	
If neither parent schizophrenic		6.7–9.7
If one parent schizophrenic		12.5–17.2
Parent	0.50	4.2–5.5
Child	0.50	9.7–13.9
If both parents schizophrenic		35.0–46.0
Aunt or uncle	0.25	2.0–3.6
Half-sibling	0.25	3.2–3.5
Niece or nephew	0.25	2.2–2.6
Grandchild	0.25	2.8–3.5

Sources: S. Kessler. (1975). Psychiatric genetics. In D. Hamburg & S. Brodie (Eds.), *American handbook of psychiatry: Vol. 6. New psychiatric frontiers.* New York: Basic Books; E. Kringlen. (1976). Twins—still our best method. *Schizophrenia Bulletin, 2,* 429–433.
[1] Identical twins are genetically identical, as indicated by a 1, and unrelated people are scored 0. The values given assume that people mate randomly, but in fact many choose genetically similar mates, so the true genetic similarities are probably higher than those indicated here. Ranges are given because results vary across studies.

identical twins, who have identical genetic makeup, and fraternal twins, who do not. Family environment is assumed to be as similar for fraternal twins as for identical ones, which may not be the case. Twins who are identical in appearance are very likely to be mistaken for each other and hence treated more similarly than are fraternal twins whose resemblance is less (Kringlen, 1976). If one twin has schizophrenia, then so does the other in 25 to 50 percent of identical twins but just 5 to 15 percent of fraternal twins (Kessler, 1975; Kringlen, 1976). Some controversial research indicates that even when they are placed with nonschizophrenic adoptive parents, children of schizophrenic biological parents are at risk.

Comparing Conceptual Models

Each of the theories of child psychopathology described in this chapter has some merit and clearly derives from the theorist's own training, experiences, and skills. Freud's theory stemmed from his clinical work with highly verbal middle-class people with neurotic complaints. It does not apply easily to the retarded, to the brain-damaged, or to slum-dwellers of low socioeconomic status. Skinner's early studies of animal learning influenced his straightforward interpretation of the causes of complex human behavior, and Rogers's counseling work with unhappy middle-class adults helped to form his vision of children's needs and their proper treatment.

Each theory seems best suited to the type of problems upon which it was originally based, and extensions to dissimilar groups do not always succeed completely. Some theories of adult psychopathology seem strained when they are applied to children. For example, the humanists' belief in the power of self-actualization and the beneficial effects of nondirective counseling simply cannot be applied to seriously psychotic children or retarded or highly antisocial ones. Rogers's writings are not particularly helpful in teaching children necessary social or academic skills. Skinner's learning approach works well with the preceding groups of children, but is less helpful in dealing with crises in self-identity and other private concerns. The physiological explanations have revolutionized our understanding of some of the genetic disorders, but provide only hints about a biological cause of such major psychological disorders as depression, schizophrenia, autism, and hyperactivity. Recent achievements in molecular biology suggest that research in this area will prove illuminating and may have practical clinical significance in the future. At present, theories specialize in the explanation of particular types of behavior disturbances, and no theory adequately covers them all. An all-embracing theory probably would have to consider both physical and social contributors to problems throughout the life span.

SUMMARY

Theories provide general explanations for events such as the occurrence of abnormal behavior. Criteria for evaluating theories include extensiveness, parsimony, empirical validity, internal consistency, testability, and practical utility. In addition, developmental theories differ in their views (1) of maturation as qualitative or quantitative change, (2) of an organic or mechanistic concept of the child, and (3) of the degree to which early experiences affect development.

Freud's psychoanalytic theory views personality as composed of id, ego, and superego systems. Psychic energy for mental activity arises in the primitive, selfish id. The more realistic ego balances the id's impulses, situational constraints, and the perfectionistic superego's demands to determine behavior. Defense mechanisms help the ego reduce tension to a bearable level. Personality development can be halted or impeded by overgratification or trauma at any early stage of personality development (oral, anal, or phallic). Erikson's ego theory extends psychoanalytic models to include social and cultural factors, and provides a developmental view of the healthy personality.

The experimental, learning-based approaches of Skinner and Bandura stress the continuous contribution of environmental events in determining behavior. Skinner's operant conditioning approach sees the ultimate causes of behavior in reinforcing and punishing events. Bandura and the cognitive social learning group maintain that a degree of self-control is possible, and that both one's expectations of self-efficacy and the probability of success determine behavior.

Rogers's humanistic, person-centered theory stresses the achievement of self-understanding, self-acceptance, and self-actualization. This goal is brought about through parents' unconditional acceptance of the child and positive regard from others, which lead to the child's self-regard.

Physiological explanations speculate that genetic or other physical defects lead to abnormal behavior. Known genetic abnormalities produce X-linked, autosomal dominant, autosomal recessive, or multiple-gene disorders. Examples of known genetically based disorders are Lesch-Nyhan syndrome, Huntington's chorea, and PKU; suspected genetically based disorders include manic-depressive disorder and some speech and learning disabilities. Gross chromosome damage is known to produce Down's syndrome and other forms of severe mental retardation. The widely accepted diathesis-stress hypothesis states that both a physical or psychological disposition and some type of stress are necessary for the formation of psychopathology.

chapter

3

Social Conditions and Children's Problems

KEY TERMS

Abuse Dwarfism.   Condition beginning in infancy in which severe physical abuse causes a
failure in the secretion of growth hormone (Hyposomatotropinism), which produces
growth delay, mental retardation, and other problems.

Compensatory Education.   Educational programs especially designed to serve children
who are likely to fail to thrive in school, such as very-low-income groups.

Socioeconomic Status (SES).   Sociological term referring to a person's or family's
relative social standing in terms of formal education, income, and residence.

OVERVIEW

This chapter depicts the family factors and environmental conditions that interfere with children's
physical and psychological growth; describes their

effects on children; and suggests how such tragedies can be averted through individual, group, and
governmental action. In particular, we consider
the debilitating impact of such factors as extreme

poverty; social, racial, and religious prejudice; family discord and dissolution; and child abuse and neglect. Although these problems are considered separately, it is important to realize that they are often combined to devastating effect in people's lives. For example, discrimination is strongly associated with economic and educational victimization, poor health care, limited education, and a high rate of mental and physical disorders. It is easy for the victims of one type of socioeconomic ill to fall prey to others also, and it is extremely difficult for those at the bottom of the social ladder to make their way up to a more privileged position. Ironically, of all who suffer, it is usually infants and children who suffer the most.

Although it is impossible to pinpoint the causes of many childhood problems, we know that children exposed to *greater numbers* of adverse factors have increased chances of developing academic-intellectual retardation and behavioral problems of some sort. British studies (Rutter, 1978; Rutter et al., 1975) identified six family problems associated with children's psychiatric disorders. The family risk factors were (1) marital discord or a broken home; (2) low income, as indicated by the father's unskilled or semiskilled job or unemployment; (3) overcrowding in the home or a large family; (4) maternal depression, anxiety, or other emotional problems; (5) the child's ever having been removed from the home or placed in foster care; and (6) the father's having an arrest and court record. Surprisingly, none of these factors alone increased children's psychological problems. However, when the family had two of the risk factors rather than just one, the probability of the child's being disturbed rose *four* times. When even more risk factors were present, the child's chances of being disturbed rose dramatically. In short, when a family is poor and badly housed, and the parents are psychologically disturbed or have criminal records, then the child is at high risk of developing behavioral problems. The poorer the family's situation and the more stressful their lives, the greater are the child's chances of becoming disturbed. First and foremost among the cripplers are extreme poverty and

malnutrition, with their accompanying illiteracy, disease, and limited life expectancy. Other crippling conditions considered include environmental hazards such as lead, and social impediments such as prejudice, inadequate schooling, and child abuse.

Even under bad living conditions, some children escape psychological harm—perhaps because of genetic advantages, a fortunate temperament that allows them to withstand stress, or care provided by some nurturant adult. These children who miraculously manage to overcome handicaps such as severe child abuse or a strong family history of severe psychiatric disturbances have been rightly termed stress-resistant or "invulnerable" (Garmezy & Streitman, 1974). Little is yet known about how these fortunate children manage to escape the fate of many others in similar situations, because study of this phenomenon has just begun. Children's developmental prospects often improve markedly if their circumstances improve. Those whose parents' marriages improve are much less likely to develop behavior disorders than are children who continue to live with embattled parents (Rutter, 1978). The same enhanced prospects are true for malnourished and neglected children who are given improved diets and additional adult stimulation (Grantham-McGregor, 1984). It is encouraging to find that children who have received a poor start in life can be helped by improving their living situations. The following discussion attempts to show that many problems occur together and are interwoven into a fabric of physical and psychological disability. These situations are not hopeless, however. As each type of problem is presented, treatment and prevention possibilities are examined.

POVERTY AND LOW SOCIOECONOMIC STATUS

The poor woman having a baby may be at risk because of her age, her nutritional status, her probable poor growth, her excessive exposure to infection in the community she inhabits, her poor housing, and her inadequate medical supervision, as well as because of complex interactions between these and other potentially adverse influences (Birch & Gussow, 1970). Impoverished living conditions adversely affect children throughout development, but may have different types of effects at particular ages. The following discussion begins with prenatal life and traces poverty's influence throughout childhood.

Prenatal Development

Extreme poverty can handicap children even before birth. The statistics are unmistakable on this point. According to the U.S. Bureau of the Census (1982), only 5 percent of white upper-class infants suffer complications at birth, compared with 15 percent of low-socioeconomic-status (low-SES) whites and *51 percent* of all nonwhites (who have very low incomes as a group). This section attempts to explain some of these huge differences in infant health. Women who live in poverty are likely to begin childbearing too early and to have many, closely spaced pregnancies. Consequently, their babies may be premature, frail, and small for their gestational age (low birthweight). Undernourished babies who are small, weigh little, and have a small head circumference for their gestational age have higher mortality and sickness rates, have more congenital anomalies (birth defects), are growth-delayed in childhood, and have more neurological disorders than normal (Magrab, Sostek, & Powell, 1984). Babies can also suffer from their mothers' childhood dietary insufficiencies. Malnourishment early in their lives produces mothers who are shorter, weigh less, and are less adequately developed physically than average. During pregnancy and later during labor, these women are more likely to have complications that may damage their babies. Women who live in poverty also continue to have children long after their prime childbearing years. Mothers over the age of 40 are themselves at greater risk during childbearing, and the incidence of certain chromosomal abnormalities in the baby increases with maternal age. For example, as Chapter 9 explains, the chances of a woman's bearing a Down's syndrome child increase rapidly after the age of 30. Risks to mothers and infants are increased further because the poor often have grossly inadequate prenatal health care, which leads to higher infant and maternal mortality rates for women regardless of age. Many such women have been malnourished throughout their lives, and their inadequate diets have continued during their pregnancies. These women are subject to dangerous complications during pregnancy and delivery. Thus, the poor mother's age, medical care, past and present diet, and number of pregnancies all can adversely affect her children.

Maternal malnutrition especially endangers the baby's developing brain. These ill effects occur whether the pregnant woman is nutritionally deprived throughout pregnancy or is deprived only during the last trimester (3 months). Autopsies of U.S. babies who were stillborn or who died within 2 days after birth have revealed that maternal diet may affect the size of the baby's brain. Brains of babies of impoverished, underfed American mothers weighed 15 percent less than the brains of stillborns of wealthier, more adequately nourished women (Naeye, Diener, & Dellinger, 1969). In extreme cases, gross maternal malnourishment during early pregnancy may cause spontaneous abortion. If born alive, the baby may die in early infancy (Stein & Susser, 1976). These conditions are almost unknown in the wealthy industrialized countries, but are tragically common in portions of Africa, India, some South American countries, and other less fortunate parts of the world.

Prevention and Treatment of Early Malnutrition Dismayed by the extent of the hunger problem, many people believe that little can be done. In fact, however, modest efforts can produce major benefits for the needy. Better nutrition alone is insufficient to help malnourished children much (Beaton & Ghassemy, 1982; Joos & Pollitt, 1984), but improved diets combined with home stimulation programs have proven to produce rebound growth in the children, both physically and cognitively (Grantham-McGregor, 1984; Grantham-McGregor, Stewart, Powell, &

Severe malnourishment often results in death. This child is clearly endangered. Many of the world's children are malnourished because of maldistribution of food supplies.

Schofield, 1979). A study conducted in an impoverished Guatemalan village showed a relationship between babies' birthweights and the mothers' health care and diets (Lechtig et al., 1975). When a program of prenatal care and nutritional supplements was given to pregnant village women, their likelihood of producing low-birthweight babies was reduced from a very high 31 percent to less than 15 percent, as shown in Figure 3-1. That is, the incidence of low birthweight was decreased by over one-half! The program's benefits were most striking among the poorest of the women who had taken high levels of food supplements during pregnancy. Such special nutrition and care programs significantly benefit children who have suffered chronic malnutrition in the first few years of life, and improve the circumstances of their entire families, who become better able to help themselves (Christiansen, 1984). It is ironic that so few nutrition and stimulation programs exist when

FIGURE 3-1. Influence of caloric supplementation on relationship between socioeconomic score and proportion of babies with low birthweight. Number of cases given in parentheses.

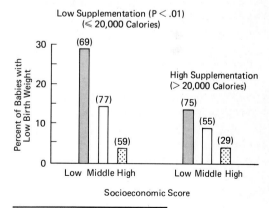

Source: A. Lechtig, H. Delgado, R. Lasky, T. Yarbrough, R. Klein, J. P. Habicht, and M. Behar. Maternal nutrition and fetal growth in developing societies. *American Journal of Diseases of Children,* 1975, *129,* 436.

they are technically and economically within the reach of most of the world's governments. Improved grains and farming methods have made many countries self-sufficient in food (such as Bangladesh), and some have actually become net food exporters (such as India). Yet political and economic forces leave significant portions of their populations starving (Schneider, 1986). The World Bank estimates that 35 million people, most of them children, die from starvation and associated diseases each year, and that 700 million more are severely malnourished (Schneider, 1986).

It is possible that raising education levels will improve infant health and survival rates. Among high-risk impoverished groups, those with the best-educated mothers have the healthiest infants. In the context of world poverty, maternal education may consist of only a few years of formal schooling, yet even this limited amount of formal education is associated with lower infant mortality and illness rates (Grossman, Coote, Edwards, Shakotko, & Chermichovsky, 1980). The better-educated women are more likely to seek prenatal care (Zill, 1983), and their children are generally healthier than the children of less-educated neighbors. We do not know why even a few years of schooling should so greatly benefit a woman and her children. The finding may be an *artifact* of some type (a result due to some extraneous factor). Perhaps there is some selection factor in education, such that the healthier and more vigorous women are more likely to receive schooling; or perhaps education provides subtle psychosocial advantages such as an interest in family health, even though incomes of the educated are no higher than those of their neighbors.

Summary To sum up, poverty is associated with high infant morbidity and mortality, and with a variety of dangers to mother and baby alike. Young and poorly nourished mothers are likely to have low-birthweight babies who are vulnerable neurologically and in other ways. Extreme prematurity and very low birthweight (1500 grams or less) endanger a baby's life. Babies who have subnormal birthweights (below 2500 grams or about

Table 3-1
Handicaps Sometimes Associated with Low Birthweight and Prematurity

Cerebral palsy
Congenital anomalies
Epilepsy
Severe mental retardation
Brain damage
Autism and other serious behavior disorders
Defects of vision
Hearing deficits
Retarded physical growth
General ill health
School achievement problems
Hyperactivity
Neurological disorders, seizures, spasticity

Source: H. G. Birch and J. D. Gussow. (1970). *Disadvantaged children: Health, nutrition and school failure.* (New York: Harcourt Brace Jovanovich).

4 pounds) and who do survive are more likely than normal-weight babies to develop serious physical, mental, and behavioral problems during childhood. Table 3-1 summarizes some of the handicaps associated with low birthweight. Children born into poverty suffer a disproportionate number of these disabilities, in part because of their greater likelihood of entering life small, ill-nourished, vulnerable, and unusually immature.

Poverty and Infant Development

The risks to impoverished children do not cease at birth. Infants weakened by malnutrition, infections, and diarrhea cry incessantly and are apathetic and unresponsive toward others. Consequently, they do not stimulate normal parenting interactions and emotional bonding (Barrett, 1984). Infants of inexperienced, economically disadvantaged mothers may receive less than optimal mothering if they are separated even briefly from their mothers after birth so that maternal bonding to the baby fails (Klaus & Kennell, 1976). However, such postdelivery separations have no apparent ill effects on babies of more experienced or higher-income, better-educated mothers (Svejda, Campos, & Emde, 1979). In addition, early health problems and ineffective parenting seem to handicap low-SES children the most. The outlook is poor for the lower-SES child who is premature or oxygen-deprived at birth (Sameroff & Chandler, 1975).

In the Kauai study described in Chapter 1, there was a heightened incidence of retardation among lower-SES children with birth complications, compared to birth-injured children of more prosperous and stable families (Werner, Bierman, & French, 1971). Among poor children, those who came from unstable families, had histories of birth complications, or had mothers with low IQs were disadvantaged. They scored from 19 to 37 points lower on an intelligence test than did poor children without birth complications or adverse family factors (Werner et al., 1971). In contrast, birth complications were associated with only a small (5- to 7-point) reduction in IQ scores for the more advantaged, higher-SES children with stable families or whose mothers had higher IQs. Premature babies of the economically secure were given good medical care and the extra attention and stimulation required to promote healthy development. This superior care enabled low-birth-weight or injured infants to thrive, despite their initial handicaps. These findings indicate that a safe, supportive, and intellectually stimulating environment can compensate for early physical damage. In contrast, a disorganized and impoverished household may further endanger poor children who have had a poor start in life.

Malnutrition and IQ   Malnutrition is particularly harmful when babies' brains are developing rapidly during the first 2 years of life. Severe protein-calorie (also called protein-energy) malnutrition during the first 12 months of life can produce mental retardation. One study found that extremely poor Mexican children who had been severely malnourished as infants had continuing problems; at the age of 5 years, the previously malnourished children had lower IQ scores than did other equally poor children who had not been starved during infancy (Delicardie & Cravioto,

1974). As described previously, the ill effects of dietary insufficiency can be successfully counteracted by a food supplement and improved care program introduced during the infant's first 6 months (Ricciuti, 1977a; 1977b; Stein, Susser, Saenger, & Marolla, 1975). Unfortunately, most such children continue to receive inadequate diets. Those who experience longer and more severe malnutrition are at greater risk of developing mental retardation than are those who are less nutritionally deprived (Ricciuti, 1977a; 1977b).

It is often difficult to determine the effects of malnutrition alone, because miseries of various types usually occur together. Malnourished children are most often raised in teeming slums with filthy water, inadequate shelter from the elements, parasites, contagious diseases, family stress, little or no medical care or schooling, and few prospects for improvement. Box 3-1 portrays the despair of Brazilian slum families as they endure the early deaths of their children.

Environmental Toxins: Lead Poisoning
Among the extra perils for American slum children is exposure to health-endangering levels of lead. About 678,000 American children under the age of 6 years (most of them from minority groups) are lead-intoxicated (Annest, Mahaffey, Cox, & Roberts, 1982; Needleman & Bellinger, 1984). High lead levels are dangerous because they damage body organ systems, including the kidneys, liver, gastrointestinal tract, and nervous system; the results include convulsions, brain damage, and mental retardation (Thurstone, Middlecamp, & Mason, 1955). Black children between 6 months and 17 years of age have blood lead levels four times greater than white children (National Center for Health Statistics, 1982). Proportionately more black children than whites live in aging slum buildings that have old lead-based paint; they also inhale leaded dust from vehicle emissions, drink water from pipes soldered with a lead mixture, and live near lead-emitting smelters and manufacturing plants. Smaller amounts of lead may produce classroom distractibility and disorganization resulting in general lowered functioning (Needleman et al., 1979). Low levels of lead may

---

BOX 3-1 • *Psychological Aspects of High Infant Mortality*

In some ways daily life in a Brazilian shantytown slum resembles that of European peasants in previous centuries (described in Chapter 1). Poor South American parents are fatalistic about high infant mortality. They may not name their babies until they are 6 months to a year old and it appears that they will live, and treat infant deaths with resignation. A psychological anthropologist Nancy Scheper-Hughes studied the attitudes toward childbearing and children of mothers in Alto do Cruzeiro, a hillside settlement of bitterly poor, displaced farm laborers. She found that the average woman had experienced 9.5 pregnancies, 1.4 miscarriages, abortions, or stillbirths, and 3.5 deaths of children younger than 5 years. (These statistics underestimate lifetime fertility rates since some informants were only 19 years old).

Like many other women around the world, Brazilian mothers dislike breastfeeding and discontinue it as soon as possible, preferring to feed their infants a less healthful gruel of cereal, milk, and sugar. With only foul and contaminated water, unprotected against parasites and infectious diseases, and given inadequate shelter and food, infants have a limited life expectancy. How do mothers cope with the probable deaths of their babies? Scheper-Hughes found that they withdraw their interest and minimize their contact with babies who appear weak or unresponsive, develop severe diarrhea, or otherwise seem to lack "the will to live." Thus, one way in which these mothers deal with infant death is not to fight the high odds against a weakened child's survival. These parents believe that fragile youngsters or retarded ones cannot hope to survive in the harsh world of the slums, so it is futile and a waste of scarce family resources to fight a baby's wish to die. The mothers told Scheper-Hughes that "if a baby *wants* to die, it *will* die." Thus shantytown parents become reconciled that what they must do out of dire necessity is what they should do because some babies are fighters and some are not.

Interestingly, these mothers also recognize that their children are being killed by their miserable living conditions (e.g., "The water we drink is filthy with germs"; "They die because we can't keep them in shoes or away from this human garbage dump we live in"). These city slum dwellers know that they must suffer miserable and unsafe conditions and they know that only the healthiest and most resolute will survive. Their explanations of child mortality reflect both what they know about health effects of their adverse physical conditions and their need to defend themselves from blame about exposing their children to conditions they cannot control.

Source: Based on N. Scheper-Hughes. (1985). The 1985 Stirling Award Essay. Culture, scarcity, and maternal thinking: Maternal detachment and infant survival in a Brazilian shantytown. *Ethos, 13*, 291–317.

---

also contribute to the development of certain forms of hyperactivity (David, Hoffman, Sverd, & Clark, 1977) and may aggravate the psychotic behavior of autistic children (Cohen, Johnson, & Caparulo, 1976). Some studies have found that small to moderate amounts of lead poisoning are associated with lowered intelligence test scores, but the relationship is not a strong one (Barrett & Zigmond, 1979; Needleman & Bellinger, 1984). Toxic wastes are increasing in children's neighborhoods, and they are harmful both physically and psychologically. As Box 3-2 shows, children are not the only victims; even famous adults have been poisoned by toxic metals.

Poverty and Child-Rearing Practices

In addition to the physical dangers imposed by their environments, many poor children receive less than optimal care. Very young and inexperienced mothers may simply not know how

---

BOX 3-2 • Historical Note on Metal Poisoning

Sir Isaac Newton had discovered calculus and the nature of white light, and later was to formulate the theory of gravitational attraction. He was the foremost scientist of his day and one of the most inventive minds in the history of Western scientific thought. But then in 1693, he deteriorated dramatically, breaking with his associates, accusing friends of plotting against him, becoming insomniac, and reporting imaginary conversations. His was not a case of simple de mentia, however, but stemmed from some laboratory work he had undertaken. He became fascinated with *alchemy* (the attempt to turn base metals into gold) and spent long nights experimenting with metal compounds, sometimes dropping off to sleep next to a bubbling retort containing a toxic mixture. The result was metal poisoning, perhaps primarily mercury poisoning. Mercury poisoning causes tremors, flaking skin, and hallucinations. Its use in the felt hat industry produced many cases of "mad hatters," inspiring Lewis Carroll's character in *Alice in Wonderland,* and mercury was probably responsible for Newton's aberrant behavior. A recent analysis of Newton's hair revealed 197 parts per million of mercury, whereas the normal level is 5.1. Nevertheless, 5 years after his bout of acute intoxication, Newton finished his *Principia,* which established the gravitational laws of the universe. Newton's case reveals the long history of metal poisoning and the diversity of its victims.

Source: W. J. Broad. (1981). Sir Isaac Newton: Mad as a hatter. *Science, 213,* 1341–1344.

---

to treat their babies. Disadvantaged teenage mothers have been found generally to be as warm to their infants as older mothers, although they may have less realistic expectations concerning their babies' abilities (Brooks-Gunn & Fursten-berg, 1986). Field (1980) found that a group of lower-SES black teenage mothers with premature babies did not know what to expect of their infants and treated them rather like dolls that could neither see nor hear but could only eat, cry, and wet. The situation was not hopeless, however. A further project (Field, Widmayer, Stringer, & Ignatoff, 1980) successfully taught such mothers about the actual abilities and needs of newborns and how to interact with them more positively. Nevertheless, the children of disadvantaged teen mothers have elevated rates of activity, hostility, and impulsiveness, and they tend to develop intellectual and school achievement problems as they grow older (Brooks-Gunn & Furstenberg, 1986). The boys are more adversely affected than are the girls.

Other groups of poor mothers are not inexperienced in child care, but are so overburdened that they have little time for it. Noisy and crowded homes may interfere with children's ability to process information, so they perform poorly on tasks requiring concentration and sustained attention (Parke, 1978). Poor children with many brothers and sisters may be deprived of the adult attention and stimulation needed for them to achieve high IQ scores (Zajonc, 1976; see Box 3-3). Impoverished households are likely to be headed by stressed and overworked parents who cannot adequately supervise or enjoy their children. The mothers may place their children in playpens or infant seats, where they receive less attention than children who are held or allowed to crawl on the floor. Even when held on their mothers' laps, lower-SES children are spoken to less by their mothers than are middle-class babies (Lewis & Freedle, 1977).

Many lower-SES children suffer intellectually from lack of sufficient parental stimulation. The more responsive, accepting, and imaginative mothers (who are more likely to be middle-class) are more successful at teaching their children skills that help them succeed at school. Moreover,

---

BOX 3-3 • Do Large Families Limit Children's Intellectual Attainment?

The Scholastic Aptitude Test (SAT) scores of the nation's youths fell markedly between 1963 and 1980, from an average of 490 to only 445. Many people found the trend disturbing and wondered about its causes. Social psychologist Robert Zajonc (pronounced "Zions") has formulated an explanation he terms the *confluence theory*. Zajonc speculates that family factors have a profound influence on children's intellectual development. Particularly important in his view is family configuration—the number, order, and spacing of siblings. Each child is exposed to a total family intellectual milieu. The family's intellectual environment is most stimulating for the only or oldest child, who interacts mostly with adults—the parents. The least intellectually stimulating home environment occurs when there are many, closely spaced children. Confirmatory research data indicate superior intellectual performance for only and older children and depressed performance for later children in large families (see Zajonc, 1986, for references). Population trends may account for students' poor SAT results between 1963 and 1980. This group came from larger families and were more likely to be later-born than those preceding or following them, which may have adversely affected their achievement levels as a group. Zajonc suggests that the continued decline in family size should produce a rise in SAT scores until the year 2000 and a possible decline thereafter.

Source: R. B. Zajonc. (1986). The decline and rise of scholastic aptitude scores: A prediction derived from the confluence model. *American Psychologist, 41,* 862–863.

---

responsive mothers provide the stimulation that enables their children to maintain or increase their IQ scores over the first 3 years of life (Bradley & Caldwell, 1978). Preschoolers' psychological development thrives in homes with the following features: (1) The mother is emotionally and verbally responsive to and involved with the child; (2) the child has appropriate play materials; (3) the mother avoids restricting or punishing the child; (4) the child's schedule and physical surroundings are well organized; (5) variety in the child's routine is provided by outings, visitors, and parties (Bradley & Caldwell, 1978). The first two of these features (the mother's involvement and responsivity, and the availability of play materials) are the best predictors of children's IQ scores at 54 months (Bradley & Caldwell, 1976).

It is much easier for privileged middle-class women to provide this type of family atmosphere than for hard-pressed low-SES mothers to do so. Lower-SES (or working-class) mothers often do not explain to children just how to perform tasks or

how to reason out problems, do not tell them the names of things, and do not positively encourage children to try to solve problems. Instead, when a child gives an incorrect response, a low-SES mother may simply indicate that it is wrong: "This is not a horse. What's this?" This type of response is much less encouraging and informative than the typical educated mother's reaction: "Well, it looks like a horse, but look here, what are these? Horns! Does a horsie have horns? Who has horns?" (The child says "Cow.") "That's right, Torrey, it's a cow!" The latter mother takes the toddler's error as an opportunity to teach her child something about the identifying marks of animals; she encourages a correct response; and she praises the child for it. In general, less educated parents tend to stress children's obedience to authority and to the rules. They are more likely to command than to explain how to perform a task, and are more likely to begin teaching the child without reflecting on how best to do so or taking the child's developmental level into account (Hess & Shipman,

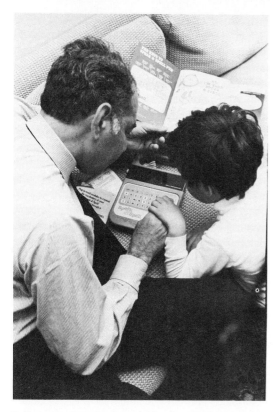

American mothers may believe that life is so harsh that they must avoid spoiling their children or making them "soft" and overly dependent on others. These mothers may ignore their children at times in order to prepare them to live in uncaring, neglectful environments. This attitude is greatly at odds with the recommendations of child care authorities and with middle-class practices and beliefs. Middle-class mothers value frequent verbal and physical interactions with their babies and are hypervigilant caretakers who attempt to protect their children from all forms of real and imagined danger (Feshbach, 1973; Hess & Shipman, 1967; Streissguth & Bee, 1972). But would such training be equally valuable for slum children? The less protected impoverished children may indeed be better prepared for life's difficulties.

This little girl is a voracious reader who may become a scholar or a professional. Children who have access to many books have the opportunity to learn more about the world than do those who get their information solely from television and the experience of everyday life.

Fathers are important to children's cognitive development and academic achievement. Children whose parents value learning and spend time helping them tend, as a group, to be high achievers.

1967). However, much of our evidence on SES differences in child rearing comes from fairly contrived laboratory observations. If the same differences hold true in well-controlled studies conducted in children's everyday surroundings, then we can understand why many poor children fail to achieve their academic and cognitive potential.

Why do poorer and less-educated parents react in ways that handicap their children cognitively? Previously we suggested that many factors may interfere with effective child rearing, including parental stress, ill health, lack of time, having to cope with many children, and inadequate education. Like the previously discussed parents from the Brazilian slums (see Box 3-1), poor North

However, maternal unresponsiveness may have unanticipated, negative effects as well. Early family teaching experiences appear to be important in the child's development of language and other skills assessed by standard intelligence tests. Carew (1977) found that children's tested intelligence at age 3 was highly correlated with the degree to which the parents spoke with and instructed their toddlers. Higher-SES children had higher intelligence test scores, and those who scored the highest of all were high-SES and had stimulating homes (i.e., had parents who read to them, named things for them, and provided other educational experiences). Scoring at the bottom were the lowest-SES toddlers whose parents provided them with little cognitive stimulation. It should be stressed that not all poor children are cognitively disadvantaged, nor are all richer ones intelligent, healthy, and indulged by their parents. Nevertheless, as a group, economically disadvantaged children lag behind their age-mates in cognitive development. A later section of this chapter describes some programs designed to aid the cognitive and social development of America's poor children.

ETHNIC MINORITIES AND DISCRIMINATION

In 1984, only 11.5 percent of the U.S. white population lived below the poverty level, as compared with 33.8 percent of blacks and 28.4 percent of those of Hispanic origin (U.S. Bureau of the Census, 1985). This means that as compared to whites, two times as many of the Hispanics and three times as many of the blacks were classified as very poor. As Table 3-2 indicates, many minority children grow up in poverty. However, since the great majority of the U.S. population is white, there are many more impoverished white children than those of other ethnic groups. Unlike their minority counterparts, though, white children tend to be poor temporarily when their parents divorce or become unemployed, and then to become more financially secure again later. Black children can expect to spend more than 5 years in poverty, contrasted with less than 10 months for the average white child (Subcommittee on Public Assistance and Unemployment Compensation, 1985). The heritage of racial discrimination in employment and education produces sustained

Table 3-2
Persons Below Poverty Level, by Race, Spanish origin, Region, and Age: 1984

	Percent Below Poverty Level			
Region and Age	All Races[1]	White	Black	Spanish Origin[2]
Total	14.4	11.5	33.8	28.4
Northeast	13.2	10.7	33.2	38.7
Midwest	14.1	11.5	37.9	30.1
South	16.2	12.0	33.6	26.0
West	13.1	11.8	26.6	25.3
Under 16 years	22.0	17.0	47.8	39.6
16 to 21 years	17.5	14.1	35.5	31.5
22 to 44 years	11.7	9.6	26.1	22.8
45 to 64 years	9.9	8.2	24.0	17.7
65 years and over	12.4	10.7	31.7	21.5

Source: U.S. Bureau of the Census. (1985). Current population reports (Series P-60, No. 149). Washington, DC: U.S. Government Printing Office.
[1] Includes races not shown separately.
[2] Persons of Spanish origin may be of any race.

want and economic hardship for minority children. As we have seen, this poverty results in excess infant and child deaths; widespread physical, intellectual, and social handicaps; and wasted lives.

The conditions associated with poverty are responsible for America's embarrassingly bad showing in international comparisons of infant mortality rates. The United States has ranked between 13th and 18th in the world in the control of infant mortality for the past decade. Japan and the northern European nations have regularly surpassed the United States on this important indicator of child welfare. Very significantly, the United States ranks only 25th in the world in preventing low-birthweight babies; in this category it is bettered even by mainland China, despite its poverty and nonindustrialized economy. China's surprisingly good showing may be attributable to its population control programs, which discourage early marriage, early childbearing, and large families. In the United States, the high birth rates among nonwhites, inadequate prenatal care for the poorer mothers in these groups, and the youthfulness of many minority mothers work together to produce excess stillbirths, premature and underweight babies, and high infant mortality rates. Nonwhite children's high-risk status continues in later years. Deaths from childhood diseases such as measles, diphtheria, and scarlet fever are six times higher among blacks than whites. Black children also have far higher rates of general ill health, abandonment, father absence, and excess levels of learning problems, as well as more school dropouts, malnutrition, neglect, dental problems, lead poisoning (as previously noted), drug abuse of some types, and teenage pregnancies (Scott & Winston, 1976).

As adults, blacks can anticipate far higher rates of psychiatric disorders than whites. For each 100,000 people, 344 blacks are admitted to mental hospitals as compared with 161 whites, according to a recent report by the U.S. Public Health Service (USDHHS, 1985). Black men consistently show the highest rates of mental disorders of any group. The vast majority of the preceding problems stem from poverty, undered-

ucation, and discrimination, and middle-class blacks fare much better in all respects.

Race, SES, and IQ

Economically advantaged whites are sometimes impatient with the inability of the permanently poor to improve themselves and better their lot. It is tempting to attribute abject poverty and passivity to some failure of personal character, or to racial differences favoring the majority group. Black, Hispanic, and Native American families tend to be among the poorest in the nation; their school attainment is generally low, high proportions of their children receive special education, and these groups are at the very bottom of the SES scale (Laosa, 1984). Within each ethnic minority group, a few middle-class individuals and families attain higher education, wealth, and social recognition, but such cases are disappointingly few. Why don't the poor and the minorities "better themselves"? One presently discredited explanation was that such groups are constitutionally less able than the more successful whites. This type of explanation was freely offered by the 19th-century middle and upper classes to account for the miserable lot of poor whites and minorities alike, as Chapter 1 notes. More recently, Jensen (1969) suggested that genetic differences between the races accounted for the lower IQ scores of blacks. Predictably, this argument was challenged by most psychologists and educators, who pointed out the overriding influence of environment in determining IQ scores (e.g., Bee, 1978; Scarr, 1981). Other social scientists stressed the bias of existing intelligence tests favoring middle-class white children (Kamin, 1974). Eventually Jensen (1977) conceded that environmental influences do depress black children's IQ scores, because impoverished black children's IQs decrease with age and length of time in an intellectually unstimulating environment. Environmental factors seem to explain the limited social and educational achievement of other minority groups as well. Hispanic youngsters whose parents have little formal education and those whose families primarily speak Spanish are particularly likely to have low scores on standard intelligence tests, to experience school achievement problems, to be retained rather than promoted, and ultimately to drop out of school (U.S. Bureau of the Census, 1977).

Unemployment and Minority Youths

In an industrialized, technologically advanced society, poorly educated young people who lack family connections helpful in finding employment are eligible for only the poorest-paying, lowliest jobs. Their chances for advancement are almost nil, and lack of capital prevents them from starting their own businesses. They are also likely to live in urban slums located far away from the most desirable jobs, because many companies have moved to the suburbs. Lingering vestiges of racial discrimination in employment further handicap nonwhite job seekers. It is difficult to advance under such circumstances, and it is even difficult to find a job, particularly for teenagers.

Unemployment rates for nonwhite youths regularly are twice or more the rates for comparable whites (U.S. Department of Labor, 1979), and unemployment rates for young people are inevitably higher than those of their elders. Black youth joblessness often exceeds 40 percent (and unemployment rates are based solely on those currently seeking work, not those who have become discouraged and stopped looking) (Laosa, 1984; Reveron, 1982). Permanently high unemployment rates breed crime, psychological disturbance, and social unrest. Unemployed people tend to view their failure to get a job as a personal shortcoming rather than the result of an adverse socioeconomic condition, so high unemployment is associated with increased rates of suicide, homicide, alcoholism, and physical and emotional breakdown (Brenner, 1973; Knapp, 1975; Okun, 1972).

As disturbing as this social portrait is, there have been some distinct improvements for minority children. Table 3-3 indicates that since 1960, and perhaps due to the nation's War on Poverty, nonwhite children have gained considerably in education. Now most children of all races complete high school. Those of Spanish origin (from the Ca-

ribbean, Mexico, and Central and South America), especially females, lag behind the other groups in number of years of school completed, perhaps because of language and cultural differences and the relatively short time many have been in the United States. They are making rapid progress, however, as shown in the table.

Linguistic Differences

Although no language is inherently superior to any other, some environments are better able than others to foster children's academic progress. In a technologically advanced society people benefit from having families that foster cognitive development and individual achievement. Cultural differences may help to explain minority children's lower average IQ scores and more limited educational attainment relative to whites. Even speakers of English vary in their native dialects and language conventions. Dialects are nonstandard speech styles that are functional and stylistic rather than deficient. Nevertheless, children who speak dialects are sometimes viewed as academically and socially undesirable, and their language forms may handicap them at school as well and limit their job prospects. Black English is an example of a genuine dialect with a vocabulary, rules of pronunciation, and a grammar of its own (Folb, 1980; White, 1984). Not all black children speak or understand black English, which tends to be the language of the poor. Table 3-4 gives examples of verb forms typical of black English as compared to standard English. These forms are not simple mistakes, since they follow structural rules (some of which resemble west African languages) and are accepted as correct by all competent speakers of the dialect. But such differences in speech make it difficult for young children to learn to speak standard English and to perform well at school. Many educational authorities (Bee, 1978; Ginsburg, 1972) and even a federal judge (Chief U.S. District Judge Robert Peckham in *Larry P. v. Riles,* 1972) have concluded that standard intelligence tests are grossly inadequate measures of nonwhite children's mental capacity. Judge Peckham concluded that the tests were developed for white children and do

Table 3-3

Years of School Completed, by Race, Spanish Origin, and Sex: 1960 to 1984

Year, Race, Spanish Origin, and Sex	Population (1000)	Percent of Population Completing—							Median School Years Completed
		Elementary School			High School		College		
		0–4 Years	5–7 Years	8 Years	1–3 Years	4 Years	1–3 Years	4 Years or More	
1960, all races	99,438	8.3	13.8	17.5	19.2	24.6	8.8	7.7	10.6
White	89,581	6.7	12.8	18.1	19.3	25.8	9.3	8.1	10.9
Male	43,259	7.4	13.7	18.7	18.9	22.2	9.1	10.3	10.7
Female	46,322	6.0	11.9	17.8	19.6	29.2	9.5	6.0	11.2
Black	9,054	23.8	24.2	12.9	19.0	12.9	4.1	3.1	8.0
Male	4,240	28.3	23.9	12.3	17.3	11.3	4.1	2.8	7.7
Female	4,814	19.8	24.5	13.4	20.5	14.3	4.1	3.3	8.6
1970, all races	109,899	5.5	10.0	12.8	19.4	31.1	10.6	10.7	12.1
White	98,246	4.5	9.1	13.0	18.8	32.2	11.1	11.3	12.1
Male	46,527	4.8	9.7	13.3	18.2	28.5	11.1	14.4	12.1
Female	51,718	4.1	8.6	12.8	19.4	35.5	11.1	8.4	12.1
Black	10,375	14.6	18.7	10.5	24.8	21.2	5.9	4.4	9.8
Male	4,714	17.7	19.1	10.2	22.9	20.0	6.0	4.2	9.4
Female	5,661	12.0	18.3	10.8	26.4	22.2	5.8	4.6	10.1
Spanish origin	3,938	18.9	17.1	10.2	17.7	22.0	7.9	6.0	9.6
Male	1,923	18.3	16.3	10.0	17.5	20.9	9.2	7.8	9.9
Female	2,014	19.6	17.9	10.4	18.0	23.1	6.7	4.3	9.3
1980, all races	132,836	3.6	6.7	8.0	15.3	34.6	15.7	16.2	12.5
White	114,290	2.6	5.8	8.2	14.6	35.7	16.0	17.1	12.5
Male	53,941	2.8	6.0	8.0	13.6	31.8	16.4	21.3	12.5
Female	60,349	2.5	5.6	8.4	15.5	39.1	15.6	13.3	12.6
Black	13,195	8.2	11.7	7.1	21.8	29.3	13.5	8.4	12.0
Male	5,895	10.0	12.0	6.7	20.5	28.3	14.0	8.4	12.0
Female	7,300	6.7	11.6	7.3	22.9	30.0	13.2	8.3	12.0
Spanish origin	6,739	15.5	16.6	8.1	15.8	24.4	12.0	7.6	10.8
Male	3,247	15.2	16.2	7.7	15.5	22.6	13.4	9.4	11.1
Female	3,493	15.8	17.1	8.4	16.1	26.0	10.6	6.0	10.6
1984, all races	140,794	2.8	5.0	6.6	12.4	38.4	15.8	19.1	12.6
White	123,103	2.2	4.5	6.6	11.7	39.1	16.1	19.8	12.6
Male	58,476	2.3	4.7	6.6	11.1	35.1	16.3	23.9	12.7
Female	64,627	2.1	4.4	6.6	12.2	42.8	15.8	16.0	12.6
Black	14,369	7.0	8.7	6.7	19.0	34.3	13.8	10.4	12.2
Male	6,334	8.8	8.9	6.6	18.6	32.9	13.8	10.5	12.2
Female	8,035	5.7	8.6	6.8	19.3	35.4	13.9	10.4	12.3
Spanish origin	7,269	13.9	15.9	8.5	14.6	27.3	11.6	8.2	11.3
Male	3,388	13.6	15.6	8.1	14.1	26.2	12.9	9.5	11.7
Female	3,880	14.1	16.2	8.9	15.0	28.2	10.5	7.0	11.0

Source: U.S. Bureau of the Census. (1960, 1970, 1980). *U.S. census of population* (Vol. 1). Washington, DC: U.S. Government Printing Office; U.S. Bureau of the Census. (1985). *Current population reports* (Series P-60). Washington, DC: U.S. Government Printing Office.

Note: Persons 25 years old and over. Persons of Spanish origin may be of any race.

not accurately test the competence of nonwhite children, many of whom receive misleadingly low scores and then are placed in separate, inferior, and dead-end classes for the academically limited. Previously, when IQ scores were used as the basis for assignment, about 15 percent of blacks but

Table 3-4
Conjugation of the Verb *To Be* in Standard English and in Black English or Ebonics

Mainstream American English	Black English (Ebonics)
We are	We is
We were	We was
You will be	You gon be
He has been	He have been or he done been
I had been	I been done been
They will have been	They should'a done been

Source: B. Smith. (1979). It ain't what you say, it's the way you say it: Exercises for teaching mainstream American English to Ebonics-speaking children. *Journal of Black Studies, 9,* p. 491.

only 2 percent of whites were placed in such classes (Bryson & Bentley, 1980; Finn, 1982). Of course, not all blacks or other nonwhites are penalized by IQ tests; the upper-income, higher-SES minority children have access to the same body of information as whites, and consequently they perform well in formal testing.

Because many minority children were unfairly penalized by traditional, white-oriented testing procedures, the U.S. Congress has specified in the Education for All Handicapped Children Act of 1975 (P.L. No. 94-142) that educational testing and evaluations must be conducted in a child's native language. There must be annual retesting to determine whether the child's educational placement continues to be appropriate, which guards against a child's being permanently misassigned on the basis of a single inadequate testing. In addition to language differences, many low-SES minority children come from environments far different from the white middle-class world of the school. They are particularly intimidated by white psychological examiners, and so may perform poorly on tests. When testing conditions are more inviting, the same child may earn a much higher score. Low-SES children's test scores are increased by roughly 10 points when (1) easy and difficult test items are intermixed, rather than presented in the usual order from easy to difficult; and (2) the examiner gives the child greater encouragement to try to answer the questions (Zig-

ler, Abelson, & Seitz, 1973; Zigler & Butterfield, 1968). Being tested by an examiner of the same race and culture also makes children feel more relaxed and comfortable and boosts their test performances (Labov, 1970; Laosa, 1984; Silverstein & Krate, 1975).

How do minority children succeed in the white-dominated world? The task is neither easy nor simple, because black, native American, and Hispanic children from poor families must become bilingual and bicultural, learning the speech and customs of white middle-class society as well as their own. This is a formidable task, for the children's culturally traditional families can provide few resources and little guidance on how to succeed in the modern world. A child's teachers may believe that the task is hopeless, and so they discourage the attempt (Wagner, 1972). With deprivation and cultural difference both playing a role, it is hardly surprising that few escape the hard life of the barrio, the black ghetto, or the reservation. For most families, the cycle of poverty goes on. As shown in Figure 3-2, one type of deprivation generates another in a cyclical manner. Impoverished parents living in a harsh and inadequate environment have less healthy children who

FIGURE 3-2. The relationship of poverty, school failure, and unemployment or underemployment.

Source: H. G. Birch and J. D. Gussow. *Disadvantaged children: Health, nutrition, and school failure.* (New York: Harcourt Brace Jovanovich), p. 268. Reprinted by permission.

are at high risk for school failure, dropout, very low incomes, and the other problems of their parents. The cycle repeats itself with each new generation. Recognition of this forbidding cycle of poverty has led to the development of many intervention programs aimed at improving the lot of the poor.

Antipoverty Programs

From the 1960s until approximately 1980, there was a national commitment to fighting poverty in the United States, and major social reform programs were implemented. New services for the poor included rent assistance, food supplements, income supplements, job training, medical assistance, and compensatory education programs. Although funding levels were much reduced subsequently because of increased federal debt, priority given to military spending, and growing political conservatism, many more poor families and elderly poor have received assistance than ever before. There have been improvements in the health, early education, and general standard of living of the poorest people in the nation; yet the income gap between the rich and the poor may have widened (Lynn, 1977). The aged have made greater gains than have poor children, leaving children as the poorest age group. Because of reduced government spending, poverty rates among children climbed more than 50 percent from 1973 to 1983, reaching the highest level since before the antipoverty programs were introduced in the mid-1960s (Subcommittee on Public Assistance and Unemployment Compensation, 1985). Poverty has proved stubbornly persistent for children in female-headed families, particularly blacks.

Compensatory education programs were developed to increase the upward social mobility of the poor. Head Start for preschool children, Follow Through in the early elementary school grades, and services offered under the Elementary and Secondary Education Act of 1965 all provided special services for poor students to give them a more nearly fair start in life. Although it was originally feared that such programs were not helpful (Levin, 1977), subsequent evaluations revealed that children at risk for educational and so-

cial failure benefited significantly (Magidson, 1977; Mann, Harrell, & Hurt, 1978; Seitz, Apfel, & Efron, 1978). Head Start children outperform other low-income children in preschool and elementary school. They are less likely to be retained in a grade, to be inappropriately placed in special education, or to drop out. Their language development is better, and they sometimes maintain their superiority on achievement test scores into the later grades (Collins, 1983; Lazar & Darlington, 1982). Moreover, the children who benefit the most from Head Start are the most needy—those with the least educated parents, those from single-parent families, and those who began Head Start with the lowest IQ scores. Head Start has proved to be a heartening success, with solid bipartisan political support in Congress (although not always in the White House), reflecting the program's great popularity among children, parents, educators, and the people.

Effects of School Desegregation

In 1954, the U.S. Supreme Court struck down racially segregated schools, ruling that they are inherently unequal. This and subsequent judicial decisions and antidiscriminatory legislation led to increased mixing of ethnic groups in the schools. It was presumed that all children must be given roughly equivalent educational opportunities, and that school desegregation would boost the self-esteem of minority students and give them greater opportunities. Since the 1950s, a number of studies have investigated the effects of school desegregation.

With a program as complex as desegregation, it is not surprising that research results have been mixed and sometimes ambiguous. However, the major conclusions are (1) that neither white nor nonwhite children's achievement is typically set back when schools become integrated (St. John, 1975), and black children's learning is sometimes facilitated (Stephan, 1978); (2) that even though they attend the same school, white and nonwhite children may have little social contact (Gerard & Miller, 1975); and (3) that desegregation alone does not significantly enhance the self-esteem of minority students (Minuchin & Shapiro, 1983).

Mere physical proximity of whites and minorities has little positive effect on their attitudes about each other, as observations of any tense but racially integrated neighborhood will attest. More encouraging are the positive effects of curricula designed to enhance interracial relations. Positive changes in attitudes and behaviors have been produced by such innovations as multiethnic curricula featuring projects on racial issues, mixed work groups, and supportive principals and teachers (Epstein, 1980; Forehand, Ragosta, & Rock, 1976). Research shows that race relations improve when high school students are assigned to work together or to participate in multiracial sports teams.

FAMILY DISCORD AND DIVORCE

Family strife may be no more common now than in the past, but today's unhappy marriages are more likely to be dissolved through separation and divorce. In 1978 there were 90 divorced persons for every 1000 with intact marriages, which was an astounding increase of 157 percent in the divorce rate during the preceding 18 years (U.S. Bureau of the Census, 1978). As Figure 3-3 illustrates, the marriage rate is declining while the divorce rate is increasing (U.S. Bureau of the Census, 1985). However, two-parent families continue to be the rule; in 1984, 78.4 percent of households with children were headed by married couples, as compared with just 21.6 percent with a single parent (U.S. Bureau of the Census, 1985). Nevertheless, more than a million children each year witness the divorce or separation of their parents (Select Committee on Children, Youth, and Families, 1983). Since 60 to 70 percent of divorces occur in families containing children and adolescents (Bane, 1979; Rohrlich, Ranier, Berg-Cross, & Berg-Cross, 1977), there is widespread

FIGURE 3-3. Marriages and divorces: 1960 to 1984.

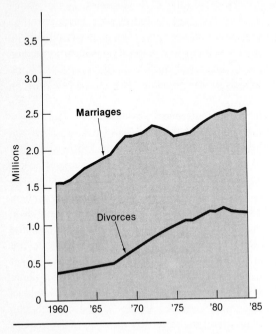

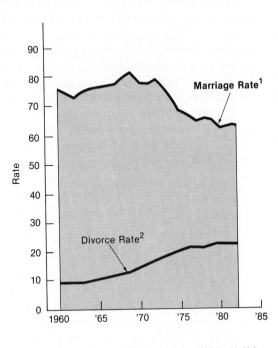

Source: U.S. Bureau of the Census. (1987b). *National data book and guide to sources. Statistical abstract of the United States* (107th ed.). U.S. Department of Commerce, Bureau of the Census. Washington, DC: U.S. Government Printing Office.
[1]Rate per 1000 unmarried women, 15 years old and over.
[2]Rate per 1000 married women, 15 years old and over.

concern about possible deleterious effects of divorce on child adjustment and development. It is estimated that by the end of the 20th century, one-third of the children less than 18 years of age will have divorced parents (Glick, 1979).

Certain groups are more likely than others to be affected by separation, abandonment, and divorce. This means that these children will need to be especially resilient in order to adjust well. Black children, poor children, and those whose parents have never completed high school are particularly likely to live in single-parent, mother-headed households (Glick, 1979). These families are among the nation's poorest, least healthy, and least well served, lacking the money for adequate housing, food, clothing, and medical expenses. Although they represent the entire range of intellectual ability, these children receive the nation's least adequate schooling.

Why Are Single-Parent Families Increasing?

Many children live with their mothers and rarely or never see their fathers. In contrast, fewer than 3 percent of U.S. children live in single-parent households with their fathers (U.S. Bureau of the Census, 1985). Ethnic groups differ in household composition. In 1984, a slight *majority* (50.2 percent) of black children were living in single-mother-headed households, compared with 15.1 percent of whites and 25.9 percent of Hispanics (U.S. Bureau of the Census, 1985). There are several possible explanations for the increasing trend toward single-parent families:

1. Motivation for marriage. Romantic love and individual fulfillment are the currently popular reasons for marriage. Previously, couples married largely for economic and family reasons (Keniston, 1977), which might have provided less exciting but more stable bases for marrying. Since marriage is now supposed to bring happiness, people are more likely to abandon their partners when they fall out of love or fail to find sufficient happiness. Today's motivations for marriage seem to be transitory and inherently unstable.

2. Employment options. Increased employment opportunities for women make them more financially independent. In the past, the husband, wife, and several children may have been needed as workers in order to provide a living. Now women can find work or welfare payments to support themselves and their children. They need not stay in unhappy marriages to survive.

3. Divorce is sanctioned. A divorce is now less expensive and easier to obtain because of more permissive legislation, and divorce is widely socially accepted. Previously, powerful religious, legislative, and financial obstacles effectively prevented couples from seeking divorces.

4. Illegitimacy is increasingly accepted. It is becoming increasingly common for unmarried women to keep and rear their babies, often with the help of welfare payments and the help of their own parents. From 1960 to 1977, the number of children living with never-married mothers increased by 700 percent (Glick, 1979). This marked trend toward unmarried motherhood is found in most groups of Americans—among devout churchgoers and movie stars, whites and minorities, and the poor and the rich alike. However, unmarried parenthood is especially prevalent among blacks, with 22.5 percent of black children under the age of 18 living with their single mothers. Neighbors, their own families, friends, and popular entertainers set the example, and teenagers follow their lead to become unmarried mothers.

5. Increased divorce rate. Changes in the composition of the U.S. population increase the overall divorce rate at present. The great population increase produced by the post-World War II baby boom first put increased demands on the school system, and then, as the baby boomers grew, on the colleges, as more schools and teachers were required to educate an unprecedented number of young people. In the 1970s this horde of baby boomers married and had children, and subsequently they began to divorce and remarry. As this group passes through the divorce-prone years, the national divorce rate will be very high, simply because there are so many people in this age group. Thus population demographcs alone account for some portion of the high divorce rate.

Thus there are powerful social forces working to produce high rates of single parenthood. Some of these factors, such as the increased employability of women and the possibility of leaving a miserable relationship, seem very positive for the individuals involved. Others, such as marrying and divorcing casually or impulsively deciding to have a baby, appear to be immature and unrealistic. Together, these changes are creating a social revolution that may prove beneficial for some children and harmful for others.

Effects of Divorce on Children

Divorce is not a simple act, and its effects may vary, depending upon factors such as the amount of acrimony between the wife and husband before and after the divorce, the divorced father's availability to the children, the family's financial situation, how well the mother copes with the situation, and the ages and sexes of the children. With such a diversity of possible family situations, it is not easy to predict how divorce will affect children. After the divorce, the vast majority of children live with their mothers. If living with just one parent has any harmful effects, then many children may be at risk. Unless they have other sources of emotional support, black children may be at high risk for adjustment problems, because they are more likely to live in low-income households with their divorced or single mothers (Select Committee on Children, Youth, and Families, 1983). However, minority groups rightly question whether the greater share of minority youths can rightly be classified as disturbed simply because they are reared in single-parent households. Perhaps the support provided by the many extended families in the black community and the help of grandmothers in child rearing counteract the possibly harmful effects of fathers' absence (Peters & McAdoo, 1983). Alternatively, children may possibly tolerate their parents' divorce quite well. Some children of divorced parents are neither highly distressed nor psychologically handicapped (Bernard & Nesbitt, 1981; Kurdek & Siesky, 1980). But the overwhelming research evidence is that parental conflict and divorce may well disturb children, at least temporarily (Emery, Hetherington, & Dilalla, 1984).

First, it should be stressed that the intense friction between the parents, rather than the divorce itself, upsets children. Compared to daughters, sons are more likely to develop disturbed behavior in response to parental combat, perhaps because the boys are more likely to be witnesses to or participants in parental confrontations. During sometimes lengthy periods when parental conflict is building prior to divorce, boys may develop problems in controlling their aggression, behave very impulsively, and become overactive and disorganized (Block, Block, & Gjerde, 1986). Problems in impulse control occur among boys whose parents are at odds and those whose parents have divorced (Hetherington, Cox, & Cox, 1979), which suggests that the boys' problems are caused primarily by parental strife. In general, girls seem to have fewer divorce-related adjustment problems, and their response patterns feature anxiety and withdrawal rather than aggression (Guidubaldi, Perry, & Cleminshaw, 1984). Perhaps boys have a greater tendency to respond aggressively to stress of any type. More boys than girls are referred to psychiatric and psychological clinics, where the most common presenting complaints are about boys' aggression and hyperactivity (see Chapter 1 for a discussion of this point). Boys' greater tendencies to develop problems in aggression control seem to be potentiated by the stress surrounding the breakup of their parents' marriages. To exacerbate the problem, there is evidence that following a divorce mothers have particular problems in managing their newly defiant and disobedient sons. The erratic, inconsistent parental discipline that often accompanies divorce, and the overstressed mothers' inability to provide firm and reasonable management, may stimulate the development of boys' conduct problems (Emery et al., 1984; Hetherington et al., 1979).

There is less consensus about age differences in children's reactions to parental divorce. Adolescents may be better able to cope with the divorce than younger children (Kurdek & Berg, 1983; Zill, 1983), perhaps because they are more independent from the family. In a clinical study of age differences in children's responses to divorce, Wallerstein and Kelly (1974) found that the ado-cents who were least affected by their parents' divorce were able to maintain some distance from their parents' problems, and their parents either willingly or reluctantly allowed them to do so. Their psychological independence from their embattled parents helped to insulate them from the stressful family situation. School-age children may develop academic problems as well as social ones. Their grades and their ability and achievement test scores may decline after the divorce when their fathers leave (Hetherington et al., 1979). Children in the late elementary school grades are particularly likely to experience school achievement problems and emotional disturbances (Shinn, 1978). Divorce upsets preschool children, too; clinical reports indicate that they respond with bewilderment, fretfulness, and heightened aggression (Wallerstein & Kelly, 1975). Stress is likely to produce temporary regression in toddlers and preschoolers, so that they develop problems in eating, sleeping, and toileting. The adjustment and skills of many preschool children significantly deteriorate during the first year after their parents' divorce (Hetherington, Cox, & Cox, 1978; Hetherington et al., 1979).

Parents naturally will wish to know how long their children's postdivorce adjustment difficulties may last. One carefully conducted study by Hetherington and her associates (Hetherington et al., 1978; Hetherington, Cox, & Cox, 1982) revealed that the first year was the worst for both parents and children, with fewer child problems thereafter. However, some children continued to have adjustment problems 2 years or more later. Some of the boys studied by Wallerstein and Kelly (1980) still seemed troubled as long as 5 years after their parents had divorced. On the more positive side, many adolescents approved of their parents' decision to separate, and reported that they matured faster as a result of the divorce (Reinhard, 1977). In retrospect, most adults interviewed in one study concluded that having their parents divorce during their childhood had little if any effect on their own subsequent adult adjustment (Kulka & Weingarten, 1979). Most children eventually adjust to their new family situations, whether they live in a mother-headed home, with a stepparent, or in some other arrangement.

Adjustment to Divorce

It may be a contradiction in terms to speak of an amicable divorce, yet some are less contentious than others. The more reasonable, less hostile divorcing couples tend to have less disturbed children. The fathers' attitude is very important for boys' postdivorce adjustment. Hetherington's group found that divorced fathers who were warm toward their sons and who spent time with them immediately following the divorce seemed to help their sons' adjustment (Hetherington et al., 1978, 1979). These boys had higher IQ scores and fewer achievement problems than did those whose fathers were less warm and less available. The divorced fathers' influence declined over time, and after 2 years the mothers' adjustment seemed to be the most important influence on the children. Mothers who were ineffective and under stress had children with problems; women who were disorganized and poor disciplinarians had children, especially boys, who were inattentive and distractible, obtained lower IQ scores, and had poorer school grades than other children of divorced mothers.

Sometimes a harmful cycle of maternal mishandling and child disobedience sets in. The overworked and worried mother becomes irritable, demanding, and punitive toward her children (especially sons). Her haphazard attempts at controlling her children, and her annoyance at their failure to obey, stimulate rebellion. Soon she and her children are caught in an escalating cycle of mutual punishment. With the passage of time and additional experience in handling the children by herself, the divorced mother usually becomes a more effective manager, and mother-child conflict decreases (but may not disappear).

Programs for Divorced Parents and Children

Because divorce is so prevalent, one might expect to find numerous programs designed to help those affected by divorce. In fact, there are surprisingly few such aids, especially for low-income black families who may need them the most (Minuchin & Shapiro, 1983). Helpful programs might assist divorced mothers in providing warm, firm, and consistent guidance for their children, especially the boys. In one such effort (Hetherington & Parke, 1979), Hetherington and her associates developed a behaviorally oriented counseling program for divorced mothers, who received instruction in child management. The mothers also had access to a 24-hour telephone consultation service for crisis advice and psychological support. These services increased the divorced mothers' feelings of competence and control and helped them to interact with their children in a more reasonable, controlled, and effective manner. Their sons responded with improved, better-controlled, and more acceptable behavior. This approach shows great promise and could be made widely available if funding were provided.

Schools also provide a location for special psychological services for children affected by parental divorce. Although children from one-parent homes represent the full range in intelligence and academic ability, their school achievement may suffer (Hetherington, Featherman, & Camara, 1981). Their school absences increase, and when in school they are more disruptive and have less effective study patterns than their classmates. Ordinary schools can improve the adjustment and achievement of such children. The boys profit from a predictable, organized school environment with consistent standards, and the girls require a warm, responsive setting in which they are expected to act maturely (Minuchin & Shapiro, 1983). Special school programs for children from one-parent families may be helpful. One school in a black ghetto trained teachers in the special needs of such students and provided the children with male teachers, on the assumption that they had few interactions with male adults. More such social experiments should be attempted and carefully evaluated. Other support services have been organized by single parents themselves. Parents without Partners is a national organization with local chapters in most major cities. This group is operated by single parents who wish to gain emotional support and to exchange information with others in their situation. Many participants find such self-help groups inviting and useful.

Sometimes divorcing couples quarrel so violently over child custody, finances, and visitation rights that they are referred for counseling by the court. Some clinics specialize in the treatment of these chaotic families (Suarez, Weston, & Hartstein, 1978). Often the parents are initially interviewed separately, then seen together to help them negotiate with each other more reasonably and effectively. Children who are troubled by a divorce may be included in the joint treatment sessions with their parents, but only after the parents have gained some measure of emotional control. Group therapy (discussed in Chapter 14) is used with parents who cannot be seen jointly with their ex-spouses or who require additional treatment with other divorced people. The intervention of trained therapists can help family members to gain objectivity in dealing with a difficult situation.

CHILD ABUSE AND NEGLECT

In recent years the United States has awakened to the plight of neglected and abused children. As recently as 1976 few people realized that child abuse was a serious social problem, but less than 10 years later a 1983 Louis Harris survey found that 90 percent of those interviewed were seriously concerned (Magnuson, 1983; Wolfe, 1985). Millions of dollars are now spent in an attempt to prevent child abuse and neglect and to provide treatment for maltreated children and their abusive caretakers. In this section, we describe the scope of the problem, the characteristics of affected families, and what is known about their rehabilitation.

Child abuse is legally defined as follows: "Child abuse and neglect means the physical or mental injury, sexual abuse, negligent treatment, or maltreatment of a child under the age of eighteen by a person who is responsible for the child's welfare under circumstances which indicate that the child's health or welfare is harmed or threatened thereby" (Child Abuse Prevention and Treatment Act of 1973, p. 626). Some authors go on to define mental abuse or psychological abuse as a concerted attack by an adult on a child's developing self-esteem and social competence. The adult's psychologically destructive behavior can take five forms (Garbarino, Guttmann, & Seeley, 1986):

1. *Rejecting,* **in which the adult systematically ignores the child and the legitimacy of the child's needs.**
2. *Isolating,* **in which the adult cuts the child off from others and suggests that the child is alone in the world.**
3. *Terrorizing,* **when the adult bullies, frightens, and verbally assaults the child.**
4. *Ignoring,* **in which the adult stifles the child's emotional and intellectual growth by depriving the child of ordinary stimulation and responsiveness.**
5. *Corrupting,* **as when the child is stimulated to engage in destructive antisocial behavior or other deviant behavior and becomes unfit for normal social living.**

It is important to realize, however, that it may be difficult to distinguish between psychological abuse and severe but traditional child-rearing practices in some cases. It is only when the severity and the deviance of the child's treatment clearly and consistently exceeds culturally acceptable standards that it is appropriate to speak of psychological abuse. Child *sexual abuse* is further defined as "[the] obscene or pornographic photographing, filming, or depiction of children for commercial purposes, or the rape, molestation, incest, prostitution or other such forms of sexual exploitation of children under circumstances which indicate that the children's health or welfare is harmed or threatened thereby" (National Center on Child Abuse and Neglect, 1979).

Although the preceding definitions seem clear, borderline cases are not always easy to identify. For example, one study classified "borderline abuse" as administering daily or weekly spankings that did not cause bruises or caused red marks that disappeared—disciplinary behavior that other people might term harsh but normal (Hunter & Kilstrom, 1979). Some definitions of psychological abuse are so loose and overinclusive as to include many commonly used parental disciplinary practices. Ideally, the child-rearing customs of established social and cultural groups are used in identifying cases of abuse. Abusive acts

violate community standards concerning the treatment of children (Parke & Collmer, 1975).

Estimates of child abuse and neglect prevalence differ widely. The National Center on Child Abuse and Neglect (1981) estimated that approximately 5.7 of each 1000 children are abused by caretakers each year, yielding over 350,000 known abuse cases annually in the United States. This conservative estimate is contradicted by one derived from a nationwide survey that yielded a much higher figure, approximating 2,000,000 child abuse cases per year (Straus, Gelles, & Steinmetz, 1980). In either case, many children are suffering needlessly, and they require protection.

Causes of Child Abuse and Neglect

Characteristics of Abusing Families One might think that people who abuse children are monsters who are easily recognized by their appearance and manner as being sadistic and emotionally unstable. Yet in most cases this characterization is inaccurate. Child abuse is a very complex problem with many roots. Family factors contribute to abuse, as well as external stressors, child characteristics, and cultural beliefs and practices, all of which combine to account for the maltreatment of children. In fact, abusive parents only rarely meet diagnostic criteria for psychopathology (Starr, 1982; Wolfe, 1985). A review of many research studies on abuse has revealed no identifying personality attributes or traits of abusers, beyond general displeasure with the parenting role and stress-related complaints (Wolfe, 1985). Parents who are economically deprived and of low SES are more likely to become classified as child abusers than are wealthier parents, but this may reflect their social and legal disadvantages more than significant social class differences. Some research suggests that white upperclass parents who abuse their children are not as likely to be reported to authorities as are less affluent, less influential parents ("Child Abuse Incidence and Reporting by Hospital," 1985). Thus it is difficult to determine whether the poor are more likely to be abusers or whether their crimes simply are more likely to be detected and reported.

It was long believed that a history of abuse as a child predisposed people toward abusing their own children, but this belief may be untrue. It now appears extremely difficult to separate the adverse effects of poverty, stress, and social isolation from the effects of having been abused as a child. All are closely linked, and each factor alone predicts child abuse at a very modest level. Taken together, these family factors relate to child abuse, but the experience of having been abused oneself does *not* predict abusiveness independent of the other background factors (Kaufman & Zigler, 1986). Few abused children later abuse their own children. Those who were abused but who are not abusive are more likely to have had one emotionally supportive parent or foster parent in their childhood, to have a good relationship with a spouse or partner, and to be experiencing little stress (Egeland & Jacobvitz, 1984).

A family's social isolation and high stress level may create a situation conducive to spouse and child abuse. Child abuse seems more likely to occur when a parent is undergoing a stressful role transition—for example, when there is intense marital discord, separation, an unwanted pregnancy, job loss, health problems, financial insecurity, or difficulties associated with moving to a new neighborhood (Garbarino, 1977). Box 3-4 describes some neighborhood characteristics associated with high child abuse rates. Abusers tend to be socially isolated, having no close friends and little contact with relatives and neighbors. Such isolation may itself create stress; it certainly reduces the parents' opportunities to observe how to handle children and what to expect of children of various ages, as well as the chance for shared babysitting with neighbors to relieve the constant burden of child care (Garbarino, 1977).

Let us try to picture the family interactions in an abusive household. First, over 90 percent of interactions in abusive families are either positive

---

BOX 3-4 • Neighborhood Differences in Child Abuse Rates

A "socially rich" neighborhood is not necessarily a wealthy one, but it is an attractive place to live. The residents take some pride in their neighborhood, rate the quality of life in the area as high, and describe their neighbors as friendly and supportive. When a parent is ill, neighbors step in to care for the children and give other help in an informal exchange system. Neighborhood children frequently play together. People are likely to remain as long-term residents in the "socially rich" area, in contrast to a more "socially impoverished" locale, where movement in and out of the neighborhood is more frequent. In the less desirable area, there are many "latchkey" children who return to empty homes after school, while more of the children from the more favored neighborhood are cared for by their parents or relatives. Child abuse and neglect rates are significantly higher in the high-risk, socially impoverished area, although the two neighborhoods may well comparable in terms of family income, ethnic composition, and parental education levels.

Researchers James Garbarino and Deborah Sherman believe that socially impoverished neighborhoods are stressful places inhabited by struggling families with little time or energy left over to establish and maintain social ties with their neighbors. The inhabitants correctly believe that theirs is a poor place in which to rear children, and they shun their neighbors rather than establish supportive relationships with them. Child mistreatment seems to thrive in this atmosphere of dislike and social isolation. A socially supportive community composed of families of competent and caring parents may effectively discourage child abuse and neglect.

Source: J. Garbarino and D. Sherman. (1980). High-risk neighborhoods and high-risk families: The human ecology of child maltreatment. *Child Development, 51,* 188–198.

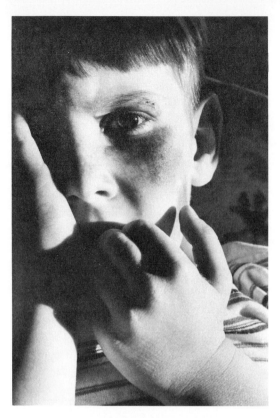

Child abuse is a personal tragedy and a national disgrace. Abused children are harmed emotionally as well as physically, and some of them die of their injuries. By law, teachers, mental health workers, and medical personnel are required to report suspected abuse to child protection authorities.

or neutral. However, there are much higher frequencies of negative, angry, coercive, threatening encounters among family members than are typical of nonabusive families (Reid, 1984). Parents who behave abusively not only are more hostile and irritable toward their children, but also are more unpleasant toward each other than are most couples. No children completely escape their wrath. Their coercive and explosive behavior usually extends to their treatment of their nonabused children, as well as to the primary child targets of their rage (Reid, 1984). When negative parent-child exchanges are relatively frequent over time, it is easy for the parent to lose control and engage in harmful, abusive discipline. There are higher

proportions of negative interactions in families with low incomes and large numbers of children, and those that are headed by single parents or include stepparents (Burgess, 1978; Daly & Wilson, 1980; Garbarino & Ebata, 1981). All of these factors are related to child abuse rates, perhaps because any of them can be highly stressful. It should be recalled, however, that only a tiny fraction of parents become abusive, whether they are stressed or not.

Cultural Factors   Child abuse is unknown in some cultures, which leads to the speculation that cultural beliefs and practices can either promote or inhibit cruelty toward children. Gil (1970) has argued that cultural approval of the use of force against children encourages physical abuse, since abuse is absent in cultures that prohibit physical punishment of children. By contrast, parents in the United States and England advocate corporal punishment to discipline children. The vast majority of parents interviewed in one study (71 to 97 percent) claimed that at times they had used physical punishment with their children (Gelles, 1979). The high intensity of the punishment these parents used is startling. Twenty percent (or one in five) said that they had hit their children with an object; 8 percent had kicked, bit, or hit their children with their fists; and nearly 3 percent had threatened their children with a knife or gun or had actually used a weapon on the children (Gelles, 1979). Because some of the parents may have been reluctant to admit to their violence, these statistics doubtless underestimate the extent of physical force used in American families.

Parents' use of force is generally approved by their neighbors, according to one finding that 86 percent of a sample of American adults agreed that young people require strong discipline from their parents (Stark & McEvoy, 1970). Half of the respondents approved of teachers' striking their students for minor offenses, such as destroying school property, hitting someone, or simply for being noisy in class. Adults are generally encouraged to use a certain amount of physical force with children, but they must be careful not to cross the line separating legitimate discipline from physical abuse. Making such a fine discrimination is difficult for some, especially when they are upset and angry. What began as an ordinary spanking can all too quickly become abusive behavior.

Child Characteristics   Children whose appearance or behavior irritates or displeases their parents are at greater risk for abuse than are other children. All of the following features have been found more often in abused than in nonabused children: prematurity (with early separation from the mother), weakness and unresponsiveness, an irritating high-pitched cry, severe illness during the first year of life, and physical unattractiveness or malformation. Mistreated children may also be psychologically disturbed or psychotic, developmentally delayed, brain-damaged, or mentally retarded, or may have serious speech disorders (Cicchetti, Taraldson, & Egeland, 1978; Friedrich & Boriskin, 1976; Smith & Hanson, 1974). Unfortunately, most of our information on child characteristics is obtained only *after* the abuse, so it is nearly impossible to determine whether the problems preceded or resulted from the mistreatment. It is clear that prematurity, low birthweight, and mother-baby separation in early life are all associated with higher risk of child abuse, especially among low-SES groups (Daly & Wilson, 1980; Klaus & Kennell, 1976). However, these factors in themselves are not sufficient to produce abuse, and many premature babies are tenderly cared for by their parents.

Child Sexual Abuse   Child protection workers have always been aware of the existence of child sexual abuse, but only recently has that concern become widespread. Although most incidents are unreported, child protection organizations estimate that between 100,000 and 1 million children are sexually abused each year, and sexual abuse is sometimes accompanied by violence (Collins, 1982). Most victims are girls between the ages of 11 and 14 years; male victims have been little studied (Browne & Finkelhor, 1986). About 75 percent of the reported cases of sex crimes against children involve members of the victim's household, neighbors, relatives, or acquaintances,

rather than strangers (DeFrancis, 1969). Most offenders are heterosexual, and they do not use physical force (National Center on Child Abuse and Neglect, 1979). The types of abuse that seem to be most psychologically damaging involve fathers or stepfathers, genital contact, and the use of force (Browne & Finkelhor, 1986). Sexual offenses committed by strangers are usually brief, are rarely violent, and mostly consist of single episodes of exhibitionism or fondling the child's genitals. In contrast, sexual abuse by household members or associates is more likely to occur over an extended time period. In the case of incest in particular, other family members may know or suspect what is happening, but take no action or even accuse the victimized child of lying.

Little trustworthy evidence is available concerning the emotional effects of sexual abuse on children. Certainly people who have been abused report some impairment. Of those who had been abused by a family member, 53 percent reported that they had suffered from at least some long-term effects on their lives, although fortunately few developed serious psychological problems (Browne & Finkelhor, 1986; Russell, 1986). When evaluated by a clinician following detection of the abuse, 20 to 40 percent of the children reportedly show emotional disturbance (Tufts, 1984). Thus it appears that emotional trauma is present in a sizable minority of sexual abuse victims. Child protection groups have been active in presenting sexual abuse prevention educational programs at schools and on television, but it is too early yet to determine the effects of these efforts.

Effects of Abuse and Neglect

In the most serious cases, children die from their caretakers' ill treatment; others sustain serious burns, cuts, or brain damage. In certain cases involving infants, abuse and neglect leads to *abuse dwarfism (hyposomatotropinism).* In this condition, serious abuse and neglect produce failure of growth hormone secretion, with resulting growth delay, mental retardation, and other problems. Up to a point, the condition is reversible when the maltreatment is ended (Money & Annecillo, 1976).

Serious maltreatment during later childhood and adolescence may be accompanied by the child's aggressive, destructive, conduct-disordered behavior, especially in boys (Rogeness et al., 1986; Williams, 1983). Abused girls also may develop conduct disorders, but neglected girls usually do not, though they may have lowered IQs (Rogeness et al., 1986). Young abused children may show a general wariness of adults. One group of battered toddlers and preschoolers displayed simultaneous approach and avoidance behaviors toward friendly adults (George & Main, 1979). They turned their heads away while moving toward an adult, or actually turned around and backstepped toward the adult. In addition, they were inappropriately aggressive and uncooperative toward both adults and other children. However, no one knows for sure how well adjusted these young children were prior to the abuse.

Prevention of Child Mistreatment

Child abuse prevention programs could be mounted at the level of the individual child and family, the school, the neighborhood, or the nation. Because the causes of child abuse and neglect are so numerous and complex, efforts at all levels may be required in order to achieve a significant reduction of cruelty toward children. However, let us first consider what might be done to aid parents and children who are caught in abusive patterns of interaction.

Parent education might be feasible and effective. Reid (1984) has reported that parents who abuse their children physically are very poor managers. They issue frequent coercive instructions to their children, but are often met with noncompliance and even defiance, so they sometimes resort to force. Abuse is more likely when parents lack the skill to terminate aversive interchanges quickly in a controlled manner. As Reid has suggested, relatively simple parenting instruction programs that would teach the parents more effective and rewarding tactics for dealing with their children could reduce their motivation to punish their children severely. Sometimes parents lack knowledge about children's abilities and needs.

High-risk mothers of premature infants could be instructed in how to stimulate and enjoy their vulnerable babies, as Field (1983) has done with low-SES black teenage mothers.

Parent support groups for those with severely developmentally delayed, retarded, and physically handicapped youngsters might also prove informative and helpful for parents who must rear difficult children. Programs such as these would educate parents about their children's needs and capabilities, teach them effective methods of child rearing, and relieve their social isolation. Because child abuse tends to be more prevalent in closed, unwelcoming low-income neighborhoods with large numbers of unsupervised, "latchkey" children (see Box 3-4), community services such as prevention programs, neighborhood centers, and supervised activities could reduce residents' stress (Garbarino & Sherman, 1980). Other preventive services could be directed toward avoiding and treating alcohol and drug abuse among parents and potential parents. Abusive and neglectful parents have been found to have a higher rate of alcoholism and drug abuse, and more diagnosed psychopathology, especially major depression (Kaplan, Pelcovitz, Salzinger, & Ganeles, 1983). It is possible that preventing or alleviating parents' drug, alcohol, and mental health problems would also reduce the probability of their abusing or neglecting their children.

Several types of interventions are presently aimed at parents who abuse their children or fear they might do so. Free telephone "hotlines" available in many cities provide parents an opportunity to express their frustration and offer them advice and information about relevant community services. Some localities offer short-term child care for desperate or impatient parents who voice concern about possibly losing control and attacking their youngsters. These child care centers allow professional staff members to observe the parents and children while they provide the children a safe haven, although a temporary one. Unfortunately, there is little or no research evidence on the effectiveness of either the "hotlines" or the shelters, although they appear to be useful community services.

In theory, cruelty toward children should be preventable to some degree. There is widespread public concern about the problem, as well as increased research support and activity. It is reasonable to expect some notable progress in prevention and treatment within the next few decades if the societal support for research and clinical services continues and intensifies.

SUMMARY

All elements of their social and physical surroundings affect children's welfare. Children are most likely to develop health and behavioral problems, and intelligence and achievement deficits, when they are subjected to several different types of stress at the same time. Prenatal factors causing developmental delays, retardation, and serious health problems include inadequate prenatal care, maternal disease, and malnutrition. Birth complications can be largely overcome in favorable environments, but can lead to future physical and psychological problems if associated with low maternal IQ, low SES, unstable families, and low child IQ. Poverty, lack of education, and neglect intensify the ill effects of the child's early health problems.

Poverty and prejudice may combine to limit the development and socioacademic achievement of minority children. This effect is especially evident when their performance is measured against culturally biased standards. Some progress has been made in promoting the early academic achievement of minority students through the federally financed Head Start and Follow Through programs, although as yet too few of these students receive college educations to prepare them for the most desirable jobs. Marital conflict also adversely affects many children. Although most children adjust to the parents' troubles and the divorce after a year or two, some remain troubled for a long time. Single-parent families are among the poorest in the nation, especially if they are black. Financial problems, poor mother-son relations in some cases, and lack of time to spend together all make life difficult for the growing number of single-parent families, most of them mother-headed.

Child abuse and neglect are significant social problems with many contributors. Abusive parents describe themselves as unusually stressed and as disliking the parental role, but most do not suffer from obvious, severe psychopathology. Low-SES caretakers who are under many forms of stress are more likely than other groups to be abusive, but most parents in such situations do not abuse their children. Middle-class families' rates of abuse may appear misleadingly low, because such abuse is unlikely to be reported. Sexual abuse victims are most likely to be preadolescent girls, and abusers are most often adult male family members and acquaintances and friends. Sexual abuse may be concealed by the family and the child, and so is difficult to detect. The victimization is upsetting to the child and may result in diagnosed emotional disturbance in as many as 40 percent of the cases. It is too early to advocate the use of physical and sexual abuse information programs for children, because little is yet known about their effectiveness and possible unintended negative effects. As in so many other areas, the need for interventions has outstripped our knowledge of their individual worth.

chapter

4

Stress and Negative Emotions: Their Role in Psychological and Physical Disorders

KEY TERMS

Bipolar Affective Disorder.   Serious mood affliction in which depression alternates with excited, seemingly elated periods and with normal mood. Formerly called Manic-Depressive Disorder.

Childhood Depression.   An affective disorder thought to occur rarely in childhood. Resembles adult depression in involving sadness, pessimistic attitudes, fatigue or overactivity, and somatic complaints.

Desensitization.   Treatment technique that introduces feared and avoided stimuli gradually, either in real life *(in vivo)* or in imagination (systematic desensitization), while the client remains calm and relaxed.

Guided Participation.   A form of therapy in which the client imitates a fearless model and is helped to make progressively closer approximations to engaging in the feared act.

Hysterical Contagion.   Group emotional reaction resulting in an apparent epidemic of symptoms mimicking physical disease, usually among adolescents.

Learned Helplessness.   A state of passivity and impaired problem solving brought about by forced exposure to inescapable, insoluble problems.

Obsessive-Compulsive Disorder.   Recurrent, unwanted ideas (obsessions) and unwilling engagement in repetitive, stereotyped actions (compulsions).

Psychological Factors Affecting a Physical Condition.   A diagnosis given when emotional factors contribute to the origin or exacerbation of a physical condition or symptom.

School Phobia.   Extreme reluctance to attend school arising from fear of some school-related situation, such as evaluation apprehension.

School Refusal.   Fear and avoidance of school stemming from home influences, school-related situations, or other factors. Includes, but is not limited to, school phobia.

INTRODUCTION

No life is free from stress—not even a child's. Stress and anxiety themselves are unavoidable, but children do differ in the amount of stress they experience; in how well their families and friends help them to cope with difficulty; and in how well equipped they are to respond to such challenges, both genetically and through their prior experience. In the most serious cases, children suffer the emotional and physical effects of exposure to such devastating events as violence or abuse, warfare, and serious diseases. At the other end of the continuum of stress, even healthy, loved, and materially advantaged children may suffer the pangs of rejection by their peers, achievement problems in school, or the consequences of parental marital discord.

This chapter deals with the problems experienced by children who are not psychologically hardy; children who cannot manage pressures effectively; and children who develop problems such as anxiety reactions, exaggerated physical complaints, phobias, obsessive compulsive disorders, depressed mood, and related problems. These types of pathological reactions may stem from hereditary vulnerability or from faulty child rearing or other past experiences. Vulnerable children respond to stress with marked anxiety, depression, physical complaints, or other maladaptive behavior patterns. They may develop generalized anxiety or a specific *phobia* (extreme, unwarranted fear of something innocuous, such as dogs). Others may develop persistent unreasonable worries and feel compelled to engage in repetitive rituals *(obsessive-compulsive disorder)*, or

may become profoundly depressed. Phobias are the most common of the preceding types of childhood disorders, and obsessive-compulsive disorders and childhood depression are the least frequent. In fact, as we explain later, depression is so rare among young children and is so little understood that experts disagree about the existence of a true syndrome of childhood depression.

Anyone who has developed stomach pains, a headache, or a stiff neck on a particularly difficult day can appreciate the fact that stress and anxiety can disrupt physical as well as psychological functioning. Sometimes psychological and social factors contribute to the development and maintenance of such chronic physical illnesses as gastric ulcer, migraine headache, and bronchial asthma. In other instances, emotional arousal produces states similar to but not identical to physical illness. For example, in the *somatoform disorders* or *functional disorders,* the adolescent has many physical complaints suggesting some physical disorder. However, thorough medical examination reveals no known physiological basis for the complaints, which may increase and decrease together with factors such as the current intensity of the parents' battles or requirements that the child attend school.

This chapter describes some of the emotional disorders of childhood and adolescence, and what is known or conjectured about their prevalence, etiology, treatment and prevention. We begin with a description of the most prevalent of these disorders—anxieties and phobias—and explain how these syndromes differ from common childhood worries and fears, both in when and how they develop and in their intensity and persistence. Next, compulsive rituals and obsessive thoughts are described and compared with similar but normal childhood behaviors. The controversial concept of childhood depression receives major attention because of the considerable debate which the problem has generated.

Research findings have helped to determine the organization and content of this chapter. Large-scale multivariate studies of parents' and teachers' ratings of many different types of children's behavior problems have provided a useful approach to categorizing child psychopathology. Achenbach and his coworkers (Achenbach & Edelbrock, 1978) have reported that such ratings tend to fall within two large categories: *internalizing* and *externalizing* disorders. The externalizing or conduct disorders feature antisocial aggression and hyperactivity, whereas the internalizing or emotional disorders are characterized by anxiety, fear, social withdrawal, and stress reactions. It is readily apparent that this chapter deals with the emotional (internalizing) disorders of childhood.

CHILDHOOD ANXIETIES AND PHOBIAS

It is normal for youngsters to be afraid in many situations that seem harmless to adults. Children may be fearful because of their physical weakness, limited knowledge of how to defend themselves, and skill deficits relative to older children and adults. Toddlers can be physically overpowered easily by older children or even by an enthusiastic medium-sized dog. They lack mature cognitive skills, so they do not know what to do when lost, how to find their way home, or even how to report their name and address to helpful strangers. These physical and intellectual limitations may make children apprehensive in unfamiliar situations.

Children also learn specific fears from others. Their parents try to protect them by teaching them to avoid dangerous situations—for example, to avoid high places where they might fall, not to play in the street, not to wander off, and to fear hot objects. Indirectly, parents often transmit their own fears to their children through their anxiety about such events and objects as thunderstorms, insects, snakes, or dentists. Other children can also transmit fears. The power of peer influence was illustrated when the preschool daughter of one of us inadvertently learned to fear insects. One day she was observed running about the playground with her friends, imitating them as they spotted harmless insects and then ran away, shrieking, "Bugs, bugs!" This experience and perhaps others like it produced what has proved to be an enduring antipathy to insects. As a college student, she still expects her nonphobic parents to eradicate unsuspecting flies and beetles trapped in her bathroom.

Fears may be easier to acquire than to overcome. There are many ways to become afraid, and many children do so. It has been estimated that 90 percent of all children develop specific fears during their early years (Macfarlane, Allen, & Honzik, 1954). Most readers can recall their own childhood fears of strangers, animals, darkness, storms, people associated with pain such as medical and dental personnel, and even imaginary ghosts and monsters. Children commonly fear more than one thing. Lapouse and Monk (1959) found that mothers reported that 43 percent of their elementary school children had as many as *seven* different fears and worries! According to other studies, however, this estimate is unusually high (Gittelman, 1985; Orvaschel & Weissman, 1985). Regardless of the true rate, since children most probably keep some of their concerns to themselves, mothers' estimates tend to be too low. Most children suffer from feelings of fear and anxiety at least occasionally.

The types of situations dreaded by children are very similar worldwide. Wherever there are formal school systems, children fear various aspects of school, and the particular nature of their fears varies with their ages (Granell de Aldaz, Vivas, Gelfand, & Feldman, 1984). The youngest students are likely to be apprehensive about separation from parents, about the teachers, and about being abandoned at school at the end of the day, while older students are more likely to fear doing poorly in academic evaluations (Granell de

Table 4-1
Age-Related Changes in Children's Fears

Age Range	Types of Fears
0–12 months	Loss of support, loud noises, unexpected, looming objects, strangers
12–24 months	Separation from parent, injury, strangers
24–36 months	Animals (especially large dogs), darkness, separation from parent
36 months–6 years	Animals, darkness, separation from parent, bodily harm, strangers
6–10 years	Imaginary beings, injury, darkness, being alone, snakes, separation from parent
10 years–adolescence	Evaluations at school, injury, death, electrical storms, being teased
Adolescence	Peer rejection, school achievement, political situation, family worries, future plans (especially in boys)

Sources: M. Rutter and N. Garmezy. (1983). Developmental psychopathology. In P. H. Mussen (General Ed.), *Handbook of child psychology* (4th ed.): *Vol 4. Socialization, personality, and social development* (E. M. Hetherington, Vol. Ed.). New York: Wiley; R. Morris and T. Kratochwill. (1983). *Treating children's fears and phobias.* New York: Pergamon Press.

Aldaz et al., 1984) (see Table 4-1). Older children have fewer specific fears (Coleman, Wolkind, & Ashley, 1977), and the situations, objects, and things feared change with increasing age. Infants generally fear particular stimuli, such as loud noises, falling, the sudden appearance of strange objects, and strange persons (Bauer, 1976, 1980), but older children's fears are likely to be more general and include fear of bad school grades or other negative evaluations, of illness in the family, and of injury (Lapouse & Monk, 1959). A knowledge of typical fears permits psychologists to determine whether a particular child's fear is normal at that age or represents a phobia.

Whether children's fears are normal can be assessed by their age of occurrence, duration, intensity, and type.

1. Unusual age of onset. Fears may require clinical assessment and treatment when the age of onset is highly unusual, as when an adolescent unaccountably develops a strong fear of the dark or of friendly strangers. Such fears are common among preschoolers, but seldom arise for the first time in adolescence. When a fear reaction first occurs at a developmentally unusual or inappropriate time, it may represent a phobia rather than a normal fear of childhood.

2. Persistence. A fear reaction that persists long after the usual age of occurrence could be a phobia. The older child who inexplicably continues to dread loud noises or strangers may have a phobia rather than one of the usual childhood fears.

3. Intensity. The stronger the fear, the more likely that it is pathological. Even developmentally common fears may be abnormal if they are sufficiently intense. Fear of dogs is the most prevalent specific fear during early childhood, but it is relatively short-lived, and is overcome by almost all children by the time they are 8 years of age (Macfarlane et al., 1954). However, if a child is so overwhelmed by panic in the presence of dogs that she is virtually housebound, the reaction clearly merits professional attention.

4. Type of fear. Some types of fear are so unusual that their very occurrence signals abnormality. Very rarely, older children and adolescents may develop *agoraphobia* (literally, fear of open places), or the incapacitating fear of leaving the safe confines of their homes and families for any activities on the outside. This disorder precludes school attendance, interferes with social relationships with peers and with holding a job, and clearly represents psychopathology whatever the person's age (Rutter & Garmezy, 1983).

Some fears are more tenacious than others, but it is not known why. Those that tend to persist throughout life include fears of physical illness or of social situations (Miller, Barrett, Hampe, & Noble, 1972). Fears that often decrease or disappear with age center around storms, darkness, ghosts and monsters (Bauer, 1976). Fortunately, children stand a good chance of overcoming most fears. One of the more common and potentially damaging childhood phobias is an extreme fear of school.

School Phobia and School Refusal

Definitions and Description   Many children become apprehensive about attending school. School entry presents formidable challenges for most first-graders. For the first time in their lives, they are required to perform difficult tasks for strangers and are judged objectively by a class standard. Classmates are not always kind and may taunt them for their unusual accents or manner of dress, for being different in their physical appearance, or for other such transgressions against the peer group's codes and values. In mild cases, reluctant students can attend school because of their parents' or teacher's support and encouragement, but in actual school refusal no ordinary measures will tempt the child to attend.

This chapter presents two technical terms for abnormal reluctance to go to school: *school refusal* and *school phobia. School refusal* is the more general term and refers to persistent refusal to attend school because of the child's intense fear and anxiety about school. Perhaps the child fears leaving home and mother, failing in school, or being bullied or teased by classmates. In *school phobia,* however, the fear must be centered around some specific aspect of the school, such as fear of a particular teacher, of being asked to give a report in class, or of the school bully. Thus school refusal is the more general term, while school phobia is reserved for cases in which some specific aspect of the school is feared. In both school refusal and school phobia, the child appears to suffer overwhelming anxiety when required to attend school. For instance, the child may wake up with a painful stomachache or headache on the Monday after a school vacation or after being kept home by a minor illness. When his mother says that he can stay home from school, the child's physical complaints diminish dramatically, since avoiding school reduces his anxiety. He predictably becomes anxious and symptomatic again whenever he prepares to attend school. As a result, the school-refusing child stays home a great deal.

It is difficult to estimate the number of school refusers, because there are no standard criteria for diagnosing the condition. When fairly loose requirements are used to identify school refusers, estimates may be as high as 17 per 1000 school children (Kennedy, 1965). Almost certainly this is an overestimate of serious school refusal, since other studies have reported rates as low as 1.4 to 4 per 1000 (Granell de Aldaz et al., 1984; Rutter, Tizard, & Whitmore, 1970) when very stringent definitions have been used. The demanding criteria used by Granell de Aldaz et al. (1984), for example, required that the child's absences be statistically significantly above average and that the child, parents, and teacher all report that the child was phobic. Unlike other types of phobias and specific fears, school refusal is equally prevalent among girls and boys (e.g., Gordon & Young, 1976; Granell de Aldaz et al., 1984), although girls typically report more general and school-related fears than boys do.

School refusal is far different from truancy (Johnson, Falstein, Szurek, & Svendsen, 1941). The child with school refusal has an emotional disorder. He is anxious, depressed, and fearful, especially in social situations (Berg, 1981). The school refuser typically remains at home when avoiding school, and probably has average grades and academic achievement scores. In other words, the school refuser does not have a conduct disorder, but the truant may. In contrast, truants avoid both home and school when they are supposed to be at school. They tend to be angry and defiant, and to have poor grades (Galloway, 1983; Hersov, 1960). Poor attendance in itself indicates nothing about the nature of the child's problem, and it is necessary to collect information on other aspects of the child's life (such as the quality of the relationship with his parents and his general emotional adjustment) so that the nature of the child's problem can be determined.

Every child is unique, but it is possible to

characterize school refusers as a group. They are mostly of at least average intelligence and earn average grades in school. They may be perfectionistic and worry about school performance. Some children are concerned about getting bad grades or failing a test (Ficula, Gelfand, Richards, & Ulloa, 1983). School refusal may develop at any age during which school attendance is mandatory. It is most likely to appear during at least minor stress or challenge, for example, when the child is entering a new school, as in the transition to high school (see Box 4-1). School refusal also may strike at the beginning of the school year, when a child transfers from one school to another, after a school holiday, or after some minor illness has kept the child home for a few days. Typically,

---

BOX 4-1 • New Kid in School: Preventing School Problems

Emotionally based school problems are likely to strike children at particular times, rather than being distributed evenly throughout the academic year. Therefore, preventionists can use the *milestone* approach to identify students with potential problems and to intervene to prevent the problems' occurrence (Roberts & Peterson, 1984). Prevention milestones occur at developmentally important periods when risk for problem occurrence is high and intervention is feasible. Particular life events are critical for the child's future development, and prevention efforts can center around these occurrences. School transitions represent one such set of critical events. Each year, as many as 30 percent of U.S. school children transfer to new schools (Holland, Kaplan, & Davis, 1974), requiring them to undergo the stress of meeting new teachers, attempting to enter new social groups, and coping with unfamiliar surroundings and with different school rules and schedules. Understandably, these stressful experiences can result in poorer academic achievement (Felner, Primavera, & Cauce, 1981), heightened anxiety, and adjustment problems for some children (Felner, 1984). Such problems are particularly likely to arise at around the transition into high school (Felner *et al.,* 1981), particulary for ethnic minority students (U.S. Department of Health, Education & Welfare, 1975).

The preceding statistics suggest that intervention initiated at the time of school transitions may prevent the occurrence of the achievement problems and emotional turmoil that can result in school refusal. Psychologist Robert Felner and his team devised a successful program to ease the emotional stress of entering high school. First, since a part of the intimidating confusion of the high school schedule relates to encountering a different group of fellow students in each class, the program provided a more stable peer support system by moving students through the classes together as a group. Thus, the bewildering diversity of classmates was reduced, and the new student could perceive the school as a more stable, safe, and predictable place. A second measure was to assign guidance functions to the homeroom teachers in order to make them more supportive and helpful to entering students. As a result of these relatively simple changes, the students had better attendance, better grades, and more stable self-concepts than did students encountering the regular school routine. Moreover, they viewed the school more favorably. These positive changes probably reduced the likelihood that they would develop negative attitudes toward education or would become school refusers.

Sources: R. D. Felner. (1984). Vulnerability in childhood: A preventive framework for understanding children's efforts to cope with life stress and transitions. In M. C. Roberts and L. Peterson (Eds.), *Prevention of problems in childhood* (New York: Wiley); R. D. Felner, J. Primavera, and A. M. Cauce. (1981). The impact of school transitions: A focus for preventive efforts. *American Journal of Community Psychology, 9,* 449–459; J. V. Holland, D. M. Kaplan, and S. D. Davis. (1974). Interschool transfers: A mental health challenge. *Journal of School Health, 44,* 74–79; M. C. Roberts and L. Peterson. (Eds.). *Prevention of problems in childhood* (New York: Wiley); U.S. Department of Health, Education and Welfare. (1975). *Dropout prevention* (Washington, DC: Educational Resources Information Center; ERIC Document Reproduction Service No. ED 105-354).

on the morning when the child is supposed to re-turn to school, she develops physical complaints such as acute stomachache, nausea, headache, or sore throat. She may also report that the other children are mean to her or that her teacher hates her (Hersov, 1960). The parents' attempts to re-assure her only create more distress until they re-lent and allow her to remain home from school. As the specter of school attendance is removed, the child typically reports feeling better.

Staying home from school creates other serious problems, however. Even home study programs may not meet all of the school refuser's academic and social needs. Prolonged school ab-sence can retard academic achievement, create problems in relating to peers and other people, and increase feelings of depression and low self-esteem (Ficula *et al.,* 1983). Eventually, the ado-lescent's career opportunities are severely cur-tailed (McDonald & Sheperd, 1976). The long-term adjustment outlook is good for younger children with acute, short-term school refusal (Kennedy, 1965), but adolescents with intense, chronic school refusal have a poor prognosis (Berg, Butler, & Hall, 1976; Rutter & Garmezy, 1983). Older children with persistent and intense school refusal later develop emotional problems as young adults, particularly debilitating agora-phobia (Waldron, 1976; Waller & Eisenberg, 1980). The prognosis is particularly bad for the future psychosocial adjustment of children whose school refusal and other problems are so severe as to require hospitalization (Berg *et al.,* 1976).

Types of School Refusal   School refusers are not all the same. The third edition of the *Diagnos-tic and Statistical Manual of Mental Disorders* (DSM-III; American Psychiatric Association, 1980) views school refusal as a symptom of separation anxiety. This approach appears correct in part, since many school refusers express great appre-hension about leaving home and being separated from their mothers. Yet this is not true of all re-fusers, particularly older ones.

Marine (1968) has identified four basic types of school avoidance. The first of these types is *simple separation anxiety,* a mild reaction fre-

Separation anxiety reactions, such as this one, can be-come persistent problems if not handled properly. This mother is attempting to interest her little girl in the nur-sery school, while keeping a firm grip on her and not permitting her to escape from the situation. What would you do in this mother's place?

quently overcome without professional help. In simple separation anxiety, the young child may become distressed at parting from his mother to enter school. The mother may be unwilling or un-able to help the child become more independent and may keep him at home, thus unwittingly help-ing to create school refusal. Separation anxiety may be found in older students as well, although less commonly. The older child may fear that something bad might happen to his mother while he is away at school and stays at home in order to protect her. This type of reaction may be more common in single-parent families, or when there is parental strife, or when the father's job keeps him away from home for long periods of time and the child and mother develop strong mutual dependency. In the second type of school avoidance, *neurotic* or *mild acute school refusal,* initial onset is sudden in a child in the lower elementary school grades, and there is little family discord. Here the prognosis is excellent, since the child's primary or only problem is school attendance. The treatment approach is direct and often successful with little prospect for the recurrence of the problem.

When properly carried out, treatment of recent-onset school refusal is strikingly effective. Supportive psychotherapy and planned school attendance produced regular, successful school attendance in 89 percent of a sample of children younger than 11 years (Rodriguez, Rodriguez, & Eisenberg, 1959). When attendance is required, care must be taken to evaluate the child's physical complaints to ensure that any genuine illness is properly treated by scheduling medical examinations before or after school hours. Thus possible physical illness receives prompt attention, but the child's complaints do not serve as a means for evading school.

The return to school may be gradual. Kennedy (1965) has recommended that parents praise their child for attending school for at least 30 minutes on the first day he returns, and that longer attendance be required on each succeeding day. Parents are also advised to ignore the child's physical complaints (and thus not to reinforce them), other than to schedule the after-hours medical appointments and to be firm but not punitive. On the first day of treatment, they announce simply that David will return to school the next day. Then they praise him for his daily attendance, and on the third day they hold a little family party to celebrate David's recovery. This rapid treatment method produced regular school attendance without any reported ill effects in 100 percent of a group of school-phobic children (Kennedy, 1965). It is important to note that all of these children had school refusal of the mild acute type, and that this was their first occurrence of the disorder. Additional interventions, such as psychotherapy, relaxation training, participant modeling, or other procedures, may be required to treat more severe cases.

Severe chronic school refusal, the third type

identified by Marine (1968), is a very different form of the disorder and has a much poorer prognosis than those discussed previously. Chronic school refusal typically is found in children older than 11 years who come from unstable families. These children have many problems that often include other aspects of emotional disorder, such as feelings of depression, negative self-image, difficulty in getting along with family members, and somatic complaints (Ficula et al., 1983). The prognosis is particularly bad when the parents have behavioral problems or when they express negative attitudes toward school (Marine, 1968). Such parents are unlikely to encourage or support the youngster's attempts to return to school. Over half of these older children remain out of school, despite varied treatment attempts (Rodriguez et al., 1959). Of those half who return to school, only about one-third appear well adjusted. Another third have problems, particularly in relating to classmates and teachers, and the remainder experience severe adjustment difficulties (Berg, 1970). Thus the chances are just one in six that a young person with severe chronic school refusal eventually will achieve satisfactory psychological adjustment. In a very small minority of the cases, school refusal is combined with childhood psychosis in the fourth type of school avoidance *(child psychosis with school refusal symptoms).* Here, the child's prognosis is especially poor, as it is in all childhood psychotic reactions (see Chapter 10).

To summarize, there appear to be several different forms of school refusal, varying in severity and prognosis. These range from the less severe simple separation anxiety and mild acute school refusal, which are relatively easily treated, to the more formidable severe chronic and the psychotic forms. Because some forms of school refusal can have serious repercussions and all forms can be troublesome, it might be best to develop prevention programs to prevent the disorder's occurrence in the first place.

Theoretical Explanations of Phobic Reactions

There are relatively few well-articulated explanations of children's anxieties and phobias. Consequently, we describe just two major approaches to childhood disorders, the psychoanalytic and the learning theory positions. Each of these theories features similar explanations of phobias and of other emotional disorders. Therefore, we do not repeat this etiological material when we later consider obsessive-compulsive and somatoform disorders. Depression presents an exception to this rule; there are many competing theories of depression, which require later consideration.

Psychoanalytic Theory   Sigmund Freud (1909/1950) originally attributed phobias to psychologically created tension, anxiety, guilt, sexual jealousy, and rage (see Chapter 2 for a description of psychoanalytic theory). Even young children were not considered exempt from these destructive emotions. In his famous psychoanalytic interpretation of the horse phobia displayed by a 5-year-old boy named Hans, Freud traced Hans's fear of horses to the boy's Oedipal sexual desires for his mother and his rage toward and fear of his father, all of which were displaced upon an animal that reminded the boy of his father— the horse. His fear also benefited the boy by keeping him at home with his mother, while at the same time he avoided the horse-ridden 19th-century European streets. Under Freud's direction, the boy's father interpreted the psychological nature of his fear to Hans, and the horse phobia was overcome. This case provided the model for the psychoanalytic interpretation of children's phobias.

Sigmund Freud's daughter Anna (A. Freud, 1977) was herself a noted scholar who wrote extensively on child psychoanalysis. She described children's anxieties as originally diffuse and vague, but later compressed into anxiety about one symbolic object, such as a dog, which represents the actual unconscious fear. The child believes she fears the symbolic figure (e.g., the animal), but actually she fears becoming overwhelmed by her sexual and aggressive feelings and experiencing probable retaliation from her parents for acting on these inappropriate feelings. Once the child's anxiety is directed toward the symbolic, external object, she can reduce anxiety by avoiding that object. Psychoanalysts

believe that the choice of phobic object is not random, but depends upon some actual or fancied resemblance to persons or events featured in the psychological conflict. For example, Hans was believed to fear male horses because their size, strength, and genitalia reminded him of his father. Freud even believed that the horses' blinkers and bridles represented Hans's father's eyeglasses and mustache. Fearing his father's anger and possible physical retaliation for his Oedipal attachment to his mother, Hans warded off his real fear of and desire to hurt his father by believing he feared horses instead. The Freudian view is that feared objects are external symbols representing some serious unconscious wish or conflict. The conflict could be Oedipal, as in the case of Hans, or could represent superego (primitive, punitive conscience) or social anxiety, or separation anxiety focused on the mother might be at work. Most 20th-century Americans find this aspect of Freudian theory unconvincing.

Because psychoanalysts do not view the phobic behavior itself as the child's central problem, they shun direct treatments based on encounters with feared situations. Rather, analytic therapists first build a trusting relationship with the child (as do therapists of all theoretical persuasions) and then use play as a vehicle of communication. The child is encouraged to act out fears and fantasies in play within the context of the warm, accepting atmosphere of the play sessions as the analyst interprets the child's fantasies, play themes, and dreams. The parent's role is limited to supplying information about the child's problem that the child may be unwilling or unable to discuss. Most such parents are in analysis themselves with another therapist.

The child's phobic reaction is considered likely to disappear without further intervention when his basic psychological conflicts have been resolved and his troublesome misconceptions have been corrected by the analyst. Psychoanalytic treatment is very expensive and time-consuming, sometimes requiring 2 or more years of regular individual treatment sessions (Sterba, 1959), which makes it prohibitively expensive for most families. As a consequence, it is used only infrequently. There have been a number of therapists' reports of successful psychoanalytic treatment of children with phobias, but, as noted in Chapter 11, uncontrolled case studies do not provide scientifically acceptable evidence of treatment success. Therefore, the relative effectiveness of the psychoanalytic approach remains open to question.

Learning Theory Approaches   The earliest and best-known learning-based interpretation of children's phobias is the classical conditioning view of the early 20th-century behaviorist John B. Watson. Watson maintained that irrational fears are learned or conditioned through exposure to unpleasant stimuli in the presence of some other, actually harmless stimulus, such as an animal. Through such conditioning or pairing with frightening or painful events, harmless events come to be feared. Obviously, this is a much-simplified description of classical (Pavlovian) conditioning; successful conditioning requires careful control of the stimulus intensity, timing of the stimulus presentations, and number of paired stimulus presentations. Ignoring such methodological considerations, Watson purported to use a conditioning procedure to train a previously fearless infant named Albert to fear a white rat (Watson & Rayner, 1920). After ascertaining that little Albert did not initially fear the rat, Watson and his assistants presented the rodent to the child while striking a steel bar with a claw hammer to create an awful noise. The child cried and became distressed, and after seven such presentations Watson believed that he had established a fear of rats and other furry objects. Generations of college students have read about the edifying example of little Albert and his conditioned rat phobia, but unfortunately they were probably misled because Watson had grossly overstated his claim (Harris, 1979; Samuelson, 1980). In fact, there is very little scientifically acceptable evidence that fears can be conditioned in this manner. Watson's procedure was slipshod and uncontrolled, and his observations failed to convince skeptical readers that the infant actually consistently feared the animal or that any fear shown by the child was due to classical conditioning. Other attempts to condition

children's fears using this type of procedure have failed (Bregman, 1934; English, 1929), or laboratory conditioning of children's fears have not fared well (Rachman, 1977). As a result, psychologists have looked toward other learning mechanisms to account for the development of phobias.

A more generally accepted alternative is provided by social learning theory, which emphasizes the role of *modeling* or *observational learning* in the development of fearful reactions. Social learning suggests that the child observes and imitates the fearful reactions of other people, even of television characters. There may be verbal warnings from others (e.g., "Stay away from that snake! Snakes are so slimy; I can't stand them!"), as well as physical cues, such as grimacing, gesturing, or running away. Fears can be acquired through direct experience such as encounters with barking or biting dogs, but more through imitation or observational learning (Bandura, 1969). Ironically, children do not necessarily fear things that could harm them. For example, they are much more likely to be hit by automobiles or to drown in a river or swimming pool than to be bitten by a wolf or a snake. Yet they tend to fear snakes and wolves more often than they develop realistic fears of accidents involving cars or bodies of water. Their parents must make special efforts to teach children many of the more useful fears through the use of verbal instructions and either planned or unwitting modeling of the fears themselves.

Research has supported the observational learning view rather than the conditioning explanation of children's fears. Children tend to suffer from the same fears as their parents and siblings, particularly as regards insects and electrical storms (Jersild & Holmes, 1935), dogs and other animals (Bandura & Menlove, 1968), and school refusal (Granell de Aldaz, Feldman, Vivas, & Gelfand, 1987; Granell de Aldaz et al., 1984). When children have frightening encounters, they tend to look at their adult companions; for example, infants who notice a strange and possibly threatening situation look toward their mothers, apparently for cues as to how to behave (Campos, Campos, & Stenberg, 1981). If the mother laughs and expresses amusement at the strange happening, the infant does the same, but if she appears frightened, her baby is likely to become alarmed. As social learning theory would predict, fearful mothers tend to have fearful children, and specific fears seem to be transmitted within families.

The two major learning-based methods for treating fear reactions are *systematic desensitization* and *modeling* (and their variants). Systematic desensitization was first developed for phobic adults (Wolpe, 1958) and later was adapted for younger clients. The client first is asked to help construct a hierarchy ranking his fears from the least to the most severe. For example, a mild fear item for a test-anxious child might be "You hear about a friend who has a test soon," and the most intense fear item might be "You are taking a test and you don't remember any of the answers and you know you won't be able to finish in the amount of time left." Then the therapist teaches the client a set of exercises to deeply relax the different muscle groups throughout the body. The relaxation is used to counteract the muscular tension associated with fear and anxiety, because it is impossible to be tense and anxious and yet relaxed at the same time.

Various clever methods have been worked out to teach children how to relax, including training in following simple instructions (e.g., "Stand up and sit down"), playing the child's favorite music, and using bubble blowing to induce deep breathing (Morris & Kratochwill, 1983). Nevertheless, some children cannot be induced to relax, and they may giggle, yawn, squirm, clench or tap their fingers, etc. Others may be unable to conjure up the needed mental images from the hierarchy when instructed to do so, and consequently require other treatment approaches. Ideally, the client first imagines the least potent of his fears (e.g., his friend's taking a test) while relaxing his body completely. Then he is helped to imagine increasingly frightening scenes while maintaining a state of relaxation. At the conclusion of treatment, the client should be able to maintain relaxation even while contemplating the most intimidating situations and should be equally calm while encountering these situations in person. Although

the imaginal or systematic desensitization procedures have successfully counteracted the fears of adults, there is only mixed research evidence for their effectiveness in the treatment of children's fears (Graziano, DeGiovanni, & Garcia, 1979; Morris & Kratochwill, 1983).

Some children have trouble in imagining fear-provoking situations on cue, so they may respond better to *in vivo* desensitization, in which they practice relaxation in the actual feared situations. All desensitization takes place in gradual steps. For example, the child who fears some aspect of the school first is brought to the school building while school is not in session, then visits the building for a few minutes during her favorite school activity, and finally tolerates a complete school day. However, neither systematic desensitization nor *in vivo* desensitization teaches the child how to deal with the situations or objects she fears. Simple desensitization may not benefit children who lack necessary skills, such as how to handle animals or make presentations. Because children so often lack needed social, athletic, or cognitive skills, they may require treatment other than desensitization.

Modeling and guided participation have proved to be very effective methods for treating children's fears (Bandura, 1969; Rosenthal & Bandura, 1978). This treatment approach uses one or more people who serve as models to demonstrate increasingly direct and bold encounters with whatever the child fears. The child can see that there are no untoward results for the models and that there is nothing to fear. Moreover, the child learns effective methods for dealing with the dogs, snakes, injections, or other dreaded stimuli. This treatment method is particularly effective when a variety of adult and child models participate and they encounter several different examples of the feared stimulus (Bandura, Blanchard, & Ritter, 1969; Bandura & Menlove, 1968). To illustrate, two adults and three children can act as models and demonstrate how to interact with dogs of three different breeds. This is more reassuring and instructive for the dog-phobic child than if just one adult model plays with one dog. Modeling displays can conveniently and effectively be presented on film or videotape, making it unnecessary to assemble a large cast of models and snakes, dogs, medical personnel, thunderstorms, or whatever is needed in the child's treatment.

It is also extremely helpful to provide the fearful child with carefully supervised confrontations with the feared situations, gradually increasing the child's performance requirements. In one study, snake-avoidant children were shown fearless models and then were helped successively to touch the arm of a person who was petting the (nonpoisonous) snake, to stroke the snake with gloved hands, and finally to lift and handle the reptile (Ritter, 1968). Comparative treatment studies have indicated that this combination of modeling and guided participation is more powerful than other treatments such as desensitization or modeling alone (Bandura et al., 1969). Unlike slow and expensive psychoanalytic therapy or other forms of play therapy, the modeling and desensitization therapies require only approximately 4½ hours of treatment over a series of about four sessions (Gelfand, 1978). These latter forms of treatment often are combined with reinforcement for the children's courageous behavior. A limitation is that most of the research evidence concerns specific fears, such as those of animals, social encounters, medical or dental treatment, or academic evaluation. More evidence is needed concerning treatment effectiveness with other types of fears, such as of nightmares, separation anxiety, loud noises, heights, or school (Morris & Kratochwill, 1983). Here is another excellent opportunity for clinical research.

COMPULSIVE RITUALS AND OBSESSIVE THOUGHTS
Definitions and Description

Obsessions and *compulsions* have been defined as abnormal thoughts (obsessions) or acts (compulsions) that are (1) unrealistic, (2) experienced as irresistible, (3) experienced as internal rather than external in origin, (4) ritualistic and stereotyped, and (5) disruptive of everyday activ-

ities (Rachman & Hodgson, 1980). *Obsessions* are recurring thoughts, doubts, or fears that the person cannot repress, despite their unpleasant nature. They are not constructive and may even prevent the person from engaging in effective problem solving. In contrast, *compulsions* are repetitive acts that the person feels forced to carry out over and over again. Either obsessions or compulsions or both must be present and must constitute the person's major psychological problem for the diagnosis of obsessive-compulsive disorder (Rachman & Hodgson, 1980).

Constituting fewer than 1 percent of psychiatric referrals for adults (Adams, 1973; Rutter et al., 1970), obsessive-compulsive disorders are even rarer in children. This low rate in childhood is somewhat surprising, since most very young children insist on certain rituals that apparently reassure them and provide a sense of security, such as a familiar bedtime routine of nursery rhyme recitation or singing and a favorite stuffed animal or ragged old security blanket. Older children may feel compelled to touch certain objects, to avoid stepping on sidewalk cracks, or to wear particular items of clothing, and may object to minor changes in home routine. Playground games and chants have come down to us intact over many centuries, thanks to children's insistence on preserving them unchanged (Opie & Opie, 1959). In contrast to the normal rituals of childhood, pathological compulsive behavior often involves maintaining extreme cleanliness and repeated handwashing, bathing, and cleaning already spotless surroundings, as described in Box 4-2. Also, childhood rituals are dropped naturally as the child becomes older, while pathological routines typically persist together with phobic behaviors. Some phobic children later develop obsessions, and for others obsessions may be followed by phobias (Rutter & Garmezy, 1983). In fact, obsessions more often occur together with other problems (such as depression or phobias) than alone. This has led some authors to question whether obsessive and compulsive behaviors truly constitute a separate entity (Rutter & Garmezy, 1983). It is known that obsessions are persistent and that when emotional

---

BOX 4-2 • The Development of Compulsive Rituals—A Case History

Leon (1977) has recounted the story of Ruth Langley (not her real name), a woman who developed various compulsive rituals early in life. Ruth was the lonely only child of wealthy but neglectful parents. Her mother insisted that Ruth's clothing be kept spotless and that the child occupy herself quietly for many hours each day when she was just 4 or 5 years of age. The little girl arranged and rearranged her dolls in particular postures and locations and felt uncomfortable if she was interrupted before completing the precise arrangements she had planned. Each evening and each morning she placed her pillow, blankets, clothing, and furniture in special locations, and during the day she repeatedly washed herself and changed her clothing. Whenever she touched books or other objects that she considered unclean, Ruth felt compelled to wash her hands.

At the age of 10, the girl was referred by her teacher for psychological assessment because her compulsive rituals had begun to interfere with her school performance. Also, the other children had begun to tease her about her strange behavior.

Her compulsive behavior became even more burdensome and incapacitating as Ruth grew older. Repeated scrubbing with strong disinfectants had rubbed her hands raw, and more and more of her time was spent in trying to avoid contamination. Fortunately, she benefited from a course of desensitization treatments in which she was led to tolerate gradually increasing amounts of contaminants. She was also helped to interact more positively with others through individual counseling and group therapy. Even after years of practice of compulsive rituals and of seclusion, it was possible to improve this woman's life in a dramatic fashion.

Source: G. R. Leon. (1977). *Case histories in deviant behavior: An interactional perspective* (2nd ed.) (Boston: Holbrook Press).

---

disorders that include obsessions continue into adulthood, the obsessions are very likely to be maintained (Rutter & Garmezy, 1983).

Etiology and Treatment of Obsessive-Compulsive Disorder

For many years, psychoanalytic theory provided the generally accepted explanation of obsessive-compulsive disorder. Maladaptive thoughts and rituals were thought to be caused by anxiety resulting from unconscious psychological conflict. Compulsions were seen as avoidance maneuvers engaged in to reduce anxiety and magically prevent some dreaded event, such as the death of a parent. In the psychoanalytic view, performing the compulsive ritual prevents the occurrence of a threatening event and produces some relief from anxiety. The compulsive act is thought to be an attempt to control the child's unconscious hostility toward others, particularly the parents (Breuer & Freud, 1895/1955).

More recent, learning-based explanations stress that compulsive behavior can arise from various sources an can be continued for many different reasons. Factors other than anxiety may contribute to compulsive actions. In some cases, seemingly compulsive behavior is actually maintained by its sensory consequences—the sounds it produces.

In one study (Rincover, Newsom, & Carr, 1979), retarded and psychotic children repeatedly switched the room lights on and off. These light-switching rituals were largely eliminated by removing the sensory consequences of operating the light switches. The switch either was made inoperative or was padded so it no longer clicked. These changes dramatically decreased the children's operation of the switches, thus demonstrating that the light switching was maintained by its reinforcing consequences rather than because it reduced anxiety. The children did not appear anxious about the interruption of their light switching, which cast further doubt on the role of anxiety in causing their ritualistic behavior.

It may be argued that although the light switching was ritualized and persistent, it did not constitute true obsessive-compulsive behavior. Other psychological treatment methods have proved effective for persons who better fit traditional diagnostic criteria for obsessive-compulsive disorder. Under the guidance of behaviorally oriented therapists, adults have overcome their compulsive behavior through guided, prolonged exposure to the feared stimulus (Foa, Steketee, & Milby, 1980), and through mutually agreed upon prevention of their excessive hand washing or other ritualistic behavior (Mills, Agras, Barlow, & Mills, 1975; Walton & Mather, 1963). Foa et al. (1980) found that after one woman was reassured about her own safety and had consented to the procedure, her prolonged exposure to dirt and other feared contaminants greatly reduced her anxiety. However, anxiety reduction alone did not necessarily control her compulsive behavior, which required interruption. Active nonviolent interference with a person's performance of a compulsive act has proven effective in overcoming compulsions. With a compulsive hand washer, for example, the water may be turned off, making the ritual impossible to perform; or a compulsive object arranger may be deprived of objects to manipulate. It is not clear whether similar methods should be used with children. Here again, there is much to be learned. At present, emotionally disturbed children's compulsive behavior is most often treated through some form of play therapy.

DEPRESSION

Depression is one of the most common behavior disorders of adulthood (Weissman, Meyers, & Harding, 1978), occurrring in 17.5 percent of all people who receive mental health treatment (Na-

tional Institute of Mental Health, 1973). *Depressed affect* or *dysphoric mood* is a milder and more common malady than clinical depression, and occurs in reaction to stressful events such as the termination of an important relationship, the death of a loved one, a serious illness, or impending financial difficulties. In fact, nearly everyone experiences some depressed affect, but this type of reaction is time-limited and quite normal. However, when the person's depressed emotions are devastating, persistent, and out of proportion to the loss, or when there is no apparent accompanying loss, then the person may be suffering true depression of clinical proportions. In cases of *exogenous depression,* there is an identifiable loss or severe stress from external events, but *endogenous depression* strikes in the absence of an obvious external reason. The types of moods or affect experienced may vary also; in major affective disorder when only depression is experienced, the person is diagnosed as having a *unipolar affective disorder.* In contrast, in *bipolar affective disorder* depression is more severe, typically recurring over time, and depressed states may alternate with normal mood and with manic states characterized by inexplicable exhilaration, greatly increased activity, impulsivity, irritability, hilarity, and grandiose, unrealistic thinking. Bipolar affective disorder is sometimes referred to as *manic-depressive disorder.*

Among older teenagers and adults, signs of clinically significant depression include such marked behavior changes as lack of enjoyment in formerly preferred activities *(anhedonia);* withdrawal from friends and customary social activities; sad facial expression and demeanor; and pessimistic statements about self, others, and the world. Depression adversely effects the person's social, cognitive, and physical functioning—in fact, all aspects of life. The victim may complain of fatigue; disturbed sleeping patterns, such as prolonged sleep or worrisome early-morning wakefulness; difficulty in concentrating and remembering; and changed eating habits, with either constant gorging and weight gain or indifference to food resulting in a loss of weight. There also may be vague physical complaints, such as nausea, dizziness, stomachache, or shortness of breath. A formerly competent, decisive person may become hesitant, confused, troubled, and unable to make simple decisions.

Depressed children resemble depressed adults in many ways. Table 4-2 presents some of the features of the juvenile forms of depression. For adults, among the most characteristic signs of depression are preoccupation with personal deficiencies, excessive self-reproach for imagined wrongs, and a general, unrealistically pessimistic view of life. In extreme cases, the person may conclude that death is the only answer and may become actively suicidal. Dysphoric or sad mood, general pessimism, self-criticism, inability to enjoy oneself, and physical complaints are all aspects of adult and late adolescent forms of depression.

Childhood Depression

Does Childhood Depression Exist? Despite an increasing volume of research reports, chapters, and books on *childhood depression,* some authorities remain unconvinced that there is such a condition separate from other disorders. This attitude can be traced to the commanding influence of psychoanalytic theory in the first half of the 20th century. Psychoanalysts viewed children as too psychologically immature to become depressed. For example, the influential child psychoanalyst Margaret Mahler (1952) maintained that the immature child ego is incapable of producing adult-style depression and instead takes rapid defensive actions against the loss. The child uses denial and repression to defend against the

Table 4-2

Developmental Continuities and Discontinuities in the Diagnosis of Major Depression

A. Adult Diagnosis: DSM-III-R Criteria for Major Depressive Episode
For a period of at least 2 weeks, the person must have sad, dysphoric mood or loss of interest or pleasure and at least *four* of the following:

1. Poor appetite or significant weight loss or gain
2. Disturbed sleep or sleeping too much
3. General inactivity or agitation
4. Chronic fatigue, loss of energy
5. Self-devaluation, excessive guilt
6. Difficulty in concentration and inability to think decisively
7. Recurrent thoughts of death or suicide
8. No organic basis, no psychosis, not normal bereavement

B. Criteria for Children under 6 Years (Depression Is Very Rare)
For a period of at least 2 weeks, the child must have dysphoric mood, as inferred from a persistently sad facial expression, and at least *three* of the preceding eight symptoms. For this age group, item 1 applies if the child drops below weight gain age and sex norms. Item 3 is scored if the child becomes lethargic or much less active than usual. Also, depressed young children may develop toilet-training problems, withdrawn or aggressive behavior, or separation problems (extreme reluctance to be parted from a parent even briefly).

C. Criteria for Prepubescent Children (Depression Is Rare)
In addition to the previously listed DSM-III criteria, this age group may develop vague physical complaints, school and social problems, or strong fears or phobias.

D. Criteria for Adolescents (Depression Increases but Is Less Prevalent than in Adults)
Negativistic and antisocial behavior may appear, especially in boys, with sulky withdrawal from family and peer activities. School problems and substance abuse may begin. Oversensitivity, especially to rejection in love relationships, may be seen.

Sources: American Psychiatric Association. (1987). *Diagnostic and statistical manual of mental disorders* (3rd ed., revised). Washington, DC: Author; D. B. Herzog & J. M. Rathbun. (1982). Childhood depression: Developmental considerations. *American Journal of Diseases of Children, 136,* 115–120; E. Poznanski, H. Mokros, J. Grossman, & L. Freeman. (1985). Diagnostic criteria in childhood depression. *American Journal of Psychiatry, 142,* 1168–1173.

This boy clearly exhibits depressed mood. Depressed children may be lethargic, unhappy, and have problems associated with eating, sleeping, and health. It may be difficult to distinguish a depressed child from one who is physically ill.

emotional pain, and so does not develop true clinical depression.

Perhaps since the prevailing theory denied the existence of childhood depression, clinicians failed to observe it. Some clinicians agreed that children do not develop depressive symptoms, but claimed that a wide variety of problems, ranging from hyperactivity to phobias, constituted "masked depression" (Cytryn & McKnew, 1974). However, the concept of masked depression proved clinically unhelpful, because it was ill defined and overinclusive. Nearly any deviant behavior could be attributed to masked depression. Finally, in view of the mounting volume of clinical accounts of depressed children, the American Psychiatric Association (1980) recognized the legitimacy of the diagnosis for children, provided that the adult diagnostic criteria were met. Since young children are notably different from adults in their verbal and cognitive abilities, unmodified

adult psychiatric criteria fit them no better than adult clothing would. Instead, clinicians are beginning to formulate age-appropriate diagnostic criteria (Carlson, 1984; Cicchetti & Schneider-Rosen, 1984; Gelfand & Peterson, 1985; Kashani, Ray, & Carlson, 1984).

Clinicians have observed that depressed affect is a frequent accompaniment of such disorders as school refusal, separation anxiety, obsessive-compulsive disorder, or psychosis (Lachenmeyer & Gibbs, 1982; Rutter & Garmezy, 1983). Consequently, it is difficult to distinguish between depression and other types of disorders. Critics of the concept of juvenile depression also contend that normal children experience a high rate of sadness, somatic complaints, school aversion, and other presumed symptoms of childhood depression. Such problems are transitory, but could be mistaken for childhood depression (Lefkowitz & Burton, 1978). A major diagnostic problem is that adult depression is detected mostly through the complaints and self-reports of the sufferers. Children are much less skilled in recognizing and reporting their feelings, especially if they are under the age of 6 or 7 years (Cicchetti & Schneider-Rosen, 1984; Kovacs & Beck, 1977).

Use of the adult criteria from DSM-III results in extremely low rates of major affective disorder in young children. Of a large group of preschool children referred for assessment in a psychiatric clinic, 4 percent had possible depression and only 1 percent clearly had a major depressive disorder (Kashani et al., 1984). Rates of diagnosed depression rise during middle childhood. Estimates are that 0.85 percent of child psychiatric patients under the age of 10 years have a primary diagnosis of depression. In the same study, the rate rose with age and doubled (to 1.7 percent) for 10- to 14-year-olds, and more than doubled again to 7.6 percent among 18- to 19-year-olds. This compares with an adult rate of 14.8% for a primary depressive diagnosis among adult 25- to 44-year-old clinic clients (Orvaschel, 1983). Depression increases among disturbed adolescents, with almost one-third (28 percent) or more of teenage clinic patients found to be significantly depressed (Carlson & Cantwell, 1980).

Sex differences in the prevalence of depression also change markedly over the life span. Depression rates for adult women are approximately twice as high as for men (Lewinsohn & Amenson, 1981). Yet, in childhood, males' and females' depression rates do not differ (Gelfand & Peterson, 1985; Orvaschel, 1983). In the middle and late teens, the sex ratio in depression begins to approximate the female predominance in adulthood. The reason for the different sex composition of child and adult depressed groups is unknown at present.

Prognosis for Depressed Children The research results are scanty and only tentative at present, but children's depression seems to be relatively persistent and may become more severe over time. In one study, the great majority (69 percent) of a group of clinic children with dysthymic (less serious) affective disorder developed major depressive disorder within 5 years (Kovacs, Feinberg, & Crouse-Novak, 1984). The depressed child's long-term prognosis probably depends upon the type of illness. One study (Welner, Welner, & Fishman, 1979) found that one-third of a small sample of adolescents who were hospitalized with unipolar depression recovered completely and without further recurrences. However, those with bipolar reactions typically are more seriously incapacitated, and almost all of them continue to be disturbed. It would be accurate to say that childhood depression is rare but seriously incapacitating.

Theories of Depression

Psychoanalytic Theories The early work of Sigmund Freud (1917/1965) and of his colleague Karl Abraham (1966) dealt only with depression in adults, but these theories were late modified and revised to apply to children as well. The basic features of psychoanalytic theory are described in Chapter 2 and so will not be repeated here. Freud believed that depression begins with a constitutional predisposition toward overreliance on oral stimulation as the source of pleasure and reassurance (see Table 4-3, which contrasts the major theories of depression). The person with such a predisposition is thought to develop excessive needs for physical contact and reassurance (Malmquist, 1977). The child's unusually strong needs for love and affection make him highly vulnerable to any form of real or perceived rejection. Events such as the birth of a sibling, harsh weaning methods, or more subtle forms of loss of love and attention from parents may constitute traumatic events, which leave a psychological scar. Consequently, the child experiences both love and hate for the mother, whom he feels has rejected him. Later in life, when he once again experiences some blow to self-esteem, the basic conflict will recur and be manifested in depression.

The superego system (or harsh, primitive conscience), which develops at around the age of 5 years, is thought to be essential for the child's feelings of self-esteem. However, the superego system is supposed to be indiscriminately self-punitive, causing the child to turn his rage at being

Table 4-3
The Major Theories of Depression

Theory	Predisposing Event	Precipitating Events	Probability of Occurrence in Childhood
Psychoanalytic	Constitutional overreliance on oral stimulation	Real or imagined loss	Mixed opinion[1]
Beck's cognitive theory	Early rejection, loss, or failure	Major loss or disappointment	Can occur
Reinforcement theory	Unnecessary to have predisposing event	Serious loss of reinforcement for behavior	Can occur
Seligman's learned helplessness theory	Unavoidable pain or failure	Major loss or traumatic event	Can occur
Genetic model	Genetic transmission within families	Not specified	Can occur

[1]Bibring (1953) maintains that depression can occur in childhood; Wolfenstein (1966) disagrees and believes that depression occurs during adolescence at the earliest.

rejected inward as punishing feelings of guilt and despair. Self-punishment is thought to represent an attempt to placate the menacing superego (Schafer, 1960) and to arouse the concern of others.

The psychoanalytic explanation of depression has long had proponents, but is very difficult to verify. Private mental events that take place early in childhood are proposed to play a causal role in later depressive reactions. Troubled people are very suggestible, and it is possible that subtle suggestions from psychoanalysts are reflected in their patients' reports of their early experiences. When there is so much opportunity for memory failure and for distortions, patients' recollections may prove unreliable indicators of the causes of depression. However, other theories of depression also rely heavily on the patients' reconstructions of early childhood events, and so most theories are difficult to verify.

Beck's Cognitive Theory Disordered thinking is also an important factor in cognitive theories of depression, but, unlike the psychoanalysts, the cognitive theorists place no emphasis on unconscious conflict. Early experiences are thought to be important in both types of theories. In Beck's (1974) cognitive theory of depression, the individual is predisposed toward depression by some early trauma (such as rejection or the loss of a parent), or by her own unrealistic and perfectionist self-expectations.

There is some research support for the view that early loss predisposes children to depression. McKnew and Cytryn (1973) studied the backgrounds of children who developed affective disorders and found that some of the children had frequent separations from their families and received care from substitutes who were indifferent toward them or who provided atypical, unstable homes. Other depressed children had been exceedingly attached to a parent whom they lost through death, divorce, or separation. Some children remained at home, but their parents became preoccupied with a new spouse, a new baby, a serious illness, or employment problems. Of course, in most instances these family situations are stressful, but do not lead to childhood depression.

Beck believes that in later life depressive reactions may be triggered by stressful events, such as another major loss or disappointment. The depression-prone person mistakenly blames the loss on some personal shortcoming and becomes convinced that she herself is unlovable, incompetent, and unworthy. Kovacs and Beck (1977) describe a "cognitive triad" of distorted depressive thinking regarding (1) oneself, (2) the situation, and (3) the future. Depressed people believe that they suffer from some type of basic defect or character flaw that causes others to reject them. At the same time, they view others as making tremendous, impossible demands on them. They conclude that the situation cannot be improved and that the future is hopeless. Beck maintains that the disordered and distorted thinking typical of depression can be found in children as well as in adults, but fails to explain exactly how early stress produces distorted thinking. In addition, early loss does not always portend later depression, and highly distressing events such as the death of a parent are not invariably found among people who become depressed (Crook & Eliot, 1980). More information is needed about the various types of factors that produce depression, including possible genetic or constitutional factors, environmental stresses, and personality characteristics.

Learning Theories   The learning approaches emphasize the importance of different learning mechanisms in the production of depressed behavior. The *reinforcement* approach maintains that loss of predictable, earned positive reinforcement can produce depressed behavior. Ferster (1974) and Lewinsohn (1974) have suggested that depression may stem from a serious decrease in reinforcing events that have previously maintained the person's behavior. A high school graduate may enter college but be unable to achieve the good grades that have previously reinforced and maintained studying; a child may lose a preoccupied parent's reinforcing attention. In

such cases, there may be a significant loss of reinforcement for the individual, and this may ultimately lead to apathy and depressed affect. Complaints about feelings of worthlessness, guilt, and suicidal talk may elicit attention and concern from others, which may, in part, compensate for the decrease in reinforcement for more appropriate behaviors.

Lewinsohn and his associates (Lewinsohn, 1974) have demonstrated that depressed people are socially awkward. They fail to initiate conversation and do not respond to others' attempts to initiate interactions, which leads other people to avoid them, thus intensifying their isolation. In Lewinsohn's view, depressed people first suffer *extinction,* or near-total loss of reinforcement for their efforts. Consequently, they display emotional outbursts at first and ultimately become passive and withdrawn. Only changed behavior, such as seeking new sources of reinforcement or re-establishing familiar ones, can terminate the depressive reaction. One of the major problems of the reinforcement explanation is that it is not always possible to identify major losses of reinforcement preceding depressive episodes, as is the case in the endogenous form of depression.

A second learning-based approach to depression is Seligman's (1975) theory of *learned helplessness.* This model portrays early learning of helpless reactions to unavoidable stress as causing depression. Seligman observed that laboratory animals that had earlier encountered unavoidable shock later could not learn to escape when avoidance was possible. The inescapable shock had apparently interfered with adaptive responding, causing a reaction Seligman termed "learned helplessness." Similar reactions have been demonstrated in a much less extreme form in children who have encountered unsolvable problems (Dweck, 1977). Seligman reasoned that the passivity, helplessness, and hopelessness of depressed people might be analogous to the learned helplessness demonstrated in laboratory experiments (Abramson, Seligman, & Teasdale, 1978). People who experience inescapable and uncontrollable tragedies may become convinced that they cannot control their lives, so they give up helplessly. At this point, it is impossible to predict which children will become vulnerable to learned helplessness and which will resist (Miller & Norman, 1979). Also, there are wide individual differences in how people respond to inescapable noxious events. No inescapable major stress is observable in the life histories of some depressed people, which presents difficulties for Seligman's theory.

Genetic and Biochemical Factors in Depression   Some affective disorders tend to run in families, which suggests a possible genetic-biochemical basis for these disorders. Some research indicates that the more closely people are related, the more likely they are to share affective disturbance. For example, one study found that both members of pairs of identical twins had an affective disorder in 69.2 percent of the cases, as compared with only 13.3 percent for fraternal twins (Gershon, Bunney, Leckman, Van Eerdewegh, & De Bauche, 1976). Thus twins with identical genetic makeup are much more similar in mood disorder than are fraternal twins, who are no more genetically similar than any other pair of siblings. Such evidence suggests that there may be a genetic basis for at least some types of depression. Nevertheless, the finding that only one identical twin had an affective disorder in at least 30 percent of the cases indicates that other, nongenetic factors also contribute to the development of affective problems.

Studies of adoptees also indicate a possible genetic basis for affective disturbance. In one study, groups of persons adopted at birth were diagnosed by examiners unaware of their biological parents' psychiatric status. Affective disorder was found to be significantly more frequent among adoptees with a depressed biological parent than was the case for people with normal parents or those with parents suffering from other types of psychological disturbance (Cadoret, 1978).

Particular types of affective disorder seem to be transmitted within families. Close relatives of a person with unipolar depression are at greater risk for developing a unipolar disorder than are others, including relatives of those with bipolar

(manic-depressive) diagnoses. People with close relatives suffering from bipolar affective disorder are at the greatest risk of developing a serious major mood disturbance, although many in this high-risk group never develop such a disturbance. The risk of developing an affective disorder is nearly twice as great for females who have clinically depressed relatives as for males (Gershon et al., 1976; Johnson & Leeman, 1977). This sex difference is difficult to interpret and may only reflect the twice-greater depression prevalance among females than among males. Although it is generally agreed that there is a hereditary component to adult depression, there is controversy about exactly what is inherited and by what mechanisms (Baron, Klotz, Mendlewica, & Rainer, 1981; Jakimow-Venulet, 1981; Rutter & Garmezy, 1983). Moreover, there is scarcely any research on the genetics of childhood depression.

The advent of effective antidepressant medication in the late 1950s suggested that at least some types of depression might have a biochemical basis. Considerable research was directed toward identifying the types of affective problems most amenable to drug treatment. Today there is good research evidence that antidepressant medication is most beneficial for appetite and weight changes, middle-of-the-night and early-morning insomnia, and morning mood worsening; indications for its use include acute onset of the depression, family history of good response to antidepressant medications or electroconvulsive therapy, and the patient's previous good response to antidepressant medication (see review by McNeal & Cimbolic, 1986). A poorer drug response is found in people who have chronic rather than acute depression, schizophrenia in the family, or a poor family history of success with antidepressant drugs (Schoonover, 1983).

Scientists have speculated that depression stems from some malfunction of the neurotransmitters (such as norepinephrine, serotonin, and dopamine) in the brain. During the past three decades the neuropsychological explanation of affective disorders has become increasingly complex, and it is now thought that there may be both receptor and neurotransmitter involvement in hormonal responses in depression. It is very likely that there are various forms of depression, and that these forms may vary biologically. As one review concluded, "There may be multiple biochemical as well as psychological pathways to depression" (McNeal & Cimbolic, 1986, p. 372).

Treatment for Depression

Various types of play therapy (see Chapter 14) may be used to help depressed youngsters (Mosse, 1974), and individual or group psychotherapy is used with adolescents. Seriously depressed or suicidal youngsters must be hospitalized in order to protect and treat them, and antidepressant medications may be administered. Sometimes the entire family is referred for counseling and family therapy. The dearth of research information concerning the effectiveness of different forms of psychotherapy for treating childhood depression imposes a severe limitation on treatment efforts.

Children and adults often respond differently to antidepressant drugs. Lithium carbonate has been dramatically effective in the treatment of adult manic-depressive disorders, and other drugs, such as the tricyclic antidepressants and the monoamine oxidase (MAO) inhibitors have relieved depressive symptoms in adults. Disappointingly, all of these drugs have produced mixed results with children (Kramer & Feiguine, 1981; Puig-Antich & Gittelman, 1982; Rutter & Garmezy, 1983), perhaps in part because the diagnostic criteria used to select the depressed child subjects have varied widely from study to study, while the diagnostic guidelines for adults are relatively invariant. In addition, some drug treatment evaluation studies are methodologically flawed, possibly leading to mistaken conclusions. After reviewing the research literature, Petit and Briggs (1977) reported that tricyclic antidepressants are often ineffective in treating depression in persons younger than 18 years, and advised against prescribing these and other drugs, which could prove lethal in suicide attempts. Recent studies have provided more optimistic findings indicating that the expert administration of imipra-

mine can improve depressed children's cognitive and social functioning (Petti & Conners, 1983).

SUICIDE

Contrary to popular belief, children attempt suicide, and some of them succeed. Fortunately, suicide is very rare in children younger than 12 years (Shaffer & Fisher, 1981), although the rate rises significantly at about the age of 14 years. In the United States, the suicide rate increases dramatically from only 0.3 per 100,000 for 5- to 14-year-olds to 8.8 per 100,000 for 15- to 24-year olds (U.S. Bureau of the Census, 1985). As Table 4-4 indicates, in the general population 12.2 of each 100,000 people commit suicide each year (U.S. Bureau of the Census, 1985), and suicide rates are highest among the elderly, with 21.4 per 100,000 for people over 75 years (Diggory, 1976). According to the National Office of Vital Statistics, suicide rates are increasing among 10- to 14-year-olds. Although still extremely low, the suicide rate for this age group *tripled* from 0.4 per 100,000 children in 1955 to 1.2 per 100,000 in 1975 (Pfeffer, 1981). This increase may reflect physicians' greater alertness to the possibility of juvenile suicide and their increased willingness to diagnose it, so that more cases come to the attention of the authorities.

In the adult population more women than men attempt suicide, but more men actually succeed in killing themselves, perhaps because men tend to use more lethal methods such as firearms. Women more commonly choose less deadly methods such as overdoses of barbiturates or other drugs, which act slowly and permit victims to save themselves or to be rescued by others. Nevertheless, women's use of firearms in suicide attempts has increased dramatically in the past 25 years (U.S. Bureau of the Census, 1985). Children younger than 12 years of age tend to choose less lethal methods; there are no reports of children this age using firearms for suicide (Pfeffer, 1981). Perhaps the preferences related to age and gender arise from men's greater access to and proficiency in the use of guns. In addition, traditional sex-role differences may play a part, and men

Suicidal thoughts and actions are rare during childhood, but become increasingly common during adolescence. This police officer is using all of his training, skill, and experience in an attempt to convince the adolescent to come inside and talk.

Table 4-4

Suicide Rates by Sex, Race, and Age Group: 1982

Age	Total	Male		Female	
		White	Black	White	Black
5–14 years	.6	.9	.8	.3	.1
15–24 years	12.1	21.2	11.0	4.5	2.2
25–34 years	16.0	26.1	20.3	7.5	3.7
35–44 years	15.3	23.6	15.6	9.2	4.0
45–54 years	16.6	25.8	11.8	10.4	3.1
55–64 years	16.9	27.9	11.9	9.5	2.2
65 years and over	18.3	38.9	12.4	6.6	1.8
All Ages	12.2	20.7	10.1	6.1	2.1

Source: *Statistical Abstracts of the U.S.: 1986* (106th ed.). *National Data Book and Guide to Sources.* U.S. Bureau of the Census (1985). Table No. 122.

may be more likely to consider suicide only when they seriously intend to succeed (Lester, 1979). During childhood, however, there is no marked preponderance of male suicides, although rates may be slightly higher for boys (Pfeffer, 1981).

Children's Motives for Suicide

To some extent, children and adults have similar reasons for attempting suicide. Most suicides occur among depressed adults, and depression is also one major correlate of suicidal behavior in children (Pfeffer, 1981; Pfeffer, Conte, & Plutchik, 1979). Completed suicide is more often associated with depression, but attempted suicide more often reflects revenge, jealousy, demands for attention, and other hostile and manipulative motivations (Lumsden, 1980). What makes some children contemplate taking their own lives? Having parents and other family members who are depressed, otherwise psychiatrically disturbed, or suicidal; the death of someone close to them; and children's own adjustment problems are all associated with suicidal threats and behavior (Shafi, Carrigan, Wittinghill, & Derrick, 1985). Suicidal family members create emotional turmoil at home, and they can unknowingly serve as models for suicidal threats and behavior. Alternatively, the child or adolescent may be unwanted or abused, may feel valueless, or may be locked in serious conflict with parents. Whatever the reason, the child comes to feel a deep, hopeless despair and a doubt that improvement is possible. Some suicidal teenagers display antisocial reactions and other forms of psychopathology. In one small group of suicidal 12- to 19-year-olds (Shafi et al., 1985), 70 percent engaged in drug or alcohol misuse, and 70 percent showed serious antisocial behavior. An additional 65 percent were abnormally overcontrolled, withdrawn, and inhibited. Thus, most of these children had multiple problems in addition to becoming suicidal.

Younger children's motives for suicide may appear bizarre, but they are understandable given the children's cognitive developmental levels. Toolan (1968) has described several different causes of youthful suicide, including irrational thinking and revenge. Most children under 9 years

of age do not understand that death is universal, irreversible, and unavoidable (Childers & Wimmer, 1971). They may envision returning to be with their families, may think that they have magical recuperative powers, and may believe they can return after death to enjoy witnessing their parents' remorse about mistreating them. Nearly half of a small group of children who committed suicide had previously discussed, threatened, or attempted suicide (Shaffer, 1974). At least some of their threats and dangerous activities seemed designed to wring sympathy from unresponsive adults. It has been suggested that feelings of depression are less important precursors of suicide in young children than in adults (Gittelman-Klein, 1977), although only recently has it been possible to assess children's depression accurately enough to answer this question.

Suicide is a social as well as a psychological phenomenon. Suicide rates vary considerably across chronological age groups, as we have described, and they also differ dramatically in different historical periods and different cultures. There even have been highly localized outbreaks of suicide, as when several teenagers at the same school commit suicide during a short time period, or among intellectual groups, as in the *Sturm und Drang* literary movement when young men in 19th-century Germany considered suicide a romantic death. More recently there has been an epidemic of suicide among young Native American men on the Wind River Indian Reservation in Wyoming. In these occurrences, suicide becomes viewed by many group members as a reasonable and honorable solution to overwhelming problems. Cultures and nations also vary in suicide rates. When suicide is honored as a tradition, as in Japan, rates understandably tend to be high, but in Catholic countries, where suicide is prohibited by law and by religion, suicides are rare by world standards (see Box 4-3). Suicides are increasing in many parts of the world, perhaps partly because of improved case reporting, partly because religious and cultural prohibitions against suicide are loosening, and partly because of the influence of social and cultural changes in general.

BOX 4-3 • Cultural Differences in Juvenile Suicide Rates

It is difficult to compare suicide rates for different populations because of variations in record-collecting methods, thoroughness, and accuracy. Nevertheless, when there are extremely large differences between groups, it seems likely that their rates truly differ. For example, suicide appears to be less prevalent among young people in England than in the United States and Japan. Until 1977 the Japanese police did not keep records of the number of suicides occurring among their young people, but they were known to be numerous. In response to general concern about a perceived increase in child suicides, record keeping was initiated. During the first few months of record keeping, from March to August of 1977, an alarming total of 398 suicides were reported for Japanese children (Reuters News Agency, 1977). In the early 1950's, Japan's suicides for 15- to 24-year-olds were estimated to be 2½ times the rate of the next highest country (Iga, 1967).

Perhaps the Japanese cultural tradition that suicide is not only acceptable but is an honorable death in an intolerable situation is responsible for the country's high suicide rate. Moreover, Japanese children experience highly stressful academic competition from very early ages. The most desirable Japanese employers make a lifetime commitment to employ and to care for their employees, who are carefully chosen. Potential employees must have outstanding total academic records, preferably from the best schools; as a result, even kindergarten children are urged to study and perform well so that they become eligible for enrollment in the most desirable schools throughout their academic careers. Concerned families provide their children with additional tutoring to ensure their success, and urge them to work harder than their classmates. In addition, scapegoating by their classmates can be severe. When children cannot succeed and cannot bear the consequences of their lack of success, they may turn to suicide.

High youth suicide rates may prevail even in the absence of a strong cultural tradition. When there is little possibility for individual success of any type, wholesale destruction of cultural tradition, and pervasive discouragement and despair, suicide may be unusually frequent. This is the case in certain Native American tribes (but not in all tribes). Suicide rates for Native American adolescents average a shockingly high 18 per 100,000 in some tribes, and

---

Prevention of Suicide

Those who work with adolescents should know how to deal with young people who have threatened or attempted suicide. Even when threats appear highly manipulative and designed to let the adolescent get his own way, they are associated with a significantly increased rate of suicidal behavior, and so cannot be dismissed. In one study of suicide victims, 55 percent had previously made suicidal threats, 85 percent had expressed suicidal ideas (as opposed to 18 percent of a group of nonsuicidal adolescents), and 40 percent had made previous suicide attempts (Shafi et al., 1985). Such findings indicate that any suicidal talk, threats, or suspicious "accidents" should be taken seriously. Table 4-5 presents some suggestions for the management of teenagers who may

be suicidal. Mental health professionals should be contacted immediately, and the person's family and friends must insist that the potentially self-destructive teenager go for assessment and treatment. The pain of depression and suicidal impulses is not permanent, although it seems so to the victim; it can be overcome, given sufficient time and proper medical and psychological care.

PSYCHOLOGICAL FACTORS IN PHYSICAL PROBLEMS

Diagnosis of physical ills is complicated by the interaction of biological and psychosocial factors in many types of disorders. This section describes various types of disorders, ranging from those that

Box 4-3 (Continued)

are five times higher for males than for females (Berlin, 1986). Significantly, in the southwest the highest rates of adolescent suicide occur in the tribes whose cultural and religious traditions have been most devastated and whose unemployment rates are the highest (Van Winkel, 1981). Parental alcoholism, being forced to live away from home, having had more than one substitute caretaker, and having trouble with the law are all related to Native American adolescent suicide (Dizmang, Watson, May, & Bopp, 1974). The young people have suffered parental mismanagement and insensitive government policies, and lack knowledge of their cultural roots. They find that they are neither truly Indian nor treated like whites.

The most promising treatment and prevention efforts have been based upon tribal traditions. One program attempts to prevent suicide among young men who have been jailed for committing minor crimes, often when they had been drinking, and who may prefer death to being shamed before their families and tribes. A tribal elder is assigned to stay with the boy overnight in jail and to provide emotional support for him. The elder speaks to him in the traditional language, whether or not the boy understands it well, and attempts to convince him of the importance of his practicing and transmitting the tribal traditions (Shore, Bopp, Waller, & Dawes, 1972). The many alcoholism treatment centers on the reservations also attempt to prevent suicide by controlling Native Americans' inadvertent self-destruction through alcohol dependency.

Sources: I. N. Berlin. (1986). Psychopathology and its antecedents among American Indian adolescents. In B. B. Lahey and A. E. Kazdin (Eds.), *Advances in clinical child psychology* (Vol. 9) (New York: Plenum); L. H. Dizmang, J. Watson, P. A. May, and J. Bopp. (1974). Adolescent suicide at an Indian reservation. *American Journal of Orthopsychiatry, 44,* 43–49; Iga, M. (1967). Japanese adolescent suicide and social structure. In E. S. Shneidman (Ed.), *Essays in self-destruction.* New York: Science House; Reuters News Agency. (1977). Children's suicides show increase in Japan. *The Salt Lake Tribune,* November 11, p. 4D. J. H. Shore, J. H. Bopp, T. R. Waller, and J. W. Dawes. (1972). A suicide prevention center on an Indian reservation. *American Journal of Psychiatry, 128,* 1086–1091; N. Van Winkel. (1981). *Native American suicide in New Mexico: A comparative study, 1957–1979* (unpublished master's thesis, University of New Mexico).

mimic physical illnesses but apparently are purely psychological to those that have a clearly physical basis but are affected by socioemotional factors and can be ameliorated by psychological means.

Somatization Disorders

First, there are the *somatization disorders*, in which the person expresses recurrent and multiple somatic complaints over a several-year period and repeatedly seeks medical attention. However, no physical disorder can be identified by any means (American Psychiatric Association, 1987). In order to qualify for this diagnosis, the complaints must be numerous and exaggerated, comprising at least 14 symptoms for women and 12 for men. The person complains of having been sickly for a long time and has a dazzling array of symptoms, which may include apparent neurological involvement (such as unverifiable paralysis or blindness), gastrointestinal pain, gynecological problems (such as painful menstruation), sexual problems (such as loss of desire), dizziness, palpitations, and other apparent cardiopulmonary difficulties. The number and type of complaints, their exaggerated quality, and the constant seeking of attention from numerous physicians and clinics mark this reaction as psychopathological. Somatoform disorders are extremely rare in men, and are thought to occur in approximately 1 percent of females (American Psychiatric Association, 1980). Almost nonexistent in childhood, somatoform disorders are believed to begin in the preadolescent and adolescent years.

Table 4-5
Psychological First Aid for Use with Adolescents at Risk of Committing Suicide

The following are preventive steps for the mature adult dealing with the suicidal youngster:

Step 1: Listen.
The first thing a person in a mental crisis needs is someone who will listen and really hear what he is saying. Every effort should be made to understand the feelings behind the words.

Step 2: Evaluate the seriousness of the youngster's thoughts and feelings.
If the person has made clear self-destructive plans, however, the problem is apt to be more acute than when his thinking is less definite.

Step 3: Evaluate the intensity or severity of the emotional disturbance.
It is possible that the youngster may be extremely upset but not suicidal. If a person has been depressed and then becomes agitated and moves about restlessly, it is usually cause for alarm.

Step 4: Take every complaint and feeling the patient expresses seriously.
Do not dismiss or undervalue what the person is saying. In some instances, the person may express his difficulty in a low key, but beneath his seeming calm may be profoundly distressed feelings. *All* suicidal talk should be taken seriously.

Step 5: Do not be afraid to ask directly if the individual has entertained thoughts of suicide.
Suicide may be suggested but not openly mentioned in the crisis period. Experience shows that harm is rarely done by inquiring directly into such thoughts at an appropriate time. As a matter of fact, the individual frequently welcomes the query and is glad to have the opportunity to open up and bring it out.

Step 6: Do not be misled by the youngster's comments that he is past his emotional crisis.

Often the youth will feel initial relief after talking of suicide, but the same thinking will recur later. Follow-up is crucial to ensure a good treatment effort.

Step 7: Be affirmative but supportive.
Strong, stable guideposts are essential in the life of a distressed individual. Provide emotional strength by giving the impression that you know what you are doing and that everything possible will be done to prevent the young person from taking his life.

Step 8: Evaluate the resources available.
The individual may have both inner psychological resources, including various mechanisms for rationalization and intellectualization that can be strengthened and supported, and outer resources in the environment, such as ministers, relatives, and friends whom one can contact. If these are absent, the problem is much more serious. Continuing observation and support are vital.

Step 9: Act specifically.
Do something tangible; that is, give the youngster something definite to hang onto, such as arranging to see him later or subsequently contacting another person. Nothing is more frustrating to the person than to feel as though he has received nothing from the meeting.

Step 10: Do not avoid asking for assistance and consultation.
Call upon whoever is needed, depending upon the severity of the case. Do not try to handle everything alone. Convey an attitude of firmness and composure to the person so that he will feel something realistic and appropriate is being done to help him.

Source: C. J. Frederick. (1976). Trends in mental health: Self-destructive behavior among younger age groups. *Keynote, 4,* 3-5.

Hysterical or Emotional Contagion

Quite different are group outbreaks of seeming physical disease. In such instances, there seems to be emotional rather than physical contagion. Usually this group contagion occurs at schools among groups of adolescents. Typically, at first one or two students fall ill, and then a few onlookers and finally many others suffer the same fate. They may complain that they feel dizzy and have severe headaches or nausea; some may become frightened and hyperventilate (begin to breathe rapidly and shallowly), causing them to faint. *Hysterical contagion* is suspected when many students are affected but thorough inspection reveals no detectable toxic or infectious agent. Often the victims' recovery is extremely rapid once the fear abates. In the representative episode, the initiator is a popular and influential group member who is taken ill and receives sympathetic attention from followers. The rumor arises that the initiator's illness is due to some poison or infection. Others develop similar symptoms and are comforted and treated, and health services are brought in. The strange behavior of the young people and the absence of any apparent physical cause convince the authorities that group

emotional contagion is at work. Conviction grows that no one is in danger, there are no new cases, and the "epidemic" is over (Gehlen, 1977; Stahl & Lebedun, 1974). Box 4-4 describes one such occurrence of hysterical contagion.

Physical Illnesses with Emotional Components

Finally, there are genuine physical illnesses with emotional components. Psychological factors such as stress and negative emotions can contribute to the formation, continuation, or exacerbation of many physical conditions. Common examples of physical conditions thought to be affected by psychological influences include migraine headache, bronchial asthma, gastric and duodenal ulcers, painful menstruation, and irregular heart

BOX 4-4 • **Hysterical Contagion in an Elementary School**

It all started when Sandy, a pretty and popular fifth-grade girl, slipped away from chorus practice at school and collapsed on a couch in the clinic room. The school secretary found her there, tried to revive her without success, and then called the fire department. An emergency team arrived quickly, put Sandy on a stretcher, and took her to the hospital. This happened just as the 9:00 classes let out, so many children saw Sandy being carried away, still unconscious. Minutes later another child complained of feeling sick; then others began to report stomachache, headache, dizziness, chills, and feelings of weakness, and some began hyperventilating (breathing fast and deep). A nearby doctor arrived, saw the fire department rescue team, noticed the children who were feeling ill, and also noticed a peculiar odor. The doctor mentioned that the children might have been affected by some toxic gas.

Some 73 children in the school reported feeling ill; the illness seemed to strike girls and fifth- and sixth-graders in particular. Members of the school board, the town council, and the public health department began to arrive. Neighbors, parents, and others in the vicinity all joined the anxious group. Seven other children were sent to the hospital.

Then something happened to relieve the problem. A public health doctor noted the curious variety of symptoms the children displayed and saw that some of them were hyperventilating. He knew that hyperventilation can occur when people feel very anxious or panicky. He called the hospital and discovered that the children from the school were feeling better and seemed to be in normal health. The strange smell was traced to an adhesive used in laying down a new carpet.

Then the doctor took decisive action. He announced to the assembled crowd that there was no gas poisoning or disease. He said there was an outbreak of mass hysteria. The children were sent back to their classes, the visitors departed, and the emergency was over. And Sandy recovered from her *genuine* illness, some sort of viral infection that had triggered the whole problem at the school.

Source: B. Rouché. (1978, August 21). Annals of medicine: Sandy. *The New Yorker*, pp. 63-70.

rates (American Psychiatric Association 1980). Many other physical disorders are thought to have psychological components as well (e.g., Dohrenwend & Dohrenwend, 1974). As yet, researchers have studied the possible psychological contributors to only a few of the more common childhood physical conditions. The two considered here are insulin-dependent diabetes mellitus (juvenile-onset diabetes) and bronchial asthma.

Diabetes Mellitus Diabetes mellitus is a serious chronic disorder in which insulin secretion is abnormal, disrupting the normal metabolism of carbohydrates, proteins, and fat. Eventually this metabolic abnormality produces cardiovascular and neurological damage (Santiago, 1984). When a patient's prescribed insulin administrations are omitted, severe insulin deficiency can induce coma and result in death. The juvenile-onset form typically develops during childhood, but can appear as early as infancy. Diabetes is difficult to manage in children, because the treatment procedure requires careful monitoring of blood and urine glucose levels, exercise, and strict dietary control. Young children understand neither the procedures they must follow nor the consequences should they fail to do so. Therefore, their parents must monitor their conditions very carefully. The best control is achieved when patients closely monitor their own condition.

Apparently there is no "diabetic personality" typical of diabetics as a group. Nor are particular family characteristics associated with juvenile diabetes (Delamater, 1986). Nevertheless, life circumstances are important to children's adherence to the demanding treatment regimen. Many studies have found that children whose diabetes was under good metabolic control came from more harmonious and cohesive families, whereas the families of those in poor metabolic control experienced more strife, had more financial problems, and were less stable (Anderson, Miller, Auslander, & Santiago, 1981; Koski & Kumento, 1977; Swift, Seidman, & Stein, 1967). Other types of long-term and significant stress may also disrupt maintenance of the treatment program, particularly for children who have unrealistic, avoidant coping styles (Delamater, 1986).

Not surprisingly, many children fail to comply with their doctors' instructions to complete the unpleasant blood and urine glucose testing several times each day, and they may not understand the complex balancing of nutrients required in their diets. Few diabetic children get a sufficient amount of exercise, which has been found to be beneficial for adult diabetics (Delamater, 1986). Now, however, intervention methods from behavioral psychology are being used to benefit these children: Precise instructions and positive reinforcement contingencies are used to increase their treatment compliance rates, and children are taught self-regulation skills so that they can take care of themselves (Carney, Schechter, & Davis, 1983; Lowe & Lutzker, 1979). Such measures are at least temporarily effective. In time it will be possible to determine whether these interventions will permanently improve children's compliance and health.

Bronchial Asthma Asthma is a potentially serious respiratory disorder characterized by periodic attacks of constriction of the bronchial passages in the lungs. The victim wheezes, coughs violently, and gasps for air. In the most severe attacks, the oxygen supply to the brain may be interrupted, and respiratory failure may lead to death. Asthma is somewhat more common in childhood than later in life, and about 60 percent of all asthma patients are children. Boys are more likely to develop asthma than are girls (Purcell, 1975).

Asthma attacks can be brought about by infections or exposure to allergens, and can be intensified by emotional stress in some cases. Faulty relationships with parents sometimes play a role. A few asthmatic children seem to improve when temporarily separated from their parents, even when the children remain in their homes and customary surroundings (Purcell et al., 1969). Since the children remain at home and are exposed to the same allergens as usual, their improvement clearly seems related to some aspect of the parent-child relationship.

Nevertheless, there is no research evidence that *either* asthma or diabetes *originates* from psychological factors (Alexander, 1977). Neither dis-

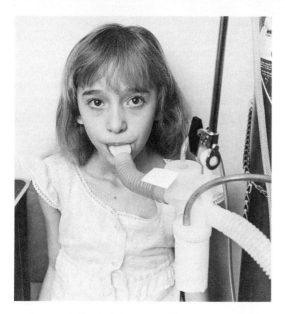

Asthmatic children's behavior problems may result from their illness and treatment. This girl has severe bronchial asthma and requires mechanical assistance so that she can breathe easily.

ease favors children of particular personality types, nor do these diseases produce characteristic personality features in their victims. Different children respond to the challenge of disease in their own styles, aided or impeded by their families, friends, and physicians. Compared to their former selves, though, children who develop chronic diseases can become more demanding, hypersensitive, and dependent on their parents (Alexander, 1977).

The treatment of asthma involves both medical and psychological management. Medications usually must be taken several times a day to produce bronchial dilation and to prevent spasm; like all potent drugs, these can produce unpleasant and even dangerous side effects. Children may also be taught voluntary muscle relaxation techniques to reduce wheezing and to improve pulmonary functioning during asthma attacks (Alexander, Miklich, & Hershkoff, 1972). Alternatively, they may participate in relaxation training to reduce their apprehension about asthma attacks or medical treatments. Training in relaxation skills has been found to be helpful for children with

asthma and other clearly delineated problems, especially when the children learn how to use relaxation techniques in everyday situations (Richter, 1984). If family discord aggravates the child's asthma, then family therapy may prove beneficial (Minuchin et al., 1975). The emerging fields of behavioral medicine and health psychology are proving increasingly helpful in the reduction and control of disease.

SUMMARY

It is normal for children to develop fears, but anxiety disorders are suspected when fears are unusual in their age of onset, intensity, persistence, and type. Phobias are thought to stem from experiences featuring observational learning, direct instruction, classical or Pavlovian conditioning, or internal psychological conflict (the psychoanalytic explanation). Most childhood phobias are overcome with or without professional treatment. An exception is chronic, severe school refusal, which is difficult to treat and has a poor prognosis for future adjustment. School refusal is found all over the world, and in its simple, acute form it is easily treated by a carefully managed return to school. Imipramine drug treatment has potentially dangerous side effects but has been reported to be successful, as have learning-based treatments such as *in vivo* desensitization and modeling. Participant modeling appears to be one of the most effective and least costly therapies for children's specific fears.

Obsessive-compulsive disorders are extremely rare during the childhood years, but become more common during adolescence. Compulsive rituals may be motivated by anxiety, by the sensory consequences they produce, or by their attention-commanding effects on other people. There has been little scientific study of the treatment of obsessive-compulsive disorders in early life.

Childhood depression is not unanimously recognized as a true syndrome separate from other emotional disorders, although clinicians are increasingly subscribing to this view. Depressive symptoms may vary with age, making it inappropriate to use adult diagnostic criteria with children. Specialists estimate that one-third or more of patients in child psychiatric clinics are depressed. Depression is variously attributed to unconscious conflict originating early in life (psychoanalytic theory), to cessation of customary reinforcing activities (operant learning explanation), to learned helplessness (Seligman's theory), or to distorted thinking linked with early loss (Beck's cognitive theory). The condition is rare, and little is known about treatment effectiveness. Preliminary studies indicate the utility of antidepressant drug treatment and of reinforcement contingency management.

Suicide is virtually unknown among children before the ages of 10-12 years, but the rate rises dramatically in early adolescence. Juvenile suicide is associated with depressed mood, but also arises from other types of motivation, such as anger and a naive belief that ordinary life contin-ues after death. Suicide rates are affected by religious, cultural, and socioeconomic factors as well as by peer group influences. Self-destructive behavior can be prevented by alertness to suicidal talk and to ineffectual attempts, and by firm insistence that the youth obtain professional help.

Physical illnesses may have emotional components. Although no particular personality characteristics seem to lead to physical illness, stress can exacerbate existing conditions and interfere with carrying out the complex and demanding daily treatment programs for chronic diseases such as diabetes mellitus and bronchial asthma. These two serious chronic diseases can arise early in childhood, and they appear responsive to family conflict and other sources of stress. The psychological treatment approaches found useful in such situations include family therapy and behavioral methods such as relaxation training.

chapter

5

Disorders of Social
Behavior

KEY TERMS

Attention Deficit Disorder with Hyperactivity (ADD-H).   A disorder-involving primary behavioral difficulties in (1) not being able to attend to tasks for extended periods of time, (2) acting before thinking about the consequences (impulsivity), and (3) fidgety or excessive motor activity.

Conduct Disorder.   A disorder involving primary behavioral difficulties in (1) rule-breaking behavior, (2) aggression, and (3) noncompliance.

Juvenile Delinquent.   A child or adolescent who usually displays some of the behavior of ADD-H and conduct-disordered children, but has also broken some type of law.

Coercion.   The process in a negative interaction between a child and an adult in which increasing aversive behavior occurs. At some point in the interaction, the child may become so aversive (e.g., tantrums, arguing, aggression) that the adult withdraws the demand and thus negatively reinforces the child's aversive behavior.

CHAPTER OVERVIEW

Problem behaviors that affect society, the environment, and other people directly are particularly difficult to prevent or to treat. These problem behaviors have been called *externalizing* behaviors because they are directed outwardly toward the social environment (Achenbach, 1982). They can be contrasted with *internalizing* problem behaviors (such as anxiety, fears, and depression), which primarily affect the child and have less obvious impact on the social environment. Examples of externalizing behavior might be a student who physically attacks a teacher, a child who deliberately sets a home on fire, or a neighborhood gang who robs a store. These are all examples of externalizing behaviors that are likely to bring a strong negative reaction from the community. Frequently, this reaction enmeshes a child or adolescent in a correctional system or results in his expulsion from school.

Externalizing problem behaviors are the most common reason for a child's referral for help by teachers and parents (Kazdin, 1985; Patterson, 1964; Wiltz & Patterson, 1974). But treatment success is modest. Children who are aggressive, argumentative, and noncompliant have poorer long-term outcomes than most children with other behavior disorders (Morris, Escoll, & Wexler, 1956; Robins, 1979; Rutter, Tizard, Yule, Graham, & Whitmore, 1976; Walker et al., 1986). Yet many professionals and educators tend to underestimate the long-term seriousness of externalizing/social disorders (Carter, 1987; Jenson, 1978). These children are not likely to outgrow their problems. The reverse is actually true, because adults who were socially disordered as children are more likely to develop such serious adjustment problems as hospitalizations for a mental disorder, arrest, multiple job changes, and divorce (Robins, 1979).

The terms commonly used by schools, juvenile courts, and mental health clinics to describe externalizing/social disorders include *antisocial personality, hyperactivity, attention deficit disorders, aggression, conduct disorder,* and *delin-quency.* These labels are not mutually exclusive and overlap in many cases. This chapter reviews the major types of externalizing/social disorders: attention deficit disorder with hyperactivity, conduct disorders, and juvenile delinquency. All of these conditions are related to some extent. However, we define each condition precisely, and review possible causes, the effectiveness of current treatments, and long-term outcome.

ATTENTION DEFICIT DISORDER WITH HYPERACTIVITY

Attention deficit disorder with hyperactivity (ADD-H) is one of the most frequently referred psychological disorders of childhood (Herbert, 1978; Langhorne, Loney, Paternite, & Bechtoldt, 1976), although a great deal of confusion has existed about the condition's definition and name. However, writers agree that ADD-H is more prevalent in males than in females, with the ratios ranging from 3:1 to 9:1, depending on the definition used by a particular research group (Ross & Ross, 1982). Similarly, the overall prevalence of ADD-H is estimated to be approximately 3 to 5 percent of the school-age population, but varies widely, depending on the criteria used to define the condition (Barkley, 1985). The developmental course of ADD-H is fairly stable, with onset of the condition probably occurring at 2 to 3 years of age in 50 to 60 percent of the cases (Barkley, 1985). The majority of the cases are not referred for professional help until the children first enter school and experience difficulty in that setting. A sizable minority of mothers (30 percent) report early difficulties with infants who later develop ADD-H. These infants are described as colicky, irritable, and hard to manage, and as having a difficult temperament (Barkley, 1985). Most children who develop ADD-H in childhood continue to have some adjustment difficulty in adolescence and early adulthood (Wallander & Hubert, 1985; Weiss & Hechtman, 1986). It is a myth that ADD-H changes dramatically in adolescence. However, to understand this condition better, it is first important to understand how it is defined.

Defining ADD·H

This condition has had several different names, including *hyperkinesis* (high rate of movement), *minimal brain dysfunction* (MBD), and most recently ADD-H. The plethora of names has been unfortunate and confusing. These terms have implied high rates of motor activity, some type of brain dysfunction, and difficulty in paying attention. However, since the third edition of the *Diagnostic and Statistical Manual of Mental Disorders* (DSM-III-R) was published by the American

Psychiatric Association in 1987 (*see* Chapter 12), the primary focus of this condition has been on poor attending skills. Table 5-1 lists the currently accepted definition of ADD-H.

Inattention   It can be seen from the definition in Table 5-1 that *inattention* is a central characteristic of ADD-H (Weiss & Hechtman, 1986). Descriptions of ADD-H children often include such statements as "He can never concentrate on his school work because he is staring out the window

Table 5-1
DSM-III-R Definition of Attention Deficit Hyperactivity Disorder

Note: Consider a criterion met only if the behavior is considerably more frequent than that of most people of the same mental age.

A. A disturbance of at least six months during which at least eight of the following are present:

(1) often fidgets with hands or feet or squirms in seat (in adolescents, may be limited to subjective feelings of restlessness)
(2) has difficulty remaining seated when required to do so
(3) is easily distracted by extraneous stimuli
(4) has difficulty awaiting turn in games or group situations
(5) often blurts out answers to questions before they have been completed
(6) has difficulty following through on instructions from others (not due to oppositional behavior or failure of comprehension), e.g., fails to finish chores
(7) has difficulty sustaining attention in tasks or play activities
(8) often shifts from one uncompleted activity to another
(9) has difficulty playing quietly
(10) often talks excessively
(11) often interrupts or intrudes on others, e.g., butts into other children's games
(12) often does not seem to listen to what is being said to him or her
(13) often loses things necessary for tasks or activities at school or at home (e.g., toys, pencils, books, assignments)
(14) often engages in physically dangerous activities without considering possible consequences (not for the purpose of thrill-seeking), e.g., runs into street without looking

Note: The above items are listed in descending order of discriminating power based on data from a national field trial of the DSM-III-R criteria for Disruptive Behavior Disorders.

B. Onset before the age of seven.

C. Does not meet the criteria for a Pervasive Developmental Disorder.

Criteria for severity of Attention-deficit Hyperactivity Disorder:

Mild: Few, if any, symptoms in excess of those required to make the diagnosis and only minimal or no impairment in school and social functioning.

Moderate: Symptoms or functional impairment intermediate between "mild" and "severe."

Severe: Many symptoms in excess of those required to make the diagnosis and significant and pervasive impairment in functioning at home and school and with peers.

Source: American Psychiatric Association. (1987). *Diagnostic and statistical manual of mental disorders* (3rd ed., revised) (Washington, DC: Author), pp. 52-53. Reprinted by permission.

or disturbing his neighbor," or "She never listens to instructions. It goes in one ear and out the other." Clearly, when compared to nonhandicapped children, ADD-H children have more difficulty attending to a task for a sustained period of time and working independently (Barkley, 1985; deHass & Young, 1984). In addition, these children may also have difficulty screening out irrelevant or extraneous stimuli (Cantwell, 1975). Even if an ADD-H child tries to attend, he may be distracted by a common classroom noise, such as a truck passing outside the school window or another child tapping her pencil.

Impulsivity   Inattention is important, but it does not completely define ADD-H. Other characteristics are also important. For example, the definition of ADD-H in Table 5-1 lists several impulsive characteristics (i.e., difficulty waiting, blurts out answers, or interrupts) that help define ADD-H. The word "impulsivity" suggests poor self-control, excitability, and the inability to delay gratification or to inhibit urges. Examples of impulsivity include jumping into the deep end of a pool despite not knowing how to swim, darting in front of traffic, risking falls by climbing along rooftops and ledges, and making tactless statements without stopping to think (Cantwell, 1975). Some of these behaviors are dangerous and result in accidents (Barkley, 1985), such as automobile accidents for ADD-H adolescents (Hechtman, Weiss, Perlman, & Amsel, 1984). In essence, impulsivity is characterized by acting before weighing alternative responses (Kagan, 1966). One approach to assessing impulsivity is to have a child scan an array of different line drawings and identify the one that is identical to a comparison drawing (see Figure 5-1). For instance, children would be shown the picture in Figure 5-1 and would have to pick a bear from the bottom group that exactly matches the sample bear at the top. This test is called the Matching Familiar Figures Test, and ADD-H children generally make decisions faster and with more errors than nonhandicapped children (Messer, 1976).

Overactivity   The terms *hyperactivity* and *hyperkinesis* refer to high levels of activity and energy. ADD-H children are frequently described as "always on the move" or "bouncing off the walls." ADD can be diagnosed either with or without hyperactivity. However, the vast majority of cases of ADD involve hyperactivity.

The actual methodological measurement of hyperactive children's motor activity ranges from simple observations of behavior to sophisticated measuring devices such as ultrasonic sensors, actometers (self-winding wrist watches), and pneumatic cushions which measure movement. Interpretation of activity level measures is difficult, because we lack norms specifying average rates of activity for children at different ages (Ross & Ross, 1982). In the absence of norms, researchers usually compare motor activity of identified ADD-

FIGURE 5-1. Sample item from the Matching Familiar Figures Test.

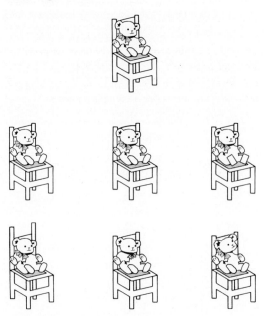

Source: Kagan, J. (1966). Reflection–impulsivity: The generality and dynamics of conceptual tempo. *Journal of Abnormal Psychology, 71,* 17–24.

H children with that of nonhandicapped children. The results are perplexing. It appears that ADD-H children are generally indistinguishable from nonhandicapped peers in unstructured free-play situations (Barkley & Ullman, 1975; Routh & Schroeder, 1976).

Perceived activity, however, seems to vary with the type of environment. Situations differ in their structure and in the demands they place on a child. As the structure and demand characteristics of an environment increase, then ADD-H children begin to stand out and be perceived as being overactive (Jacob, O'Leary, & Rosenbald, 1978). The type of activity must be considered in the assessment of ADD-H children. Overall levels of activity may not be the critical element in identifying hyperactive children; instead, it may be whether their activities bring them into conflict over rule breaking with their caretakers (Ross & Ross, 1982; Routh, 1980). A child who fidgets, taps his foot, is unable to keep his hands to himself, and talks out of turn may constantly come to the attention of the teacher and be perceived as overly active. A child who is engaged in the same amount of motor activity but who is diligently working is judged to be normally active. Support for the idea that an ADD-H child is primarily off-task and impulsive (see also Box 5-1), instead of just overly active, is found in the checklist items that are used to identify ADD-H children (see Table 5-3). Many of these rating scales have a predominance of items dealing with behavior problems such as "quarrelsome, destructive, distractible, or temper outbursts" (Conners, 1969) rather than just simple activity level (Lahey, Hobbs, Kupfer, & Delamater, 1979).

Other Characteristics of ADD-H Although the defining characteristics of ADD-H primarily include inattention, impulsivity, and fidgety motor behavior, there are also other characteristics that are common to this condition. For example, ADD-H children commonly have social difficulties, particularly with peers (Cunningham, Siegal, & Offord, 1980; Whalen, Henker, Collins, Fink, &

Dotemoto, 1979). They are viewed as being immature, uncooperative, self-centered, and bossy. Most ADD-H children have few close friends, and they tend to play with younger children (Barkley, 1985). These children are frequently judged as more aggressive, uncooperative, and easily led (Campbell and Paulauskas, 1979). Aggressive behaviors are also found in a sizable subgrouping of ADD-H children (Campbell, Breaux, Ewing, & Szumowski, 1986; McGee, Williams, & Silva, 1984; Prinz, Connors, & Wilson, 1981). When aggression is associated with ADD-H, the prognosis is generally poorer (Loney, Whaley-Klahn, Kosier, & Conboy, 1981). ADD-H children also tend to be academically deficient (Barkley, 1985; Cunningham & Barkley, 1979) and to have reading deficiencies (Halperin, Gittelman, Klein, & Rudel, 1984). A 5-year follow-up study showed that 70 percent of ADD-H children repeated at least one grade, as compared to 15 percent of nonhyperactive children (Weiss, Minde, Werry, Douglas, & Nemeth, 1971). A high proportion (ranging from 40 to 80 percent) of children labeled as ADD-H have also been identified as learning-disabled (Lahey, Stempniak, Robinson, & Tyroler, 1978; Lambert & Sandoval, 1980; Safer & Allen, 1976).

Possible Causes of ADD-H

There is probably no one cause of ADD-H. In the past decade, a great deal of effort has gone into researching possible causes of ADD-H. Some of the research is highly controversial, such as that on the effects of food additives and sugar. But most of the work has followed more conventional lines of research, such as genetics and other biological causes.

Organic Brain Damage Overactivity and poor impulse control have long been associated with the diagnosis of organic brain damage in children. As early as 1908, Tredgold suggested that hyperactivity was linked with brain damage caused during birth by injury or deprivation of oxygen. These

BOX 5-1 • Impulsivity and Mediating Fidgety Behaviors in Hyperactive Boys: A Possible Link

An aspect of impulsivity is the inability to wait in order to earn a reward (reinforcer). Often ADD-H children are described as being unable to delay gratification and needing instant gratification. Gordon (1979) conducted a study with hyperactive and nonhyperactive boys in which they had to learn to wait and withhold a response to earn a candy. To earn a candy, the boys had to first press a button, then wait a period of time (6 seconds), and then press the button again. If they pressed the button too quickly, they lost the candy. This type of procedure is called *differential reinforcement of low rates of behavior* (DRL)—in this case, DRL on a 6-second schedule.

The nonhyperactive boys did much better on the waiting task than the hyperactive boys, who seemed unable to wait. For example, the nonhyperactive boys (1) made fewer responses than did hyperactive boys, (2) earned more candies than hyperactive boys, and (3) were overall more efficient in their responding (see Figure 5-2).

Table 5-2
A list of observed mediating behaviors used by hyperactive boys to delay their responding

Circling DRL response button with finger 9 times
Swinging legs 11, 12, or 20 times
Counting with lip movements
Counting out loud—numbers or ABCs
Blowing on reward box
Singing out loud
Shaking reward box 10 times
Hitting knee with right hand 20 times
Foot-tapping 16 times
Tapping finger 10 times on button box
"Walking" fingers around DRL button 9 times
Stomping with foot 9 or 10 times
Running around table once
Hitting side of box
Jumping jacks 4 times
Hitting collateral (other nonfunctional buttons on console)
  buttons

Source: M. Gordon. (1979). The assessment of impulsivity and mediating behaviors in hyperactive and nonhyperactive boys. *Journal of Abnormal Child Psychology, 7,* 317–326. Reprinted by permission.

One interesting aspect of the study by Gordon (1979) was the behaviors that the boys used to help themselves wait (mediating behaviors) between button pushes. Ninety percent of the hyperactive boys used one of the observable motor behaviors listed in Table 5-2 to help them wait, but only 30 percent of the nonhyperactive boys used behavior mediators. Most (80 percent) of the nonhyperactive boys used nonbehavioral mediators, or some type of thinking strategy to pass the time. The more behavioral mediators a child used, the poorer his performance on the waiting task. The more covert or nonbehavioral mediators a child used, the better his performance. The behavioral mediators listed in Table 5-2 are closely related to the fidgety, restless behaviors commonly described in hyperactive children. Gordon (1979) suggests that such physical mediating responses may actually be used by hyperactive children to help control their own impulsivity.

FIGURE 5-2. The performance of hyperactive and nonhyperactive groups over three time blocks of a DRL 6-second schedule. Top: responses; middle: reinforcements; bottom: efficiency score.

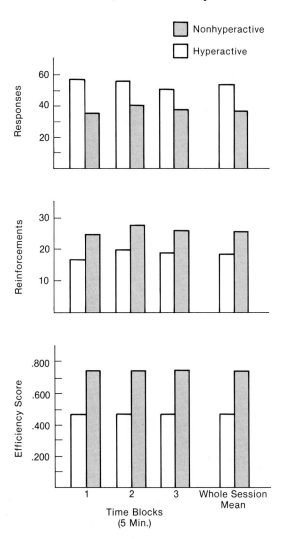

Source: M. Gordon. (1979). The assessment of impulsivity and mediating behaviors in hyperactive and nonhyperactive boys, *Journal of Abnormal Child Psychology, 7,* 317–326. Reprinted by permission.

early injuries were assumed to go unnoticed until school age, when increased demands were placed on the child (Ross & Ross, 1976). The brain damage hypothesis received additional support from the effect of an encephalitis epidemic that occurred in the United States in 1918. Upon recovery from this disease, many children showed a major shift in behavior and general personality changes. Children who had previously been compliant were now hyperactive, distractible, irritable, deceptive, and generally unmanageable in school (Ebaugh, 1923; Hohman, 1922; Strecker, 1929).

Other evidence of the possible link between hyperactive behavior and brain damage was provided by brain-injured soldiers (Goldstein, 1942) and children who had suffered head injuries (Strecker & Ebaugh, 1924). Since the injury through disease, birth trauma, or head injury was mostly of a minimal nature without being health- or life-threatening, the term *minimal brain damage* was coined. Some researchers went so far as to assume that the presence of hyperactive behaviors and their associated characteristics was sufficient to justify the diagnosis of minimal brain damage (Strauss & Kephart, 1955; Strauss & Lehtinen, 1947). This approach was severely criticized (Sarason, 1949), and attempts to empirically demonstrate the link between brain damage and ADD-H have not been successful. Most children with ADD-H do not show "hard" signs or histories of brain damage (Rie & Rie, 1980; Rutter, 1977; Taylor & Fletcher, 1983). Stewart and Olds (1973) estimated that only 10 percent of the referrals for hyperactivity showed a clear history of brain damage. Similarly, most children with brain damage do not develop ADD-H characteristics (Rutter, 1977, 1982).

Because of the lack of credible evidence supporting brain damage as a major cause of ADD-H, the Oxford International Study Group on Child Neurology recommended in 1962 that the term *minimal brain damage* be changed to *minimal brain dysfunction* (MBD), and that brain damage should not be inferred from behavioral signs alone (Kessler, 1980). But the new definition of minimal brain dysfunction has also led to confusion and difficulty (see Box 5-3).

The neurological diagnosis of MBD is difficult to make on the basis of any one clearly defined factor, as indicated in Box 5-3. A modern expla-

Table 5-3
The Conners Teacher Rating Scale

Listed below are descriptions of behavior. Place a check mark in the column which best describes this child. ANSWER ALL ITEMS.

Observation	Degree of Activity			
	Not at All	Just a Little	Pretty Much	Very Much
Classroom Behavior				
1. Constantly fidgeting				
2. Hums and makes other odd noises				
3. Demands must be met immediately—easily frustrated				
4. Coordination poor				
5. Restless or overactive				
6. Excitable, impulsive				
7. Inattentive, easily distracted				
8. Fails to finish things he starts—short attention span				
9. Overly sensitive				
10. Overly serious or sad				
11. Daydreams				
12. Sullen or sulky				
13. Cries often and easily				
14. Disturbs other children				
15. Quarrelsome				
16. Mood changes quickly and drastically				
17. Acts "smart"				
18. Destructive				

Table 5-3 (Continued)

Observation	Degree of Activity			
	Not at All	Just a Little	Pretty Much	Very Much
Classroom Behavior				
19. Steals				
20. Lies				
21. Temper outbursts, explosive and unpredictable behavior				
Group Participation				
22. Isolates himself from other children				
23. Appears to be unaccepted by group				
24. Appears to be easily led				
25. No sense of fair play				
26. Appears to lack leadership				
27. Does not get along with opposite sex				
28. Does not get along with same sex				
29. Teases other children or interferes with their activities				
Attitude toward Authority				
30. Submissive				
31. Defiant				
32. Impudent				
33. Shy				
34. Fearful				
35. Excessive demands for teacher's attention				

Table 5-3 *(Continued)*

Observation	Degree of Activity			
	Not at All	Just a Little	Pretty Much	Very Much
Attitude toward Authority				
36. Stubborn				
37. Overly anxious to please				
38. Uncooperative				
39. Attendance problem				

Source: C. K. Conners. (1969). A teacher rating scale for use in drug studies with children. *American Journal of Psychiatry, 126,* 884–888. Copyright 1969 by the American Psychiatric Association. Reprinted by permission of the author and the publisher.

BOX 5-2 • **Steven on the Move: A Case Study**

Steven's mother cannot remember a time when her son was not into something or in trouble. As a baby he was incredibly active—so active, in fact, that he nearly rocked his crib apart. All the bolts and screws became loose and had to be tightened periodically. Steven was also always into forbidden places, going through the medicine cabinet or under the kitchen sink. He once swallowed some washing detergent and had to be taken to the emergency room. As a matter of fact, Steven had many more accidents and was more clumsy than his older brother and younger sister. Even though Steven was less well-coordinated and more clumsy than other children, he always seemed to be moving fast. His mother recalls that Steven progressed from the crawling stage to a running stage with very little walking in between.

Trouble really started to develop for Steven when he entered kindergarten. Since his entry into school, his life has been miserable and so has the teacher's. Steven does not seem capable of attending to assigned tasks and following instructions. He would rather be talking to a neighbor or wandering around the room without the teacher's permission. When he is seated and the teacher is keeping an eye on him to make sure that he works, Steven's body still seems to be in motion. He is either tapping his pencil, fidgeting, or staring out the window and daydreaming. Steven hates kindergarten and has few long-term friends; indeed, school rules and demands appear to be impossible challenges for him. The effects of this mismatch are now showing in Steven's schoolwork and attitude. He has fallen behind academically and has real difficulty mastering new concepts; he no longer follows directions from the teacher and has started to talk back. Steven is scheduled for an evaluation next week by the school psychologist, and his parents are coming for a placement conference. The professionals at the school have mentioned medication, but Steven's parents think he is too young. They want a special program to help Steven behave, attend, and learn the basic academic material needed for the first grade. Possibly what the parents and school staff will develop is an in-school program, in which Steven will earn points for appropriate behavior and the points will be exchanged for in-school privileges (such as free time and honorary jobs) and for home privileges (such as television time and a later bedtime).

BOX 5-3 • Minimal Brain Dysfunction: The Difficult Diagnosis

Minimal brain dysfunction or MBD is extremely difficult to diagnose because of the confusion and ambiguity surrounding the concept. An early definition of minimal brain dysfunction was not only confusing but all-encompassing:

> The term "minimal brain dysfunction syndrome" refers in this paper to children of near average, average, or above average intelligence with certain learning or behavioral disabilities ranging from mild to severe, which are associated with deviations of function of the central nervous system. These deviations may manifest themselves by various combinations of impairment in perception, conceptualization, language, memory, and control of attention, impulse, or motor function. (Clements, 1966, p. 9)

Later definitions of MBD have speculated about altered brain functions and neurological dysfunctions without specifying the exact locations or details of these problems (Klein & Gittelman-Klein, 1975). These neurological problems are generally identified by incidents in a child's medical history such as birth complications, head injuries, perceptual deficits such as clumsiness, or a family history of similar behavior problems. A neurological examination may reveal an abnormal electroencephalogram (EEG) pattern (Rosenthal & Allen, 1978). No conclusive indicators of MBD exist, however, and a number of the "soft" neurological signs (such as clumsiness) can disappear as the child matures. Often clinicians seek to explain a child's hyperactivity by reference to MBD; at the same time they use the hyperactivity as proof of the existence of MBD—a completely circular argument. The confusion surrounding the MBD concept has led some researchers to abandon the term. Ross and Ross (1976) have stated, "It is our opinion that the use of the term *minimal brain dysfunction* should be discontinued because it contributes more than its share to the morass of confusion in this area" (p. 12).

Sources: S. D. Clements. (1966). *Minimal brain dysfunction—terminology and identification* (U.S. Public Health Service Publication No. 1415) (Washington, DC: U.S. Government Printing Office); D. F. Klein and R. Gittelman-Klein. (1975). *Problems in the diagnosis of minimal brain dysfunction and hyperkinetic syndrome* (unpublished manuscript); R. H. Rosenthal and T. W. Allen. (1978). An examination of attention, arousal, and learning dysfunctions of hyperactive children. *Psychological Bulletin, 85,* 689–715; D. M. Ross and S. A. Ross. (1976). *Hyperactivity: Research, theory, and action* (New York: Wiley).

---

nation of the MBD theory as given by Wender (1971, 1972) and as reviewed by Rie (1980) involves the brain's limbic system, which is directly involved in arousal and reward (positive reinforcement). Supporters of this theory propose a deficit in the metabolism of neurotransmitters. Simply stated, a balance generally exists between neurological excitation and inhibition. The MBD child is presumed to have a defective inhibitory system, which results in the child's being more active and less sensitive to the effects of positive reinforcement than the normal child. The behavior problems experienced by MBD children are assumed to be caused by their inability to learn effectively through positive reinforcement. Wender (1971) recommends the use of stimulant medication with MBD children to restore the balance between the excitatory and inhibitory systems; this balance enhances the effects of positive reinforcement so the learning and behavioral adjustment is facilitated. Reviewers have questioned the research on neurotransmitter balance and MBD children and the effects of stimulant medication's ability to restore a theorized imbalance (Barclay, 1985; Ross & Ross, 1982). Ross and Ross (1976) concluded, "There is little empirical support for this theory, and some of its assumptions about high arousal level and defective reward system have been questioned or contradicted" (p. 71).

Genetics   Several researchers have sought to explain the behavioral characteristics of ADD-H children through some type of genetic mechanism. Scientific work in this area is difficult to conduct, because the causal effects of heredity and environment are difficult to separate. Researchers have used two basic approaches. First, the incidence of psychiatric disorder in parents of ADD-H children is compared to that of families of non-handicapped children. Researchers assume that a higher incidence of psychiatric disorder in the families of ADD-H children would indicate a possible basis for heritability of the condition. Cantwell (1975) interviewed parents of ADD-H children and found that 10 percent of the ADD-H children's parents reported they had been ADD-H themselves. In addition, 45 percent of these parents said they had some type of psychiatric problem (such as alcoholism, sociopathy, or hysteria). Other studies have reported similar results (Morrison, 1980; Morrison & Stewart, 1971), but caution is necessary in interpreting these studies. For instance, parents who suffer from psychiatric conditions may provide a marginal home life, which may also contribute to the development of ADD-H. But in answer to this criticism, comparisons of the biological and adoptive parents of ADD-H children have been made. In these studies the ADD-H children were adopted in infancy and had no contact with their biological parents after adoption. A higher incidence of psychiatric disturbance was found in the ADD-H children's biological parents than in their adoptive parents (Morrison & Stewart, 1971, 1973).

The second approach to the study of genetic causes has been to compare genetically identical *(monozygotic)* twins and nonidentical (*dizygotic* or fraternal) twins. Willerman (1973) studied 54 monozygotic and 49 dizygotic twin pairs by sending their mothers a questionnaire that assessed child activity levels. There was a significant correlation for activity level between the monozygotic

twins, but no such correlation between the dizygotic twins, supporting a genetic basis of activity levels. High levels of activity, however, are not synonymous with ADD-H (see discussion above). Other, more recent studies, however, have assessed more than motor activity and found significant correlations for ADD-H between monozygotic twins (Hefferon, Martin, & Welsh, 1984).

Genetic studies of ADD-H children indicate that heredity probably plays a role in the development of the condition. The exact role of genetics, however, is still difficult to determine. Specific genes may cause higher activity levels, inattention, or impulsivity, or there may be an interaction effect between combinations of genes. There is no simple answer. Probably there is an interplay of multiple causes among genetics, biological factors, environmental variable, and family stresses that increases the vulnerability of a child to ADD-H (Barkley, 1985).

Environmental Factors   Children are subject to a number of stresses—environmental pollution, exposure to low levels of radiation, ingestion of foods with man-made chemicals, and high divorce rates—that did not exist 50 years ago. These environmental stresses have been implicated in the increase in the number of ADD-H children. Poisons are a threat to all young children but pose an even higher threat to hyperactive children. Stewart, Thach, and Freidin (1970) have found that a significantly greater number of preschool children who accidentally poisoned themselves were later diagnosed as ADD-H. The connection between poisonings and hyperactivity, as pointed out by Ross and Ross (1976), is not an unreasonable one, since ADD-H children are more likely to "get into things." The "things" may be toxic substances such as paint that affect health and behavior.

A common source of lead poisoning is lead-based paint in old buildings. However, lead is also spewed into the environment from industrial pollution, such as smelting plants and from the use of leaded gasoline used in automobiles (see Chapter 3). The use of leaded gasoline alone puts approximately 240,000 tons of lead into the air each year in the United States (Ross & Ross, 1982). David, Clark, and Voeller (1972) found that a group of ADD-H children whom they studied had greater lead stores in their blood than nonhandicapped children. The lead in the bloodstream was not at toxic levels, but at a subtoxic level that might cause minimal poisoning and contribute to the behavioral symptoms of ADD-H. In a similar study, concentrations of metal toxins (lead, arsenic, mercury, cadmium, and aluminum) were studied as trace elements in the hair of school-aged children in Wyoming (Marlowe et al., 1985). In this study, a significant relationship was found between the accumulation of metals (particularly lead) and increased problematic behaviors as measured by a behavior checklist.

Food additives and diet have recently been given a great deal of publicity as causes of ADD-H, particularly by parents and children who value natural or organic foods. The "Feingold diet" has received the most attention (Feingold, 1975b). This diet restricts artificial food colorings, flavorings, and natural salicylates (aspirin-like compounds). Although others have been unable to replicate his results, Feingold (1975a) has written that a large percentage (50 percent) of ADD-H children show favorable results from the diet and has testified to the U.S. Senate Subcommittee of Health:

> Following management of children whose primary complaint was hyperkinesis or MBD (minimal brain dysfunction) with diet eliminating all artificial colors and flavors, we again observe the rapid and dramatic response in about 50 percent of cases reported by our earlier patients. Within a few weeks and sometimes days, a complete reversal of the behavioral pattern was observed. (Feingold, quoted in Swanson & Kinsbourne, 1980, p. 133)

Feingold has assumed that the ADD-H child is allergic to or genetically predisposed to react negatively to these compounds. The problem with Feingold's diet hypothesis is that much of its support has been anecdotal without adequate scientific evidence. Recent reviews of diet research have generally indicated that diet can play a role in ADD-H (Conners, 1980; Harley & Matthews,

1980; Swanson & Kinsbourne, 1980; Trites, Tryphonas, & Ferguson, 1980; Tryphonas, 1979; Varley, 1984). However, the effects are far less dramatic than those reported by Feingold, and the vast majority of ADD-H children do not show an improvement on the Feingold diet. As stated by Conners (1980), "On the basis of all the evidence available at this time, in answer to the question, 'Is there anything to Dr. Feingold's hypothesis?' " one might answer, "Yes, something—but not much and not consistently" (p. 107).

In a similar vein, numerous parents report that sugar has a profound effect in producing ADD-H behaviors in their children. Some studies have been conducted with sugar ingestion and ADD-H symptoms (Conners, 1986; Prinz, Roberts, & Hantman, 1980); there is no evidence that controlling sugar significantly affects the behavior of ADD-H children (Varley, 1984). Sugar should be viewed as energizing an already existing behavioral pattern. Instead of causing a behavior to happen, sugar may merely amplify an already existing behavior pattern, whether the behavior is appropriate or inappropriate.

Family Factors   Some studies with ADD-H children have shown that their mothers are generally critical, disapproving, and unaffectionate, and use severe punishment (Battle & Lacey, 1972). There has been some concern that this type of parenting style may actually cause the condition. However, it is now generally agreed that this type of behavior probably is a response to the ADD-H child's inappropriate behavior rather then the cause of it (Weiss & Hechtman, 1986). For example, when ADD-H children are treated or get older and their behavior improves, then their mothers become less controlling and more responsive (Barkley & Cunningham, 1979; Barkley, Karlsson, & Pollard, 1985). However, ADD-H children do leave a mark on parents, particularly their mothers, who tend to be less confident, under more stress, more socially isolated, more self-blaming, and more depressed than mothers who do not have ADD-H children (Mash & Johnston, 1983). These faults in parenting style and self-confidence do not cause

ADD-H, but they can exacerbate the child's behavioral problems (Barkley, 1985).

Treatment of ADD-H

Few childhood behavior disorders have raised such controversy and heated debate as ADD-H. The treatment of this condition has covered a wide range of approaches, including medication, psychotherapy, educational interventions, and diet. Each approach has supporters who are sure that their intervention is the most effective; over time, however, few treatments have been scientifically documented to be highly effective (Weiss & Hechtman, 1986). Traditional psychotherapy, counseling, and play therapy for ADD-H children are considered relatively ineffective in altering the child's behavior problems (Mendelson, Johnson, & Stewart, 1971; Menkes, Rowe, & Menkes, 1967; Safer & Allen, 1976). Educational approaches that have stressed quiet and nondistracting classroom environments and cubicles (Cruickshank, Bentzen, Ratzeburg, & Tannhauser, 1961) have also not been significantly effective (Ross & Ross, 1982). The two most promising approaches have been stimulant medications and behavior management techniques.

Stimulant Medication   The use of stimulants (such as amphetamines) with emotionally disturbed children was first introduced by Bradley (1937). Bradley was a physician at a residential treatment center for children, and he first used benzedrine with children in an attempt to treat severe headaches. To Bradley's surprise, the medication did not affect the children's headaches, but instead had a dramatic impact on their behavior. Their work habits and school performance improved, and their behavior problems decreased. The children referred to the benzedrine tablets as their "arithmetic pills" because the medication improved their classroom performance (Ross & Ross, 1976). Bradley's discovery went relatively unnoticed until the 1950s, when stimulant drugs started to be widely prescribed for ADD-H children. Controversy erupted over the use of stimulants with ADD-H children when as many as 10

percent of all the elementary-age children in Omaha, Nebraska were erroneously reported to be on the drug. The debate continues today and includes such topics as the general usefulness of stimulants (Barkley, 1977), their effects on mother-child interactions (Barkley & Cunningham, 1979), their effects on academic performance (Barkley & Cunningham, 1978), their side effects (Safer, Allen, & Barr, 1972), and their possible abuse (Weiss & Hechtman, 1986).

Even with the scientific debate, today such medications as methylphenidate (Ritalin) and dextroamphetamine are recognized as changing the behavior of ADD-H children. On average, 75 percent of ADD-H children on stimulant medication show a behavioral improvement, and 25 percent either do not change or get worse (Barkley, 1977). The main immediate improvements for stimulants include improved attending behavior and reduced impulsivity (Barkley, 1985; Douglas, 1974). Fidgety behavior has also been reported as improved, depending on the dosage of the drug (Barkley & Jackson, 1976). However, the medication has failed to reduce activity measures, such as the number of times a child is out of his seat or away from his desk. Barkley and Cunningham (1979; Cunningham & Barkley, 1978) reported that mothers needed to exert less control over their ADD-H children and responded to them more positively after the children were medicated. One recent study (Abikoff & Gittelman, 1985) found that after ADD-H children were placed on the medication, they were "indistinguishable" from their nonhandicapped peers in a classroom.

Academic achievement is critical to the adjustment of ADD-H children, both in school and later as adults. As indicated previously, most ADD-H children are academically deficient. The exact effects of stimulant drugs on learning and academic performance are unclear; however, preliminary evidence indicates that stimulants *do not* improve children's academic performance (Barkley & Cunningham, 1978; Ross & Ross, 1982). In one series of studies, it was found that stimulant drugs increased attention to work and reduced distractibility in underachieving children (Rie &

Rie, 1977; Rie, Rie, Stewart, & Ambuel, 1976a). Academic improvement (as measured by a standardized achievement test), however, was not improved by medication, even though both parents and teachers rated the children as academically improved. It appears that ADD-H children placed on medication may show an initial improvement in academics (that is, over the first week's trial; Pelham, Bender, Caddell, Booth, & Moorer, 1985) but in the long term (1 to 10 years), there is essentially no effect of stimulants on academic achievement (Charles & Schain, 1981; Weiss & Hechtman, 1986). Rie, Rie, Stewart, and Ambuel (1976b) warned that stimulant medication may mask academic problems, because increased attending behavior and reduced classroom behavior problems may be misperceived by teachers as positive changes in achievement. In actuality, the children's learning problems and deficits may be left untreated and unimproved.

The side effects that accompany the use of stimulant medication include insomnia, rebound irritability, decreased appetite, and headaches, all of which are relatively minor and generally temporary. Suppressed growth in height and weight have also been reported (Safer et al., 1972). However, when children are taken off the drug for the summer there can be a "rebound" effect, in which the children tend to grow quickly and compensate for some of these growth deficiencies.

More serious side effects include *attributional effects*. With attributional effects, people ascribe their behaviors to some particular factor. For example, many people believe that a rabbit's foot controls their luck. ADD-H children may show a similar attribution effect with stimulant medication (Bugental, Whalen, & Henker, 1977; Whalen & Henker, 1976). An ADD-H child may forget her medication in the morning, and then assume that she will have a terrible day at school. Rosen, O'-Leary, and Conway (1985) reported a case of an ADD-H child named Tom who had attributional difficulties in withdrawing from medication. Tom spontaneously stated, "My mother couldn't get me my pills from the hospital. My pills make me get done with my work," and "I get angry without

my pill." With a great deal of training and some setbacks, Tom was weaned from the medication and began to attribute his successful behavior to his own self-control. Furthermore, attributional errors can be made by parents and teachers as well as by the child. If a child and her parents and teacher attribute all behavioral control to a pill, a lack of teaching or learning can result; those involved may stop expecting that the ADD-H child will develop alternative coping behaviors which may be critical to later adjustment.

Possibly the greatest drawback to the use of stimulant medication with ADD-H children is its lack of long-term effectiveness. Clearly, the positive short-term effects of stimulants encourage teachers and parents to use them. A 1-year follow-up of ADD-H boys receiving stimulant medication together with psychotherapy has been encouraging (Satterfield, Cantwell, & Satterfield, 1979). In the long term, stimulant medication had its greatest effects in the following areas for the boys receiving treatment: (1) reducing serious automobile accidents in adolescence, (2) producing higher self-esteem, (3) providing a more positive view of the children by adults and peers, and (4) improving social skills. It does not, however, improve children's overall academic achievement or the number of grades passed or failed (Weiss & Hechtman, 1986). In virtually all comparisons (social, academic, behavioral) with nonhandicapped peers, ADD-H children who were treated and ADD-H children who were not treated with stimulants did more poorly. A basic implication from much of this research is that in the long run children who receive medication may be only slightly better off than children who received no medication. Clearly, stimulant medication is a short-term management tool (Barkley, 1977).

Behavior Therapy Behavioral techniques used with ADD-H children have largely been used in classrooms and homes (O'Leary & O'Leary, 1980). Techniques vary, but the most frequently used interventions include (1) positive reinforcement for on-task behavior, for remaining seated, and for completing assignments; (2) *response cost* (loss of reinforcement) for inappropriate behaviors such as noncompliance, refusal to sit down, and aggression; and (3) *cognitive-behavior modification,* which emphasizes self-control and self-reinforcement (see Chapter 14).

In an early study, Patterson, Jones, Whittier and Wright (1965) demonstrated that the nonattending behavior and inappropriate body movements of two mentally retarded hyperactive children improved through the use of positive reinforcement in the form of candy for appropriate behaviors. Similarly, numerous studies have demonstrated that reinforcement techniques can be used to improve on-task behavior in ADD-H children (as reviewed by Hendersen, Jenson, & Erken, 1986). However, like medication alone, reinforcement techniques that improve on-task behavior do not necessarily improve academic performance. Ayllon and Rosenbaum (1977) have suggested that behavioral programs that directly improve academic performance often have the beneficial side effects of reducing disruptive behaviors in ADD-H children. Cognitive-behavior modification approaches that teach self-control, problem solving, and self-reinforcement for appropriate behavior have been promising with ADD-H children; however, the overall effectiveness of this approach has not been demonstrated (Whalen, Henker, & Hinshaw, 1985). Teaching the parents of ADD-H children to design behavioral programs for their children has been demonstrated to be effective. O'Leary, Pelham, Rosenbaum, and Price (1976) trained parents to be part of the treatment team and utilize a reward system in the home to reinforce both academic and social achievement of ADD-H children in school. Similarly, Dubey, O'Leary, and Kaufman (1983) used behavioral parent training procedures to reduce the severity of behavior problems in ADD-H children. A 9-month follow-up with this study showed that the children maintained their gains and that the parents viewed the children more positively than parents in a control group viewed their children.

Virtually no long-term follow-up data exist documenting the effectiveness of behavioral approaches to the treatment of ADD-H (O'Leary, 1980; Ross & Ross, 1982). The cost of doing follow-up studies and the difficulty in locating subjects are barriers to conducting extensive follow-up research (Mash & Dalby, 1979). This situation is unfortunate, since cost-effectiveness comparisons are needed to evaluate the different interventions. Clearly, behavioral approaches involve more time and cost more money than do stimulant medication interventions. Both stimulant medication and behavioral techniques appear to be effective in the short term and may be more effective when used in combination (Chase & Clement, 1985; Gittelman-Klein et al., 1976; Wolraich, Drummond, Salomon, O'Brien, & Sivage, 1978). Stimulants may be more cost-effective and better in controlling impulsivity. Behavior therapy may be more effective in improving academic deficits and has fewer negative side effects than stimulants. Both appear to reduce disruptive behaviors and improve attending. However, no treatment has been demonstrated to be truly effective in the long term.

CONDUCT DISORDER

The term *conduct disorder* is a broad label used to identify a number of aversive and socially disruptive behaviors in children. The definition of *conduct* is "a mode or standard of personal behavior especially based on moral principles" (*Webster's Ninth New Collegiate Dictionary,* 1983, p. 274). The key to this definition is a "standard of personal behavior." A breakdown in the social control of a child's personal standard of behavior by a parent, teacher, or society in general leads to insufficiently controlled behavior excesses referred to as a *conduct disorder.* This disorder is an externalizing disorder that affects all the people that deal with the child. The types of problem behaviors associated with conduct-disordered children include aggression (Loeber & Schmaling, 1985b; Patterson, 1976a, 1982, 1986), noncompliance (Forehand, King, Peeds, & Yoder), temper tantrums (Bernal, 1969; Bernal, Duryee, Pruett, & Burns, 1968), stealing (Loeber & Schmaling, 1985a); fire setting (Patterson, 1982), and destructiveness (Wolf, 1971).

Characteristics of Conduct-Disordered Children

The behaviors listed above are clearly aversive to parents and teachers; however, they are not unique to conduct-disordered children. Virtually all children have engaged in some of these behaviors at one time or another during their development. The qualities separating the conduct-disordered child from a nonhandicapped child are the intensity and frequency (excesses) of these behaviors (Quay, 1972). Behavioral excesses such as frequent aggression and noncompliance are the most obvious characteristics of conduct-disordered children. Along with the excesses, however, come a series of deficits. It is easy for parents, teachers, and professionals to focus only on the aversive behavioral excesses and miss treating the behavioral deficits.

One of the most disturbing deficits of conduct-disordered children is their poor moral development and lack of empathetic behavior (Goldstein, Glick, Reiner, Zimmerman, & Coultry, 1987; Jurkovic & Prentice, 1977). Many conduct-disordered children show little guilt or conscience concerning their destructive behavior. Other writers have described this flaw as more of a deficit in *rule-governed* behavior (Barkley, 1985). A child is usually directed by a social rule that guides behavior in different situations. For instance, a rule might be "Honest people do not steal." Conduct-disordered children, however, appear to be *contingency-governed* (Skinner, 1954) because they respond to the immediate rewards in the environment (for example, "I will steal it if I can get it now") instead of a social rule. This contingency orientation is reflected in many conduct-disordered children's questioning what will happen to them if they misbehave, rather than reflecting on the effect the behavior may have on some other person.

Other deficits associated with conduct disorders include poor social skills and academic deficiencies, particularly poor reading skills (Rutter & Yule, 1973; Semier, Eron, Myerson, & Williams, 1967; Wells & Forehand, 1985). Researchers have shown that one of the strongest correlates

with antisocial behavior in adolescents is a deficiency in academic skills (Dishion, Loeber, Stouthamer-Loeber, & Patterson, 1984). This deficiency has important implications for later adjustment as an adult, when basic academic skills are necessary for employment. In their social relationships, conduct-disordered children are frequently described as being inappropriately competitive, uncooperative, bossy, and defensive about criticism. These children do not know how to be appropriate leaders, how to initiate conversations, and how to socially reward other adults and peers. Loeber and Patterson (1981) reported that 72 percent of the conduct-disordered children referred to the Oregon Research Institute for service had poor peer relations. Patterson (1976a) has characterized the aggressive conduct-disordered child as "retarded in the development of many of the basic social skills" (p. 289). Table 5-4 lists the behaviors, both excesses and deficits, commonly associated with conduct-disordered children. Although the behaviors listed in the table are many and diverse, the basic definitive characteristics of the conduct-disordered child are excesses in aggression and noncompliance, with deficits in rule-governed, social, and academic behaviors (see Box 5-4 for a case example).

Antisocial-Aggressive Behavior We cannot give a concise definition of aggression in the conduct-disordered child, because experts disagree on its exact definition and causes. However, Table 5-5 lists the definition of "conduct disorder" from DSM-III-R (American Psychiatric Association, 1987). This definition emphasizes the fact that aggressive behavior is intended to do either physical harm or psychological injury and may involve property damage. Aggression can be further broken down into *overt* and *covert* aggression (Loeber & Schmaling, 1985a, 1985b). Overt or confrontive aggression involves such behaviors as arguing, temper tantrums, and fighting. The aim of the hostile or angry type of aggression is to do harm or injure another person. Covert aggression generally involves more of a concealed act, as in stealing, truancy, or fire setting. With this covert type of aggression, injury or harm is an incidental

Table 5-4
Behavioral Characteristics of Conduct-Disordered Children

Behavioral Excesses	Specific Behaviors
Aggression	Physically attacks others (peers and adults)
	Verbally abusive
	Destroys property
	Sets fires
	Vandalizes
	Cruel to animals
	Revengeful
Noncompliance	Breaks established rules
	Does not follow commands
	Argues
	Does the opposite of what is requested

Behavioral Deficits	Specific Behaviors
Moral behavior	Shows little remorse for destructive behavior
	Appears to have no conscience
	Lacks concern for feelings of others
Social behavior	Has few friends
	Lacks affection or bonding
	Has few problem-solving skills
	Acts aggressively and impulsively rather than cooperatively
	Constantly seeks attention
	Poor conversation skills
	Does not know how to reward other peers and adults socially
Academics and school	Generally behind in the academic basics, particularly reading
	Has difficulty acquiring new academic information
	Truant

by-product of the child trying to reach a goal; for instance, the child may steal to get money, engage in truancy to get a day off from school, set a fire to produce excitement, or engage in a mugging or gang fight to gain power. Overt aggression is more a reactive, often impulsive action, whereas covert aggression is more a planned act for gain.

Aggression as a means of controlling others has been investigated by Patterson, who labeled it *pain control* or *coercion* (Patterson, 1976a, 1982). Pain control involves the use of aversive behaviors such as hitting in order to control another person. A common example is frequently seen in grocery stores when a child wants a small toy and the parent refuses. The child may escalate the hostilities and start to engage in a screaming and kicking tantrum until the parent buys the toy to quiet the child and escape the disapproving

stares of the other customers. Here the child has perhaps unwittingly used aggression (a tantrum) as an instrument to coerce and shape the parent's behavior. Pain control is so common in conduct-disordered children and their families that on average a hit or tease occurs every 30 minutes in these families (Patterson, 1982; Patterson, Reid, Jones, & Conger, 1975).

The aggression of the younger conduct-disordered child should be contrasted with the socialized aggression of the juvenile delinquent. Conduct-disordered children have been referred to as having solitary aggressive type or *unsocialized* aggressive reactions (American Psychiatric Association, 1987). These labels indicate that the conduct-disordered child shows a lack of concern and feeling for others and is socially deficient—so deficient that the child has no significant friendships

BOX 5-4 • Bobby, a Conduct-Disordered Child (Solitary AggressiveType)

Bobby Jones is the type of boy who makes his teacher regret Mondays when he has to go back to teaching. This child seems to be the opposite of what adults want in a child. Bobby goes out of his way to do the opposite of what was requested. Adults have to repeat and repeat what they want; then Bobby argues and fights back. He seems to have a million excuses why he should not do the simplest of tasks. When pushed, Bobby responds by fighting or trying to get even. He once destroyed an art project by another boy because he thought he should get a prize. He is also suspected of setting a fire in the classroom last year, but it could not be proven. What is most frustrating about Bobby is that he does not seem to care about others. As long as he gets his way, that is all that matters. He never shows guilt or remorse for a behavior that hurts another person, even when he is caught red-handed.

Because he is such a troublemaker, the other children in the classroom do not like Bobby. They simply stay away from him and would rather not include him in any of their activities because he takes charge and tries to push them around. Bobby's schoolwork also suffers. It is so much trouble to get him to do something that most teachers have given up on Bobby. He is now 2 years behind in reading.

At home, Bobby rules the household. His mother is permissive and has trouble handling Bobby. She just cannot set a limit. Bobby's father is seldom home; when he is home, he is overly strict and wants things changed immediately. Bobby is constantly a source of conflict between his mother and father, and they talk of getting a divorce.

Things have gotten so difficult with Bobby at school that he has been referred to a special education classroom. The incident that seemed to provoke the referral involved Bobby beating a smaller boy for a collection of scratch-and-sniff stickers. He will be sent to the classroom next week; however, his mother objects to the placement and wants a second chance for Bobby.

or relationships. A *socialized*, or *group type* aggressive reaction, however, differs in that the child or adolescent shows loyalty and concern for some people (generally a peer group, such as a gang). A socialized aggressive delinquent may show no concern for an elderly person whom he has mugged, but great concern for a gang member who has been insulted or injured. Juvenile delinquency, both socialized and unsocialized, is covered later in this chapter.

Noncompliance Simply defined, *noncompliance* is "not doing what is requested" (Patterson et al., 1975) with the request generally being made by a parent or teacher. Noncompliance is one of the most common behavior problems of childhood (Herbert, 1978) and comprises one-third of children's deviant behavior (Wahl, Johnson, Johansson, & Martin, 1974). Patterson, Ray,

Shaw, and Cobb (1969), using observers in the homes of conduct-disordered boys, found that on average, one noncompliant behavior occurred every 10 minutes. In normative studies, compliance rates of nonhandicapped children to parental requests range from approximately 60 to 80 percent of the requests (Forehand, 1977). However, compliance rates for clinic-referred children who have behavior problems range from only 30 to 40 percent. Developmentally, noncompliance decreases until approximately age 5 (Patterson, 1976a); however, for disturbed children after age 5, noncompliance is an extremely stable problem behavior.

The forms of noncompliance can be diverse. A child may simply ignore a request made by an adult, often causing the adult to wonder if the child has heard or understood the request. Noncompliance can also take the form of delaying, passive resistance, arguing, or giving excuses why

Table 5-5
DSM-III-R Definition of Undersocialized Conduct Disorder

A. A disturbance of conduct lasting at least six months, during which at least three of the following have been present:

    (1) has stolen without confrontation of a victim on more than one occasion (including forgery)
    (2) has run away from home overnight at least twice while living in parental or parental surrogate home (or once without returning)
    (3) often lies (other than to avoid physical or sexual abuse)
    (4) has deliberately engaged in fire-setting
    (5) is often truant from school (for older person, absent from work)
    (6) has broken into someone else's house, building, or car
    (7) has deliberately destroyed others' property (other than by fire-setting)
    (8) has been physically cruel to animals
    (9) has forced someone into sexual activity with him or her
    (10) has used a weapon in more than one fight
    (11) often initiates physical fights
    (12) has stolen with confrontation of a victim (e.g., mugging, purse-snatching, extortion, armed robbery)
    (13) has been physically cruel to people

    Note: The above items are listed in descending order of discriminating power based on data from a national field trial of the DSM-III-R criteria for Disruptive Behavior Disorders.

B. If 18 or older, does not meet criteria for Antisocial Personality Disorder.

    Criteria for severity of Conduct Disorder:

    Mild: Few if any conduct problems in excess of those required to make the diagnosis, *and* conduct problems cause only minor harm to others.

    Moderate: Number of conduct problems and effect on others intermediate between "mild" and "severe."

    Severe: Many conduct problems in excess of those required to make the diagnosis, or conduct problems cause considerable harm to others, e.g., serious physical injury to victims, extensive vandalism or theft, prolonged absence from home.

Source: American Psychiatric Association. (1987). *Diagnostic and statistical manual of mental disorders* (3rd ed., revised) (Washington, DC: Author), p 55. Reprinted by permission.

a behavior cannot be done. An extreme form of noncompliance is *negativism,* which is "an exaggerated form of resistance, occurring when a child becomes stubborn or contrary, often doing quite the opposite of what the parents wish" (Herbert, 1978, p. 20). Like aggression, however, noncompliance is found in both conduct-disordered and non-conduct-disordered children. The difference, however, with conduct-disordered children is that the frequency and intensity of the noncompliant behavior is much higher. When children fall into the clinical range of 40 percent compliance or less, and use extreme measures to avoid complying (such as temper tantrums or violent arguments), then they are on the path to developing an oppositional or conduct disorder.

The effects of severe noncompliance and op-

positional behavior on others are not difficult to understand; they leave adults with feelings of helplessness and frustration. The expression "out of control" has frequently been used to describe the conduct-disordered child, and its use stems directly from noncompliance. The lack of conscience and moral concern for others may be explained partially by the effects of noncompliance in early development. Herbert (1978) speculates that the development of compliance and rule-following behavior is critical to socialization and moral development. Learning to comply may be an "essential core to morality," in that a child learns to regulate her interpersonal behavior by a set of external rules and values and not by what happens to please her at the moment.

In a similar fashion, noncompliance may directly affect a child's development of social and academic skills. If the child is uncooperative with other children, then the development of basic social and interactive skills may be delayed. If a child does not follow simple directions from teachers, then the development of academic skills such as reading, which depend on drill and practice, may be retarded. Jenson, Reavis, and Rhodes (1987) have suggested that noncompliance is a "kingpin" or central behavior that controls many of the deficits and excesses found in conduct-disordered children. If compliance can be increased in these children, then many of the other difficult behaviors (such as aggression, arguing, and temper tantrums) may improve without direct treatment of these behaviors. Russo, Cataldo, and Cushing (1981) have shown that if noncompliance can be reduced in children, then other inappropriate behaviors such as crying, tantrums, and aggression will stop without being directly treated (see Box 5-5).

Other Characteristics of Conduct-Disordered Children   In addition to the characteristics already mentioned, conduct-disordered children have other common characteristics that distinguish them as a clinical group. First, boys are far more likely to be diagnosed as having conduct disorders than girls are (Kazdin, 1985; Wells & Forehand, 1985). Schwarz (1979) estimates that the likelihood for boys to develop conduct problems is four to eight times greater than for girls. Similarly, Rutter, Tizard, and Whitmore (1970) found that teachers and parents reported that boys displayed two to three times more lying, fighting, stealing, destructiveness, and bullying than did girls.

DSM-III-R lists the prevalence rate of conduct disorder as "common," and it is estimated that one-third to three-quarters of all child referrals for services include the problems associated with conduct disorder (Wells & Forehand, 1985). The exact incidence of conduct disorders in the gen-

---

BOX 5-5 • **Behavioral Noncompliance and Its Relationship to Other Problem Behaviors**

Problem behaviors for externalizing/socially disordered children seem to revolve around a common set of problems that include noncompliance, tantrums, fighting, arguing, and crying. These problem behaviors may be more than slightly related. In fact, they may revolve around one basic behavior, noncompliance. Russo, Cataldo, and Cushing (1981) investigated the effects that successfully changing noncompliance had on other problematic behaviors that were not treated directly. This study included three children who had been identified as being noncompliant, hyperactive, and uncontrollable, with at least two other negative behaviors such as aggression, self-injurious behavior (SIB), or tantrums. For example, Tom, aged 3 years and 7 months, was referred for tantrums, aggression (kicking and biting), and SIB (head banging and hand biting).

The intervention included having the experimenter give the child a command and then wait 5 seconds. If the child complied, he was reinforced with a small piece of food (candy, cereal, or raisins) and physical contact (for instance, a hug and a "Good boy" or "Good girl"). None of the other problem behaviors such as tantrums or aggression were treated. The results of this experiment for Tom are shown in Figure 5-3.

It can be seen that as compliance increased (because it was directly reinforced), the other problem behaviors (crying, SIB, and aggression) decreased, even though they were not directly treated. It appeared for Tom and the other two children in the study that improving compliance had the side benefit of spontaneously improving the other problem behaviors. This study also showed that "nagging" (repeating a request over and over) made the situations worse by decreasing compliance and increasing problem behaviors.

FIGURE 5-3. Percentage of compliance and the three untreated corollary behaviors (crying, SIB, and aggression) for Tom across experimental conditions and therapists.

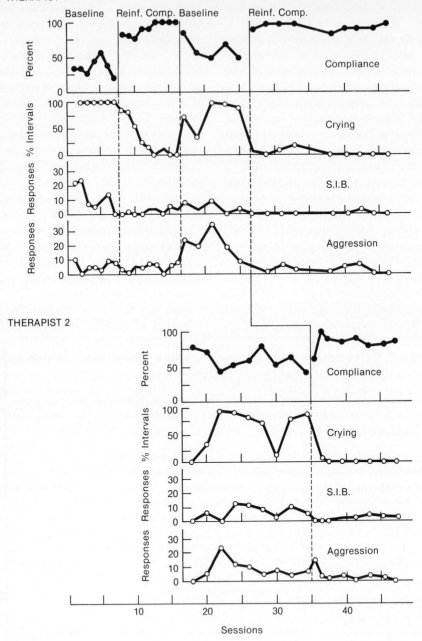

Source: D. C. Russo, M. F. Cataldo, and P. J. Cushing. (1981). Compliance training and behavioral covariation in the treatment of multiple behavior problems. Journal of Applied Behavior Analysis, 14, 209–222. Reprinted by permission.

Children must be diagnostically labeled in order to receive special education services.

eral population, however, is difficult to determine because of differences in definitions and the overlap of this condition with other conditions (such as oppositional disorder, ADD-H, and delinquency). In the Isle of Wight study, Rutter et al. (1976) studied the total population of children on a British island. The prevalence of conduct disorders and delinquency was found to be 4 percent for the 10- and 11-year old children. The Isle of Wight study was conducted in a rural setting. In a similar study in urban London, Rutter and his associates found the incidence to be as high as 8 percent.

Possible Causes of Conduct Disorder

Like ADD-H, conduct disorder probably has several different causes, all of which can lead to similar behaviors. Some of these causes are prob-

ably genetically based, represent inherited temperament characteristics, and are as old as the human race. In addition, some of the causes are undoubtedly social and involve such variables as modeled violence on television, divorce, or family stress.

As with ADD-H, there is probably no single element that causes conduct disorder, but instead an interaction among many factors. The number of elements and their interactive effects increase the vulnerability of certain children to conduct-disordered behavior patterns.

Instinct and Temperament Theories *Instinct theories* emphasize that innate, inherited behavior patterns can explain behaviors that are common to conduct disorders. Generally, the behavior dealt with by instinct theories includes aggressive behaviors such as fighting or intimidation. Psychoanalytic theory has explained senseless human aggression through an instinct that strives blindly for the destruction of life (Freud, 1933). This instinct, *thanatos,* has the opposite function in psychoanalytic theory to the life-preserving instinct, *eros* (as reviewed by Baron, 1977).

Temperament, like instinct, is assumed to be largely inherited (Torgerson, 1976). Unlike instinct, temperament is not considered a rigid behavior pattern that cannot be changed. Instead, it is more a personality style or trait that predisposes a child to act in certain ways. Recently, several researchers have investigated temperament styles in children from very early ages to adulthood (Chess & Thomas, 1983; Graham, Rutter, & George, 1973; Thomas & Chess, 1977; Thomas, Chess, & Birch, 1969). Thomas and associates (Chess & Thomas, 1983; Thomas & Chess, 1977) have conducted an extensive study of children's early temperament and the development of behavior disorders. From infancy to adulthood, the temperaments of 136 New York children were studied extensively according to nine behavioral characteristics (see Table 5-6). The individuals were scored as infants on the nine different temperament characteristics on a 3-point scale of high, medium, and low. When the children were approximately 2 years old, 65 percent fell

Table 5-6
Nine Temperament Characteristics Used to Assess Children

1. Activity Level: the motor component present in a given child's functioning and the diurnal proportion of active and inactive periods.
2. Rhythmicity (Regularity): the predictability and/or unpredictability in time of any biological function.
3. Approach or Withdrawal: the nature of the initial response to a new stimulus, be it a food, toy, place, person, etc. Approach responses are positive, whether displayed by mood expression (smiling, verbalizations, etc.) or motor activity (swallowing a new food, reaching for a new toy, active play, etc.). Withdrawal reactions are negative, whether displayed by mood expression (crying, fussing, grimacing, verbalizations, etc.) or motor activity (moving away, spitting new food out, pushing a new toy away, etc.).
4. Adaptability: responses to new or altered situations. One is not concerned with the nature of the initial responses, but with the ease with which they are modified in desired directions.
5. Threshold of Responsiveness: the intensity level of stimulation that is necessary to evoke a discernible response, irrespective of the specific form that the response may take, or the sensory modality affected.
6. Intensity of Reaction: the energy level of response, irrespective of its quality or direction.
7. Quality of Mood: the amount of pleasant, joyful, and friendly behavior; as contrasted with unpleasant, crying, and unfriendly behavior.
8. Distractibility: the effectiveness of extraneous environmental stimuli in interfering with or altering the direction of the ongoing behavior.
9. Attention Span and Persistence: two categories which are related. Attention span concerns the length of time a particular activity is pursued by the child. Persistence refers to the continuation of an activity direction in the face of obstacles to its continuation.

Source: S. Chess and A. Thomas. (1983). *Origins and evolution of behavior disorders: From infancy to early adult life.* (New York: Brunner/Mazel), p. 42. Reprinted by permission.

into three basic temperament categories. Ten percent were *difficult children,* who cried frequently, were irregular in biological functions, had a high rate of negative moods, had a predominance of intense reactions, were easily frustrated (leading to tantrums), negatively withdrew from new stimuli, and were slow to adapt to change. Fifteen percent of the children were *slow-to-warm-up children.* They adapted slowly to changes, had a low activity level, and had an initial but not long-lasting tendency to withdraw from change. Finally, the researchers identified 40 percent of the sample as *easy children,* who were regular in their habits, adapted well to change, were happy, and approached objects and people with little fear. The other 35 percent of the children studied in this group did not fit into any one of the three categories, but shared characteristics across categories.

Although the three temperament categories were broad, they were relatively stable over time

and predicted the later emotional status of the children (Chess & Thomas, 1983). Seventy percent of the difficult children studied by Thomas et al. (1969) developed behavior disorders, while only 18 percent of the easy children later developed problems. The types of problems ranged from adjustment reaction and depression to conduct disorder.

In the study of temperament by Thomas et al. (1969), parents of difficult children initially did not differ from other parents in their child-rearing practices and interactions with their children. An unfavorable difference developed, however, for some parents as the difficult children grew older. In effect, the temperamentally difficult children had shaped and molded the parent's negative reactions and attitudes toward the children. A difficult child, however, does not necessarily develop into a conduct-disordered child. What is important to note is that difficult children are more vulnerable to stress and have more difficulty adjusting and adapting (Graham et al., 1973; Rutter, 1983).

There seems to be little biological value for a difficult temperament, particularly in view of the more positive reactions elicited by children with an easy temperament. However, a report by de Vries (cited by Chess & Thomas, 1983) illustrates why a difficult temperament may have benefit for some children in some situations. In the study by de Vries, the temperament of the children of the Masai tribe (a tribe of herders in the sub-Sahara region of Kenya) was studied. de Vries assessed the infants of the Masai tribe and identified the 10 infants with the most easy temperament and the 10 with the most difficult temperament. He returned to the tribe 5 months later and found that a severe drought had killed 97 percent of the tribe's cattle herd. When he tried to locate the families of the children he had assessed for temperament, he found seven of the families with easy babies and six of the families with difficult ones. The families of the other infants had moved away to escape the drought. Interestingly, of the seven easy infants, five had died, and of the difficult infants, all had survived. When times get difficult, there may be survival value in being a difficult infant; in other words, the "squeaky wheel infant may get the grease (milk)."

Physiological and Genetic Variables Several physiological variables may account for the aggression and noncompliance found in conduct disordered children. It has been theorized that an extra male chromosome (XYY) may result in hypermasculinity and enhanced aggression in males. Normally, humans have 46 chromosomes and males have an X and a Y chromosome, while females have two Xs, XX. The X is the female and the Y is the male chromosome. Some studies have found significantly higher rates of the rare XYY chromosome pattern in prison inhabitants than in the general population. However, on closer inspection, it was found that the criminal behaviors most frequently associated with the XYY pattern were property offenses instead of aggression or antisocial offenses (Witkin et al., 1976). Witkin et al. (1976) noted that the XYY males probably did

not engage in criminal behavior more than XY males, but they may have been caught and punished more regularly because this condition is associated with intellectual dullness.

The need for stimulation and the physiological reactions that conduct-disordered children show may explain some of the behaviors of these children. Quay (1965, 1972, 1977) has suggested that severely conduct-disordered children may be motivated by a pathological need for stimulation. Thrill-seeking aggression and rule breaking may be forms of stimulation seeking that help relieve a state of boredom. Some research has shown that delinquents high in conduct disorders do very poorly in attending to boring tasks, and that they need to relieve boredom through some behavior such as singing and talking to themselves (Orris, 1969).

The genetic model of aggression and antisocial behavior is based primarily on the same logic as described earlier for ADD-H children (see the earlier discussion). First, biological parents who have antisocial characteristics are compared to see whether their children have higher rates of antisocial behavior when the children have been adopted out at birth. Adoption studies have shown that antisocial behavior is higher in the children of antisocial parents (Cadoret, 1978; Crowe, 1974). Similarly, twin studies comparing antisocial behavior in monozygotic and dizygotic twins have found higher rates of antisocial behavior in the monozygotic twins (Christiansen, 1974; Cloninger, Reich, & Guze, 1978).

Genetic evidence and stimulation-seeking behavior suggest a biological basis for conduct-disordered children's behavior. However, some of the strongest evidence for the causes of conduct disorders comes from studies of family and social factors.

Family Factors The effects of family influences on the development of conduct disorders in children are well supported by research evidence. Factors such as child-rearing practices, the consistency of discipline, the supportive atmosphere of the family, separation, and divorce all appear to have some effect in producing aggressive, noncompliant children. Child-rearing practices can vary along several different dimensions. Hetherington and Martin (1979) have listed a series of dimensions that includes (1) a *control* dimension, from restrictiveness to permissiveness; (2) an *affective-emotional* dimension, from warmth to hostility; (3) a *discipline* dimension, from consistency to inconsistency; and (4) a *psychological* dimension, from love-oriented to power-oriented parenting styles. Some extreme forms of these parenting styles appear to influence the development of conduct disorders in children. Parents who are habitually inconsistent in rule setting and discipline can leave a child confused regarding the exact limits and consequences for the child's behavior. Parents who use erratic control and are inappropriately permissive are more likely to have aggressive and behaviorally disordered children (Hetherington, Cox, & Cox, 1977b; Hetherington & Martin, 1979; Kazdin, 1985). One particular potential pattern identified in the development of aggressive children (Bandura & Walters, 1959) or delinquent adolescents (McCord, McCord, & Zola, 1959) is that of a lax, permissive mother and a rigid, restrictive father. Other patterns include permissive parents who accept the child's aggression and parents who are rejecting and restrictive. The research findings have been summarized by Wells and Forehand (1985): "In reviewing the results of studies . . . from behavioral, social, and psychological research, it is striking that one finding is consistent across studies—the extreme importance in the etiology of aggression of parental, particularly maternal, hostility and negativism toward the child, and/or the lack of consistent limits and consequences for negative behavior" (p. 235).

Divorce, separation, and marital conflict are found more frequently in the families of conduct-disordered and delinquent children than in families of normally adjusted children. Boys are particularly affected by divorce, and they are more likely than girls to develop noncompliant and aggressive behaviors after a divorce (Hetherington, 1979; Hetherington, Cox, & Cox, 1977a). This sex difference in the development of conduct-disordered behaviors for boys may be related to the loss of the father as an appropriate sex-role model (Hetherington, 1979). The development of conduct disorders and delinquency, however, does not appear to be a direct result of divorce or separation, but stems from the marital conflict and disharmony leading up to the break between parents (Hetherington et al., 1977a) or from the poverty that follows divorce (Hodges, 1986). As Rutter (1979) has stated, "Anti-social behaviors were linked with broken homes not because of the separation involved, but rather, because of the discord and disharmony which led to the break" (p. 283). During the period of marital disharmony, the child may be forced into coalition with one parent and in return may be rejected by the other parent, causing intense conflict (Schwarz, 1979). It should also be noted that the conduct-disordered child's behavior may promote marital disharmony, which in turn is associated with more acting-out behavior in the child (Griest & Wells, 1983).

These are only some of the family variables associated with conduct disorder and delinquency; many other variables can contribute to the risk vulnerability of a child's become antisocial. A list of these factors is given in Table 5-7 (Kazdin, 1985). However, there are still two powerful contributors to noncompliance and aggression that need to be discussed: modeling and coercion.

Modeling Modeling is the acquisition of new behaviors through the observation and imitation of other people's behavior (Bandura, 1973; Kirkland & Thelen, 1977). For conduct-disordered children, acquiring aggressive and noncompliant behaviors may involve the imitation of parents, peers, and possibly some characters from television and films. Bandura and Walters (1959), in studying aggressive adolescent boys, found that their parents repeatedly modeled and reinforced aggressive behavior directed against others. These parents, however, punished aggressive behaviors if these were directed against themselves. Parents of nonaggressive boys did not generally condone aggression, and in family conflicts these parents were considerate and used reasoning to handle problems.

Table 5-7

Factors That Contribute to Antisocial Behavior

Psychopathology and Criminal Behavior in Parents. The risk factor for antisocial behavior is increased if either parent has a psychiatric illness. However, alcoholism or criminal behavior in the father is particularly associated with antisocial behavior.

Parent-Child Interactions. Inconsistent parenting and discipline practices are associated with antisocial behavior. Lax, erratic, or overly harsh punishment practices are related to antisocial behaviors. One pattern is especially associated with antisocial behavior: a lax mother and an overly severe, punishing father.

Broken Homes and Marital Discord. Divorce and broken homes can be related to antisocial behavior, particularly if accompanied by a continuing bitter conflict between parents, reduced income, reduction in the quality of living, and/or decreased child supervision.

Birth Order and Family Size. Delinquency and antisocial behavior are greater among middle children than they are for first- and last-born children. In addition, family size is related to delinquency; a greater number of children is associated with higher rates of antisocial behavior.

Social Class and Socioeconomic Disadvantage. Delinquency and antisocial behavior are related to poorer living conditions and economic and social disadvantage. However, this effect is not particularly strong across studies.

Source: A. E. Kazdin. (1985). *Treatment of antisocial behavior in children and adolescents* (Homewood, IL: Dorsey Press).

Violent films and television can provide models for children, teaching them new and more sophisticated forms of physical and verbal aggression (Liebert, Sprafkin, & Davidson, 1982; Olweus, 1984). As is well known, children are amply exposed to television programming. Nearly 98 percent of American households have television sets; 52 percent have more than one set, one of which is used primarily by children (Nielsen Television Index) (Liebert, Sprafkin, & Davidson, 1982). On average, children watch over 3 hours of television programming each day, spending more time watching television than in any other waking activity, including school (Lyle & Hoffman, 1972). In 1972, the Surgeon General of the United States concluded that there is "a causal relationship between viewing violence on television and aggressive behavior" (quoted in Eron & Huesmann, 1984, p. 141). This relationship is not difficult to appreciate when the percentage of violence on television is understood. On average, 80 percent of all television programming from 1967 to 1979 involved violent acts. There was an average of 5 violent acts per program (Gerbner, Gross, Morgan, & Signorielli, 1980; Signorielli, Gross, & Morgan, 1982). Of particular concern is the finding that weekend morning programming and cartoons (children's favorite viewing time) contain the highest level of violent programming.

The modeling effects of aggression in filmed violence are well documented (Bandura, Ross, & Ross, 1963; Eron, 1963; Leyens, Camino, Parke, & Berkowitz, 1975; Leibert & Baron, 1972). Filmed violence not only teaches new and unique ways to be aggressive, but it also has a *disinhibitory* effect on aggression in general (Bandura et al., 1963). That is, a child who is exposed to a violent film model will be less inclined to stop or inhibit aggressive behavior when given the opportunity. In addition, repeated exposure to violence over time may *desensitize* or dull a child to the effects of aggression and the signs of pain in others (Baron, 1977; Cline, Croft, & Courrier, 1973; Thomas, Horton, Lippincott, & Drabman, 1977).

New longitudinal research shows the relationship between television viewing by children and its later consequences. Eron and Huesman (1984) have reported the long-term effects of television violence on hundreds of children studied from 1960 to 1981. The results show that the effects of violent television are only small in the short run but that the cumulative effects over time can be large. Children as young as age 6 showed increases in aggressive behavior in relation to television watching, and males about 8 years old (third-graders) showed the most vulnerability to television violence.

[I]t is likely that children around age 8 in the United States are especially susceptible to the influence of violent television. From grade 1 to 5 children are becoming increasingly aggressive; also during that period the amount of television violence viewed increases from grade 1 to 3 and then starts to decline. (Eron & Huesmann, 1984, p. 143)

The long-term behavioral effects reported in this study after 22 years are even more impressive. There was a clear relationship between the amount of violent television watched and the number of criminal convictions, aggression against a spouse, and traffic violations when these children

grew up. Figure 5-4 shows the relationship between serious adult criminal acts and the frequency of television watching (measured at age 8) for males and females.

The Coercion Hypothesis   The use of aggression and noncompliance to control other people's behavior has been called *coercion* or *pain control*, as noted earlier (Patterson, 1974; 1982; 1986; Patterson & Reid, 1970). Patterson (1976a) assumes that coercive behaviors may stem from instinct, modeling, television viewing, or reinforcement. Infants use coercive pain control by crying to gain a parent's attention for care and feeding. This type of elementary pain control no doubt has survival value for the infant. More refined coer-

FIGURE 5-4. **Relation of TV viewing at age 8 to seriousness of crimes committed by age 30.**

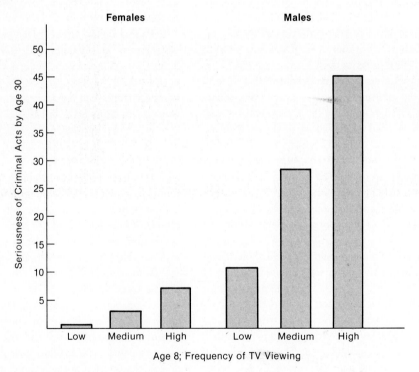

Source: L. D. Eron and R. L. Huesmann. (1984). The control of aggressive behavior by changes in attitudes, values, and conditions of learning. In R. J. Blanchard and D. C. Blanchard (Eds.), *Advances in the study of aggression* (Vol. 1) (New York: Academic Press), p. 150. Reprinted by permission.

cive behaviors such as tantrums, teasing, or aggression are learned through modeling and reinforcement for the behaviors. What is important, however, is not necessarily how the aversive behaviors are acquired, but rather how they become so intense and destructive.

All children are coercive at some point; however, conduct-disordered children use coercion much more frequently and intensely than other children. Coercive control follows a typical sequence of behaviors in which a demand or request is made to a noncompliant child by either an adult or another child. The child responds to the demand with aversive behaviors rather than compliance. The person who made the original demand withdraws it in order to avoid the child's aversive behavior. Withdrawing the request or demand reinforces (negatively) the problem child and increases the chances that in the future he will respond with more intense and aversive forms of behavior. The problem child also learns that requests are not to be taken seriously and can be avoided by show of ferocity (see Table 5-8).

The escalation of pain control results in interactions in which family members exchange punishment at high rates (Patterson, 1982, 1984). The communication patterns in the family are altered, in that the family is not open and a general atmosphere of hostility exists. Parents who are caught in this coercive trap are inconsistent disciplinarians. The evidence indicates that children from such families are nearly twice as resistant to changing their problem behaviors when punished as normal children are (Patterson, 1976a). Moreover, the children are not as responsive to social praise and reinforcement, and they lag behind in the development of age-appropriate social skills.

Childhood tantrums may be viewed by many adults as a disturbing behavior that is difficult to understand. Recent research, however, suggests that tantrums may be a form of pain control used by children in a coercive process.

Table 5-8

The Coercive Process of an Aggressive Child with Peers and Parents

Peer Request	Aggressive Child's Response	Request Is Withdrawn	Reinforcement
"Please give me the truck you have."	Hits and pushes the → requesting child	→ Hitting and pushing stops	1. The aggressive child is reinforced by the → request ↓ 2. The peer is reinforced by the cessation of → hitting and pushing 3. The result is an → increase in aggression in the future when requests are made of the problem child

Parent Request			
"Clean up your dirty bedroom."	Has a tantrum, slams → doors, and throws more toys around the bedroom	→ Tantrum stops	1. The aggressive child is → reinforced by the ↓ parent's withdrawing the request for a clean room → 2. Parent is reinforced for the withdrawal of the request by a cessation of the tantrum → 3. The result is an increase in tantrums in the future when requests are made by the parent

Treatment of Conduct Disorders

The very diverse nature of the behaviors that constitute conduct disorders makes the condition difficult to treat. Aggression can take several different forms, ranging from physical and verbal aggression to property destruction (such as fire setting). Noncompliance can range from simply ignoring requests to doing the exact opposite of what was requested. In addition, deficits such as poor social skills, a lag in moral development with little consequence, and poor academic skills make each conduct-disordered child a unique and individual case. Clinicians from different backgrounds may set entirely different priorities in treating these problems.

Traditional Treatment Approaches Traditional approaches to the treatment of conduct disorders have involved techniques such as therapeutically induced insight into the origin of the problem, play therapy, and *catharsis* (see below). Psychodynamic approaches to the treatment of conduct disorders have generally included insight into the development of an underlying conflict usually involving the child's parents and a psychosexual theme (Aichhorn, 1964). In one case study, unstructured play therapy was used to discover the underlying motivations of a 5-year-old girl, Jane, who had developed violent temper tantrums and noncompliance (Seeberg, 1943). Through 69 play therapy sessions in which Jane could freely express her feelings, a basic unconscious sexual conflict involving her mother was uncovered. Jane was encouraged to release her aggression and jealousy toward her mother in the play therapy situations. Her aggression ceased to be a problem after the play therapy sessions; however, her noncompliance continued.

Catharsis is defined as a therapeutic release

of pent-up aggressive drives in a socially acceptable manner. The hypothesis is that aggressive energies build up in a child and must be discharged in some form of aggressive behavior. In treatment, the therapist assumes that one form of aggression can be substituted for and is equivalent to other forms of aggression. For example, a frustrated child who is restrained from hitting a peer who has taken his toy can alternatively release the built-up aggressive impulses by hammering pegs. In this example, hammering pegs is substituted for hitting the other child. The two acts are considered equivalent in that once the pegs are hammered, the aggressive energies are assumed dissipated. In treatment contexts, a therapist may urge a conduct-disordered child who is violent to punch a Bobo doll or fight with rubber foam bats.

The research evidence indicates that catharsis does not significantly reduce the aggressive behavior of children (as reviewed by Parke & Slaby, 1983). Rather, as Bandura (1973) has stated, "Evidence from research studies of children indicates that, far from producing a cathartic reduction of aggression, participation in aggressive activities within a permissive setting maintains or increases it (Feshbach, 1956; Freeman, 1962; Kenny, 1952; Mallick & McCandless, 1966; Nelsen, 1969)" (p. 148).

Traditional therapeutic approaches to the treatment of conduct-disordered children have not been well researched, and those that have been researched have not been found to be particularly effective (Herbert, 1978; Kazdin, 1985). Some approaches that on first inspection seem reasonable, such as catharsis therapy, may actually be counterproductive in controlling aggression and noncompliance. Medication approaches have also not been extensively used with conduct-disordered children, because no drug effectively reduces noncompliance or aggression.

Social Learning and Behavioral Approaches

The most promising approaches to the treatment of conduct disorder are social learning and behavioral approaches. These approaches, in contrast to traditional psychotherapy, emphasize changing observable behavior through direct interventions.

Instead of trying to interpret underlying conflict or release stored aggressive impulses, behavioral methods utilize environmental consequences, parent training, contingency contracting, and conflict resolution training to change disruptive behavior (Wells & Forehand, 1981). Techniques such as point systems, reinforcement, precision request making, time out (brief withdrawal from a positive environment), and relaxation training (see Box 5-6) are commonly used to deal with aggressive and noncompliant behavior.

Gerald Patterson and his colleagues at the Oregon Research Institute have spent two decades researching effective behavior change techniques with conduct-disordered children. Patterson's research group has seen over 200 families with children who were primarily aggressive and noncompliant. Approximately 50 percent of these children also engaged in truancy, stealing, and fire setting. The primary treatment approach used with these children has been to train parents to effectively reduce their children's "noxious" behaviors (Fleischman, 1981; Patterson, 1974, 1976b; Patterson & Fleischman, 1979). Treatment in the home has consisted of training parents to define and track both deviant and appropriate behaviors; to withdraw reinforcement, or to ignore inappropriate responding, and to use time out for inappropriate behaviors; to construct contracts with specified contingencies for behaviors and to catch the child being good and reinforce him for appropriate behaviors. Figure 5-5 shows that in one study the rate of obnoxious behavior before treatment averaged 0.7 responses per minute for aggressive boys, as compared to 0.45 responses per minute for nonproblem boys. After treatment and a 12-month follow-up, the observed rate of obnoxious behaviors for the aggressive boys was within normal limits.

The investment of professional time in the Patterson studies was relatively small, particularly when compared to the significant therapeutic gains. Other behavioral approaches have concentrated on improving compliance and reducing aggression by using precision request making and other behavioral techniques (Forehand & McMahon, 1981). It appears that these parents get caught in coercive interactions because they do not use appropriate requests systematically followed by consequences. The variables that affect child compliance are listed in Table 5-9. Parents are taught to be specific, to give the child time enough to comply, to use a neutral voice, to make eye contact, not to use a question format (e.g.,

"Wouldn't you like to clean your room?"), not to nag, and to follow compliance or noncompliance with an appropriate consequence (Jenson et al., 1987). The outline for a precision request is given in Figure 5-6 (Webster-Stratton, 1983).

Improving compliance and reducing aggres-

BOX 5-6 • The Turtle Technique to Control Impulsive Aggression

The turtle technique is a form of behavioral self-control and muscle relaxation that is used with elementary school children to control impulsivity and aggression (Schneider, 1974; Schneider & Robin, 1973). The technique starts by telling the child a story about a little turtle and an old tortoise:

> Once upon a time there was a handsome, young turtle. He was six years old and he had just started first grade. His name was Little Turtle. Little Turtle was very upset about going to school. He preferred to be at home with his baby brother and his mother. He didn't want to learn school things; he wanted to run outside and play with his friends, or color in his coloring book. It was too hard to try to write letters or copy from the board. He wanted to play and giggle with friends—he even loved to fight with them. He didn't like sharing. He didn't like listening to his teacher or having to stop making those wonderful loud fire engine noises he used to make with his mouth. It was too hard to remember not to fight or make noise. And it was just too hard not getting mad at all the things that made him mad.
>
> Every day on his way to school he would say to himself that he would try his best not to get in trouble that day. But, despite that, every day he would get mad at some-

The turtle technique reduces impulsive responding.

sion is insufficient in treating conduct-disordered children. The child's deficiencies must also be treated if a conduct-disordered child is to make long-term improvements. Social skills training programs that improve problem solving, conflict negotiation, acceptance of negative feedback, and

giving of positive feedback to others can be effective with behaviorally disordered children (Morgan & Jenson, in press). When the children master these skills, they are assigned homework to ensure that they practice the skills. Similarly, academic problems must be corrected if a conduct-

Box 5-6 (Continued)

body and fight, or he would get mad because he made a mistake and would rip up his papers. So he always would get into trouble, and after a few weeks he just hated school. He began to feel like a "bad turtle." He went around for a long time feeling very bad.

One day when he was feeling his worst, he met the biggest, oldest tortoise in his town. He was a wise old turtle, who was 200 years old and as big as a house. Little Turtle spoke to him in a very timid voice because he was very afraid of him. But the old tortoise was as kind as he was big and was very eager to help him. "Hey there," he said in his big bellowing voice, "I'll tell you a secret. Don't you realize you are carrying the answer to your problem around with you?" Little Turtle didn't know what he was talking about. "Your shell—your shell!" he shouted. "That's why you have a shell. You can hide in your shell whenever you get that feeling inside you that tells you you are angry. When you are in your shell, you can have a moment to rest and figure out what to do about it. So next time you get angry, just go into your shell." Little Turtle liked the idea, and he was very eager to try his new secret in school. The next day came, and he again made a mistake on his nice clean paper. He started to feel that angry feeling again and was about to lose his temper, when suddenly he remembered what the old tortoise had said. He pulled in his arms, legs, and head, quick as a wink, and rested until he knew what to do. He was delighted to find it so nice and comfortable in his shell where no one could bother him. When he came out, he was surprised to find his teacher smiling at him. He told her he was angry about the mistake. She said she was very proud of him! He continued using his secret for the rest of the year. When he got his report card it was the best in the whole class. Everybody admired him and wondered what his magic secret was. (Schneider & Robin, 1973, pp. 10–11)

The story is used to teach a child to respond like the wise old tortoise by closing his eyes, putting his chin on his chest, and pulling his arms close to his body when the cue word "turtle" is given. After the child has mastered the turtle response through modeling and rehearsing, a relaxation process of tensing and relaxing body muscles is taught. The child now can control his own impulses by going into the turtle response and while in this posture the child can relax, which is incompatible with feeling angry. The next step is to teach the child problem solving, in which he assesses alternative solutions and consequences to conflict while he is in the turtle posture. This gives the child a chance to choose alternative behaviors and not to act impulsively while in a relaxed state. The teacher can use the word "turtle" to prompt a child to go into the turtle response to avoid impulsive aggression. Eventually the child is reinforced for using the turtle response spontaneously in conflict situations. Some children report doing "turtle in my head" without prompting and without going through the physical turtle response for self-control. The results reported by Schneider and Robin (1973) indicate that aggression and tantrums decreased by 46 percent and 54 percent in two elementary school classrooms for the emotionally disturbed after 8 weeks of training using the turtle technique.

Sources: M. Schneider and A. L. Robin (1973). *The turtle manual* (Technical publication, Point of Woods Laboratory School, State University of New York at Stony Brook), quoted by permission of the authors; M. Schneider, (1974). Turtle technique in the classroom. *Teaching Exceptional Children, 7,* 22–24.

BOX 5-7 • Comprehensive Treatment of Chronic Fire Setting in a Severely Disordered Boy

Jim was a 10-year-old boy enrolled in a mental health day program that treated severely behaviorally disordered children. In this program, he was treated for a major fire-setting problem (Koles & Jenson, 1985). Jim's developmental history was characterized by deprivation, inadequate parenting, chaotic home life, and a series of foster home placements. He was diagnosed as having both conduct disorder and ADD-H. His list of referral problems included stealing, hyperactivity, tantrums, learning disabilities, aggression, noncompliance, zoophilia, and fire setting. The fire setting had been a problem since Jim was 3, when he burned down the family home. Since this, in his foster placements, Jim had averaged approximately one fire setting every 2 weeks.

It was assumed that Jim set fires partly because he enjoyed seeing the fires and partly as a reaction to stress. The stress was related to a series of skill deficits in the social and academic areas. In addition, it was assumed that Jim did not fully realize the dangerous consequences of his behavior. The therapy involved a multiple-treatment approach that served to educate Jim, relieve his stress, and consequate his fire setting.

1. *Social problem-solving skills* were taught to Jim; these involved positive relationships with others, successful classroom adjustment, peer interaction skills, and problem-solving skills.
2. *Relaxation training* was implemented, using basic muscle relaxation techniques to help reduce anxiety.
3. *Oversensitization,* in which Jim visited a hospital burn unit and interviewed a depressed 10-year-old boy who had suffered burns over 80 percent of his body while playing with matches, was used. He was also given additional information from the Burn Unit social worker and a fire investigator.
4. *A fire safety education program,* in which Jim participated through a local fire department, involved film and lecture materials on the destructive effects of fire.
5. *Overcorrection procedures,* in which Jim collected combustible material in a metal container and set it on fire, were used. He recited a series of statements over and over again during the safe fire (for example, "Fires can kill people," "This fire is safe because it cannot spread"). He was then required to scrub the container. The overcorrection procedure served to oversatiate Jim with the fascination of fire setting.
6. *Behavioral contracts* were used to reward no fire setting or to punish Jim mildly when a fire was set (e.g., by making him go to bed early).

After treatment, Jim's fire setting dropped from an average to once every 2 weeks to virtually zero fires at a 1-year follow-up. Jim improved his basic social skills and appeared better prepared to handle stressful situations, although some of his inappropriate behaviors such as stealing and family problems continued.

Source: M. Koles and W. R. Jenson. (1985). A comprehensive treatment approach for chronic firesetting in a boy. *Journal of Behavior Therapy and Experimental Psychiatry, 16,* 81–86.

FIGURE 5-5. Total deviant behaviors in the home for the treated sample of deviant children (solid line) before, during, and after treatment and their nondeviant peers (represented as a grid showing the range of normative behaviors).

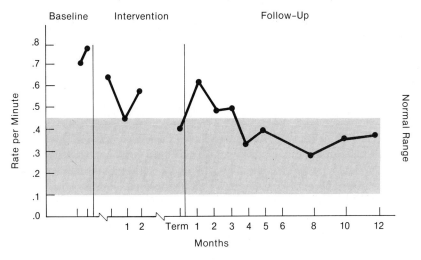

Source: G. R. Patterson. (1974). Interventions for boys with conduct problems: Multiple settings, treatments, and criteria. *Journal of Consulting and Clinical Psychology, 42,* 476. Copyright 1974 by the American Psychological Association. Reprinted by permission of the author.

disordered child is going to make a successful adjustment to a school setting. Behaviorally based direct instruction programs have been proven effective in teaching basic academic skills to conduct-disordered children (Kesler, 1987). However, deficits in rule-governed behavior, empathy, and moral behavior are difficult to remedy. A new program has been developed for conduct-disordered children that emphasizes social skills training, aggression control, and moral education (Goldstein et al., 1987). This program is discussed in more detail in the section on juvenile delinquency.

Table 5-9
Factors That Affect Compliance During Request Making

1. *Question Format:* It is better not to use a question format such as "Isn't it time to . . . ?". It is better to state "It is now time to . . . ". Questions reduce compliance with conduct-disordered children.
2. *Eye Contact:* It is better to make direct eye contact with a child when making a request.
3. *Distance:* It is better to be 1 meter or less from a child when making a request.
4. *Two Requests:* More than two requests (i.e., nagging) reduces compliance.
5. *Loudness of Request:* It is better to give a request in a soft but firm tone instead of a loud voice.
6. *Time:* Children should be given approximately 3 to 5 seconds to comply once a request is given. During this interval, the adult should not give another request, repeat the request, or engage in an argument with the child.
7. *Nonemotional Requests:* It is better to give a request in a nonemotional manner, instead of yelling or calling the child names.
8. *Descriptive Requests:* It is better to give a specific descriptive request instead of a global request (for instance, "Clean your room" may not be as effective as "Clean your room by stacking the toys in the box, books on the shelf, and clothes in the closet.").
9. *Consequate Compliance:* Consistently reinforce compliance and mildly punish noncompliance.

FIGURE 5-6. Parental command-consequence procedure.

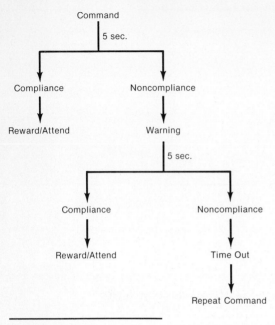

Source: C. Webster-Stratton. (1983, May). Intervention approaches to conduct disorders in young children. *Nurse Practitioner,* pp. 23–34. Reprinted by permission.

JUVENILE DELINQUENCY

Juvenile delinquency is a problem associated with adolescence in the public's mind and in media presentations. It is often portrayed as part of a stage of adolescent rebellion that will pass. However, delinquency is not an isolated product of adolescent development. Many of the problems associated with delinquent behavior, such as aggression, destructiveness, noncompliance, and demands for attention, have their roots in childhood and as externalizing/social disorders. Many adolescent delinquents have had diagnoses of conduct disorder or ADD-H (Hollander & Turner, 1985; Robins, 1979). An American longitudinal study found that 80 percent of the children who frequently engaged in stealing, lying, and truancy later appeared in juvenile court for an offense (Robins, 1966, 1974). The children picked as most aggres-

sive by their teachers and peers in the sixth and seventh grades were most likely to become adolescent delinquents, particularly if they had academic failures (Robins, 1979).

The seriousness of the externalizing problem behaviors takes on new importance when the juvenile exhibiting the problem behaviors is adult-sized with many of the capabilities of an adult. Vedder (1979), in reviewing the area of juvenile delinquency, estimated that half of the serious crimes in the United States are committed by youths between the ages of 10 and 17. In 1984, juveniles under the age of 18 committed 17 percent of all violent crimes and 35 percent of all property crimes in the United States (Federal Bureau of Investigation, 1984). For male delinquents, robbery is the most frequent violent crime; for females, it is aggravated assault (Strasburg, 1984). The average age for the first arrest is decreasing with the peak now well below 13 years of age (Goldstein et al., 1987). Interestingly, the most frequent victim of an adolescent delinquent crime is another juvenile. The rate is seven times higher for juvenile crime against other juveniles than juvenile crime against adults.

Characteristics of Adolescent Delinquents

Several studies on delinquents have identified diagnostic categories that have several shared characteristics (Jenkins, 1973; Jenkins & Boyer, 1968; Jenkins & Hewitt, 1944; Kohn, 1977; Peterson, Quay, & Tiffany, 1961; Quay, 1964). The results of these studies indicate three broad categories of delinquents: (1) the socialized/subcultural; (2) the unsocialized/psychopathic, and (3) the disturbed/neurotic delinquent (Quay, 1964).

The *socialized delinquent* is described as having bad companions, engaging in gang activities and cooperative stealing, being truant from home and school, and staying out late. The socialized delinquent is generally portrayed on television and the movies as the gang member who is closely attached to a peer group that totally rejects conventional society. In contrast is the *undersocialized delinquent,* who is not attached to a gang or

Juvenile gang crime is often portrayed in the media and press as a particularly difficult problem. Gang members often form close social bonds with peers while rejecting the values and standards of conventional society. This type of socialized delinquency is often a path to later adulthood criminality.

set of friends but is instead a loner. This type of delinquent defies authority; is assaultive, impulsive, selfish, and boastful; and has no conscience or guilt feelings about his acts. The last type of delinquent is the *neurotic* or *overinhibited delinquent*, who is seclusive, shy, and anxious. Like the undersocialized delinquent, the neurotic delinquent has few friends and is likely to commit antisocial acts alone.

Irrespective of personality type, there are common characteristics that some delinquents share. These characteristics are not dissimilar to those already discussed for other externalizing/social disorders. Hollander and Turner (1985) found in a sample of 185 incarcerated delinquents that 85 percent met the diagnostic criteria for conduct disorder. In this sample, the greatest majority were undersocialized (69 percent) and 19 percent had a secondary diagnosis of ADD-H. Clearly, be-

havioral excesses such as aggression, noncompliance, and destructiveness are associated with delinquency (Loeber, Weissmann, & Reid, 1983; Roff & Wirt, 1984). As in other externalizing/social disorders, significant deficits are also associated with delinquency; these include lack of social skills, peer rejection, lack of problem-solving skills, and poor academic skills (Dishion et al., 1984; Loeber et al., 1983; Roff & Wirt, 1984). Two of the most potent antecedents and covariates of adolescent delinquency are early aggression (Roff & Wirt, 1984) and academic skills deficits (Dishion et al., 1984).

The academic difficulties associated with delinquency are easy to underestimate, because delinquents have difficulty both socially and academically in adjusting to school. These youths have high rates of truancy; many drop out of school because of academic retardation, which puts them far below their peers in achievement levels. Rutter and Yule (1978) suggest that not all antisocial behavior leads to academic failure, but in some cases the reverse may be true—that is, academic failure may lead to antisocial behavior. In particular, reading difficulties have been associated with delinquency in youths (Rutter & Yule, 1973). In our society, reading is a critical skill for employment and other aspects of everyday life. A childhood reading failure may substantially contribute to loss of self-esteem, discouragement, and delinquent behavior (Rutter & Yule, 1978).

Causes of Adolescent Delinquency

The causes of delinquency are similar to the causes already reviewed for ADD-H and conduct disorder. Genetics, temperament, and family factors are all similar for these children. For example, genetics plays a role in the development of antisocial and delinquent behavior (Mednick & Hutchings, 1978). Social factors such as poverty, broken homes, parental psychiatric disturbance, poor parental discipline, and lack of supervision are also associated with delinquency (Farrington, 1978; Glueck & Glueck, 1950, 1959, 1970; Hetherington & Martin, 1979; Lewis & Balla, 1976; Offord, Allen, & Abrams, 1978).

The casual and descriptive factors related to delinquency in the United States are best summarized in the conclusion of the report by the President's Commission on Law Enforcement and Administrative Justice (1967). This report was prepared two decades ago, but the descriptive and risk factors still fit well (Kazdin, 1985).

Delinquents are concentrated disproportionately in the larger cities. Arrest rates are next highest in the suburbs and lower in rural areas.

Delinquency rates are higher among children from broken homes. They are similarly high among children who have numerous siblings.

Delinquents tend to do badly in school. Their grades are below average. Large numbers have dropped one or more classes behind their classmates or have dropped out of school entirely.

Delinquents tend to come from backgrounds of social and economic deprivation. Their families tend to have lower than average incomes and social status. But perhaps more important than individual family situation is the area in which the youth lives. One study has shown that a lower class youth has little chance of being classified as delinquent if he lives in a predominantly upper class neighborhood. (President's Commission on Law Enforcement and Administrative Justice, 1967, pp. 56-57)

Treatment of Delinquents

Controversy surrounds the types of interventions that should be used with delinquent youth, particularly the issue of punishment versus rehabilitative treatment. Should youths who commit serious crimes be punished as adults, or should the basic approach assume that a youth does not have the experience or judgment of an adult, and thus should be treated rather than punished? Should the treatment be aimed at a psychopathological underlying cause, or should the treatment be aimed at teaching the adolescent replacement skills for inappropriate behaviors?

Juvenile Corrections and Institutions   Society has the right to be protected from crime and property damage. Fagan and Hartstone (1984) have observed that America is getting tough and that the approach of "aid, encouragement, and guidance" to juveniles is giving way to punishment, "just deserts," and "secure confinement." This view, however, may not be a productive approach. Research has indicated that just keeping young delinquent offenders out of the juvenile corrections systems (*diversion*) may be relatively as effective as a specific intervention (Gensheimer, Mayer, Gottschalk, & Davidson, 1986). However, juvenile offenders are often placed in institutional settings.

Institutional placements include large state training schools, forestry camps, detention centers, and long-term youth correctional facilities. Most institutions serve the multiple purposes of holding juveniles awaiting court action, administering diagnostic evaluations, providing temporary housing, and giving correctional punishment. The effectiveness and appropriateness of institutional treatment are questionable. The data on general effectiveness from institutional programs indicate that approximately half of all juveniles from training schools will later be rearrested and incarcerated (Griffin & Griffin, 1978). Instead of being seen as rehabilitation centers, institutions have been characterized as "crime training schools" in which inmates learn new criminal techniques from their peers (Haskell & Yablonsky, 1970; Stumphauzer, 1979). Frequently youths are themselves victimized in institutional placements through violence and homosexual exploitation (Bartollos, Miller, & Dinitz, 1976).

Achievement Place   The Achievement Place or teaching-family model is a community-based, family-style program which serves six to eight delinquents in each group home (Phillips, 1968). The program assumes a behavior deficiency model, in which delinquent's behavior problems are caused by a lack of essential adjustment skills rather than by internal psychopathology (Kirigin, Wolf, Braukmann, Fixsen, & Phillips, 1979). The group home parents are called "teaching parents" because the program emphasizes the teaching of social skills, academic competency, prevocational skills, and self-care skills through modeling and direct instruction. Each group home has four main components: (1) a motivational system (token economy and level system), (2) a self-government system, (3) a behavioral skills training program, and (4) a relation-building program between the youths and the teaching parents. Initially, each youth in the program must earn daily privileges such as television time or extra snacks; later, as the youths advance through the program, they earn privileges on a weekly basis. Close contact is maintained between the teaching parents and the community, particularly the neighborhood school. Each youth brings home a daily report card indicating school performance and behavior, and earns points at home for positive report cards.

The Achievement Place program is rigorously evaluated, and the teaching parents must be certified. In addition, the community evaluates the program, as do the adolescents in the program. For example, the adolescents rate the program on the fairness of teaching parents and the effective-

ness of the self-government. The initial results from Achievement Place have been impressive, particularly when compared to institutional placement. Figure 5-7 shows the percentage of reinstitutionalized youths 1 and 2 years after release from a boys' school (the comparison group) or Achievement Place. This study was based on only a small number of adolescents. A more extensive study of 150 Achievement Place group homes evaluated the number of offenses and the reinstitutionalization rate 3 years after boys' participation in the program. The basic finding was that the Achievement Place participants did not significantly differ in recidivism from the participants from traditional programs (Jones, Weinrott, & Howard, 1981; Kirigin, Braukmann, Atwater, & Wolf, 1982). It appears that the youths make consistent progress while they are in the program (Kazdin, 1985), but that these gains fade when the youths are returned to their old environments.

FIGURE 5-7. The cumulative percentage of youths who were institutionalized 1 year and 2 years following release from treatment in an institution (boys school group) or Achievement Place.

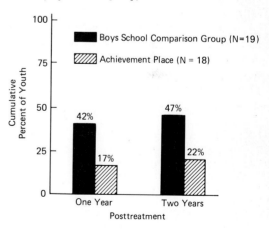

Source: K. Kirigin, M. M. Wolf, C. J. Braukmann, D. L. Fixsen, and E. L. Phillips. (1979). Achievement Place: A preliminary outcome evaluation. In J. S. Stumphauzer (Ed.), *Progress in behavior therapy with delinquents* (Springfield, IL: Charles C Thomas), p. 131. Reprinted by permission of the publisher.

Table 5-10
General Overview of Anger Control Training

Week 1: Introduction
1. Explain the goals of anger control training and "sell it" to the youngsters.
2. Explain the rules for participating and the training procedures.
3. Give initial assessments of the A-B-Cs of aggressive behavior: (A) What led up to it? (B) What did you do? (C) What were the consequences?
4. Review goals, procedures, and A-B-Cs; give out binders.

Week 2: Cues and Anger Reducers 1, 2, and 3
1. Review first session.
2. Introduce the Hassle Log.
3. Discuss how to know when you are angry (cues).
4. Discuss what to do when you know you are angry.
   - Anger reducer 1: deep breathing
   - Anger reducer 2: backward counting
   - Anger reducer 3: pleasant imagery
5. Role play: cues + anger reducers.
6. Review Hassle Log, cues, and anger reducers 1, 2, and 3.

Week 3: Triggers
1. Review second session.
2. Discuss understanding what makes you angry (triggers).
   - External triggers
   - Internal triggers
3. Role play: triggers + cues + anger reducer(s).
4. Review triggers, cues, and anger reducers 1, 2, and 3.

Week 4: Reminders (Anger Reducer 4)
1. Review third session.
2. Introduce reminders.
3. Model using reminders.
4. Role play: triggers + cues + reminders + anger reducer(s).
5. Review reminders.

Week 5: Self-Evaluation
1. Review fourth session.
2. Introduce self-evaluation.
   - Self-rewarding
   - Self-coaching
3. Role play: triggers + cues + reminders + anger reducer(s) + self-evaluation.
4. Review self-evaluation.

Week 6: Thinking Ahead (Anger Reducer 5)
1. Review fifth session.
2. Introduce thinking ahead.
   - Short- and long-term consequences
   - Most and least serious consequences
   - Internal, external, and social consequences
3. Role play: "if-then" thinking ahead.
4. Role play: triggers + cues + reminders + anger reducer(s) + self-evaluation.
5. Review thinking ahead.

Week 7: The Angry Behavior Cycle
1. Review sixth session.
2. Introduce the angry behavior cycle.
   - Identifying your own anger-provoking behavior
   - Changing your own anger-provoking behavior
3. Role play: triggers + cues + reminders + anger reducer(s) + self-evaluation.
4. Review the angry behavior cycle.

Week 8: Rehearsal of Full Sequence
1. Review seventh session.
2. Introduce using new behaviors (skills) in place of aggression.
3. Role play: triggers + cues + reminders + anger reducer(s) + SL skill + self-evaluation.

Table 5-10 *(Continued)*

Week 9: Rehearsal of Full Sequence
1. Review Hassle Logs.
2. Role play: triggers + cues + reminders + anger reducer(s) + SL skill + self-evaluation.

Week 10: Overall Review
1. Review Hassle Logs.
2. Recap anger control techniques.
3. Role play: triggers + cues + reminders + anger reducer(s) + SL skill + self-evaluation.
4. Reinforce for participation and encourage to continue.

Source: A. P. Goldstein, B. Glick, S. Reiner, D. Zimmerman, and T. M. Coultry. (1987). *Aggression replacement training: A comprehensive intervention for aggressive youth* (Champaign, IL: Research Press), pp. 80–81. Reprinted by permission.

Aggression Replacement Training The aggression replacement training (ART) approach to juvenile delinquency is based on the premise that juvenile delinquents are lacking in the "broad array of personal, interpersonal, and social-cognitive *skills* that collectively constitute effective prosocial behavior" (Goldstein et al., 1987). It is assumed that delinquents are essentially deficient in these "prosocial" skills, and that these skills can be taught to and will be used by the youths. A structured learning approach to *social skills training* is first taught, in which the adolescents learn basic interaction skills such as conversation skills, asking for help, appropriately expressing feelings, dealing with stress, and self-control (Goldstein, Sprafkin, Gershaw, & Klein, 1980). The social skills are taught through modeling, role playing, performance feedback, and transfer training to new situations. After the social skills training component, the juveniles are taught the second component of the program, *anger control training.* Anger control teaches specific alternative skills to respond to hassles and provocations. The youths are taught to recognize anger triggers, physiological cues that signal anger arousal, reminders of how to produce anger-reducing self-statements and social skills, relaxation techniques, and a self-evaluation component (called the Hassle Log) to judge how well the techniques are being used in different situations. Table 5-10 lists the basic components of the anger control training.

The last training component of the ART program involves *moral education empathy training.* The adolescents are assessed to determine their current level of moral development. The assessment is based on Kohlberg's (1969, 1973) six stages of moral development. The youths are then given a series of moral dilemma exercises, such as the "Heinz dilemma," in which a woman is dying of cancer and an expensive drug could save her life but the husband has no money. The question is this: Should the husband steal the drug or not? The moral training consists of several different dilemmas that are presented in group sessions to youths from a lower stage of moral development who are mixed with youths from a higher stage. The youths are encouraged to argue and debate each case, with the assumption that the adolescents who are operating at the lower moral level will improve their prosocial moral behavior and move to a higher level.

Certainly the ART treatment approach includes the basic skills that most delinquents appear to need: social skills training, anger control, and enhancement of moral empathy. However, the research on the effectiveness of this approach is only preliminary. Field studies at the Annsville and MacCormick facilities of the New York State Division of Youth show that delinquents can learn and benefit from the social skills training and anger control components. However, the results are less clear on the effectiveness of the moral training component and the long-term effectiveness of the program.

FOLLOW-UP

Children and adolescents who have externalizing/ social disorders generally do not outgrow their difficulties and many have more difficulties as adults. Ironically, professionals tend to underestimate the long-term seriousness of externalizing/social disorders (Carter, 1987; Jenson, 1978). ADD-H children appear to have the best outcomes of children with social disorders (Wallander & Hubert, 1985; Weiss & Hechtman, 1986). As young adults, approximately 30 to 40 percent of the sample in one study functioned essentially normally; 40 to 50 percent continued to have significantly more social and emotional problems than controls; and 10 percent were significantly disturbed, requiring intensive services (Hechtmann, Weiss, Perlman, & Tuck, 1981).

The outlook for conduct-disordered children and juvenile delinquents is poorer. An earlier study found that 80 percent of a group of 1000 delinquents had been arrested at least once by early adulthood (Glueck & Glueck, 1940). Antisocial children continue to have problems in school (Walker et al., 1986) and have poorer outcomes in adulthood than their age-mates (Robins, 1979). The estimates vary, but from 70 to 80 percent of antisocial children are thought to have poor outcomes (psychiatric problems, multiple jobs, multiple marriages, substance abuse, incarceration) as adults (Morris et al., 1956; Robins, 1974, 1979).

One variable that seems to predict a particularly poor outcome for children with ADD-H, conduct disorder, or delinquency is an early history of aggressive behavior (Campbell, et al., 1986; Eron & Huesmann, 1984; McGee et al., 1984; Roff & Wirt, 1984). Aggressiveness is not stage-related and appears to be a very stable problem behavior over time (Kazdin, 1985; Olweus, 1979). The more intense and frequent the aggressive behavior, then the poorer the outcome for any type of externalizing/social disorder.

SUMMARY

Social disorders of children are some of the most common behavior disorders referred for treatment and special education services. The social disorders presented in this chapter include attention deficit disorder with hyperactivity (ADD-H), conduct disorder, and juvenile delinquency. ADD-H is characterized by poor attending, impulsivity, and fidgety motor behavior. The conduct-disordered child is a rule breaker who is noncompliant and aggressive. The juvenile delinquent has many of the characteristics of ADD-H and conduct-disordered children; however, the delinquent has also engaged in some type of law breaking.

The childhood social disorders stand out because the behaviors that define these disorders are primarily behavioral excesses. All children fight, are sometimes inattentive, and sometimes break rules. However, socially disordered children engage in these behaviors excessively, compared to their peers. It is easy to focus just on the excesses of these children, but the youngsters also have significant deficits. These deficits include poor academic skills, inappropriate social skills, and inadequate moral or rule-governed behavior. If the deficits are not treated along with the excesses, these children will have a poor outcome in adolescence and adulthood.

c h a p t e r

6

Drug Usage by Children and Teenagers

KEY TERMS

Addiction. In Physical Addiction, the drug user develops tolerance for the drug, requiring increasingly larger doses to achieve an effect. Also, drug cessation creates a characteristic withdrawal syndrome, with effects ranging from the unpleasant to the life-threatening, depending upon the drug involved. In Psychological Addiction, the user feels compelled to take the drug, but there is no withdrawal syndrome.

Delirium Tremens (DTs). A traumatic withdrawal reaction produced by abrupt cessation of drinking in the final stages of alcoholism; the condition is characterized by fever, tremors, hallucinations, and convulsions, sometimes resulting in death (20 percent of the cases).

Fetal Alcohol Syndrome. A condition in which alcohol consumed by the pregnant woman acts as a toxin for her fetus, causing physical deformities and mental retardation. This condition is most common among children of heavy drinkers and alcoholics, but the safe amount of alcohol for pregnant women to consume is presently unknown.

Prevalence. The frequency of a particular condition within a population, most often given as the number of persons per 1000 (or for rare conditions as the number of persons per 100,000) who have the disorder. Can be presented as Annual Prevalence, or the number of cases found within a specific year, or as Lifetime Prevalence, which is the number of cases within the lifetime of a particular group (such as high school seniors).

Stimulant Psychosis.   A toxic reaction caused by an overdose of some stimulant drug, such as amphetamine. The user becomes excited, irritable, aggressive, irrational, and sometimes dangerous. One such incident makes future ones more likely.

THE DRUG PROBLEM— INTRODUCTION

Parents and legal authorities continue to be alarmed by the extent of illicit drug use, smoking, and drinking among the young. This chapter is devoted to exploring a number of basic questions regarding young people's drug usage: (1) Why are adolescents and young adults so attracted to potentially toxic and illegal drugs, and why do older people not share this attraction to the same degree? (2) Which harmful or illegal drugs are currently popular and why? (3) How do these substances affect adolescents psychologically, educationally, socially, and physically? (4) What can be done to prevent, control, and treat drug misuse?

Let us consider the first question listed, about the seemingly unique attraction of drugs to young people. Is this true or not? Perhaps the premise is wrong, and adults seek drugs as avidly as their juniors. In fact, youthful drug users will be the first to point out that mature adults have used very dangerous drugs for centuries. Adults' attraction to harmful drugs is clearly evident today. Despite widespread dissemination of information about the health perils associated with tobacco, large numbers of adults continue to smoke. Comfortably seated before their television sets, they shun exercise and puff away on their cigarettes, preferably while sipping an alcoholic beverage or a highly sugared soft drink. But this form of the good life exposes them to significant long-term health risks from killing diseases, such as cancer, stroke, and cardiovascular disease. The temptation to worry about the health risks they are creating can be calmed by taking over-the-counter or prescription drugs to relieve tension, depression, fatigue, or insomnia. The legal distribution of *psychoactive* (mind-affecting) drugs is a huge and ex-

tremely profitable business, with gigantic advertising and promotional budgets directed toward physicians and the public. The black market for illegal drugs is flourishing as well. Consequently, adults have developed a keen appetite for chemical substances of various types. Their children may note and resent their parents' apparent hypocrisy in relying on many types of psychoactive drugs themselves while they condemn teenagers' drug use. Adults' prohibitions accentuate rebellious teenagers' eagerness to use the forbidden psychoactive compounds.

Even though both younger and older people consume sizable quantities of drugs, most would agree that the two groups differ in their reasons for drug usage. Most adults recall their teens as the time when they lived dangerously, if they ever did so. Young people are more likely to take risks of all types. Their motor vehicle accident rates are notoriously high. Drunken drivers cause over 25,000 deaths and 75,000 injuries in the United States each year (Milgram & Nathan, 1986); many of the dead and injured and their victims are juveniles. In fact, drunk driving is a leading cause of death among the young. This highway carnage associated with drunkenness caused the creation of a Presidential Commission on Drunk Driving in 1983, and several states and the U.S. Congress are taking steps to stiffen penalties for drunk drivers and to raise the minimum drinking age. Unfortunately, the U.S. data do not unequivocally indicate that tougher laws and increased minimum drinking ages will significantly improve the situation (Milgram & Nathan, 1986). When culture and custom decree uncontrolled teenage drinking, the ill effects are very difficult to control.

By their very nature, young people like danger and excitement. Not only do teenagers drive fast and carelessly, but they take other types of

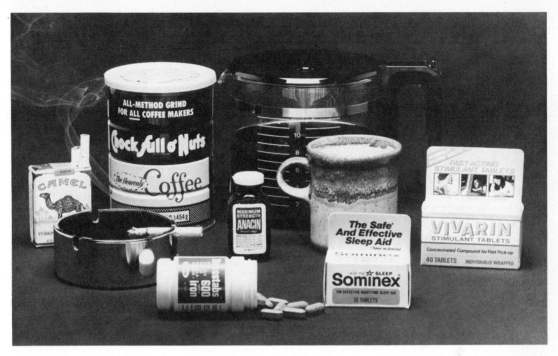

Many people take psychoactive drugs during the course of a typical day. Some of these substances are addicting, and many present long-term health hazards. For many children, drug misuse begins at home.

risks as well. Many endanger their long-term career prospects by playing rather than studying, skipping school, and reassuring their parents that their school failures are unimportant because they don't care about going to college. Of course, at the same time, other young people are working industriously and effectively and are compiling good academic, social, and work records. Yet the fact remains that many youths who will later become good citizens and dependable workers drink and smoke too much, use illegal drugs, and are a menace on the roads. Why?

The answer is not known completely, but there are some research indications that teenagers may not yet realize that the laws of physics and biology do apply to them personally. They believe that older and less clever people will get hurt but that they will not. Consequently, they may ignore the evidence regarding the link between smoking and grave illness of many types, because they feel personally invulnerable to the health haz-

ards associated with tobacco (Botvin, 1982). Many teenagers believe that other people might develop cancer from smoking, but not them. Besides, they reason magically that by the time they personally need it there will be a cure for cancer, or they may claim that the risks are exaggerated because they know of some 85-year-old who is in good health after having smoked for 70 years, or they may offer some other equally illogical rationalization. Teenagers' ability to ignore facts and deny the dangers associated with hazardous courses of action makes it somewhat risky to base prevention and treatment programs for them on the dire long-term outcomes of presently attractive activities such as drug usage (Albino, 1984). As we describe later, prevention efforts directed at adolescents have instead pointed out the *present* disadvantages of substance misuse. For example, smoking prevention programs feature information about smokers' bad breath, yellow teeth, loss of physical fitness, and related negative effects of smoking

(Evans et al., 1978). Because youthful drug users fail to appreciate the long-range danger involved in their favorite activities, they may continue to experiment with ever more potent and potentially toxic chemicals, especially if they have never personally experienced any serious negative consequences.

This chapter uses the terms *drug misuse* and *substance misuse* to describe the excessive, destructive, or illegal use of psychoactive drugs. Drug misuse can apply to heavy cigarette smoking and to alcoholism as well as to the ingestion of heroin or cocaine, because any of these agents can prove destructive and all of them are illegal for minors. By this definition, many people might be classified as substance misusers: That is, they imbibe a substance that is illegal; is harmful psychologically, physically, or both; is addictive; and/or is used in a societally disapproved fashion. Consider the example of a 12-year-old boy who has recently begun to smoke cigarettes. His teenaged brother keeps him supplied with cigarettes and conceals his smoking from their parents. The 12-year-old would qualify as a drug misuser under our definition, because his activity is legally prohibited; it is also severely disapproved by his parents, teachers, and other adult caretakers; and smoking is addictive and very harmful to the boy's health. Although he would be the last to agree, this boy is misusing a powerful, addictive, dangerous substance. In contrast, if he takes a psychostimulant drug prescribed by a physician for the control of his attention deficit and hyperactivity, no drug misuse is involved. In the case of the prescribed drug, the boy's drug use is medically supervised; the drug is likely to benefit the boy; it is legal; and is generally socially condoned.

Substance misuse is somewhat different from *addiction. Physical addiction* or dependence occurs when a drug (1) produces *tolerance,* or the need to take increasing quantities in order to produce a noticeable *effect;* or (2) produces *withdrawal* or an *abstinence syndrome,* a characteristic grouping of unpleasant, sometimes dangerous physical symptoms, when use is discontinued. Substances that are *psychologically addictive* and create strong cravings for their continued use *(ha-*

bituation) are often physically addictive as well. Some nonaddictive drugs can be misused—for example, marijuana. Also, someone may use an illegal substance once or twice, and this would constitute substance misuse but certainly not addiction. In contrast, addiction to nonprescribed drugs necessarily involves substance misuse. Addicts are, by definition, substance abusers, and virtually all addictions endanger health.

DEVELOPMENT OF SUBSTANCE MISUSE

Will today's experimentation with marijuana lead to tomorrow's tragic death from an overdose of cocaine? Many drug education programs have low credibility among students because they grossly overstate the perils of using the milder illegal drugs. Most young people know, or believe they know, that experimentation with relatively innocuous drugs does not lead to dependence on dangerous ones. Yet there is an element of truth to the accusation. Typically, people do not begin their drug careers with narcotics or injected cocaine; they try more easily obtained, less formidable drugs instead. Those who have tried and liked some of the minor drugs are more likely to be drawn to other, potentially more harmful ones than are teens who have never used any illegal substance. Long-term studies of drug use among large groups of high school students show that students' drug usage follows a predictable course (Kandel & Faust, 1975). Most begin by using alcohol and tobacco, which are easily obtained because adults use them freely. Often beer or wine are tried first, and then cigarettes or hard liquor. Those students who progress to the next stage of substance usage usually next try another readily obtainable substance, marijuana. Some adolescents then graduate to more potent drugs, such as LSD, psychostimulants, cocaine, or narcotics. Only a small minority of teenagers eventually obtain the most dangerous drugs, but the route to heavy drug use is highly predictable. Most begin with familiar substances of abuse and stop there, but a few are drawn to increasingly dangerous and expensive drug habits.

Who are the few who assume terrible risks in order to experience psychoactive drug effects? Parents want to know whether this could happen to their child, and how it might be prevented. One predictor of progressing to more serious drug usage is the person's *heavy use* of a substance at the preceding stage. Thus, the teenager who becomes a frequent smoker or drinker is more likely to progress to the use of marijuana than is the classmate who only rarely smokes or drinks. Once a person has become aware of and likes consciousness-altering drugs, she is likely to seek other types. However, this happens to relatively few young people. As Louria (1977) observed, "Very few (well under 1 percent) of those who start with tobacco and cannabis (marijuana) ever reach the stage of injecting heroin and likewise very few become habituated to injected stimulants" (p. 110).

Tobacco

Only in the past 20 years has it been realized how dangerous tobacco is. The leading illnesses causing death in the United States are cancer, heart disease, and stroke, and cigarette smoking has been proven to be a major risk factor in all three (U.S. Department of Health, Education and Welfare [DHEW], 1979). Consequently, the prevention of smoking by young people is an important public health concern, and a successful prevention campaign could save some 27 billion dollars in tobacco-caused medical care, absenteeism, decreased work productivity because of illness, and accidents (U.S. DHEW, 1979).

Table 6-1 presents some recent data concerning young people's smoking habits and their alcohol and drug usage. The rates cited in the table may appear high because they represent any reported use of the various substances ever *(lifetime prevalence).* Smoking rates for all age groups have decreased during the last two decades, perhaps because widely publicized information about the serious health risks related to smoking seems to be having some effect on those younger than 21 years as well as on their seniors. More than 60 percent of youths now believe that smoking one or more packs of cigarettes per day involves great

risk (Johnston, O'Malley, & Bachman, 1985). Nevertheless, large numbers of teenagers continue to take up the habit. Young women in particular are acquiring a taste for cigarettes, perhaps in part because of advertising campaigns designed to add them to the group of smokers. Women's smoking arouses particular concern because it significantly increases their risk of giving birth to vulnerable premature or low-birthweight babies (Frazier, Davis, Goldstein, & Goldberg, 1961; Meredith, 1975). Prior to 1977, a much higher percentage of boys than girls were smokers, but national survey data show that since that time the sex differences in smoking have virtually disappeared (Johnston et al., 1985). In the same national survey of nearly 16,000 high school seniors, a sizable majority of 69.7 percent claimed to have smoked a cigarette at some time. This means that only about one student in three has never lit up.

In previous decades, casual experimentation with tobacco resulted in lifelong smoking habits in about 70 percent of the people who had smoked more than a single cigarette (Hamilton-Russell, 1971). However, with more people quitting smoking than ever before, the addiction prospects for casual smokers may not be so grim as previously. Nevertheless, it is much more difficult to attain the status of ex-smoker than most young people think. Nicotine is a powerfully addicting drug; habitual smokers experience strong cravings for nicotine, as well as physiological tolerance requiring them to smoke increasing numbers of cigarettes each day. When they decide to quit, smokers suffer a withdrawal syndrome consisting of irritability, distress, and inability to concentrate. Cigarette advertising and adolescent values both portray smoking as sophisticated, daring, and sexy, so some young people decide to try it for a while and then believe that they will simply stop when they decide to do so (Lieberman Research, Inc., cited in Brecher & the Editors of *Consumer Reports*, 1972). However, large numbers of aspiring ex-smokers of all ages revert to smoking within a few weeks, months, or even years of swearing off cigarettes (Flaxman, 1976). Smokers are unpleasantly surprised to find that the habit is tenacious,

Table 6-1
Lifetime Prevalence of Use of Sixteen Types of Drugs by Subgroups, Class of 1983

	Marijuana	Inhalants[1]	Amyl/Butyl Nitrites	Hallucinogens[1]	LSD	PCP	Cocaine	Heroin	Other Opiates	Stimulants[2] (adjusted)	Sedatives	Barbiturates	Methaqualone	Tranquilizers	Alcohol	Cigarettes
All seniors	57.0	13.6	8.4	11.9	8.9	5.6	16.2	1.2	9.4	26.9	14.4	9.9	10.1	13.3	92.6	70.6
Sex:																
Male	59.9	16.6	11.9	13.4	10.4	6.9	18.6	1.5	10.7	26.0	15.6	10.7	11.6	13.7	93.5	69.0
Female	53.4	10.4	5.2	9.9	6.9	4.2	13.4	0.8	8.1	27.3	12.9	8.8	8.5	12.7	91.6	71.6
College plans:																
None or under 4 years	61.2	14.9	10.5	14.4	11.0	8.8	18.3	1.7	11.2	31.7	18.0	12.9	12.8	15.3	93.3	76.0
Complete 4 years	52.2	12.3	7.2	9.0	6.5	3.5	13.6	0.8	8.0	21.8	11.3	7.4	7.7	11.3	92.0	65.8
Region:																
Northeast	63.7	13.0	8.4	14.0	8.7	6.0	20.5	1.1	9.0	26.9	12.4	8.4	8.7	12.3	95.4	72.9
North Central	57.0	14.4	8.6	15.1	11.7	6.2	12.5	1.3	10.0	29.8	15.9	11.9	10.8	13.4	94.8	74.3
South	50.8	12.4	9.0	7.8	6.7	4.3	12.0	1.4	8.5	23.4	15.9	9.9	11.8	13.9	90.5	69.2
West	59.2	15.3	6.9	11.2	8.4	6.1	25.1	0.9	10.8	28.4	11.9	8.7	7.3	13.2	88.4	63.6

Source: L. D. Johnston, P. M. O'Malley, and J. G. Bachman. (1984). *Drugs and American high school students, 1975–1983* (DHHS Publication No. ADM 85-1374). Washington, DC: U.S. Government Printing Office.
1. Unadjusted for known underreporting of certain drugs.
2. Adjusted for overreporting of nonprescription stimulants.

and that quitting is difficult even when it is unmistakably and seriously endangering their health. It is chilling to watch someone who is seriously ill with chronic lung disease light up a cigarette, but it is not yet an uncommon sight.

Somewhat different types of factors seem to be associated with starting and later with maintaining the practice of smoking. Since so many young students try smoking at least once or twice, it would seem that no particular, enduring personality pattern characterizes those who become smokers. However, researchers have found that when teenagers begin to smoke they are more rebellious, curious, and socially confident than their classmates (Jarvik, Cullen, Gritz, Vogt, & West, 1977; Lichtenstein, 1982). At the same time, tobacco must be available and be used by the youth's family members or friends. Peers undoubtedly encourage their nonsmoking friends to take up the practice, and family members may purposely or unwittingly provide attractive models of tobacco use. When both a parent and an older sibling are smokers, the child is *four times* as likely to smoke as is the child from a home in which no one smokes, suggesting that family influences may be prime determinants of tobacco use (U.S. DHEW, 1977). Later, we point out that the influence of groups such as families and friends extends to the use of alcohol and illicit drugs as well. Thoughtfully devised prevention programs are being introduced to counteract the powerful social influences of close associates who are smokers, of certain adolescent values, and of tobacco industry advertisement campaigns. Several such prevention efforts are described in Box 6-1.

Once a teenager begins to smoke, new factors maintain the habit, and physiological effects become important (Lichtenstein, 1982). As in other addictions, there are immediate positive physical consequences from smoking, produced by the nicotine. The smoker develops physical dependence on nicotine, and experiences both relief and mild exhilaration upon beginning to smoke a cigarette. Certain times of day or situations, such as social gatherings, after meals, while watching television, or while drinking coffee or alcohol, will become powerful cues for smoking. An additional consideration is that smoking helps the person avoid the negative psychological and physiological effects of withdrawal. It is understandable that most smokers want to quit but that their attempts to do so have been unsuccessful (U.S. Public Health Service, 1976). It is all the more impressive that the vast majority who are highly motivated to quit eventually succeed, but often only after many attempts (Lichtenstein, 1982). Tobacco use is best avoided completely, because addiction is so difficult to prevent and to treat.

Alcohol

Large numbers of high school students have decreased their use of illicit drugs, but they continue to drink alcohol to excess. There have been few changes in the lifetime prevalence (ever having tried alcohol) over the past decade, with the rate varying between 90.4 percent in 1975 to a peak of 93 percent in 1979 and a slight decline thereafter. The proportion of heavy party drinkers (potential problem drinkers) among high school students has decreased slightly. In 1979, 41 percent of high school seniors sampled said that at least once in the past 2 weeks they had drunk very heavily (had five or more drinks in a row). The first decrease in that statistic was a drop to 39 percent of those who had drunk heavily in 1984 (Johnston et al., 1985). The reason for this diminution is unknown.

Although both sexes are equally likely to have sampled alcohol at some time, more boys became heavy drinkers, at least during the high school years. In the 1985 survey (Johnston et al., 1985), 6.6 percent of the boys reported daily use of alcohol, as compared to only 2.7 percent of the girls. Also, nearly half of the boys (48 percent), but only less than a third (30 percent) of the girls, said they had five or more drinks on some occasion in the past 2 weeks. It appears that during adolescence, at least, heavy drinking is a masculine prerogative. This is fortunate, because a young woman's heavy drinking can result in serious damage to her unborn child. *Fetal alcohol syndrome* occurs in prenatal life among the babies of alcoholic mothers or, to a lesser degree, among the babies of nonaddicted heavy drinkers who

BOX 6-1 • How to Prevent Teenage Smoking

Information about why and when teenagers begin to smoke cigarettes can be used to prevent other young people from smoking. We know that adolescents tend to be risk takers, and are less affected than adults by information on the negative long-term health consequences of smoking. Thus, scare tactics alone are unlikely to prevent students from taking up smoking. An appeal to the immediate unattractive and unwanted effects of smoking is more likely to meet success. Moreover, as parents and teachers have found, adults may be ineffectual influence agents for adolescents as compared with friends. The power of peers is felt more in the areas of dress, hair style, music preferences, and minor purchases than in educational, religious, and career choices, where parents may exert more influence. However, the more rebellious teens, who are especially likely to try tobacco and drugs, probably do not listen a great deal to their parents in any respect, at least not until they mature.

Perhaps prevention programs should be geared to peer rather than adult influences and to immediate rather than future effects, as several moderately successful antismoking programs have done. One of the first such intervention packages was directed toward junior high school pupils and featured videotapes with peer actors providing basic information on smoking dangers and the greater attractiveness, fitness, and good health of nonsmokers (Evans et al., 1978). Other tapes also exposed the manipulations of tobacco advertising and the power of parental modeling of smoking. Finally, small groups of students participated in discussions of methods to use in coping with social pressures to smoke. Later, few members of either the videotape-discussion group or the control group began to smoke, perhaps because both had seen a videotape of a saliva test for smoking that focused on the immediate ill effects of nicotine on the body.

In another prevention effort, popular high school students led a program for sixth- and seventh-graders in which participants first were given information about smoking and encouraged to make a commitment not to smoke. In a series of later meetings, they discussed how to analyze and to counteract efforts to get them to smoke. At the end of a year of periodic meetings, 9.9 percent of the control group but only 5.6 percent of the treatment group reported having smoked in the previous week (McAlister, Perry, Killen, Slinkard, & Maccoby, 1980). Other effective prevention interventions have utilized 5-minute television spot presentations of antismoking propaganda, combined with peer-presented classroom activities and homework assignments involving parents who had also viewed the programs (Flay, D'Avernas, Best, Kersell, & Ryan, 1982; Flay, Johnson, & Hansen, 1984). Once again, only half as many participating children began smoking as did nonparticipants. Surprisingly, at least one smoker was reported to have quit in 23 percent of all the viewing homes.

The studies cited here have demonstrated some success in preventing cigarette usage— over nearly a 2-year period, in some cases. If there were as much money available for prevention research as there is devoted to tobacco advertising, fewer people would die prematurely.

Sources: R. I. Evans, R. M. Rozelle, M. B. Mittelmark, W. B. Hansen, A. L. Bane, and J. Havis. (1978). Deterring the onset of smoking in children: Knowledge of immediate physiological effects and coping with peer pressure, media pressure, and parent modeling. *Journal of Applied Social Psychology, 8,* 126–135; B. R. Flay, J. R. D'Avernas, J. A. Best, M. W. Kersell, and K. B. Ryan. (1982). Cigarette smoking: Why young people do it and ways of preventing it. In P. McGrath and P. Firestone (Eds.), *Pediatric and adolescent behavioral medicine* (New York: Springer-Verlag); B. R. Flay, C. A. Johnson, and W. B. Hansen. (1984). Evaluation of a mass media enhanced smoking prevention and cessation program. In J. P. Baggaley and J. Sharpe (Eds.), *Experimental research in TV instruction* (Vol. 5) (Montréal: Concordia University); A. L. McAlister, C. Perry, J. Killen, L. A. Slinkard, and N. Maccoby. (1980). A pilot study of smoking, alcohol, and drug abuse prevention. *American Journal of Public Health, 70,* 719–721.

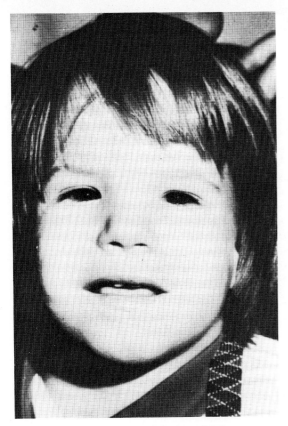

A retarded fetal-alcohol-syndrome child. Note the epicanthic folds on eyelids, the low nasal bridge, and the thin upper lip.

consume 1 ounce or more of pure alcohol daily (Streissguth, Martin, Martin, & Barr, 1981). The fetal alcohol syndrome is described in Box 6-2.

The past few years have witnessed no marked changes in the age at which students begin drinking alcohol. However, over the longer term, the average age of first drinking has dropped somewhat. One estimate is that during the 1940s and 1950s the average age of first drinking was 13 or 14 years, but that in the mid-1970s the age was closer to 12 years (Demone & Wechsler, 1976). Now by the ninth grade (at about age 15 years), 55 to 56 percent of American students have been introduced to alcohol (Johnston et al., 1985).

Drinking patterns are usually established early in life. "If an individual is ever going to drink, he or she will likely have begun prior to graduation from high school" (Demone & Wechsler, 1976, p. 207). Alcohol proves addicting for a smaller proportion of users (2 to 10 percent) than do nicotine and most other addictive substances, according to Barry (1977). But alcohol addiction is disastrous. Alcoholism is the most common and one of the most harmful forms of addiction in the United States today. However good their previous adjustment, alcoholics typically become erratic, undependable, and belligerent; lose their jobs; destroy their marriages; drive away their nonalcoholic friends; and terrorize their children. When deprived of alcohol, they experience convulsions, hallucinations, and other, potentially fatal withdrawal symptoms (*delirium tremens* or DTs). Every city has a dilapidated slum section that harbors large numbers of alcoholics. Unlike addiction to narcotics or most other psychoactive drugs, long-term alcoholism can result in extensive physical deterioration, such as permanent brain damage *(Korsakoff's psychosis)* and cirrhosis of the liver.

It is ironic that one of the most potentially dangerous of the addictive drugs, alcohol, is also one of the most socially condoned when taken in moderation and is perhaps the easiest to obtain. Many teenagers seek new sensations and do not find moderation attractive, so their drunkenness endangers themselves and others. Communities have found that one way to prevent some of the harmful effects of teenagers' immoderate drinking is to increase the minimum legal drinking age. This strategy is unpopular with those under 21 years, but is sometimes effective. One study reported the effects of both lowering the legal drinking age in some states and increasing it again in others (Wagenaar, 1983). Such changes are not controlled experiments, so it is difficult if not impossible to gauge their effects. The rate of alcohol-related auto crashes immediately increased by 10 to 30 percent when the drinking age was decreased so younger individuals could legally drink. States that raised their legal drinking age immediately decreased their alcohol-related auto accidents by the same margin. However, the lower

BOX 6-2 • Maternal Alcoholism and Prenatal Development

When she was serving as a pediatric resident at a county hospital, Christy Ulleland noticed that some babies had low birthweights and failed to thrive. Their failure to develop normally was puzzling, because the babies were receiving adequate diets and good medical care. Nevertheless, they remained weak, and puny, and did not gain weight normally. When Dr. Ulleland looked carefully into the backgrounds of these infants, she found one common feature—their mothers tended to be alcoholic (Ulleland, 1972). Moreover, as illustrated below, babies of alcoholic mothers often have a deformed facial appearance characterized by a small head, small eyes, short nose, flattened nasal bridge, narrow upper lip, small chin and flat midface. Many have abnormally small heads (microcephaly), and deformed hearts and joints, and virtually all of them are small and developmentally delayed (Streissguth, 1976; Streissguth, Landesman-Dwyer, Martin, & Smith, 1980). This array of disorders, which is called the *fetal alcohol syndrome,* commonly results in borderline or below-normal intelligence and retarded academic achievement when the child becomes older. Furthermore, follow-up studies of babies born to alcoholic mothers have shown that even those with no apparent physical deformities have significantly lower IQs than do children born to women who are not alcoholic but who are similar to the alcoholic mothers in most other respects. It is true, however, that the alcoholic mothers' offspring who have the most physical deformities also tend to be the most severely mentally retarded.

What causes fetal alcohol syndrome? Beyond the fact that the mother was alcoholic while pregnant, little is known about the mechanisms responsible for this disorder. It is known that when a pregnant woman consumes alcohol, the alcohol passes into the fetus where it is retained for long periods of time. But why alcohol in large quantities (for instance, two bottles of wine per day) should so profoundly affect the developing fetus has not yet been discovered. Nor is it known how much alcohol for the mother is too much for her unborn baby.

Sources: A. P. Streissguth. (1976). Maternal alcoholism and the outcome of pregnancy: A review of the fetal alcohol syndrome. In M. Greenblatt and M. Schuckit (Eds.), *Alcoholism problems in women and children* (New York: Grune & Stratton), photograph reprinted by permission of Grune & Stratton, Inc., and A. P. Streissguth; A. P. Streissguth, S. Landesman-Dwyer, J. C. Martin, and D. W. Smith. (1980). Teratogenic effects of alcohol in humans and laboratory animals. *Science, 209,* 353–361; C. N. Ulleland. (1972). The offspring of alcoholic mothers, *Annals of the New York Academy of Sciences, 197,* 167–169.

rates were typically not maintained (Milgram & Nathan, 1986). Thus, although eliminating legal drinking in younger people would seem to be a very simple preventive intervention, its value in reducing accidents is still under study.

More likely than not, a drinking teenager has parents and siblings who drink as well. Certain types of family constellations foster abstinence, moderation, or misuse. Husbands and wives who agree in their attitudes about drinking and who have similar patterns of drinking tend to have children who emulate their alcohol use (Zucker, 1976). Thus, parental and cultural values greatly influence young people's drinking. Antisocial val-

ues also can be transmitted to one's children. When parents are heavy drinkers, when they create tension and conflict in the family, and when they hold antisocial attitudes, then the teenaged children are likely to drink heavily (Zucker, 1976). This is a family pattern that is also seen in the backgrounds of heavy illicit drug users. Since family customs, values, and practices can encourage children to drink, it seems likely that prevention efforts should involve family members.

Marijuana

The popularity of illicit drugs changes over time, and marijuana is no exception. Marijuana and the more potent hashish have been very popular among high school groups for the past 20 years, and remain the most widely used of the illicit drugs. The psychoactive ingredient in marijuana is *tetrahydrocannabinol* (THC), and marijuana with a high concentration of THC is called *hashish*. Both are readily obtainable at most high schools and even junior high schools. Nevertheless, as with other illegal drugs, their popularity among students has decreased somewhat in recent years. The peak lifetime prevalence (those who have *ever* used marijuana) of 60.4 percent of high school students was reached in 1979, but the prevalence rate decreased to 54.9 percent in 1984 (Johnston et al., 1985). The possible reasons for this continuing decline are explored later. Nevertheless, marijuana usage levels remain extremely high. About 1 in every 20 high school seniors in a recent representative sample reported using marijuana on a nearly *daily* basis during the past month (Johnston et al., 1985).

Pharmacologists generally consider marijuana in its pure form to be a mild and nonaddictive drug, with less potential for misuse and overdose than alcohol and many other drugs. However, marijuana has been found to be a significant factor in motor vehicle accidents and fatalities (Peterson, 1984). Taken repeatedly and in high dosages, as it could be by impetuous high school students, marijuana may create tolerance, requiring increased dosages to achieve an effect, and a withdrawal syndrome (sleep disturbances, restlessness, irritability, decreased appetite, sweating, and weight loss from abrupt elimination of retained body fluids). After quitting, the user typically experiences no intense craving for marijuana (Tinklenberg, 1977). Some studies report neither tolerance nor withdrawal effects. However, there may be psychosocial effects. Some users become preoccupied with the drug experience and lose interest in other activities; in their preoccupation they may reject non-drug-using friends and family members, which creates interpersonal friction. In the sociology of teenage drug use, peers provide models, sources, and encouragement for dangerous experimentation and continued substance misuse. An additional negative factor in marijuana and hashish use is that the street drugs available to adolescents are sometimes mixed with contaminants and other drugs that can prove dangerous.

Given the hazards of even the seemingly mild illicit drugs, their widespread use among the young presents something of a puzzle. It is possible that their psychosocial as well as their pharmacological effects support their use. Experimentation with drugs is considered sophisticated and daring by some adolescents, and students can gain status by becoming users. In support of this argument, it has been found that when teenagers are surveyed, they tend to overestimate their smoking and drug usage (Schinke & Gilchrist, 1985; Severson & Ary, 1983). They undoubtedly also exaggerate their drug involvement when talking with their friends, so that they appear tougher and more sophisticated. An additional incentive is provided by marijuana's pharmacological properties. Users praise its ability to produce a relaxed, mild euphoria (although they do not use precisely these words). Smoking marijuana becomes a pleasant group experience, and some people report increased pleasure in music and other sensual experiences, enhanced sexual performance, increased appetite, and mild hilarity. Among the less pleasant effects and those that are less obvious to users are interference with immediate memory and ability to perform classroom tasks, and also dangerous and erratic driving (Secretary of Health, Education and Welfare, 1980). Other temporary physical effects include disruption of normal sperm production and slight reduction of testosterone production, especially in younger men. Longer-term health effects can include impaired lung function, probably resulting from smoking as the method of ingestion.

Because such a large portion of the population uses marijuana, it appears that attempts to outlaw it have proved futile. Harsh laws have simply been circumvented by the drug dealers, who have become big, though illegal, businessmen. Initial attempts to frighten young people into shunning drugs were easily detected as lies and gross exaggerations. The 1936 film *Reefer Madness*, which was designed to deter drug use, has been laughed at for several years now as an unintentional comedy. Such scare tactics left the more daring young people with an abiding scorn for drug prevention programs (Horan & Harrison, 1981). And yet there is some indication that teenagers are not impervious to the good-health movement that has captured their elders. The emphasis on improved nutrition, weight reduction, and vigorous physical exercise may be affecting younger people's attitudes toward illicit drug use. Since 1979, more and more high school seniors have begun to consider regular (but not experimental) marijuana use to be physically and generally harmful. At present, 67 percent of high school seniors judge regular use of marijuana to involve great risk. Perhaps the widespread publicity about the health hazards of cigarette smoking have affected attitudes about smoking marijuana as well, or perhaps social and cultural trends as yet unknown are at work. Whatever the reasons, a decrease in the use of marijuana seems to be occurring.

Inhalants

Inhalants are appealing to children who seek a drug experience but lack the money to buy illicit drugs. Volatile hydrocarbons such as airplane glue, gasoline, cleaning fluid, and aerosols provide poor and younger boys with a way to get high. Inhalants typically are used by 11- to 15-year-olds (Schonberg & Schnoll, 1986), especially by whites and Hispanics (Cohen, 1977). Very few older teenagers use inhalants often. Only 5.1 percent of the seniors in the national high school study reported that they had used an inhalant even once in the preceding year (Johnston et al., 1985).

These substances are readily available everywhere. Inhaling volatile hydrocarbons requires no special skills or paraphernalia, and children can easily learn how to do it from friends or even from magazine articles warning about the hazards involved. The effects are quick and potent, and include impairment of judgment and feelings of dizziness, elation, drunkenness, and weightlessness (Cohen, 1977). Repeated use can produce dizziness and hallucinations, and long-term, continuous use can damage vital organs (Schonberg &

Schnoll, 1986). As in any form of intoxication, accidents can occur. Especially dangerous is the practice of sniffing inhalants inside plastic bags placed over the head, which can lead to death by asphyxiation. Gasoline sniffing can produce sudden death from heart rhythm irregularities (Bass, 1970) or respiratory failure (Comstock & Comstock, 1977). Little research has been done on these products' toxicity, because they are not intended to be ingested. Apparently there is no physical addiction, although users can develop tolerance to solvents, which can be perilous and lead to death by poisoning.

Also included as inhalants are the amyl and butyl nitrites, which are sold legally and are referred to as "poppers" or "snappers." These have been tried by 1 in every 12 high school seniors (8 percent) (Johnston et al., 1985). Somewhat older youths tend to use these inhalants; the aerosols and glue tend to be discontinued as young people enter their teens.

Hallucinogens

Humans have perhaps always sought drug-induced elation, strange visual effects, and spiritual experiences by consuming certain plants, mushrooms, and liquids. Today these substances are termed *hallucinogens* (hallucination-producing agents), even though their effects seem to be primarily emotional and they rarely produce faulty perceptions like those in psychosis. Those who ingest LSD-25, PCP or "angel dust," mescaline, peyote, psilocybin, and related compounds experience certain sensations which they term "consciousness-expanding." Some hallucinogens, such as peyote, continue to be used in religious ceremonies by certain Native American groups. Following widely publicized experimentation with LSD and other hallucinogens by well-known artists and intellectuals in the 1950s, the use of these substances spread to colleges during the 1960s, and eventually included secondary school pupils, although not in large numbers. In the 1985 national high school study, just 4.7 percent of the students had used LSD during the past year, and 6.5 percent had used other hallucinogens (Johnston et al., 1985).

The decline in young people's use of LSD since the late 1960s is probably due to news reports that it can produce chromosome breakage, suicide, psychosis, and repeated, uncontrollable LSD experiences despite discontinued use. However, most of these ill effects have been found to be exaggerated, rare, or nonexistent (Brecher & the Editors of *Consumer Reports*, 1972). Nevertheless, they are widely believed and may have discouraged the use of hallucinogens.

LSD stimulates the central nervous system and the sympathetic division of the autonomic nervous system. Users report weird visual sensations (flashes of light, enhanced appreciation of colors, blurring or distortion of vision), mood swings, inability to gauge time, dizziness, weakness, tremors, drowsiness, and uncontrollable thoughts. Some people find this experience exciting and seek it repeatedly, but others are terrified. The reasons for these individual differences in reaction may be due to a host of different factors, including the drug type, dosage, and purity; the user's drug history and other personal characteristics; and the setting for drug use.

Hallucinogens are not addicting, but do create some degree of tolerance, requiring increasing dosages to produce an effect. There is no perceived compulsion to continue their use, and there are no withdrawal symptoms. A major danger is that street drugs may be adulterated with dangerous substances. Many young people experiment with hallucinogens only once or a few times, and then, having satisfied their curiosity, turn to other drugs.

Stimulants

Cocaine   Since the publication of this book's first edition in 1982, cocaine has assumed much greater prominence in the illicit pharmacopia of adolescents and young adults. In 1982 we stated that cocaine was seldom used by adolescents because of its cost, but the recent introduction of cheaper products, such as the impure but potent coca paste and crack, have put it within the reach of the young; 43 percent of high school seniors in the 1985 survey reported that it would be fairly easy or very easy for them to get cocaine (Johnston et al., 1985). Initial use of cocaine occurs at an older age than first use of most other illicit drugs. In some samples of adults, the average age of first experimentation was 21 years (Kandel, Murphy, & Karus, 1985). The great majority of adolescent users first try it in the 10th, 11th, or 12th grade (O'Malley et al., 1985), in contrast to their much earlier sampling of alcohol, cigarettes, inhalants, and marijuana. Cocaine users tend to smoke tobacco and marijuana heavily and to be heavy drinkers, and they may use all three substances together. Adolescents who use marijuana heavily are particularly likely to become cocaine users in young adulthood (Kandel et al., 1985).

Cocaine can be sniffed, injected, or smoked, and it has become a very popular illicit drug, as Box 6-3 indicates. It acts as a central nervous system stimulant and as a euphoriant or mood elevator. In small dosages, stimulants increase work output, help people resist fatigue, and create a temporary good mood; users also believe that stimulants enhance their intellectual, physical and sexual performances. Sigmund Freud once mistakenly recommended it to his fiancée. Freud later changed his opinion when the drug's dangerous side effects became apparent to the scientific community (Austin, 1978; Freud, 1884). In intravenous doses of 16 to 32 milligrams, cocaine produces an intense, very brief euphoria that peaks in 8 to 12 minutes and dissipates in 30 to 40 minutes. Smoking the rock crystal form called *crack* has similar effects. Intranasal ingestion is slower-acting and less preferred by heavy users. Habituation or tolerance develops after the first few doses, creating strong cravings for the drug. Typically users experience a stimulant effect for a 2- or 3-hour period after cocaine ingestion, with rapid heartbeat, high blood pressure, and rapid breathing, followed by a precipitous drop in mood. Chronic cocaine snorters may develop nasal congestion and dripping *(rhinitis),* as well as nasal irritation, ulceration of the mucous membranes of the nose, and ultimately perforation of the nasal septum.

Ironically, even successful professional and business people can be attracted to the "status

---

BOX 6-3 • What's New in Drugs—Crack

During 1986, a new form of cocaine was distributed on a large scale. Drug users love it because it is powerful, but does not need to be injected; it is also easy to obtain and remarkably inexpensive, priced at as little as $10 per use. In the form called *crack,* the cocaine is processed into lumps, and then is pressed into a pipe and smoked. The psychological effects include a powerful euphoria or "rush," which lasts only about 3 minutes, followed by a lower-level stimulant effect called an "afterglow" for perhaps 20 minutes. These properties plus its relatively low cost have made crack popular among drug users of all ages and in all areas of the country.

Like other forms of cocaine, crack is addictive. Addiction makes its cost soar to approximately $200 a day for heavy users, leading to all types of crime, from white-collar embezzlement to burglary and prostitution. Crack sales are enormous in volume and enormously profitable, because the cocaine can be purified at little cost and then sold at high prices. Dealers can carry very small amounts of crack pellets on their persons, which is wise in terms of the law. When they are arrested, the crack they possess is not very expensive, which limits legal charges against them to misdemeanors rather than the more serious felonies. In consequence, they are arrested frequently, but resume business within a short period of time. At the same time, on the national level, there are large budget cuts in the agencies that combat the illegal drug trade (such as the U.S. Customs and Immigration Service and the National Institute on Drug Abuse), and crippling cuts have impeded drug use prevention and treatment services at all levels of government. In the near future, at least, it will be business as usual for the drug dealers.

Sources: E. Greene. (1985, November 13). Cocaine, glamorous status symbol of the 'Jet Set,' is fast becoming many students' drug of choice. *Chronicle of Higher Education,* pp. 1, 34–35. R. B. Resnick and E. B. Resnick. (1984). Cocaine abuse and its treatment. *Psychiatric Clinics of North America,* p. 1, 713–728.

---

drug" cocaine, and can become uncontrollable addicts if they continue to use it. Like other stimulants, cocaine in high dosages can be dangerous or even fatal. People poisoned by cocaine may develop a reaction in which they become highly suspicious and paranoid, have hallucinations, may become violent, and experience extreme depression as the drug wears off. With overdoses, tremors, delirium, and convulsions develop. Emergency room episodes involving cocaine have increased dramatically in recent years. For example, in Los Angeles, cocaine admissions in hospital emergency rooms increased 274 percent and cocaine-involved deaths were up 282 percent in the 3-year period from 1981 to 1984 (National Institute on Drug Abuse [NIDA], 1985). Similar though less striking increases have been reported in other geographical areas.

Virtually all Americans now know that co-

caine overdoses can be life-threatening. The growing list of athletes and entertainers who have been hurt or killed by cocaine accidents includes John Belushi, Len Bias, Richard Pryor, and Mackenzie Phillips. Its expense and its use by the rich and famous have lent glamour to cocaine and made it a status symbol. Tragically, a planned or inadvertent overdose can also kill, causing acute respiratory failure or circulatory collapse. Moreover, it is addicting, although withdrawal reactions are different from and less severe than those associated with narcotics. Young people with low incomes must produce large sums of money regularly in order to support a cocaine habit costing perhaps $200 a day, so they must steal from family, friends, and strangers, and many become dealers themselves.

As a class of drugs, stimulants can prove addicting. The abstinence syndrome following withdrawal is characterized by intense depression, agitation, insomnia, nausea, and headaches, all of which can be relieved by proper medical care. Addicts often attempt to self-medicate by taking sedatives to ease the agitation produced by the cocaine. Usually they become addicted to the sedatives as well as to the cocaine, thus only increasing their woes.

Other Stimulants In addition to cocaine, the stimulants include ephedrine, the amphetamines, methylphenidate (a mild stimulant, trade name Ritalin), and related compounds. Their effects are similar to those described for cocaine, and cocaine users may resort to the less costly, longer-acting amphetamines when they cannot afford the more expensive drug. At the height of the 1960s drug craze, "speed freaks" injected large quantities of amphetamine over an extended period of wakefulness. The results were dramatic, but hardly desirable, and included all of the nasty aspects of **stimulant psychosis,** with agitation, paranoia, and violence. The psychotic behavior disappears days or weeks after stimulant use is discontinued, but can resume if stimulants are used once again. In any single year, 18.29 percent of the high school girls and 16.8 percent of the boys have used stimulants (Johnston et al., 1985).

Depressants

Teenaged sensation seekers most commonly try intoxicants, stimulants, and hallucinogens, but occasionally they add a sedative or depressant, such as pentobarbital (Nembutal) or secobarbital (Seconal). Less frequently, they may use one of the minor tranquilizers, such as meprobamate (Miltown or Equanil), chlordiazepoxide (Librium), or diazepam (Valium). Tranquilizers and sedatives were used daily by only about 0.1 percent of seniors in the 1985 national high school sample (Johnston et al., 1985). The students chose methaqualone (Quaalude) for use nearly as often as all of the other barbiturates combined, possibly because of its greater availability.

Like alcohol, which is also a depressant, these drugs can produce intoxication, loss of coordination, nausea, giddiness, and aggressive behavior.

They are highly addictive, and produce severe and physically dangerous withdrawal symptoms. Users develop tolerance, and thus require increasing dosages, but the fatal dose level (the amount that proves deadly) remains constant. Thus it is easy for users to take fatal overdoses, particularly in combination with alcohol (Cooper, 1977).

Narcotics

Products of the opium poppy (*opiates,* such as opium, morphine, heroin, and paregoric) and synthetic narcotics have long been used to induce relaxation, soothe fussy babies, relieve anxiety, and counteract intractable pain. Many patent medicines of the 19th century contained morphine, and large numbers of Americans became addicted to these narcotic elixirs. Ironically, some who were addicted to morphine were treated with another highly addicting drug, which was named *heroin* to denote their heroism in taking the cure, but of course this treatment was doomed to fail. Parents with infants who failed to thrive could give them *laudanum,* a potent and highly addicting mixture of morphine and alcohol. The passage of legislation prohibiting nonprescriptive use of opiates probably prevented addiction for many, but also had the unintended effect of creating a flourishing illegal trade, so opiate prices soared (Brecher & the Editors of *Consumer Reports,* 1972). Today, drug addiction continues to be a major social problem, and is implicated in much criminal activity by users and dealers.

The addictive power of narcotics is legendary, but perhaps exaggerated. Certainly, there is habituation and a withdrawal syndrome, but very few of the U.S. servicemen who used heroin in Vietnam became or remained addicted after they returned home; they simply stopped taking heroin. In addition, a greater number of ex-addicts have been discovered in the United States than had previously been thought possible:

> Current epidemiological research . . . documents that while fairly large numbers of persons in the more general community may experiment with heroin or other opiates, they do not necessarily proceed to compulsive use. . . . [E]ven for those who move on to regular use of heroin or other opiates,

continual addiction is not inevitable, so that many regular users either moderate or even cease altogether using heroin or other opiates. (Lukoff, 1977, p. 199)

Opiates other than heroin were reported to have been used at least once by about 10 percent of the high school seniors in the 1985 survey (Johnston et al., 1985)—a rate that undoubtedly would have been higher if the less conservative high school dropouts had also been included in the survey. In contrast, only 1.3 percent of the seniors admitted to having tried heroin. Because heroin is a highly illicit drug, students may have concealed its use, so these statistics may represent an underestimate of unknown magnitude. Certainly, with widespread drug experimentation and increased availability, narcotics consumption could increase sometime in the future. Recent trends are toward a decrease in illicit drug use in general, however.

MOTIVATION TO USE ILLICIT DRUGS

What draws young people to illicit drugs, although they are expensive and sometimes difficult to obtain, and their use can bring trouble with parents, teachers, and the law? Many teenagers recognize that drug use can endanger their health and can even prove fatal. Yet there have been only very slight decreases in the use of most illicit drugs in recent years, and many youngsters persist in experimenting with whatever drugs are available and in vogue. A number of factors may help to account for drug use, including the drug experience itself, the need to appear daring or adult, and the influences of friends and family members. We consider each of these potential determinants of drug usage here.

The Drug Experience

The use of psychoactive drugs is an ancient human tradition. Most societies have discovered mind-affecting drugs and used them in ritual observances, or smoked or eaten them as a part of everyday life. The altered consciousness itself is commonly enjoyed and granted high social status, especially when drug use is controlled by cultural conventions so that it involves only particular peo-

ple at prescribed times and places. Thus, in most traditional cultures, drug use is neither excessive nor noticeably harmful. When drugs are used in defiance of established social customs, however, as in today's developed nations, use tends to be immoderate and is more likely to be physically harmful.

Transition to Adulthood

Some children consider drinking, smoking, and consumption of illegal drugs to be indicators of adulthood. Young teenagers can mimic adults and can share some of their experiences vicariously by using illicit drugs long before their parents consider it appropriate for them to do so. It is not unusual to see 13- and 14-year-olds wearing grotesque imitations of the makeup, hair styles, and clothing of well-known rock performers. They copy their cigarette, tobacco, and drug habits as well. It has been suggested that among some groups in the United States, using drugs is just one aspect of growing up (Jessor & Jessor, 1977). This interpretation of juvenile drug consumption (described in Box 6-4) emphasizes the tumultuous nature of American adolescence—a time during which some teenagers flout religious and conventional values, defy moral and legal strictures, and declare their independence in a very unmistakable fashion. It should be emphasized that many young people do *not* go through such a phase, much to the relief of their parents, and that many of those who do are later indistinguishable from their more conforming neighbors. We must also point out that some substances, such as tobacco, alcohol, and marijuana, are so widely used by adolescents that no particular personality features or family background could possibly typify all of the youths who use them.

Influence of Parents and Peers

It is extremely rare for a youngster to try drugs unless she associates with drug users. Thus the greater the frequency of drug use in the population, the more likely the child is to become a user herself. The social learning theory approach to child development (Bandura, 1977) stresses the influence of others who act as models for the child

---

BOX 6-4 • **Coming of Age in America**

Adults have certain rights and prerogatives barred to children. If you want to drive cars, hold attractive jobs, marry, smoke cigarettes, drink alcohol, or take drugs, you had better be an adult. Children are not supposed to do these attractive things until they make the transition to adulthood. How and when does this happen? To answer these questions, Richard and Shirley Jessor (1977) conducted a long-term study of a group of teenagers in a small college town in the mountain West. They found that one socially conservative group of teenagers never began to smoke or drink, and that another, rather rebellious group did so very early—in the early junior high school years. Of most interest to the Jessors were the students who did not initially smoke marijuana or use alcohol, but who began to do so in the course of the 4-year study (at or before their senior year in high school). These students were characterized by a number of features. They became more tolerant of socially deviant beliefs and practices and less regular in their church attendance; they began putting less emphasis on achievement in school; became more independent from their parents, and associated with other youths who used drugs. At about the same time that they began to drink, these teenagers began to smoke marijuana, have sexual intercourse, and report increases in their own lying, stealing, cheating, and aggression.

The Jessors interpreted these data as suggesting that "the normal course of developmental change in adolescence is in the direction of greater problem proneness. This . . . implies that problem behavior may be viewed, at least in part, as an aspect of growing up" (1977, p. 238).

Source: R. Jessor and S. L. Jessor. (1977). *Problem behavior and psychosocial development* (New York: Academic Press).

---

to emulate. Even socially condoned parental drug usage can promote children's drug experimentation. When parents use alcohol and tobacco, as well as prescribed barbiturates and amphetamines, their children are more likely to become drug users, even despite their parents' disapproval (Miller & Cisin, 1983; Newcomb, Hula, & Bentler, 1983). In such circumstances, the children may come to view their parents as drug-using hypocrites who apply a more lenient standard to themselves than to their offspring. In other families, drug-using parents are lenient about their children's use, or simply do not care. Either way, family members are extremely influential models of conduct for young people.

Friends are very important, too; nearly every study of teenage drug use has reported that users have friends who are users, and abstainers have abstaining friends. This suggests that parents are correct to be disturbed if their children want to associate with the wrong crowd. Friends' use of

drugs is one of the most powerful predictors of drug use, and teens are more likely to resemble their friends in drug use than in any other feature except age and sex (Kandel, 1978; Petersen, 1984). However, it is very difficult for parents to dictate their older children's choice of friends. When parents are heavy users of legal or illegal psychoactive substances, and when a teenager's friends use illicit drugs, he is overwhelmingly likely to do so as well (Huba, Wingard, & Bentler, 1979). He has the models, the motivation to imitate them, and the access to the drugs. It is a rare teenager who can say no to such powerful social influences.

Other Family Influences

There are exceptions to this rule, but on the whole young illicit drug users tend to come from less traditional families, and abstainers are more often found in families with traditional religious and moral values. A possible drawback of being a

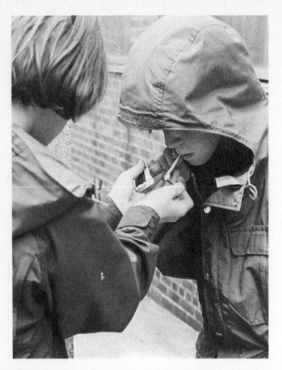

Younger children want to try the illicit drugs that are popular with high school students and adults. Some children become drug users at shockingly early ages.

Personality Characteristics

Intense clinical and research scrutiny over many years has failed to identify any unique personality characteristics that predict drug use or dependence. Narcotics addicts have frequently been described as immature, irresponsible, insecure, and egocentric, living only for the moment. However, it is impossible to determine whether they become this way because of their narcotics addiction or whether pre-existing personality features have made them susceptible to addiction. That is, we cannot say which comes first—the behavioral characteristics or the drug dependence. In earlier times, psychotherapists were convinced that drug usage stems from a flawed, addictive personality. The psychoanalysts (such as Freud and later Fenichel) tied drug addiction to masturbation; homosexual impulses; unconscious, unresolved needs for dependency and oral stimulation; and an unconscious drive toward self-destruction (Salmon & Salmon, 1977). Even some contemporary psychoanalysts view addiction as caused by personality defects, particularly low self-esteem and a craving for unceasing praise and approval (Greenspan, 1977). Early developmental deprivation or overindulgence is presumed to result in a resort to the use of drugs.

A problem with this theory is that the most searching objective research has failed to identify any particular child or parent characteristics that actually do lead to the use of drugs. Some children with particular sensation-seeking personalities choose to try drugs, and others with exactly the same characteristics do not. The personality differences found between users and abstainers tend to be very modest in magnitude, and include a taste for risk taking, rebelliousness, dislike for and avoidance of school, and feelings of alienation (Glantz, 1984; Kandel et al., 1978). This syndrome could be termed *acute adolescence,* because it well describes the stormy transition from childhood into adulthood followed by many young people in industrialized nations. However, these behavioral characteristics prove transitory in most cases, and hardly constitute a personality type. At present, it appears that social and environmental

liberal, permissive, and democratic parent is that this attitude allows children more latitude for all types of experimentation, including using drugs. Among white middle-class families, youthful heavy drug users tend to come from households that are generally less religiously observant, less cohesive, more permissive, and less strict. Such families undoubtedly are less restrictive about their children's choice of friends. They emphasize the child's individuality, freedom, and personal adjustment more than do families of abstainers, who value discipline, family cohesiveness, conventional patriotism, and religion (Blum & Associates, 1972). These are only trends, however; many readers may be aware of counterexamples in which defiant, heavily drug-using sons and daughters emerge from the most authoritarian, conventional, and pious families in their communities.

factors may prove to be better predictors than personality features. The present consensus is that problematic substance use and addiction may be accompanied by various adjustment problems, but are probably caused by a combination of factors, such as family influences, peer practices, and the popularity of psychoactive drugs.

DIVERSITY OF DRUG USE DETERMINANTS

As Table 6-2 indicates, predicting adolescent drug use is not an easy matter, and the accuracy of prediction is far from perfect. However, the greater the number of risk factors present in a child's life, the more likely it is that she will try drugs. As has been described, the acute adolescent syndrome, marked by rebelliousness and alienation from adult values, seems to accompany other predictors of susceptibility to drugs. Associated with this behavioral syndrome is a particular type of relationship with one's parents. Abstainers are more likely to come from homes in which parents espouse traditional values, have a warm relationship

T a b l e 6-2
Correlates of Adolescent Drug Use

Adolescents' Characteristics
  Anticipation of adulthood
  Curiosity
  High in social confidence
  Rejection of traditional social values
  Poor school attendance and achievement
  Expectation of positive consequences from drug use
  Rebelliousness
  Being male (boys are generally more likely to be users than are girls)
  Delinquent activity

Family Characteristics
  Modeling of the use of alcohol, tobacco, and psychoactive drugs
  Permissive discipline
  Nontraditional values and tolerance of deviance
  Less closeness between parents and children

Peer Influences
  Friends who are drug users
  Peers being more important influences than parents

Characteristics of General Environment
  Ready availability of drugs

with their children, and provide a structured home environment; drug users are more likely to stem from less traditional, less accepting families (Brook, Whiteman, Gordon, & Cohen, 1986). In abstainers' homes, mothers have mutually good relationships with their children, but of course a child's drug use can destroy a previously close relationship with a parent. In fact, it would be highly unusual for a warm, accepting parental attitude to extend to a child's drug involvement. It should also be pointed out that the differences between the homes of users and nonusers are extremely small (although statistically significant in Brook et al.'s study). More influential is parental use of tobacco, alcohol, and drugs, because this provides a direct example for the children. If one adds drug-using friends to these factors, the odds become extremely high that a young person will try and will probably like using drugs. Teenagers are inclined to use drugs, drink, and behave deviantly when their family backgrounds, personal beliefs and values, and perceived social environments all support and encourage problem behaviors.

Furthermore, engaging in deviant behaviors with like-minded companions may produce additional changes in adolescents' values and surroundings that, in turn, foster even more antisocial behavior. Jessor and Jessor (1977, 1978) have suggested that illicit drug usage, delinquent acts, truancy, and other socially disapproved behavior may all serve the same function of expressing independence from the constraints imposed by family and social institutions. The use of outlawed drugs is just one way among many in which autonomy and rebellion may be expressed.

TREATMENT OF DRUG ADDICTION

Drug addiction is very difficult to treat effectively, and relapses are common. The types of treatment available range from inpatient detoxification and group therapy to outpatient methadone or drug-free treatments. Some programs are supervised by physicians and other professionals, and others stress self-help in groups of former addicts. Many programs, such as the nonprofessionally directed Alcoholics Anonymous, serve adults rather than children or adolescents. We now describe the major types of treatments available and assess their effectiveness. Although some of these treatments are chiefly for adults, the emphasis here is on treatment for the young.

Hospitalization and Detoxification

Formerly, narcotics addicts were sent or volunteered to go to federal hospitals in Lexington, Kentucky, and Fort Worth, Texas, to be withdrawn from drugs. These programs featured withdrawal (detoxification) using decreasing doses of morphine, and several months of inpatient treatment. Despite their great cost, these programs proved to be nearly useless. Most of those who were treated resumed their narcotics habits soon after their release. Even had hospital programs proved effective, there are now too many addicts to attend to in this fashion.

A similar program for adolescents at Riverside Hospital in New York produced the same disappointing results. Despite 3 years of inpatient and outpatient treatment, 95 percent of those treated later resumed using narcotics (National Clearinghouse for Drug Abuse Information, 1975). Scandals concerning the availability and use of illicit drugs inside the hospital helped lead to its closure. Treatment authorities now agree that hospital-based, long-term treatment programs have failed. Nevertheless, short-term hospitalization and detoxification are necessary to manage the dangerous withdrawal symptoms associated with alcohol and barbiturate dependence.

Methadone Maintenance

During the past 20 years, methadone maintenance has been one of the most widely used treatments for narcotics addiction. Proponents of this treatment method view physiological dependence as the most important aspect of narcotics addiction (Dole, Nyswander, & Warner, 1968). To combat the physical dependence and prevent withdrawal symptoms, addicts are given daily dosages of methadone, a synthetic narcotic. Methadone must be taken daily, and patients who are

doing well may take home 2- to 3-day supplies. However, methadone itself presents some serious problems. It is highly addicting, can seriously harm a fetus, and must be consumed for years, perhaps for life. Methadone's advantages over heroin are that it is legal and it is cheap. Nevertheless, a certain amount of methadone is diverted to the black market, and there have been methadone-related deaths, some of which occurred when children or other family members mistakenly drank a mixture of orange juice and methadone stored in the home refrigerator. A longer-acting opioid alternative to methadone, LAAM (levo-alpha-acetylmethadol), may prevent such accidents, and may allow addicts to travel.

Even its proponents are forced to admit that methadone maintenance has its drawbacks. In addition to the possibilities of accidental poisoning and of harm to unborn children, another problem is that methadone does not prevent users from combining it with other non-narcotic drugs. Thus, they can treat themselves to a potent chemical cocktail including methadone, alcohol, and stimulants if they wish, and thus continue their illicit drug use. Here are the observations of a former addict:

> They take methadone and they also use other things (alcohol and liquid amphetamine). . . . You see methadone keeps you straight, but some fellas are not satisfied with that. Some are. They like the rush and they like the needle. They miss that. You take methadone orally. And some go along with it, usually the old timers, because the kick of the needle and the hustle and all is over for them. They just want to be well. . . . But guys who are still looking for something extra; they want to do something. (Lander, 1973, p. 191)

Because methadone is a potent narcotic drug, it is not typically used by minors. By law, methadone use is prohibited for those under 16 years of age who have not been dependent on narcotics for at least 2 years. Teenagers younger than 18 years must have their parents' written consent and must have tried and failed in at least two previous attempts at detoxification (National Clearinghouse for Drug Abuse Information, 1975). Despite these precautions, adolescents obtain black-market methadone, and some inject it and become addicted. In any case, methadone may not be the treatment of choice for the young. Youthful addicts seem to require treatment in a highly structured environment emphasizing instruction in academic, interpersonal, and vocational skills (Biase, 1973). Simply giving them methadone fails to meet their social, academic, and job-training needs. In addition, methadone treatment has been significantly less effective for younger addicts than for older ones (Simpson, Savage, Lloyd, & Sells, 1978). In older addicts, methadone decreases use of narcotics, reduces criminal activity, and promotes employability (Simpson et al., 1978). Methadone is less commonly used with people younger than 40 years because its long-term health effects are unknown, and because of the greater range of treatment and educational needs of the young.

Chemical Antagonists

Methadone blocks the euphoria produced by large doses of narcotics only when the methadone is given in even larger dosages (the *blockade effect*). Consequently, scientists have searched for drugs that would prevent addicts from getting any psychological effects from narcotics but that, unlike methadone, would not themselves be addictive. Several narcotic antagonists, such as naloxone, naltrexone, and cyclazocine, have been tested for effectiveness, safety, and appeal to addicts. All have some unpleasant side effects, such as nausea, dizziness, drowsiness, depression, and constipation. The chemical antagonists do not appeal to most addicts, and have acquired a bad street reputation (Julius & Renault, 1976), so they have limited promise at present.

Antabuse has long been taken by alcoholics as a deterrent to drinking. Antabuse induces feelings of intense sickness and nausea if taken with alcohol, and so prevents drinking. Unfortunately, it is easy for an alcoholic to defeat Antabuse treatment either by stopping taking Antabuse or by drinking until the effects of Antabuse are overcome by intoxication. A central and still unsolved problem with substance abuse is that it is terribly difficult to motivate addicts to abstain, particularly for a long period of time and without backsliding.

Perhaps it would be more profitable to develop appealing types of treatments and to train sympathetic, concerned therapists than to concentrate on temporarily disrupting drug distribution systems and to blame treatment failures on the lack of motivation of the addicts (Miller, 1985).

Therapeutic Communities

Therapeutic communities are based on the assumption that all addicts are manipulative and have antisocial personalities. Addicts are presumed to require residential treatment and close supervision in which they encounter harsh confrontations with the unpleasant reality of their drug habits. The first of the residential treatment programs was Synanon, which was founded in 1958 by Charles Dederich, himself a former addict. Like Alcoholics Anonymous, Synanon viewed addiction as deriving from a personal weakness. Addicts' manipulativeness was attacked in group sessions featuring confrontations, demands for confessions of hypocrisy and cheating, and group support for abstention. Only highly motivated applicants were accepted following a rigorous screening process, and even then they could not always tolerate the restrictive program, which was run autocratically by ex-addicts and their admirers within the group. There are many variants of the therapeutic community approach. Other programs, such as Odyssey House, use professional therapists as staff members as well as former addicts, and feature group therapy, tutoring sessions, adult education, and vocational training. Length of stay is individually determined, but varies from 6 to 18 months in most settings. The older therapeutic communities typically barred all psychoactive drug use, but some multimodal treatment programs now prescribe methadone maintenance as a treatment aid.

Despite its rigor, therapeutic community treatment is largely unsuccessful. Approximately 75 percent of those who enter programs such as Odyssey House, Phoenix House, Gateway House, and Daytop Village drop out within the first month (National Clearinghouse for Drug Abuse Information, 1975). Many addicts, especially young ones, are unwilling to make the required commitment to long-term, possibly permanent residence in the therapeutic community. Addicts who profit most from these programs are white, middle-class, and better educated, being high school graduates rather than academic dropouts (Louria, 1977). As with other drug treatments, the success rate is disappointingly low. Of 2500 addicts treated in the Phoenix House program, only 130 overcame their addiction, and 90 percent of the successful group did not have regular jobs. They worked in addiction programs rather than in the community (Wald & Hutt, 1972). A recent review of effectiveness revealed that fewer than 15 percent of admissions to all types of therapeutic communities graduate from treatment, and over half drop out in less than 3 months (De Leon, 1984). Nevertheless, the therapeutic communities are counted among the most successful of the addiction treatment efforts (Sells, 1979).

Drug-Free Counseling Treatments

A number of outpatient counseling programs have been developed to help addicts who are reluctant to become dependent on methadone or unwilling to become a permanent resident of a dictatorial therapeutic community. Outpatient counseling on either a group or an individual basis is the form of treatment offered to most adolescent substance abusers (82.5 percent) (NIDA, 1985). The procedures used in the drug-free treatments include individual and group counseling, educational and recreational activities, and vocational guidance. Participants are helped to become and to remain free of drug use. However, like the alternative approaches, the drug-free services have an exceedingly high dropout rate. They are probably more suitable for nonopiate drug users than

When skillfully presented, group therapy is a popular, safe, and moderately effective form of treatment for juvenile substance misusers. No form of treatment, however, is sufficiently powerful to prevent or treat compulsive drug use.

for narcotics addicts, because the client is largely unsupervised and is left in his or her customary environment with access to an array of illicit drugs. Drug-free counseling may be the most appropriate and effective treatment for non-narcotics users now available (Sells & Simpson, cited in Sells, 1979), but still leaves much to be desired.

All of the drug treatment programs just described seem to have some, though limited, beneficial effects. The therapeutic communities and drug-free treatments produce the lowest rates of readmission to drug treatment programs (Sells, 1979). These treatments also decrease both narcotic and non-narcotic drug use and improve employment rates. Those addicts who have the best outcomes in all treatments comply better with treatment demands, stay in treatment longer, and do not have criminal records.

PREVENTION

Because there has been only limited success in treating drug use and addiction, prevention assumes added importance. Yet prevention has also proved to be extremely difficult. The early prevention programs were particularly ineffective, and featured ludicrous scare tactics portraying all illicit drugs as highly addictive and physically and socially ruinous. These lies and exaggerations were obvious to young people, who then dismissed all official pronouncements as falsehoods even when drug control agencies later presented accurate information regarding drugs that were truly dangerous (Horan & Harrison, 1981). In the early 1970s, information issued by federal agencies became less alarmist and more trustworthy, thus gradually gaining young people's confidence. However, even accurate drug information may not deter children from experimentation with psychoactive drugs. In fact, one accurate drug information program evaluated by Stuart (1974) actually seemed to increase drug use. As a result of the educational program, the adolescents became curious about drugs and tried them in increased numbers. Programs limited to providing students with information about drugs are at best ineffec-

tive. As one reviewer concluded, "Most such programs increase knowledge about drugs, a few change attitudes in desirable directions, but virtually none reliably reduce drug usage" (Smart, 1977, p. 274). It seems that something more than information is needed.

Most present-day prevention programs address participants' emotional and social needs, in addition to providing information about drug effects. For example, a school-based alcohol use prevention program for 7th- to 10th-graders (Goodstadt, Sheppard, & Chan, 1982) succeeded in decreasing students' alcohol consumption. The prevention program was broadly conceptualized and dealt with myths about alcohol; alcohol advertising tactics; reasons for drinking; and effects on family, fitness, sexual behavior, and driving performance. The more successful programs make effective use of social science information regarding influence processes, while the ineffective ones merely present the information in a traditional classroom fashion (Nathan, 1983). An alternative prevention tactic is to distract youngsters by introducing activities to replace substance use (Schinke & Gilchrist, 1985). One such project, called Channel One, was a national program to prevent adolescent drug use by providing alternative recreational and community projects (Stein, Swisher, Hu, & McDonnell, 1984). Unfortunately, this ambitious and well-intentioned project failed in its major objective. The results revealed "significant improvement in democratic patterns and alternative [activity] participation, but also indicated increased use of some substances and in the frequency of drunkenness" (Stein et al., 1984, p. 251). Thus success is not assured, even for well-planned efforts.

Federal and state authorities often have preferred the seemingly more direct route of cutting off young people's access to prohibited substances and providing penalties for their sale and use. Thus, there are minimum age limits on the legal use of alcohol and tobacco, and these limits are sometimes changed to modify young people's access to these substances. In addition, there is a continuing, unsuccessful effort to cut off the supply of illegal drugs, both nationally (by crackdowns on dealers) and internationally (as in the Reagan administration's sending U.S. military personnel to Bolivia in 1986 in an attempt to destroy cocaine processing plants). Earlier, Mexican marijuana fields were sprayed with the health-endangering herbicide paraquat in order to interrupt the marijuana trade, but to no avail: Dealers turned to numerous alternative sources of marijuana, including many within the United States.

There are powerful economic reasons for the continuing use of illegal substances; there are many purchasers; and enforcing the law has proven impossible. So long as the demand and the supply exist and cannot be permanently decreased, our national drug problem can be expected to persist. The days in which young people were safe from drugs have passed. Just as Prohibition laws against the use of alcohol in the 1920s failed to curb alcohol use, laws against nonmedical use of narcotics and other psychoactive drugs have not eliminated illicit drugs. Law enforcement efforts resulting in reduced supplies may cut experimentation by new users, but do not deny illegal drugs to addicts. The addicts simply must steal more in order to support their habits when drugs are in short supply. This is not to say that legal measures always fail. It is probable that legal deterrents virtually eliminated amphetamine abuse in Japan following World War II, and opiate use in mainland China ceased, by law, after the Communists gained control. However, legal remedies have been less successful in combating drug use in North America, despite the increasing harshness of the antidrug laws. Probably, particular historical times and cultures requires their own prevention approaches, and there is no single best solution for all nations at all times.

As we have pointed out earlier, there is a ray of hope. Over the past several years, there has been a small but continuing nationwide decline in teenagers' use of potentially harmful substances (Johnston et al., 1985). This drug use decrease preceded such national prevention efforts as the "Just Say No" program and may be a part of a personal health improvement trend that has Americans adopting healthier styles of life. They are exercising more, eating more fresh fruit and vegetables, and shunning fats and sweets. A natural accompaniment would be for young people to decrease their drinking, smoking, and illicit drug use, as they seem to be doing. In addition, the many antidrug information programs under way may be having some effect, as the information offered is now generally perceived to be trustworthy. Youngsters are not immune to concerns about their health; in the past, they came to avoid drugs with bad reputations (such as LSD) because of their apparent ill effects. Thus, information and health dangers associated with drug use could affect the prevalence rates. Many of the prevention efforts do produce limited but significant benefits for participants (Schinke & Gilchrist, 1985), and it may be that the combined effects of the many separate programs teenagers encounter are now becoming apparent in decreased drug abuse. Finally, the life-threatening properties of some drugs, particularly cocaine, have received widespread press coverage because of the deaths of celebrity users. Children cannot dismiss news about the tragic deaths of young star athletes and entertainers as adults' exaggerations about the danger of drugs. Significantly, cocaine had the reputation of an exciting glamour drug, and many young users anticipated no adverse effects. In this case, it appeared that the authorities were right about the danger and the users were wrong, which may have bolstered teenagers' confidence in drug officials' pronouncements. Any or all of these factors may be producing a welcome decrease in young people's drug consumption.

SUMMARY

Psychoactive drugs, which affect users' perceptions and emotions, are found in most households. Drug misuse occurs when these drugs are overused or used inappropriately, and when outlawed drugs are consumed. Some drugs produce physical addiction and require increasing dosages to produce an effect or withdrawal symptoms when the drug is discontinued. Addicting drugs include nicotine; alcohol, in some cases; stimulants, including cocaine; depressants; and narcotics. Some illicit drugs are not addictive, such as marijuana, hallucinogens, and inhalants.

Some substances such as tobacco, alcohol, and marijuana are used by many high school students. The typical sequence is to proceed from heavy alcohol and tobacco use to marijuana, with some students going on to use cocaine, inhalants, and hallucinogens. Those teenagers who misuse drugs are most likely to have parents and siblings who drink, smoke, and indulge in prescribed or illicit psychoactive drugs. Drug-using adolescents also have drug-using friends, and they and their families tend to be somewhat less traditional and more permissive than are abstainers and their families. Drug users show accentuated signs of adolescent turmoil, rejecting school and adult authority, although it is difficult to determine whether the rebellion precedes or follows their drug use. There are no particular personality types predictive of drug addiction.

Addictions are extremely difficult to break permanently, especially in the young. Nearly any form of treatment produces decreased use if the full course is followed, but dropout rates are high for all treatments. Methadone maintenance is effective, but is seldom used with young addicts; therapeutic communities are aimed mostly at older addicts; and teenagers are mostly given outpatient counseling. The relatively little success of treatment efforts has heightened interest in prevention. Here again results are significant but limited, with the more psychologically sophisticated programs producing greater success. Fortunately, youthful drug use appears to be decreasing, possibly because of prevention programs and the widely publicized drug-related accidents and deaths of celebrities.

chapter
7

Habit
Disorders

KEY TERMS

Anorexia Nervosa.   A condition of self-inflicted starvation accompanied by compulsive exercising.

Articulation Disorder.   A disturbance in speech-sound production that results in chronic abnormal vocalization.

Bulimia.   Uncontrolled binge eating followed by purging (often vomiting).

Elective Mutism.   Selective speaking under certain circumstances but with no physical defect and without a deficit in general intellectual ability.

Encopresis.   Abnormal or unacceptable patterns of fecal expulsion by children who are beyond the age of toilet training and who lack organic pathology.

Enuresis.   Chronic inappropriate wetting by children who do not evidence physical disorders and who are old enough to be toilet-trained.

Narcolepsy.   A disorder involving involuntary and inappropriate sleeping spells.

Obesity.   A condition in which an individual is extremely overweight (20 percent or more), to a degree that it impairs health and social interactions.

Somnambulism.   Episodes of activity during sleep, more commonly known as "sleepwalking."

Stuttering.   A disturbance in the fluency and rhythm of speech, with intermittent blocking, repetition, or prolongation of sounds, syllables, words, or phrases.

INTRODUCTION

The disorders examined in this chapter have been viewed in a variety of ways in the literature on child psychopathology. Emphases have ranged from primarily physiological to psychological, as theorists have explored both causation and resulting behaviors or symptoms. It is also not unusual to encounter perspectives representing a mixture of organic and psychological components. All of these views are correct to some degree, because the disorders presented here have varying elements, depending on the particular case. We have chosen to discuss these problems as *habit disorders* because of the strong perspective of learning that emerges in one fashion or another in each. In so doing, it is not our intent to discount the influence of physiology where relevant, and the reader will encounter considerable attention to such factors. In many cases research has indicated that the most effective treatment is found in a combination of physiological and behavioral intervention.

Some habits are very desirable and important to human functioning (for instance, the nearly automatic behavioral movements involved in typing a paper). Other habitual behaviors may not be desirable but are so inconsequential that they would not be viewed as disorders (for example, nail biting). The topics reviewed here represent extreme deviations from normal behaviors, are unusual in their form or frequency, and usually require treatment. They are also behavioral patterns that parents frequently identify as topics of concern.

SLEEP DISORDERS

At one time or another, many parents voice dissatisfaction or concern about their children's sleep patterns. Bakwin and Bakwin (1972) have stated that "disturbances of sleep are *common* during childhood" (p. 546; emphasis ours), and Schaefer and Millman (1977) have noted that "children show a very high incidence of sleep problems" (p. 223). Some evidence suggests that as many as 30 to 45 percent of very young children exhibit sleep disturbances (Van Tassel, 1985). From these statements it seems that sleep behavior is of considerable concern to parents, although the prevalence of sleep problems is not clearly documented. Fortunately, about half of all sleep disorders are considered minor (Schaefer & Millman, 1977).

Sleep is comprised of several different states and stages; we examine these briefly prior to discussing sleeping disorders. Sleep consists of two distinct states. One, called *REM sleep*, is a period during which rapid eye movements occur and an individual dreams. The other state, known as *NREM sleep*, is not characterized by rapid eye movements and is made up of four distinguishable stages based on electroencephalographic (EEG) activity. Stage 1 of NREM sleep represents the transitional period between wakefulness and sleep; stages 2, 3 and 4 are characterized by differences in amount and type of EEG activity and are generally spoken of as increasing "depth" of sleep. Normal sleep patterns begin with NREM sleep and progress from stage 1 through stage 4 during the first 90 minutes or so of the night. At about this point the first period of REM sleep occurs and is typically brief, lasting from 5 to 15 minutes. Normal sleep is characterized by repeated cycles of REM and NREM sleep as well as by the various stages of NREM sleep. Stage 1 usually accounts for only about 5 percent of a total night's sleep; stage 2 accounts for about 40 to 60 percent; and the remainder consists of stages 3 and 4. Most of the stage 3 and stage 4 sleep occurs during the first two cycles of NREM sleep. In normal sleep the cycles are not random and are, in fact, cyclic. Mendelson, Gillin, and Wyatt (1977) described the early portion of a night's sleep as "waking, stage 1, stage 2, stage 3, stage 4, stage 3, stage 2" (p. 7). At this point the first REM period occurs, and the NREM stages recycle (2, 3, 4, 2), followed by another REM period. These sleep cycles and stages, illustrated pictorially in Figure 7-1, are important in the following discussion, since certain sleep disturbances tend to occur predominantly during particular sleep states.

Nightmares and Night Terrors

There is considerable dreaming during normal sleep, and dream sleep continues to be of theoretical interest (Crick & Mitchison, 1983; Evans, 1984). As all of us know from experience, dreams can be either pleasant or unpleasant. Most children have occasional bad dreams and nightmares that result in wakefulness and fear. However, these sleep disturbances are frequent, persistent, and intense for some children. We discuss two sleep disorders in this section: *nightmares* and *night terrors*. Nightmares and night terrors may appear somewhat similar, but only on the surface. As we examine them more closely, distinctions become quite evident.

Nightmares and night terrors tend to happen at different times of night and during different sleep stages. Nightmares generally occur during REM episodes, stage 1 sleep, and during the latter part of the night. This is the stage when dreaming typically occurs, which may suggest that nightmares differ from other dreams mainly in content. On the other hand, night terror incidents seem to occur during the first 2 hours of sleep and arise out of stage 4, a NREM state. As indicated above, stage 4 NREM sleep is not a period during which dreaming normally takes place; it is considered to be the stage of deepest sleep. This suggests that night terrors are distinctly different phenomena from ordinary dreams.

There are a number of differences between a child's behavior during nightmares and night terrors. For example, children experiencing night terrors typically sleep through the episode, even though their behavior is extremely agitated. Often their eyes are wide open, as though they were staring at something in terror; they make grimaces, exhibit considerable physical movement, sometimes running about the room frantically; they may also shout and scream. Parents often watch such activity helplessly, unable to quiet their children with reassurances or awaken them. Nightmares present a very different picture. Children's movements and verbalization are much more subdued, typically restricted to moaning and slight movements in bed. Beyond this, children

FIGURE 7-1. The thick bars above the EEG sleep-stage lines indicate periods of REM coinciding with emergent stage 1 EEGs. The arrows mark the successive EEG pattern cycles.

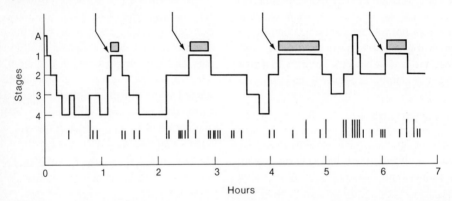

Sleep problems are more common during childhood than one might expect.

having nightmares most often are already awake by the time their parents arrive.

From this description, one might conclude that night terrors are merely more fearful episodes of nightmares, perhaps more dramatic in content. Further examination of such events would not support such a deduction. Nightmares are usually followed by a period during which the child is awake, recognizes people and surroundings, can provide a coherent account of what has transpired, and can remember the contents of the dream. Night terrors are followed by instant and peaceful sleep, lack of recognition of people and surroundings, and, frequently, complete amnesia regarding both contents and occurrence. Furthermore, children experiencing night terrors often hallucinate; those with nightmares do not. Night terrors may be rather prolonged (15 to 20 minutes), whereas nightmares tend to be of a much shorter duration (1 to 2 minutes).

At this point, there is little question that nightmares and night terrors are distinctly different phenomena. Either may, however, present a serious difficulty, depending on the circumstances and the persistence of the problem. The cause is largely unknown at this time (Knopf, 1979), al-though some theories (such as psychoanalytic) have proposed a variety of rather elaborate notions such as sexual impulses that are not understood by the individual or have been rejected with condemnation (Keith, 1975). The literature has not discussed treatment to any extent, aside from reports of the use of such medication as imipramine and diazepam (Boller, 1976; Fisher, Kahn, Edwards, & Davis, 1973) and psychotherapy (Keith, 1975). Knopf (1979) has suggested that the relative absence of attention to such problems may be due to their infrequent occurrence, al-though Kales, Jacobson, and Kales (1968) have indicated that at least one night terror incident occurs in about 1 to 3 percent of all youngsters 5 to 12 years of age. Incidence of serious sleep problems in the general population remains undocumented, and the figures noted by Kales and associates shed little light, as the report of just one episode would not give strong indication of serious problematic behavior.

Somnambulism

It is estimated that about 6 percent of all children have episodes of *somnambulism* or sleep-walking (Bakwin & Bakwin, 1972). Somnambulism and night terrors have a number of common features, and it is not unusual to find both problems in the same child. Sleepwalking occurs during NREM sleep in stages 3 and 4. (Unlike normal children, somnambulist children will often start to sleepwalk if they are stood upright during stage 3 and 4 sleep—something that will not occur in normal children.) Sleepwalkers typically do not remember the incidents and are very difficult to awaken. Their eyes are open and they appear to be walking with a definite purpose, although they show very little emotion. Somnambulism can create particular problems, because children can place themselves in danger by walking in unsafe places such as balconies and stairways. Essentially, their senses are not functioning in a manner that would protect them from falling or other types of accidents.

Somnambulism is most often attributed to some type of emotional stress. Frequently, some specific accident or other stressful incident is reported to have preceded the sleepwalking (Kurtz & Davidson, 1974). Treatment has taken a number of approaches with varying degrees of success. It is generally agreed that pharmacological treatment is of little benefit (Bakwin & Bakwin, 1972; Knopf, 1979). Both psychoanalytic and behavioral therapies have been employed with variable success, often treating both the parents and the child. The treatment of somnambulism remains largely unexplored relative to that of many other childhood disorders, perhaps because the problem "is rarely brought to the attention of the physician" (Bakwin & Bakwin, 1972, p. 551). It may be that some of our seemingly most typical and simple problems, such as sleepwalking, are actually more complex than they appear on the surface.

Narcolepsy

Narcolepsy is a disorder in which individuals encounter "sleep attacks" at times when they are trying to stay awake (such as during the day). Narcolepsy has often been thought of as excessive sleep, but more correctly should be viewed as inappropriate sleep incidents (Mendelson et al., 1977). The term "inappropriate" is not meant to suggest a value judgment; the fact is that narcoleptic incidents can prove physically dangerous and socially embarrassing. They may take place at any time or place, when the individuals are walking, standing, driving an automobile, or at the dinner table. Often the episodes are brief, lasting about 15 minutes or even much less. Patients usually describe the incidents in terms of an irresistible urge to sleep. Some are aware that an attack is about to occur, whereas other patients experience the episodes without any warning. Still others are able to avoid sleep by concentrating intensely on remaining awake.

Estimates regarding the prevalence of narcolepsy vary from 0.02 to 0.097 percent in the general population, or about 10 in 1000 at the most. These figures would suggest that there are as many as 250,000 individuals in the United States suffering from narcolepsy (Kiester, 1976; Mendelson et al., 1977). It is unclear how many narcoleptics are children, although the onset of the problem seems to occur predominantly between the ages of 10 and 20. The cause of narcolepsy has largely eluded researchers to date. One factor that has been identified relates to disturbances of REM sleep. Unlike most people, narcoleptics seem to begin their nocturnal sleep in a REM state. As indicated earlier, sleep begins in normal people with several NREM stages, followed later in the cycle by REM sleep. Narcoleptics do, however, seem to have relatively normal *amounts* of REM and NREM sleep during the night. Treatment of narcolepsy has primarily focused on drug therapy, with benefits reported from using stimulants such as amphetamines, although some complications and side effects may appear (Guilleminault, Carskadon, & Dement, 1974; Parkes & Fenton, 1973).

TOILETING PROBLEMS

Periodically, most parents express concern regarding their children's toileting behavior, particularly when the youngsters are being trained to perform this natural function in a socially appropriate manner. The process of toilet training often generates a certain amount of frustration and

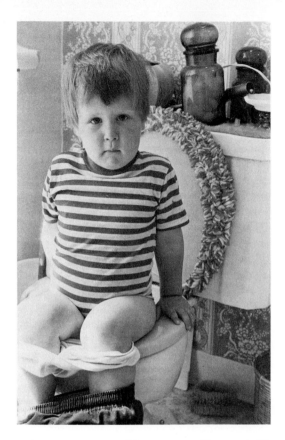

Toilet training may not be easy even with normal children, and it often seems to be a concern of parents.

stress for parents and children alike. For the most part, problems encountered in toilet training are transient, and appropriate patterns of behavior are developed by the time a child is 2 to 4 years of age. However, for a small percentage of children this does not occur: For them, toileting remains problematic beyond the normal age at which we expect these behaviors to have been habituated, and may continue into and beyond the elementary school years.

It is somewhat surprising that more research has not been undertaken on toileting behaviors. The question of the best time for beginning training has not yet been completely resolved. Around age 2 seems to be the commonly accepted time when serious efforts should be directed toward

shaping these behaviors. However, some evidence indicates that children may be amenable to training as early as 16 to 18 months of age (Madsen, Hoffman, Thomas, Koropsak, & Madsen, 1975). Obviously the appropriate age will vary from child to child—a statement that holds true for all behaviors. The study by Madsen et al. (1975) also suggested that parental expectations as well as the individual child's characteristics may be determining factors. These investigators found that most parents' methods were generally inefficient when compared to systematic treatment procedures aimed at teaching appropriate toileting behaviors. Thus, in many cases, problems with waste elimination should perhaps include a view that extends beyond the child to consider the family. Such a notion is not unusual in a discussion of habit disorders generally and has received considerable attention in the literature on toileting problems.

Encopresis

Encopresis is a general term that refers to abnormal or unacceptable patterns of fecal expulsion by a child beyond 3 years of age who does not exhibit organic pathology (Doleys, 1979a). This generic label includes several different types of conditions. On one dimension, encopresis can be viewed in terms of *retentive* and *nonretentive* problems. Retentive encopretics are characterized by an excessive retention of fecal material, whereas nonretentive encopresis involves uncontrolled expulsion of feces *(incontinence),* resulting in soiled clothing and bedding. Another dimension relates to whether or not control of fecal expulsion has been established and then ceased (known as *discontinuous* or *secondary* encopresis), or whether control has never been reliably established (*continuous* or *primary* encopresis). It is easy to see how such subcategories represent very different disorders, even though the behaviors may appear similar in some cases. These distinctions are very important when we are trying to establish causation and treatment.

Some authors have estimated that about 3 percent of the population is encopretic (Levine, 1975; Yates, 1970). Some types of encopresis, which affect more boys than girls, do not occur primarily at night. A rather substantial proportion of encopretics seem to be of the discontinuous type. Although statistics differ depending on the source, well over half of all cases of encopresis may involve children who have established control and then cease to exercise it (Doleys, 1979a). Obviously encopresis represents a difficult and frustrating problem for all involved, including the child, parents, and peers. Some difficulties extend far beyond the unpleasant process of cleaning up the mess and the embarrassment of having an accident. For example, Keilbach (1976) reported on a discontinuous encopretic, 8 years of age, who used fecal material as an aggressive "missile" against family members, as a gift offering, and as material for artistic expression. Certainly this was a bizarre case that involved other complications. It takes little imagination, however, to see how encopresis can generate a myriad of negative emotions in caretakers that can work against treatment.

Treatment of encopresis has generally followed one of the three major theoretical perspectives on the problem: medical, psychoanalytic, and behavioral. Medical treatment tends to emphasize direct physical control of fecal matter, using enemas, laxatives, stool softeners along with modified diet, and sometimes pediatric counseling (Landman & Rappaport, 1985). In some cases, medication has also been employed to control bowel actions. An antidepressant drug (imipramine) has been employed because of its presumed relaxing influence on muscle structures. The drug is assumed to inhibit the internal anal sphincter, which would reduce the frequency of defecation. A certain amount of success has been obtained so long as medication is continued, although it is clear that such treatment would not be appropriate for retentive encopretics, since it reduces the frequency of bowel movements. Other medications have also been tested (such as Senokot), but have been found to be of little help in relieving problem soiling (Berg, Forsythe, Holt, & Watts, 1983).

Doleys (1979a) has noted that clinicians must attend to environmental as well as physical factors in order to effect a cure. The psychoanalytic view

of encopresis regards the behavior as a symptom of inner conflicts and tends to employ psychological treatment that emphasizes interpretation of the child's play, the older child's acquisition of insight, and counseling of parents and the child. Evidence regarding the success of psychotherapy is very sketchy, primarily because of the virtual absence of adequate research on the approach.

The primary focus of behavioral treatment is the establishment and maintenance of appropriate toileting behavior through manipulating environmental consequences. For the continuous encopretic, this becomes a process of teaching control skills that presumably have never been learned. For the discontinuous cases, it becomes a matter of re-establishing and maintaining such behaviors. Many procedural variations have been used with an impressive success rate. For the most part, treatment studies can be grouped into three general categories: (1) those that primarily give positive reinforcement for appropriate control, but no punishment for soiling; (2) those that punish the child who soils; and (3) those that employ a combination of positive reinforcement and punishment. One of the major strengths of the behavioral studies is that they provide specific procedural descriptions for use by clinicians and caretakers. The specificity of behavioral approaches makes evaluation and replication of treatment procedures easier than with other theoretical perspectives.

Behavioral treatments of encopresis appear promising, as noted earlier. Over 93 percent of the cases in studies reviewed by Doleys (1979a) were successfully treated using behavioral procedures. Wright (1980) found that results were even more striking when behavioral treatment was combined with systematic compliance monitoring to check on the degree to which parents and children adhered to the treatment program instructions. Wright reported only 1 unsuccessfully treated case among over 500 patients who had consulted him and his colleagues during an 8-year period. Although these are impressive statistics, further research is clearly needed. Encopresis is not a simple problem. There is great variation in the circumstances surrounding each case, and interventions are successful to the degree that every individual case is precisely evaluated and an individualized treatment program is implemented.

Enuresis

Enuresis is probably more widely recognized as a toileting problem than encopresis. Certainly it is a more frequent topic of informal conversation among parents as well as a subject examined in the professional literature. In part there is a good reason for this, because enuresis is more common. Doleys (1979b) has cited incidence figures as high as 15 to 20 percent for children 5 years of age. Once again, this disorder seems to be more evident in males than females (with about a 2:1 ratio) and declines more rapidly with age in females than males (Verhulst et al., 1985). *Nocturnal enuresis* refers to chronic inappropriate nighttime bedwetting by children who do not exhibit evidence of physical disorders. There is considerable difference of opinion regarding the minimum age at which such behavior should be considered problematic. However, most clinicians view urinary incontinence after about 3 to 5 years of age as a problem.

Early literature considered encopresis as the fecal equivalent of enuresis (Doleys, 1983). However, there is no solid evidence of a relationship between the two disorders, and some researchers have obtained results suggesting that they are *not* related (Doleys, McWhorter, Williams, & Gentry, 1977). That is, an enuretic child may or may not also be encopretic. Another point should be made here regarding enuresis: While enuresis often occurs at night, encopresis may occur either during the day or night. Some evidence indicates that over 50 percent of encopretics are incontinent both day and night (Levine, 1975). The major focus of research on enuresis has been on nocturnal occurrences, and the disorder has often been labeled as *functional nocturnal enuresis*. Because of this trend in the literature, the present section emphasizes the nighttime behavior. This is not meant to suggest that inappropriate urination may not also occur during the day; however, in this context, it is interesting to consider the connection between sleep and urinary incontinence.

There are three generic classes of theories regarding causation and related treatment: medical, psychodynamic-psychoanalytic, and behavioral. Considerable attention has been given to enuresis in relation to the influence of sleep patterns. It is reasonable to think that enuresis might occur only during deep sleep, when a child is unaware of and does not react to the physiological need to void. Certainly there are individual differences which would explain why some waken and void themselves in the toilet, and others do not. There is another notion, however, which is related to waking but is quite separate from sleep depth. Some people are aroused from sleep more readily than others. With a child who is particularly difficult to arouse (regardless of relative sleep level), then it is easy to see how bedwetting might occur. Despite the appealing logic (and the anecdotal reports), neither of these notions has been conclusively supported by research (Doleys, 1979b, 1983). They remain as areas in need of further investigation.

The psychodynamic perspective interprets enuresis as a symptom of some inner conflict. This notion is consistent with the fundamental psychoanalytic view of disorders and has been encountered in our earlier discussion of encopresis. Effectiveness of psychoanalytic treatment has been poorly documented, and there is little research evidence to support a success rate significantly different from that of subjects receiving no treatment (Quay & Werry, 1979). Medical explanations of enuresis have included developmental or maturational lag, genetic influences, abnormalities of the urinary tract, and a deficit in cortical control. Obviously some of these may be interrelated, and treatment can be implemented only with some.

Many different medications have been tried over the years, but only two types have generated continued interest. One of these types, amphetamines, is related to the sleep factors noted above. Amphetamines are stimulants and are thought to make it easier for the enuretic to awaken, either by raising the average depth of sleep or by making the individual more easily aroused. This line of reasoning connects enuresis with deficiencies in cortical inhibition (Crosby,

1950) and arousal deficits in sleep (Finley, 1971; Kales & Kales, 1974). Although the logic is reasonable, the evidence does not suggest that stimulants are effective in the treatment of enuresis (Blackwell & Currah, 1973). A second drug, imipramine, has previously been encountered in our examination of encopresis. As noted earlier, imipramine presumably has a relaxing influence on the muscles. In treating enuresis, this effect is assumed to permit greater than usual bladder expansion and would thus reduce the frequency of the need to void. This approach to treatment is thought to offset small bladder capacities indicative of developmental lag. Results of treatment with imipramine for enuresis are inconclusive at present. While some research has shown success that is superior to that of inactive placebo treatments with a limited number of enuretics (for instance, Doleys & Wells, 1975; Forsythe & Merrett, 1969; McConaghy, 1969; Starfield & Mellits, 1968), the success rate is often below 30 percent, and relapses are common after termination of the medication (Houts, Liebert, & Padawer, 1983). In addition, such intervention must be viewed with caution because certain side effects have been noted, even occasional toxic death in children (for instance, see Rohner & Sanford, 1975).

Behavioral approaches to treating enuresis mainly focus on the environmental contingencies related to urination. Specific treatment procedures have been combined with varying degrees of success. Doleys (1979b) has classified behavioral treatments into three general types: (1) specific contingency manipulation, such as positive reinforcement or punishment; (2) reinforcement to attempt to expand bladder capacity, and (3) urine alarm systems (either singly or in combination with other procedures). Electric devices have been developed to sound a bell or buzzer when urine causes a circuit to close. These devices have been used in mattress pads and in training pants. Alarm devices have long been popular for the treatment of enuresis. They have been used and studied since the 1930s (Mowrer & Mowrer, 1938), are inexpensive, and are easy and safe to use (for example, see Finley & Wansley, 1976; Nettelbeck & Langeluddecke, 1979; Wagner & Matthews

1985). However, another reason for their popularity can be attributed to their relatively high success rates, often between 80 and 90 percent (Doleys, 1977; Lovibond & Coote, 1970; Turner, 1973; Yates, 1970). It should be noted that the use of alarm systems to treat enuresis has often been plagued by relapse of the inappropriate wetting behavior. This has been a continuing problem. Doleys (1977) reviewed studies between 1960 and 1975 and reported a 41 percent relapse rate by subjects receiving treatment for 5 to 12 weeks. However, treatment success seems improved and relapse rate reduced when alarms are used repeatedly to strengthen the conditioning (for instance, Houts et al., 1983; Jehu, Morgan, Turner, & Jones, 1977); when there is intermittent scheduling of alarm activation (Finley, Besserman, Bennett, Clapp, & Finley, 1973; Finley & Wansley, 1976); and when attention is paid to family stress factors (Berg, 1981; Dische, Yule, Corbett, & Hand, 1983).

In most instances, it appears that combining various procedures is the most effective approach to treating enuresis. Here again, the nature of any given program is best determined by a careful analysis of the specific child's characteristics. It should be noted, however, that all treatment approaches suffer from less than complete success and that a certain percentage of cases can be expected to relapse and need retreatment.

EATING PROBLEMS

Nearly all parents periodically complain about their children's eating behavior. Such concerns often focus on the parents' beliefs or preferences about proper eating habits for children. The parents complain that their youngsters do not eat enough, that they do not eat the "right" food, or that they do not eat at the proper time or place or with the prescribed implements. It is important at this point to return briefly to one of the thoughts expressed in Chapter 1: Individual behaviors vary substantially within the range of what would be considered normal. More often than not, child eating behavior falls within the normal range of variation, even though parents are concerned.

Obesity

Obesity presents a number of problems for those so affected. Evidence has long suggested that obesity is related to health problems (Committee on Nutrition, 1967) as well as to psychological and social difficulties (Bruch, 1957; Bullen, Monello, Cohen, & Mayer, 1963; Hammar et al., 1972; Monello & Mayer, 1963; Weil, 1977). In fact, Winick (1975) characterized obesity as "one of the main health problems in America today, . . . [and it] also constitutes a significant health hazard in developing countries" (p. v). Thus we address obesity as a serious problem to both physical and mental health.

Part of the gravity of obesity lies in the fact that it is not easily treated. Theories regarding causes of obesity are conflicting, and treatment attempts have been relatively unsuccessful. With regard to treatment, Coates and Thoresen (1978) stated that "in general, strategies have been limited in number . . . [and] have produced very modest outcomes" (p. 144). They further noted in an even more pessimistic vein that "once overweight occurs it tends to persist and even worsen despite our best attempts to alter its course" (p. 147).

Causation Theories regarding causation of obesity vary and often appear to be in conflict, as noted above. One view suggests that obesity is a hereditary or constitutional condition. Support for this perspective is partially derived from findings indicating that there are cellular differences between obese and nonobese individuals, as well as between those who are obese as children and those who become overweight as adults. For example, there seem to be two physiological types of obesity, hyperplastic and hypertrophic. *Hyperplastic obesity* occurs when an individual has an abnormally high number of fat cells (nonobese people tend to have about three billion such cells, whereas hyperplastic obese counterparts may have double that number). *Hypertrophic obesity* occurs when individuals are overweight primarily because of extremely enlarged fat cells rather than because of a larger-than-normal number of fat cells. Obesity that is primarily hyperplastic seems to develop in childhood, whereas hypertrophic obesity is more an adult disorder (Hirsch, 1975; Winick, 1975). Such findings, however, remain only suggestive, as the distinction regarding onset does not always hold (Grinker, Price, & Greenwood, 1976; Hirsch, 1975).

Biological or physiological explanations feature the inheritance of a tendency toward obesity or slimness. Many times we hear statements such as "Johnny inherited his fatness from his parents" or "Sally is slender just like her mother." But these are just unsubstantiated popular beliefs, involving oversimplified explanations. New evidence on obesity illustrates both the importance of research and the need for more sophisticated theoretical perspectives that can tolerate multiple and interactive causation (e.g., genetic and environmental). As an example, obesity is common among a Native American tribe of Arizona, the Pimas (Brody, 1980), as described in Box 7-1.

Obesity is often a lifelong problem. This young boy may grow up to be obese or overweight.

Box 7-1 • Obesity in the Pima Tribe of Arizona

The prevalence of obesity in adult Pima males is approximately 77 percent, and in Pima females about 88 percent. Such statistics are most striking when compared with the general population of the United States, where adult obesity is found in about 14 percent of the males and 24 percent of the females. This Native American tribe is highly inbred and thus shares a great deal of genetic material as well as the same environment. Researchers investigating the Pimas suspect that certain genetic material may be present in this population that was very adaptive in the past but contributes to obesity today. A "thrifty gene" may have allowed the Pimas to store calories in times of plenty and to survive during droughts and times when food was scarce. Those without such genetic makeups may have succumbed during famine periods (which are known to have been characteristic of the early environment of this population). Thus, what may have been a very adaptive genetic composition is now creating problems as food supplies are more constant—an interesting potential interaction between inheritance and environment. Further reporting of evidence on people such as these is clearly of great interest and importance to scientists studying obesity.

Source: J. E. Brody. (1980, February 5). Tending to obesity, inbred tribe aids diabetes study. *New York Times,* pp. C1, C5.

Many researchers and therapists working in the area view learned behavior as an important causal factor in obesity. There is little question that food consumption in contemporary society serves social as well as physiological purposes, for both children and adults. Many aspects of adult eating appear automatic and involuntary, even though eating is a behavior that is under voluntary control. On the surface, one is not immediately prompted to imagine how obesity might be the outcome of childhood learning. However, close examination of eating in a newborn infant may suggest how parents' attitudes may influence this behavior. Jordan and Levitz (1975) have described such a hypothetical scenario:

For example, the breast-fed child sucks until satisfied and the mother does not know how much milk [has been consumed]. . . . [T]he mother produces milk according to the demands of the child. This important biological feedback system is completely disrupted when the breast is replaced by a bottle. Now the mother . . . can see how much milk the child has ingested. She can use this cue to shape the child's eating behavior according to her own attitudes about how much the child should eat. It becomes possible for her to overfeed or underfeed her child. Beginning with this process, the parent assumes a much

greater role in teaching and shaping feeding behavior. (p. 142)

This statement suggests how food consumption may be influenced by environmental contingencies at a *very* early age. It takes little imagination to extrapolate such influences beyond infancy. Many parents socially reinforce their children for eating. Often children are admonished to "clean their plate" for one reason or another (for instance, it is socially appropriate, the cook may feel hurt, or some convoluted logic is invoked regarding necessary guilt because of depriving "all those starving children" elsewhere). Can such influences contribute to obesity? Does obesity developing during childhood destine an individual to obesity as an adult? The interaction between learning and the physiological components of obesity also requires examination.

A substantial part of the literature suggests that obesity in youngsters predicts adult obesity. Some have argued that this is not always the case (for example, Garn, Clark, & Guire, 1975). However, evidence suggests that overweight infants tend to be obese during childhood and adolescence (Heald & Hollander, 1965) and that this progression continues to adulthood (Knittle, 1972; Mullins, 1958; Rimm & Rimm, 1976). Stunkard and Burt (1967) gave an obese adolescent only 1 chance in 28 of being of normal weight when reaching adulthood. Abraham, Collins, and Nordsieck (1971) found that 86 percent of obese boys and 80 percent of obese girls were also obese as adults. For youngsters of average weight, only 42 percent of the boys and a mere 18 percent of the girls were obese as adults. Thus the evidence does not suggest an optimistic outlook for the obese youngster.

We have indicated earlier that there may be cellular differences between obese individuals who become overweight as youngsters and those who become heavy as adults (that is, the former tend to have an abnormally high *number* of fat cells, whereas the latter are characterized more by *enlarged* fat cells). If the infant-feeding scenario presented previously (Jordan & Levitz, 1975) results in an obese infant, such a child may develop a high number of fat cells. In fact, Knittle (1975) has found that some obese children already have the normal adult number of fat cells by the time they are 3 years of age. This becomes particularly important in view of the fact that losing weight does little to reduce the number of fat cells (Coates & Thoresen, 1978; Leon & Dinklage, 1983; Winick, 1975). Certainly, more research is needed in this area, but the seriousness of what has just been noted is compelling. It may be that once one develops an overabundance of fat cells, little can be done to reduce that number. Consequently, reduced intake alone does not produce significant weight loss. This fact, combined with the implication that such conditions seem to be developed very young, highlights the importance of treatment and control of obesity in children.

Treatment Procedures   Perhaps in testimony to its difficulty, there are many different weight loss approaches. Coates and Thoresen (1978) have indicated that treatments can generally be classified as representing one or a combination of six basic approaches: (1) reduced caloric intake, (2) appetite-suppressant drugs, (3) increased physical exercise, (4) therapeutic starvation, (5) intestinal by-

pass surgery, and (6) changes in eating habits based on social learning theory. Varying degrees of effectiveness have been reported with each approach, and certain health risks are also associated with some techniques.

Caloric restriction would seem to be the simplest treatment for obesity. One would think that weight reduction should result if energy intake is reduced below energy expenditure. Unfortunately, the success of such an approach to treating obesity has been disappointing. Asher (1966) studied 269 youngsters being treated for obesity in Great Britain using caloric restriction and found that none was able to reach an appropriate weight level. In fact, only about one-fourth of the children reduced their weight to as little as 25 percent *above* the appropriate level. Somewhat greater success has been reported by employing frequent contact and combinations of hospitalization and outpatient treatment (Coates & Thoresen, 1978). However, long-term maintenance of weight loss remains problematic for caloric restriction, with 70 to 80 percent of the patients regaining the weight they had lost (Hammar, Campbell, & Woolley, 1971; Lloyd, Wolff, & Whelan, 1961).

Appetite suppressant medication has not been very successful in treating obesity (Bauta, 1974, Collipp, 1971; Court, 1972; Lorber, 1966, Lorber & Rendleshort, 1961). Drug therapies have included the use of stimulants (amphetamines), some medications that are not amphetamines, and hormonal treatments. In all cases, results seem disappointing, and the risks may be sufficient to argue against the use of such medication with juveniles. Beyond the minimal weight loss achieved, there is a considerable danger of abuse and dependence with some drugs (such as the amphetamines), and a risk of detrimental effects on health and growth with others (such as hormonal treatments) (Rivlin, 1975). In all treatments such as these there seems to be a continuing problem with patient adherence to the program regimen, which may contribute to the low success rate (Marston, 1970; Wright, 1980).

It is possible that obese youngsters may be less active than their nonobese counterparts. Some early research evidence has suggested no differences between the populations (Stunkard & Pestka, 1962). However, other investigators have found that obese individuals are significantly less active than those of normal weight (Bullen, Reed, & Mayer, 1964). Mayer (1975) reported that obese girls were considerably less active than thin girls, even when they were engaged in the same vigorous sports such as tennis, volleyball, and swimming. Exercise treatment for obesity has had variable success. People enrolled in structured exercise programs have most often shown little actual weight loss but have reduced their body fat (Coates & Thoresen, 1978). However, Mayer (1975) reported considerable success in a 4-year program of nutrition education and physical exercise conducted with several hundred obese children. Approximately 60 percent of the youngsters lost weight, although it was unclear how much loss had occurred. Follow-up data on these subjects after the program terminated were disappointing. Mayer noted that "the effect that we had instilled and that persisted for four years while the program was going on had been completely obliterated in the three years" since the program ceased to operate (1975, p. 80).

Therapeutic starvation has been employed in extreme cases of obesity for both adolescents and adults and requires hospitalization. Advocates of this approach exercise great control of caloric intake and attempt to demonstrate that weight reduction is possible for patients who seem unable to achieve loss by other procedures (Wadden, Stunkard, Brownell, & Day, 1984). Starvation therapy tends to result in short-term reduction, but regaining weight seems to be a serious problem (Nathan & Pisula, 1970; Wadden, Stunkard, & Brownell, 1983). Also, certain health hazards have been reported with adolescents, such as lowered adrenal functioning and growth retardation (Brook, Lloyd, & Wolff, 1974; Garces, Kenny, & Drash, 1968).

Intestinal bypass surgery also represents a rather extreme form of treatment for obesity. This procedure typically involves surgically altering the length of the small intestine in order to reduce the amount of absorbing surface. Such techniques have primarily been used with adults, although some work of this type has been undertaken with adolescents (Coates & Thoresen, 1978). Weight reductions have resulted, although most patients do not achieve normal weight levels. Health risks must also be considered, for complications have been reported for both adults and adolescents (Scott, Dean, Shull, & Gluck, 1976; White, Cheek, & Haller, 1974).

Behavioral treatment of obesity overlaps other approaches to a degree, but has been so popular in recent years that it warrants special emphasis. Stunkard (1979), writing about behavioral medicine, contended that "more people are receiving behavioral treatment for obesity than are receiving behavioral treatment for all other conditions combined" (p. 279). He estimated that 400,000 people receive some form of behavioral treatment for obesity weekly.

Behavioral treatment of obesity does not completely discount physiological factors, such as cellular formations and genetic influences. It does, however, focus on those contingencies in the environment that can be manipulated to alter habits related to energy intake and expenditure. There have been far more specific variations in the procedures used in the behavioral treatment of obesity than can be discussed here. The interested reader may wish to examine other sources that address this topic in depth (for instance, Ferguson, 1975; Mahoney & Mahoney, 1976a, 1976b; Varni & Banis, 1985).

Early reports on behavioral treatment of obesity tended to concentrate on energy intake or eating (for example, Stuart, 1967). Stunkard (1979) has described such a program that includes four basic elements. The first involves a precise and ongoing description of the behavior to be controlled. This means that the individual being treated must keep careful records of what is eaten, when it was eaten, who was present, and how the individual felt at the time. Such surroundings and circumstances can become cues for eating.

The second element involves control of the stimuli preceding food consumption. This element is based on one of the fundamental principles of behavioral analysis and modification—those contingencies contiguous to an act often become related to the event through conditioning. As such factors are identified, they become targets for control and modification.

The third element is related to developing techniques for control of eating behaviors. In this context, behavior modification procedures are employed to alter food consumption patterns, such as the speed with which clients eat. The last component focuses on modification of the consequences of eating, which essentially refers to rewarding eating behavior that will promote weight reduction. Although this program relates to eating, it is easy to see how such fundamental principles can be generalized to other factors that may influence weight control, such as energy expenditure (exercise). In fact, other work has included attention to a variety of environmental dimensions in addition to eating, such as investigation of family, personality, and social variables related to obesity (Leon & Roth, 1977; Schilson & Van Valkenburg, 1984; Wooley, Wooley, & Dyrenforth, 1979); self-initiation of treatment (Loro, Fisher, & Levenkron, 1979); and self-regulation behaviors

(Cohen, Gelfand, Dodd, Jensen, & Turner, 1980). It has become increasingly evident that obesity is a complex problem requiring such a broad perspective.

Behavioral patterns leading to obesity are not developed overnight, but over a considerable period of time. Furthermore, as time progresses and the condition persists, such habits become a part of one's life. This is clear from the limited success regarding weight loss in many cases, and even more so from the incredible difficulty obese children experience in maintaining a weight loss. The phenomenon of dieters' regaining excess weight has continually plagued therapists. Even less is known about how to alleviate this problem than about how to achieve initial weight loss; in fact, it may be the most critical focus of study. Some researchers have begun to study factors associated with long-term weight loss maintenance, such as the study by Cohen and associates (1980) described in Box 7-2. A more complete understanding of weight maintenance will surely contribute significantly to the knowledge of obesity in general.

BOX 7-2 • A Study of Weight Level Maintenance

Cohen and her associates studied two groups of youngsters who had participated in a weight reduction program: those who had lost weight but regained it, and those who had lost and maintained the reduced weight. Choosing subjects from friends of the two groups, the researchers also sampled youngsters who had never been overweight. This investigation focused on a number of interesting variables relating to maintenance of weight level as well as to weight gain and reduction. Of particular interest were factors relating to self-discipline (that is, regulation of food intake and exercise), parental control, reported *level* of food intake, and social activity. A variety of interesting differences were noted among the groups. Those who had maintained weight loss reported more self-regulation of weight and more physical exercise than either the "regainers" or those who had never been obese. The subjects that were considered to have regained excessive weight reported more parental control than the normal-weight youngsters but were no different from the "maintainers." None of the groups differed in the amount of food intake or in social activity. Although certain questions have been raised (even by the researchers themselves) concerning the data from this single study, the results are certainly provocative in terms of future research and treatment of childhood obesity. A solid knowledge base and reliable treatment implications await further study.

Source: E. A. Cohen, D. M. Gelfand, D. K. Dodd, J. Jensen, and C. Turner. (1980). Self-control practices associated with weight loss maintenance in children and adolescents. *Behavior Therapy, 11,* 26–37.

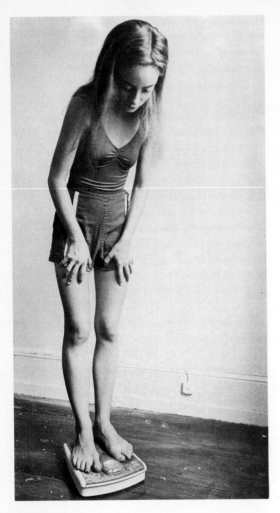

This young woman is recovering from anorexia nervosa. Treatment can prevent long-term, serious health problems in those affected by this and other eating disorders.

Anorexia Nervosa

Anorexia nervosa is a condition of self-inflicted starvation that occurs most often in adolescent females, with most cases developing before age 25 (Halmi, 1985). Only about 4 to 6 percent of anorexics are male; about 96 percent are female (Halmi, 1978). Although anorexia nervosa used to be very rare, it appears to be occurring much more frequently in recent years (Bruch, 1978; Maloney & Klykylo, 1983). Some writers

have estimated that for females between 12 and 18 years of age, the prevalence may be as high as 500 in 100,000 (Crisp, Palmer, & Kalucy, 1976), although others place the prevalence at only 0.24 to 0.61 per 100,000 (Halmi, 1974). The increased prevalence may result from the tremendous influence of the broadcast media and the value contemporary society places on slenderness. This reasoning is persuasive, given the predominance of female patients. It also seems to occur more frequently in families that are above average socioeconomically, and further evidence suggests that individuals in higher social classes have a greater desire to be thin (Dornbusch et al., 1984). The slogan "You can't be too rich or too thin" appears on T-shirts and other items in expensive catalogues. Although the societal line of logic is compelling and likely accurate to some extent, it is too easy to chastise society. The disorder is complicated and can be life-threatening in some instances (as in the case of the well-known singer Karen Carpenter). As we make clear in the following discussion, causation may be complex and difficult to identify. Also, anorexia nervosa is not totally a phenomenon of recent vintage. One of the most often cited and most graphic descriptions of the disorder was published in 1689. In this work, Morton characterized an individual as being so thin that she was "like a Skeleton only clad with Skin" (cited in Halmi, 1978, p. 137).

For the most part, individuals identified as suffering from anorexia nervosa seem to be driven by a need to be thin or, more specifically, by an obsession to avoid being fat. This results in a sharp reduction of food intake and is often accompanied by an almost frantic, compulsive exercise routine (Gilbert & DeBlassie, 1984; Leon & Dinklage, 1983). These behaviors occur despite the fact that few patients have a history of being overweight. In fact, most descriptions of them as children include terms such as "the perfect child"; they are almost overly docile and conforming. Often they are excellent students and appear to have few problems or disorders of any kind. They are frequently characterized as intellectually superior; they are overly sensitive; they hold a negative perception of themselves; and they manifest compulsive behaviors such as repetitive cleaning rituals (Kolb, 1977; Leon, Lucas, Colligan, Ferdinande, & Kampe, 1985). Not all cases of anorexia nervosa have compulsive features, although such elements are very prominent in the literature on this disorder.

After they recover, most anorexics can describe the environmental contingencies that prompted and precipitated their unusual eating behavior. Often the behavior was triggered by some rather common or trivial event that made them feel too heavy or not respected. The onset of the disorder is usually quite sudden; eating is reduced and a rigorous exercise regimen is begun. Frequently, as weight loss and exercise compulsively continue, family members repeatedly make note of the fact that the youngster is becoming too thin or is beginning to look emaciated. Despite these cues, anorexics often deny such viewpoints, continue to exercise, and eat very little. The high activity level typically continues until the individual reaches such a weakened state that it can no longer be continued. Weight loss may range from 15 to 50 percent below normal (Chess & Hassibi, 1978; Muuss, 1985). Physiological changes go far beyond the reduction of body fat to include a wasting of muscle tissue and alterations of the bone marrow, as well as a variety of other problems associated with starvation (Halmi, 1978). Menstruation ceases in female patients or becomes extremely painful, and often the protective layers of flesh diminish so completely that it is painful to sit on a hard surface such as a wooden chair or in a bathtub. Frequent bruising also occurs as the disorder progresses. Clearly, anorexia may become a serious problem; it is not one that can easily be dismissed. In 15 to 21 percent of the cases, death through starvation occurs (Halmi, 1978).

A very interesting problem is how youngsters can be victimized by anorexia nervosa. Most of the clinical descriptions of such individuals would lead us to believe that they should receive a great deal of reinforcement for all of their "good" and conforming behavior. Furthermore, the events that reportedly precipitate the disorder often seem too trivial to trigger such a dramatic outcome (Bruch, 1978). The causation of anorexia nervosa remains somewhat unclear. Some writers have attributed the disorder to genetic factors (Garfinkel & Garner, 1982), hormonal and endocrine problems (Dippe, 1978; LaGrone, 1979), or as malfunction of the hypothalamus (Gold, Pottash, Sweeny, Martin, & Davies, 1980; Kolb, 1977). Others have postulated psychological problems (Boskind-Lodahl, 1976; Gilbert & De-Blassie, 1984). Perhaps the most common view of causation stresses environmental influences, often including parental behaviors and the impact of family relations or other life stress situations (Bruch, 1978; Halmi, 1978; Muuss, 1985). One theory related to development and environmental influences suggests that anorexics have not learned to label the sensation of hunger appropriately. Support for this notion was indicated in the results of a study by Agras, Barlow, Chapin, Abel, and Leitenberg (1974), who found that informative feedback regarding the effects of eating or not eating was the most potent factor in treatment. While further research is clearly needed, this line of work may be important in terms of both causation and treatment.

Many of the physiological problems associated with anorexia nervosa will reverse under treatment, but treatment is often complex and must focus on both physical and psychological factors. One of the immediate needs is to correct the individual's nutrition problem. This can be difficult, because many patients will resist, but it is essential in order to begin reversing the physical deterioration. A variety of therapeutic procedures have been employed for this process, including hospitalization, psychotherapy, drug treatment, force-feeding, behavior modification, and information feedback to the patient regarding the effects of eating (Agras et al., 1974; Colligan, Ferdinande, Lucas & Duncan, 1983; Halmi & Larson, 1977; Liebman, Minuchin, Baker, & Rosman, 1975; Peake & Borduin, 1977; Tolstrup, 1975; Van Buskirk, 1977; Werry & Bull, 1975). Treatment must address a variety of factors, because the weight and nutrition problems may be symptomatic of other difficulties. Therapists often focus on the relationships among family members, particularly if the youngster is still living at home (Caille, Abrahamsen, Girolami, & Sorbye, 1977). Often such treatment is aimed at changing parental expectations for conforming, obedience, and achievement striving, since these children seem to try too hard to meet parental expectations. Therapy approaches seem to include combinations such as those noted above, and also family counseling in most cases. Clearly, anorexia nervosa is not a simple disorder, and treatment seems most effective when a combination of methods is used to address the many problems of an anorexic teenager.

Bulimia

Bulimia is an eating disorder in which there are frequent episodes of uncontrolled binge eating alternating with purging of what has been consumed. During such eating binges, a person may ingest enormous quantities of food in a very short time period. Although estimates vary widely, it has been reported that bulimics may consume between 1500 and 15,000 calories in a single binge (Barrios & Pennebaker, 1983), with "bad days" involving from 3 to 27 times the recommended daily energy consumption (Abraham & Beumont, 1982). The individuals may not be able to control such eating binges, although they typically view them as abnormal. The fear of being unable to stop eating may then lead to purging (through vomiting or laxatives) and periods of fasting. This disorder has been referred to as *bulimia nervosa, bulimarexia, dysorexia, purge-vomiting, binge-purge syndrome,* and *abnormal weight control syndrome* (Maloney & Klykylo, 1983; Schlesier-Stropp, 1984).

Bulimia is often thought to be closely related to anorexia nervosa. Although it does occur separately (Fairburn, 1981; Halmi, Falk, & Schwartz, 1981), it is also often found in conjunction with or as a variant of anorexia nervosa (Garfinkel, Moldofsky, & Garner, 1980; Pyle, Mitchell, & Eckert, 1981; Schlesier-Stropp, 1984). For example, Casper, Eckert, Halmi, Goldberg, and Davis (1980) studied the incidence of bulimia in anorexics and found that 47 percent of subjects with anorexia nervosa also exhibited bulimic behaviors. Both dis-

orders occur together, but not in all cases, and there are certain characteristics that distinguish the two. Common to both anorexia nervosa and bulimia is an extreme concern with body weight and fear of becoming fat. Bulimic individuals exhibit a considerable fluctuation between gaining and losing weight, whereas anorexics are characterized only by extreme, life-threatening weight loss (Schlesier-Stropp, 1984).

It is very difficult to accurately determine the prevalence of bulimia, because affected individuals are extremely secretive about the extreme binging and purging, and social eating behavior is usually controlled and appropriate (Fairburn & Cooper, 1982). Unless an individual admits that a problem exists, the disorder is difficult to detect, as bulimics' body weight and condition are typically within the normal range. Nevertheless, a limited number of prevalence studies have been attempted. Diagnostic records of 22 students at the University of Washington receiving outpatient services for eating disorders were evaluated, and 19 (86 percent) were found to have bulimia diagnoses (Stangler & Printz, 1980). This would represent a very small prevalence in the general student population of 37,000 but probably reflects a substantial underestimate, because these were only the individuals who sought treatment. Halmi et al. (1981) conducted a survey of students enrolled at a New York university and found 13 percent reporting bulimic symptoms. Thus, evidence regarding the prevalence of bulimia in the general population is largely lacking, although it seems to be substantial in those already identified as having eating disorders.

Like anorexia nervosa, bulimia seems to be much more common among women than men (Halmi et al., 1981; White & Boskind-White, 1980). Some reports indicate that the disorder is limited to females (e.g., Fairburn & Cooper, 1982; White & Boskind-White, 1980), although a few bulimic males have been identified (Hawkins & Clement, 1980; Herzog, 1982). Bulimia occurs most often in young adults, primarily during the 20s, although reported ages have ranged from the midteens to the early 50s. It also seems that bulimia occurs at a similar rate among black and white populations, at least during the adolescent years (VanThorre & Vogel, 1985). The disorder seems to begin most often during the late teen years and rarely after 30 years of age. It is interesting that purging (vomiting) typically begins substantially after the overeating, often from 1 to 3 years (Fairburn & Cooper, 1982: Pyle et al., 1981). It is difficult to determine accurately how frequently episodes of bingeing and purging occur in bulimics, once again because of the solitary nature of these behaviors. Investigations have reported that episodes may occur weekly, daily, and many times daily (one study—Fairburn, 1980, 1981—indicated episodes occurring from 3 to 30 times daily).

The causes of bulimia are somewhat unclear at this time. There seems to be a preoccupation with food and a persistent urge to eat. Schlesier-Stropp (1984) noted that "A bulimic's day revolves around food and eating," and that bulimics "consistently report that their minds are filled almost constantly with thoughts of food, eating, and vomiting such that their concentration and everyday activities are impaired" (p. 250). Nearly any incident may trigger an episode of bingeing; in this respect, bulimia is not unlike the behavior of alcoholics. Strober (1981) suggested that anorexics who also exhibit bulimia seem to have more evidence of affective disturbance and alcohol use than individuals with anorexia nervosa alone. In addition, depression and anxiety play a prominent role (Russell, 1979), and life stress is frequently reported as having a relationship to bulimia (Strober, 1984). These areas would seem to be important for further research, particularly because suicide has been noted as the most common cause of death for bulimics (Crisp, 1982; Maloney & Klykylo, 1983).

Treatment of bulimia is an area that clearly illustrates the importance of sound research methods (addressed in Chapter 11). Early treatment of the disorder often focused on medication with the use of anticonvulsant drugs, because there seemed to be a link between EEG abnormalities and compulsive eating disorders (Green & Rau, 1974, 1976; Rau & Green, 1975). The effectiveness of this treatment appeared promising, with success as high as 90 percent (Green & Rau, 1974), although the research methods were weak. Wermuth, Davis, Hollister, and Stunkard (1977) followed up on these drug investigations but employed a placebo condition in which inactive pills were given to some participants. These investigators found no improvements as a result of the drugs. These findings raise serious questions regarding the use of anticonvulsant medication to treat bulimia, and they warrant further investigation.

Other treatment approaches to bulimia have included group therapy (Boskind-Lodahl & White, 1978; White & Boskind-White, 1981) and various behavioral interventions (Brooker, 1982; Fairburn, 1980, 1981; Linden, 1980; Rosen & Leitenberg, 1982; Turner, Hersen, Bellack, & Wells, 1979). Each of these approaches to treatment included differing elements, and results indicated that they were effective, although the effectiveness was based to varying degrees on individual patient differences. Those bulimics exhibiting the most severe symptoms over a longer period of time are the most difficult to treat. Continued intervention research is clearly needed, perhaps focusing on the different components of this disorder, early identification, and assessment procedures (Swift, 1985). The latter points will, however, remain problematic as long as the behavior is so hidden from public view.

SPEECH DISORDERS

Definitions of speech disorders have varied considerably in type and specificity. The definition used here represents a synthesis of definitions derived from several authorities (for example, Perkins, 1977; Van Riper & Emerick, 1984). For our purposes, *defective speech* or *speech disorder* (which are terms often used interchangeably) refers to speech behavior that is sufficiently deviant from normal or accepted speaking patterns that it attracts attention, interferes with communication, and adversely affects communication for either the speaker or listener. As before, we are focusing on behavior deviations that clearly exceed the normal range of variations.

Estimates of how many children suffer from defective speech have varied greatly; consequently, many authors either avoid this topic or are extremely vague in their discussions. The most frequently quoted figure in the speech pathology literature suggests that about 7 to 10 percent of the population is affected (Emerick & Hatten, 1979). These figures do not differ greatly from other general estimates (e.g., Perkins, 1977), although some studies have shown considerable variation between locales—for example, from 21.4 percent in Fresno, California, to 1.0 percent in Philadelphia (Milisen, 1971). The American Speech-Language-Hearing Association (ASHA) estimated that in 1979 one out of every 20 Americans (or 5 percent) had a speech or language impairment (ASHA, 1979). Incidence and prevalence consistently vary as a function of age. Milisen (1971) indicated that speech disorder incidence is roughly 12 to 15 percent for children in kindergarten through fourth grades, reduces to about 4 to 5 percent in fifth through eighth grades, and remains somewhat constant thereafter unless therapeutic intervention is undertaken. In some cases treatment results in a change, whereas in others the children outgrow a disorder or "self-correct" their problems (Evans, 1985). Service patterns vary over time and between types of disorders and grade levels, as we shall see. Estimates are also confounded by service regulations and laws, such as the overall 12 percent ceiling for services to be provided to the handicapped under the Education for All Handicapped Children Act of 1975 (P.L. 94-142). A recent report to Congress reflected this type of estimate in noting that 2.86 percent of those *enrolled* in school (aged 3 to 21) during 1983–1984 were classified as speech-impaired (U.S. Department of Education, 1985). Once again, we are faced with the reality that prevalence is socially rather than absolutely defined.

Identification and classification approaches to speech disorders have also varied, depending on etiology and the treatment perspective being employed (Diedrich & Carr, 1984). Rather than examine classifications completely, we select from rather traditional categories and attend to speech disorders that are related to habit. Specifically, we

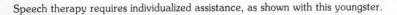

Speech therapy requires individualized assistance, as shown with this youngster.

discuss problems of delayed speech, elective mutism, articulation, and stuttering. Readers interested in a more comprehensive examination of speech disorders should consult other sources (for example, Emerick & Hatten, 1979; Hutchinson, Hanson, & Mecham, 1979; Perkins, 1977; Schiefelbusch, 1978; Van Riper & Emerick, 1984).

Delayed Speech

Very young children are typically able to communicate to some degree through gestures, noises, and other means prior to the learning of speech and language (Tiegerman, 1985). Most such behaviors tend to be dropped as they learn the process of speaking. However, in some cases children develop speaking skills much later than is normally expected. As we begin this discussion, it is important to remember that we are examining deviations from normal that are *significant* or *extreme*. As we listen to children and adults, we note considerable variation in speaking ability or performance: Some people are quite skilled and articulate (those "silver-tongued" individuals), whereas others are less facile ("tongue-tied"). This normal range of skill is *not* the focus of the current discussion. In order to examine delayed speech, it is helpful to review the typical development of speech. Box 7-3 summarizes certain landmarks of normal language and speech development in children.

We have noted previously that, in some cases, maturation may serve as a natural cure for certain speech problems. Most young children make a certain number of errors in their speech that do not typically persist. For example, they may delete final consonants (*buy* for *bike*) or unstressed syllables (*nana* for *banana*), and they often substitute certain sounds for others (*tit* for *sit, dup* for *soup*) (Ingram, 1976). Often these errors are considered amusing and cute, and it is not uncommon for parents, siblings, or other individuals to focus attention on such errors, for example, by imitating the child's pronunciation to others or by speaking in "baby talk" with the child (Dunn & Kendrick, 1982). These behaviors may inadvertently promote speech disorders. Although the precise nature of the impact remains under

exploration, there seems to be a relationship between parental communication-speech patterns and those of their children (see, for example, D'Odorico & Franco, 1985; Fernald, 1985; Lawrence, 1984; Schaffer, Hepburn, & Collins, 1983; Shipley, Kuhn, & Madden, 1983; Smolak & Weinraub, 1983).

Delayed speech represents a failure of speech to develop at the expected age. Some children with delayed speech develop little or no expressive speech beyond vocalizations that are not interpretable as conventional language. Such children may continue to communicate nonverbally through gestures, or they may use nonspeech vocalizations extensively long after such behavior is typical. Others can speak a little, but their proficiency is limited for their age, and they mainly use nouns without qualifying or auxiliary words.

Etiology of Speech Delays   The term *delayed speech* is applied to inadequate proficiency that may be caused by any of a number of influences, ranging broadly from heredity to environment (Blegvad & Hvidegaard, 1983; Mather & Black, 1984). Such disorders may stem from experience deprivation, such as when a child is raised in an environment that provides little opportunity for learning to speak or circumstances that actively interfere with mastering speaking skills. Delayed speech may also be the result of sensory deprivation from an anatomical defect such as a hearing loss. Other factors that may contribute to cases of delayed speech include neurological problems (such as cerebral palsy) and emotional disturbances (such as childhood schizophrenia or autism), or less severe problems (such as negativism). Our focus in this discussion is on speech delays that may be caused by the establishment of faulty habits, which in turn are the result of abnormal or unsatisfactory learning circumstances (for example, experience deprivation, reinforcement contingencies that do not promote speaking).

Negativism describes a set of behaviors that may contribute to delayed speech. When children are developing speech, their parents are exerting great pressure on them to learn many other skills

BOX 7-3 • Landmarks of Normal Language and Speech Development

CHILD'S CHRONOLOGICAL AGE	CHILD'S NORMAL SPEECH DEVELOPMENT
6 months	Repeats self-produced sounds; imitates sounds; vocalizes to other people; and uses about 12 different speech sounds (known as phonemes).
12 months	Commonly uses up to 3 words besides *mama* and *dada;* may vocalize such words as *bye-bye, hi baby, kitty,* and *puppy;* and uses up to 18 different phonemes.
18 months	Commonly uses up to 20 words and 21 different phonemes; jargon words or phrases are present, and often automatically repeats words or phrases said by others (echolalia); uses names of objects that are familiar, one-word sentences such as *go* or *eat,* and uses gestures; uses words such as *no, mine, good, bad, hot, cold, nice, here, where, more,* and expressions such as *oh-oh, what's that,* and *all gone;* the use of words at this age may be quite inconsistent.
24 months	Commonly uses up to 270 words and 25 different phonemes; jargon and echolalia are infrequent; averages 75 words per hour during free play; speaks in words, phrases, and two- to three-word sentences; averages two words per response; first pronouns appear, such as *I, me, mine, it, who,* and *that;* adjectives and adverbs begin to appear; names common objects and pictures; enjoys Mother Goose; refers to self by name, such as *Bobby go bye-bye;* and uses phrases such as *I want, go bye-bye, want cookie, up daddy, nice doll, ball all gone,* and *where kitty.*
30 months	Commonly uses up to 425 words and 27 different phonemes; jargon and echolalia no longer exist; averages 140 spoken words per hour, says words that name or identify items such as *chair, can, box, key,* and *door;* repeats two digits from memory; average sentence length is about $2\frac{1}{2}$ words; uses more adjectives and adverbs, demands repetition from others (such as *do it again*); almost always announces intentions before acting; begins to ask questions of adults.
36 months	Commonly uses up to 900 words in simple sentences averaging three to four words per sentence; averages 15,000 words per day and 170 words per hour; uses words such as *when, time, today,* and *not today,* and can repeat three digits, name one color, say name, give simple account of experiences, and tell stories that are understandable; begins to use plurals and some prepositions; uses commands such as *you make it, I want,* and *you do it;* verbalizes toilet needs.

as well. During this period children are expected to learn how to eat properly, to go to bed when it is expected, to control excretory functions, and to begin exhibiting many other behaviors that char-acterize adults. These demands exceed some children's tolerance level, so that they may be unable to perform as expected by parents and others. Certain children respond negatively to such a sit-

Box 7-3 *(Continued)*

CHILD'S CHRONOLOGICAL AGE	CHILD'S NORMAL SPEECH DEVELOPMENT
42 months	Commonly uses up to 1200 words in mostly complete sentences that average between four and five words in length; 7 percent of the sentences are compound or complex; averages 203 words per hour; rate of speech is faster; relates experiences and tells about activities in sequential order; can say a nursery rhyme; asks permission (such as Can I? or Will I?).
48 months	Commonly uses up to 1500 words in sentences averaging 5 to $5\frac{1}{2}$ words in length; averages 400 words per hour; counts to three, repeats four digits, names three objects, and repeats nine-word sentences from memory; names the primary colors, some coins, and relates fanciful tales; enjoys rhyming nonsense words and using exaggerations; demands reasons why and how; questioning is at a peak, up to 500 a day; passes judgment on own activities; can recite a poem from memory or sing a song and uses such words as *even, almost, now, something, like,* and *but.*
54 months	Commonly uses up to 1800 words in sentences averaging $5\frac{1}{2}$ to 6 words but now averages only 230 words per hour and is satisfied with less verbalization; does little commanding or demanding; about 1 in 10 sentences is compound or complex, and only 8 percent of the sentences are incomplete; can define 10 common words and count to 20; asks questions for information and learns to control and manipulate persons and situations with language.
60 months	Commonly uses up to 2200 words in sentences averaging six words; can define *ball, hat, stove, policeman, wind,* and can count five objects and repeat four or five digits, definitions are in terms of use—can single out a word and ask its meaning; makes serious inquiries (such as *what is this for, how does this work,* etc.); uses all types of sentences, clauses, and parts of speech; reads by way of pictures and prints simple words.
66 months	Commonly uses up to 2300 words in sentences that average $6\frac{1}{2}$ words in length; grammatical errors continue to decrease as sentences and vocabulary become more sophisticated.
72 months	Commonly uses up to 2500 words in sentences averaging 7 words in length; relates fanciful tales, recites numbers up to 30; asks the meaning of words; repeats five digits from memory, can complete analogies such as as the following: A table is made of wood, a window of _____. A bird flies, a fish _____.

Source: C. D. Weiss and H. S. Lillywhite. (1976). *A handbook for prevention and early intervention: Communicative disorders* (St. Louis: C. V. Mosby), pp. 56–58.

uation by refusing to perform, and one very effective type of refusal is refusing to talk. It is quite easy for a parent to punish some types of refusal (such as refusal to eat or to go to bed), but it is not as simple to handle a refusal to talk. A child cannot easily be forced to talk and may be able to communicate needs quite adequately through gestures. In other circumstances, children are frequently punished for talking because parents view it as inappropriate or inconvenient (for instance, it is too loud or badly timed because the parents are conversing, watching television, or reading). Consequently, it is easy to see how the habit of not speaking may be learned: It is reinforced at times; it is a method of avoiding punishment at others; and it may be a means of expressing refusal to perform that does not place one in great jeopardy of being punished. If such circumstances persist over a sustained period of time when speech is typically developed, the result may be a child with a significant delayed speech problem. Not only has the child failed to learn speaking skills, but in some cases she has learned *not* to speak.

If the child's failure to speak is a form of rebellion, the reward contingencies in the environment must be altered. It must be made more reinforcing for the child to speak than not to do so. In addition, the child must be taught the skills of speaking that have not heretofore been learned. It may also be necessary to alter child behavior patterns that are only indirectly related to the speech delay, such as eating and going to bed. Clearly, if the problem persists over a period of years, it becomes increasingly difficult to treat because the delay is more pronounced and the behaviors become more firmly habituated by continued and increasingly complex reinforcement contingencies.

In some ways, delayed speech caused by negativism sounds like *voluntary mutism* or *elective mutism,* in which the child can speak but does not. Certainly the behaviors are similar and analogies may be drawn between the causes. However, the terms *voluntary* or *elective mutism* are more often associated with problems other than negativism or battles of will between parents and child. Consequently, we examine such speech disorders later.

Another category of causation in delayed speech is experience deprivation, in which the environmental circumstances limit the opportunity to learn speaking skills and/or actually interfere with such learning. Environmental contingencies must exist in a configuration that will permit and promote children's learning to speak. This cer-

tainly does not mean that the family home life has to become a contrived miniature language class on a continuing basis. Most households function routinely in a manner that will foster a child's speech acquisition (for example, encouragement to name objects and reinforcement for response). There are, however, some households that do not promote language acquisition, and significantly delayed child speech may result. In some cases conversation is unusually infrequent in a child's home. Such circumstances may exist if parents rarely speak with each other or the child. Consequently, the child does not have much speech modeled, and perhaps receives little reinforcement for speaking and vocalizing. The basic principles of learning would suggest that learning will be retarded in such an environment and that the outcome may well be delayed speech. There may be additional difficulties in the family, which may contribute to the child's problems in learning to speak. The relationship between the parents may be rather tense or troubled, which results in a low frequency of verbal communication and also causes anxiety or fear in the child. Perhaps the talking between the parents that *does* occur consists largely of arguing and threatening. This may easily compound the difficulty of infrequent modeling by adding a component of punishment or aversive stimulation. The child's learning may be further interfered with if speaking is often associated with punishment (for example, often when the father speaks, the mother shouts obscenities in response).

In some cases, an environment where there is little talk may be observed that is quite unlike that described above, although the net result may be quite similar. Such a situation may exist when a child who can hear perfectly well is born to parents either one or both of whom are deaf. The parents' major mode of communication may be via signs and gestures. There may be little speech learning by the child in this type of environment, or, at best, the child's speech proficiency may be significantly delayed. It should be emphasized that the outcomes of such circumstances are extremely variable. As a personal example, one of us knows of four brothers with normal hearing who were born to parents who were deaf and had been so from a very early age. The parents used sign language but little or no verbal communication. All of the boys (now adults) learned to speak quite well, and although they experienced some minor problems in school, they have distinguished themselves in a variety of fashions. One holds a Ph.D. in special education from a major university. A second has both an M.D. and a Ph.D. (the latter earned at a well-known European university); the third is an able public servant; and the fourth began his rise to the heights of achievement as an inventor and has become a millionaire. We would all be fortunate to be so successful, but it is important to remember that this is an exceptional story. An introspective recollection by one of the brothers, published in Hardman, Drew, and Egan (1987), suggested a variety of exceptional influences (such as unusually close relationships with the grandparents) that led to a favorable outcome in this particular case. Substantial speech delay is not uncommon in hearing children born into an environment where verbalization is unusually infrequent on account of parental deafness.

Delayed speech caused by experience deprivation may occur in situations much different from those described above, where verbal conversation is infrequent. There are some homes where there is a great deal of verbalization and noise, but it occurs in a very confused and unsystematic fashion. From a perspective of habit or learning disorder, such an environment may seriously impede the acquisition of speech at the time when it is normally learned. Learning a skill is a rather delicate process, particularly in its early stages. Stimuli must be presented in an uncomplicated, systematic fashion and without competing or distracting stimuli, so that a child can focus on the important features and discriminate those that are central from those that are not important. In addition, when an appropriate behavior occurs, it needs to be reinforced (and this process must be repeated consistently if learning is to progress). A chaotic environment probably will not provide such contingencies and may produce delayed speech.

Children learning to speak will tend to take the route that requires the least effort. Thus, if

there is little need to speak it is unlikely that the child will do so, and in some homes a child has little need to speak. Such conditions are often described in other terms (for instance, the "overprotective parent"), but from a learning perspective there simply may be little need to learn speech. Let us use a fictitious illustration to complete this examination, although many readers have probably informally observed situations that may have similar features. As children begin to develop speech and interact with those around them, they communicate in several ways. They may imitate; express pleasure or displeasure; and request with sounds, gestures, facial expressions, and body posture. It is not uncommon to encounter parents who want to satisfy all of their child's needs (after all, in a civilized society, this exemplifies being a "good" parent). There are extremes wherein parents anticipate a child's desires or needs and quickly provide for them by responding to gestures or nonspecific vocalizations. They may rush to feed their child, procure toys for him or her, and meet a multitude of other needs in response to a mere gesture or cry. By doing this they may teach (reinforce) such behaviors and delay speech development, whereas the child might have to perform more exacting tasks (such as asking for water) to obtain reinforcement in other circumstances. It is easy to see how such behaviors, in extreme form, could teach a child to meet needs in a fashion other than speaking. Delayed speech can result from this type of situation, although it does not necessarily do so (Acredolo & Goodwyn, 1985).

Treatment of Speech Delays   Speech delay caused by experience deprivation can be treated through the fundamental principles of learning; in theory this is a simple task, but implementation can be very difficult. Alteration and precise control of stimuli and reinforcement contingencies may be quite complex. Considerable success has been evident in direct teaching interventions that alter the stimulus-reinforcement contingency in order to promote more normal speech development (Bricker & Bricker, 1974). Obviously, alternative methods, procedures, and perspectives may be useful (for example, see Fay, 1984; Richardson, 1983), and these may well involve collaboration among speech clinicians, teachers, and parents (Hornby & Jensen-Proctor, 1984). The approach will always depend on the specific details of the problem(s) and the viewpoint of the therapist.

Elective Mutism

The term *elective mutism* is not new and has usually been attributed to Tramer (1934), who used it in describing two youngsters who would only speak under certain circumstances. The fact that elective mutes may speak in certain situations represents one of the distinctions between this problem and extreme delays in speech development. As indicated earlier, some children with severe speech delays may not have learned to speak. In such cases they either do not have speaking skills or the skills may be very limited. Elective mutism, as a learned behavior, presents quite another situation. The child who is electively mute "may be defined as a child who does not speak but who has *no speech or language disorders . . . no physical defect of the speech mechanism . . . is not aphasic, nor . . . of sufficiently deficient general intelligence so as to be unable to formulate speech and language*" (Friedman & Kargan, 1973, p. 249; emphasis ours). Thus electively mute children generally do have speaking abilities but choose not to utilize them. It is important to reiterate that electively mute children typically do speak in particular situations and to certain individuals, but these circumstances are limited — often involving only certain members of the child's immediate family.

The obvious question is why or under what circumstances a child would elect not to speak. Some of the previous discussion on negativism has relevance here. A child may choose to remain silent in order to control or manipulate others. Children may also remain mute because it is not reinforcing to speak, and speaking may even be punishing or anxiety-producing. Electively mute children are often described as being shy, socially withdrawn, and anxious with others; therefore, they do not wish to draw attention to themselves by speaking (Dollard & Miller, 1950; Friedman & Kargan, 1973).

Elective mutism may occasionally be confused with what is known as *reluctant speech* (Straughn, Potter, & Hamilton, 1965). However, as described in the literature, reluctant speech occurs when there "is a normal frequency of speech under one set of stimulus conditions . . . [and] a very *low* frequency of speech in others" (Williamson, Sewell, Sanders, Haney, & White, 1977, p. 151). This is perhaps a difference in degree, in that elective mutism would be viewed as *no* speech under certain circumstances. Treatment of reluctant speech may follow basic principles of modifying the child's reinforcement contingencies. However, it may be easier to initiate than treatment of elective mutism, in which the child speaks not at all in some settings, thus leaving nothing to reinforce (Williamson, Sanders, Sewell, Haney, & White, 1977). Eliciting initial verbal output when the child is nonverbal has presented problems in treatment, but behavioral procedures have been fairly successful in modifying elective mutism (Bauermeister & Jemail, 1975; Calhoun & Koenig, 1973; Colligan, Colligan, & Dillard, 1977; Griffith, Schnelle, McNees, Bissinger, & Huff, 1975; Van Der Kooy & Webster, 1975; Wulbert, Nyman, Snow, & Owen, 1973). Often such treatments have emphasized reinforcement of verbal activities (such as storytelling or reading) in the child's verbal environment and efforts to generalize these contingencies to the nonverbal situations. Such reinforcement often results in increased spontaneous speech. On some occasions, response cost procedures (taking away points for being nonverbal) have been combined with reinforcement when subjects are not responsive to the latter condition alone (Griffith et al., 1975).

Articulation Disorders

Articulation problems represent the largest category of all speech disorders. By far the majority of cases encountered by public school speech clinicians involve articulation disorders (Emerick & Hatten, 1979), with some estimates ranging as high as 75 percent (Van Riper & Emerick, 1984). An articulation disorder is basically a disturbance in speech-sound production. In most instances, such problems in children are *functional articulation disorders*—that is, they are not caused by any readily apparent organic defect (Dworkin & Culatta, 1985; Powers, 1971). In a certain number of cases, articulation difficulties follow a developmental path: As the child grows, older articulation errors often diminish or are eliminated. This has led some public school officials to contend that speech clinicians should not give as much attention as they do to articulation problems, particularly when children are very young. Certainly there is some logic to such a position as fiscal and human resources become increasingly scarce. However, some articulation errors are not caused merely by immature speech development. Articulation performance is likely to improve with development until about the age of 9 or 10. Problems that exist beyond that point are likely to persist unless therapy intervenes; such disorders can become increasingly difficult to remedy if permitted to continue untreated (Milisen, 1971).

Like other speech disorders, defective articulation may be caused by a variety of factors. Some cases are due to brain damage or nerve injury (often referred to as *dysartia*); others are caused by physical deformity (such as malformed mouth, jaw, or teeth structures); some are thought to be due to heredity (Mather & Black, 1984); and many cases represent learned behaviors (Hutchinson et al., 1979). Those caused by defective learning (functional disorders) constitute a significant problem, because only a small proportion of articulation errors can be attributed to identifiable organic flaws. However, there are also many causes for functional articulation disorders. The stimulus and reinforcement contingencies that result in such problems are as variable as those that promote or permit speech development in general. Perhaps the modeling by parents is inappropriate, such as baby talk; although the influence of baby talk has been questioned (Cromer, 1981), the literature suggests that the nature of parental speech is influential on children's linguistic maturity (for instance, see Fernald, 1985; Lawrence, 1984). It may be that household reinforcement for accurate speech production is unsystematic.

In many instances, it is less important to precisely determine the causes of functional articulation disorders than the causes of organically based disorders, which may be amenable to surgical correction. However, the influential contingencies cannot be ignored, because treatment must focus on altering the causal factors in the environment if these still exist. The essential task is one of rearranging learning contingencies so that more appropriate speech patterns can be acquired. A variety of behavior modification procedures have been successful in improving articulation problems of habit (for example, Johnston & Johnston, 1972; Mowrer, Baker, & Schutz, 1968; Ryan, 1971b; Wolfe & Irwin, 1975). Costello and Bosler (1976) found that children will speak appropriately in situations outside the treatment sessions if the setting for these sessions is systematically varied. Generalization of appropriate learning is obviously important to the child's overall speech performance (Olswang & Bain, 1985), and treatment may, once again, involve collaboration among teachers, parents, and speech therapists (Nigram, 1983).

Stuttering

Stuttering is perhaps the most widely recognized of all speech disorders. Stuttering represents a disturbance in the fluency and rhythm of speech, with intermittent blocking, repetition, or prolongation of sounds, syllables, words, or phrases. Nearly all of us at one time or another have known or encountered an individual who stutters, and most of us personally exhibit such behaviors occasionally even though we are not stutterers. Furthermore, nearly all young children stutter at times as they develop their speaking abilities. For the most part these are normal nonfluencies that disappear as the child grows older and progresses in speech development. However, these normal behaviors play a prominent role in certain theories of stuttering.

Most of us think of stuttering almost automatically when we consider speech disorders in general. This is not surprising, as in stuttering the interruptions in the flow of speech are very evident and easily remembered. In addition, stuttering makes listeners very uncomfortable. Often listeners try to "help" the stutterer by filling in the relevant words when a block occurs. It is clear that the communication process creates a considerable degree of discomfort for both the stutterer and listener. Consequently, people tend to remember stutterers better than those with other speech disorders. Despite the prominence of stuttering, it is among the least prevalent of speech disorders. For example, Perkins (1977) presented estimates indicating that articulatory disorders occur with nearly six times the frequency of stuttering. Although prevalence statistics are notoriously variable and inaccurate, stuttering consistently appears as a speech disorder that occurs rather infrequently when compared to other problems.

Etiology of Stuttering   The causes of stuttering have been investigated for many years. Scientists in the past have often searched fruitlessly for a single cause. Fortunately, more current thinking has discarded this oversimplified perspective (Clutter & Freeman, 1984). Present theories about the causes of stuttering can basically be divided into three types: those that address it as an emotional or neurotic problem (that is, wherein stuttering is a behavioral manifestation of some emotional difficulty); those that view it as a constitutional or neurological problem (once a widely accepted position); and those that view stuttering from a learning perspective (Homzie & Linsay, 1984). What appears clear is that stuttering is a behavior that may have many or differing causes (Helm, Butler, & Benson, 1977).

There is decreased interest in attempting to find a constitutional cause of stuttering, although a few such studies still appear in the literature. Some investigators have explored neurological dysfunction generally whereas others have focused more specifically on such factors as cerebral dominance problems and cortical organization. Results have been mixed. For example, Cohen and Hanson (1975) studied 20 matched pairs of stutterers and fluent speakers ranging from 8 to 16 years of age and found support for the theory that the cortical organization of stutter-

ers might be different from their fluent counterparts. Moore and Lang (1977) pursued this line of research and found that stuttering and nonstuttering subjects seemed to make predominant use of different hemispheres of the brain to process the same material. Other researchers have found support for the notion that cerebral dominance problems may be present in stutterers to a greater degree than in individuals with fluent speech (Blood, 1985; Brady & Berson, 1975; Greiner, Fitzgerald, & Cooke, 1986; Sommers, Brady, & Moore, 1975). On the other hand, investigators have also found cerebral hemispheric factors *not* to be a significant influence in stuttering (Brutten & Trotter, 1985; Gruber & Powell, 1974; Slorach & Noehr, 1973). Thus some research has continued to attend to neurological causation of stuttering, with variable results.

Studies have also explored a variety of possibilities other than the major ones listed above. Some literature has examined the notion that heredity may play a role in stuttering and linked this line of thinking to sex differences in the incidence of the disorder (male stutterers outnumber females about four to one). Some authors have suggested that the hereditary influence exists because of higher incidence of stuttering within certain families, studies of parental disfluency, and twin studies where shared genetic material exists (for example, see Sheehan & Costly, 1977). As we know, however, it is often difficult to separate the impact of heredity and environment generally as well as in speech disorders (Mather & Black, 1984). Often this can only be accomplished under specific genetic analysis (such as in certain types of Down's syndrome). Other researchers have studied quite different etiological possibilities. For example, Perkins, Rudas, Johnson, and Bell (1976) conducted an investigation with subjects ranging from 14 to 67 years of age. They concluded that stuttering is a function of poor coordination among voice control, articulation, and respiration processes. While this seems to support a physiological influence, it does not specifically implicate neurological dysfunction and it may relate to learning, as we will see later when we examine a treatment study by Azrin and Nunn (1974). Other evidence has also suggested an interaction between physiological and behavioral or learning factors, such as behavioral mismanagement or behavioral abnormalities of the laryngeal system (Conture, Schwartz, & Brewer, 1985; Healey, 1984).

The learning theory approach to stuttering is not new but has attracted increased attention over the years. Some writers have contended that stuttering, in its fully developed form, is a learned and more severe outgrowth of normal nonfluency in the early years that increases (Bloodstein, Alper, & Zisk, 1965). The obvious question at this point concerns how one learns to stutter. Certainly this behavior is not something that an individual would want to learn. Different answers to this question have been proposed, but most often they are variations on the basic principles of learning theory. One particularly relevant description was published many years ago by a prominent speech pathologist. Wendell Johnson wrote a communication to parents to illustrate one view of how stuttering may be learned by children. An abridged portion appears in Box 7-4; space limitations do not permit its reproduction in full. Johnson elaborated on how to generate stuttering and how to avoid such behavior, illustrating the principles of learning theory in dramatic and practical terms.

The publication of Johnson's letter indicates that a learning perspective on stuttering is far from being a new idea. It is presented in this volume, over 45 years after its original publication, because of the graphic clarity with which it describes how a child may learn to stutter. Research on the causes and treatment of learned stuttering has continued. Although not all authorities subscribe to Johnson's position (for instance, see Cooper & Cooper, 1985), considerable evidence in the literature supports the notion that at least some stutterers are the victims of habit disorders like those Johnson describes (Avari & Bloodstein, 1974; Bourdon & Silber, 1970; Manning, Trutna, & Shaw, 1976; Ryan, 1971a; Silverman, 1976; Wahler, Sperling, Thomas, & Teeter, 1970). As

we have suggested, this view holds that most young children exhibit a certain amount of nonfluency as they learn and develop speaking skills and that stuttering disorders may often be an outgrowth of that nonfluency. The difference between normal nonfluency and stuttering may be indistinguishable at first, as noted in Johnson's letter. However, when attention is drawn to the nonfluencies rather than the fluent statements, an unfortunate set of learning contingencies may be formed that result in stuttering. Even within the learning theory view of stuttering, there is considerable difference of opinion concerning the functional and precise form of these contingencies. Each case must be examined and treated individually.

Treatment of Stuttering   Treatment of stuttering has been as varied as the theories of causation. Psychotherapy has met with limited success (Van Riper & Emerick, 1984). Other procedures have been used to focus on the rhythm process of speech such as using a metronome to establish a beat (Wohl, 1968), as well as relaxation therapy to overcome tenseness (Gray, 1968). In all cases results have been mixed. Treatment of stuttering has increasingly included behavioral therapy that attempts to teach the affected individual fluent speaking patterns as well as to minimize relapses (Evesham & Fay, 1985; James, 1983; Shenker & Finn, 1985). Although some approaches have used the fundamental principles of learning as a basis, others have combined these principles with a neurological and physiological view of the problem (Boberg, Yeudall, Schopflocher, & BoLassen, 1983). Box 7-5 presents a rather complex series of behavioral treatment procedures reported by Azrin and Nunn (1974); these authors indicated impressive results from a study that included attention to certain physiological characteristics of stutterers (such as breathing and physical movements), as well as behavior modification principles. Because the results of this study are so striking, the method in modified form has been employed for a variety of habit disorders (Azrin & Nunn, 1977). Continued research is crucial in the

---

BOX 7-4 • An Open Letter to the Mother of a Stuttering Child

My dear Mrs. Smith:

I thoroughly appreciate your concern over the speech difficulty of Fred, your four-year-old boy. You say that he is in good health, that he is mentally alert, and is generally normal by any standards you know about. I note that you have been careful not to change his handedness, and that he is now generally right-handed. But in spite of all this he stutters.

It will interest you to know that the majority of four-year-old stutterers just about fit that description. I want to say to you very nearly the same things I should say to the mothers of thousands of other "Freds." There are some stuttering children who are not like your boy, and their mothers need somewhat different advice. But the "Freds" make up the majority. . . .

First of all, I want to put you at ease if I can by stressing that the most recent studies have tended strongly to discredit the popular view, which perhaps you share, that stutterers are generally abnormal or inferior in some very fundamental sense. Concerning this point, I should like to make as clear a statement as possible—and I make it on the basis of over one hundred scientific studies of stuttering in older children and adults, and five recent investigations involving over two hundred young children, stutterers and non-stutterers. . . .

I do not know of any way of examining a child so as to determine, with any degree of certainty, whether he will ever come to be regarded as a stutterer. So far as I know, stutterers generally are not significantly different from non-stutterers aside from their speech, and aside from the way they feel about their speaking experiences. So far as I know, in fact, even the speech of young stutterers is quite normal until they are diagnosed as stutterers.

We found, for example, that two-, three-, and four-year-olds—all the children of these ages in a large nursery school, somewhat better than average children by most standards—spoke, on the average, in such a way that one out of every four words figured in some kind of repetition! The whole word was repeated, or the first sound or syllable of it was repeated, or it was part of a repeated phrase. One out of four words was the average; about half of the children repeated more frequently than that. Another way to summarize the findings is to say that the average child makes 45 repetitions per thousand words. This was the average—the norm. . . .

Investigation seemed to show that a rose by any other name doesn't smell the same at all. If you call a child a stutterer you get one kind of speech—and personality—development,

---

examination of this and other procedures for the treatment of stuttering.

SUMMARY

In this chapter, we have examined a very diverse range of habit disorders that present significant difficulties in a child's development. Many of these create problems that sorely test the resources and patience of families as well as professionals. In discussing the causes and treatments of habit disorders, we have all too often had to rely on words such as "unclear," "unknown," and "unsuccessful." We are painfully aware that parents who seek assistance in solving their children's problems frequently receive conflicting opinions and advice. This further emphasizes the need for systematic and rigorous research that will provide a more solid information base for effective clinical treatment—a need that is encountered repeatedly in this book.

We begin our discussion of habit disorders with sleep problems, a common difficulty. Researchers have studied several different stages of

Box 7-4 (Continued)

and if you call him a normal or superior speaker you get another kind of development—within limits, but they seem to be rather wide limits.

I can illustrate what I mean by telling you briefly about two cases. The first case is that of Jimmy, who as a pupil in the grades was regarded as a superior speaker. He won a number of speaking contests and often served as chairman of small groups. Upon entering the ninth grade, he changed to another school. A "speech examiner" saw Jimmy twice during the one year he spent in that school. The first time she made a phonograph record of his speech. The second time she played the record for him, and after listening to it, told him he was a stutterer.

Now, if you have ever tried to speak into a phonograph recording machine you probably suspect what is true. Practically all children who have done this—in studies with which I am familiar—have shown a considerable number of hesitations, repetitions, broken sentences, etc. It is easy to see how the apparently untrained teacher misjudged Jimmy who was, after all, a superior speaker as ninth-graders go.

He took the diagnosis to heart, however. The teacher told him to speak slowly, to watch himself, to try to control his speech. Jimmy's parents were quite upset. They looked upon Jimmy's speech as one of his chief talents, and they set about with a will to help him, reminding him of any little slip or hesitation. Jimmy became as self-conscious as the legendary centipede who had been told "how" to walk. He soon developed a quite serious case of stuttering— tense, jerky, hesitant, apprehensive speech.

The second case was Gene, a three-year-old boy. His father became concerned over the fact that now and then Gene repeated a sound or a word. Gene didn't seem to know he was doing it, and he wasn't the least bit tense about it. But the father consulted the family doctor and told him that Gene was stuttering. The doctor took his word for it. (Practically all stutterers are originally diagnosed by laymen—parents and teachers—and "experts" almost never challenge the diagnoses!) He told the father to have Gene take a deep breath before trying to speak. Within forty-eight hours Gene was practically speechless. The deep breath became a frantic gasping from which Gene looked out with wide-eyed, helpless bewilderment. . . .

Source: This open letter was originally published as an article in the April 1941 issue of the magazine entitled *You and Your Child* (Conner Publications, Inc., Harrison, New York). It is presented in abridged form; our source was W. Johnson, S. F. Brown, J. F. Curtis, C. W. Edney, and J. Keaster. (1948). *Speech handicapped school children* (New York: Harper & Row), pp. 443–451. Reprinted by permission.

sleep that may be involved in different ways with sleep disorders. Night terrors, nightmares, and somnambulism are particularly difficult problems. Research seems to indicate that different stages of sleep are related to these conditions, as well as to different types of sleep disturbance, such as narcolepsy. More research in the area of sleep disorders is clearly needed, as the behaviors can be quite pronounced in some cases and are difficult to treat.

We also discuss toileting problems, with a particular focus on encopresis and enuresis. En-copresis represents problematic patterns of fecal expulsion, whereas enuresis refers to wetting difficulties. These disorders have been thought to be related, although evidence for this view is lacking. Treatment can be very difficult, and relapses are frequent.

A great deal of attention has been given to eating problems, particularly obesity. Although obesity is a seemingly simple problem on the surface, both physiological and psychological research has shown that it is an extremely complex disorder. A variety of treatments have been em-

BOX 7-5 • Azrin and Nunn's Treatment Procedures for Stuttering

Table 7-1 summarizes information regarding the subjects as well as data on stuttering frequency. Treatment procedures included the following:

1. *Inconvenience review.* The client reviews the inconveniences and annoyances that have resulted from stuttering.
2. *Awareness training.* The client deliberately stutters and is required to describe in great detail the nature of the episode, including the type of words stuttered, the situations or persons which provoke stuttering, and associated body movements such as blinking or facial or hand movements.
3. *Anticipation awareness.* The client is taught to alert himself to the likelihood of a stuttering episode.
4. *Relaxation training.* Several procedures are used to teach the client to relax himself when he becomes tense, as tension is generally associated with stuttering.

Table 7-1
Individual stuttering frequencies of 14 clients before and after treatment

CLIENT			PRETREATMENT FREQUENCY OF STUTTERING (PER DAY)	ONE-MONTH POSTTREATMENT FREQUENCY OF STUTTERING (PER DAY)	NO. OF WORDS STUTTERED ON TELEPHONE FOLLOW-UP
AGE (YR)	SEX	NO. OF YEARS STUTTERED			
25	female	12	10	0	0
37	female	23	45	0	0
23	male	17	30	0	0
44	female	34	500	8	0
25	female	17	2	0	0
44	male	36	10	2	0
30	male	27	1000	4	0
37	male	34	100	7	0
67	male	65	250	7	5
64	male	24	20	0	0
4	male	2	1000	0	0
19	male	15	100	4	0
9	female	6	150	0	0
26	male	23	1000	0	0
		Mean $\bar{x} = 24$	$\bar{x} = 372/day$	$\bar{x} = 2/day$	$\bar{x} = 04$

5. *Incompatible activities.* The client is taught activities that are incompatible with stuttering. The activities competing with stuttering are to stop speaking, to take a deep breath by exhaling and then slowly inhaling, to consciously relax one's chest and throat muscles, to formulate mentally the words to be spoken, to start speaking immediately after taking a deep breath, to emphasize the initial part of a statement, and to speak for short durations. As the speech becomes more fluent, the client gradually increases the duration of speech.
6. *Corrective training.* The client is given practice in initiating the competing activities the instant he starts stuttering. If necessary, the counselor reminds him to stop speaking and to carry out the competing activities.

Box 7-5 (Continued)

7. *Preventive training.* The client is given practice in engaging in competing activities when he anticipates that he will stutter.

8. *Symbolic rehearsal.* The client imagines himself in stuttering-prone situations and describes and demonstrates to the counselor the activities prescribed for such circumstances.

All of the procedures listed above were incorporated into a single counseling session of about 2 hours duration. No additional counseling sessions were given, although follow-up telephone contact provided encouragement and answered questions. A telephone group was also established among the patients to provide a network of support, information, and practice.

Figure 7-2 shows the degree of stuttering after treatment, expressed as a percentage of the pretreatment level as recorded by the clients. The figure shows that stuttering decreased by 94 percent on the first day and with minor variation continued to decline for the duration of the follow-up.

FIGURE 7-2 **Frequency of stuttering for 14 clients. The pretreatment level was obtained just prior to treatment. The frequency after treatment was obtained from the record kept by the clients each day. The data points are expressed as a percentage of the clients' pretreatment level. Accordingly, the pretreatment level is 100 percent. The treatment occurred during a single 2-hour session designated by the slash mark at the arrow. Fourteen clients are included in all of the data through the first month; the fourth month includes eight clients. The data are given for each day of the first week, for each week of the first month, and monthly thereafter.**

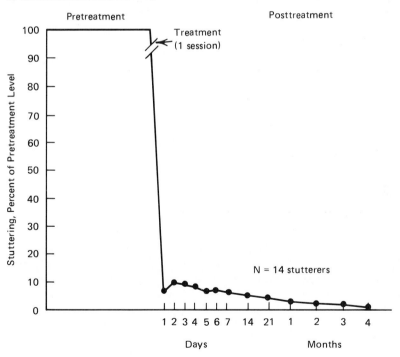

Source: Adapted and abridged from N. H. Azrin and R. G. Nunn. (1974). A rapid method of eliminating stuttering by a regulated breathing approach. *Behavior Research and Therapy, 12,* 279–286. Copyright 1974 by Pergamon Press, Ltd. Reprinted with permission.

ployed for obesity, and evidence of effectiveness has largely been disappointing. Anorexia nervosa is a complex eating disorder that has received increasing attention in the recent literature. Primarily a problem occurring in adolescent females, anorexia nervosa is a condition of self-inflicted starvation. Health complications can be extremely serious, even resulting in death in a certain percentage of cases, and treatment is quite difficult. Bulimia, or the "binge-purge" syndrome, is characterized by episodes of gorging followed by purging via vomiting or laxatives. Thought to be related to anorexia nervosa, bulimia is beginning to emerge as a distinct disorder. Research on and treatment of bulimia are difficult, partially because this covert behavior is guarded in a shroud of secrecy by those affected.

Speech disorders are the last topics discussed in this chapter. Speech disorders reportedly affect 7 to 10 percent of the general population, although research evidence has suggested great geographic variation. Delayed speech, elective mutism, and articulation disorders are discussed. Stuttering is probably the most widely recognized speech difficulty; however, it actually is found in a much smaller percentage of the population than other types of speech disorders, such as articulation problems. Treatment of speech disorders varies greatly, depending on the type and often the characteristics of the individual case. In some instances it is relatively simple, whereas in others it may be complex, lengthy, and of limited effectiveness. Learning-based treatments have met with particular success in the treatment of selected speech disorders.

chapter

8

Learning Disabilities

KEY TERMS

Auditory Association. The act of associating or relating ideas or information that is presented verbally.

Auditory Blending. The process of blending the parts of a word into an integrated whole.

Auditory Discrimination. The ability to distinguish between different sounds.

Dyslexia. A severe type of learning disability that impairs the ability to read; sometimes dyslexic individuals cannot read at all.

Hyperactivity. An excess of activity in inappropriate circumstances; also referred to as Hyperkinesis; often accompanied by attention deficits.

Neurological Dysfunction. Presumed malfunctioning of the neurological system; often the affected individual exhibits behavioral signs of brain injury.

Perceptual Disorder. A deficiency or abnormality in the reception and/or interpretation of stimuli.

Visual Discrimination. The process of distinguishing among visually presented stimuli.

INTRODUCTION

Learning disabilities, as a formally recognized category of disorders, are relatively new when compared to most childhood disorders. Although teachers and students have certainly encountered such difficulties for many decades, the label itself was first proposed in 1963 by Dr. Samuel Kirk, one of the pioneers in a field now known as "special education." Kirk's statement on learning disabilities defined the field. He described a type of disorder that had been recognized and studied (to some extent) before, but had never been given sufficient organized, formal attention to provide a solid information base. In recent years the concept of learning disabilities has had a phenomenal influence on special education, which makes the study of learning-disabled youngsters all the more exciting. To complete the background for this chapter, we need to briefly review the history of what we now call *learning disabilities.*

In a very significant sense, much of the progress made in working with children's problems has been initiated by parents. This may be even more true with learning disabilities than with other types of problems. Kirk's (1963) remarks on learning disabilities were part of a major address at a conference in Chicago—a meeting convened by parents to examine problems of "perceptually handicapped children." It would probably be a gross understatement to say that these parents were frustrated. The children being discussed did not fit neatly into any major category of handicapping condition at the time. They could not be considered as mentally retarded; in fact, they often were of normal or above-average intelligence. They exhibited a wide variety of behavioral characteristics. However, a common theme recurred in the stories that their parents exchanged. These youngsters were largely failing in school; they were often having difficulty in reading, spelling, and mathematics. Frequently, too, they were rather awkward and clumsy, and many were unable to participate adequately in a variety of

Communication between the teacher and the parents of a learning disabled child is essential. It may begin with just a note but to be effective will involve much more as time goes on.

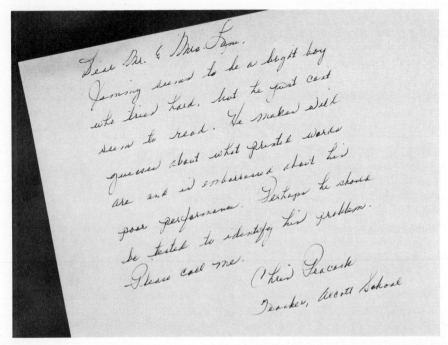

sports (but they were not physically handicapped by any traditional definition). In many cases there was a long history of disruptions and difficulty, such as that illustrated in Box 8-1. Simply stated, these children had learning disabilities; their problems largely defied the existing diagnostic and treatment techniques available at the time the label was proposed. In many ways our expertise

---

BOX 8-1 • *Home Wrecker: Tyke Leaves Trail of Terror*

GRAND RAPIDS, Mich. (UPI) It's not difficult to follow the trail of toddler Robin Hawkins—it's strewn with disasters.

In the last two months the 2-year-old has chalked up $2,296.37 in damages, including a wrecked car, television, dishwasher, and refrigerator.

Robin's trail of terror began with the toilet. Alice the cat got dunked, drowned, and flushed.

Her father . . . neatly tallied the expenses in a yellow tablet: $62.75 for the plumber, $2.50 for Alice.

That was only the beginning.

Robin decided to give teddy bear a bath—atop the heating element in the dishwasher. That cost her father $375 for repairs, $25 for smoke damage, and, of course, $8 for the teddy bear.

Then there was the refrigerator. Robin stuck some magnetic letters in the vents just before the family left home for the weekend, causing the motor to burn out. The cost: $310 for the refrigerator, $120 in spoiled food, and $3.75 for the magnetic letters.

"That evening, we sat down to watch TV," said Hawkins, an East Grand Rapids police officer. "Robin had twisted the fine tune so far that it broke inside."

Cost: $115.

The next day Mrs. Hawkins went to pick up her husband from his second job as a part-time security officer. Robin was left asleep in her safety seat; the keys were in her mother's purse inside the car.

"We heard the car start up and we ran outside, just in time to watch the car start down the street," Hawkins said.

Robin ran into a tree. Cost: $1,029.52 in repairs.

A few days later, Robin tried to play some tapes in the family stereo. Cost: $36 for tapes and $35 for tape deck repairs.

Shortly afterwards, the couple parked their car halfway in the garage after a shopping trip because they were planning to unload groceries. Robin was strapped in her safety seat.

"My wife had the keys, so we figured everything was OK," Hawkins said.

Everything was OK, until they heard a loud noise and went outside to find the automatic garage door bouncing off the hood of the car with you know who locked inside, pushing the remote control. Cost: $120.

Robin also lifted $620 out of the cash register at the supermarket, drilled 50 holes in the walls of a rental property owned by her parents, painted walls with nail polish, and slipped the garden tractor out of gear so it rolled down the driveway, narrowly missing a neighbor out on a walk.

The grand total, including miscellaneous damage of $53.85, comes to $2,296.37.

"Some day when she comes and asks me why she isn't getting any allowance, I'll show her this," Hawkins said, waving the yellow pad containing his daughter's damages.

---

has not progressed greatly since that time, although some advances have been made.

It is not difficult to see why parents attending the Chicago conference were frustrated. Many of them had exhausted their resources attempting to seek a "cure" or simply *some* help for their children. They could not be satisfied with the advice and assistance provided to parents of mentally retarded children, or to those with blind or deaf children. Their youngsters had none of these handicaps. It was not uncommon to encounter an individual child who, by virtue of measured IQ, could be considered "bright," yet was unable to learn. Consequently, the parents were doing the only thing they could at this point — attempting to marshal an organized effort, with a common goal, in order to promote funding for research and training of professionals who could better teach their children.

The common goal was crucial and necessitated having a common language or diagnostic label. Prior to 1963 (and to some extent, today), people working with these children had a variety of names for their problems: *perceptually handicapped, brain-injured,* or *minimal brain dysfunction* to name a few. Although terminology may seem rather unimportant, the various labels served to split the people engaged in research and professional training into factions that were not collaborating or even cooperating toward a productive end. Each perspective viewed the child narrowly, with some concentrating on supposed developmental delays and others on perceptual problems. No one faction wanted to consider other approaches, and zealous efforts often generated more debate than serious comprehensive study of the problem. Lerner (1981) has characterized this situation in terms of the familiar fable of the six blind men from India attempting to describe an elephant. Early predominant conceptions of the learning-disabled child were almost as dramatically disparate and narrow as the blind men's descriptions in the fable. Thus it is not surprising that parents were eager for a label — a term that would give them a common focus and unify their efforts.

The label of learning disabilities was enthusiastically accepted. As Hallahan and Cruickshank noted, "In some cases it was accepted with religious fervor" (1973, p. 7). The notion of learning disabilities was simple — in fact, deceptively simple, as we shall soon see. The label was essentially positive and did not carry the stigma associated with other terms, notably *mental retardation.* However, it also created some immediate and serious difficulties that continue to plague the field.

Many of the participants at the Chicago meeting were so intent on terminology that they virtually ignored the long series of qualifiers and cautionary statements presented by Kirk. He strongly desired that these children be conceptualized mainly in terms of descriptions of their behavior, rather than as members of a labeled category associated with technical jargon. Instead, a category and a labeled entity emerged in full bloom, and behavioral descriptions were often neglected. To make matters worse, the category of *learning disabilities* had yet to develop a solid conceptual base utilizing a foundation of research data. Although some research had been conducted, it was very limited, sporadic, and so unsystematic that a cohesive body of knowledge about the problem did not exist. Also, there were practically no personnel trained in the area who could help the children and train others to do so.

PREVALENCE

In this professional context, the field of learning disabilities was born and began to grow at a phenomenal rate. Because of imprecise use of the label, it is difficult to determine how many children were and are identified as learning-disabled at any one time. Epidemiological studies that would provide empirical evidence concerning prevalence of learning disabilities have not been undertaken to the same degree as in other areas of disabilities. As we indicate later, definitions of learning disability have varied greatly over time and between geographical locations. This imprecision, of course, makes even gross estimates of frequency very unreliable. However, it is clear that the learning disability area experienced an explosive growth as illustrated by statistics cited in the 1975–1976 *Yearbook of Special Education*. This volume indicated that over 42,000 schools in the United States had identified learning-disabled children by the spring of 1970, and that nearly 28,000 of the schools were providing specialized instruction. This represents a substantial proportion of the total number of 81,000 operating schools at the time, and is impressive in view of the fact that only 7 years had passed since the term *learning disabilities* had been coined. A further indication of this early rapid growth is found in the following quotation from this same volume: "The handicapped subset that has had the most dramatic growth rate at the elementary level during the last 5 years is special learning disabilities. In many local education agencies, the . . . annual rate of increase (for this group) still exceeds 250 percent" (*Yearbook of Special Education,* 1975–1976, p. 415).

In addition to a phenomenal growth rate, the prevalence figures for learning disabilities have always varied greatly depending on the source, with some being so high as to be questionable. For example, Wallace and McLoughlin (1979) found prevalence figures ranging from 1 to 28 percent of school children, whereas at about the same time the National Advisory Committee on Handicapped Children estimated the prevalence at between 1 and 3 percent of school-age children. Regardless of which prevalence rate one accepts, learning disabilities clearly represent a very large proportion of all exceptional children served in the schools. During the 1983–1984 school year there were over 4.3 million children identified as exceptional being served, and nearly 2 million or about 42 percent of these were labeled as learning-disabled (U.S. Department of Education, 1985).

The history of the learning disabilities field can provide at least two important lessons. First of all, the power of organized parent groups became evident as perhaps never before. Certainly this was not the first group of parents ever to organize, but it may well have been the most potent. Parents of the mentally retarded had achieved a good deal of progress, but they had the advantage of a field that was relatively well established. Parents of the learning-disabled created a massive

focus of activity nearly overnight, and from a point that virtually had no focus. This brings us to our second point: While the growth of the field of learning disabilities was indeed rapid, it was undisciplined. There was no solid, systematic program of scientific investigation on which to base programs of personnel preparation. However, there was an increasing demand for qualified personnel, as suggested by the statistics cited above. Frequently the individuals pressed into service had little or no training. This occurred in all institutions and professional groups—teachers, psychologists, and university faculty. Consequently, instructors were often hired more on the basis of their interest in the problem than because of their actual knowledge or experience. This situation led to some very predictable outcomes. Programs were more often based on misconception than on solid principles of instruction or diagnosis derived from research. And the children involved suffered. Classes for the learning-disabled quickly became dumping grounds for children with all types of difficulties. The second lesson that the development of the field of learning disabilities teaches us, therefore, is the danger of developing a massive program of activity without a firm conceptual base and a foundation that will facilitate scientific knowledge acquisition. The field of learning disabilities is still plagued with the residue from these early errors, as becomes evident in the following sections.

DEFINING LEARNING DISABILITIES

In the context of our previous discussion it is not surprising that there is little agreement on the definition of learning disabilities. The term was introduced, as noted earlier, in response to growing pressure for a common term. Kirk (1963) was very cautious with his language as he proposed the term *learning disabilities.* He was extremely concerned about the intended purpose—the need for a label that would be useful for research, behavioral management, or training. His concerns went largely unheeded, and the field expanded in an uncontrolled fashion. Children with a wide variety of problems were labeled as learning-disabled, and often definitions either were very loose and vague or were tailored to cover those who were already being served, in order to justify their special treatment. Kass (1969) noted five different definitions that had emerged over a 6-year period, whereas Vaughn and Hodges (1973) used 10 definitions in a survey to determine the amount of agreement among special educators. Cruickshank (1972) indicated that there were over 40 different terms in the English language to describe what was basically the same child behavior. It was his opinion that the variation in terminology was "in itself a significant barrier to the development of a coherent program." Added to this was what he called "no common denominator of understanding," which further compounded the difficulties of a field lacking conceptual clarity and experiencing unprecedented growth (Cruickshank, 1972, p. 382).

It is clear from the discussion presented thus far that defining learning disabilities is not a simple task. In fact, some have viewed the definition of learning disabilities with a very jaundiced eye. For example, Divorky (1974) has stated, "The truth is that learning disabled are whomever the diagnosticians want them to be" (p. 21). Despite such views and the difficulty in being precise, we attempt to provide a definition here. Perhaps the most widely accepted legal definition was presented in the Education for All Handicapped Children Act of 1975 (more commonly known as Public Law 94-142):

> Specific learning disability means a disorder in one or more of the basic psychological processes involved in understanding or in using language, spoken or written, which may manifest itself in an imperfect ability to listen, think, speak, read, write, spell, or to do mathematical calculations. The term includes such conditions as perceptual handicaps, brain injury, minimal brain disfunction, dyslexia, and developmental aphasia. The term does not include children who have learning problems which are primarily the result of visual, hearing, or motor handicaps, of mental retardation, or of environmental, cultural, or economic disadvantage. (1975, Section 5(b)(4))

In many ways, this definition resembles the statement with which the term *learning disabilities*

began in 1963. It is clearly very broad and quite vague in many respects. It would certainly make a behaviorist uncomfortable, for it fails to specify the behaviors characteristic of learning disabilities. However, it is important to remember that this definition is set in the form of a law—one that must necessarily be broad in order to apply to many different settings, children, and purposes.

Learning disabilities is a general educational term. Although it may serve certain administrative and other purposes satisfactorily, it is insufficiently specific for research purposes (Harber, 1981) and must even be more precisely and behaviorally defined for instructional uses. The term can be effectively used only as a generalized referent or umbrella term, in that it encompasses a variety of specific types of problems (Hammill, Leigh, McNutt, & Larsen, 1981). In fact, some of the narrowly defined *types* of learning disabilities, such as dyslexia, have themselves been characterized as a collection of different syndromes (Benton & Pearl, 1978; Healey, 1984; Hynd & Cohen, 1983; Hynd & Hynd, 1984). This notion is further emphasized in an article by Rosenthal and Allen (1978), in which they reviewed research attempting to distinguish among children with hyperkinesis, minimal brain dysfunction, and learning disabilities. They asserted that "there is probably such a degree of overlap between these categories that perhaps half of the subjects in a learning disability study might also be labeled either minimally brain dysfunctional or hyperkinetic" (p. 693).

Rosenthal and Allen's point highlights the difficulty of discussing such disorders in terms of highly specific labels or categories. Definitions, causes, and behavioral characteristics often become confusingly intertwined. In some instances children may exhibit similar behavior, but each child's behavior stems from a different cause. In other cases the reverse is true: The same cause may generate different behaviors. Perhaps nowhere is the complexity of the human organism as evident as it is with learning disabilities. In order to minimize this difficulty, we now focus on children's behavioral characteristics and attempt to speak in specific behavioral, biological, and observable terms as much as possible.

DESCRIBING AND CLASSIFYING LEARNING DISABILITIES

Learning-disabled children have been described as having a mild disorder (Idol-Maestas, Lloyd, & Lilly, 1981). They have also been long noted for exhibiting many different behaviors. As isolated incidents, such behaviors may not be abnormal except when they recur or when they occur in combinations that substantially handicap children's daily performance. It has been said many times that all of us are learning-disabled to some degree or in some fashion. This may be an attempt to counteract any harm done by labeling some children as learning-disabled. There are some striking differences between the literature on learning disabilities and that focusing on other disorders. It is not uncommon for descriptions of learning-disabled children to be void of references to actual research; instead, it often appears to be based on unsystematic clinical observations that are presented as "common knowledge" and marked by ambiguities (Kavale & Nye, 1981). In some cases the actual behavior of the children seems to be ignored in favor of relying on stereotypes (Bryan,

1974). On the other hand, agreement on behavioral descriptions by parents, teachers, and psychologists is sufficiently frequent to suggest that learning disabilities do exist. In any case, readers should try to maintain an appropriate perspective as we describe the characteristics of learning disabilities on the following pages. We describe behaviors that are commonly discussed by those who are working with children labeled as learning-disabled. Often these syndromes do not have a firm empirical base, although where such evidence exists we so indicate (with relief). Furthermore, it is useful to remember that normality is socially defined by many sources, as we have discussed in Chapter 1.

As noted earlier, learning disabilities have often been viewed as mild disorders (Idol-Maestas et al. 1981; Ysseldyke & Algozzine, 1979). This perspective has received relatively little attention with respect to empirical validation, despite some attempts to develop such a conceptualization (Deloach, Earl, Brown, Poplin, & Warner, 1981; Torgesen & Dice, 1980; Weller, 1980; Weller, Strawser, & Buchanan, 1985). In addition to severity, literature trends in learning disabilities

Learning disabilities can lead to intense frustration, as suggested by this youngster's behavior. Identifying the actual problem is often not easy.

have begun to address subtypes of the generic disorder (e.g., Healey, 1984; Hynd & Cohen, 1983; Hynd & Hynd, 1984; Strawser & Weller, 1985), although emergence of a widely accepted classification scheme for subtyping has not occurred.

Hyperactivity

Hyperactive behavior or *hyperkinesis* has been examined in considerable depth in Chapter 4, which addresses social disorders in children. However, hyperactivity must also be briefly considered in the context of learning disabilities, because it is perhaps the most common behavioral characteristic associated with children who are labeled as learning-disabled (Bryan, 1974). In fact, hyperactivity is frequently the first behavioral characteristic mentioned in descriptions of learning disabilities by teachers (Hardman, Drew, & Egan, 1987). It is often reported that such children cannot sit still for more than a very short time, fidget a great deal, and are in general excessively active. Such behavior is often viewed as one of the "soft" signs indicating neurological dysfunction.

It is important to note that not all children labeled as learning-disabled are hyperkinetic. In addition, the stereotype of hyperkinesis seems to have led many to expect and consequently to see hyperactivity in children with learning problems. Although hyperkinesis is commonly viewed as involving a general excess of activity, evidence suggests that this may be incorrect and that we might find it more fruitful to look at the appropriateness of a child's behavior in particular settings. Hyperkinetic children do seem to exhibit higher levels of inappropriate activity than their normal counterparts under structured circumstances, such as might be found in the usual type of classroom instruction. However, most research indicates no difference between hyperactive and other children in unstructured situations, such as play and other nonacademic settings (Baxley & LeBlanc, 1976; Whalen & Henker, 1976).

Clearly, hyperactivity is common in learning-disabled children. However, observations of hyperactivity alone are not sufficient to lead to a diagnosis of learning disabilities, and not all learning-disabled children are hyperactive. Furthermore, a generalized superficial view of hyperactivity is not likely to be of great value in treatment, because it seems to be somewhat situation-specific; that is, in some contexts these children may be overly active, but not in others. Research aimed at clarifying the relationship between hyperactivity and the other constellation of attributes associated with learning disabilities is essential if we are to advance our understanding and treatment of this population.

Perceptual Problems

Children who are labeled learning-disabled often have perceptual problems. Abnormalities of perception have played a historic and prominent role in clinical and research descriptions of such youngsters. In fact, the field of learning disabilities seems to have grown out of the early work of Werner and Strauss (e.g., 1939, 1941) and Goldstein (1936, 1939), who were studying the perceptual, cognitive, and behavioral effects of brain injury. The notions relating perceptual disorders to learning disabilities enjoyed considerable popularity over the years. Interest in this view has diminished somewhat recently, because of failure to establish a clear connection between such problems and neurological dysfunction. However, attention to perceptual difficulties in learning-disabled children has not completely dissipated. As recently as 1977, Cruickshank contended that perceptual factors were the key to defining learning disabilities. In a somewhat earlier statement, he asserted that "irrespective of the presence or absence of diagnosed neurological dysfunction, learning disabilities are essentially and almost always the result of perceptual problems based on the neurological system" (Cruickshank, 1972, p. 383).

Despite the assessment and conceptual difficulties, perceptual problems represent a rather appealing explanation for some of the behaviors exhibited by learning-disabled children (for example, the inability to copy from a chalkboard or to recognize properties that distinguish geometric shapes such as circles and triangles). In a general sense, children with perceptual disorders do evidence behaviors that suggest "a disturbance in the awareness of objects, relations, or qualities, in-

Reversal of letters is characteristic of some type of learning disabilities.

volving the interpretation of sensory stimulation" (Lerner, 1981 p. 30). Regardless of the particular etiology involved, learning-disabled children have a number of difficulties in processing sensory information.

Visual Perception Problems Humans receive information from the environment through a number of sensory systems with varying degrees of efficiency and accuracy. The area most often identified as problematic for learning-disabled children is visual perception. Children with visual perception problems may exhibit a variety of specific deficiencies that can seriously interfere with school achievement. They may see a visual stimulus only as unrelated parts rather than as a whole or integrated pattern. Lerner (1981) provides the following example, which may have particular relevance to school performance at an early age. She notes that "when asked to identify the capital letter 'A,' the child with perceptual disorders may perceive three unrelated lines rather than a meaningful whole" (p. 30).

Children with visual perceptual disorders may also have difficulty with *figure-ground discrimination*. Figure-ground discrimination, which

most of us master easily, is the process of distinguishing a visually presented object from its background. In school, a child with this type of disorder may have problems focusing on a given word or line on a printed page. This particular example raises certain questions that recur throughout this chapter, and that have plagued the perceptual theorists specifically and workers in learning disabilities generally. Does the inability to focus on or to identify a particular word provide substantive evidence of a perceptual problem—specifically, a figure-ground discrimination difficulty? It is conceivable that the child merely has an attention problem (another characteristic often attributed to children labeled as learning-disabled). It is also possible that the child cannot remember the word (memory problems have also been frequently attributed to such children). Perhaps the child has not been effectively taught the word (an instructional deficiency). There is no question that these all may be reasonable explanations for the same behavior, and it is difficult to determine which of them are operative in an individual case. This discussion also emphasizes the relative scarcity and imprecise nature of research information currently available. Clearly, research efforts in the

227

area of learning disabilities must be intensified and become more analytical than has been the case previously.

Children labeled as having learning disabilities are frequently described as having difficulty in *visual discrimination* (the ability to discriminate one visual stimulus from another). Such problems may result in several behaviors that are often encountered by teachers of these youngsters. The children may not be able to discriminate between certain letters or words (e.g., *W* and *V*, *sit* and *sat*). They may exhibit letter reversals, which logically relate to a visual discrimination problem (for instance, horizontal reversals of such letters as *b* and *d*, or vertical reversals of letters such as *b* and *p*). Discrimination errors such as those noted above are not unusual in all younger children and normally decrease with age. The question then becomes one of determining when a "problem" exists. Hallahan, Kauffman, and Lloyd (1985) have noted, "It is the child who continues to have difficulty and who even makes frequent errors on easily discriminable letters who should be given extra attention" (pp. 33–34). Evidence suggests that reversal and rotation errors of artificial graphic forms drop dramatically with age and are relatively infrequent by ages 7 or 8 (Gibson, Gibson, Pick, & Osser, 1962). Since letter reversal may represent a process similar to reversing artificial figures, a child who continues to transpose letters frequently beyond the age of about 7 or 8 may have a potential problem warranting investigation.

We have described a number of problem behaviors shown by learning-disabled children and often attributed to disorders of visual perception. Certainly we have not examined all visual perception problems that have appeared from time to time in the literature; our purpose is to be illustrative rather than exhaustive. Some youngsters have also been characterized as having problems of perception in other sensory areas, notably auditory and haptic. Although these have received somewhat less attention, they warrant brief discussion to provide a more complete picture of the perceptual difficulties associated with learning disabilities.

Auditory and Haptic Perception Problems *Auditory perception* involves the ability to recognize, organize, and interpret stimuli that are received through the sense of hearing. *Haptic perception* involves the process of obtaining information via the tactile (sensation of touch) and kinesthetic (body sensation from movement and/or position) systems. We now discuss behaviors which are regarded as problems in both auditory and haptic perception. As we examine these disorders, it will become evident how they can create difficulties in school as well as in other environments.

Singly or in various combinations, difficulties in four different components of auditory perception have often been reported in children who are labeled as learning-disabled: difficulties in *discrimination, association, memory,* and *blending*. Since auditory stimuli represent a substantial source of information in school (as do visual stimuli), problems in auditory perception may be a significant performance handicap in this environment. For example, children with difficulties in *auditory discrimination* may not be able to distinguish between the sounds of certain syllables or words. They may also have problems in identifying particular other sounds such as the doorbell, and in distinguishing between that sound and another. Children who have difficulties in *auditory blending* may be unable to blend the phonic elements of a word together into a consolidated whole as they say the word (for example, an inability to blend the phonemes *m-a-n* to form the word *man*). Auditory association and memory are of obvious significance because of the way in which much of our schooling occurs. A child who has difficulty in *auditory memory* may not be able to recall information that is presented verbally, such as is often the case with the alphabet, the days of the week, and the months in the year. Children with *auditory association* deficits often cannot make simple associations between ideas or information items that are presented verbally (such as simple analogies).

Clearly, we may encounter children who have a particularly difficult time with information presented either through the visual or the auditory

sensory systems. When such problems are identified it often becomes necessary to teach material
through alternate modes of presentation. Depending on the nature of the disorder, one may choose
to present material predominantly in an auditory
mode (such as using tape recordings of books for
an individual who has visual perception problems).
Such a notion has been employed for some learning-disabled individuals at school when they are
required to read or to take tests that represent
visual stimuli. For those with deficiencies in auditory perception, other alternatives are obviously
needed. Unfortunately, we seldom find individuals
with a "pure" deficit in one perceptual system,
which complicates instructional and therapy approaches rather substantially.

Learning-disabled children may also have
problems in *haptic perception,* which includes
both tactile and kinesthetic sensation. These deficiencies are not common (Mercer, 1983), but are
thought to play important roles in certain school-
related activities (Ayres, 1975; Wedell, 1973). As
stated earlier, tactile perception involves information obtained via body movement or position.
Handwriting is thought to rely partially on haptic
perceptual abilities, in that a child must receive
tactile information relative to holding the pencil
and kinesthetic sensation regarding movement
during the process of writing. Children with difficulties in this area may be unusually slow writers,
may have problems with regard to spacing and
forming letters, may not be able to stay on the
lines, and may show a variety of other difficulties
that combine with perceptual disorders described
earlier.

Comments Earlier in the chapter, we raised
questions concerning the amount of empirical evidence available pertaining to children labeled as
learning-disabled. As we conclude the discussion
of perceptual problems, this issue must be mentioned once again. *Perceptual dysfunction* is a theoretical construct used to explain certain types of
behavioral deficits. Such behavioral deficits have
often been reported by teachers and other clinicians working with these children (Bryan, 1974).

Perceptual-motor difficulties have often been associated
with learning disabilities.

However, the reader must be cautioned that explanatory theories such as neurological dysfunction are largely deduced by analogy and are not
directly observable. We know that certain children exhibit various constellations of behaviors
that are similar to the behavior of other subjects,
such as adults with known cerebral injury. However, they also resemble younger children more
than ones their own age, suggesting that general
physical immaturity may play a role. For the children who are our immediate concern, knowledge
is mainly inferential.

Memory/Information Processing

The ability to remember what one learns is
essential to daily life and central to successful performance in school. Memory and other cognitive

processes are complex phenomena that have been studied by experimental psychologists for decades. Because it is difficult to study cognition directly, we theorize about the manner in which these functions occur, based on a person's observable behavior. Most of our theories are several steps removed from what is observed. Memory may be one of the best examples of the intuitive process of theory construction and the difficulties involved in developing and studying such theories. Memory is the end product of several cognitive steps. In a very simplified sense, one must perceive a stimulus and process (encode) the information; store the information; and, finally, retrieve the information and somehow indicate that it has been retrieved (recognize or recall the information). Thus in order to study memory an experimenter must be reasonably certain, *at a minimum,* that the research particpant has perceived and encoded the material to be remembered.

Short- and Long-Term Memory Despite nearly a century of study, memory still is only partially understood. This limited understanding must be kept in mind as we discuss this topic in the present chapter. Theories regarding the manner in which the memory functions have varied over the years. Earlier theories focused a great deal of attention on differences between long-term memory (LTM) and short-term memory (STM). Initially, the concepts were defined simply in terms of the time interval between learning and recall. These distinctions soon became viewed as primitive, and much contemporary memory research no longer examines performance simply in terms of STM versus LTM. The learning/memory phenomenon is now more often conceptualized in terms of information processing, which involves consideration of the interrelationships of perception, attention, storage, and retrieval of information.

Children labeled as having learning disabilities have long been informally characterized as having memory and other information-processing problems (Hall, 1980). Frustrated teachers continually bemoan the fact that such children may learn something one day but will have forgotten it by the following day. Certainly such forgetting has

happened to all of us. However, this type of behavior occurs so often in learning-disabled children that some consideration is clearly warranted here. The clinically reported memory difficulties have been so frequent that they have led to a variety of common-sense theories (such as the "leaky bucket" hypothesis, in which the child is taught a fact, but memory failures result in performance failure later). In some cases there have been reports of poor ability to recall material that was recently learned, but reasonable or good ability to remember events or material encountered in the more distant past. (A clinical account of this phenomenon is found in the final pages of this chapter.) All of these factors make the study of memory in the learning-disabled even more fascinating, and also make the problems of such individuals more perplexing.

It is paradoxical that memory problems have been so evident in the clinical descriptions of learning-disabled children, and yet formal research examining this topic has been rather scanty. This research deficit is even more striking, because the memory research efforts in normal and other deviant populations have been so intense. Memory characteristics of learning-disabled children remain relatively unexplored or, at best, examined in a piecemeal manner. Some research has found no differences between the STM performance of learning-disabled youngsters and their nondisabled counterparts, while LTM performance has appeared deficient (for instance, Bauer, 1977; Swanson, 1979). Other investigations have indicated LTM (24 hours) to be similar between learning-disabled and normal children (Raskin, 1968, 1971). Thus in the face of continuing clinical reports of poor memory, research results remain mixed. This type of evidence base has led some to suggest that children labeled as learning-disabled may have *different* rather than generally deficient memory and cognitive abilities (Hall, 1980)—a notion that has held considerable appeal in the field for some time. Keener analysis than a LTM–STM perspective is likely to be more successful in pinpointing specific instructional emphases for the learning-disabled than viewing them as generally cognitively deficient (for example, see Finch & Spirito, 1980; McKinney & Haskins, 1980).

Attention Problems   It has been suggested earlier that learning-disabled children may have an attention problem. This hypothesis has also been suggested in relation to their information-processing abilities. Teachers frequently report that these children are unable to sustain attention to lengthy tasks (short attention span), and some research evidence has supported this conclusion (for instance, Sykes, Douglas, & Morgenstern, 1973). However, much of the experimental research related to cognition has addressed the issue of *selective* attention problems—that is, an inability to focus attention on important stimuli and screen out or ignore irrelevant stimuli. This has been examined by studying what is known as *incidental learning.* In most learning tasks, there are certain stimuli that are important and central to acquiring the information (such as the idea presented in the narrative on a printed page). In addition, there are usually some stimuli that are unimportant—in fact, irrelevant—to acquiring the information (such as the page numbers, the location of a certain passage on a page, or the color of the book cover). Individuals who use selective attention will tend to ignore the irrelevant stimuli (or at least to attend to them to a lesser degree) and to focus on the stimuli that are central to the task. Evidence suggests that learning-disabled children do not employ selective attention to the same degree that normal children do (Hallahan, Kauffman, & Ball, 1973; Pelham & Ross, 1977; Tarver, Hallahan, Kauffman, & Ball, 1976). These studies consistently found that normal children recalled more central information than did their learning-disabled counterparts. On the other hand, the learning-disabled children either equaled or surpassed their normal classmates in their recall of *irrelevant* information. This evidence suggests that learning-disabled children focus attention approximately equally on relevant and irrelevant stimuli, and thus may not employ selective attention. Data also suggest that selective attention abilities improve with age for both learning-disabled and normal children, but that learning-disabled children

may be 2 to 4 years behind their normal peers. Such findings have been interpreted as supporting the idea that a developmental delay accounts for learning disabilities (Pelham & Ross, 1977; Tarver et al., 1976).

Material Organization   The effect of the degree of organization of material on the memory of learning-disabled individuals has been examined in a series of studies. The notion is quite simple: Material that is organized in some fashion (for example, words in conceptual categories, such as examples of fruit, occupations, and the like) should be more easily learned and remembered than material that is not organized (for instance, randomly ordered words). This effect has been clearly demonstrated with both normal and mentally retarded populations (Drew & Altman, 1970; Simpson, King, & Drew, 1970). However, studies with learning-disabled subjects indicated that there were no differences between groups receiving organized material (words presented in lists that were conceptually categorized, such as animals, flowers, and foods, and groups receiving unorganized material) (Freston & Drew, 1974; Parker, Freston, & Drew, 1975). These results were surprising and particularly interesting in view of performances observed in the other populations. This line of research was extended by Dumaresq (1976), who found that when multiple learning trials were provided and the subjects were given specific categorization cues ("Tell me all the animals you remember"), learning-disabled children profited from material organization. These results seem to suggest that the learning-disabled may require more practice and explicit cues to improve their learning and recall of material. The word organization studies just reviewed used auditory stimuli. Suiter and Potter (1978) further pursued this research with learning-disabled children but employed visual stimuli. Their results indicated that subjects receiving organized material performed better than those receiving unorganized material. Thus, with these subjects, memory performance may be similar to that of normal and mentally retarded subjects when visual stimuli are used.

Reinforcement/Incentives   In a different line of research, Freibergs and Douglas (1969) compared hyperkinetic and normal children on a concept-learning task under two conditions of reinforcement: continuous and partial (intermittent) schedules. No performance differences were evident between the groups under the continuous-reinforcement condition, in which *every* correct response was reinforced. However, the hyperkinetic children performed more poorly under the intermittent-reinforcement schedule. Subjects were retested 2 months after the cessation of training—an interval that can easily be considered as a test of LTM. Results of the retest were similar to those obtained earlier, with no differences between hyperkinetic and normal subjects receiving continuous reinforcement. However, the performance of the hyperkinetic children under intermittent reinforcement had deteriorated in comparison to their normal counterparts. These results, once again, suggest an interesting line of investigation needing further work.

The employment of reinforcement and incentives with learning-disabled children has also received attention as a means of potentially altering the manner in which they apply learning strategies (Torgesen, 1982). This line of work has emerged out of rather consistent observations that learning-disabled youngsters have what some would term *attitudinal* or *motivational* problems; they often appear to be rather inactive learners and do not engage in many learning tasks with strategies that are effective for mastery. Although it is not evident that performance incentives influence strategies that they can apply (that is, modify strategies), incentives do seem to "increase the rate and consistency with which these children apply strategies already in their repertoire" (Torgesen, 1982, p. 49). This perspective is receiving continuing attention (for example, Licht, 1984; Licht & Kistner, 1986) and may provide important information pertaining both to the learning difficulties of learning-disabled children and to their treatment.

Comments   As we conclude this section, it seems important to restate a notion that has been mentioned previously. We have discussed several characteristics that have been attributed to and studied in learning-disabled children. We have not, however, elected to *characterize* such individuals. It is our opinion that in doing so we would inevitably err in some fashion. It remains our contention that the term *learning disabilities* is a broad, umbrella-type label that may include many different specific problems. Clinicians and researchers alike may observe any of a variety of difficulties, in combination or singly, in an individual child carrying such a label.

DEVELOPMENTAL FACTORS

Theories of human development have played an important, although not always pre-eminent, role in learning disabilities for many years. In many cases, developmental delay perspectives have been involved in researchers' frustrated attempts to derive a single, comprehensive theory relating to the causation of learning disabilities. Developmental theory has also emerged because performance of such children in a number of areas resembles that of younger normal children (for instance, see Bryan & Bryan, 1982; Houck, 1984; Smith, 1983).

It has been suggested that learning-disabled youngsters show a lag in neurological development (Goldstein & Myers, 1980). In some cases, evidence supporting such a developmental lag has been found as a peripheral result in studies focusing primarily on other topics (such as language ability, hyperactivity, or attention); this is not surprising, because for the most part neurological status can only be inferred from behavior. Others, however, have assessed behavior with the basic intent of studying neurological involvement (for instance, Dykman, Ackerman, Clements, & Peters, 1971; John et al., 1980). Although it is seldom that separate investigations consistently examine precisely the same factors, there is considerable evidence suggesting neurological immaturities and development lag in learning-disabled children. It also appears that such youngsters are most different from their normal counterparts at younger ages. It is suggested by some that certain areas of neurological maturation deficiency tend to diminish or "catch up" with time, whereas others do not. Denckla (1979) has indicated that the immaturities most likely to catch up involve early-maturing skills, which need only reach a certain developmental "floor" to permit academic progress (such as left-right letter reversals). In contrast, late-emerging, more complex skills that require a relatively high level of development often seem to remain immature (such as rapidly recalling names or words from memory) (Rourke, 1976).

Learning-disabled children have often been described as exhibiting extremely uneven abilities across skill areas. Their mental development progresses in "fits and starts" and thereby proceeds very unevenly in some cases (Kinsbourne & Caplan, 1979). The skill areas that are significantly delayed often appear quite like those of younger normal children (Abrams, 1968).

ETIOLOGY

In our examination of the learning-disabled, we have described a wide variety of specific problems that may apply to an individual. It is hardly surprising that a variety of known and hypothesized factors may cause or contribute to the disability. If, in fact, we are examining many different specific disabilities in this chapter, it is logical that many different causes may be involved, all of which contribute to learning problems. The behaviors found in learning-disabled children have been explained in several fashions. Hypothesized causes of learning disabilities have included such factors as birth injuries, nutritional abnormalities, developmental delay, poisoning by environmental elements, genetic defects, and poor teaching. In addition, some authors have suggested that learning disabilities are no more than the extremes of biological variation. Consider the following quote from Lynn, Gluckin, and Kripke (1979, p. 139): "In fact, the causes of learning disabilities are unknown. If we knew what caused a learning disability, we would call it by another name." They continue, "No *honest* classification of learning disabilities can be based on causes, because the causes are unknown" (p. 158, emphasis ours).

Thus, as we discuss causation in learning disabilities, it is important for the reader to remember that precise knowledge is largely absent and that much of what we are describing represents theory, hypotheses, analogies, and inferences drawn from other populations, situations, or information. Someday, though, we expect that the disorder will be defined more precisely and that there will be a better understanding of its etiology and how to treat it.

Neurological Damage

We have already mentioned the assumption held by some that learning disabilities may be caused by brain damage, or at least by some type of neurological problem (Adelman, 1979; Gaddes, 1980; Hynd & Cohen, 1983; Ramirez, 1982). Opinions regarding this perspective vary greatly. Some authors have taken a very strong position favoring a neurologically based explanation. For example, Hallahan and Cruickshank (1973) have stated that "the problems of the great majority of children described as 'learning disabled,' in our opinion, are fundamentally based in neurological function or dysfunction" (p. 12). In most circumstances, the existence of neurological damage as a cause is presumptive. This has led many professionals to discontinue the pursuit of neurological bases of learning disabilities. Until technology advances permit more precise assessment of neurological status, neither of the theoretical extremes described above can be verified. Most likely, there are some children labeled as learning-disabled whose problems are based on neurological damage. It is also probable that others with the same global label and similar abnormal behavior do not have any neurological dysfunction.

Many factors could result in the neurological damage suspected in some learning-disabled children. For example, difficulties encountered in prenatal development could result in such damage (such as low birthweight or inadequate gestational age at birth, Rh blood incompatibility between the mother and fetus, or serious maternal infection). Similarly, abnormalities during the birth process may also cause neurological damage (inadequate oxygen supply to the baby or abnormal positioning of the fetus during delivery), or damage may occur after birth, as when a child has convulsions from a high fever. These are merely examples of factors that may have a significant impact on the neurological status of an individual. They are also relevant to childhood disorders other than learning disabilities and are discussed more completely in Chapter 9, which examines mental retardation, and Chapter 3, on poverty-related risks to development.

There has been some empirical link between neurological dysfunction and learning disabilities. For example, Frank and Levinson (1973) studied 115 children identified as having a particular type of learning disability called dyslexia (inability to read). They found brain dysfunction in over 97 percent of their subjects. Efforts have also included using the electroencephalograph (EEG) to study the learning-disabled. This instrument measures the electrical energy generated by the cerebral cortex and provides some information regarding the functioning of the brain. Results have been mixed; some learning-disabled children exhibit abnormalities, whereas others do not (Myklebust & Boshes, 1969). Such results may be explained by the wide variety of problems that are grouped together under the term *learning disabilities*. However, results of this nature may also be caused by imprecise measurement; many questions have been raised regarding the utility of the EEG for this purpose (Page-El & Grossman, 1973). The EEG has also been combined with digital computers for purposes of collecting and analyzing brain-wave information on learning-disabled individuals (Ahn et al., 1980; John et al., 1980). This process, termed *neurometrics,* has even been recommended as a convenient screening approach for learning disabilities (Ahn et al., 1980), although it is rather unlikely that the necessary equipment and procedures will be available in school settings, where screening assessment most often occurs.

Genetic Causation

The possibility that learning disabilities are inherited often concerns parents. There is some evidence that genetic factors may play a role, but once again it is unlikely that any cause can be

identified for all of the learning disabilities (Houck, 1984). In an early study, Hallgren (1950) examined 276 children and their families. Of these children, 116 were labeled as dyslexic because of problems with certain academic tasks (spelling, reading, and writing). In examining the families of these children, Hallgren found that 88 percent of the subjects had relatives who were learning-disabled. Dyslexia has also been investigated in studies of twins. For example, Hermann (1959) studied 12 sets of identical twins (as we know, identical twins have the same genetic composition); in all 12 pairs, both children were diagnosed as dyslexic. Hermann also examined 33 pairs of fraternal twins (who have different genetic composition). With these subjects, 11 pairs were found where both children were dyslexic, whereas in the remaining 22 sets only one of each pair was so diagnosed.

The higher concordance or agreement rates for identical twins than for fraternal twins suggest that there may be some genetic contributions to the development of dyslexia. However, the problems of separating the influence of genetics and environment always persist. A case could also be made that abnormal behaviors in one family member may be reflected by other family members as a result of learning or family expectations and standards. Even the results for identical twins could be caused by their very similar environment. It is true that such children have the same genetic composition, but it is also true that they share the same environment, even prenatally. Identical twins "most often . . . [share] a single chorionic membrane and single placenta" (Chinn, 1979) and prenatal damage (such as oxygen insufficiency) could easily affect both twins similarly. With fraternal twins, "there are always two chorions and two placentas" (Chinn, 1979, p. 222), and such damage might not affect both babies in the same manner. This point is important, because if subjects (twins) are selected on the basis of one being dyslexic, and this condition proves to be due to a prenatal accident of some sort (such as oxygen deprivation or nutrition abnormality), the identical sibling of that fetus would probably have been subjected to the same condition, whereas a fraternal sibling may have developed in a different environment. It has also been observed that identical twins tend to be treated more similarly after birth than fraternal twins as they grow up, especially since they cannot be easily discriminated from each other (Ausubel, Sullivan, & Ives, 1980). Any or all of these possibilities *might* explain the results of twin studies such as Hermann's. Although the evidence suggests some genetic influence, one certainly cannot ignore environmental explanations.

Environmental Influences

As we have reviewed child behavior disorders throughout this text and in this chapter, it is clear that the environment may influence a child in many significant ways. Although the area of learning disabilities involves certain intriguing notions of a neurological and developmental nature, the environment must also be viewed as a potentially important contributor. In this sense, "the environment" is perceived quite broadly. If, in fact, maternal condition is significant during the prenatal period, then such factors create the environment of the unborn child. The environment after birth has also been identified as causing learning disabilities. In this context, general diet inadequacy and the influence of food additives have been of some interest over the years (Cott, 1972; Feingold, 1976; Lockey, 1977; Spring & Sandoval, 1976; Swanson & Kinsbourne, 1980; Wunderlich, 1973). General sensory stimulation, specific language stimulation deficiencies, and poor teaching have also received considerable attention as potential causes of learning disabilities (Smith, 1983; Wallace & McLoughlin, 1979).

The environment also appears to play a significant role in learning disabilities in regard to the motivation with which such youngsters approach much of their schoolwork. Poor motivation has long been prominent among descriptions of these children, with characterizations of inattentiveness, poor concentration, and minimal task persistence (Licht, 1984). Such behavior has led to characterizations of learning-disabled children as *inactive learners* who, because of long-term, repeated academic failures, develop feelings of helplessness about schoolwork and do not actively engage in learning tasks (Licht & Kistner, 1986; Torgesen & Licht, 1983). Whether this is a cause (etiology) or effect (resulting behavior) remains unclear, and some would claim that the distinction is unimportant. These children have probably entered school with certain difficulties, and the environment has contributed to a vicious cycle of failure that exacerbates the problem. Further applied research along this line of reasoning is clearly important.

TREATMENT

The area of learning disabilities has sorely tested the definitional and explanatory capability of education and behavioral science. It is our contention that this testing process has also provided a substantial service to the field. Throughout history, behavioral scientists and educators have sought that single concept that efficiently explains all of the behaviors exhibited by a particular group of individuals. In most cases such efforts are destined to fail. This may be more evident with learning disabilities than any other behavior disorder. Thus the conceptual and explanatory problems associated with this area have served as a constant reminder to behavioral scientists that it is probably not useful to search for *one single* theory or *one single* treatment for use with a diverse group of individuals. We are dealing with many specific disabilities and must approach the field in that manner.

Drug treatment has been frequently used for learning disabilities, especially to control hyperactivity. Some type of psychostimulant, such as Ritalin (methylphenidate) or Dexedrine (dextroamphetamine), is frequently chosen although a number of different drugs may be used depending on the response of the individual child. Medication is effective in some cases, such as increasing children's ability to focus on the task at hand (Henker & Whalen, 1980), but not in others, such as benefiting the acquisition of new skills (Pelham, 1983); medication may also have unfavorable side effects. The complexity of determining which medication to administer highlights both our poor understanding both of the disorders and of the drugs and their action. In a book written for parents, Wender (1973) noted, "It is impossible to predict beforehand to which medication a child will respond." He continued, "It may be necessary to try several [drugs] before the best one is found" (p. 59). Identifying an effective medication and an appropriate dosage level can prove difficult. In many cases, psychostimulants have been administered in very high doses. Pelham (1983) has noted that "children in these studies have received mean doses of stimulants that improve *social behavior* but are 50 percent to 400 percent higher than the dose . . . recommended as the maximum to improve *cognitive abilities*" (pp. 15–16, emphasis in the original). Very high dosage levels can produce bothersome side effects. Like other forms of treatment, drug therapy requires much individual tailoring. We should also emphasize another point here: Even if a medication controls the hyperactive behavior, we have not "cured" a learning disability by administering the drug. The hyperactivity has been controlled, but the child most likely still has learning problems, if for no other reason than that he is behind academ-

ically. In addition, research results have seriously questioned the assumption that drug treatment results in academic improvement (Rie, Rie, Stewart, & Ambuel, 1976a, 1976b).

Because medical treatment by itself is not sufficient, the next logical step is behavioral treatment. It would be a gross understatement to say that a variety of instructional techniques and materials have been developed for children labeled as learning-disabled. One only has to peer briefly into the special education journals to be overwhelmed by both the number and variety of interventions. For the most part, these materials and techniques have been based on some theory of causation or are adapted from treatments for other types of childhood learning disorders. Some, such as precision teaching, are firmly grounded on empirical evidence, whereas others are founded in clinical intuition and lack a sound research basis.

From an instructional perspective, perhaps the most soundly empirically based treatment approach involves the use of applied behavior analysis principles. As we know from other portions of this text, applied behavior analysis permits iden-

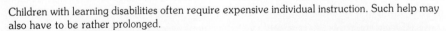
Children with learning disabilities often require expensive individual instruction. Such help may also have to be rather prolonged.

tification and modification of a wide range of behaviors. Based on the pioneering work of B. F. Skinner, this approach focuses primarily on observable performance (or behaviors) and de-emphasizes underlying causation, such as internal mental, anatomical, or biochemical abnormalities. Such a treatment approach has great appeal, because its specific format can be modified and applied to a wide variety of problems and in many contexts. This approach is very useful in remedying academic deficits and sociobehavioral abnormalities of the learning-disabled. Furthermore, attention to and restructuring of incentives and other motivational aspects of the academic environment may have a significant impact on the field of learning disabilities from an educational perspective (Licht & Kistner, 1986). Obviously, behavior analysis techniques cannot remedy a biochemical imbalance or other neurological problem. In such cases treatment must come from several sources, perhaps including medication to address one problem and behavioral treatment to address behavioral performance difficulties. Box 8-2 presents an example of treating digit reversal using behavioral procedures.

There has been a considerable shift in approaches to instructional intervention with the learning-disabled in the past few years. The field of learning disabilities has, since its inception, been one of the most controversy-ridden areas in education and psychology with regard to instructional intervention. The various theories of causation have had enthusiastic proponents and have often represented "warring" factions competing for funding and public favor. This tendency continues to date, although, without an apparent formal declaration of truce, a movement has begun toward focusing on each child's specific instructional problems rather than insisting on a generalized concept of learning disabilities. Treatment literature in learning disabilities is now beginning to address topics such as "writing disabilities" (Walmsley, 1984), "arithmetic and mathematics disabilities," "cognitive disabilities," and others (Hallahan et al., 1985). Intervention has been even more specific *within* such areas as cognitive

training, where problem solving (McKinney & Haskins, 1980), problem attack strategy training (Lloyd, 1980), and retrieval difficulty in reading disability (Kagan, 1983) have received attention. Such a trend is promising in one sense, because the generic *learning disabilities* label represents so many different difficulties. There is, however, some question regarding the ability of the major treatment agencies (public schools) to conceptualize and handle intervention effectively. Time and priorities (deciding what to focus on, and in what order) become even greater problems (Deshler, Schumaker, Lenz, & Ellis, 1984).

Perceptual-motor training has also received considerable attention in the treatment of learning disabilities. A variety of perceptual-motor interventions have been developed, each with somewhat different procedures. The basic notion is that higher-level processes, such as reading and writing, can evolve only after adequate development of the motor and perceptual systems. These intervention systems frequently include a number of physical and movement exercises (such as walking and jumping), which purportedly promote the development of motor and perceptual systems. The underlying theory holds that such development then influences the growth of cognitive skills.

Perceptual-motor training has enjoyed widespread popularity among some practitioners working with a variety of handicapped children, including the mentally retarded and learning-disabled. Unfortunately, the acceptance of such programs has been based more on clinical intuition than on solid scientific evidence regarding their effectiveness. Research on the efficacy of perceptual-motor training is probably most notable for methodological flaws and errors. Hallahan and Cruickshank (1973) reviewed the research on such training and concluded, "No persuasive empirical evidence has been brought to the fore in support of perceptual-motor training, [and] neither has there been solid negative evidence" (p. 216). This negative conclusion re-emphasizes the problems regarding the field of learning disabilities that we have noted earlier in the chapter, and highlights the need for rigorous research efforts.

BOX 8-2 • Treatment of Digit Reversal in an 8-Year-Old Boy

Bob, an 8-year-old boy, was enrolled in a Basic Skills class in the Ontario-Montclair (California) School District. While considered by his teacher to be one of her most capable students, Bob had specific difficulty in adding numbers yielding a two-digit sum. Almost invariably, he would reverse the order of digits in the sum, for instance, writing 21 as the sum of 5 + 7. He had exhibited this behavior for approximately one year before the present study began. As a result of this behavior, Bob received several neurological and visual examinations, and was given considerable extra help by his present and previous teachers. The failure of this extra help to modify the behavior led his present teacher to consider her role in maintaining the behavior.

Several factors suggested that teacher attention might be reinforcing Bob's digit-reversal behavior. First, Bob was able to discriminate easily between numbers containing the same but reversely ordered digits, such as 12 and 21. Second, he often pointed out reversals on his own paper to the teacher when she failed to notice them. Finally, he was observed on several occasions erasing correct . . . sums and reversing the order of the digits. . . .

PROCEDURES

The basic datum of the study was the number of digit reversals made by Bob each day. For the duration of the study, Bob (along with other class members) was given 20 addition problems at the same time each morning. It was common classroom procedure to do a number of such problems daily, and hence, the study necessitated few deviations from normal classroom routine. All problems were designed to yield two-digit sums. Numbers yielding a sum of 10 or sums composed of two identical digits, such as 11 or 22, were not used. This left a population of 80 sums composed of different digits. Addition problems were designed by first dividing these 80 sums into four groups: 12 to 32, 34 to 54, 56 to 76, and 78 to 98. Five sums from each group were chosen to comprise the problems for a given day. By choosing five different sums from each group on consecutive days, over a four-day period all 80 sums were used and none were repeated. Over the four weeks of the study, each sum was thus used seven times. On a given day, sums were chosen from each group such that no reversely ordered sums, such as 18 and 81, appeared. For any sum, the possible permutations of numbers yielding that sum is equal to the sum minus one. Thus, even for the lowest sum used, that of 12, eleven permutations of numbers exist that will yield that sum when added. By randomly selecting permutations without replacement, it was thus possible to provide 20 different addition problems each day, even though each sum was repeated seven times in the course of the study.

On each day of the study, Bob would raise his hand as soon as he had completed all 20 problems. The teacher would then proceed to Bob's desk and check his worksheet. For the first seven days of the study, the teacher marked all correct responses with a "C." All digit reversals were marked as incorrect with an "X," and were pointed out to Bob by the teacher with the comment: "This one is incorrect. You see (pointing), you reversed the numbers in the answer." After all 20 problems had been scored in this manner, all digit reversals were returned to, and Bob was provided with extra help in solving each problem. This extra help had two basic components: one, Bob was taken through the adding process involved in each problem, using a variety of teaching aids, such as counters and number lines; and two, verbal and

Box 8-2 (Continued)

physical prompting of correct response forms for those problems was provided. This constituted Baseline Period 1 of the study.

For the next seven days, all digit reversals were marked as correct with a "C." This procedure was adopted in consideration of the fact that marks for incorrect responses might have developed conditioned reinforcing properties. No other comments were made concerning the reversals, no "extra help" was given with them, and statements pointing out such errors were ignored. Correctly written sums were likewise marked as correct with a "C," but were also followed by characteristic teacher consequences, consisting of a smile, a pat on the back, and the comment: "This one is very good." This combination of procedures had the effect of withholding all teacher attention for digit reversals (other than marking item as correct) and making more attention contingent upon correct response forms. After each problem had been scored and responded to, the teacher returned to her desk without further comment to Bob. This constituted Experimental Period 1 of the study.

Baseline Period 2 and Experimental Period 2 followed. Each was seven days in length and replicated the previous baseline or experimental period.

It should be emphasized that throughout the study, Bob's daily performance was evaluated and responded to only after all 20 problems were completed. Hence, any change in the digit-reversal behavior would not be evident until the day(s) following a change in the teacher-attention contingency.

RESULTS

All of Bob's worksheets were rescored by an independent judge on each day of the study. Before rescoring, all of the teacher's marks were removed from the worksheets. Worksheets were then scored for correctly and reversely ordered sums. Two other scoring categories were possible, but were never used. These categories were for correctly and reversely ordered, inappropriately added sums. Reliability was computed by dividing the number of agreements between teacher and judge in scoring correctly and reversely ordered sums by 20, the number of possible agreements. This fraction was then multiplied by 100 percent to determine the percentage of agreement between scores. In all cases, the percentage of agreement was 100 percent.

The number of digit reversals made by Bob on each day of the study is graphed in Figure 8-1. It can be seen that in the first baseline period, digit reversals were made at a significantly high rate, varying between 18 and 20 and averaging 19.4 per day.

When the teacher-attention consequences of this behavior were discontinued, Bob continued to make reversals at a high rate for three days (Days 8 through 10 in Figure 8-1). The rate then dropped off dramatically, varying between 0 and 5 and averaging 2.5 reversals per day for the next four days (Days 11 through 14 in Figure 8-1). It should be noted that on Days 8 and 9, Bob failed to order any digits correctly. Consequently, the teacher was unable to respond differentially to correct response forms until Day 10. The significant drop in rate on

Box 8-2 (Continued)

240   CHAPTER 8

Box 8-2 (Continued)

FIGURE 8-1. Number of digit reversals per day under baseline and experimental conditions.

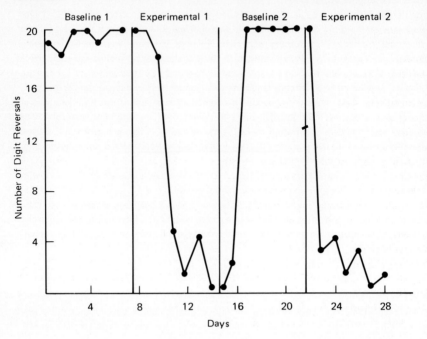

Day 11 is thus indicative of the sensitivity of the behavior to the consequences provided by the teacher.

    After the sixteenth day, when teacher attention was again made contingent upon digit reversals, the number of digit reversals jumped to 20 and remained at that level for the duration of the second baseline period. The average number of reversals per day for the last five days of this period was thus slightly higher than the daily average observed during the first baseline period.

    The second experimental period (Days 22 through 28 in Figure 8-1) was also characterized by a drop in the rate of reversals. By the second day of this period, the number of reversals had dropped to three. The average number of reversals per day for the last six days of this period was two, slightly lower than during the final four days of the first experimental period. The significant changes in the rate of reversals occurring in the second baseline and experimental periods provide further evidence of the strong control exerted over this behavior by teacher attention.

Source: J.E. Hasazi and S. E. Hasazi (1972). Effects of teacher attention on digit-reversal behavior in an elementary school child. *Journal of Applied Behavior Analysis, 5,* 157–162. Copyright 1972 by the Society for Experimental Analysis of Behavior, Inc. Reprinted by permission.

BOX 8-3 • **Roa Lynn's Story**

"That is to say, I was completely frustrated, completely at odds with my environment, a sort of fake who believed he was somebody, but could furnish no evidence to prove it."

—Henry Miller

I was twenty-five years old when I came across the above lines one Sunday in the *New York Times Book Review*. Miller was wearing the hat of a reviewer that day; I no longer remember the name of the book he reviewed, but the words hit me hard because I knew, somehow, that he was describing me. I copied down the words carefully and put them away.

For years I had hidden from parents, sisters, teachers, friends, even my husband, the fact that I can read only a few minutes at a time before becoming confused and exhausted. My problems extend beyond the inability to read well. Although I managed to earn a bachelor's degree and attend graduate school, I can neither recite the alphabet straight through nor do I know the multiplication and division tables. I add by surreptitiously counting on my fingers, and my spelling is bizarre. I have difficulty writing down the simplest note when someone gives me information—even a telephone number gets twisted in my hands. I am frequently bewildered by complex stimuli such as large parties, some kinds of music, and cluttered rooms. Although I have a good memory for events more than a few days old, I often cannot recall what I have most recently learned. When I move to a new city, it takes years before I can walk out the door confident that I will be able to find my way home. Despite such disabilities, I chose journalism as a career, and pursued it with intermittent successes.

Quite by chance some years later, Miller's words came back to me. At age 38 I was watching a news program on WNBC-TV in which Dr. Frank Field demonstrated a device to test for dyslexia. It struck me instantly that I had the symptoms discussed on the program. The very next day my self-diagnosis was confirmed by a psychiatrist specializing in dyslexia; and, somewhat later, it was reconfirmed after extensive testing by an educational specialist. She preferred to say that I was "learning disabled."

I cannot overemphasize the enormity of my relief when I finally had a name other than "stupidity" for the problems that were so painful and so central to my life. I had always feared

Box 8-3 (Continued)

THE PROGNOSIS

Throughout this chapter, we have stressed that the term *learning disabilities* is, at best, an umbrella label that encompasses many different specific disorders. Consequently, the prognosis for the child diagnosed as learning-disabled is as variable as the many problems that the term covers. Some who were learning-disabled as children survive only marginally as adults, supported by welfare or perhaps employed in jobs that are well below their potential. There are remarkable exceptions such as the late Nelson Rockefeller, who had a moderately severe learning disability (dys-

lexia) but who was able to achieve political prominence through personal perseverance in combination with fortuitous family circumstances.

The learning-disabled themselves—those who are most directly affected—do not usually describe publicly what their life is like. Only the impersonal accounts of psychologists and educators are widely available. The quotation in Box 8-3 is an unusual exception. It is a statement by Roa Lynn, excerpted from the preface to a book entitled *Learning Disabilities: An Overview of Theories, Approaches, and Politics* (Lynn et al., 1979).

A postscript to Lynn's statement seems ap-

Box 8-3 (Continued)

that despite my high scores on intelligence tests, I was really stupid. Yet, at the same time, relief was mixed with despair and I sank into depression when I realized that the learning struggles, and therefore the life struggles, that had so tormented me would never go away.

Although I have managed to work for publications such as *Time* and *Newsweek,* my attempt to make a living as a reporter was, as one doctor put it, "like a paraplegic trying to become a professional football player." In fact, I was often unable to read through my own stories once they were published. Due to the exhaustion I experienced trying to keep pace with my peers, my career performance was extremely uneven; but it was consistent: I would start a new job after about six months of recuperation from the last one. In the first few months I would manage to do good, even outstanding, work. Taking note of my performance, my editors would naturally expect more of the same. For a short period I would succeed in meeting both my own high standards and those of my bosses. But then as the pressure to produce mounted while my ability to produce diminished, I would find myself unable to go on with my work. At this point (usually about four months into a job), I would panic and find some reason to quit so that I could leave before anyone realized that I was no longer productive. My most vivid memory of every work experience was the daily fear that the boss was going to call me into his office and fire me because he knew, just as I did, that I was too dumb to do the job.

Groping in the dark, terrified that I was really stupid, sometimes without money to buy the bare essentials of life because of my inability to hold a job, there were times when I considered suicide.

When I found out that I was not stupid, but dyslexic, I tried to rescue myself using the reporter's tools I have been able to master. I thought that an odyssey around the country, talking my way through a field I couldn't read my way through, might produce a more valuable statement pulling together a controversial field than would a conscientious literature review; and I hoped by understanding my condition to save my own life.

Source: R. Lynn, N. D. Gluckin, and B. Kripke. (1979). *Learning disabilities: An overview of theories, approaches, and politics* (New York: Free Press), pp. ix–xi. Reprinted by permission.

propriate, in order to emphasize the theoretical and practical importance of research. Obviously it is a significant achievement for someone with Roa Lynn's problems to have done all that she has done, and even to have completed a book. In addition to that success, Lynn and Dr. Bernard Kripke undertook what turned out to be a 4-year search for some type of treatment that would ease her difficulties. Often such ventures meet with disappointment and result in only limited success. Their efforts were frustrated at the beginning, but they finally achieved considerable success. Lynn is currently receiving medical treatment (involving none of the medication mentioned in this chapter) and describes her disability rather cautiously as being "in a state of remission" (R. Lynn, personal communication, January 7, 1980). She can now read for extended periods of time and can perform many of the tasks that were previously impossible for her. She has continued her research on learning disabilities. In this case, the current prognosis appears promising. Only more intense interdisciplinary research efforts will result in similar gains for others who have been labeled as learning-disabled. We hope that some readers of this book will someday contribute to this effort.

SUMMARY

Learning disabilities is a label of relatively recent origin that has generated considerable confusion and controversy. The individuals so labeled exhibit an extremely diverse set of learning and behavioral problems. They may be average or above in intelligence, but often have pronounced difficulties in reading, math, and other school subjects. They are often, but not always, characterized as hyperactive as children. The learning-disabled have also been described as having perceptual difficulties, memory problems, and attention deficits. Learning-disabled individuals may exhibit various combinations of these characteristics and may be handicapped to varying degrees, depending on the nature of their problem(s) and the setting. Research to date has been somewhat unsystematic and often not sufficiently rigorous to yield progress in understanding and treating these conditions.

This chapter concludes with the same plea that began it: Researchers in the learning disabilities must dedicate themselves to rigorous scientific investigation of the phenomena. Practitioners in the school and other service agencies are desperately attempting to cope with the problems of the learning-disabled, largely without a solid knowledge base from which to operate. Diagnostic and treatment procedures remain relatively primitive, and often techniques are embraced when their effectiveness has not been objectively evaluated (or when there is, at best, only scanty evidence regarding their effectiveness). The future of the field of learning disabilities will depend upon the formulation of useful behavioral definitions of the various types of learning disabilities, and then on their objective and systematic study.

chapter

9

Mental Retardation

KEY TERMS

Adaptive Behavior. The ability to respond constructively and independently to demands of the social environment in relation to general expectations of one's age level and cultural group.

Developmental Period. The time between birth and the 18th birthday; terminology used by American Association on Mental Deficiency (AAMD) for the purpose of defining mental retardation.

General Intellectual Functioning. Results obtained by assessment on an individually administered standardized intelligence scale; terminology used in the AAMD definition of mental retardation.

Incidence. The rate of occurrence (number of new cases) of a disorder that are identified during a specified time period (for example, 1 year).

Prevalence. The total number of cases of a disorder existing at a particular point in time.

Significantly Subaverage. Measured IQ more than two standard deviations below the test mean; terminology used in the AAMD definition of mental retardation.

INTRODUCTION

Mental retardation is a disorder that has been recognized perhaps longer than any other that we currently study in psychology. Written documents from ancient Egypt made oblique references to the condition as early as the 1500s B.C., and it may have been implicit in law codes of Babylonia nearly 1000 years earlier (Scheerenberger, 1983). In addition to its lengthy history, mental retardation is relatively common. It occurs in the families of the wealthy and prominent (including that of the late President John F. Kennedy), as well as in less advantaged families. Although prevalent, mental retardation is often misunderstood. Many have a stereotyped notion that all mentally retarded children are extremely dull and physically different, as is the case with some but not all retarded people (such as individuals with hydrocephalus and Down's syndrome). Many retarded children can cope with the demands of daily life and have no distinctive physical characteristics that would set them apart from others.

DEFINING MENTAL RETARDATION

Defining mental retardation is not as simple as it might seem on the surface. In the past, many definitions became popular and then faded into scientific obscurity as others emerged. Part of the difficulty in defining the condition relates to the central role of intelligence in mental retardation. It has been commonly accepted that the mentally retarded have a lower level of intelligence than is typical in the general population. Consequently, definitions of mental retardation have reflected many facets of the long-standing controversy regarding the nature of intelligence and the degree to which it can be altered by experience. In addition, the many disciplines operating in the field have each yielded different perspectives, definitions, and terminology regarding mental retardation, further complicating the issue. Psychologists, sociologists, anthropologists, educators, medical personnel, and others have undertaken research in the area, but only relatively recently have seri-

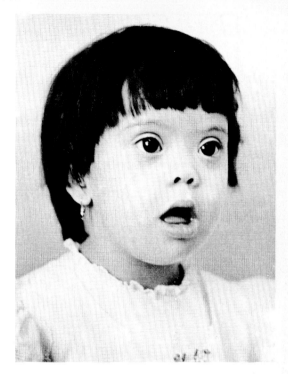

Down's syndrome is a type of retardation that often comes to mind for lay people thinking about mental retardation.

ous efforts been made to conceptualize mental retardation from a multidisciplinary viewpoint. As we will see in later sections, classification systems still vary to some degree from one profession to another; each system emphasizes the treatment orientation or scientific perspective associated with its specific profession.

Perhaps the most widely accepted definition of mental retardation has been presented by the multidisciplinary American Association on Mental Deficiency (AAMD) (Grossman, 1983). This definition has undergone many revisions and refinements over the years, and these have yielded the following formulation: "Mental retardation refers to significantly subaverage general intellectual functioning existing concurrently with deficits in adaptive behavior and manifested during the developmental period" (Grossman, 1983, p. 1).

BOX 9-1 • AAMD Definition of Mental Retardation

General intellectual functioning is defined as the results obtained by assessment with one or more of the individually administered general intelligence tests developed for that purpose.

Significantly subaverage is defined as IQ more than two standard deviations below the mean for the test.

Adaptive behavior is defined as the effectiveness or degree with which an individual meets the standards of personal independence and social responsibility expected for age and cultural group.

Development period is defined as the period of time between birth and the eighteenth birthday.

COMMENTARY

Mental retardation as defined denotes a level of behavioral performance without reference to etiology. Thus, it does not distinguish between retardation associated with psychosocial or polygenic influences and retardation associated with biological deficits. Mental retardation is descriptive of current behavior and does not necessarily imply prognosis. Prognosis is related to such factors as associated conditions, motivation, treatment, or training opportunities more than to mental retardation itself.

The two-dimensional nature of this definition, orginally formulated in earlier published versions of AAMD manuals, represents a fundamental conceptualization of the mental retardation symptom complex and is a crucial aspect of the classification scheme. Knowledge of the relationship between intelligence and adaptive behavior is still incomplete. It has not been determined with a high degree of precision what level of intelligence individuals need to cope adequately with the environmental demands of their subcultures or of the larger society. Intellectual functioning is assessed with one or more of the individually administered general intelligence tests. Such assessments measure current intellectual functioning only. Intellectual status may change, as may adaptive behavior. Adaptive behavior is a product of the interactions of an individual's abilities and skills with the expectations of society and of the opportunities to learn. Thus, individuals of the same level of measured intelligence may differ meaningfully in their social adaptation. For a person to be diagnosed as being mentally retarded, impairments in intellectual functioning must coexist with deficits in adaptive behavior.

Significantly subaverage intelligence refers to performance which is more than two standard deviations below the mean (usually 100) of a standardized general intelligence test and is represented by an IQ of 67 or below on the Stanford-Binet and an IQ of 69 or below on Wechsler's scales. For several reasons, these upper IQ limits are proposed only as guidelines rather than as rigid limits. The assessment of intelligence is subject to some variation because of such factors as test construction, circumstances of administration, and measurement errors. Despite these limitations, intelligence test scores represent more reliable and valid measures of ability and performance than do either adaptive behavior measures or clinical judgment.

The arbitrary IQ ceiling values are predicated on data supporting a positive correlation between intelligence and adaptive behavior. This correlation declines in significance at the upper levels of mild retardation, and some individuals with an IQ below the ceilings may not demonstrate impaired adaptive behavior. Conversely, other individuals with scores slightly above these ceilings may be diagnosed as mildly retarded during a period when they manifest

Box 9-1 (Continued)

serious impairments of adaptive behavior. In such cases, the burden is on the examiner to avoid misdiagnosis with its potential stigmatizing effects, and to rule out such factors as emotional disorders, social conditions, sensory impairment, or other variables that might account more readily for observed deficits in adaptive behaviors.

In combination, and in the hands of qualified professionals, use of measures of intelligence and of adaptive behavior and of clinical judgment may minimize errors in the diagnosis of mental retardation. Since these expectations of adaptive behavior vary for different age groups, *deficits in adaptive behavior* will vary at different ages. These may be reflected in the following areas:

During *infancy and early childhood* in:

1. *Sensory-motor skills development*
2. *Communication skills* (including speech and language)
3. *Self-help skills*
4. *Socialization* (development of ability to interact with others)

During *childhood and early adolescence* in:

5. *Application of basic academic skills in daily life activities*
6. *Application of appropriate reasoning and judgment in mastery of the environment*
7. *Social skills* (participation in group activities and interpersonal relationships)

and

During *late adolescence and adult life* in:

8. **Vocational and social responsibilities and performances**

During infancy and early childhood, sensory-motor, communication, self-help, and socialization skills ordinarily develop in a sequential pattern reflective of the maturation process. Delays in the acquisition of these skills represent potential deficiencies in adaptive behavior and become the criteria for mental retardation.

The skills required for adaptation during childhood and early adolescence involve complex learning processes. This involves the process by which knowledge is acquired and retained as a function of the experiences of the individual. Difficulties in learning are usually manifested in the academic situation but in evaluation of adaptive behavior, attention should focus not only on the basic academic skills and their use, but also on skills essential to cope with the environment, including concepts of time and money, self-directed behaviors, social responsiveness, and interactive skills.

In the adult years, vocational performance and social responsibilities assume prime importance as qualifying conditions of mental retardation. These are assessed in terms of the degree to which the individual is able to maintain himself independently in the community and in gainful employment as well as by his ability to meet and conform to standards set by the community.

It is these deficiencies in adaptive behavior which usually determine the need of the individual for programs or services or legal action as a mentally retarded person.

Box 9-1 (Continued)

Box 9-1 (Continued)

FIGURE 9-1. Intellectual functioning.

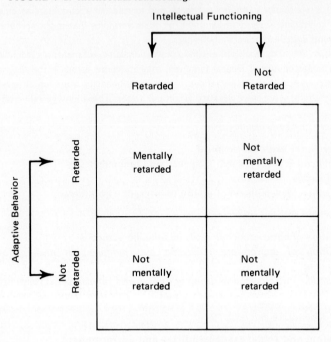

In *infancy and early childhood,* deficits in sensory-motor development, in acquisition of self-help and communication skills, and development of socialization skills point to the needs for medical services, for early childhood education, or for family guidance.

During *childhood and early adolescence,* deficits in learning and coping skills indicate needs for specialized educational, prevocational, and recreational programs.

In the *late adolescent and adult years,* deficits determine the needs for vocational training, placement, and a variety of supportive services.

The relationship between intellectual functioning, adaptive behavior, and mental retardation is illustrated in Figure 9-1.

Within the framework of the definition of mental retardation, an individual may meet the criteria of mental retardation at one time in life and not at some other time. A person may change status as a result of changes or alterations in intellectual functioning, changes in adaptive behaviors, changes in the expectations of the society, or for other known and unknown reasons. Decisions about whether an individual is classified as mentally retarded at any given time are always made in relation to behavioral standards and norms and in comparison to the individual's own chronological age group.

Source: H. J. Grossman. (Ed.). (1977). *Manual on terminology and classification in mental retardation* (Washington, DC: American Association on Mental Deficiency), pp. 11–15. Reprinted by permission.

Some of the terminology in this definition seems rather general and abstract. However, the AAMD manual includes definitions of each key term and a rather complete commentary on the concepts. This material is reproduced in Box 9-1.

The AAMD definition departs from earlier efforts in several ways. One important difference involves the manner of viewing intelligence measures. The AAMD definition treats intelligence as an individual's behavioral functioning level at the time of evaluation. This approach avoids defining mental retardation as an incurable condition. The AAMD definition also circumvents another concept that has historically created considerable difficulty—the assumption that retardation is of constitutional origin. Mental retardation was once thought to be caused by biological pathology, although no physical basis for the condition has been found for the largest segment of the population (the functionally retarded). The concept of adaptive behavior represents another departure from early definitions. Social adaptation or adjustment has long been recognized as an area of deficiency of the retarded. However, only during the last 25 to 30 years has socially maladaptive behavior been included as a criterion for the diagnosis of mental retardation (Heber, 1959). It is important to note the requirement that deficits in adaptive behavior must exist *concurrently* with reduced intellectual functioning. Thus, according to the AAMD, individuals cannot be classified as mentally retarded unless they are deficient in both intellectual and social areas simultaneously. However, as with many other conceptual changes, actual adherence to this requirement in practice has been somewhat slow.

DESCRIBING AND CLASSIFYING MENTAL RETARDATION

Classification systems are invariably based on factors such as type of causation, performance level, or physical manifestations. Because of the different definitions in the mental retardation field over the years, there have been similarly varied bases for describing and classifying such individuals. Chapter 12 addresses classification of child be-

havior disorders in a more complete and general fashion; the present section specifically examines descriptive classifications of mental retardation. Such examination emphasizes the multifaceted nature of the mental retardation problem, as well as the multidisciplinary nature of the field. Readers should remember that all descriptions and classifications are useful in some circumstances but may be less functional in others, in which case they should not be used.

The term *mental retardation* is an extremely general label that includes a very heterogeneous population. Scientifically, it is necessary to specify the type of individual being studied. From a practical standpoint, there is also a need to be more specific, since different types of retardation require different approaches to treatment and service delivery. Classification schemes in mental retardation provide a common vocabulary and serve as a convenient means for communication about the work under way, whether it be research or clinical treatment. Mental retardation involves many fields of study, each with its own terminology and descriptive system, and so several classification schemes warrant discussion.

Historically, the characteristic most typically associated with mental retardation has been reduced intellectual functioning. The *severity* of the intellectual impairment has long been a common means of describing and classifying those who are retarded and remains in use today. As we mentioned earlier, the AAMD uses measured intelligence as one part of its definition of mental retardation and employs a severity scheme for classification. The AAMD system includes four groupings based on the severity of intellectual deficit as follows: (1) IQ of 50–55 to approximately 70—*mild mental retardation;* (2) IQ of 35–40 to 50–55—*moderate mental retardation;* (3) IQ of 20–25 to 35–40—*severe mental retardation;* and (4) IQ below 20 or 25—*profound mental retardation.* The AAMD classification scheme is stated in terms of degree of departure from the average, as indicated previously. However, diagnosis cannot be based on IQ scores alone. The IQ ranges above are illustrative, and are based on the Wechsler Intelligence Scales. Other tests yield dif-

BOX 9-2 • AAMD Classification of Adaptive Behavior Levels

AGE AND LEVEL INDICATED	ILLUSTRATIONS OF HIGHEST LEVEL OF ADAPTIVE BEHAVIOR FUNCTIONING
3 years and above: **Profound** (Note: all behaviors at greater degree of impairment would also indicate **Profound** deficit in adaptive behavior for persons 3 years of age or above.)	*Independent functioning:* Drinks from cup with help; "cooperates" by opening mouth for feeding. *Physical:* Sits unsupported or pulls self upright momentarily; reaches for objects; has good thumb-finger grasp; manipulates objects (e.g., plays with shoes or feet). *Communication:* Imitates sounds, laughs, or smiles back (says "Da-da, buh-buh" responsively); no effective speech; may communicate in sounds and/or gestures; responds to gestures and/or signs. *Social:* Indicates knowing familiar persons and interacts nonverbally with them.
3 years: **Severe** 6 years and above: **Profound**	*Independent Functioning:* Attempts finger feeding; "cooperates" with dressing, bathing, and with toilet training; may remove clothing (e.g., socks) but not as act of undressing as for bath or bed. *Physical:* Stands alone or may walk unsteadily or with help; coordinates eye-hand movements. *Communication:* One or two words (e.g., Mama, ball) but predominantly vocalization. *Social:* May respond to others in predictable fashion; communicates needs by gestures and noises or pointing; plays "patty-cake" or plays imitatively with little interaction; or occupies self alone with "toys" few minutes.
3 years: **Moderate** 6 years: **Severe** 9 years and above: **Profound**	*Independent functioning:* Tries to feed self with spoon; considerable spilling; removes socks, pants; "cooperates" in bathing, may indicate wet pants; "cooperates" at toilet. *Physical:* Walks alone steadily; can pass ball or objects to others; may run and climb steps with help. *Communication:* May use four to six words; may communicate many needs with gestures (e.g., pointing). *Social:* Plays with others for short periods, often as parallel play or under direction; recognizes others and may show preference for some persons over others.
3 years: **Mild** 6 years: **Moderate** 9 years: **Severe** 12 years and above: **Profound**	*Independent functioning:* Feeds self with spoon (cereals, soft foods) with considerable spilling or messiness; drinks unassisted; can pull off clothing and put on some (socks, underclothes, boxer pants, dress); tries to help with bath or hand washing but still needs considerable help; indicates toilet accident and may indicate toilet need. *Physical:* May climb up and down stairs but not alternating feet; may run and jump; may balance briefly on one foot; can pass ball to others; transfers objects; may do simple-form board puzzles without aid. *Communication:* May speak in two- or three-word sentences (Daddy go work); name simple common objects (boy, car, ice cream, hat); understands simple directions (put the shoe on your foot, sit here, get your coat); knows people by name. (If nonverbal, may use many gestures to convey needs or other information.) *Social:* May interact with others in simple play activities, usually with only one or two others unless guided into group activity; has preference for some persons over others.

Box 9-2 (Continued)

AGE AND LEVEL INDICATED	ILLUSTRATIONS OF HIGHEST LEVEL OF ADAPTIVE BEHAVIOR FUNCTIONING

6 years: **Mild**
9 years: **Moderate**
12 years and above: **Severe**
15 years and above: **Profound**

Independent functioning: Feeds self with spoon or fork, may spill some; puts on clothing but needs help with small buttons and jacket zippers; tries to bathe self but needs help; can wash and dry hands but not very efficiently; partially toilet-trained but may have accidents.

Physical: May hop or skip; may climb steps with alternating feet; rides tricycle (or bicycle over 8 years); may climb trees or jungle gym; play dance games; may throw ball or hit target.

Communication: May have speaking vocabulary of over 300 words and use grammatically correct sentences. If nonverbal, may use many gestures to communicate needs. Understands simple verbal communications including directions and questions ("Put it on the shelf." "Where do you live?"); some speech may be indistinct sometimes. May recognize advertising words and signs (ice cream, STOP, EXIT, MEN, LADIES). Relates experiences in simple language.

Social: Participates in group activities and simple group games; interacts with others in simple play ("Store," "House") and expressive activities (art and dance).

9 years: **Mild**
12 years: **Moderate**
15 years and older: **Severe**

Independent functioning: Feeds self adequately with spoon and fork; can butter bread (needs help with cutting meat); can put on clothes and can button and zipper clothes; may tie shoes; bathes self with supervision; is toilet-trained; washes face and hands without help.

Physical: Can run, skip, hop, dance; uses skates or sled or jump rope; can go up and down stairs alternating feet; can throw ball to hit target.

Communication: May communicate in complex sentences; speech is generally clear and distinct; understands complex verbal communication including words such as "because" and "but." Recognizes signs, words, but does not read prose materials with comprehension.

Social: May participate in group activities spontaneously; may engage in simple competitive exercise games (dodge ball, tag, races). May have friendship choices which are maintained over weeks or months.

Economic activity: May be sent on simple errands and make simple purchases with a note; realizes money has value but does not know how to use it (except for coin machines).

Occupation: May prepare simple foods (sandwiches); can help with simple household tasks (bed-making, sweeping, vacuuming); can set and clear table.

Self-direction: May ask if there is "work" for him to do; may pay attention to task for ten minutes or more; makes efforts to be dependable and carry out responsibility.

12 years: **Mild**
15 years and over: **Moderate**

Independent functioning: Feeds, baths, dresses self; may select daily clothing; may prepare easy foods (peanut butter sandwiches) for self or others; combs/brushes hair; may shampoo and roll up hair; may wash and/or iron and store own clothes.

Box 9-3 (Continued)

Box 9-2 (Continued)

AGE AND LEVEL INDICATED	ILLUSTRATIONS OF HIGHEST LEVEL OF ADAPTIVE BEHAVIOR FUNCTIONING
	Physical: Good body control; good gross and fine motor coordination.
	Communication: May carry on simple conversation; uses complex sentences. Recognizes words; may read sentences, ads, signs, and simple prose material with some comprehension.
	Social: May interact cooperatively and/or competitively with others.
	Economic activity: May be sent on shopping errand for several items without notes; makes minor purchases; adds coins to dollar with fair accuracy.
	Occupation: May do simple routine household chores (dusting, garbage, dishwashing; prepare simple foods which require mixing).
	Self-direction: May initiate most of own activities; attend to task 15–20 minutes (or more); may be conscientious in assuming much responsibility.
15 years and adult: **Mild** (Note: individuals who routinely perform at higher levels of competence in adaptive behavior than illustrated in this pattern should NOT be considered as deficient in adaptive behavior. Since by definition an individual is not retarded unless he shows significant deficit in *both* measured intelligence and in adaptive behavior, those individuals who function at higher levels than illustrated here cannot be considered to be retarded.)	*Independent functioning:* Exercises care for personal grooming, feeding, bathing, toileting; may need help in selection of purchase of clothing.
	Physical: Goes about hometown (local neighborhood in city, campus at institution) with ease, but cannot go to other towns alone without aid; can use bicycle, skis, ice skates, trampoline, or other equipment requiring good coordination.
	Communication: Communicates complex verbal concepts and understands them; carries on everyday conversation, but cannot discuss abstract or philosophical concepts; uses telephone and communicates in writing for simple letter writing or orders but does not write about abstractions or important current events.
	Social: Interacts cooperatively or competitively with others and initiates some group activities, primarily for social or recreational purposes; may belong to a local recreation group or church group, but not to civic organizations or groups of skilled persons (e.g., photography club, great books club, or kennel club); enjoys recreation (e.g., bowling, dancing, TV, checkers, but either does not enjoy or is not competent at tennis, sailing, bridge, piano playing or other hobbies requiring rapid or involved or complex planning and implementation).
	Economic activity: Can be sent or go to several shops to make purchases (without a note to shopkeepers) to purchase several items; can make change correctly, but does not use banking facilities; may earn living but has difficulty handling money without guidance.
	Occupation: Can cook simple foods, prepare simple meals; can perform everyday household tasks (cleaning, dusting, dishes, laundry); as adult can engage in semiskilled or simple skilled job.
	Self-direction: Initiates most of own activity; will pay attention to task for at least 15–20 minutes; conscientious about work and assumes much responsibility but needs guidance for tasks with responsibility for major tasks (health care, care of others, complicated occupational activity).

Source: H. J. Grossman. (Ed.). (1977). *Manual on terminology and classification in mental retardation* (Washington, DC: American Association on Mental Deficiency), pp. 25–33. Reprinted by permission.

ferent scores at each level of retardation severity. Clearly, these are viewed as approximations, and the AAMD manual cautions users against viewing them as solid points of distinction. Furthermore, there is obviously a certain amount of overlap, which emphasizes that these categories should be used as guides only and that clinical judgment should be exercised in viewing *all* diagnostic information available.

For many years severity of intellectual impairment has been a predominant means of classifying retarded individuals. In fact, identification of children who were "truly dull" was the basic purpose of Binet and Simon's (1905) early work in developing a method of measuring intelligence. Classification groupings and their labels have varied greatly over the years and still differ considerably between disciplines. We have chosen to focus on the AAMD scheme, because it is current and is used by several disciplines.

The AAMD also considers *adaptive behavior* in diagnosing mental retardation. Readers will recall from our earlier discussion that an individual must exhibit deficits in adaptive behavior *and* measured intelligence to be considered mentally retarded by AAMD standards. The AAMD classification of adaptive behavior levels is based on a developmental framework, as indicated by the material in Box 9-2. A child's level of skill development is observed and compared to the skills of other children of the same age. Older children who attain the same level of adaptive behavior functioning as younger children are classified as more retarded than the younger children.

Etiology (cause) provides another basis for classification of mental retardation. Physicians have often used etiology as a basis for classification, and this approach has typically been referred to as the *medical classification system.* The etiological classification scheme has also been included in the AAMD perspective and follows, in general, the systems of both the World Health Organization (1978) and the American Psychiatric Association (1980). As presented by the AAMD, etiology of mental retardation is divided into the following 10 categories (Grossman, 1983, pp. 130–154):

1. **Following infection and intoxication (e.g., syphilis, congenital rubella).**
2. **Following trauma or physical agent (e.g., mechanical injury during birth).**
3. **With disorders of metabolism or nutrition (e.g., [phenylketonuria or] PKU, galactosemia).**
4. **Associated with gross brain disease, postnatal (e.g., neurofibromatosis).**
5. **Associated with diseases and conditions resulting from unknown prenatal influence (e.g., hydrocephalus, anencephaly).**
6. **Associated with chromosomal abnormality (e.g., Down's syndrome).**
7. **Associated with other perinatal (gestational) disorders (e.g., prematurity).**
8. **Following psychiatric disorders (e.g., autism).**
9. **Associated with environmental influences (e.g., cultural-familial retardation).**
10. **Associated with other conditions (e.g., known conditions such as blindness, unknown causes).**

By far the largest portion of mentally retarded individuals would be classified in categories 9 and 10. These two categories account for 75 to 85 percent of the retarded population, with the other eight categories accounting for the remaining 15 to 25 percent. The largest segment of the retarded thus represents a group about which we know the least with regard to causation.

The *educational classification system* provides another basis for grouping those with mental retardation. This classification scheme (sometimes called the *educability expectation system*) describes retardation in terms of expected academic achievement. It generally includes three categories of mental retardation: *educable, trainable,* and *custodial.* In some cases, however, a fourth category is included, known as the *dull-normal.* Table 9-1 summarizes this classification system and presents educational expectations typical of individuals at each level.

Each classification system discussed here has certain strengths and weaknesses. Clearly, each has a different purpose, and its usage may be limited to a particular discipline or situation. Although there may be some overlap, the systems

Table 9-1
Educational Classifications and Achievement Expectations

Category	Approximate IQ Range[1]	Educational Expectation
Dull-normal	IQ 75 or 80 to 90	Capable of competing in school in most areas except in strictly academic areas, where performance is below average. Social adjustment that is not noticeably different from the larger population, although in the lower segment of adequate adjustment. Occupational performance satisfactory in nontechnical areas, with total self-support highly probable.
Educable	IQ 50 to 75 or 80	Second- to fifth-grade achievement in school academic areas. Social adjustment that will permit some degree of independence in the community. Occupational skills that will permit partial or total self-support.
Trainable	IQ 20 to 49	Learning primarily in the areas of self-help skills, very limited achievement in areas considered academic. Social adjustment usually limited to home and closely surrounding areas. Occupational performance primarily in sheltered workshop or an institutional setting.
Custodial	IQ below 20	Usually unable to acquire even sufficient skills to care for basic needs. Will usually require nearly total care and supervision for duration of lifetime.

[1]IQ ranges represent approximately ranges; high vary to some degree, depending on test administered. *Source:* P. C. Chinn, C. J. Drew, and D. R. Logan (1979). *Mental retardation: A life cycle approach* (2nd ed.) (St. Louis: C. V. Mosby), p. 23. Reprinted by permission of the publisher.

presented differ in many ways. A retarded individual may be classified in several different fashions at different times, depending on the system employed, the situation, and any of a multitude of other contingencies (for instance, the services available in a particular community; evaluation by a psychologist as opposed to a physician). Some who would prefer a single approach to classification have criticized this practice. However, a single approach to classification is not possible, given all of the different reasons for classifying mental retardation (legislative, administrative, instructional).

Professionals using applied behavior analysis have achieved perhaps the closest approximation to a uniform scheme in this respect. This approach focuses on functional skill descriptions (the retarded person's actual skills) rather than on the other dimensions discussed above (although it is somewhat similar to the AAMD system of adaptive behavior dimensions). Treatment is essentially based on the fundamental principles of learning theory, which have been presented earlier in this text (see Chapter 2). Often, the mildly mentally retarded are taught language, as well as basic academic and social skills. Those with more severe handicaps are typically taught self-help skills related to personal hygiene, such as grooming. One major strength of this perspective is that classification, description, and diagnosis are integrally tied to instruction and treatment. Because of this characteristic, the behavioral approach is particularly useful in the development and evaluation of individualized instructional and treatment programs.

PREVALENCE

How many children are mentally retarded? As is the case in defining the condition, answering this question is not as simple as it may seem on the surface. First of all, a complete census of the population would be neither simple to conduct nor economically feasible. Some direct census investigations have been undertaken over the years (for instance, Birch, Richardson, Baird, Horobin, & Illsley, 1970; Lemkau & Imre, 1969; Mercer, 1973), although for the most part we have relied on estimates based on expected percentages of retardation in the general population. Regardless of approach, the definition of retardation plays a central role in the outcome. Obviously, if the definition is altered, there may be a substantial difference in the number of individuals considered as retarded.

As we examine the magnitude of the mental retardation problem, it is important to distinguish briefly between two terms that are used in epidemiological research—*incidence* and *prevalence*. This is important here, because much of the literature about mental retardation has either ignored the distinction or used the terms loosely and interchangeably. There is, however, a substantial difference between the two. *Prevalence* refers to the number of cases identified in a given population at a particular point in time. *Incidence* refers to the rate of occurrence or the number of new cases identified within a specified period of time (for instance, in 1 year). Those cases counted in an incidence study would include new births (babies who were identified as retarded at birth) and older individuals who are newly diagnosed as retarded (such as those mildly retarded children who reach school age, begin to encounter problems, and are therefore tested and diagnosed). Those cases counted in a prevalence study would include all of the examples above, as well as individuals who were previously diagnosed and are still retarded at the time the study is conducted. These two types of measures clearly do not result in the same figures, which makes the distinction between them important. The number of people considered to be retarded is therefore somewhat variable. Particularly with the mildly handicapped, a person may be identified as retarded at one point in time (for example, school years) and no longer functionally retarded at a later time (during adulthood). In addition, it should be noted that precise data regarding either prevalence or incidence are very difficult to obtain.

Recent estimates of the prevalence of mental retardation have typically ranged from 1 to 3 percent of the general population (Grossman, 1983). The U.S. Department of Education stated in a 1985 report to Congress that more than 750,000 individuals with mental retardation between the ages of 3 and 21 were receiving services in America's public schools and that over 19,000 of these were between the ages of 3 and 5 (U.S. Department of Education, 1985). The 3 percent estimate has been most commonly cited in the literature, although some writers have advocated a figure closer to 1 percent. Tarjan, Wright, Eyman, and Keeran (1973) estimated prevalence using the 1 and 3 percent figures alternately for a hypothetical community of 100,000. Their figures with the 1 percent assumption were strikingly similar to actual observations collected by Mercer (1973) in a California city of 100,000.

Despite such evidence, we are still faced with an imprecise answer to the question regarding mental retardation prevalence. That is, prevalence rates may vary in different geographical locales. Mercer emphasized the impossibility of generalizing her findings directly to other communities (1973). Other surveys conducted in different settings have more closely approximated the 3 percent prevalence level (Lemkau & Imre, 1969). Thus, estimates and actual data regarding prevalence have varied between 1 and 3 percent (Baird & Sandovnick, 1985; Cooper, Wilton, & Glynn, 1985). While these estimates are most common, some controversy continues (for example, see Baird & Sandovnick, 1986; Richardson, Koller, & Katz, 1986). Clearly, the prevalence estimate depends on the frame of reference (that is, distinctions between incidence and prevalence), the environmental setting, and perhaps other unknown factors.

DEVELOPMENTAL FACTORS

As noted earlier, development is a central factor in the AAMD definition of mental retardation (Grossman, 1983). One can hardly discuss the disorder without heavy reference to child development. Study of retardation's causation, classification, treatment, and prognosis immediately immerses one in the developmental process. The purpose of this section is to examine the manner in which development plays a role in mental retardation.

In the section that follows this, we examine the etiology of mental retardation during prenatal, neonatal, and childhood periods. The prenatal period is vital to normal development. During gestation, toxins, accidents, or other unfavorable events may occur that place the unborn baby at risk for mental retardation. These often involve maternal health problems or genetic abnormalities that influence fetal growth and development.

In diagnosing child psychopathology, it is important to establish *when* the onset of a particular problem occurs. Very often the timing of an infection or of a chromosomal or physical accident will determine the impact of that incident. For example, *when* a debilitating accident occurs often affects the manner in which a youngster adapts to being paralyzed. It may also dictate the type of treatment administered and its success rate. These same types of considerations are evident in mental retardation. When a mother contracts German measles *(rubella)* determines the impact of the disease on her unborn child. If rubella is contracted by the pregnant mother during the first 3 months of gestation, there is considerable risk that the developing fetus will become mentally retarded. There is somewhat less danger later in the pregnancy, although such diseases usually involve some risk.

During the first trimester (3 months) of pregnancy, the tissue development of an unborn baby is progressing very rapidly. It is during this time that the foundation of physical development is primarily established, although the rest of the period should certainly not be discounted. The basic material for what will later become the *central nervous system* (the brain and the spinal cord) is rapidly being established, along with the visual and auditory systems, and many other parts of the young baby that are extremely important to its ability to function. When the tissue is developing at its most rapid rate, it is *most* vulnerable to the effects of detrimental influences such as rubella. If the central nervous system tissue being formed

at this time is damaged by infection, genetic accident, or factors such as maternal nutrition, all such tissue that subsequently develops may be damaged. For example, if the mother contracts German measles at the time that her unborn child is first (and most rapidly) developing tissue related to visual organs, the child has a much higher probability of being born with a visual defect than if the disease is contracted at a later time. This same child may also be mentally retarded, perhaps severely, because the essential foundation for the central nervous system development is also being formed at that time and all prenatal development beyond that point is affected. Thus the prenatal basis of the physiological development of a child is crucial and is affected by the timing of both fortunate and less fortunate events. This timing rule is very important in the prenatal study of mental retardation. It is important to determine when a vital organ system is developing most rapidly and when the foundation for later development is being established.

Mental retardation also may arise during early childhood. Physiologically, the baby is obtaining essential substances for life, such as nutrition and oxygen, from the environment. The baby is also affected by environmental stimulation (noises, light, and persons), which has great importance for subsequent development of mental functioning, speech, and social development. If the child's environment is basically supportive and stimulates proper development, there is a high likelihood that the child will develop normally. However, if the environment retards or interferes with development, the child may become retarded. As before, although from a different standpoint, the timing of unfortunate circumstances (or accidents) may have serious consequences. For example, if some infection is contracted by the newborn or young child that causes deafness prior to development of language, it may well affect all subsequent language development. Similarly, if the early environment is insufficiently stimulating, mental retardation may result.

Mental retardation can be prevented by timely treatment in some cases. An illustration of this can be found in phenylketonuria (PKU), which is an inherited metabolic disorder. In this condition, infants are unable to process phenylalanine properly. Phenylalanine is found in many common foods such as milk; the inability to metabolize it results in an accumulation of substances that damage the central nervous system, and mental retardation develops. However, if dietary treatment is implemented early, before the damage occurs or is serious, mental development can proceed normally.

ETIOLOGY

The causes of mental retardation are many and varied. In some cases, pathology of a physiological or biological nature can be identified; however, in many more, causation is unknown. The purpose of this section is to provide an overview of the origins of mental retardation.

Prenatal and Neonatal Causation

Genetic Factors   Genetic abnormalities are discussed in Chapter 2 in relation to a variety of disorders, including certain types of mental retardation. Briefly, the normal individual has 23 pairs of chromosomes, with one of each pair being contributed by each parent. Genetic *anomalies* (abnormal genetic makeup) may present various prob-

Slightly over two months and about one-and-one-half inches long, this fetus is developing very rapidly and is also very vulnerable.

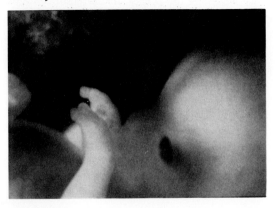

FIGURE 9-2. Chromosome configuration of a Down's syndrome female with trisomy 21.

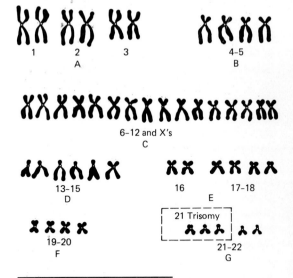

Source: D. W. Smith and A. A. Wilson. (1973). *The child with Down's syndrome (mongolism)* (Philadelphia: W. B. Saunders), p. 6. Reprinted by permission of the publisher.

lems that ultimately result in mental retardation. *Down's syndrome* is one of these prenatal conditions. Actually, there are three types of Down's syndrome, each resulting from a different type of chromosomal error.

The most common cause of Down's syndrome is known as *nondisjunction,* in which an extra chromosome exists at the 21st position in the G group. This condition is also known as *trisomy 21* because of the three chromosomes in that position. Figure 9-2 illustrates a chromosomal configuration for a Down's syndrome female with trisomy 21. Such a condition occurs because of improper cell division during the formation of the egg or the sperm. Because the error occurs prior to fertilization, its impact on the developing embryo is substantial and the damage severe. The probability of a nondisjunction error resulting in trisomy 21 is dramatically elevated for mothers over 40 years of age. Evidence suggests that the risk of a Down's syndrome birth after age 40 is approximately 1 in 65, whereas it is only 1 in

1500 under the age of 30 (Mikkelsen & Stene, 1970). Even higher risk levels were found by Lindsjö (1974) in a Swedish study: an incidence of 1 in 16 for women over 45, 1 in 67 between ages 40 and 44, 1 in 267 between ages 35 and 39, 1 in 687 between ages 30 and 34, and 1 in 1133 between ages 29 and 25. These figures are similar to those of more recent research that found incidence rates of 1 in 2000 at maternal age 20 and 1 in 20 over age 45 (Miller & Erbe, 1978). It should be noted that recent years have witnessed improved fetal diagnostic techniques and a reduction in pregnancies among older women. There has been a resulting decline in the incidence of Down's syndrome births (Penrose, 1967; Richards, 1967). Investigation of trisomy 21 continues, including basic research using animal models (mouse trisomy 16), which may provide further information regarding the chromosomal errors (Cox & Epstein, 1985; Epstein, Cox, & Epstein, 1985).

Down's syndrome may also be caused by a second chromosomal aberration involving material in the 21st pair in the G group. This condition is known as *translocation* and occurs when material from the 21st pair breaks off and fuses itself to another chromosome pair. For example, the material may fuse with the 14th or 15th pair of the D group. This imbalance of genetic material causes about 9 percent of all Down's syndrome infants of mothers under 30 years of age and 2 percent of Down's infants born to mothers over 30. This represents a very different incidence pattern from that of nondisjunction Down's syndrome. Nondisjunctions may well be genetic accidents that occur as a function of age or health. Translocation has been demonstrated to be inherited in about one-third of the cases (Robinson & Robinson, 1976).

The third type of genetic abnormality resulting in Down's syndrome is known as *mosaicism*. This condition is distinctly different from nondisjunction and translocation, in that it represents an accident that occurs after fertilization and that produces an infant with a mixed chromosomal makeup: Some tissue has cells that are affected, whereas other tissue has cells with the normal genetic configuration. Often cells with an abnormal

makeup involve the 21st pair, as in the conditions discussed earlier. However, the involved tissue and resulting damage are highly dependent on when the error occurs during the development of an embryo. The level of mental retardation may vary from mild to more severe impairment. Some cases of mosaic Down's syndrome have even been reported in the normal range of functioning, which illustrates dramatically the interaction between genetic and environmental influences.

Maternal Characteristics   Maternal age seems to be associated with aspects of the baby's health other than Down's syndrome. Spontaneous abortions occur more frequently in mothers who are very young (under 15), particularly if there have been multiple pregnancies. Likewise, the risk to both mother and infant is substantially increased for mothers over 35 to 40 years of age. Spontaneous abortion is **least** likely to occur between the maternal ages of 20 and 30; this has been translated by many to mean that these are the prime childbearing years.

Although the mother's age is certainly important, other maternal influences also appear related to infant prematurity. For example, adequate nutrition may be one of the most important factors influencing general fetal health and well-being. Maternal nutrition deficiencies may have a significant impact on fetal development, as discussed in Chapter 3. Logic and the most fundamental knowledge of physiology would suggest that poor maternal nutrition endangers early mental development. Despite such logic, and fragmentary evidence, the precise nature and degree of risk remain unclear.

Sometimes the unborn fetus may be inadequately nourished, regardless of the mother's nutritional status. Conditions such as maternal thyroid deficiency, chronic diabetes, and anemia may substantially affect the development of the fetus and result in premature birth. Problems associated with prematurity substantially increase the possibility that the baby will be intellectually impaired. If, for example, the mother has a vascular insufficiency, the blood supply to the fetus may be inadequate, limiting the basic flow of nutrients and

Maternal age seems related to certain causes of mental retardation.

oxygen. Maternal diabetes may have similar effects. The impact is mainly dependent on the severity of the mother's condition and on the success of its medical treatment. However, maternal diabetes is always considered to create some degree of risk to the baby, who should be monitored for birthweight and gestational age problems as well as for other complications (Babson, Pernoll, Benda, & Simpson, 1980).

Serious damage to the fetus may be caused by incompatible blood types between the mother and the unborn baby. Perhaps the best-known form of this problem involves the *Rh factor*. This difficulty may be encountered if the mother's blood is Rh-negative and the fetus has Rh-positive blood. The mother's system may become sensitized to the fetus's Rh-positive blood and begin to produce antibodies that cause serious damage to the fetus. Sensitization of the mother may occur if the Rh-positive blood from the fetus enters her circulatory system, which commonly happens during

delivery, or if Rh-positive blood has been used in a transfusion given to the mother. Typically, the firstborn child is not at risk unless maternal sensitization occurs following a transfusion to the mother. However, subsequent pregnancies present considerable fetal risk unless the mother receives medical treatment. The babies in these successive pregnancies are often damaged in the later stages of gestation as the mother's antibodies seek to destroy the Rh-positive red blood cells, which are essentially a foreign substance in the maternal system. This can result in several conditions, including *erythroblastosis fetalis* (a severe form of anemia) and *hyperbilirubinemia.* The latter condition results in an "accumulation of bilirubin from the hemoglobin in the red blood cells" (Robinson & Robinson, 1976, p. 120), which may be so concentrated that it damages the brain tissue and causes mental retardation. Fortunately, treatment for Rh incompatibility has advanced substantially, and many babies have been saved.

A variety of maternal infections may also increase the risk of harm to the unborn fetus, particularly if they occur during the first trimester of pregnancy. The likelihood of spontaneous abortion or severe defect in the infant is considerably greater when the mother has an infection accompanied by elevated fever *(febrile infection)*. Such conditions may be especially problematic, as the mother's illness may be very mild or even not recognizable but still may result in fairly serious harm to the fetus. This makes both research and treatment difficult. Also, viral infections may result in serious difficulties during pregnancy, although they do not always damage the fetus. Hellman and Pritchard (1971) reported that approximately 5 percent of all pregnancies have problems with infections that can be attributed to identifiable viruses.[1] German measles (rubella) is perhaps the viral infection most widely recognized as causing mental retardation. As noted earlier, the risk to the fetus is greatest in cases in which the mother contracts rubella during the first trimester of pregnancy. Evidence suggests that there is a 50 percent chance that the fetus will be infected if the mother has rubella during this time (Cooper & Krugman, 1966), and there is continued but lesser risk if she contracts it during the later months of pregnancy (Hardy, McCracken, Gilkeson, & Sever, 1969). It should be noted that mental retardation is not the only damage that results from congenital rubella. Deafness is the most frequent outcome; others include cerebral palsy, cardiac difficulties, blindness, seizures, and other neurological problems. However, data collected on the 1964 rubella epidemic indicated some impairment in intellectual functioning in half of the infected children (Chess, Korn, & Fernandez, 1971).

Syphilis is an infection caused by bacteria (the spirochete bacterium) transmitted by sexual contact. Maternal infection with syphilis may have a serious impact on the development of a fetus, particularly if the infection continues past the 18th week of gestation. In this condition the bacteria cross the placenta and actually infect the developing fetus, causing damage to the central nervous system and circulatory system tissue. Although treatment of syphilis has progressed over the years, venereal disease in general remains a serious problem. Often conditions are unreported, either because of embarrassment or because the symptoms are mild and subside. The danger to the fetus remains, however, and may result in spontaneous abortion, stillbirth, mental retardation, and many other difficulties for the infected baby. Treatment may prevent such outcomes *if* implemented prior to the 18th week; the damage inflicted after this time is likely to be permanent.

Toxoplasmosis is another infection that may result in severe problems for the unborn fetus. This condition is caused by a protozoan infection that is carried in raw meat and fecal material. One of the major hazards of toxoplasmosis is that in the mother, the infection may be so mild that it does not cause serious concern—perhaps no more so than a common cold. Fetal impact may be dramatic, however. Evidence suggests that nearly 85 percent of surviving newborns may be mentally retarded and may have other complications, such as blindness, convulsions, and a variety of other difficulties (Sever, 1970). It should be noted that if the mother is exposed prior to conception, the danger to the fetus is minimal, but toxoplasmosis becomes a problem if the exposure occurs during pregnancy.

Clearly, maternal infection may cause a wide variety of complications, leading to mental retardation, other defects, and even stillbirth. The fetus may also be endangered by a number of other substances introduced into the mother's system from the outside. Chemicals, drugs, alcohol, smoking, and radiation all may cause difficulties for the fetus. In some cases the detrimental effects are well known, whereas in others the data are only suggestive. However, it seems that the prenatal risk is heightened whenever almost any foreign elements enter the mother's system.

---

[1] Illnesses associated with viruses that are known to reach the fetus include smallpox, chickenpox, measles, mumps, hepatitis, encephalitis, poliomyelitis, and herpes simplex, as well as others. However, not all of these have been clearly identified as causing lasting impairments in the fetus.

Atypical Birth   Thus far, we have discussed several factors that may operate during the prenatal period to place the fetus in danger of retardation. A comprehensive examination of all possible influences that may operate during this period is far beyond the scope of this chapter; complete volumes have been written on this crucial part of life development (see, for example, Abramson, 1973; Arey, 1974; Babson et al., 1980; Balinsky, 1981). The final period of this phase, the birth process, also subjects a baby to risk of mental retardation. Historically, certain schools of thought have viewed the process of birth — even an easy birth — as an extremely traumatic psychological event. Early psychoanalysts (notably Sigmund Freud) attributed many later life difficulties, such as anxiety and depression, to repercussions from the shock of birth trauma. Birth is stressful to mother and infant alike. However, current thinking focuses much more narrowly on the physical trauma of atypical births than did earlier theories.

FIGURE 9-4. Example of breech fetal position.

Source: *Dorland's illustrated medical dictionary* (25th ed.) (1974). (Philadelphia: W. B. Saunders), p. 1253. Copyright 1974 by W. B. Saunders Company. Reprinted by permission of the publisher.

FIGURE 9-3. An example of normal fetal position.

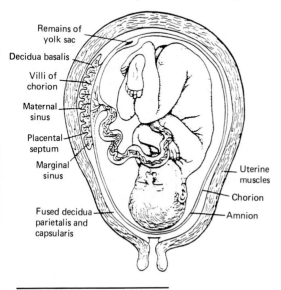

Remains of yolk sac
Decidua basalis
Villi of chorion
Maternal sinus
Placental septum
Marginal sinus
Fused decidua parietalis and capsularis
Uterine muscles
Chorion
Amnion

Source: P. L. Chinn. (1979). *Child health maintenance: Concepts in family-centered care* (2nd ed.) (St. Louis: C. V. Mosby), p. 109. Reprinted by permission of the publisher.

The position of the fetus *in utero* is very important in terms of potential birth problems. Figure 9-3 illustrates a normal fetal presentation, with the head positioned toward the cervix and the face down (it is assumed that the mother is lying on her back). Other fetal positions substantially raise the probability of damage. For example, the problematic *breech presentation* occurs when the buttocks (rather than the head) are positioned toward the cervix. Figure 9-4 illustrates the breech fetal position. Several difficulties may result from a breech birth. Unless the fetus can be turned, the head will exit through the birth canal last rather than first. This occurs during the later stages of labor, when the contractions are stronger and more rapid than during early labor. Breech birth may place a great deal of stress on the head of the fetus. In a normal delivery, the head moves through the birth canal slowly, permitting a gradual process of molding of the skull. But in a breech presentation, molding of the head may be rather rapid and perhaps incomplete, causing mechanical damage to the brain tissue. Damage may also occur because of the abnormal pressure (it is more intense and is brought to bear on a head that is in a reversed position).

The breech position may cause difficulties other than possible mechanical damage. Since the fetal head is the last portion to exit, the baby must obtain its oxygen solely from the umbilical cord until delivery is completed. This may cause two difficulties. First, the cord may be too short to remain attached while the head is expelled. Under such circumstances the placenta may become detached from the uterine wall, eliminating the oxygen supply to the fetus. This becomes particularly problematic if the head does not pass through the pelvic girdle fairly easily and quickly. The fetal head will be tightly confined in this portion of the birth canal, especially since the normal molding process is not occurring. If such difficulties arise, the baby may become *anoxic* (oxygen-deprived) and experience severe tissue damage. Anoxia may also occur if the cord is long enough but becomes pinched between the baby's head and the pelvic girdle. In such circumstances, the oxygen supply may be cut off in the same manner as if the placenta had become detached. In current medical practice, a breech baby is seldom delivered through the birth canal because of the risk described above. Even turning the fetus is dangerous, both because it is difficult and because of the possibility of entangling the umbilical cord and the body. In many cases a breech baby will be safely delivered by cesarean section.

Figure 9-5 illustrates another abnormal fetal position that results in serious difficulties. In the *shoulder presentation,* a shoulder or arm proceeds down through the pelvic girdle before the rest of the fetus. This type of presentation makes delivery through the birth canal difficult and frequently impossible. Sometimes it is possible to reposition the fetus, which may make delivery rather routine. However, as noted previously, *in utero* repositioning may prove difficult; cesarean section is often favored when extremely unusual fetal positions are present.

FIGURE 9-5. Example of shoulder fetal presentation.

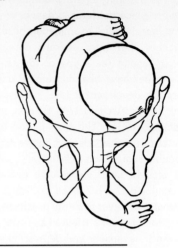

Source: Dorland's illustrated medical dictionary (25th ed.) (1974). (Philadelphia: W. B. Saunders), p. 1253. Copyright 1974 by W. B. Saunders Company. Reprinted by permission of the publisher.

In this discussion of the birth process and mental retardation, we should mention yet another area of risk. (Prospective parents should take heart, however, because advances in medicine have made childbearing safer than ever before.) Even if the fetal position is normal in all respects, the time the delivery takes can be very important. It has been noted previously that during early stages of labor, contractions are typically less frequent and intense than those occurring later in delivery. This progression of intensity and frequency serves a very important purpose. In the early stages of labor, the fetus begins to move into the birth canal and the pelvic girdle begins to stretch. For a normally positioned fetus, the head also begins to be molded to fit through the birth canal. This is possible because the fetal skull is not solid. There are seams in the bony structure that have yet to grow together; these facilitate the molding process (thus, the temporarily misshapen heads often observed in newborn infants). The lower intensity of early labor permits the molding to occur gradually. The pressure of molding is absorbed by fluid surrounding the baby's brain, protecting it from injury. However, if labor proceeds very rapidly, time may not permit adequate molding of the skull. Generally, a delivery following a labor of less than 2 hours is considered a *precipitous birth*. In these instances, there is an increased risk of brain injury and mental retardation.

The average labor time for a normal delivery is about 7 to 12 hours. Difficulties may also result in deliveries in which labor is unusually prolonged. One of the problems that may accompany prolonged labor is similar to that associated with precipitous birth. If advanced labor (intense and frequent contractions) continues for a long period, a great amount of pressure is placed on the skull of a fetus. This pressure may rupture membranes and blood vessels, causing tissue damage and mental retardation. A second danger of prolonged labor is oxygen deprivation (anoxia) to the fetus, or even a stillborn baby. Labor that continues substantially beyond the normal time span may place a fetus at risk if the placenta begins to become detached, cutting off the baby's oxygen supply before delivery is completed.

Neonatal Characteristics   Two neonatal characteristics are highly related to a child's risk of developing retardation—*birthweight* and *gestational age*. (*Gestational age* refers to the age of a fetus calculated from the time of conception.) Low birthweight and inadequate gestational age are perhaps the most common risk factors. Infants with these two characteristics may be endangered in a wide variety of ways. They may be mentally retarded or retarded in their physical development; they may be highly vulnerable to infections or other diseases and thus have a higher probability of dying as infants. Figure 9-6 shows infant mortality risk in relation to gestational age and birthweight. Premature infants have inadequate birthweight and low gestational age.

Comments   The preceding discussion may have been anxiety-provoking for the reader who is studying mental retardation for the first time, or is a prospective parent. We regret provoking anxiety, but it may be unavoidable or even helpful. The student of mental retardation cannot ignore these anxiety-arousing topics, but must maintain an appropriate objective perspective. *The vast majority of pregnancies proceed normally and produce normal babies.* Today, more than ever, medical advances have increased the safety of the mother and baby. Readers will recall that the prevalence of mental retardation is estimated as between 1 and 3 percent of the population. Mental retardation that is caused by prenatal influences, including abnormalities in the birth process, is quite infrequent; some is now preventable, as we point out later.

Causation during Infancy and Childhood

In some cases, a newborn infant may already be in serious difficulty, even though damage is not apparent at birth. A number of genetic disorders cause problems during infancy and later in a child's development. The first genetic disorder we discuss actually overlaps the prenatal and early stages of infant development. PKU, mentioned earlier (see p. 256), is an inherited metabolic disorder that occurs in about 1 of every 10,000 live births. Affected infants lack the ability to process phenylalanine, a substance found in certain foods such as milk. This results in an accumulation of toxic levels of phenylpyruvic acid, which severely damages the central nervous system. If the condition remains untreated, dramatic and serious intellectual impairment results. Most individuals with untreated PKU have IQs below 50 and are unable to speak. Many cannot master such basic tasks as bowel control and walking; they often exhibit generally aberrant behavior (Knox, 1972; Wright & Tarjan, 1957).

We have mentioned that PKU causes damage in both prenatal and neonatal stages of development. Prenatal damage occurs with pregnancy in mothers who themselves have PKU. In such circumstances the fetus is exposed to a high level of phenylalanine, which damages the fragile developing nervous system. The neonatal PKU condition presents a different situation, one in which great treatment progress has been achieved. In these circumstances the mother is a carrier but does not have PKU herself. PKU children born to such mothers develop symptoms after birth. When they encounter phenylalanine in their diet, their enzyme deficiency prevents proper processing of the substance, and toxic-

FIGURE 9-6. Neonatal mortality risk based on 14,413 live births from 1974 to 1980 at the University of Colorado Health Sciences Center.

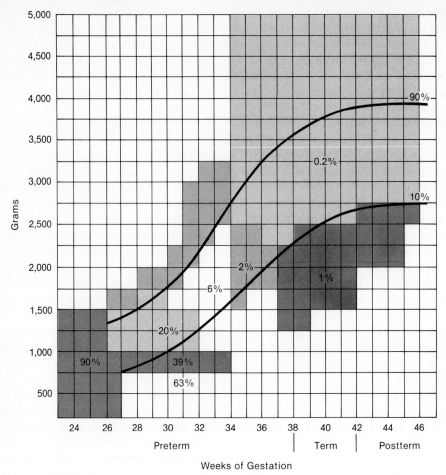

Source: B. L. Koops, L. J. Morgan, and F. C. Battaglia. (1982). Neonatal mortality risk in relation to birthweight and gestational age: Update. *Journal of Pediatrics, 101,* 972. Reprinted by permission.

level accumulations occur as described before. As we have noted, the resulting damage will be severe if the condition is untreated. Fortunately, such outcomes are unnecessary today because of advances in early diagnosis and treatment.

Maple syrup urine disease is another genetic disorder where there is metabolic deficiency. In this case, the diagnostic label is more representative of a symptom than of the disease process. Affected infants tend to excrete urine that has a dis-

tinctive odor resembling maple syrup. Maple syrup urine disease may cause severe intellectual impairment, although more often than not the condition is fatal. Menkes, Hurst, and Craig (1954) originally described a family in which four out of six infants died of the disorder during the first few weeks of life. These babies exhibited a variety of difficulties, and their urine had the distinctive odor of maple syrup. Researchers traced the cause of this condition and linked metabolic deficiencies of three separate amino acids to extreme central nervous system damage in the newborn (Silberberg, 1969; Snyderman, Norton, Roitman, & Holt, 1964; Westall, Dancis, & Miller, 1957). As with PKU, treatment may require dietary control, although it is complicated by the fact that three amino acids found in many different foods are involved in the problem. In an untreated state, maple syrup urine disease is lethal—few untreated infants survive more than a few weeks. Even treatment is risky, because so little is known about it.

Galactosemia is another genetically linked metabolic disorder that may produce mental retardation during early infancy. With this condition there is difficulty in carbohydrate metabolism, unlike the two previously discussed disorders, which involve protein and amino acid metabolism. Infants with galactosemia are unable to process certain sugar elements in milk properly. The result of such a condition, if untreated, is toxic damage to the infant's liver, brain, and other tissues. Again, treatment consists of dietary control (elimination of milk and other foods containing lactose) at a very early age, which may successfully prevent substantial damage. Untreated, galactosemia may cause permanent and serious intellectual impairment.

The reader should not interpret the discussion thus far as suggesting that all postnatal genetic disorders are metabolic in nature. Some are sex-related; that is, the aberration occurs in the sex chromosome portion of the genetic material (as in *Turner's syndrome, Klinefelter's syndrome,* and *Lesch-Nyhan syndrome*). Other genetic disorders may produce a variety of physical and functional manifestations. The interested reader may wish to consult a medically oriented volume for more complete information (for instance, Carter, 1978, 1979), since a comprehensive examination of genetic disorders related to mental retardation is quite technical and is beyond the scope of this chapter.

Most schemes for classifying events have certain failings in common: There are nearly always examples that do not neatly fit the classification system. This is exemplified by the first disorder

discussed here, PKU. Although we have chosen to examine the topic in the subsection on postnatal disorders, we have seen that it also occurs prenatally in certain cases. The same is true of the next few conditions to be discussed: some overlap exists between prenatal and postnatal causes of retardation.

In the very early stages of prenatal development, tissue begins to differentiate, setting the stage for formation of various organs. We have mentioned in the earlier section on developmental factors that this is a very vulnerable period for the unborn because of the vital development under way at the time. One event of great importance is the development of the neural tube, which eventually becomes the spinal and brain areas. This occurs quite early, with a groove being evident by the 17th or 18th day of gestational age; closure of the tube is normally completed between the 25th to 28th day. Substantial deviations in the closure process can result in serious outcomes, which are generally called *clinical defects.* The causes of such problems are unclear.

One closure-related clinical defect is known as *anencephaly,* which appears when there is improper closure at the head end of the neural tube. Anencephaly occurs early and results in incomplete development of the forebrain portion of cerebral tissue (in fact, the tissue often degenerates as gestation proceeds). Infants born with anencephaly typically die shortly after birth. Improper closure at other parts of the neural tube may also cause major damage to the central nervous system. For example, incomplete closure in the lumbar or thoracic spinal region may permit the spinal cord tissue and *meninges* (tissue covering) to protrude or bulge from their normal position. The type and extent of damage may vary, depending on the longitudinal position of the affected area. Paralysis of the body below the damaged area is not uncommon and may prevent control of excretory functions. Infections may result and progress up the spinal cord tissue, causing brain damage. Although typically not as serious as anencephaly, any incomplete closure of the neural tube may produce mental retardation as well as other disabilities.

Hydrocephalus is a clinical defect that may or may not be related to improper closure of the neural tube. In a generic sense, *hydrocephalus* refers to an increase in cerebrospinal fluid volume in the skull from any cause. With incomplete neural closure, the cerebral tissue does not assume its proper position in the skull cavity and is replaced by fluid. In such conditions, an excess of fluid in the skull is merely a symptom and is not the major difficulty in terms of brain damage. The primary problem results from the improper neural closure, wherein the spinal cord begins to fuse with surrounding tissue at the opening. As the body grows in length, the upper cerebral tissue is actually pulled into the spinal area.

Hydrocephalus more commonly results from defects in the production or absorption of cerebrospinal fluid. The central nervous system has a circulatory system for the distribution of cerebrospinal fluid. This fluid plays a number of important

Hydrocephalus is a clinical defect often resulting in mental retardation.

roles, one of which is to provide a protective layer between the brain tissue and the bony structures of the skull and spine. As this fluid circulates, a certain amount is produced anew and a similar amount is absorbed. If more is produced than is absorbed, an excess of fluid accumulates, putting pressure on the brain and causing brain damage and mental retardation. This may occur in two fashions, depending on age and skull development. During early infancy, as noted earlier, the skull is in sections and is not solid. An excess of fluid accumulating in the skull cavity at this time will place outward pressure on the skull, spreading the sutures and enlarging the head. The fluid production-absorption imbalance may also occur after the suture lines have begun to fuse. Obviously, in such circumstances, an adequate expansion of the skull cavity will not be possible. Hydrocephalus under both of the preceding situations places excess pressure on the brain, typically resulting in damage and mental retardation. The degree of impairment may vary from very severe to only mild. In some cases treatment is possible if the problem is discovered early and immediate surgery is undertaken to implant devices to drain excess fluid.

Psychosocial Factors

Infancy and the early childhood years are extremely important periods in an individual's development in a number of ways. Certain aspects of physiological development must be completed during these years, or they will never occur. In addition, during this time the infant is acquiring many of the skills and behaviors essential to intelligent behavior. The environment plays a vital role in this development, although we know painfully little regarding its *precise* impact in many cases (Wright, 1971). Our most solid evidence of environmental infuence has been found in situations where there is severe abuse and neglect. Clearly, such deprivation has a serious impact on the young child's development and may result in severe developmental lag and mental retardation (see Chapter 3). Our knowledge about the precise influence of less extreme environmental conditions is more limited. During the postnatal period, a complex constellation of social and physical factors comprises the child's environment. These factors include socioeconomic status, verbal and teaching interactions typical in the family, achievement motivation, exposure to toxic substances such as lead, and nutrition, to name only a few.

The list of potential psychosocial causes of retardation is nearly endless, and many risk factors occur together, so that it is often difficult to trace the origins of retardation in mild cases. This is particularly unfortunate, because, as noted earlier, the majority of mental retardation cases fall into the mild range. Many individuals who are mildly retarded come from low-socioeconomic-status environments, with circumstances of poverty and other characteristics described in Chapter 3. In the absence of other evidence (such as identifiable physiological abnormalities), and with the potency of sheer numbers, it is difficult to avoid drawing strong conclusions regarding environmental causation. However, as MacMillan (1982) has noted, "we must be careful to avoid class stereotyping" (p. 111). Investigation of causes with this part of the retarded population quickly becomes very complex and involves sociological as well as psychological influences. Furthermore, satisfactory resolution of the historical "nature-nurture" question remains forthcoming.

TREATMENT

This section examines a variety of techniques employed in working with mentally retarded children and adolescents. The term *treatment* should be interpreted cautiously, not in a literal sense, for it does not necessarily lead to a *cure*. Substantial progress has been made in preventing certain types of mental retardation, notably those with biomedical causes (Koch, 1979). (Prevention of retardation where there appears to be an environmental cause is a serious societal problem that is discussed fully in Chapter 15.) In addition, in some cases we are now able to arrest the progress of damage that would become more serious if untreated, as in the case of dietary treatment for PKU. However, although some prevention is pos-

sible, mental retardation is not amenable to *cure* as the term is generally interpreted.

The medical profession has played a significant role in the field of mental retardation. This is particularly true in cases that are identified prior to the beginning of formal schooling. Several factors contribute to this involvement. First of all, mothers are typically under the care of physicians during pregnancy, and the newborn infant is also under close medical scrutiny. Difficulties that arise during this time naturally come to the attention of the physician, especially as they usually stem from physiological problems of some nature—the type that the medical profession is trained to work with. Medical personnel are influential during a child's early years for yet another reason. Prior to the time the child enters school, the family is more likely to have a relationship with a physician than with a representative of any other discipline. Whereas it is not uncommon to have a family doctor, it would be rather unusual to have a family psychologist, and unless the family is very poor, they would probably not have a family social worker. Consequently, if a child of 3 or 4 years of age seems a little slow in mental development, the family physician is a probable contact even if the problem seems more mental than physical.

Prenatal Intervention

Earlier we have discussed Down's syndrome, a form of mental retardation caused by chromosomal abnormalities that can be diagnosed *in utero*. This diagnosis is accomplished by drawing a sample of the amnionic fluid *(amniocentesis)* and performing a chromosomal analysis. Such procedures carry some risk to the baby and are not recommended on a routine basis for every pregnancy. Amniocentesis may, however, be undertaken if certain risk factors are present (such as advanced maternal age or prior birth of a Down's child).

When we speak of *treating* Down's syndrome, the term is being used loosely and arouses a certain amount of controversy. If diagnosis indicates that the fetus has Down's syndrome, nothing can be done to *treat* the baby to prevent retardation. The genetic error exists in the cell structure, and subsequent cell division will include the chromosomal aberration. The parents may decide to terminate the pregnancy through a therapeutic abortion in order to avoid giving birth to a Down's child. Recent years have witnessed a decrease in the prevalence of Down's syndrome babies, which has partially been attributed to the availability of amniocentesis and legal abortions. Preventive measures of this type have become increasingly popular because of the emotional distress and financial expense involved in rearing a permanently disabled child.

The issue of abortion is, of course, highly controversial. Even more debatable are practices of allowing such children to die once they are born by withholding medical treatment (unrelated to their retardation) that would permit them to continue living (for example, simple surgery to correct an intestinal obstruction). These practices, as well as others (such as active termination of life of non-viable neonates), are not uncommon (Drew, Logan, & Hardman, 1984; Duff & Campbell, 1973). A decision involving such alternatives raises many moral and legal questions and is agonizing for both parents and professionals (Hardman & Drew, 1978). The physical and emotional outcomes of a decision to terminate life in such circumstances must be carefully measured against the impact of giving birth to and raising a child with Down's syndrome or some other serious disability that is identifiable at or before delivery. Medical personnel must be extremely sensitive to the needs of parents during the decision-making process; the parents should also be made aware of the resulting medical actions and potential legal ramifications (Hardman & Drew, 1980). In many cases, other professionals (such as psychologists and members of the clergy) are called in to assist in this difficult time.

We have previously noted that Rh incompatibility between mother and fetus can lead to mental retardation. Fortunately, over the years medical science has made dramatic progress in treating this condition. When an Rh incompatibility exists, doctors can monitor the fetal condition by periodically analyzing the amnionic fluid. If the fetus reaches a critical state, one of several actions may be taken. In the later stages of pregnancy, it may be possible to induce labor and deliver the baby early. As soon as delivery is completed, the infant is usually treated with an exchange transfusion, which supplies fresh and healthy blood. Obviously, such a procedure may not be possible if gestation has not progressed sufficiently to permit the infant to survive. But in such a situation the fetus must still have fresh blood. In some cases this has been successfully accomplished by conducting an exchange transfusion through surgically extending a fetal leg. However, perhaps the most dramatic development has involved transfusions conducted completely on an intrauterine basis. This is typically accomplished by inserting a long needle through the mother's abdomen directly into the peritoneal cavity of the fetus. The fetus then receives a transfusion of blood that is compatible with the mother's antibodies, and fetal development can proceed without damage to the unborn child.

An additional treatment has been developed in which an Rh-negative mother is injected with Rh_o immune globulin (commercially known as RhoGAM). As we have mentioned earlier, Rh incompatibility often does not present a problem during the first pregnancy if the mother has not become sufficiently sensitized to produce antibodies in damaging quantities. The mother should be injected with RhoGAM within the first 72 hours after she gives birth to her first baby. She will then be desensitized and can begin a subsequent pregnancy without antibodies being present. Treatment with RhoGAM is necessary for each pregnancy for Rh-negative mothers.

We have also discussed PKU, an inherited metabolic disorder that can lead to mental retardation. Recall that PKU infants cannot properly process phenylalanine, which then accumulates in the body to a point at which the central nervous system is damaged. PKU can be diagnosed early through routine screening procedures. If a baby is identified as having PKU early (within the first few days after birth), the level of phenylalanine in the system can be carefully *controlled* through dietary restrictions.[2] If it is initiated in time, control of the phenylalanine may prevent an accumulation from seriously damaging the central nervous system (Berman & Ford, 1970; Knox, 1972). If, however, treatment is not initiated promptly, irreparable damage may occur. Although PKU may be one of the most extensively studied genetic disorders related to mental retardation, the exact manner in which accumulated phenylalanine damages the central nervous system tissue is currently unclear. At least research on this disorder has led to an effective clinical diagnosis and treatment program, and to a consequent reduction in the number of impaired individuals.

Medical personnel often serve important roles in the general prevention of high-risk pregnancies. As we have noted earlier in this chapter, many conditions (such as maternal malnutrition) may contribute to such circumstances, and when they occur the probability of mental retardation is increased. Routine health care becomes very important in identifying and treating high-risk mothers and infants. The medical profession is joined in such efforts by social workers, nutritionists, and others who work as a team to provide comprehensive care for needy families.

Postnatal Intervention

There is a great deal of interest in infant stimulation programs for those children who are identified early as having problems. In some cases, such efforts are used with children who are at risk because of prenatal or later environmental circumstances. In others, the infants may be clearly identified as retarded because of a condition present at birth (such as Down's syndrome). This type of treatment often involves psychologists, behavioral therapists, educators, and parents. Although each program has different characteristics, the basic notion is to provide the infant with a stimulus-rich environment through systematic, planned stimulation of all sensory modalities. The goal of such treatment is to accelerate development beyond what may be expected in the normal environment. Research on infant stimulation is logistically difficult, and there is limited evidence regarding its lasting impact. However, the concepts have great intuitive appeal, and some long-term results appear promising (Hayden & McGinness, 1977; Strickland, 1971). Perhaps the two most prominent efforts to date have been the Milwaukee Project (Heber, Dever, & Conry, 1968; Heber & Garber, 1971) and the Carolina Abecedarian Project (Ramey & Campbell, 1977). Both projects involved comprehensive interventions in a variety of family environmental areas, as well as direct infant stimulation. As with most research of this nature, results are still emerging, but they seem to be favorable with respect to improving intellectual and social functioning (Garber & Heber, 1977; Ramey & Campbell, 1979a, 1979b).

Mentally retarded children frequently show distinct deficits in language development. Research efforts in this area have emphasized establishing an imitative repertoire of language skills (Baer & Guess, 1971; Baer, Peterson, & Sherman, 1967; Garcia, Guess, & Byrnes, 1973; Schumaker & Sherman, 1970), as well as generalization of language skills from one environment to another (Murdock, Garcia, & Hardman, 1977). Although results have varied to some degree, language treatment appears to offer a promising line of investigation and potential treatment, and more retarded children are learning to speak appropriately than was thought possible in the past. Teaching procedures have included demonstrating the required sounds and then rewarding children's closer and closer approximations to normal speech. Although effective, the process is extremely tedious and requires a devoted set of teachers and parents who are willing to spend a

[2] The term *controlled* is emphasized above because care must be taken in how treatment is implemented—simple elimination of phenylalanine is not sufficient. *Mass screening* procedures using blood samples result in the misidentification of a certain percentage of infants as PKU children who actually are not (*false positives*, in diagnostic terminology). When this occurs, the initiation of a highly restrictive diet results in a variety of impairments that otherwise would not occur. The preferred approach includes mass screening combined with follow-up evaluations of those infants who are suspected of having PKU.

great deal of time teaching their retarded children. Some evidence regarding the effectiveness of parent teaching programs is available (for instance, Cheseldine & McConkey, 1979), although highly structured programs conducted by trained professionals seem most efficient. Box 9-3 presents a study investigating the effectiveness of a treatment program aimed at modifying *echolalic speech* (the inappropriate repetition of the speech of others) in retarded children.

BOX 9-3 • A Treatment Program for Echolalic Children

Three subjects participated in this investigation. Their scores on the Vineland Social Maturity Scale (Doll, 1953) and the Alpern-Boll Developmental Profile (Alpern & Boll, 1972) are included in Table 9-2. Because echolalia is a unique language disorder, communication scores included in Table 9-2 are of questionable validity.

Each child's speech functioning had been labeled by referring agencies as developmentally delayed and echolalic. Subject 1 was 5 years, 7 months (5–7) old. She exhibited a repertoire of autistic-like behavior and was an independent child who preferred solitary ritualistic play to adult or peer interaction. Subject 1 often tantrumed when requested to take part in preschool activities. Although she was retarded in all areas of functioning, major delays were observed in the language, cognitive, and social areas. She had been echolalic for over 2 years.

Subject 2 (age 3–8) exhibited delayed development in all areas. His echolalic language behavior had been interpreted to be the result of emotional disturbance with concomitant mental retardation of an unknown etiology. Subject 2 would respond to many adult-directed requests, but his echolalic speech made it difficult to evaluate his cognitive capacity. When left alone, he played primitively with preschool toys while he repeated nonsense phrases over and over. He was frequently observed vocalizing a television commercial jingle for several consecutive hours. He had been echolalic for over a year.

Subject 3 (age 4–2) was diagnosed as having a pituitary-related hormone deficiency, which had delayed his physical growth; he was .91 m tall and weighed about 20 kg. His delayed development in cognitive functioning had been interpreted to be caused by a hormonal imbalance. Subject 3 demonstrated high rates of manipulating objects, but his interest in a single object lasted only for a short time. Because of this and his brief attention span, he had been described as hyperactive. Subject 3 generally made his desires known by posing questions to adults as he had heard the adult question him in the past. For example, he often asked to go to the bathroom by saying, "John, you want to go to the toilet?" Adults typically responded, "Oh John, you want to go to the toilet," and Subject 3 would immediately echo, "Oh John, you want to go to the toilet." Subject 3 had been echolalic for well over a year. A speech

Table 9-2
Vineland social maturity scale and Alpern-Boll developmental profile results

| SUBJECT | VINELAND SOCIAL QUOTIENT | ALPERN-BOLL IQ | ALPERN-BOLL DEVELOPMENTAL AGE EQUIVALENTS[1] | | | | |
			PHYS-ICAL	SELF-HELP	SOCIAL	ACA-DEMIC	COMMU-NICATION
1	63	61	4–6	4–6	2–2	3–8	2–0
2	68	73	3–0	3–4	2–6	2–10	1–10
3	70	57	2–6	3–6	1–10	2–2	2–0

[1]In years–months

Treatment takes on a different character as the mentally retarded child begins formal schooling. As we have mentioned earlier, many children are not identified as being retarded until they enter school. This is particularly true for a large portion of those who are mildly handicapped. Although their development may have been somewhat slow, their skills have been adequate to adapt (if only marginally) in the preschool environment. However, as they enter the schools, they

---

Box 9-3 (Continued)

therapist had worked with him for 10 months prior to this investigation, with no changes in his echolalic responding.

All three subjects had received comprehensive medical and psychological evaluations prior to referral to the experimental preschool. These reports indicated that each subject's hearing and vision were normal.

A list of 25 questions were compiled and used to assess echolalic behavior. Questions selected included those used in previous studies (Lovaas, 1976; Risley & Wolf, 1967), those that parents of subjects indicated as important, and those frequently used in criterion-referenced language-assessment instruments. All three subjects consistently echoed each of the 25 questions prior to the initiation of training. The sentences were:

Trained Response Probes

1. What's your name?
2. Where do you live?
3. Are you a boy or a girl?
4. How old are you?
5. What do you drink with?
6. What goes "meow, meow"?
7. What do you want? (while holding a cup of juice)
8. Is this a ball? (while holding a ball)
9. Is this a cat? (while holding a pencil)
10. What do you do when it's cold outside?
11. What do you do when you're thirsty?
12. How are you today?

Untrained Response Probes

13. What's his name? (pointing to a friend)
14. Is this an apple? (holding up an apple)
15. What do you want? (while withholding a favorite toy)
16. Is this a car? (holding up a ball)
17. What do you do when you are hungry?
18. What goes "ruff-ruff-ruff"?
19. What goes "tick-tock-tick-tock?"
20. What goes "moo"?
21. What do you cut with?
22. What are you doing? (while subject is eating)
23. What are you doing? (while subject is writing)

Box 9-3 (Continued)

are expected to perform in those skill areas that are most difficult for them.

Depending on the type and extent of the child's mental retardation, some of the medical and behavioral treatments discussed earlier may still be going on during the school years. Medication may be administered on a continuing basis if the child has difficulties that warrant such treatment. The behavioral therapist may continue working with children of school age to shape social

---

Box 9-3 (Continued)

24. What are you writing with?
25. What did you have for breakfast? (after asking parents)

Training and generalization data were collected in three areas of the school facility. Most of the training was conducted in individual study booths (1.5 × 2 m) designed to minimize extraneous stimuli from the classroom (10 × 4 m). Generalization data were collected in the booths and also in indoor and outdoor free-play areas (5 × 7 m and 20 × 40 m, respectively). The indoor area contained typical preschool materials (e.g., building blocks, puzzles, balls, miniature cars), while the outdoor area contained gross-motor toys (e.g., tricycles, balls, jungle gym, sandbox, wagons).

TRAINING PROCEDURE

The trainer prerecorded the correct responses targeted for training on a standard cassette tape recorder. These responses were repeated 25 times on the tape, with a 1- to 2-second pause between each repetition.

Training sessions occurred once each school day and lasted 10 to 30 minutes. Working in an enclosed study booth, the trainer and subject were seated face to face across a .65 × .9 m table. The trainer held an edible reinforcer (M&M, corn chip, pretzel, raisin, or cup of juice) approximately .5 m away from the subject's face and presented a targeted stimulus question (e.g., "What's your name?"). If the child echoed the stimulus, gave an incorrect response, or was silent for 10 seconds, the trainer said "no" loudly, removed the reinforcer from view, and turned away from the subject. The trainer simultaneously turned on a tape recorder and played the correct response at an audible volume. When the subject echoed the correct response, the trainer immediately switched off the recorder, turned back to the subject, smiled, and issued the edible reinforcer and verbal praise. In all cases the experimenter waited until a correct response was emitted, either directly in response to a question or echoed to the taped stimulus, before issuing reinforcement. If the child did not echo the taped response following any of the 25 prerecorded repetitions, the trainer rewound the tape and replayed it. This process was repeated until the taped stimulus was echoed. The training procedure is outlined in Table 9-3.

To maintain responding, the trainer delivered edibles and praise intermittently during baseline sessions. Reinforcers were issued on a variable ratio 5 schedule [reinforcing, on the average, every fifth correct response] 10 seconds following each child's response to a question stimulus. This procedure was similar to that reported by Carr and associates (1975). Subjects 1, 2, and 3 received 90, 113, and 118 training sessions, respectively.

Sessions were audiotaped at least once during baseline and at least three times during each training experiment and generalization probe for each subject. Independent raters worked

skills or to teach them to speak appropriately. The type of treatment and instructional programming will be largely determined by an assessment of individual needs.

One of the traditional approaches to instruct-

ing mentally retarded children in school has been to separate them from their nonhandicapped classmates. This has been accomplished by the use of both special schools and self-contained classes in regular schools. In the former arrange-

Box 9-3 (Continued)

TABLE 9-3

Tape-recorder training procedure for correct and error responses

STIMULUS 1	RESPONSE	CONSE-QUENCE	STIMULUS 2	RESPONSE	CONSE-QUENCE
Question (e.g., "What's your name?")	Correct	Reinforcer(s)			
	Error: Echo Incorrect Silence (5 sec.)	Loud "No" Edible removed Experimenter turns away	Taped answer (e.g., "Al Smith")	Echo (e.g., "Al Smith")	Reinforcer(s)

from these tape-recorded response data on a trial-by-trial basis. In addition, the raters monitored the trainer's behavior by direct observation. The raters' data were compared for reliability purposes. Reliability was calculated by dividing the number of agreements by the number of agreements plus disagreements using only cells in which entries had been coded. . . .

METHOD

During this phase of the investigation, each of the subjects was trained to emit four appropriate responses to question stimuli. Data were collected on the frequencies of correct responses and echolalic responses. Echolalic responses were defined as repetitions of the total stimulus question excluding the articles *a* and *the*. A response that included both the stimulus questions and the correct answer was not correct and was scored echolalic.

BASELINE

The trainer individually asked each subject four targeted questions. Each question was repeated 10 times in succession, with a 10-second pause between questions. Baseline conditions lasted 3 days for each subject.

Box 9-3 (Continued)

ment, mentally retarded children receive instruction in a separate school, operated exclusively for the handicapped. Self-contained classes represent a somewhat less dramatic separation, with classes for mentally retarded children being operated within a school that also houses nonhandicapped children. In past years these arrangements were the primary service delivery patterns for most, if not all, children identified as mentally retarded. Most recent trends have substantially altered the

---

Box 9-3 (Continued)

INTERVENTION

The trainer applied the tape-recorder procedure to the first trained response probe, "What's your name?" in individual sessions with each of the subjects. Next, intervention conditions were

FIGURE 9-7. Frequency of correct and echolalic responses for Subject 1.

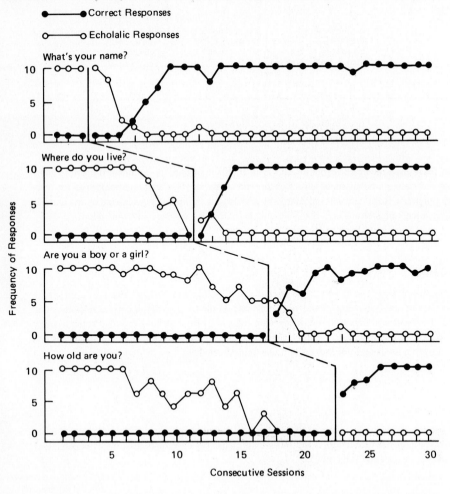

---

use of segregated approaches such as special schools and self-contained classes.

The favored means of instruction now aims to minimize the separation of handicapped and non-handicapped children. With this system, the men-tally retarded are instructed with their normal classmates to the degree that is feasible. The extent to which such integration occurs is presumably based on an individual child's level of functioning. Mildly handicapped children may receive

---

Box 9-3 (Continued)

successively introduced for three other stimulus questions with each subject according to multiple-baseline designs across responses.

RESULTS

Interobserver reliability for correct responses was 95 percent, with a range of 88 to 100 percent. Mean reliability for echolalic responses was 92 percent, with a range of 85 to 100 percent.

As can be seen in Figures 9-7, 9-8, and 9-9, each subject's frequency of correct responses increased after training. Three to seven sessions were required before correct responses were emitted to the first stimulus question, but each subsequent application of the procedure to a new question required fewer sessions. Additionally, by the completion of training on the first stimulus question, concurrent reductions were noted in echolalic responding by all three subjects on each of the three as yet untrained stimulus questions. Correct responses increased only when training was introduced.

FIGURE 9-8. Frequency of correct and echolalic responses for Subject 2.

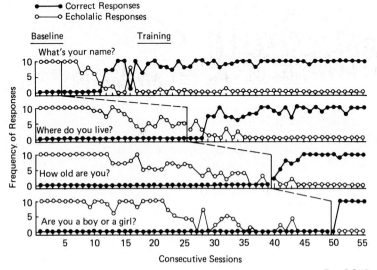

Box 9-3 (Continued)

instruction in a regular classroom with additional special assistance, or they may be in the regular class part of the time and receive specialized instruction part of the time in what is known as a *resource room*. In general, the more severely handicapped the child, the greater the likelihood that instruction will be undertaken in a setting apart from the regular educational environment. However, most recent thinking and practice have advocated working with even the more severely

Box 9-3 (Continued)

FIGURE 9-9. Frequency of correct and echolalic responses for Subject 3.

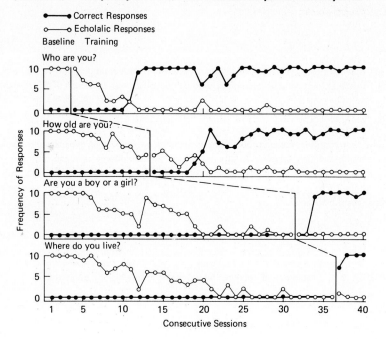

DISCUSSION

These data indicated that the training procedure effectively increased the subjects' correct responding to stimulus questions and decreased their echolalic responding. Additonally, there was evidence that the procedure resulted in a generalized decrease in echolalic responding to untrained questions. The deceleration tactics included in the procedure (loud "No" and removal of edible reinforcer) may have been responsible for this phenomenon. The reduction in the number of training sessions required to increase the frequency of correct responses indicated a cumulative effect. . . .

Source: W. J. Palyo, T. P. Cooke, A. L. Schuler, and T. Apolloni, (1979). Modifying echolalic speech in preschool children: Training and generalization. *American Journal of Mental Deficiency, 83,* 480–489. Reprinted by permission of the American Association on Mental Deficiency. References cited in the box text may be found in the References section of the present chapter.

Great effort is often required to teach simple tasks to retarded children.

retarded youngsters in instructional settings as close as possible to those of their nonhandicapped peers (Stainback & Stainback, 1985; Wehman & Hill, 1982; Wilcox & Bellamy, 1982).

The more integrated pattern of instruction has become a major focus of attention for educators since the mid-1970s. The popularity of this perspective is often attributed to the enactment of Public Law (P.L.) 94-142, the Education for All Handicapped Children Act of 1975 (described in more detail in Chapters 8 and 15). Certainly the idea was promoted by this act, but the integration movement predates P.L. 94-142 by a considerable 'period of time. In fact, P.L. 94-142 is probably best viewed as the culmination of a trend that began long before the law was conceived.

In 1970, Evelyn Deno presented a model that has been termed the *cascade system* of special ed-

ucation service. This model suggests a continuum of services ranging from segregated to integrated, based on the functioning level of the child. Figure 9-10 illustrates Deno's scheme. Her idea suggests that retarded children should receive the least restrictive possible instruction and placement; that is, their schooling should be like that of normal children to the degree that this is possible. As this notion gained popularity, and P.L. 94-142 was enacted, the terms *least restrictive alternative* and *mainstreaming* began to emerge and are now

FIGURE 9-10. The cascade system of special education services. The tapered design indicates the substantial difference in numbers of children involved at the different levels. The most specialized facilities and treatment are likely to be needed by the fewest children on a long-term basis.

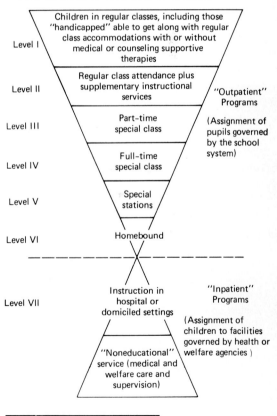

Source: E. Deno. (1970). Special education as developmental capital. *Exceptional Children, 37,* 229–237. Copyright 1970 by The Council for Exceptional Children. Reprinted with permission.

commonly found in the literature (Polloway, 1984). As these concepts have gained popularity, integration efforts have been undertaken with more severely retarded children that would not even have been considered a decade ago (Stainback & Stainback, 1985).

As we examine the *least restrictive alternative* concept, it is important to realize that the notion has many legal connections outside the context of education for mentally retarded children. The principle has its basis in criminal law (for instance, the case of *Jackson* v. *Indiana,* 1972), holding that it is cruel and inhumane ot dispense punishment disproportionately harsh in relation to the crime committed. The link between criminal law and educating mentally retarded children may seem tenuous at first glance. However, legal scholars have placed a great deal of emphasis on the relationship of this law to treatment of the mentally retarded (Kindred, Cohen, Penrod, & Shaffer, 1976). Throughout the years there have been many cases of litigation involving education of the mentally retarded. Furthermore, federal legislation such as P.L. 94-142 is not as innovative in educating the handicapped as some would suggest. Drew et al. (1984) catalogued over 200 different major pieces of federal legislation enacted between 1827 and 1981 that have focused on this area, and the number has surely grown since that time.

Dramatic changes such as integrating instruction for the handicapped into the educational mainstream never occur without controversy. The movement toward mainstreaming can be traced to research evidence that indicated few, if any, positive effects of placement in isolated special classes (for instance, Cegelka & Tyler, 1970; Goldstein, Moss, & Jordan, 1965; Vacc, 1972). Furthermore, some have openly suggested that segregated facilities are not justifiable on either financial or ideological bases (Orelove & Hanley, 1977). Interestingly, evidence is mixed regarding the effectiveness of integration (for example, see Brinker, 1984; MacMillan & Semmel, 1977; Stainback & Stainback, 1985). Thus one must ask why such a massive change would occur in the absence of a solid data base. Such a trend should

not be surprising, given today's climate of education in general and services to the mentally retarded in particular. Education of children is an enterprise in which society has traditionally had a great interest. It is a field "where changes and the initiation of new practices are often due to philosophical or social shifts in perspective. . . . P.L. 94-142 was enacted as a result of our social conscience" (Drew & Buchanan, 1979, p. 51). Such an observation explains the concern of the courts and lawmakers with education of the retarded. It does not, however, diminish controversy and debate. Wide-ranging and intense arguments on both sides have dwelled on issues of poor conceptual definitions (specifically of the least restrictive alternative), economics, and professional and parental resistance. It is simply not clear what is best for the children.

Educational integration of the retarded with normal children is part of a larger issue relating to the mentally retarded that has been called *normalization*. The normalization principle goes far beyond the context of education and refers to placement, residential arrangements, and treatment for retarded individuals at all ages. First espoused by Nirje (1969) and Bank-Mikkelsen (1969), the concept means "making available to the mentally retarded patterns and conditions of everyday life which are as close as possible to the norms and patterns of mainstream society" (Nirje, 1969, p. 181). This notion has been most prominent in arguments against mass institutionalization of large segments of the retarded population.

Debate regarding the placement of the retarded in residential institutions has been intense and continuing. Often the arguments have been based on compassion or on practicality. There is great variation from one institution to another; some provide good treatment, whereas others are quite dismal. Those that fall in the latter category have prompted much of the antiinstitutionalization furor. Many of those against institutional placement for the retarded have focused on the extremely bad conditions and treatment (Blatt & Kaplan, 1966), in "warehouses for human beings" (Burt, 1976, p. 441). Others have been more specific in demonstrating the negative effects of continued institutionalization on performance of a variety of tasks (Ohwaki & Stayton, 1978). Such literature raises the immediate question of how the mentally retarded fare outside an institutional setting. Research results are mixed regarding this question. Some of the retarded manage rather well, whereas others encounter some or great difficulty (Birenbaum & Re, 1979; Edgerton, 1967, 1984; Edgerton & Bercovici, 1976). The debate becomes further clouded as we look at retarded residents' views of the institution when they are elderly and have been institutionalized for many years. Drew et al. (1984) cited evidence indicating that older residents of institutions are largely happy with their lives and, in some cases, quite fearful of moving into the mainstream of society. Thus this issue remains unresolved, as do many other related to the mentally retarded.

PREVENTION

Prevention of mental retardation has been a goal of professionals in the field for many years. Because of the varied causes of mental retardation, prevention efforts have been extremely diverse, and some approaches have involved controversial methods. In some cases, preventing mental retardation requires courses of action that are unacceptable to some segments of the population.

As we have seen, there are a number of prenatal causes of mental retardation. In some cases these involve health problems or disease states that affect the developing fetus through the mother during pregnancy. Certain causes have become less of a problem than they once were because of immunizations (such as that for rubella) that are routinely undertaken with a large portion of our general population. To the extent that these are effective in reducing the occurrence of maternal difficulties during pregnancy, they become important steps in preventing mental retardation.

Maternal nutrition and personal habits may also have adverse effects on a developing fetus in certain cases. In some instances, high-risk maternal conditions have existed long before the pregnancy. Drew et al. (1984) indicated that "mater-

nal malnutrition, *which is often a life-long state of inadequacy,* has been implicated as exerting possible damaging influence on the fetus, particularly to the central nervous system" (p. 165, emphasis added). Such problems become especially severe when expectant mothers do not seek health care advice, which occurs with surprising frequency. In 1977 the President's Committee on Mental Retardation found that as many as 30 percent of all expectant women do not consult a physician during their pregnancy. In a related manner, there has long been concern regarding heavy maternal consumption of alcohol and related birth defects, which are estimated to occur in about 2 per 1000 live births (Centers for Disease Control, 1984). Abel (1984) reported that thus far media campaigns to inform women of these dangers have not reduced alcohol consumption appreciably. Furthermore, Baumeister and Hamlett (1986) found a disappointingly low commitment on the part of state governments for programs to prevent fetal alcohol syndrome, although there were notable exceptions.

A close relationship between medical personnel and new parents is important in the prevention of mental retardation. As we have seen in the section on causation, a number of problems may lead to development of mental retardation very quickly after birth unless they are recognized through monitoring, assessment, and early intervention. For example, PKU screening is now routinely undertaken when a baby is born and the family is in contact with a physician. When a baby is identified, treatment can be successfully undertaken through dietary control, thereby preventing damage to the central nervous system.

Prenatal screening and diagnosis can also lead to preventive intervention that may be highly controversial from a moral and ethical perspective. Procedures are available that permit detection of certain types of fetal damage *in utero,* which may present those involved with a difficult decision regarding continuation of the pregnancy. Although therapeutic abortion is legal and is much more accepted than it once was, such actions still present dilemmas for many people. In addition, there is greater public awareness of the problems of providing treatment to versus withholding it from newborn babies who are grossly defective at birth (Drew et al., 1984). Decisions to withhold treatment and thereby "prevent" mental retardation are difficult and have many ramifications beyond any specific case being considered (Hardman, 1984; Hardman & Drew, 1980).

SUMMARY

Mental retardation has long been recognized and studied scientifically for many decades. Despite this lengthy history, problems and variations regarding definition and classification have persisted even into recent times. However, the AAMD definition is widely accepted and includes both intellectual and adaptive behavior deficits. Although definitional differences are significantly reflected in prevalence figures, estimates of the number of retarded have generally ranged from 1 to 3 percent of the general population. Classification schemes used in the field of mental retardation have included etiology, adaptive behavior, severity of intellectual deficit, and educational expectations. Each approach to definition and classification has certain advantages and limitations, depending on its purpose.

Causation of mental retardation is as varied as the types and levels of severity of the problem. Mental retardation may result from abnormalities during pregnancy, birth, and infancy. During the prenatal period, mental retardation may result from genetic aberrations or environmental difficulties that influence the health of the mother and the fetus. Also, the birth process itself may result in damage that can cause mental retardation. After birth, mental retardation may be caused by environmental influences that limit the opportunity to develop, or by trauma or physical accident.

Treatment of mental retardation has been as diverse as its causes and behavioral characteristics. Some treatments have involved biological and medical interventions, whereas others have focused on psychological and behavioral methods. Results have been mixed; some are promising, some disappointing. Each must be assessed individually.

chapter

10

Childhood Psychosis and Pervasive Developmental Disorders

KEY TERMS

Childhood-Onset Pervasive Developmental Disorder.   A childhood disorder that occurs during middle childhood and shares a number of behavioral symptoms with infantile autism and childhood schizophrenia.

Childhood Schizophrenia.   A childhood psychotic disorder that is characterized by a late onset, thought disorder, hallucinations, and delusions.

Infantile Autism.   A pervasive developmental disorder that is characterized by an early onset and difficulties in relating socially to other people.

Pervasive Developmental Disorders.   A general classification category from DSM-III-R that includes two conditions: infantile autism and childhood-onset pervasive developmental disorder.

CHAPTER OVERVIEW

Childhood psychosis and *pervasive developmental disorders* are two general labels that have been used to describe some of the most damaging and debilitating childhood disorders. The terms *psychosis* and *developmental disorder* can be confusing, particularly if they are used interchangeably. However, there are important distinctions between the two terms. First, *psychosis* is the older of the two terms, and it has been used in the past to describe all of the conditions covered in this chapter. *Psychosis* carries many connotations of bizarre, incomprehensible behaviors that seem to be extremely abnormal, as in the case of a child who lives in a fantasy world, hears strange voices, and completely screens out reality. It also implies that a child may have been developing normally and then has developed bizarre behaviors. The term is frequently used to describe conditions such as schizophrenia with a childhood or adolescent onset.

Pervasive developmental disorders is a new term that was first used as a classification category in the third edition of the *Diagnostic and Statistical Manual of Mental Disorders* (DSM-III) (see Chapter 12). Unlike *psychosis,* the term *pervasive developmental disorder* suggests that the condition has happened early in the child's development and has affected all of the child's developing systems (social, language, and cognitive). In a sense, the child has never really been normal, but either was born with the condition or developed it very early. *Pervasive developmental disorders* is a general category from the new DSM III-R that includes two basic conditions: infantile autism and childhood-onset pervasive developmental disorder.

This chapter reviews the basic childhood psychoses and pervasive developmental disorders. Particular comparisons are made between childhood schizophrenia and infantile autism, because these are the most frequent disorders in these categories; however, other conditions (such as childhood-onset pervasive developmental disorder, Rett's syndrome, and Wilson's disease) are also briefly covered. The history, possible causes, treatments, and prognoses for each condition are reviewed.

HISTORY AND DEFINITIONS

Historically, the diagnosis of childhood behavior disorders—especially of severe forms such as childhood psychosis—has been a matter of con-

troversy (Kanner, 1971a; Ollendick & Hersen, 1983). This controversy was a function of early beliefs that bizarre forms of behavior were a result of demonic possession. Demons possessed sinners and witches, and theoretically, because children were generally too young to be sinners, they could not be possessed; their strange behaviors were thus simply ignored or denied. However, there are some early accounts of disturbed children. Some old Irish folk tales describe a fairyland of the "good people" who had the form of humans but not the "burden of the human heart." These fairy children were remote, beautiful, and in no need of human contact (Park, 1982). Autistic children have these characteristics.

Probably the most famous early child case is that of Victor, the "wild boy of Aveyron," who was found wandering naked in the woods of Aveyron, France, in 1799. When first captured, Victor acted much like a wild animal; he had few civilized behaviors, and it was assumed at the time that he had been raised by wolves. Victor was placed with a physician, Jean Itard, who worked with him using several techniques that were very similar to modern special education techniques (Itard, 1799/1962). From Itard's description of Victor, it is clear that he had not been raised by wolves, but was suffering from infantile autism. When first discovered at approximately the age of 11, Victor avoided eye contact, played with few toys, resisted any change, and had a remarkable memory but no language. These are some of the basic behavioral symptoms of childhood autism, a condition that was not recognized until 140 years later.

Although there are sketchy accounts of childhood psychosis and developmental disorders, no real advancement was made in their research or treatment until the turn of the 20th century. The study of the childhood disorders made advancements on the coattails of adult psychiatry. Kraepelin, a German psychiatrist, developed classification systems and wrote textbooks on adult psychiatric disorders. In particular, he described *dementia praecox* (early progressive mental deterioration)—a form of psychotic behavior that he assumed started in adolescence *(praecox),* and that was characterized by mental deterioration and bizarre behavior *(dementia)* (Kraepelin, 1896). Later, a Swiss psychiatrist, Bleuler (1911/1950), coined the term *schizophrenia* (a Greek term meaning "split mind") to describe this condition.

Several decades later, researchers started to describe childhood conditions that were similar to the adult conditions. Potter (1933) was the first to describe childhood schizophrenia. Later the terms *symbiotic psychosis* (Mahler, 1952) and *atypical childhood psychosis* (Rank, 1949) were introduced. These two conditions closely parallel the modern description of childhood-onset pervasive development disorder. Infantile autism was not recognized as a separate condition until 1943, when Leo Kanner discovered the remarkable similarity in behavorial characteristics of 11 children referred to Johns Hopkins Hospital for treatment (Kanner, 1943).

Childhood Schizophrenia Defined

Potter (1933) based his classification system for childhood schizophrenia on many of the characteristics of adult schizophrenia. He commented, however, that children are unlikely to exhibit psychopathology with all the elaborations of an adult. Stated simply, because children do not have the language complexity, intelligence, or maturity of adults, their psychotic symptoms are different. Potter developed a classification system that included a lack of interest in the environment; withdrawal into a fantasy world in which everyday experience has little meaning; a defect in logical thinking; and emotional reactions ranging from a stupor to extreme, unexplained excitement. What primarily characterized these children were the second and third of these symptoms (their withdrawal into a fantasy world and their illogical, disturbed thinking).

Modern classification of schizophrenia does not differ a great deal from Potter's early description of the condition. However, DSM-III-R does not have a specific category for childhood schizophrenia. The adult criteria for schizophrenia are used for children and adolescents; these criteria are listed in Table 10-1. As can be seen from this list, a great deal of emphasis is placed on hallucinations and thought disorders (illogical, disturbed thinking). For "schizophrenia occurring in childhood there are oddities of behavior; but typically there are hallucinations, delusions (unreasonable false beliefs), and loose associations or incoherence (not in a logical or proper sequence)" (American Psychiatric Association, 1980, p. 89).

Infantile Autism Defined

The term *autism* was first introduced into the psychological language by Bleuler (1911/1950) to describe adult patients who withdrew socially from their environment. It was Leo Kanner (1943), however, who first studied and applied this label to 11 children who were socially aloof and self-isolated from a very early age. He studied this same group from their early childhood through adulthood, giving detailed descriptions of their adjustment and placements.

Kanner viewed infantile autism as a distinct syndrome different from childhood schizophrenia or mental retardation. With schizophrenia, there is a withdrawal from a normal level of functioning, while autism is a syndrome in which the child has never functioned at an adequate level, suggesting an "infantile" origin of the condition (Margolies, 1977). Along with the cardinal characteristic of an inability to relate to other people, Kanner found other distinct disturbances supporting his contention that autism was indeed a separate syndrome. These characteristics included disruption of language development, or a complete failure to develop language; a need to maintain the environment with no changes ("sameness"); monotonous repetitions of behavioral sequences such as hand flapping or twirling; good intellectual abilities in very restricted areas (such as a memory for dates or names); and little spontaneous play or inappropriate play activities.

The DSM-III-R definition of autism includes most of the early characteristics described by Kanner, such as a lack of social responsiveness to other humans, disrupted communication skills, and bizarre responses to aspects of the environment. However, DSM-III-R has added the stipula-

Table 10-1
Diagnostic Criteria for a Schizophrenic Disorder

A. Presence of characteristic psychotic symptoms in the active phase: either (1), (2), or (3) for at least one week (unless the symptoms are successfully treated):
  (1) two of the following:
    (a) delusions
    (b) prominent hallucinations (throughout the day for several days or several times a week for several weeks, each hallucinatory experience not being limited to a few brief moments)
    (c) incoherence or marked loosening of associations
    (d) catatonic behavior
    (e) flat or grossly inappropriate affect
  (2) bizarre delusions (i.e., involving a phenomenon that the person's culture would regard as totally implausible, e.g., thought broadcasting, being controlled by a dead person)
  (3) prominent hallucinations [as defined in (1)(b) above] of a voice with content having no apparent relation to depression or elation, or a voice keeping up a running commentary on the person's behavior or thoughts, or two or more voices conversing with each other
B. During the course of the disturbance, functioning in such areas as work, social relations, and self-care is markedly below the highest level achieved before onset of the disturbance (or, when the onset is in childhood or adolescence, failure to achieve expected level of social development).
C. Schizoaffective Disorder and Mood Disorder with Psychotic Features have been ruled out, i.e., if a Major Depressive or Manic Syndrome has ever been present during an active phase of the disturbance, the total duration of all episodes of a mood syndrome has been brief relative to the total duration of the active and residual phases of the disturbance.
D. Continuous signs of the disturbance for at least six months. The six-month period must include an active phase (of at least one week, or less if symptoms have been successfully treated) during which there were psychotic symptoms characteristic of Schizophrenia (symptoms in A), with or without a prodromal or residual phase, as defined below.

Prodromal phase: A clear deterioration in functioning before the active phase of the disturbance that is not due to a disturbance in mood or to a Psychoactive Substance Use Disorder and that involves at least two of the symptoms listed below.
Residual phase: Following the active phase of the disturbance, persistence of at least two of the symptoms noted below, these not being due to a disturbance in mood or to a Psychoactive Substance Use Disorder.
Prodromal or Residual Symptoms:
  (1) marked social isolation or withdrawal
  (2) marked impairment in role functioning as wage-earner, student, or homemaker
  (3) markedly peculiar behavior (e.g., collecting garbage, talking to self in public, hoarding food)
  (4) marked impairment in personal hygiene and grooming
  (5) blunted or inappropriate affect
  (6) digressive, vague, overelaborate, or circumstantial speech, or poverty of speech, or poverty of content of speech
  (7) odd beliefs or magical thinking, influencing behavior and inconsistent with cultural norms, e.g., superstitiousness, belief in clairvoyance, telepathy, "sixth sense," "others can feel my feelings," overvalued ideas, ideas of reference
  (8) unusual perceptual experiences, e.g., recurrent illusions, sensing the presence of a force or person not actually present
  (9) marked lack of initiative, interests, or energy
Examples: Six months of prodromal symptoms with one week of symptoms from A; no prodromal symptoms with six months of symptoms from A; no prodromal symptoms with one week of symptoms from A and six months of residual symptoms.
E. It cannot be established that an organic factor initiated and maintained the disturbance.
F. If there is a history of Autistic Disorder, the additional diagnosis of Schizophrenia is made only if prominent delusions or hallucinations are also present.

tion that the condition must develop before 36 months of age. DSM-III-R also indicates that autism is developmental in nature, with the symptoms gradually manifesting themselves from infancy to 36 months of age. This syndrome development is described in Table 10-3 for a child from infancy to 60 months of age for the most typical type of autism, with an early but gradual onset (Freeman & Ritvo, 1984).

It should be noted that while Kanner was ac-curate in describing the autism syndrome in general, he was wrong about the intellectual ability of these children. He thought that autistic children had good intellectual development, based on the observation that some of the children had exceptional cognitive abilities *(splinter skills)* in one area, such as memory for calendar dates. However, it is now recognized that most autistic children are intellectually mentally retarded. Even the few children with exceptional splinter skills are generally

Table 10-2

Diagnostic Criteria for Infantile Autism

At least eight of the following sixteen items are present, these to include at least two items from A, one from B, and one from C.

Note: Consider a criterion to be met *only* if the behavior is abnormal for the person's developmental level.

A. Qualitative impairment in reciprocal social interaction as manifested by the following:
    (The examples within parentheses are arranged so that those first mentioned are more likely to apply to younger or more handicapped, and the later ones, to older or less handicapped, persons with this disorder.)
    (1) marked lack of awareness of the existence or feelings of others (e.g., treats a person as if he or she were a piece of furniture; does not notice another person's distress; apparently has no concept of the need of others for privacy)
    (2) no or abnormal seeking of comfort at times of distress (e.g., does not come for comfort even when ill, hurt, or tired; seeks comfort in a stereotyped way, e.g., says "cheese, cheese, cheese" whenever hurt)
    (3) no or impaired imitation (e.g., does not wave bye-bye; does not copy mother's domestic activities; mechanical imitation of others' actions out of context)
    (4) no or abnormal social play (e.g., does not actively participate in simple games; prefers solitary play activities; involves other children in play only as "mechanical aids")
    (5) gross impairment in ability to make peer friendships (e.g., no interest in making peer friendships; despite interest in making friends, demonstrates lack of understanding of conventions of social interaction, for example, reads phone book to uninterested peer)

B. Qualitative impairment in verbal and nonverbal communication, and in imaginative activity, as manifested by the following:
    (The numbered items are arranged so that those first listed are more likely to apply to younger or more handicapped, and the later ones, to older or less handicapped, persons with this disorder.)
    (1) no mode of communication, such as communicative babbling, facial expression, gesture, mime, or spoken language
    (2) markedly abnormal nonverbal communication, as in the use of eye-to-eye gaze, facial expression, body posture, or gestures to initiate or modulate social interaction (e.g., does not anticipate being held, stiffens when held, does not look at the person or smile when making a social approach, does not greet parents or visitors, has a fixed stare in social situations)
    (3) absence of imaginative activity, such as playacting of adult roles, fantasy characters, or animals; lack of interest in stories about imaginary events
    (4) marked abnormalities in the production of speech, including volume, pitch, stress, rate, rhythm, and intonation (e.g., monotonous tone, questionlike melody, or high pitch)
    (5) marked abnormalities in the form or content of speech, including stereotyped and repetitive use of speech (e.g., immediate echolalia or mechanical repetition of television commercial); use of "you" when "I" is meant (e.g., using "You want cookie?" to mean "I want a cookie"); idiosyncratic use of words or phrases (e.g., "Go on green riding" to mean "I want to go on the swing"); or frequent irrelevant remarks (e.g., starts talking about train schedules during a conversation about sports)
    (6) marked impairment in the ability to initiate or sustain a conversation with others, despite adequate speech (e.g., indulging in lengthy monologues on one subject regardless of interjections from others)

C. Markedly restricted repertoire of activities and interests, as manifested by the following:
    (1) stereotyped body movements, e.g., hand-flicking or -twisting, spinning, head-banging, complex whole-body movements
    (2) persistent preoccupation with parts of objects (e.g., sniffing or smelling objects, repetitive feeling of texture of materials, spinning wheels of toy cars) or attachment to unusual objects (e.g., insists on carrying around a piece of string)
    (3) marked distress over changes in trivial aspects of environment, e.g., when a vase is moved from usual position
    (4) unreasonable insistence on following routines in precise detail, e.g., insisting that exactly the same route always be followed when shopping
    (5) markedly restricted range of interests and a preoccupation with one narrow interest, e.g., interested only in lining up objects, in amassing facts about meteorology, or in pretending to be a fantasy character

D. Onset during infancy or childhood.

Specify if childhood onset (after 36 months of age).

Source: American Psychiatric Association. (1987). *Diagnostic and statistical manual of mental disorders* (3rd ed., revised) (Washington, DC: Author), pp. 38–39. Copyright 1987 by the American Psychiatric Association. Reprinted by permission.

Some autistic children appear physically normal and attractive.

retarded in most other areas. A case example of an autistic boy, which describes many of the symptoms of autism and their effects on a family, is presented in Box 10-1.

Childhood-Onset Pervasive Developmental Disorder — Not Otherwise Specified

The category of childhood-onset pervasive developmental disorder (COPDD) was new to the DSM-III classification system. It can also be a confusing disorder for several reasons. The first of these is its name. COPDD is a specific condition; it can, however, be easily confused with the global classification category of pervasive developmental disorders. The classification category of pervasive developmental disorders includes the specific conditions of (1) infantile autism and (2) COPDD.

The second confusing aspect of COPDD is that it shares many characteristics of both infantile autism and childhood schizophrenia (Cohen, Volkmar, & Paul, 1986). The DSM III-R diagnostic criteria are listed in Table 10-4, with impaired social relations being a primary characteristic. The primary difference between COPDD and autism and

childhood schizophrenia is the age of onset for the condition. COPDD is supposed to occur after 36 months of age, which is later than autism conditions develop, and before age 12, which is before the onset of most schizophrenic conditions. This range of acceptable onset for COPDD is like a "no child's land" for a psychosis or a developmental disorder, because few cases are diagnosed during this time period (see Figure 10-1). The low frequency and overlapping characteristics add to the confusion, because few clinicians have had experience with COPDD.

More research is needed on COPDD as a clinical condition. Is it truly a separate condition with a separate cause? Or is it a subtype of autism with an onset after 36 months of age? Because there is so little factual information on COPDD, the rest of this chapter concentrates primarily on infantile autism and childhood schizophrenia.

DIFFERENCES AND SIMILARITIES BETWEEN AUTISM AND CHILDHOOD SCHIZOPHRENIA

Several researchers have argued that autism and childhood schizophrenia are fundamentally differ-

Table 10-3
Areas of Disturbances

Ages	Sensory-Motor	Speech-Language	Relating to People, Objects, and Events
Birth 0 to 6 months	Quiet or fussy Persistent rocking Startled and/or nonresponsive to stimuli Unusual sleep cycles	No vocalizing Crying not related to needs	No anticipatory social responses (absent or delayed smiling response) Poor or absent eye-to-eye contact Fails to respond to mother's attention and crib toys
6 to 12 months	Sleeping and eating cycles fail to develop Uneven motor development Difficulty with transition to table foods Failure to hold objects and/or attachment to unusual objects Appears to be deaf Preoccupation with fingers Over- and/or underreaction to sensory stimuli	Babbling may stop Does not imitate sounds, gestures, or expressions	Unaffectionate; difficult to engage in baby games Does not wave "bye-bye" No interest in toys Flicks objects away
12 to 24 months	Sleep cycle problems Loss of previously acquired skills Sensitivity to stimuli Seeks repetitive stimulation Repetitive motor mannerisms appear: e.g., handflapping, whirling	No speech or occasional words Stops talking Gestures do not develop Repeats sounds noncommunicatively	Withdrawn No separation distress Unusual use of toys: e.g., spins, flicks, lines up objects
24 to 36 months	Sleep cycle problems continue Appears to be able to do things but refuses Delay in self-care skills Unusual sensitivity to stimuli and repetitive motor mannerisms continue Hyperactivity and/or hypoactivity	Mute or intermittent talking Echolalia: e.g., repeats TV commercials Specific cognitive abilities: e.g., good rote memory, superior puzzle skills Leads adult by hand to communicate needs	Does not play with others Prefers to be alone Unusual use of toys continues
36 to 60 months	Above continue, sensitivity to stimuli and motor mannerisms may decrease	No speech Echolalia Pronoun reversal Abnormal tone and rhythm in speech Unusual thoughts	Above continue but may become social Upset by changes in environment

Source: B. J. Freeman and E. R. Ritvo. (1984). The syndrome of autism: Establishing the diagnosis and principles of management. *Pediatric Annals, 13,* 284–296. Reprinted by permission.

ent conditions (Makita, 1966; Rutter, 1974; Schopler & Dalldorf, 1980). Studies that have specifically compared autistic and schizophrenic children have found consistent differences between them (Green, et al. 1984). It appears that the primary differences between infantile autism and childhood schizophrenia are reflected in the cardinal characteristics of the two conditions. Autism is de-

fined as a condition in which the child's ability to relate socially to other people is greatly disturbed. Childhood schizophrenia, on the other hand, is described primarily as a condition characterized by thought disorder and hallucinations.

Other fundamental differences also exist. First, there is a marked difference when the two conditions occur during childhood. Rutter (1974)

BOX 10-1 • Billy: A Case Description

Billy is a blue-eyed, blond little boy of striking beauty; he is almost too perfect physically. His parents first became aware that Billy was different and had special problems when he was 5 years old but had not yet begun to talk. Some of his other behaviors also bothered Billy's parents a great deal. Billy didn't seem to play like other children. He would rock for long periods of time in his crib, and he had little interest in toys. At best, Billy would just spin the wheels on his trucks and stare as they turned. Most disturbing to Billy's parents was the fact that he showed little affection. Billy was not a warm baby. When his mother picked him up to cuddle, Billy would start to cry and arch his back until he was put back in his crib. Billy treated other children and adults as objects of no consequence in his life. He didn't care about people; he would rather be left alone.

Since Billy's behavior became recognizable as different from normal, other changes have occurred. Billy developed language very slowly, and in a strange way. His language is what specialists call "echolalic" in nature. When Billy is asked a question, he simply responds by echoing the question. Billy also has a great deal of trouble using pronouns and prepositions correctly when he is trying to talk. He will commonly reverse pronouns and refer to himself as "you" or refer to another person as "I." The correct use of prepositions also causes Billy a great deal of difficulty. Up or down, on or under, or a yes-or-no answer to a question are very confusing concepts for Billy. He simply answers "Yes" or "No" at random. When viewed as a whole, Billy's language is not just delayed; it is also disturbed in some fundamental way. He simply does not learn. Over and over he makes the same language mistakes.

Aside from Billy's atypical language development, he now spends a great deal of time in repetitive, non-goal-oriented behavior, called *self-stimulatory* or *stereotypic* behavior. He has progressed from simple rocking and spinning the wheels on his toys to flapping his hands and twirling in circles until he falls from dizziness. If made to stop this behavior, Billy will throw ferocious temper tantrums that include screaming, biting, and often head banging. This self-destructive behavior is very disconcerting because in his tantrums, Billy not only breaks things; he hurts himself as well.

Billy also has a tremendous need to protect himself against any sort of change, including changes in his daily routine or his physical environment. Billy's mother recently rearranged the furniture in the living room while he was napping. When Billy awoke and entered the rearranged room, he immediately started to cry and whine; then he had a tantrum until the furniture was returned to its original position. Changes in his daily schedule also produce near-panic reactions that end up in tantrums. It seems as though Billy has memorized his environment and daily schedule, and any change produces the unknown for Billy. Adjustment and relearning are very difficult for him.

Billy's behavior cripples his family as well as himself. The furniture arrangement episode is only one of many incidents in which Billy requires his parent's constant attention. If he is left alone for even short periods of time, Billy can hurt himself or break something. After claiming all the attention his parents and older brother can give, Billy returns little. He is not affectionate and will not even look his brother in the eye, nor does he seek his mother's affection. Billy suffers from a rare childhood developmental disorder known as infantile autism.

---

combined the data of two other researchers (Makita, 1966; Kolvin, 1971) and came up with the distribution of cases by age that is depicted in Figure 10-1. Infantile autism has a peak age of onset before age 2½, whereas schizophrenia appears in later childhood and early adolescence. If a child has not developed autism by 5 years of age, he probably never will. The greatest age of risk for

Table 10-4
Diagnostic Criteria for Childhood-Onset Pervasive Developmental Disorder

299.80 Pervasive Developmental Disorder Not Otherwise Specified

This category should be used when there is a qualitative impairment in the development of reciprocal social interaction and of verbal and nonverbal communication skills, but the criteria are not met for Autistic Disorder, Schizophrenia, or Schizotypal or Schizoid Personality Disorder. Some people with this diagnosis will exhibit a markedly restricted repertoire of activities and interests, but others will not.

Source: American Psychiatric Association. (1987). *Diagnostic and statistical manual of mental disorders* (3rd ed., revised) (Washington, DC: Author), p. 39. Copyright 1987 by the American Psychiatric Association. Reprinted by permission.

FIGURE 10-1. Distribution of cases of child psychosis by age of onset.

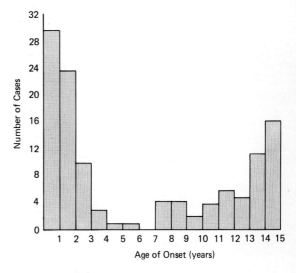

Source: M. Rutter. (1974). The development of infantile autism. *Psychological Medicine, 4,* 150. Reprinted by permission of Cambridge University Press and the author. Data from Makita (1966) and Kolvin (1971).

childhood schizophrenia, however, is from 7 to 15 years. Autism develops early, disrupts basic development areas (social relations, language, and intellect), and continues into adulthood with little change in its clinical course. Childhood schizophrenia develops late, leaves many of the developmental areas untouched, and runs a varied course with episodes of improvement and relapse. Additional differences between autism and childhood schizophrenia are listed in Table 10-5. The characteristics of these two conditions are contrasted in more detail when individual features of social skills, language, intelligence, and self-stimulatory behavior are discussed.

However, some areas of commonality be-

Table 10-5
Differential Characteristics of Infantile Autism and Childhood Schizophrenia

Infantile Autism	Childhood Schizophrenia
Early onset (before 30 months)	Late onset (late childhood–adolescence)
Early abnormal development	Develops normally and then withdraws into fantasy world
Poor social interaction skills (poor eye contact, social avoidance, lack of play skills)	Dependency on adults but interacts socially
No hallucinations or delusions	Hallucinations and delusions
Mentally retarded	Normal intelligence
Language disturbance (muteness, pronoun reversals, echolalia)	Good language development
Steady course of the disorder	Variable course
Concrete thinking	Thought is disordered (illogical, jumps from one topic to another)

tween these two conditions should also be discussed. First, these two conditions are similar in that they are both rare. The general prevalence of autism in the general population is 3 to 4 in 10,000 (Hanson & Gottesman, 1976; Hermelin & O'Conner, 1970; Lotter, 1966; Paluszny, 1979). Similarly, schizophrenia is rare in childhood and adolescence. The incidence rate for schizophrenia in adulthood and adolescence is 2 to 4 per 1000 (Babigian, 1980) and approximately 1 in 1000 for children (Petty, Ornitz, Michelman, & Zimmerman, 1984). Both autism and childhood schizophrenia occur more frequently in males; the male-female ratio is approximately 4:1. However this male-female difference disappears for schizophrenia in late adolescence, when the ratio is nearly 1:1. Possibly the most striking common feature of autism and childhood schizophrenia is that they can occur in the same child. Petty et al. (1984) have reported three cases in which children originally diagnosed as autistic were then diagnosed later in childhood and adolescence as also having schizophrenic symptoms. The three autistic children in these cases were high-functioning youngsters (they had good language and intellect) who later developed delusions, thought disorders, and hallucinations. It is not unreasonable to expect that if autism and childhood schizophrenia have different causes, they might occur on rare occasions by chance in the same children.

Social Skills

The inability to form personal relationships and to relate socially to other human beings is considered the most significant characteristic of autistic children. Autistic infants are frequently described by their mothers as being noncuddly babies who seldom laugh and who often become stiff and rigid when they are picked up. Other mothers have described their autistic infants (before they were diagnosed as autistic) as exceptionally "good" babies because they were so undemanding and did not need the mother's constant attention. This lack of social relatedness is reflected in the child's later social development. Many autistic children do not develop appropriate play skills. For instance, they would rather spin the tires or wheels on a toy than play with it ap-

propriately. Most autistic children also do not form normal friendships with other children. They are social isolates.

The research in the social behavior of autism has expanded in the past ten years (Schopler & Mesibov, 1984). This research has primarily focused on eye contact and gaze aversion, the approach and avoidance of autistic children, play skills, and social skills training. However, social interactions remains one of the most difficult research areas because of the difficulty in explicitly defining and reliably recording social behaviors.

Facing another person and making good eye contact are very important to our day-to-day social interactions. It has been suggested that abnormality of eye contact in autistic children may not be in the amount of eye contact, but rather in the way eye contact is made (Mirenda, Donnellan, & Yoder, 1983). For example, an autistic child might stare at another person's face, but not particularly the person's eyes. Or the "reciprocal" quality of eye contact during a social exchange may differentiate autistic from nonautistic children (Howlin, 1984). Others have suggested that the complexity and changing aspects of the face, particularly the eyes, are avoided by autistic children (Dawson & Galpert, 1984). The autistic child may prefer to stare at an unchanging part of the face. Avoidance of human facial patterns and a preference for more ordinary objects have been demonstrated in a classic experiment by Hutt and Ounsted (1966). These experimenters measured the amount of time autistic and nonautistic children spent looking at either room fixtures or faces drawn on the wall. The autistic children spent significantly more time looking at the room fixtures than at any of the drawn faces. The face most avoided by these children was a smiling human face with eyes (Hutt & Hutt, 1970).

A nonhandicapped child will frequently initiate social contacts and will generally not avoid contact initiated by other people (Richer, 1978). However, autistic children systematically avoid play situations and engage in solitary and uncooperative activities (Rutter, 1978a; Schreibman & Mills, 1983). These children do not show the necessary social imitation skills needed to engage successfully with other children (Varni, Lovaas, Koe-

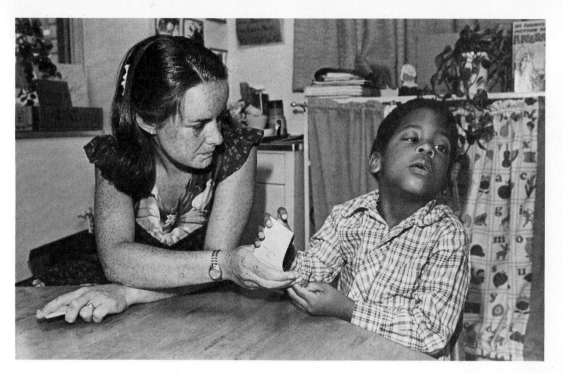

Maintaining eye contact in a meaningful social exchange is a difficult problem for many autistic children. It may not simply be a problem of making eye contact. Instead, it may be the reciprocal exchanges of appropriate glances and looking away that is the problem for autistic children.

gel, & Everett, 1979). Many autistic children relate to other people as "objects" instead of people, often pushing or pulling them by the hand to get what they want (Rimland, 1964). However, recent research has shown that social avoidance in autistic children may be a threshold phenomenon. Given enough time and exposure to accepting and initiating nonhandicapped children, autistic children spontaneously improve their social interactions by watching their peers more, improving their social responsiveness, and decreasing their interfering behaviors such as self-stimulation (Lord & Hopkins, 1986).

The social behavior of children with late-onset schizophrenia is also characterized by social withdrawal and avoidance of others. However, this social withdrawal occurs later in the child's development and is not a direct, overt avoidance of all social contact, as in autism. These children may be bizarre in their social interactions or withdrawn into a fantasy world. In Eggers's (1978) study of

late-onset childhood schizophrenia, 90 percent of the children studied had difficulty in making social contacts, and 45 percent were described as introverted. Several of these children had great difficulty in adapting socially and asserting themselves under appropriate circumstances. Likewise, Watt (1974) and Watt and Lubsensky (1976) found that many children who later developed schizophrenic conditions also had social development problems. The boys were described as negativistic, egocentric, unpleasant, and antisocial. The girls were more "quietly maladjusted," in that they were quiet, introverted, socially insecure, and dependent.

Language

Disturbance of language is a basic symptom of childhood autism (DeMyer, Hingtgen, & Jackson, 1981). The exact nature of the language disturbance distinguishes autistic children from nonpsychotic children who have language difficulties.

For example, many prelanguage skills are absent in children who are later diagnosed as autistic. Patterns of babbling that normally occur in children before 2 years of age frequently do not develop in autistic children (Bartak, Rutter, & Cox, 1975; Ricks, 1972). Many of these children who do not babble or respond to sound have intact auditory systems. Similarly, many autistic children do not show age-appropriate gesturing skills and verbal imitation skills, both of which are considered to be prelanguage skills in most children.

A significant percentage (28 to 61 percent, depending on the source cited) of autistic children do not develop language skills and are mute at some point during their childhood (as reviewed by Fay & Schuler, 1980). Sixty-five percent of the autistic children in one study who had not developed language by age 5 remained mute all of their lives (DeMyer et al., 1973). If an autistic child develops language, it is generally late, and the child shows a poor vocabulary, unusual speech content, simple speech structure, and a monotone quality. Many autistic children use language as a noncommunicating self-stimulatory behavior, or they interpret language concretely. For instance, a mother of an autistic boy asked him to "crack a

BOX 10-2 • "Yes" or "No" and Sign Language Training with an Autistic Boy

Nathan was a five-year-old autistic boy who had spoken language but a difficult language problem. He could not answer questions that required a "yes" or "no" response. He always answered "Yes" even when it was obvious that he wanted to say "No" (for instance, when offered something he did not want to eat, he would answer "Yes"). In an experiment (Walker, Hinerman, Jenson, & Petersen, 1982), hundreds of trials were used to teach Nathan to respond with a proper "Yes" or "No" response. Objects were placed in front of Nathan that he could name—for example, a toy car. When asked what the object was, he would respond, "car." However, when asked whether the object was a ball (when it was actually a car), he would answer "Yes." In essence, Nathan could correctly name objects, but when asked whether they were or were not a type of object, he failed. He always answered "Yes."

The conditions of the experiment were as follows (see Figure 10-2): A1, A2, A3, and A4 were baseline conditions with no consequences for an answer; B1 was a condition in which reinforcement was given for a correct response; B2 was a condition in which reinforcement was given for a correct response and a mild punisher (standing up and sitting down) was given for an incorrect response; and B3 was a reduced-syntax condition to reduce any confusion, in which Nathan was simply asked "Ball?" None of these conditions were successful. Nathan was unshakable and always answered "Yes," even though it appeared to the experimenters that he wanted to give the correct response.

In condition B4, Nathan was taught the correct sign-language hand signs for "Yes" and "No," using a *total communication approach* (in which the hand sign and the spoken word are paired at the same time). It took Nathan 2 days to learn the hand signs. He was still required to give the correct verbal response of "Yes" or "No" when asked a question about an object in front of him. The experimenter would ask a question, and Nathan would make the hand sign, look at it, and then give the correct spoken response. When the experimenters wanted to go back to baseline (A5) and would not let Nathan make the sign on the desk top, he would shove his hands in the desk, make the sign, and then give the correct spoken response. At a four-week follow-up, Nathan had dropped the manual signing and had no more difficulty with the spoken "Yes" and "No" responses.

This single case study shows that a total communication approach using hand signs can window" and let some air in the room. The boy actually took an object and broke the window.

Autistic children frequently exhibit *echolalic speech;* that is, they repeat sentences or questions addressed to them. A child might have *immediate echolalia* or "parrot speech" in which the most recently heard speech is repeated. For example, when an autistic child is asked her name, she might simply repeat, "What's your name?" Some autistic children demonstrate *delayed echolalia,* in which something heard hours or days ago is repeated (Carr, Schreibman, & Lovaas, 1975). A child might repeat something that was heard days

before and is totally out of context and sounds bizarre. Pronoun reversal and failure to comprehend concepts involving the idea of opposites (such as "yes" and "no" or "on" and "under" — see Box 10-2) are also problems for autistic children (Rutter, 1974). For example, with pronoun reversal, an autistic child refers to himself as "you" and addresses others as "I."

The autistic child is also much less likely to speak about things that are outside of his immediate environment or to speak as frequently as a nonhandicapped child of the same age (Rutter, 1978b). Experiences of happiness, sadness, and

Box 10-2 (Continued)

help autistic children with difficult language problems. No one knows why it works. However, it may be that a child can make a sign and hold it while she makes a spoken response. If the response is purely auditory, it lasts only a moment and then fades.

FIGURE 10-2. Mean percentage of Nathan's correct responses across sessions for each condition.

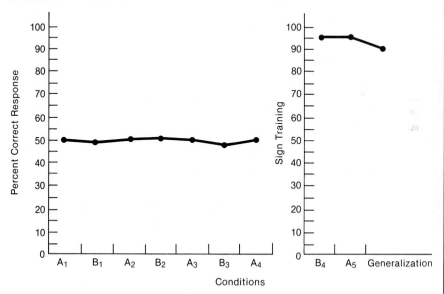

Source: G. R. Walker, P. S. Hinerman, W. R. Jenson, and P. B. Petersen. (1982). Sign language as a prompt to teach a verbal "Yes" and "No" discrimination to an autistic boy. *Child Behavior Therapy, 3,* 77–86. Figure reprinted by permission.

excitement are also absent from the language of many autistic children. Inflection and change of emphasis on certain key words containing emotional meaning are missing, which results in a flat, monotonous manner of speaking.

The type and quality of language of autistic children can be sharply contrasted with the language of schizophrenic children. First, the language of autistic children is generally delayed or disrupted in its normal development. The language of schizophrenic children is generally normally developed. Second, the language of autistic children is confused and the content is impoverished; by contrast, schizophrenic children generally use correct language structure to communicate bizarre thoughts. Unlike autistic children, whose mutism or strange use of language sets them apart as different, the bizarre meaning and fantasy of schizophrenic children's language content are abnormal.

Intelligence

The majority of autistic children are intellectually retarded as measured by standard intelligence tests (DeMyer et al., 1981). One study found that among autistic children tested in the preschool years, 74 percent had IQs below 52 and only 2.6 percent had IQs above 85. When these same children were tested 6 years later, the majority still scored in the retarded range (DeMyer et al., 1974). Even the majority of the children who had shown the most social improvement and who had received several years of treatment and special education scored in the retarded range. Intelligence appears to remain remarkably stable over time, irrespective of current treatment or educational programs (DeMyer et al., 1981; Freeman, Ritvo, Needleman, & Yokota, 1985).

However, it is easy to be fooled by some autistic children's abilities. Leo Kanner felt that autistic children were not retarded, but were unable to perform well on intelligence tests because of poor skills in relating to other people. He was particulary impressed by *idiot savant skills* or *splinter skills*. In these isolated skills, an autistic individual shows superior performance (for example in

mathematical computation, art abilities, music, or calculating exact calendar dates).

Only 10 to 20 percent of autistic individuals have these special splinter skills (Goldberg & Soper, 1963; Rimland, 1978). However, it is easy to be impressed by the one special ability and to assume that such a child has normal intelligence; generally the opposite is true. Creak (1961) first called these special abilities "islets of ability" or "splinter skills" because these special areas are surrounded by other areas of general intellectual retardation.

In contrast to the lower IQs typical of children with autism, those who develop schizophrenia later in childhood tend to show a normal range of intelligence. Although some clinicians and researchers believe that schizophrenic children are intellectually dull, the research does not support this view. In one study, Eggers (1978) found that only 10 percent of older schizophrenic children were below average in intelligence and that 23 percent were above average. Similarly, in samples of schizophrenic children Watt and Lubensky (1976) found the average IQ to be 102, and in a different study Green et al. (1984) found the average IQ to be 88. The exact nature of intelligence also seems to be different for autistic and schizophrenic children. The majority of autistic children are retarded with particular deficits in verbal and reasoning skills. Childhood schizophrenics, however, show less retardation and overall better intellectual development in all areas.

Self-Stimulatory and Self-Injurious Behavior

Self-stimulatory or *stereotypic* behavior is a repetitive, apparently purposeless behavior that occurs in nonhandicapped, psychotic, and developmentally disordered children. Self-stimulatory behavior is not unique to childhood behavior disorders. Many nonhandicapped people unconsciously pull their hair, bite their fingernails, wiggle their feet, or tap pencils. What distinguishes these common forms of self-stimulatory behavior from abnormal self-stimulation is exaggeration in form, frequency, and appropriateness of the behavior for a particular environmental setting. For example, an autistic child may spend hours spinning coins, gazing at lights, rocking, twirling, or flapping hands. All of these behaviors have a social and educational cost for autistic children.

The exact causes of self-stimulatory behavior are unclear; however, several theories and research into the area have provided some surprising findings. It has been suggested that self-stimulation is reinforcing in itself, and also that it serves to maintain the regularity of the child's environment (Lovaas, Schreibman, & Koegel, 1974). Some studies have shown that autistic children will work at one task to earn the opportunity to self-stimulate (Hung, 1978). Other studies have shown that the kinesthetic, visual, and auditory feedback received from engaging in the self-stimulatory behavior is reinforcing (Rincover, 1978). Rincover, Peoples, and Packard (1976) have experimental data that substantiate this point. For example, when the sound associated with spinning objects (auditory feedback) is blocked (sensory extinction), the frequency of object spinning decreases.

Self-stimulation helps to maintain the regularity of the environment in several ways. Autistic children engage in more self-stimulation in an unstimulating or unfamiliar environment (Runco, Charlop, & Schreibman, 1986). When tasks are frustratingly failed, self-stimulation increases (Churchill, 1971), and it decreases with correct responding (Runco et al., 1986). These results indicate that autistic children do use self-stimulatory behavior to maintain environmental regularity by avoiding boring or unfamiliar situations, or situations in which failure is probable.

Self-injurious behavior is similar to self-stimulation, but much more destructive and frightening. Common forms of self-injurious behavior in autistic children include head banging, face slapping, scratching, and biting. The motivational factors for self-injurious behaviors are similar to those for self-stimulation. For example, the sensory feedback received from self-inflicting a wound may be reinforcing (Devany & Rincover, 1982). Other important factors that may motivate self-injurious behavior include inappropriate but well-intended concern and attention from others, which may serve to reinforce the behavior as a means of avoiding compliance to requests (Carr, 1977). Using self-injurious behavior as an avoidance strategy in this way may be a particular problem (Carr, 1977; Edelson, Taubman, & Lovaas, 1983). For example, Carr, Newsom, and Binkkoff (1976) found that self-injurious head banging dramatically increased when commands were given to a psychotic child (see Box 10-3).

The problems associated with self-stimulation and self-injury include ostracism because other people are frightened or repelled by the behaviors (Devany & Rincover, 1982). In addition, self-stimulatory behavior may interfere with an autistic child's attention and learning new tasks (Koegel & Covert, 1972). It may disrupt previously learned behaviors and interfere with observational learning (Varni, Lovaas, Koegel, & Everett, 1979), and may displace socially acceptable play behavior (Koegel, Firestone, Kramme, & Dunlap, 1974). For example, Koegel et al. (1979) found that when two autistic children were allowed to self-stimulate, their rates of play with toys were very low (see Figure 10-4). However, when the self-stimulation was suppressed by a mild punishment procedure, the self-stimulation decreased; *unreinforced,* spontaneous play then increased. When the children were again allowed to stimulate themselves with no consequences, spontaneous play decreased and self-stimulation increased.

Differences in self-stimulatory and self-injurious behavior between autistic and schizophrenic children have not been well researched. Both forms of behavior can occur in both types of conditions. The basic difference is in the frequency of occurrence: Autistic children generally engage in self-stimulating and self-injurious behavior at much higher rates than schizophrenic children. However, certain types of self-stimulation also occur in childhood schizophrenia. For example, *hand regard,* or gazing at a hand, is not an uncommon form of self-stimulation for schizophrenic children.

Stimulus Overselectivity

Stimulus overselectivity is a perceptual disability in which a child responds "only to part of a relevant cue, or even to a minor, often irrelevant feature of the environment" (Lovaas, Koegel, & Schreibman, 1979, p. 1237). Overselectivity has been studied mostly in autistic children (Koegel & Schreibman, 1977; Lovaas & Schreibman, 1971) and has been found to occur in a large number of children, particularly those with lower IQs (Wilhelm & Lovaas, 1976). Stimulus overselectivity interferes with learning many of the basic stimulus discriminations needed to adjust to the environment. For example, Schreibman and Lovaas (1973) taught both nonhandicapped and autistic children to discriminate between lifelike male and female dolls. Normal children used a number of cues, including the doll's head features, to learn the discrimination. Autistic children, however, selected irrelevant cues such as the doll's shoes to learn the discrimination; when the shoes were changed, some suddenly lost the discrimination.

It has been suggested that stimulus overselectivity greatly hinders autistic children in learning complex discriminations in language and social skills (Lovaas et al., 1979). It may also help explain the common need among autistic children to keep their environments the same or unchanging. This insistence on sameness characteristically in-

---

BOX 10-3 • **Self-Injurious Behavior and Commands**

Carr, Newsom, and Binkoff (1976) investigated the effects of adult verbal statements on the self-injurious behavior of a psychotic child. The subject in this study was Tim, an 8-year-old schizophrenic boy who had been self-destructive since he was 2 years old. Tim would hit his head with a closed fist or open hand throughout the day. Although he seldom hurt himself severely, Tim would often cut or bruise his face. Various types of treatment, including drugs, electric shock, physical restraints (his hands were tied behind his back), and isolation had been unsuccessful in stopping his hitting himself.

Carr and associates wanted to study the effect of adults' comments on Tim's rate of self-injurious behavior. He was given two types of comments: (1) *Tacts* were simple declarative statements such as "The walls are white" and (2) *mands* were command statements which required some response from Tim, such as "Point to the window." All statements were made by an adult who looked directly at Tim and smiled. Two adults participated, one who was informed about the experiment and a naive adult who did not know its details. Baseline observations were made during a free-time period when no tacts or mands were given.

Figure 10-3 portrays the results of the experiment. At first, no comments were made to Tim during free time, and he hit himself infrequently. When tact statements were introduced, the number of hits remained low. However, when commands were given to Tim, his rate of hitting himself stayed high.

The researchers concluded that Tim avoided or escaped doing things required of him by hitting himself. Interestingly, in a second experiment, when adults were telling Tim a pleasant, enjoyable story, they could make mands but Tim would not hit himself. The stories presumably reduced the aversiveness of the original commands and were so pleasant he did not want to escape from the situation.

Source: E. G. Carr, C. D. Newsom, and J. A. Binkoff. (1976). Stimulus control of self-destructive behavior in a psychotic child. *Journal of Abnormal Child Psychology, 4,* 139–153. Figure reprinted by permission of Plenum Publishing Corporation and the authors.

volves requiring the house furniture arrangement to stay exactly the same or a daily schedule or travel route to remain unchanged. If they are changed, the child may have tantrums and persistently try to return the situation to its previous state. Overselectivity may help account for this need for sameness, because the child has learned to rely on an irrelevant characteristic (such as a chair's position or a particular arrangement) to help discriminate and map their environment.

Stimulus overselectivity has not been studied extensively in schizophrenic children. However, studies have shown that it is present in chronic adult schizophrenics (Broen, 1973; Meiselman, 1971).

Family Characteristics

There is much speculation concerning the families and parents of autistic and schizophrenic children. Some writers have portrayed autistic children's parents as highly intellectual, cold, and rejecting individuals with little interest in people or human warmth (Bettelheim, 1967; Eisenberg & Kanner, 1956). For example, King (1975) has suggested that autism is caused by a "double-bind" attitude of mothers who superficially appear warm but are actually cold and rejecting toward their children. Much of this speculation has been refuted by careful research (Cantwell, Baker, & Rutter, 1978; Kolvin, Garside, & Kidd, 1971) and

Box 10-3 (Continued)

FIGURE 10-3. Stimulus control of self-destructive behavior in a psychotic child.

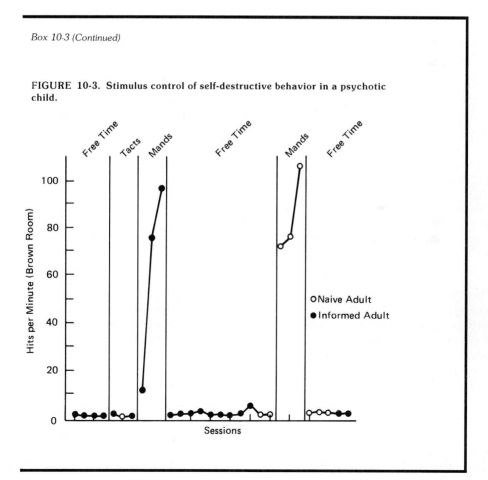

FIGURE 10-4. Percentage of time-sample intervals in which self-stimulatory and appropriate play behaviors occurred during (a) baseline, (b) suppression of self-stimulation conditions, and (c) reversal.

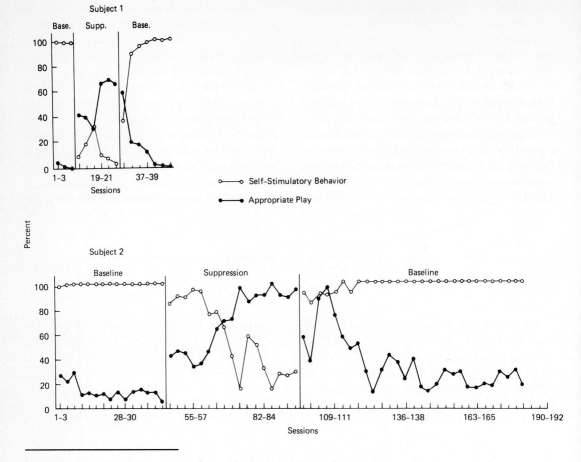

Source: R. L. Koegel, P. B. Firestone, K. W. Kramme, and G. Dunlap. (1974). Increasing spontaneous play by suppressing self-stimulation in autistic children. *Journal of Applied Behavior Analysis. 7,* 525. Copyright 1974 by the Society for the Experimental Analysis of Behavior, Inc. Reprinted by permission.

by sound clinical observations (Drotar, 1978). For example, when parents of autistic children are compared to parents of other types of handicapped children, no difference has been found on personality or interaction measures (Cox, Rutter, Newman, & Bartak, 1977; Schreibman & Mills, 1983). However, the damage to parents and families has been done with this type of unscientific speculation (Pingree, 1984; Schopler, 1969).

Other comparisons have also been made between the parents of autistic and schizophrenic children and other populations. The parents of autistic children have been reported to be of higher than average socioeconomic class and intelligence. Rutter and Lockyer (1967) found that parents of autistic children came from more professional and executive backgrounds than parents of nonautistic children. However, this finding may have been a result of bias in sampling, because parents from higher socioeconomic classes may have had better access to professional services. When whole populations of children and their parents living in a specific geographical area (such as the city of Göteborg, Sweden, or the state of Iowa) have been assessed, no socioeconomic differences have been found (Gillberg & Schaumann, 1982; Tsai, Stewart, Faust, & Shook, 1982).

Surprisingly, marital stability of the families of autistic and schizophrenic has been found to be greater than for other disturbed children (Lowe, 1966; Schain & Yannet, 1960). Lowe (1966) found that 11 percent of autistic children and 15 percent of schizophrenic children came from broken homes. This is far below the average of 50 percent for other types of emotionally disturbed children. Other studies have found similar results or rates of divorce equal to those of families that do not have handicapped children (Cantwell et al., 1978; Cox et al., 1977; Rutter & Lockyer, 1967). It is difficult to establish exactly why the rates of divorce are lower for autistic and schizophrenic children's families. The stress caused by having an autistic or schizophrenic child may draw families closer together and reduce the divorce rate.

Differences between the families of autistic and schizophrenic children are hard to pinpoint. However, autistic and schizophrenic children are rarely found in the same families (Schopler & Dalldorf, 1980). The families of schizophrenic children also have a higher incidence of adult schizophrenia among their members (Kolvin, Ounsted, Richardson, & Garside, 1971; Rimland, 1964) and on average come from lower socioeconomic levels (Kolvin et al., 1971; Rutter, 1978a) than families of autistic children.

ETIOLOGICAL THEORIES OF AUTISM AND CHILDHOOD SCHIZOPHRENIA

Theories about the causes of autism and childhood schizophrenia abound in the clinical literature. Speculation has run high concerning the role of parents in causing these disorders as compared to biological factors. Even animal ethologists (scientists who study animals in their natural environments) have not been able to resist the lure of speculation and have advanced their own theories of causation (Tinbergen, 1974). Most theories fall into two broad classes: psychological causes and biological causes.

Psychological Theories

Freud contributed some of the earlier theoretical work toward an explanation of schizophrenia. Later refinements by Abraham (1955) maintained that the development of schizophrenia is brought about by a regression or fixation of the *libido* (sexual energy) at an early primary stage. This stalling of normal development presumably produces a withdrawal of personal and object relationships into an autoerotic state of self-stimulation. Later, Abraham (1955) related schizophrenia to an overreliance on the oral and anal stages of development, in which no definite boundaries exist between a child's inner and outer worlds. This nondifferentiation between what exists in the real world and what exists in one's mind is believed to be the basis of psychosis. Freud's personality theory, which divides the personality into the ego, superego, and id, maintains that psychosis is the ego's loss of control and reality, and a total surrender to the instinctual id.

Why a personality would regress or fixate in its sexual development so drastically and produce a psychotic state is a question never fully answered by psychoanalysts. One of the more unusual causes suggested is that of the *schizophrenogenic* mother. According to this theory, the mother is the main cause of a child's retreat into the world of psychosis. The mother is depicted as detached, cold, and rejecting (Reiser & Brown, 1964). Since these mothers are described as being perfectionistic and cold, the term "refrigerator mothers" has been used to describe them.

Possibly the best-known contemporary psychoanalyst who has written about the causes of autism is Bruno Bettelheim, long-time director of the famous Orthogenic School located at the University of Chicago. Bettelheim believes that the condition of autism is the child's attempt to blot out stimuli in order to avoid psychological pain. Although organic factors may be present in the development of autism, the parents' treatment of the child primarily contributes to the development of this condition. According to Bettelheim (1967), autistic children have parents who meet their physical needs but neglect many of their emotional needs. The adults in the autistic child's life do not treasure and want the child, particularly during critical periods of development when emotional bonding is established between child and parent. In defense against pain of rejection, the child retreats into an inner world, an "empty fortress' (the title of Bettelheim's 1967 book) in which external reality and stimuli are screened out.

Bettelheim maintains that there are three basic types of autistic children, differing in the degree of withdrawal caused by the severity of the early neglect. First are the autistic mute children who have totally severed communication and contact with the real world. These children treat other humans as objects and constitute the most disturbed type. Second are the children who have some language and display occasional anger outbursts. They have some contact with reality, but still do not act independently. Last are the children commonly labeled as schizophrenic. These children have fairly good language skills and form limited social relationships; however, they have rich fantasy lives that interfere with normal functioning and serve as a defense against a capricious real world. The schizophrenic child, according to Bettelheim, is the least disturbed and has the best prognosis if placed in an accepting environment that allows redevelopment of attachments to other people.

Psychoanalysts have not been the only theorists to speculate about the psychological causes of autism. Behavioral psychologists, such as Ferster (1961), have suggested that autistic behavior is a learned operant (voluntary) behavior. Ferster believed that an autistic child's behavior is not fundamentally different in type from that of nonhandicapped children, but only in rate and amount. For example, it was demonstrated that under laboratory conditions autistic children did, indeed, learn like other children (Ferster & DeMyer, 1962).

Ferster also believed that the autistic child's behavior is not regularly reinforced. The child is presumably put on prolonged extinction or intermittent reinforcement by adults (parents) who may dislike her, who may be preoccupied, or who may be suffering from a long-standing illness.

Over time, a child in this situation fails to learn many of the normal social behaviors and language skills and develops, instead, bizarre or psychotic-like behaviors. One such replacement behavior is self-stimulation, which is thought to be used by the autistic child to replace normal social behaviors. Self-stimulation, by virtue of its disagreeable effect on adults, attracts attention, which in turn serves as a reinforcer for the child. Secondary reinforcers, such as adult praise or verbal reinforcement, have little effect on this type of child's behavior, because they have not been paired systematically in the past with primary reinforcement from the adult, such as food and comfort. Instead, abnormal patterns of behavior have been firmly established to provide for the child's needs.

Other psychoanalytic and behavioral theories of the causes of autism and schizophrenia exist (Boatman & Szurek, 1960; Szurek, 1956; Ullmann & Krasner, 1969); however, all of these are similar. Both psychoanalytic and behavioral theories emphasize a disturbance during early development, which is primarily the fault of a parent. The children in both theories retreat into inner worlds. According to the psychoanalytic theory, the retreat is into an inner-defensive psychological world; according to behavioristic theory, the retreat is into a self-stimulatory world. However, all of these theories are relatively old and are presently considered almost theoretical curiosities. Most of the modern research on causation of autism and schizophrenia is in biological theories.

Biological Theories

Biological theorists view the causes of autism and schizophrenia as functions of birth trauma, viral infections (such as German measles), metabolic problems, and genetic factors. These events also contribute to increased incidence of seizures, low birthweight, abnormal neurological measures (electroencephalograph [EEG] and computer tomographic [CT] brain scan), mental retardation, and poor motor development. These biological variables are also important in the development of conditions that are easily mistaken for autism and childhood schizophrenia, such as Rett's disease and Wilson's disease (see Box 10-4).

In recent years, major advances in computer-guided brain imaging have given scientists a literal cross-section picture of autistic individuals' brains. CT scans use a series of cross-sectional x-rays to produce lifelike pictures of the brain at different depths. The results on autistic individuals have shown some abnormal brain structures, but the results have not been consistent in the type of abnormality or consistent across autistic individuals. For example, the rate of brain structural abnormalities has varied from 18 to 20 percent of the individuals tested, depending on the ages of the autistic samples and how they were defined (as reviewed by Coleman & Gillberg, 1985). The most consistent findings have involved the lateral ventricular system of the brain (two cavities deep in the brain filled with cerebral fluid). These cavities are either enlarged or asymmetrical in size in some autistic individuals; however, these abnormalities are not diagnostic, because they can occur in some mentally retarded and schizophrenic individuals as well. Even the more advanced positron emission tomographic (PET) scans have not found definitive evidence of brain abnormalities in autistic individuals (Rapoport et al., 1983).

A number of difficulties can arise at birth, including prolonged labor, low Apgar scores (scores used to rate newborn infants), low birthweights, hemorrhaging during delivery, umbilical cord wrapped around the child's neck, and cesarian deliveries. Two large studies comparing autistic children's birth records have been conducted. Campbell, Hardesty, and Burdock (1978) compared the records of 105 autistic children against the records of nonhandicapped children, and Deykin and MacMahon (1980) did the same with the records of 145 autistic children. No single birth trauma factor was clearly associated with autism. The autistic children had a statistically significantly greater number of birth trauma factors; however, it took all the factors lumped together to make this difference. Similarly, Goldfarb (1964) and Taft and Goldfarb (1964) have found birth trauma effects for a subgroup of schizophrenic children. However, for both autism and schizophrenia, birth trauma may be a contributing factor increasing the vulnerability of the child. It is doubtful that it is a definitive factor in causing either condition.

Diseases and their effects on the central nervous system have been suspected of causing autistic-like symptoms in children. For example, mothers have reported four times the rate of influenza during their pregnancy with an autistic child than with an unaffected sibling (Deykin & MacMahon, 1979). Viral infections have been especially suspected in contributing to autism (Coleman & Gillberg, 1985; Fowle, 1968). Chess, Korn, and Fernandez (1971) studied the effects of rubella contracted by pregnant mothers. In a sample of 243 children who were born after their mothers had rubella, 10 children developed the complete syndrome and 8 children the partial syndrome of autism. Chess (1977) has indicated that out of the rubella sample of 243, the equivalent rate for autism would be 412 per 10,000 for the complete autism syndrome and 329 per 10,000 for the partial syndrome, for a combined rate of 741 per 10,000. This is in comparison to the general population rate of 4.5 autistic cases in 10,000. Clearly, there is a link between autism and the rubella virus. Other viral diseases that have also been linked to autism include congenital cytomegalovirus (a virus passed from the mother to the child *in utero* that destroys developing brain tissue), herpes simplex virus, and even the mumps (Deykin & MacMahon, 1979; Gillberg, 1986; Markowitz, 1983; Stubbs, Ash, & Williams, 1984).

Viral infections during pregnancy may be too simple an explanation for the cause of autism. For instance, not all the children whose mothers contract these viruses get autism. However, the cause may involve a general defect in the immunological system of the child. For instance, two studies have reported that autistic children have a suppressed ability to develop immune antibodies (Stubbs, Crawford, Burger, & Vandenbark, 1977; Warren, Margaretten, Pace, & Foster, 1986). These immune antibodies are used by the body to fight off infections. Higher rates of genetic and immune system abnormalites have also been reported by the UCLA Registry for Genetic Studies in Autism. There may be a link between a genetic flaw and the development of a complete immune system to

BOX 10-4 • Rett's Syndrome and Wilson's Disease

Some conditions can look very much like infantile autism or childhood schizophrenia; however, they are not. These conditions may be caused by something that can be treated, like Wilson's disease. Or the condition may be lifelong but degenerative, like Rett's syndrome, and a family should know what to expect from the disorder.

RETT'S SYNDROME

This syndrome has only recently been discovered; it was described in 1966 by an Austrian neurologist, Andreas Rett. The condition only affects females and looks very much like infantile autism. A child who is developing normally then regresses very quickly; she develops self-stimulatory movements of the arms, such as head patting; mental retardation occurs; the spine starts to curve abnormally; and the child has difficulty with walking normally (an abnormal gait). These girls also may develop several autistic-like behaviors, such as a lack of need for social contact and difficulty in making eye contact. The exact cause of Rett's syndrome is unknown, but is hypothesized to be a degenerative genetic condition.

CASE HISTORY

Jane was developing normally, and her parents were pleased with their first child. Then at 18 months several things happened. Jane started to become less loving, did not need social contact, and would not make eye contact. In the past, she had loved to play and to be held. She also started to pat her head constantly, and she had difficulty with simple things she used to do, such as picking up and using a spoon. Her walking started to be affected, in that she seemed to drag a foot. In addition, she began to lean to one side, and the doctor thought that she was developing a curved spine.

Jane seemed to be getting worse, so her parents took her to a specialist. He said that she appeared to have Rett's syndrome, which is a degenerative condition. Jane would be severely retarded. This was very hard for her parents, who remembered Jane as a normal little girl.

fight disease in autistic children. Genetics appears to be an important factor.

Genetic factors can be involved in the development of a clinical condition in two ways. First, direct damage to the genetic material itself, such as the chromosome structure that holds the genes, can cause a defect. Second, an abnormality can be coded in the genetic material and passed on as an inherited characteristic. In 1969, a new condition that has major implications for autism was discovered. The condition is known as *fragile-X syndrome*, and it results from damage to the chromosome structure (Lubs, 1969); it is now considered the second leading cause of mental retardation (Townes, 1982). Fragile-X syndrome is found in males and is caused by a breaking or splitting at the end of the X Chromosome (sites q27 and q28). Several studies have found that fragile-X syndrome occurs in a significant number of autistic males, ranging from 5 to 20 percent (Coleman & Gillberg, 1985; Watson et al., 1984). In addition, since fragile-X syndrome affects males, it may help explain why more males than females have autism. It appears that fragile-X syn-

Box 10-4 (Continued)

WILSON'S DISEASE

Wilson's disease is an inherited metabolic disorder in which the body is unable to use copper, resulting in a toxic buildup of copper in the liver, kidneys, and brain. First described by Wilson (1912), this condition generally appears in late childhood or early adolescence and is characterized by psychotic behavior in approximately half the children affected. The psychotic behaviors exhibited include disorientation, poor impulse control, paranoia, or severe anxiety or depression. Wilson's disease is easily confused with childhood schizophrenia, because many of the developing symptoms are similar and the age of onset is the same for both conditions. However, Wilson's disease results in abnormal copper levels in the blood and urine and can be definitely diagnosed by looking into the patient's eyes to see whether the iris is surrounded by a brownish-green ring (Kayser-Fleischer ring).

CASE HISTORY

John was a model student until he was 12 years old, at which time his schoolwork and behavior began to change. At first he seemed unable to concentrate for any length of time on his schoolwork, and his grades started to go down. John, aware of his difficulty, was anxious about his poor performance. He would act impulsively, trying to do too much, and when he failed he would mope around the house crying and withdrawing to his room. His parents finally arranged an appointment with a mental health specialist to try to help John out of his "slump," but things got worse. Talking with a therapist did no good. John would vacillate from periods of depression to states of extreme and unexplained anxiety, often talking incoherently. Facial tics developed. At this point John was examined by a neurologist, who flashed a beam of light into his eyes and saw a set of dimly outlined greenish rings. Later, when blood and urine analysis confirmed high toxic levels of copper, the diagnosis of Wilson's disease was made. John was started on a medication that helps wash excess copper out of his body. At the last report, his ability to concentrate and memory have improved and John no longer suffers from anxiety or despair.

Sources: A. Rett. (1966). *Über ein Zerebral-Atrophisches Syndrome bei Hyperammonamie* (Vienna: Bruder Hollinek). S. A. Wilson. (1912). Progressive lenticular degeneration: A familial nervous disease associated with cirrhosis of the liver. *Brain, 34,* 295.

drome may be an inherited characteristic and that genetic inheritance mechanisms may be important in the overall development of autism.

Major advances have been made in the research on genetics and autism in the past decade. Most of this work has been done through maintaining a large registry of families with autism at UCLA (the Registry for Genetic Studies in Autism). This registry has been used to study multiple-incidence families (families with more than one autistic child) and families with twins who have autism. Of particular interest are twin studies, in which genetically identical twins *(monozygotic)* are compared to fraternal twins (*dizygotic,* or non-genetically identical) to determine whether there are differences in autism. A higher incidence of autism for monozygotic twins would suggest a genetic base for the condition. Folstein and Rutter (1978) studied a small sample of sets of identical twins and fraternal twins in which one twin was autistic. Identical twins had a higher rate of concordance for autism (that is, *both* twins of a pair were autistic) (36 percent) than fraternal twins (0 percent). A much larger study involving twins from the UCLA registry compared 61 pairs of twins and found the concordance rate for monozygotic twins to be 95.7 percent and for dizygotic twins to be 23.4 percent (Ritvo, Freeman, Mason-Brothers, Mo, & Ritvo, 1985). Similar results with multiple-incidence families have suggested that one form of autism may be caused by a *recessive gene* (gene contribution from both parents needed), as opposed to a *dominant gene* (gene contribution from only one parent needed) (Ritvo, Spence, et al., 1985).

Two other findings from this genetics work are important. First, autism may be a *spectrum condition;* that is, the full expression of the autism condition may be found in one child in a family, but the siblings may also be affected, albeit less severely. The siblings may be mildly affected by having higher rates of mental retardation, language difficulties, and learning problems than those of other nonhandicapped children. The preliminary work in this area has found just such a higher incidence (Folstein & Rutter, 1978; August, Stewart, & Tsai, 1981). The second finding from the genetics research is that there are rare cases (four reported families) in which each family has three or more autistic children (Ritvo et al., 1986). Such a high incidence of autism in isolated familes with no significant medical histories for viral infections would suggest a strong genetic base for some types of autism.

Similar studies have been done for childhood schizophrenia. Viral infections (Torrey & Petersen, 1976), abnormal brain structures (Reider, Mann, Weinberger, van Kammen, & Post, 1983), and especially genetics have been implicated among the causes of schizophrenia (as reviewed by Mirsky & Duncan, 1986). Concordance rates for schizophrenia in identical twins have been reported to be 41 percent, as opposed to 14 and 17 percent for fraternal twins (Kallman & Roth, 1956). Studies of foster or adopted children also offer a method for studying the effects of genetics on childhood schizophrenia. The strategy in adoption studies is to identify schizophrenic parents who gave up their children for adoption to nonaffected parents. The task is then to measure how many of these adopted children later developed schizophrenia. Rosenthal (1972) and Rosenthal, Wender, Kety, Weiner, and Schulsinger (1971) studied Danish adopted children, some of whom had normal parents and some of whom had schizophrenic parents. The results showed higher rates of schizophrenia in children who had schizophrenic natural parents, regardless of whether the adoptive parents were schizophrenic or normal.

Both the autism and childhood schizophrenic genetics studies suggest a *polygenic recessive gene model* (involving many genes from both parents) as a cause for some of the cases. Although there are some researchers (Hanson & Gottesman, 1976) who are particularly skeptical about a genetic cause for autism, the scientific evidence is mounting. However, it would be incorrect to suggest that all autism and all childhood schizophrenia are genetically based. It is more likely that there are multiple causes leading to one type of condition, especially autism. Table 10-6 lists some of the probable and improbable causes of these conditions.

TREATMENT

The treatments for autism and childhood schizophrenia are varied and controversial. The controversy comes from desperate attempts to treat some of these conditions, which historically have had very poor outcomes. It is not difficult to imag-

Table 10-6

Theories of Etiology for Autism and Childhood Schizophrenia

Theory	Childhood Schizophrenia	Autism
Psychoanalytic		
Maternal conflict	Unlikely	Unlikely
Behavioral		
Loss of reinforcer effectiveness	Unlikely	Unlikely
Organic		
Birth trauma	Possible	Unlikely
Abnormal brain structure	Possible	Possible
Disease	Possible	Possible
Fragile-X syndrome	Unlikely	Possible
Recessive gene	Possible	Possible

ine trying almost any reasonable approach to save self-injurious children who are slowly destroying themselves. All the major approaches, including psychoanalytic treatment, behavioral interventions, and medical approaches, have been used with autistic and schizophrenic children.

Psychoanalytic Treatment

The basic aim of psychoanalytically oriented treatment of autistic and schizophrenic children is to repair ego damage resulting from a dysfunctional mother-child relationship. The analyst totally accepts the psychotic child's behavior and allows him to regress to earlier developmental states, so that he can re-experience the normal development that was presumably disrupted by an indifferent, rejecting mother.

In Bettelheim's Orthogenic School for psychotic children, environmental stress is reduced to a minimum for the psychotic child. Adults accept all forms of behavior, while at the same time encouraging the child to relive earlier experiences in a milieu of total acceptance. In the Orthogenic School program, it would not be unusual to see a 10-year-old child sitting on the lap of an adult, who is feeding the child from a baby bottle. While the child is in treatment at the school, which may take several years, all parental contact with the child is minimized—a "parentectomy." It is felt that the parents, particularly the mother, have to a large extent caused the child's condition. To allow the parents to visit the child or take her home on visits would only impede therapeutic progress or reinstate the problem.

Bettelheim (1967) has reviewed the effectiveness of his program by following 40 patients after discharge from the school. The results indicated that the outcomes for 40 percent of the children could be described as "good" or "cured," 38 percent as "fair," and 20 percent as "poor." This outcome evaluation, however, has been criticized by Wing (1968) as not being based on objective criteria, particularly in the diagnosis and measurement of improvement.

Individual play therapy is a common psychoanalytic treatment for psychotic children. It is felt that if a child is allowed to play with toys in an unstructured and accepting environment, he will act out symbolically many of his psychological problems. The therapist then interprets to the child the psychological basis of these disturbances and tries to facilitate solutions to these problems in an accepting and supportive manner.

Ney, Palvesky, and Markely (1971) have compared the effectiveness of psychoanalytically oriented play therapy and behavior therapy (behavior modification) in the treatment of schizophrenic children. The children ranged in age from 3 to 15 years; all were self-abusive or extremely aggressive and did not interact well with others. The behavior therapy approach emphasized increasing communication, imitating, and a knowledge of body parts, and used candy and social praise as reinforcers for appropriate behaviors. The play therapy treatment emphasized unstructured play with sand and toys and interpretation of the children's problems in an accepting fashion. Results of this study indicated that behavior therapy was effective in meeting the stated treatment goals of improving the children's overall behavior. Play therapy, however, did not significantly change the children's behavior.

Psychoanalytic treatment approaches to autism and childhood schizophrenia were among the earliest pioneering efforts at treatment. However, their overall effectiveness in improving a child's behavior is questionable. The length of time required for treatment is very long and is not considered cost-effective by most hospitals and treatment agencies. Most importantly, the psychoanalytic assumption that parents cause the conditions is fundamentally in error. Such an assumption adds a great burden to a family in treatment and separates parents from the treatment process. Parents can be valuable assets to a comprehensive treatment approach.

Behavioral Approaches

Behavior therapy is one of the most productive treatment approaches for autistic and schizophrenic children (DeMyer et al., 1981; Jenson, Preator, Ballou, Reavis, & Freston, 1987; Margolies, 1977; Paluszny, 1979). Behavioral treatment seems to be attractive to many clinicians and

Occupational therapist holds autistic child to calm her down.

the use of time out. Behavioral deficits such as poor eye contact, failure to speak, and impoverished social skills are remedied by teaching and reinforcing appropriate behavioral replacement skills.

Possibly the most dramatic effects of the use of behavior management have been seen in the treatment of severe self-stimulation and self-injury. Behaviors such as head banging, scratching, biting, and face slapping can lead to disfigurement and blindness. Behavioral techniques such as time out, overcorrection, and differential reinforcement of zero rates of behavior (DR0) have been effective in reducing self-injury (Horner & Barton, 1980). The effectiveness of these behavioral techniques has been encouraging: Schroeder, Schroeder, Smith, and Dalldorf (1978) showed in a 3-year study that behavior modification was effective in significantly reducing or eliminating self-injury in 94 percent of the cases studied. In addition, parents have rated behavioral techniques as effective and acceptable in reducing the self-injury of their autistic children (Pickering & Morgan, 1985).

One of the most dramatic applications of behavioral techniques to self-injury has been the use of physical restraints as positive reinforcers for *not* engaging in self-injury (Favell, McGimsey, & Jones, 1978; Foxx, 1979; Foxx & Dufrense, 1984). It was observed that a number of self-injurious clients appeared to like their restraints, such as arm splints and straitjackets, and became agitated and distressed when they were removed. Using the behavioral rule "Take what the client gives you and work with it," Foxx and Dufrense (1984) conducted a study in which a self-injurious client named Harry could earn access to his restraints by not engaging in self-destructive behavior when he was out of his restraints. If Harry hit himself, then the restraints were taken away for a short period of time (a form of time out). Slowly, the total amount of time in restraints, which was earned by not engaging in self-injurious behavior, was decreased, and other, more appropriate behaviors (such as working on the hospital unit) were reinforced. The results from the study are presented in Figure 10-5. It can be seen from this fig-

educators because it is evaluative in its basic approach, treats problem behaviors directly, and includes parents as part of the treatment team. The basic behavioral approaches follow a consistent pattern. First, empirical data are gathered on the target behaviors (problem or abnormal behaviors) before the treatment intervention is started. This pretreatment sample (baseline) is then used as a standard to evaluate the treatment effects. If the treatment is not effective, it is either changed or stopped. The behaviorist treats behavior that is happening here and now and can be measured. Behavioral excesses, such as self-stimulatory behavior, tantrums, bizarre speech, or aggressive behaviors, are treated by ignoring them, by reinforcing an incompatible behavior, or by using direct punishment techniques, such as a loss of tokens or

FIGURE 10-5. The effect of reinforcing periods of non-self-injury with restraints and 5 minutes of time out from restraints following any instance of self-injurious behavior. No contingencies were in effect during the baseline and probe conditions. Smaller, softer restraints were substituted during the second treatment condition for the heavy metal ones used during the first condition.

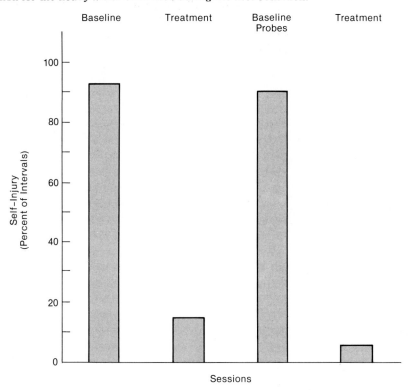

Source: R. M. Foxx and D. Dufrense. (1984). "Harry": The use of physical restraint as a reinforcer, timeout from restraint, and fading restraint in treating a self-injurious man. *Analysis and Interventions in Developmental Disabilities, 4,* 1–13. Reprinted by permission.

ure that Harry was self-injurious during baseline approximately 90 percent of the time he was out of restraints; that during the second treatment phase his self-injury fell to 6 percent; and that the self-injury was virtually eliminated at a 4-year follow-up.

Language development is critical to the prognosis of autistic and schizophrenic children. If they do not develop a means of communication, they will probably remain institutionalized for the rest of their lives. An impressive breakthrough in teaching autistic children language was made by Lovaas, Berberich, Perloff, and Schaeffer (1966) (see Figure 10-6). This intensive program took 7 hours each day and emphasized teaching spoken language in many small steps. The autistic children began by imitating an adult trainer's speech. The results of this classic experiment demonstrated that language could be taught to mute autistic children by therapists who were patient and persistent. The children received positive reinforcement for a correct response, punishment (the therapist would look away) for careless errors, and a slap on the thigh for inattention. However, few therapists use physical punishment to teach autistic children to speak; nor can they spend hours each day with each child. New techniques such as sign language have been used with verbal

FIGURE 10-6. The first 26 days of verbal imitation training for Billy and Chuck, psychotic boys who were mute before training. The sounds and words are printed in lower-case letters on the days they were introduced and in capitals on the days they were mastered.

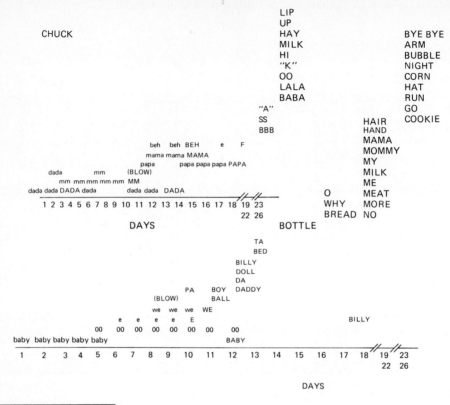

language training to help remedy the extreme language difficulties of autistic children (Carr, 1979). Most of the effective language approaches have combined the simultaneous presentation of a sign-language hand sign with the spoken word (the total communication approach) (Barrera, Lobato-Barrera, & Sulzer-Azaroff, 1980). The results have been surprising: Some mute autistic children have learned to communicate with manual signs, but a surprising number have also learned to communicate orally through total communication (Carr, 1979; Fulwiler & Fouts, 1976). Signs have also been used to help speaking autistic children learn difficult verbal concepts, such as a "yes" and "no" discrimination (see Box 10-2), color dis-

criminations (Van Wagenen, Jenson, Worsham, & Petersen, 1985), and learning to count with numbers (Worsham, Jenson, & Drew, 1984), when other procedures have failed.

Behavioral techniques are best applied in or close to a child's natural environment, instead of in a hospital or clinic setting. Major advances have been made in the cost-effective education of autistic children, using a system of behavioral techniques (Hung, Rotman, Cosentino, & McMillan, 1983; Schopler & Olley, 1980). School settings have been particularly productive because non-handicapped peers can actually be used as behavior managers and teachers, with the unexpected side benefit of socializing autistic children. In one study, the spontaneous social interactions between autistic and nonhandicapped peers at lunch, recess, and play time constituted 3 percent of all interactions at baseline. After nonhandicapped peers were used as behavioral tutors in the autism classroom, the spontaneous interactions increased to over 90 percent in the unstructured settings (Jenson, Young, Clare, & West, 1986).

Possibly the most important step in treating autistic children has been to incorporate parents actively into the treatment team. Parent training has been successful in teaching parents to decrease inappropriate behavior and to teach needed adjustment and self-help skills (Howlin et al., 1973; Koegel, Schreibman, Britten, Burke, & O'Neill, 1982). Including parents is important because it gives them the skills they need to manage their child's behavior in home settings, which decreases the probability that the child will be institutionalized. (Lovaas, Koegel, Simmons, & Long, 1973). In addition, it frees the parents. One study compared the effects of behavioral parent training in the home and direct clinic treatment for autistic children (Koegel et al., 1982). Not only was the home parent training more effective in the long term, but on average a trained parent had 115 more minutes each day for leisure than nontrained parents whose children received behavioral services in a clinic had.

Behavioral techniques are effective, but they do not cure autistic or schizophrenic children. They effectively manage problematic behaviors and teach needed survival behaviors. Their main treatment effect is in keeping children in the community with their families and not in institutions. These techniques are also more humane, because good behavior management practice incorporates whole families in the treatment process.

Medical Approaches

Medical treatment of autistic and schizophrenic children has taken a number of forms, including psychosurgery, electroconvulsive shock, and drug therapies. Most of the more drastic approaches, such as psychosurgery (Ajuriaguerra, 1971) and electroconvulsive shock (Bender, 1953), have been abandoned because of the possible harmful side effects and doubtful therapeutic effects. The more controversial drug therapies used with autistic and schizophrenic children include treatment with D-lysergic acid (LSD-25) (Bender, Corbrink, Faretra, & Sankar, 1966) and vitamin B (Rimland, 1973). Both of these drug therapies have been tested and found to have doubtful treatment effects for psychotic or developmentally disordered children.

The major advances in medication-based treatment for schizophrenic children have been in the use of antipsychotic medications, such as Thorazine, Mellaril, and Stelazine. The major antipsychotic medications work well with psychotic adults and are more effective with older autistic and schizophrenic children. These medications help reduce bizarre speech and aggression, and appear to "organize" the patients' behavior (Campbell, Anderson, Deutsch, & Green, 1984; Fish, 1976). The antipsychotic medications have also been found to be effective in reducing self-injurious behavior, particularly if they are used in combination with behavioral techniques (Durand, 1982; Singh & Millichamp, 1985). However, when antipsychotic medications are used with children, difficulties arise if the drugs are overused or relied on as a sole treatment approach. The side effects of overuse are drowsiness, which reduces the ability to learn, and (if a drug is used for an extended period of time) troublesome involuntary motor movements, or *dyskinesia*.

The newest and most promising medication for autistic children is a drug named fenfluramine (Ritvo, Freeman, Geller, & Yuwiler, 1983). Fenfluramine is more like a stimulant medication (amphetamine) than like a more traditional antipsychotic medication. In fact, fenfluramine was first developed as a diet drug. The first reported effects of fenfluramine with autistic children have included improvements in social awareness, improved communication and cognitive functioning, and reduced inappropriate behaviors. Although the effects of fenfluramine are promising, it appears that only 25 to 30 percent of autistic children show a measurable improvement. More research is needed on fenfluramine to improve its effectiveness and to study the long-term application of the drug.

As a treatment for autistic and schizophrenic children, medication is relatively inexpensive, is less time-consuming than psychological interventions, and can be administered by just a few staff members. These benefits are also the most damaging drawbacks of drugs. It is too easy to medicate a difficult child and let her languish in the back ward of a state hospital. States of stupor induced by high doses of drugs do reduce aggression and bizarre forms of behavior. However, drug-induced stupor interferes with learning and wastes precious time during which a child might be learning new language and self-help skills. Also, medication has no long-lasting effects: Once the drug is withdrawn, the symptoms reappear. Drugs are best used in moderate dosages, under close medical supervision, and in conjunction with other forms of therapy.

PROGNOSIS AND OUTCOME

Autistic children do not improve a great deal as they grow older. Several controlled studies and reviews (Eisenberg, 1957; Kanner, 1971b; Lockyer & Rutter, 1969, 1970; Lotter, 1974, 1978; Rumsey, Rapoport, & Sceery, 1984; Rutter, 1970, 1978a; Rutter, Greenfield, & Lockyer, 1967) have examined the adult status of autistic children diagnosed in childhood and followed into adulthood. Lotter (1978) reviewed 21 outcome studies and estimated that only 5 to 17 percent of autistic children had good outcomes, as assessed by near-normal social life and satisfactory functioning at school or work. Similarly, Rutter (1977) reviewed a number of follow-up studies and found that one in six autistic children (16 percent) made a good adjustment and were able to live independent lives. A quarter (25 percent) of the children made an intermediate adjustment leading to semidependent living, and 60 percent remained severely handicapped. Even higher-functioning autistic individuals tend to retain some self-stimulatory behavior and exhibited concrete thinking. It should also be recognized that even autistic adults who make a good social adjustment seldom marry,

rarely have children, and often have difficulty in forming relationships.

Autistic adults frequently change jobs or need supported employment, and they have a lower socioeconomic status than their IQ or educational level would suggest they should have. Behavior problems such as inflexibility, rather than poor work skills, cause them employment problems (Brown, 1978; Rutter, 1978a). For example, Rutter (1978a) reports that several young autistic men whom he studied lost their jobs "largely because their workmates were driven to distraction by their talk about bus routes, timetables, or other obsessional interests" (p. 504).

Intelligence is one of the most important predictors of future outcome for autistic children. Unfortunately, intelligence is a very stable characteristic for autistic children and does not improve with treatment or special education programs (Freeman et al., 1985). Near-normal intelligence while the child is young predicts good adjustment in adulthood. Intelligence scores, however, are gross indicators and predict poor outcomes better than they do good ones. For example, an IQ score below 50 in childhood means a poor prognosis, regardless of other variables in an autistic child's life (Rutter, 1974). It is not possible with higher IQ scores to make a precise prediction as to whether a child will adjust only fairly well or will make an excellent adjustment. Language seems to be the critical element in making predictions when IQs are above 50. If a child's IQ is above 50 and there is a severe language disability (but the child does speak), the prognosis is fair. If the child has only a mild language disorder and normal nonverbal intelligence, the prognosis is good (Rutter, 1974).

Institutionalization frequently harms autistic and schizophrenic children. Individual treatment programs and educational opportunities are minimal in many large hospitals. Kanner (1971b) did a 28-year follow-up study of a group of autistic children, several of whom were placed in institutions or with foster parents, some on farms. The results clearly showed that placements in large institutions led to a deterioration in social skills and general functioning, and were tantamount to "life sentence" in the institution. The farm placements, however, produced some of the best and longest-lasting adjustments: The autistic children had routine farm chores that made them useful, and they were generally accepted by small communities despite their peculiarities.

Behaviors that are difficult or dangerous for a parent to manage at home put an autistic child at particular risk for institutionalization. Soper (1987) in a survey of parents, found that such behavior problems as aggression, self-injury, tantrums, and running away were the highest-rated factors in making a decision to institutionalize an autistic child. Secondary factors for institutionalization included poor self-help skills, such as toileting problems, inabiity to dress, and feeding problems. These types of problems burden parents immensely and put an enormous strain on family resources unless the parents find help.

Trained parents and a comprehensive state-wide system of services are some of the most important outcome factors for autistic children. Lovaas et al. (1973) reported the results for autistic children who were treated and then released to either their parents or institutions. The children released to institutions lost their previous treatment gains and reverted to old abnormal behavior patterns. The children who stayed with their trained parents either maintained their original treatment gains or improved further. An even more dramatic demonstration of the effectiveness of parental involvement is the TEACCH (*Treatment and Education of Autistic and Related Communication handicapped CH*ildren) program of North Carolina (Schopler, Mesibov, & Baker, 1982). This program is a cooperative effort of parents and professionals to provide a comprehensive treatment approach that includes parent training, specialized classrooms, group homes, and research and training at a university level. Commonly reported rates of institutionalization of autistic individuals range from 40 to 90 percent of the population, depending on the study. The institutionalization rate of autistic individuals who participated in the TEACCH program over a 10-year period was only 8 percent (Schopler et al., 1982). Clearly, parents working with professionals to provide a continuum of services that focuses on early intervention and education can greatly improve the prognosis of autistic children.

Childhood schizophrenia has a course and outcome different from those of early-onset infantile autism. Eggers (1978) studied 57 children with late-onset schizophrenia in West Germany and found that 20 percent recovered completely, 30 percent made relatively good adjustments, and 50 percent made poor adjustments. Again, intelligence is a good predictor for schizophrenic children (Eggers, 1978; Pollack, 1960). Eggers (1978) found that the majority of children studied who had above-average IQs had favorable outcomes, while all of the children with low IQs had poor outcomes; interestingly, children with average IQs had about as many poor as good outcomes. Again, intelligence seems to be only a gross indicator of future outcome and does not allow precise predictions in individual cases.

The child's age and type of onset of the condition may have prognostic value for childhood schizophrenia. The earlier the onset is (before age 10) the lower is the chance of a favorable recovery. For childhood schizophrenia, a slowly developing condition that takes a great deal of time to

Table 10-7

Factors Related to Poor and Good Outcomes for Autistic and Schizophrenic Children

	Poor	Good
Infantile autism		
Language before age 5		×
IQ normal		×
IQ below 50	×	
Discharge to institution	×	
Discharge to trained parents		×
Early intervention		×
Comprehensive treatment services		×
Childhood schizophrenia		
IQ above average		×
IQ below average	×	
Onset before age 10	×	
Acute onset		×
Slow onset	×	
Identifiable precipitating event		×
Good social skills		×

manifest itself completely is associated with a poor adjustment in childhood. This slow or insidious onset is contrasted with an acute (fast) onset, which is often precipitated by a stressful event, such as a family member's death or parental divorce (Eggers, 1978; Vaillant, 1964). Table 10-7 summarizes the prognostic indicators for both autism and childhood schizophrenia.

SUMMARY

This chapter has described childhood psychosis and pervasive developmental disorders, particularly infantile autism and childhood schizophrenia. Most researchers and clinicians now consider autism and childhood schizophrenia to be separate disorders with several basic differences. Autism, which generally develops before 36 months of

age, is primarily a disorder in relating to other people. Problems in social behavior can include poor eye contact, avoidance of social interactions, and a lack of basic social skills such as smiling or showing empathy. Along with problems in social relations, autistic children also have problems with the use of language. They have high rates of self-stimulatory behavior or self-injurious behavior, and three-fourths of them are mentally retarded. High rates of self-stimulatory behavior, poor intellectual functioning, and a lack of language skills limit a child's ability to relate to other people.

In contrast to autism, childhood schizophrenia is primarily a thought disorder that develops late in childhood. Hallucinations, inability to connect thoughts logically, random jumping from topic to topic, and withdrawal into a fantasy world are common for the schizophrenic child. Unlike many

---

BOX 10-6 • Epilogue for Billy

What happens to a boy like Billy, who was discussed in Box 10-1? His parents are exhausted from years of caring for their son, who seems oblivious to their efforts. Placing him in the state hospital would be an easy answer. However, Billy's parents sense that this would be disastrous for his development and later adjustment. If he is admitted to the state hospital, he could spend the rest of his life there.

This family was lucky. When Billy was ready to start school, the school district and the local mental health center arranged to place him in a special classroom within a regular public school. The classroom was well staffed, so that he had individual instruction and treatment from a teacher who was trained to manage children with behavior disorders. Billy's disruptive self-stimulation and tantruming were decreased through the use of a time-out procedure (seclusion for a short period of time). Intense language training was implemented, and slowly he has learned more appropriate language. His echolalia has begun to disappear. When his appropriate behavior becomes stabilized in the classroom, he will begin an academic program and learn reading and writing.

There have also been changes for Billy's family. The mental health center offered a series of child management classes that taught the family, including Billy's brother, how to handle his disruptive behavior. The classes also gave Billy's family a chance to see that they were not alone and that other families had similar problems with their disturbed children. When the course was officially finished, the parents decided to continue meeting and planning for their children. The group members supported each other in times of need and worked actively to keep their children out of large institutions.

Although Billy is now making progress both behaviorally and academically, he will probably always be autistic and in need of special help. But great things are beginning to happen. The other day, just before the bus came to get Billy, he hugged his mother and kissed her good-bye for the first time, just like a normal boy.

autistic children, schizophrenic children generally develop good language skills and have near-normal intelligence. Periods of improvement and relapse are characteristic of the schizophrenic child, while autism runs a steady course, with little overall change in the behavioral symptoms from childhood through adulthood.

Like most of the severe behavior disorders of childhood, autism and childhood schizophrenia appear not to have a single cause, but are complex in their origins. Birth complications, disease, and genetics are suspected of contributing to the development of autism and schizophrenia. The origins of these conditions are primarily biological in nature, although environmental factors can interact to improve or worsen their courses. Parents do not cause autism or chidhood schizophrenia, as was once thought.

Effective treatment approaches have been slow in coming for autism and childhood schizophrenia. These children typically do not profit from long-term separation from their families and community and/or from placement in large institutions. Promising new approaches for these children emphasize getting them into treatment at a young age and including family members as part of the treatment effort. Structured behavior therapy approaches are effective in reducing many bizarre behaviors and teaching more appropriate and adaptive behaviors. Medication is also effective in reducing problematic behaviors. However, it should be emphasized that both medication and behavior therapy only manage the behavioral symptoms of these conditions and do not produce cures. The long-term effectiveness of these approaches is promising, but they have not yet been studied extensively. The variables that best predict later adjustment include the child's intelligence, language usage, and age of onset of the condition. To conclude this chapter, Box 10-6 describes the progress of the autistic boy discussed in Box 10-1.

chapter

11

Research Methods Used to Study Child Behavior Disorders

KEY TERMS

Control.   Holding all variables constant between experimental conditions except the independent variable, so that any differences observed can be attributed to the treatment influence.

Cross-Sectional Designs.   Designs in which comparisons are made between different groups of subjects at different ages. Often used in developmental studies of children.

Dependent Variable.   The behavior or performance observed to assess the impact of treatment. Multiple dependent variables are often used.

Descriptive Research.   Research that attempts to describe certain groups or situations. No manipulation is involved.

Difference Research.   Research that compares treatments or conditions to determine whether there is a difference.

External Validity.   Pertains to how well the results of a study generalize to other subjects, measures, and settings that were not actually involved in the research.

Group Experimental Designs.   Research designs in which groups of subjects are compared to determine the effects of treatments.

Independent Variable.   The factor under study and manipulated by the researcher. Also called the Experimental Variable.

Internal Validity.   The degree to which all systematic influences have been controlled or held constant except the independent variable.

Longitudinal Designs.   Designs in which a sample of subjects is observed repeatedly over an extended period of time to measure change. Often used in developmental studies.

Quasi-Experimental Designs.   A type of experiment in which a researcher compares groups that have pre-existing differences (for example, on IQ) rather than actually manipulating conditions. Those pre-existing differences represent the independent variable.

Relationship Research.   Research aimed at determining the degree to which two or more phenomena relate or vary together. Also called Correlation Research.

Reliability.   The consistency with which observers record the same behavior type, level, or performance score from simultaneous observations.

Time-series Designs.   Experimental designs in which a researcher manipulates the experimental variable over different phases of treatment conditions (for instance, baseline, treatment, baseline) and records many repeated observations. Often used with a small number of subjects or a single subject.

INTRODUCTION

Throughout this volume, there have been hundreds of references to research studies. These investigations vary in quality, some being reliable and others untrustworthy and seriously misleading. This chapter attempts to introduce readers to the essentials of research design so that they can become better-informed research consumers. After finishing the chapter, readers can expect to be able to answer questions such as these: Was an appropriate control group or condition used, or did improvement in speech occur because of maturation? Was an appropriate dependent measure employed, or did the researcher observe behaviors unrelated to drug abuse? Only well-conducted research can answer important clinical questions asked by parents and faced by professionals daily. Do children grow out of phobias, or do phobias persist into adulthood? Are drugs or psychotherapy more successful in the treatment of childhood schizophrenia? What are the most sensitive and accurate measures of children's emotions? We can guess at the answers to such questions, but children's lives are too important for us to base their treatment on such guesses. The most careful and very best research scrutiny is required.

As we study child behavior disorders, it becomes evident that most children display both desirable and undesirable behaviors from time to time. Often it is difficult to determine which actions can be considered normal and which we should be concerned about as deviant and requiring intervention. The boundaries of normality are fluid and are determined largely by societal values. In addition, the source of societal values is rather difficult to identify precisely. As mentioned in Chapter 1, a child's behavior is often judged in terms of (1) the behavior of age-mates, (2) the intensity and persistence of any problem behavior, and (3) the degree to which behaviors are culturally appropriate. Thus it seems that normality judgments are primarily made by comparing a child's behavior with that of a majority of like others. This brings us to the question of how we obtain information regarding behavioral norms (and deviations from these norms).

In order to know how most people behave, we must have information that is gathered *systematically*. We cannot rely on casual observations alone, because such procedures will not produce reliable information. Informal observation, such as we might casually undertake while shopping, is likely to be very selective and quite inaccurate. We may only notice certain individuals (such as those who dress strangely), or certain behaviors that seem different or inappropriate. Such observation will be very unsystematic, and the resulting information will be incomplete. Consequently, we must turn to a process that emphasizes the systematic acquisition of information—namely, research.

Research, like most terms, has different meanings for different people. For our purposes, *research* is broadly defined as a systematic method of inquiry, a systematic way of asking questions and obtaining information. This is a rather simple definition, with the emphasis focusing on the term *systematic,* or proceeding in a methodical, planned fashion. Certainly there are many ways for us to obtain information. Every day we make decisions and act based on information. More often than not, our attention is focused mainly on the particular decision to be made or the action to be taken, often in a limited manner (such as the driving need to buy *that* stereo equipment *today*). In research, the focus is on objective, systematic information gathering. The process may not produce a soaring emotional state for most people in the same way as impulse buying does, but it does tend to result in more rational decisions.

As noted previously, research is a process whereby we systematically gather data regarding some important practical or theoretical question. If research is planned and executed in a technically sound manner, the results should provide an objective answer to the question. In some quarters, it has become fashionable to question the value of research or to make jokes about the utility of research findings (for example, Senator William Proxmire's "Golden Fleece Award" has been given to various unfortunate investigators whose research titles might appear frivolous to untutored readers). While such pursuits are amusing, it is important to remember that many items and processes that now make our daily life easier were once the results of some research that was perhaps thought silly at one time.

We are all consumers of research, whether we are conscious of it or not. Scientific investigation has contributed immeasurably to the world around us. It influences the production of food we eat, our clothing, our modes of transportation, the medicines we take, the way we write term papers, the way we go on reducing diets, and many other products and procedures we use in daily life. Too frequently we encounter poor-quality products that we are told have been carefully developed and evaluated. Consequently, we are skeptical when advertisements say that a product has been scientifically evaluated and is of unsurpassed quality. Having been misled in the past, we may become suspicious of any scientific claims. However, with some knowledge of the characteristics of good research, consumers can make more informed choices, whether personal or professional.

This chapter attempts to increase readers' ability to evaluate the quality of psychological and educational research studies—that is, to make them better-informed research consumers. Obviously we are dependent on research of many types—not only on material products, but on educational, psychotherapeutic, and physical rehabilitation programs developed through research as well. For example, parents of a problem child must often make decisions regarding a treatment program for their child. Likewise, teachers and other professionals must make decisions concerning educational or other treatment programs for children. Box 11-1 describes an investigation on the effects of a self-recording procedure on attending and academic productivity; this procedure was implemented with two adolescent males who were described as having multiple handicaps (mental retardation and schizophrenia) (Morrow, Burke, & Buell, 1985). In addition to behavioral difficulties, they were performing poorly on academic tasks; consequently, the target behaviors chosen for treatment were attending and math problem computation. Such *comparative research studies* (in this case, the subjects' performance with and without treatment were being compared) are necessary in order to determine which treatment method is more successful with particular problems.

SCIENCE AND COMMON SENSE

There are many popular misconceptions and negative stereotypes regarding science and scientists—for example, that scientists are unrealistic dreamers, "space cadets," or arrogant "ivory-tower eggheads," incapable of relating to the "real" world. (It is surprisingly easy to think of negative stereotypes of scientists.) This view implies that there is little relationship between science and common sense (a notion explicitly stated by some). There are some important differences between the two, but it would be incorrect to conclude that they are totally unrelated.

In one sense, science and common sense are similar. Kerlinger (1973) stated that science can be thought of as a "systematic and controlled extension of common sense" (p. 3). However, Kerlinger also emphasized that there are some essential and significant differences between the two, mostly related to the concept of *systematic* procedures. Generally speaking, common sense is characterized by a much less systematic approach to problems than is the scientific method. Common sense might dictate doing things in a traditional way, such as spanking unruly children. Someone using the scientific approach would be more inclined to study the behavioral effects of spanking as contrasted with other methods of controlling disobedience. Table 11-1 summarizes some of the ways in which science and common sense differ.

FUNDAMENTALS OF THE RESEARCH PROCESS

In general, research can be conceptualized as a process that begins with a question and progresses through a systematic series of steps aimed at obtaining an answer to that question. Obviously, procedural details will vary greatly, depending on the particular discipline of the researcher involved; they may even vary between investigations within a given discipline. However, the general process remains essentially unchanged.

Research Questions

As mentioned above, the research process begins with the formulation of a question. At this point, we need to consider briefly the nature of research questions. There are as many different specific types of research questions as there are studies and investigators. We can, however, place the general types of research questions in psychology into three basic categories: *descriptive* questions, questions regarding *differences*, and questions about *relationships or correlations*.

Descriptive questions ask about the nature of a phenomenon. Such questions are aimed at describing a particular group or a type of individual with regard to certain characteristics (What are the behavioral patterns characteristic of individuals with anorexia? What is the average IQ of psychotic children? and so on.) These questions are not simple to answer, because they require samples of subjects who are truly representative of the group of interest, such as all autistic children or all depressed ones. *Difference* questions ask, "Is there a difference?" Investigations addressing difference questions may compare groups (for example, is there a significant difference in academic performance between the group that received individual tutoring and the group that received structured group instruction?), or they may compare an individual's behavior before and after treatment has been applied (as in the study described in Box 11-1). *Relationship* questions ask to what degree two or more phenomena are related or vary together. These are often termed correlational questions (after the correlational statistical analyses used). A correlational study might explore the relationship between annual family income and the frequency of mental health problems of children. Simply stated, the question might read: As family income varies, what tends to happen to the frequency of youngsters' mental health problems? (To put it another way, as income increases, does the frequency of child mental health problems tend to increase or decrease?)

It has been noted that these represent *general* types of research questions investigated in psychology and other behavioral sciences. Certainly there are many variations within these general categories of questions, many studies that in-

BOX 11-1. • **Example of a Research Study That Could Influence Treatment Decisions**

This study investigated the effects of a self-recording procedure on the attending-to-task behavior and academic productivity of two adolescent males with mental retardation and schizophrenia. The subjects were 15 and 17 years old and observed to have poor attending behaviors and unsatisfactory performance in math. Treatment phases involved using a cassette recorder close to the subjects' desks during math class; the recorder played a tape with a periodic beep

FIGURE 11-1. Percentage of attending-to-task behavior across baseline, first treatment phase, withdrawal, second treatment phase, and follow-up.

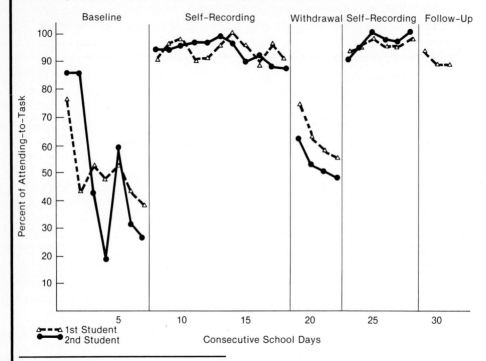

Source: L. W. Morrow, J. G. Burke, and B. J. Buell (1985). Effects of a self-recording procedure on the attending to task behavior and academic productivity of adolescents with multiple handicaps. *Mental Retardation, 23,* 137–141. Reprinted by permission.

clude combinations of these questions, and situations in which the distinctions among the types of questions are blurred. However, for initial instructional purposes regarding research methods, it is helpful to view research questions at this general level. It is important to be able to identify the type of question being addressed in order to understand a study more easily.

Research Paradigms: Descriptions, Advantages, and Limitations

Scientists working in psychology and education often classify research into two major categories: *experimental* and *nonexperimental* approaches. Each is applicable in certain situations, and selection of a particular approach or method

Box 11-1 (Continued)

signal. When the subjects heard the beep, they were to stop their work and mark a 5" × 8" card with either a plus (if they thought they were working) or a minus (if they were not working on their assignment). The experiment involved a *reversal design*—one in which data are recorded before treatment, while treatment is under way, when treatment is withdrawn, and then when treatment is reintroduced (we examine this design later in the chapter). Figures 11-1 and 11-2 indicate that self-recording improved both attending-to-task behavior and the number of math problems computed correctly for both subjects (a few follow-up data were collected on one subject with respect to attending 30 days after the experiment was terminated; the other subject had moved and was not available). These results would seem to suggest that self-recording might be helpful in academic settings for youngsters with problems such as those in this study.

FIGURE 11-2. Percentage of mathematics problems computed correctly across baseline, first treatment phase, withdrawal, and second treatment phase.

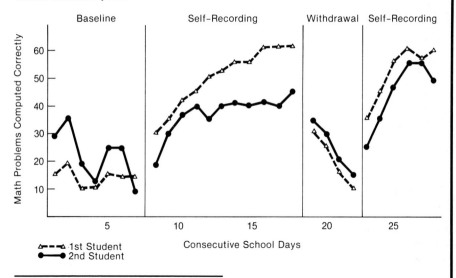

Source: L. W. Morrow, J. G. Burke, and B. J. Buell (1985). Effects of a self-recording procedure on the attending to task behavior and academic productivity of adolescents with multiple handicaps. *Mental Retardation, 23*, 137-141. Reprinted by permission.

will depend on the question under investigation and the setting in which a study is conducted. Both experimental and nonexperimental research studies have contributed substantially to our understanding of child behavior disorders. The serious student should become acquainted with both approaches, in order to be knowledgeable regarding research on children's problems.

In some ways, experimental and nonexperimental research approaches are mirror images of each other. Experimental research is most often thought of in terms of tightly controlled studies in which the investigator manipulates some treatment or condition that the subjects experience. Investigators using nonexperimental research methods tend to observe, analyze, and describe

Table 11-1

Differences Between Scientific Inquiry and Common-sense Reasoning

Area of Difference	Scientific Inquiry	Common-sense Reasoning
Use of theories and concepts	Studied systematically	Studied informally and unsystematically, if at all
Level of proof required	Very stringent and according to agreed-upon principles	Loose and variable
Control demanded	High degree	Little or none
Interest in relationships between phenomena	Systematic, constant study of relationships	Unsystematic, often only interested in those of personal relevance
Types of explanations regarding phenomena	Couched in the observable, logical, empirically testable	Often extended beyond the empirically testable to metaphysical explanations

phenomena as they exist, rather than manipulating treatments or conditions. Experiments often involve a great deal of control over the research environment and conditions under which subjects participate (for example, no strangers may be allowed to intrude; noise, light, and temperature levels may be held constant). Nonexperimental research, on the other hand, does not typically impose as much control, and data collection on a phenomenon or group of subjects more often tends to take place in a more natural environment, such as a classroom, playground, or home.

Experimental and nonexperimental research approaches each have certain advantages and limitations. Some of these are inherent in the general approaches, whereas others are specifically relevant to particular methods or strategies within these general approaches. In all cases, a researcher must weigh the merits of each procedure and determine the most appropriate method and specific procedures to be employed.

One major advantage of experimental research over nonexperimental methods involves the use of control. An investigator using experimental methods exercises a greater degree of direct control than one using nonexperimental methods. The researcher attempts to control or hold constant all influences except the treatment variable that is being manipulated. Because ex-

perimental research involves the use of control in this manner, an investigator can be more confident in attributing her results to the treatment variable. If the only known difference between two groups of children is the treatment they receive, then posttreatment differences in behavior can probably be attributed to the type of treatment received. Experimentation is also characterized by more control of the research setting, as noted above: this minimizes the possibility that results may be influenced by extraneous events, such as merely the expectation that a treatment will be effective.

The limitations of experimental research can be viewed in the same context as the advantages discussed above. Because of the high degree of control, experimental studies are frequently conducted in a rather artificial environment. Obviously the degree of artificiality varies, since experiments may be executed in a contrived laboratory setting or in a field setting that approximates the subjects' natural environment. Results may be substantially altered by an artificial environment if the setting is sufficiently unusual that subjects perform differently than they would normally. For example, children who have spent most of their time at home may be unusually active or frightened if they are brought to a laboratory or clinic (especially if they see unfamiliar adults in white lab coats, which could indicate that they are doctors who might give injections).

A second limitation of experimental research also concerns the issue of artificiality. Experimental investigations often involve people (experimenters and other subjects), activities, and materials that are unfamiliar to the subjects. Some experiments utilize exotic apparatus that would never be encountered outside a research laboratory. (How often does a rat find a lever to press for food in its normal living area?) Such stimuli might influence the subjects' performance so that they perform uncharacteristically.

As stated earlier, nonexperimental research does not involve the use of direct control to the degree evident in experiments. This is both an advantage and a limitation. On the positive side, many nonexperimental methods do not create an artificial environment that would influence subjects' responses. In fact, some nonexperimental investigations are specifically aimed at studying subjects in their natural environment. Obviously, not all nonexperimental research is conducted in this manner, and in some cases the presence of observers makes those observed somewhat uneasy and constrained in their behavior.

The relative absence of control becomes a limitation to the degree that it contributes to unreliable data. For example, it is quite likely that the data obtained in a case study are substantially influenced by the biases of the interviewer, especially if a structured protocol of questions is not used. Without the control imposed by a consistent set of questions, information may be obtained only in areas that a particular interviewer deems important, which may contribute to incomplete and perhaps unreliable data. (Also, bias can be evident in how the interviewer asks even the standard questions—for example, in how he or she gives IQ test instructions.)

An observer records children's behavior to trace progress.

Nonexperimental Research   If an investigator is observing a third-grade boy to see how he gets along with his classmates, that investigator is engaging in nonexperimental research, at least informally. Nonexperimental research methods involve observation, analysis, and description of phenomena, rather than the manipulation of treatment variables that is involved in experimentation. A variety of specific procedures may be viewed as nonexperimental. Each has certain distinctive features, as well as unique advantages and limitations. In this section, we briefly examine certain nonexperimental research methods that are of particular importance in the study of child behavior disorders.

Observation.   Observation is a data collection method that may be used in both experimental and nonexperimental research. It is discussed in this section because manipulation of a treatment variable is not inherent in the observation process. Observation has been viewed by some as a distinct research method because of its tradition of use by certain disciplines, such as anthropology.

Observation techniques vary greatly, depending on the type of investigation and setting in which a study is conducted. One variation involves the degree to which an observer participates in the activities of the group being studied. For example, anthropological research has often used what is known as *participant observation,* wherein the individual collecting the data actually participates in the setting or activities being observed. Such procedures are vastly different from investigations in which a *nonparticipant observer* collects the data. As suggested by the terminology, nonparticipant observers try to be as inconspicuous as possible and do not actually become involved in the social interactions under investigation. Researchers in psychology have tended to use nonparticipant observation procedures and often are not even seen by those being observed (when observations are made through a one-way mirror or by means of audio or video recordings). Such procedures are employed not because investigators are unscrupulous snoopers, but because they do not want the awareness of being observed to change research participants' behavior. Pre-

school and kindergarten children are delightful to observe because they adjust to nonintrusive observers' presence so rapidly. In fact, when some leaves blew against a familiar observer's shoe on the playground once, a small girl commented on the leaves on "the shoe." Not "the lady's shoe," but "*the* shoe," which indicated the child's lack of concern about being observed.

The influence of known or evident observers on subjects' behavior has been demonstrated frequently in the psychological literature. For example, White (1977) found that observer presence had a dramatic effect on family activity level. He used alternating 30-minute periods in which an observer was physically present and then absent from the room (observing from behind a one-way mirror during the "absent" periods). The self-conscious family's activity level was approximately 50 percent lower when the observer was present than when absent. Researchers employing nonparticipant observation do so because they are very concerned about the subjects' behaving as naturally as possible (a factor that is particularly important in some types of studies). This seems achievable if subjects become accustomed to the observer to the point that behavior returns to a natural state (Masling & Stern, 1969), or if such camouflaging devices as concealed video cameras, the one-way mirror (Mercatoris & Craighead, 1974; White, 1977) or radio transmitters are used. However, many people may never behave completely naturally when they are aware of being observed.

Observation procedures may also vary in the amount of structure imposed on a study by the researcher. Structure may be imposed either on the environment or on the observer. For example, data may be recorded in a completely unstructured environment, such as the natural setting in which the subjects live, while they routinely engage in their normal activities. On the other end of this continuum, data may be collected in an environment that is very structured, artificial, and foreign to the subjects, such as a contrived laboratory setting. Similarly, observer procedures may vary on a continuum of structure. Data may be recorded in a totally unstructured fashion (for example, field notes recorded anecdotally without any guidelines) or they may be recorded in a very structured and prescribed fashion (for instance, a standardized protocol or checklist used for counting disruptive behavior frequency). Usually researchers start to study some condition, such as conduct disorders, in an unstructured way and then go on to address specific questions about the disorders with more structured observations.

Case studies. Case studies represent a second nonexperimental research method. Such studies characteristically involve an in-depth examination of an individual or a small social unit such as a family. Case studies are traditionally characterized by a lack of experimental controls (Kazdin, 1980). The focus of such a study may vary, depending on the nature of the research question. Usually the researcher attempts to determine all of the factors or influences that are important in a subject's development and current behavior. Data collected often include developmental history, including physical, psychological, and social aspects of the person's development. The case study's purpose is to determine why an individual has reached his current status. An investigator describes the subject and attempts to reconstruct his past history and the nature and sources of any present problems.

For the most part, case studies address descriptive questions, either as a preliminary investigation, to verify a theory, or to understand and remedy particular problems for the subject being studied. In the latter situation, a case study may provide an in-depth clinical picture of the individual as a prelude to providing some type of intervention aimed at solving problem behavior. This purpose is illustrated by the case of Kathy K., reported by Blanco and Rosenfeld (1978), which is presented in Box 11-2.

As suggested by Box 11-2, case studies are usually quite detailed and lengthy. We have chosen to present only a part of this report. The remainder of the case study of Kathy K. included a behavioral description, an assessment of her personality functioning, a physician's report, a diagnostic summary, a report of treatment, and a follow-up report. Treatment involved a multifaceted behavioral intervention with Kathy, as well as manipulation of various aspects of her environment

thought to be contributing to her problems. Outcomes of the treatment were portrayed as "excellent," even though her parents gave only limited cooperation to the treatment program. As Kathy's story indicates, case studies are important in the study and treatment of child behavior disorders.

Case studies are rich in the depth, complexity, and quantity of information typically obtained. They also have a limitation, however: Case studies usually only describe only one subject, or, at most, a few (such as a family). The information thus may not apply to other individuals or situations different from those studied. Another limitation of the case study approach involves possible bias on the part of the investigator or of informants such as the client or family members. In most cases there are no objective records of the client's past interactions. Information must come from the individual client or perhaps from interested third parties, such as parents or other relatives. Such data may be biased, because informants are aware of the existing problem and consequently interpret earlier events differently than they would without such knowledge (for example, parents may view previous normal play incidents as abnormal because the child has now been labeled as emotionally disturbed). Data bias or inaccuracy may also occur because of faulty memory on the part of the informants. Individuals providing information may selectively remember certain types of incidents; they may be able to recall only more recent events; or they may confuse one child's reactions with those of another child. Case study data may also be biased by the investigator's or therapist's interpretations. Information for a case study comes from the patient or other informants and is necessarily filtered through the investigator before it is recorded. Such data are quite vulnerable to the biases and expectations of an investigator, and may be entered into the records in a manner that is incomplete or inaccurate to some degree (Mischel, 1968).

Experimental Research   As noted earlier, experimental research is characterized by manipulation of the treatment or condition under study. The factor under study, the one manipulated by

BOX 11-2 • The Case of Kathy K.

Kathy K., a bright junior high girl, was referred by her seventh-grade counselor to a school psychologist. The counselor reported that since school had begun a few weeks earlier Kathy had become very teary eyed and tense, having complained to the school nurse about stomachaches, head pains, and anxiety. Her mounting list of absences was viewed with alarm by her teachers and counselor, who recognized Kathy as a talented teenager now performing well below her capabilities. The diagnosis of school phobia was simple enough. The referral noted that she seemed "preoccupied" and "daydreaming" in class, "unhappy" and a "loner" with no social interests. Inquiries by teachers and the counselor produced only minimal responses from the girl. On days of attendance, she was often seen to be calling her mother on the school's public telephone. On two occasions, classmates reported that after she got to school on the school bus, she turned around "crying," to walk home alone about two miles away. The counselor had telephoned her mother, who claimed to be "very irritated" by her daughter's behavior and said that "reasoning with her" was not at all effective.

In pursuing the case with her parents, inquiry was made about Kathy's health. Mrs. K. reported that the family doctor found Kathy to be in excellent health, but since she was viewed as "shy and anxious," he had prescribed small amounts of tranquilizers. However, within two weeks he discontinued these as being ineffective.

As is frequent in such cases, Kathy was relatively relaxed and in no distress when she stayed home on school days. She occupied her time by helping her mother, reading, and watching television. The counselor reported her parents to be "at their wits' end" and definitely concerned enough to permit a psychological evaluation. The psychologist learned from Kathy's previous elementary principal that Kathy had shown an identical pattern when younger, although at a lesser intensity. Interestingly, Kathy's elementary school was directly across the street from her home, where her mother was readily accessible when she showed fear reactions previously. Kathy's new school, its associations, and its significant distance from her mother apparently provoked her current, more intense, reaction. The psychologist reviewed the causal conditions and planned a comprehensive evaluation and multifaceted attack on Kathy's problems.

SCHOOL INFORMATION

School records revealed her IQ scores of 124 and 139 on the Otis-Lennon Mental Ability Test, testifying to superior to very superior intellectual potential. Yet it appeared that Kathy had been an underachiever since entering school. Although teachers through the years had reported her to be "cooperative" and a fairly conscientious worker, Kathy had been a B and C student at best, earning only slightly above grade-level scores on most standardized achievement tests.

Lacking in confidence, timid, and reticent, Kathy was poor in attendance. She appeared sad, futilely fighting tears, and unable to sustain the normal school day without being excused

---

an experimenter, is known as the *independent variable* (also called the *experimental variable*). If, for example, we are interested in determining the effectiveness of a new treatment for childhood autism, then our independent variable may be "type of treatment." We may be comparing a new treatment with one that has been used previously—contrasting the effects of these different treatments on autistic behavior, for example. As we manipulate a treatment, we must have some way

Box 11-2 (Continued)

from class to call home. Peer relationships were minimal; Kathy had no friends and did not seek other companionship. . . .

FAMILY INFORMATION (INTERVIEW WITH PARENTS)

The members of the family include Mr. K., age 37, Mrs. K., age 36, Kathy, and two boys, ages 9 and 4. Mr. K., a sports enthusiast, is a bright, shallow, talkative individual currently employed as a junior grade statistician. He reported that he was a poor student through high school, to his father's dismay, but later was admitted to and graduated from a small, noncompetitive college, although never fulfilling his own ambition of becoming a doctor. Valuing high achievement but unable to realize it himself, he is attempting to meet this need through Kathy's school and vocational career. Attempting to "prevent Kathy from making the same mistake," he cannot tolerate any imperfection in the girl, and he has high expectations and places pressure on his daughter. His sons, he claims, "will be athletes some day!" He also expresses the view that a child "should serve the parents," regarding as secondary the child's individual needs, desires, and unique qualities.

Mrs. K., a high school graduate, appears as a self-centered, anxious, uncertain, and mildly depressed suburban housewife. A "less attractive fraternal twin" in a family of six children, she recalled that her childhood, particularly her adolescence, was unhappy and unfulfilling, because she lacked attention, social experiences, and achievement. Like her husband, she also seeks to meet her own needs of social acceptance and achievement through her daughter. Because Kathy is unable to live up to these demanding expectations, Mrs. K. in certain ways rejects the girl. In this case, such rejection takes the form of criticism or stringent demands. Ironically, the mother's behavior fosters Kathy's feelings of inadequacy and fear, the very things Mrs. K. cannot tolerate.

Although Mr. K.'s career and sports interests take him away from the home a considerable amount of time, he is quite opinionated regarding child rearing and family life and is the dominant member in the family. Although his wife resents his absence and control, she submits to the situation, yet feels angry and despondent. Kathy's anxiety and fearfulness regarding separation may, in part, be a reflection of the mother's similar feelings when her husband is absent.

Kathy's relationships with siblings, particularly her 9-year-old brother, appear poor. Being a rather aggressive, confident, and athletic boy, he receives much parental attention and praise. Kathy resents him and she sometimes hits him very hard when she is irritated. The boy, in turn, is reported to be "merciless" when he taunts her for her school absences and having "fake pains." Kathy often has voiced her desire to be left peacefully alone, as she cannot tolerate such ridicule.

Source: R. F. Blanco and J. G. Rosenfeld, (1978). Case studies in clinical and school psychology (Springfield, IL: Charles C Thomas) Reprinted by courtesy of Charles C Thomas, Publisher.

of measuring its effect. Perhaps we want to count the number of times per hour that a child exhibits what is considered "autistic behavior" (which must be defined operationally—perhaps as bizarre hand or body movements, lack of interest in other people, bizarre speech content, and so on). The measure or means by which we determine a treatment's effect is known as the *dependent variable*. So we manipulate an independent variable (treatment type) to observe its effects on the dependent variable (the frequency with which the behavior occurs under different treatment conditions, or the score an individual receives on a depression scale).

Quasi-experimental designs. The discussion presented above illustrates a type of investigation in which a researcher literally manipulates the experimental variable (treatment) and observes the effect of that manipulation on one or more dependent variables. Such a study may be conducted by sampling a group of autistic children and then randomly assigning half of them to one group and the other half to a second group. The groups will be very similar in their behavior and other characteristics (because the children have been randomly assigned to the groups) until after the two treatments are applied. There are, however, situations where a researcher cannot manipulate the independent variable in a literal sense. This may be the case if we are interested in comparing the performance of mentally retarded children and nonretarded children on some task. In this example, the focus of study is on performance differences between the two populations, and our independent variable may be labeled "subject classification" (retarded versus nonretarded). We will not actually be manipulating the independent variable, since the intelligence differences are pre-existing and impossible to alter. Investigations such as this, in which subjects cannot be randomly assigned to groups, are known as *quasi-experimental studies,* whereas those in which an independent variable is literally manipulated are viewed as *true experiments* (or, simply, *experiments*).

Quasi-experimental studies have particular limitations that do not pose problems in true experiments. We have just used the example of comparing mentally retarded and nonretarded subjects on some task performance. As we design such a study, our aim is to control or hold constant everything except the independent variable. This is no problem when we deal with certain variables, such as sex, age, and socioeconomic status. There are, however, other influences that cannot be readily controlled. Each group has a history of being retarded or nonretarded. That history carries with it a myriad of experiences that cannot be precisely assessed or controlled; for example, the nonretarded subjects are likely to be healthier and more self-confident than the retarded individuals. Thus, if we obtain results that suggest differences, we must be cautious in the way findings are interpreted. Although we will want to be able to attribute differences to the independent variable (in this case, retardation), some of the experiential factors (such as general health status, social rejection, or vitality) may also differentially affect the subjects' performance. This is a continuing problem with quasi-experimental studies and one that researchers must constantly address. It does not, however, preclude the use of such designs in psychology and other behavioral sciences; it simply requires that we proceed with caution. There are many areas of great interest where the only means of investigation are quasi-experimental designs, and they have provided enormous amounts of useful information over the years.

Longitudinal/cross-sectional designs. The study of child behavior disorders is frequently undertaken within a developmental framework. That is, we may be interested in how a particular disorder develops or in the developmental course of children's behavioral problems. In these cases, the investigations use a span of time (often several years) as the independent variable. Two basic approaches have been commonly employed in such research: *longitudinal designs* and *cross-sectional designs.* Longitudinal studies select a sample of subjects, test or observe them, and follow these same subjects for an extended period of time, repeating the assessment intermittently. For example, a researcher may be interested in observing the development of social skills in retarded youngsters as they progress from age 3 to age 15. Cross-sectional investigations, on the other hand, sample at one time different groups of subjects who are at several age levels (for example, 3 to 5, 6 to 8, 9 to 11, and 12 to 15) and compare the dependent measure scores (for instance, social skills scores or self-esteem scores) across groups. In both longitudinal and cross-sectional studies, there is an attempt to draw conclusions regarding the developmental trajectory of the dependent

Longitudinal studies of people, such as this elderly couple, may present a number of problems for investigators.

variable being measured; in both strategies, time or age is the independent variable. Classification of these approaches as experiments is not easy (illustrating that most classification schemes are somewhat arbitrary). Longitudinal studies typically do not involve manipulation of an independent variable, but only repeated observations or measurements over time. Cross-sectional investigations seem to fit the quasi-experimental mold where pre-existing differences (for instance, different age groups) are present at the time of assessment.

Longitudinal and cross-sectional designs also have certain advantages and limitations that must be considered in developmental studies. As noted previously, longitudinal investigations measure the same subjects repeatedly, usually over an extended period. This permits observation of change in the same individuals as they develop, which is a distinct strength of the longitudinal approach with regard to interpretations of a developmental

nature. Potential problems with this procedure are that subjects' development may be altered by the repeated assessments as they become more "test-wise," and that events such as war or economic depressions may affect their development (which would mean that one would not be evaluating development *only*). Another limitation often encountered in longitudinal studies is subject attrition. As an investigation proceeds over an extended period of time, it is not uncommon for a certain portion of the subjects to be lost because they move, refuse to continue, or die (if the time period is really protracted, there may also be investigator attrition). This may make data collected toward the end of a study different from data collected earlier because of the particular characteristics of the lost subjects, rather than on account of an actual developmental trend. Thus the group of subjects may not actually be the *same* at the conclusion of the study. Moreover, in really lengthy longitudinal studies, the measure originally used may become outdated and fail to address matters of contemporary concern. Finally, such studies often are prohibitively expensive, so most longitudinal studies now are limited to no longer than 4–5 years.

Cross-sectional studies are more convenient to conduct than longitudinal investigations, because subjects from several age levels are sampled and typically assessed once at about the same time. This circumvents the difficulties with subject attrition and possible effects of repeated testing. However, other problems are found in cross-sectional developmental studies. One of the most serious limitations is inherent in the cross-sectional approach—the fact that different cohorts or groups are being compared. There is a strong tendency to interpret differences between groups as representing developmental trends in the same manner as longitudinal conclusions are drawn (Achenbach, 1978). Such inferences must be viewed with great caution, because differences may be caused by factors that are not a result of development. In some cases, the age range from the youngest to the oldest groups is so great that sociocultural or historical changes have been substantial (for instance, groups were born in such different times that social mores regarding child rearing have changed, or prevailing teaching practices or permissiveness levels have changed). Consequently, differences between the groups could be due to development, sociocultural variations, or a combination of the two. Developmental interpretations from cross-sectional studies must thus be made with great care, although such designs remain an important part of our research methodology in psychology if employed prudently.

Time-series designs. Thus far, the examples of experimental research have primarily involved investigations in which groups of subjects might be studied. Traditionally, such studies have been conducted with no fewer than 10 subjects in each group (often more). There is yet another type of experiment, which characteristically does not compare groups of this size: *time-series designs*. Time-series experiments involve investigations in which an independent variable is manipulated across two or more phases. Treatment is

actually manipulated (for example, applied, then withdrawn, then reapplied), and the dependent variable is monitored. Time-series studies are often used to assess the effect of treatment on the behavior of a small number of subjects or even a single individual subject. If treatment manipulation reliably changes the subject's behavior, then one can conclude that the treatment is effective. Time-series designs have provided researchers with a powerful tool for investigating the effects of treatment in applied settings where only limited numbers of children with similar problems may be available for study—something that is not always possible in large group studies. There are several variations in time-series design formats, which we discuss more completely later.

Time-series designs have an advantage over group experiments because many more measurements are collected on the same individuals over some period of time. In group experiments, there is often only one test or measurement after treatment has been applied. In cases where multiple measurements are obtained in group studies, they often constitute only two or three repeated assessments. Even in longitudinal studies, the measurements are far fewer than those typically obtained in time-series investigations. In time-series studies, many observations are made (perhaps several daily) under both untreated and treated conditions. These experiments are occasionally termed *continuous measurement studies* because of the ongoing collection of data over time from a subject. This represents an important strength, because one can actually observe the process of change as well as determine the end product.

On the other side of the coin, time-series experiments have been criticized because of the small number of subjects that are studied (often only one). The concern here involves the generalizability of data obtained on only one or a few individuals. Can one third-grade boy with a conduct disorder tell us how children with conduct disorders will generally respond to a particular treatment? In addition, the types of subjects frequently studied in time-series research are often quite atypical—those who really need treatment because their problems are severe. How do we know that the results would be similar if other people were tested? Basically, we do not, unless several replications of the same investigation with different subjects show very similar results. For example, a particular medication may have disastrous side effects in only 1 in 10,000 patients. Testing only a few children may fail to reveal such a rare but potentially lethal reaction.

Group experimental studies represent a mirror image of time-series designs in terms of strengths and limitations. More subjects are included in the group study, so that the concern about generalization is lessened. We are more likely to obtain a representative sample of behavior from 30 to 60 subjects than we are from 1 or 3. Another issue arising from group experiments, as they are frequently executed, relates to the small number of measurements that are obtained. If, for example, an experiment is conducted on equivalent groups, different treatments are applied, and subjects are then tested, we have only one sample of behavior—that provided by the test after experimental treatments have been administered. It is certainly possible that this one assessment involves atypical performance and that the researcher may not be aware of it. This concern is somewhat offset by the fact that many subjects are usually tested. It is unlikely that all individuals (or even a substantial number) would be behaving atypically unless all had some contagious disease or all were subjected to some stress such as an earthquake or a fire.

There are strong designs and weak ones, ones that produce reliable results and others that may prove misleading. The particular advantages and limitations of specific experimental designs could more than fill this entire book. Interested readers should consult any of the various available volumes on research design (Achenbach, 1978; Bailey, 1982; Barlow & Hersen, 1984; Drew & Hardman, 1985; Goldstein, 1979; Kazdin, 1980; Kratochwill, 1978; Nesselroade & Baltes, 1979; Tawney & Gast, 1984). The limitations of experimental research cannot be discounted as inconsequential, nor should they be viewed as insurmountable difficulties. Experimentation remains

one of our most powerful tools in the search for causes and most effective treatments of behavior disorders. These limitations can be circumvented to a substantial degree if a researcher is cautious and thorough in planning prior to execution of an experiment. The goal in each study is to exploit the advantages and take precautions to minimize or eliminate the impact of methodological difficulties. Table 11-2 summarizes the advantages and limitations of different research paradigms.

FUNDAMENTALS OF DESIGNING RESEARCH

Previous sections have alluded to the process of designing or planning an investigation—an essential step in research. No investigation that is designed poorly or planned in a haphazard fashion can generate results that are very reliable or useful. The importance of this crucial step cannot be overemphasized, regardless of which approach is being employed. The purpose of the present section is to provide background regarding the fundamentals of designing experimental research. This emphasis here is not meant to discount the value of nonexperimental research in studying child behavior disorders. However, to avoid repetition, a more complete examination of nonexperimental methods as they relate to assessment is presented in Chapter 13.

The Concept of Control

Earlier, we have alluded to the concept of *control* in several areas. It warrants specific attention here because it is so central to a well-designed experiment. Many different factors can influence children's behavior, including their intelligence, language skills, motivation, relationship with the examiner, and so on. The object of experimentation is to identify those factors that actually do affect a child's task performance and to eliminate the other factors. The concept of *control* involves eliminating the systematic influence of all variables, *except the one being studied*. For example, perhaps we want to compare the effectiveness of two treatment programs. In this case we have decided to conduct a group experiment. One group

T a b l e 11-2
Advantages and Limitations of Different Research Paradigms

Paradigm/Strategy	Advantages	Limitations
Case study	Considerable depth and breadth of information on a given patient's problems.	Data may be biased or inaccurate if informant is biased or does not remember accurately, or if investigator holds a strong bias.
Cross-sectional	Much more convenient to execute than longitudinal studies.	Group differences may make developmental inferences difficult or incorrect.
Experimental (generally)	Exercises considerable control to minimize effects of extraneous factors.	Amount of control exercised may create artificiality and alter subjects' behavior.
Group experimental	Use of many subjects promotes greater confidence in generalizability of results.	Use of few measurements on subjects does not permit observation of change process.
Interview	Data may be rich and informative because interviewer can probe and interrogate further when answers are unclear or incomplete.	Data may be biased or inaccurate because of interviewer bias and interaction between respondent and interviewer.
Longitudinal	Permits observation of subjects' development over an extended period of time.	Repeated assessment may alter subjects' performance; subject attrition may be substantial over the extended time period.
Nonexperimental	Less exercise of control permits observation of subjects in a natural state.	Less exercise of control may generate unreliable or uninterpretable data.
Observational	Permits precise behavioral descriptions of subjects' behavior and changes caused by intervention.	Data may be inaccurate if observer is biased, or unreliable if observer is not trained or if target behaviors are defined ambiguously.
Quasi-experimental	Permits the study of populations that are different prior to the investigation.	Difficult to control for pre-existing differences other than the independent variable.
Questionnaire	Economical means of obtaining data from a large, geographically dispersed sample if distributed by mail.	Data obtained may be limited by format of questionnaire or biased by low response rate.
Time-series	Many measurements on same subject permit observation of change process as treatment is manipulated.	Often criticized for using small number of subjects, which may limit generalizability of results.

will receive treatment A, whereas the second will receive treatment B (the independent variable will thus be type of treatment, as discussed earlier). The concept of control dictates that all factors must be equivalent for both groups except the independent variable (treatment). That is, the groups must be equivalent with regard to any factors that may influence the results (such as age, sex, or problem severity). Procedures must also be similar for the two groups except for any procedural details that are actually part of the treatment characteristics. Unless these matters are held constant, or controlled, we will not be able to attribute any differences to the effect of our treatment. For example, we may not be able to infer that subjects in group A performed better than those in group B because they received individualized instruction (our treatment), if they also had more time to complete the task than group B did. The concept of control is basic to experimental design—a notion we encounter repeatedly.

Designing Time-Series Experiments

Time-series experiments are very powerful research tools for studying child behavior disorders. Frequently we are faced with a situation in which an individual child has a particular problem. As behavioral scientists, we are interested in exploring the nature of the problem and finding an effective treatment. At the same time, as clinicians, we have an immediate need to solve the problem for *this child*. Time-series designs are particularly well suited for situations in which there is a scientific purpose and an immediate clinical need at the same time. With disorders that strike less than 1 child in 1000, it may not be feasible to find a group of children with the same problem in order to investigate the nature of the difficulty using a group experiment. In addition, by the time that all this has been accomplished, we may have neglected a clinical responsibility for the individual child. Time-series designs provide a means by which we can treat individuals and at the same time systematically collect scientifically sound information regarding the effectiveness of a treatment. It is well beyond the scope of this chapter

to examine all the details involved in time-series research. We provide an overview of fundamental design concepts and examine a few basic design formats. Interested readers may wish to consult volumes that are devoted exclusively to time-series experimentation (for instance, Barlow & Hersen, 1984; Kazdin, 1982; Kratochwill, 1978; Tawney & Gast, 1984).

A few preliminary points need discussion before we examine design formats. As noted earlier, in time-series experiments there are usually a number of performance measures in each phase. These are typically obtained by repeated observations of the child's behavior over a period of time. The observations may be conducted over a series of sessions, days, weeks, or some other time dimension that is appropriate, given the nature of the experiment. Obviously, a researcher will not merely observe the child in a casual or unsystematic fashion. It is crucial that the investigator have a clear and detailed description of how the behavior will be observed or measured. This is known as determining the *target behavior*—the target for change that will be used as a dependent variable. Again, let us assume that we have a particular child with a particular problem—say, failure to attend to schoolwork or teacher instructions. Most likely, that problem involves a behavior or several behaviors that are causing serious difficulties. The behaviors that are selected to be modified or eliminated become the target behaviors. Our dependent variable may be the number of times those behaviors occur in a 10-minute interval.

We have mentioned that there are different phases in time-series experiments. How does a researcher determine when to change phases, such as from baseline to treatment? This is one of the most important points to consider in designing, executing, and evaluating time-series experiments. Phase changes should occur only when a researcher has obtained enough measures or observations to permit an adequate sample of behavior and when the behavior's rate is stable. The purpose of changing phases is to demonstrate behavior change in the child. Both as researchers and as clinicians, we want to be able to attribute any observed behavior change to the new condition or treatment. This cannot be done with any confidence unless the data are stable prior to phase change. Basically, this means that we cannot determine exactly how many sessions or data points will be involved in any single phase prior to beginning an experiment. The determination of when phases can be changed must be made when the data collected provide a stable estimate of behavior rate (Gelfand & Hartmann, 1984). Related to this point, it is also crucial to have reliable observations and to know the *level* of reliability present in a set of data. Without such information, one may be making judgments based on inconsistent scores or performance observations, and such judgments may lead to incorrect treatment decisions (Hartmann, 1982). Most time-series investigations that are well designed and executed will (or should) provide detailed reliability information.

The A-B Design   The *A-B design* is no longer used to any great extent because of serious weaknesses that we examine later. It is discussed here only because of its conceptual simplicity, in order to promote a basic understanding of more elaborate time-series designs.

There are two phases in the A-B design configuration: baseline and intervention. Figure 11-3 illustrates a data display from an A-B experiment. As suggested by Figure 11-3, baseline data are collected for a period of time (sessions 1 through 9) until a stable estimate of behavior is obtained. Data in this phase represent the performance level or behavior frequency exhibited by the subject in an untreated condition. After a stable rate of baseline behavior has been established, the intervention phase is begun. This is represented by sessions 10 through 17 in Figure 11-3.

A cursory inspection of the data in Figure 11-3 might suggest that the treatment being examined is effective. The baseline data are extremely stable, and as the intervention is initiated, the rate begins to decrease dramatically. It continues to decrease and stabilizes with a few minor variations. However, this data display illustrates nicely the serious problems with an A-B design. Assessment of the strength of a treatment depends on

FIGURE 11-3. Hypothetical data display from an A-B experiment in which a student's rate of disruptions is examined with and without reinforcing on-task behavior.

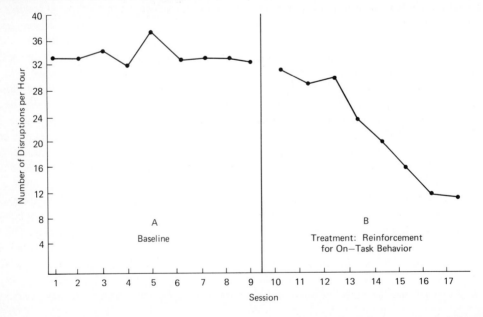

attributing a behavior change to the intervention. The major difficulty with an A-B design is the absence of supporting evidence for such an assumption. Although the behavior depicted in Figure 11-3 does change coincidentally with intervention, other influences may be occurring simultaneously that may have the same effect (if this is true, the concept of control is not operative). For example, suppose that on day 10 or 11 of the experiment in Figure 11-3 the child's parents begin to administer a medication aimed at reducing the child's hyperactive behavior. If the experimenters are unaware of this, they may believe that the reduction in disruptive behavior is explained solely by their treatment (reinforcement of "on-task" behavior). The design itself does not provide assurance that the independent variable is the influential factor.

The Reversal Design In order to circumvent the difficulties just described, behavioral researchers have extended the A-B format to include a *reversal* phase. Figure 11-4 illustrates a data display from a reversal experiment. This figure shows that a reversal design is an extension of the simple A-B design discussed above. Procedures during phases A_1 and B_1 are essentially the same as before. However, after the behavior stabilizes in B_1, a further phase change is initiated. The A_2 or reversal phase involves removal of treatment and

returning to baseline conditions, with the hope that the child's baseline performance rate will be recaptured. Following this same line of reasoning, the A_2 phase is continued until the data stabilize once again, after which treatment is reinstituted in the B_2 phase. There are a number of reversal variations, although the basic format usually involves three or four phases (that is, A-B-A or A-B-A-B).

A reversal design provides much greater evidence regarding the influence of intervention than an A-B design. Ideally, the data will follow the basic pattern of change illustrated in Figure 11-4 (although this is not always the case). If this occurs, a researcher can be relatively confident that the independent variable is *the* factor influencing behavior. It is unlikely that other events would occur simultaneously with *each* phase change.

Despite its strengths, the reversal design does have certain limitations. Confidence regarding the effect of an independent variable rests primarily on the reversal of the target behavior in phase A_2. If reversal does not occur, the researcher has little evidence regarding the influence of intervention. Suppose that an experiment is conducted using a reversal design and that the data obtained appear as shown in Figure 11-5. We have little reason to believe from these data that the independent variable (treatment) is controlling the target behavior. There may be several explanations of why the

FIGURE 11-4. Hypothetical data display of a reversal design.

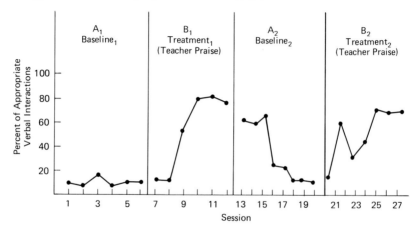

FIGURE 11-5. Example of an A-B-A experiment that does not reverse the child's behavior rate.

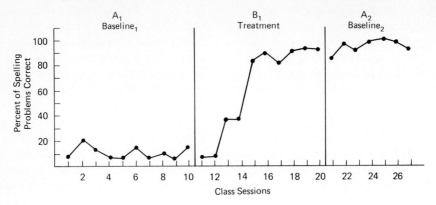

data do not reverse. First, the target behavior may not be under the control of the independent variable, and the change in rate from A_1 to B_1 may be the result of some outside influence—for example, some other program introduced by a teacher or parent. In fact, with data such as those shown in Figure 11-5, we are in a position just as weak as that of a simple A-B design. Another explanation may be that the treatment is so powerful that the influence is not reversible even when baseline conditions are re-established in A_2; for instance, the disruptive, resistant child may learn some method of self-control and may use it consistently thereafter. A third explanation may relate to the target behavior itself. Some behaviors are not reversible, particularly those that involve skill acquisition. It is extremely difficult to reverse certain skills, such as the ability to read or the familiar example of riding a bicycle or swimming. It is apparent that in Figure 11-5 the unfortunate experimenter has selected an inappropriate design to study the target behavior.

One further comment should be made regarding the use of reversal designs. The experimenter in Figure 11-5 has demonstrably used an inappropriate design, because the target behavior does not reverse. There are other occasions when a reversal design should not be employed. In some circumstances, it may be undesirable or even dangerous and unethical to reverse treatment conditions. For example, we may be working with a

child who is exhibiting self-injurious behavior. If we implement a treatment to eliminate those behaviors, it would be very undesirable to reverse the conditions so as to produce a renewed high rate of self-injury, even though only temporarily.

The Multiple-Baseline Design Multiple-baseline designs are very useful for time-series experiments in which reversal configurations are not appropriate or behaviors are unlikely to reverse. In these designs, data are recorded on two or more behaviors simultaneously or on a single behavior in two or more settings simultaneously. Treatment is introduced in a staggered or sequential fashion, as in the example in Figure 11-6, in the different settings separately. In this example, the same behavior (a retarded girl's tantrums) is treated in three different locations. First, the child receives a program to reduce temper tantrums in the classroom. Then treatment is implemented in the home setting. Reference to Figure 11-6 suggests that the multiple-baseline design resembles conducting several A-B experiments, but at different points in time. The change from baseline to treatment for each of the target settings shown in the figure is timed sequentially, so that the behavior in setting 2 (the playground) remains in baseline while treatment is applied to temper tantrums in setting 1 (the classroom), and so on. In *all* cases, the phase changes must occur only after stable data are evident in the target settings or behaviors

FIGURE 11-6. Data display from a hypothetical multiple-baseline experiment.

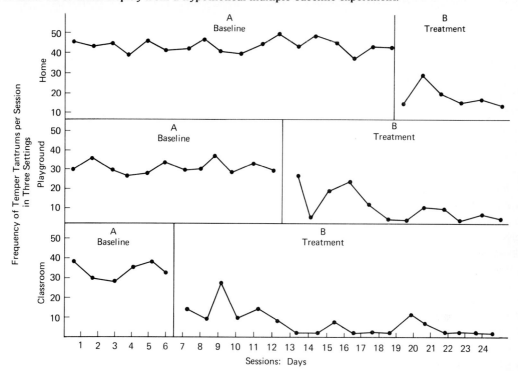

under study. The strength of multiple-baseline designs is based on the staggering of phase changes. If the independent variable (treatment) is influencing the target behaviors, there should be a pattern of sequential change that reflects the consecutive application of intervention (as in Figure 11-6). For example, if separate behaviors are studied, then the data on behavior 2 should remain stable throughout the time that baseline conditions exist for *that* behavior (or even though treatment is applied to behavior 1 during that period). If the treatment is effective, the child's behavior should improve when (and only when) that particular behavior is treated and should not reverse.

As with most basic design formats, there are a number of variations in multiple-baseline experiments. They can be used with separate behaviors and environments, as previously described. In addition, this design is also suitable in situations where the same behavior and the same treatment are studied with two or more subjects (a multiple-

baseline-across-subjects design). In this instance, treatment is applied to different children in a staggered fashion, much as we have described for settings and behaviors. The multiple-baseline design is very flexible, as is suggested by these examples. It is a very powerful design that in recent years has been of increased interest to behavioral researchers. Moreover, multiple-baseline procedures do not involve the reinstatement of troublesome behaviors—a particularly important consideration in the treatment of disturbed children.

Designing Group Experiments

Traditional group experiments have been used in psychological research for many years. As noted earlier, group experiments differ in several ways from the time-series designs just discussed. Obviously, more subjects are used; also, far fewer assessments are usually obtained. Frequently the experimental groups are formed, treatment is applied, and a single performance or behavioral

measure is then administered (we are not advocating this routinely, however). As indicated in the
diagrams presented earlier, time-series experiments usually involve many data points collected
or observations made over a number of sessions.
Various types of designs are used in group experiments; only a few of the basic formats are examined here.

　　We consider a number of factors as we explore group experimental designs. One of those
factors is whether we are discussing a comparison
of several groups or a pretest-posttest comparison
performed on the same group (*repeated measures*). In this context, a *separate-group design* refers to investigations in which a different group receives each of several experimental conditions
(i.e., group A receives one treatment and is compared with group B, which receives a second
treatment). Because the different groups are constituted of different subjects, the performance
scores in one group are not influenced by performance scores in the other and so are independent
of each other. This is distinguished from a *pretest-
posttest study,* in which the same subjects are
being assessed twice. Because the same individuals are being tested in both the pretest and the
posttest, scores in the posttest are clearly *not* independent from those on the pretest.

　　One point about terminology should be made
here. The terms *experimental variable* and *independent variable* are often used interchangeably
and refer to the same concept—the factor that
differentiates the groups or that is manipulated.
For the remainder of this chapter, we use the
term *experimental variable,* to avoid confusion
with the notion of independence as mentioned
above. An experimental variable may be independent (as in the two-group example above) or may
involve repeated measures (which makes the comparison nonindependent, as with the pretest-posttest example).

　　Another important factor in group experimental designs involves the number of experimental variables being studied. Group experimental
designs may be aimed at studying one, two, or
more experimental variables, depending on the
nature of the investigation. We discuss group ex-

**FIGURE 11-7. Diagram of a hypothetical group
experiment design with one variable (an independent comparison).**

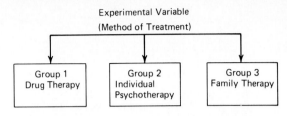

periments in terms of both the independence factor and the number of experimental variables
under investigation.

Designs with One Experimental Variable

Perhaps the simplest group design involves those
studies with one experimental variable, often
called *single-factor designs.* Figure 11-7 presents
a diagram of a single-factor study in which three
separate groups are compared. Since this experiment includes three different groups, each of
which receives a different treatment, it is a separate-group design or independent comparison. As
indicated in Figure 11-7, the experimental variable is the method of treatment, and there are
three types of treatments being compared (drug
therapy, individual psychotherapy, and family
therapy). It is important to remember that an experiment such as this requires that the groups be
equivalent on all important variables other than
the one being tested—in this case, the method of
treatment. This requirement is the important concept of control, which allows us to attribute any
significant behavioral differences observed to the
effect of the experimental variable. In this example, we randomly assign individuals to groups
prior to initiation of the treatment, administer the
treatment, and then test the subjects in each
group. If we obtain performance scores that are
substantially different between groups, then we
will probably conclude that the performance differences are due to the different treatment
methods.

　　Single-factor experiments may also include
repeated measures of a group's performance. Fig-

FIGURE 11-8. Diagram of a hypothetical experimental design with one experimental variable (learning stage) and three repeated measures.

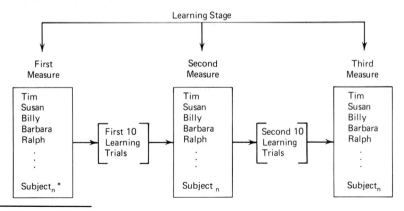

*Subject$_n$ is a notation that refers to the last subject in a group.

ure 11-8 illustrates a study with one experimental variable in which a single group's performance is measured repeatedly. The experimental variable in this example is learning stage (early, midway, late); the same subjects' performance is assessed three times (at the beginning of the study, after the first 10 learning trials, and again after the second 10 trials), which generates three data points that will be compared. The scores from each of the three measurements are conceptually the same as our conditions in the earlier example of an independent comparison. As before, the concept of control requires that, to the degree possible, the only difference among the first, second, and third measures is the experimental variable—learning stage. Such experiments have often been used to determine whether children make different types of errors at different stages of learning new material.

Group Designs: Multiple Experimental Variables Group experiments may also include two or more experimental variables (these are also termed multifactor designs). Although there are many variations of multifactor designs, we examine only a few basic ones here. Figure 11-9 illustrates a study that investigated the effects of two experimental treatments (variables) on the perfor-

mance of mentally retarded adolescents: (1) reward anticipation (subjects anticipated a reward for good performance in one condition, whereas those in the second condition were not anticipating

FIGURE 11-9. Diagram of an experimental design with two experimental variables (both independent comparisons).

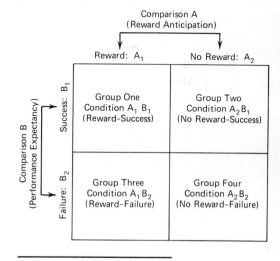

Source: R. F. Welch and C. J. Drew (1972). Effects of reward anticipation and performance expectancy on the learning rate of EMR adolescents. *American Journal of Mental Deficiency, 77,* 291-295. Reprinted by permission.

a reward), and (2) performance expectancy (in one condition subjects were given information that led them to believe they would surely succeed, whereas subjects in the second condition were given information that would suggest that success was unlikely). Thus there were two conditions under each of these experimental variables. As shown in the figure, there were four separate groups, one for each condition: this indicates that both experimental variables (reward anticipation and performance expectancy) represented independent comparisons.

Occasionally, it is desirable to have repeated measures on one experimental variable while the second is independent. Figure 11-10 illustrates a study using this type of design. This experiment was conducted with children diagnosed as having learning disabilities (see Chapter 8). The two experimental variables were degree of organization of the material (organized versus unorganized) and level of difficulty of the material (low versus intermediate versus high difficulty). In this study the experimental variable of material organization was an independent comparison, because separate groups were used for each condition. The second experimental variable was one in which repeated measures were taken, because all subjects received the low-, intermediate-, and high-diffi-

culty materials. Designs that employ both independent and repeated measures on experimental variables are known as *mixed designs*.

As noted earlier, there are a great many variations in group experimental design. It is possible to study more than two experimental variables simultaneously, with many combinations of independent and repeated comparisons. We have also mentioned the use of quasi-experimental designs with pre-existing differences (such as the child's age or gender) as a focus of the study. A complete examination of all such topics is beyond the scope of this chapter, and readers are referred to volumes devoted exclusively to experimental design (for instance, Cook & Campbell, 1979).

COMMON DESIGN MISTAKES

Classic textbook examples are seldom found outside the environment in which they were contrived—in classroom lectures and textbooks. This is the case in research design just as it is in other areas of study. The designs we have presented must often be altered to answer a particular research question or to suit a set of circumstances. In many cases, factors are encountered during research execution that may threaten the soundness of an investigation and require design or proce-

FIGURE 11-10. Diagram of an experimental design with two experimental variables (one independent and one repeated).

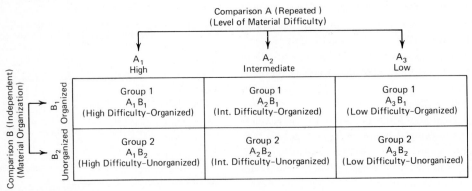

Source: T. B. Parker, C. W. Freston, and C. J. Drew (1975). Comparison of verbal performance of normal and learning disabled children as a function of input organization. *Journal of Learning Disabilities, 8,* 386–393. Reprinted by permission.

dural changes. This section examines some common design mistakes.

Internal and External Validity

Validity is a term used in many different contexts, and it is misused perhaps as often as it is properly employed. We are limiting the use of this term to two aspects of research design. *Internal* and *external validity* represent two crucial concepts in research design and are major criteria by which investigations are evaluated. These concepts were initially presented by Campbell (1957) and later popularized by Campbell and Stanley (1963). *Internal validity* refers to the technical soundness of an investigation in terms of control: that is, how well designed is this study? Experiments that are internally valid are those that have controlled all systematic influences except the one under investigation (the experimental variable). *External validity*, on the other hand, speaks to the issues of generalizability — "[t]o what populations, settings, treatment variables and measurement variables" results can be generalized (Campbell & Stanley, 1963, p. 175).

Both internal and external validity are important, although they may be incompatible in certain circumstances. In some situations, the achievement of adequate internal validity requires conducting an investigation in a controlled or contrived laboratory setting. For example, one might best assess the social perception of juvenile delinquents in a laboratory, but at the risk of their giving uncharacteristic performances. To the extent that such efforts create an artificial environment and influence subjects' performance, the generalizability of results may be reduced. That is, subjects may respond differently in a laboratory than they do in their homes or schools. The reverse may also be true, and studies may be representative but poorly controlled. Research is a process of constant compromise in order to achieve an appropriate balance between internal and external validity. The notion of an "appropriate balance" may well vary greatly from study to study. Particularly in the early stages of a research program, internal validity may be the primary concern, whereas later, as the fundamental knowledge base grows, more attention may be given to external validity and the issue of to whom the results will apply. In all cases, however, care must be taken not to sacrifice internal validity to such an extent that the value of any knowledge gained is diminished. Campbell and Stanley (1963) emphasized the importance of internal validity by noting that *"internal validity"* is the basic minimum without which an experiment is uninterpretable" (p. 175, emphasis in the original).

A number of factors can threaten the internal validity of an investigation, and total elimination of all possible threats is often impossible. Nearly every study can be strengthened in some fashion. From a practical standpoint, a researcher's task is to eliminate or minimize the influence of as many problems as possible. Those internal validity problems that cannot be eliminated in a particular study must be accounted for as the results are interpreted.

Internal validity pertains very specifically to the important concept of control, described previously. Without control of confounding extraneous influences, a researcher will not be able to attribute results to the experimental variable. For example, suppose we are investigating the effects of a new treatment for obesity. Certainly, if differences are evident, we want to be able to say that our treatment has probably generated the participants' weight loss. This will not be possible if, say, some other treatment for obesity is also carried out at the same time (which is common for the overweight), and thus becomes a rival explanation for the results. For example, in addition to a reducing diet, a subject may try fasting. Similarly, we will not be able to determine the effects of our treatment if the scales are adjusted (changed or recalibrated) between two measurements of the subjects' weight. In either case, differences may be caused by our treatment or by the other factors, which will not permit us to say with confidence what has caused the change. We have mentioned only a few threats to internal validity. Interested readers should consult texts that examine these topics more completely (for example, Campbell & Stanley, 1963; Drew & Hardman, 1985).

Related to internal validity concerns are the influences of *placebo effects*. Placebo effects are changes in subjects' behavior or performance that may occur simply because they are in an experiment and not because of any particular impact of a treatment or intervention. Kazdin (1980) examined placebo effects and noted that "the fact of participation alone may lead the client to expect and evince improvement and account for change independently of the specific techniques that are implemented" (p. 322). Because of such influences, it may be difficult to attribute changes in subjects to treatment. Such a situation was evident in a study by Wermuth, Davis, Hollister, and Stunkard (1977), which investigated a treatment for bulimia (see Chapter 7). These investigators found a substantial effect when they administered inactive pills to subjects; therefore they were not able to determine that improvement was due to actual medication. Placebo effects present a substantial challenge to researchers studying child behavior disorders, because they are likely to be present in some form and to some degree in nearly all therapeutic interventions. In addition, they may be quite potent, in some cases showing influences that overpower and oppose a medication's actual pharmacological properties (for instance, see Wolf, 1959).

As stated earlier, *external validity* refers to the generalizability of results, which can also be threatened by a number of factors. The basic notion of external validity is that the experimental results must be applicable to subjects, materials, and settings other than those used in the particular experiment. We may not be able to accomplish this if there are substantial differences between the subjects, materials, or setting of the experiment and those in the world outside the experiment. For example, if the sample of subjects is different from the population at large (or the population to which a researcher wishes to generalize), then the results will probably *not* be generalizable. This is a problem when only a few people from a target group, such as mothers of autistic children, volunteer to participate in a study. The volunteers may be more highly educated and their children less seriously disturbed than the remainder of the group of interest. Similarly, the environment in which a study is conducted, such as a brightly lit, sparsely furnished, sterile laboratory, may be unusual or different from the subjects' routine environment. If this is the case, subjects may behave differently than usual, and the results will probably not generalize to their homes, schools, and neighborhoods. As before, several major types of factors have been identified as threatening external validity, and interested readers may wish to consult more detailed discussions of these topics (for instance, Campbell & Stanley, 1963; Drew & Hardman, 1985).

The examination of threats to internal and external validity highlights the importance of thorough planning prior to the execution of a study. Often more time is spent in planning than in actually conducting an investigation. Without such initial efforts, an investigation may provide inaccurate information that is of little or no value in the treatment of behavior disorders in children. As a consumer of research, one must keep possible threats to internal and external validity in mind when examining the results of a study. Often the use of common sense alone can help readers to spot errors that invalidate research studies.

Avoiding Pitfalls

Researchers have several methods of avoiding the threats to validity described above. Employing the appropriate experimental design can be useful, because some designs are particularly vulnerable to certain problems. Procedures employed during the actual execution of a study can also be very important in minimizing weaknesses in internal and external validity. Techniques for subject selection and assignment to groups or treatments are vital and powerful procedural tools to strengthen the internal and external validity of investigations.

Behavioral researchers seldom study an entire population. In most cases, it is necessary to select a sample of individuals from a given population to serve as subjects. This immediately increases the importance of carefully defining and describing the subject population. Unless this is accomplished, an investigator does not know which individuals are potential subjects and to what population the results should generalize. Population definition is of crucial importance as a foundation of external validity and for selecting an appropriate sample. Many sampling procedures are available, and choice of an appropriate procedure depends on the specific nature of an investigation. Space restrictions preclude a detailed examination of all sampling techniques that may be employed. Once again, interested readers may wish to consult one of the volumes that are solely devoted to sampling (for example, Cochran, 1977; Sudman, 1976).

One of the most generally used methods of selecting subjects is known as *simple random sampling*. This procedure, like sampling in general, is aimed at obtaining a sample of subjects that will be representative of the population under study. To accomplish this goal, researchers use a selection process in which each individual in the population has an equal chance of being chosen to participate in the investigation. Since each person has an equal chance of selection, it is assumed that the subject sample characteristics will represent those that exist in the population. Certainly this is an assumption and random sampling does not totally *ensure* a representative sample. However, random sampling procedures do decrease the probability that some systematic bias is operating in the selection process. Even if the resulting sample is found to be unrepresentative in some important way, statistical corrections can be used to control for the differences. The most simple and effective technique for selecting a random sample involves using a *random number table* (available in most statistics texts).

We have repeatedly stressed the importance of group equivalence on the characteristics other than the experimental variables (the fundamental concept of control, which is essential to internal validity). The basic tool that a researcher can use to accomplish group equivalence is subject assignment. Two general techniques have been used in behavioral research for assigning subjects to groups: *random assignment* and *experimental matching*. Experimental matching basically involves procedures wherein a researcher forces

group equivalence on some characteristic(s) thought to be important for the particular study being conducted. For example, if chronological age is thought to be important, groups may be formed by matching children on chronological age. This is often accomplished by replacing subjects or switching group assignments for given subjects until the average chronological age is the same for the treatment and control groups.

Random assignment procedures (usually accomplished by using random number tables) have become favored over experimental matching. In fact, some researchers believe that matching should be employed only as a last resort, if ever. There are many reasons for favoring random assignment over experimental matching. Perhaps the most compelling relates to the characteristics on which equivalence is desired. Experimental matching requires a clear knowledge of those factors on which control is to be exercised. In one sense, it is nearly a declaration that "these are the important factors and others are not." By selectively placing subjects (switching or replacing), there is a substantial possibility that the groups will be made different on some factors in addition to those being matched. The major strength of random assignment procedures is that, because of the nature of the process, there is little reason to expect any *systematic* differences between the groups. Thus the researcher is probably forming equivalent groups on those factors that are known to be important and those that are as yet unidentified as being important for control (a nice touch, and good insurance for the durability of internal validity).

ETHICAL ISSUES IN CONDUCTING RESEARCH

Ethical issues are vitally important in psychology, because the field centrally involves people working with other people. When children's behavior is given a diagnostic label and is treated, ethical problems may arise. Psychologists come in many specfic forms; however, from a broad view, people in this and related fields are caretakers and treatment specialists, and generally constitute the

Are these children old enough to decide whether or not to participate in a research study?

professionally authorized arm of society that addresses human concerns. As such, they must be especially concerned about fairness and avoiding harm to clients. Psychologists as human beings have desires and personal agendas, but if those involve taking unfair advantage of their responsible positions, they are not acting ethically. They may be punished by their professional societies, and/or state licensing offices, and they may be liable to lawsuits.

Ethical concerns hold a place of particular importance in psychological and other behavioral research because of the nature of the research undertaking. We do look and explore into—some might say "invade"—the lives of others. We do this in order to find causes of problems and more effective treatments; however, because psychological research involves people, great care must be taken to ensure fairness to those being studied. A researcher's task is not limited to the design and execution of a technically sound investigation. Constant vigilance must be maintained regarding ethical issues as they pertain to research procedures and related professional activities, especially in the area of child behavior disorders. Institutional review boards or human subjects committees oversee research ethics, as do federal offices, school district research participation com-

mittees, and others. The typical child research project is scrutinized by at least three such bodies in order to protect the welfare of participating children and their families.

Concern for research ethics is not new, although it has emerged more prominently in recent years. Most professional organizations now have ethical codes of conduct for their members. Some (such as the American Psychological Association) have made a practice of investigating allegations and expelling individuals from membership for breaches of ethical conduct. In addition, federal agencies funding research activities typically have regulations regarding appropriate and ethical treatment of subjects. Complete volumes have appeared regarding research ethics (for instance, Diener & Crandall, 1978); as we shall see, the issues are complex ones, far exceeding the scope of this chapter. Interested readers may wish to consult any of a number of references for a more complete examination of ethical issues in research (for example, Diener & Crandall, 1978; Keith-Spiegel, 1976).

Probably the most conspicuous concern in research ethics is the protection of the physical and psychological welfare of subjects. This concern has emerged because of two major influences: periodic cases of flagrant abuse of research participants' rights, and a generally heightened societal sensitivity regarding individual rights. Ethical issues related to subjects are of particular concern in psychological research, especially in terms of subjects' consent to participate in a research project.

Consent in research may be viewed simply as a means by which subjects openly declare whether or not they wish to participate in an investigation. Upon further inspection, this apparently simple process involves a number of complexities. To be valid, consent must include three elements: *capacity, information,* and *voluntariness.* All three elements must be present for consent to be meaningful; the researcher must also be aware that consent is not permanent. It may be withdrawn at any time, which means that participants must be allowed to discontinue their participation whenever they wish to do so and without penalty of any type, whether psychological or material.

Capacity refers to a person's ability and legal authority to consent to participate in a research project. Although a 12-year-old boy who is a juvenile delinquent may have the ability to decide whether to agree to participate in an investigation, he does not have the legal authority to do so, because he is considered a minor. His parent or legal guardian must grant consent for him to participate, but he must also agree that he wants to do so. This issue is even more sensitive and difficult when psychotic, retarded, or very young children are studied. Because they lack the ability to determine whether they should participate, their caretakers and the investigators must take special pains to protect them from exploitation. At the same time caretakers must bear in mind that progress in treatment can come about only through research, and so participation is desirable in the public interest.

The second element of consent is *information.* Speaking in the context of mental retardation research, Turnbull (1977) has explained:

> [T]he focus is on *what information is given and how it is given* since it must be effectively communicated (given and received) to be acted upon. The concern is with the *fullness* and *effectiveness* of the disclosure: is it *designed to be fully understood, and is it fully understood?* The burden of satisfying these two tests rests on the professional. (p. 8, emphasis in the original)

This places a great burden on behavioral researchers and causes particular problems with certain types of studies in which examination of the consent information may alert subjects to what the hypothesis is, which may make them act unnaturally.

Voluntariness, the third element of consent, is once again more complex than it may appear on the surface. Clearly, a generalized notion of voluntariness would suggest that subjects in a study must agree to participate of their own free will. This also places a great deal of responsibility on researchers in the study of child behavior disorders. Certainly there should not be any constraint or coercion, either explicit or implicit. In some in-

stances, even a reward for participation may be coercive; for example, this might be the case with monetary rewards for destitute families or altering time of probation for prisoners serving as subjects.

Researchers working in the area of child behavior disorders must be particularly cautious regarding ethical practices. In many cases, meeting the requirements of the three elements of consent presents considerable difficulty (Siegel & Ellis, 1985). First, consent must be obtained from a child's parents, a guardian, or some other agent who is legally responsible and authorized to act on the child's behalf. Even then, a researcher must be confident that the consentor's interests coincide with what may be the best interests of the child, which is not always the case (Drew, Logan, & Hardman, 1984). In nearly all cases it is also necessary to obtain consent from the child as well, despite the fact that there is no legal requirement to do so. Ethical appropriateness often goes far beyond what is legally necessary, as illustrated by the material presented in Table 11-3.

Thus far we have discussed ethical considerations related to subjects' consent for participation. This is an important topic, but one must keep in mind *why* consent is addressed so centrally when examining research ethics. One of the major concerns in behavioral research ethics is the possibility of harming participants. Individuals must not be harmed by serving as subjects in any study. Obviously we do not want to physically harm subjects, but the notion of harm also extends to such matters as psychological stress, social embarrassment, and many other areas. This is a difficult and complex consideration involving several questions. Ordinary living is not stress-free. As researchers, we must judge how much additional stress would prove harmful; whether we cannot create *any* stress; and many other issues. If pushed to their conceptual limits and interpreted in an extremely literal manner, these considerations would significantly detract from our ability to conduct psychological research (or perhaps would eliminate it). Of course there is *some* stress for subjects participating in most investigations, and we cannot take a position that there must be absolutely *no* psychological infringement. It is necessary for us to bal-

Table 11-3
Ethical Considerations Presenting Particular Problems in Research with Behavior-
Disordered Children

Consent Element	Guideline	Problem	Potential Solution
Capacity	Subjects must be mentally and psychologically able to give consent and also of legal age to give consent.	Behaviorally disordered children are typically not of the legal age to give consent. In many cases, they are also unable to give consent by virtue of mental or psychological limitations.	Consent must be obtained from the legal guardian of the child who has the authority to make legal decisions for the child. The child should also give consent, despite the fact that it is not legally required in most cases.
Information	Subjects and legal guardians must be fully informed regarding purposes and procedures of the study. The information communicated must be understood.	Behaviorally disordered subjects may have particular difficulty understanding the information, regardless of how well it is communicated.	Researchers must be certain that legal guardians understand the information and make every attempt possible to make the children understand.
Voluntariness	Subjects and guardians must give consent of their own free will without explicit or implicit coercion of any type. They must be aware that they can withdraw consent at any time.	Subjects and guardians may feel some degree of coercion simply because the researcher may represent a power figure for them. Similarly, the children may feel coerced if guardians consent.	Researchers must be very sensitive to any evidence of reluctance to consent or desire to discontinue participation. This is true for both subjects and guardians.

Note: In addition, subjects and guardians have the right to expect guaranteed confidentiality of information obtained by a researcher, as well as the right to nonharmful treatment, to knowledge of results, and to full compensation for the time the subjects spend participating.

ance carefully the concept of harm and the potential risk for harm as we undertake each study. For this reason, we have independent review boards (human subjects committees, institutional review boards) operating in most agencies that examine research proposals and attempt to protect subjects' rights. The questions involved are complex, and there are no simple answers. We must turn to professional guidelines, such as those of the American Psychological Association (1981), and to our colleagues in a cooperative fashion for help.

Another ethical issue in psychological research (related to harm in some senses) involves the degree to which we invade our subjects' privacy. Privacy has been long treasured in Western society. When we collect and analyze information (data) on subjects, we are invading their privacy to some degree. Although total privacy does not exist, each of us has some concept of the degree to which we want to share certain matters with others outside our close circle of family and friends, and of the form in which that sharing is acceptable. As we have seen with harm, issues of privacy must be carefully balanced with a need to conduct research that will help us solve people's problems. Once again, there are no simple answers, and the best that we can do is to be sensitive and remain alert to procedures that may unduly or unnecessarily invade privacy.

Deception is also a topic that often surfaces in examining research ethics. *Deception,* in this content, is a misrepresentation of information regarding the purpose, nature, or consequences of an investigation. Such a misrepresentation may occur because information is omitted or because false information is given. Either, if serious and potentially harmful to subjects, is unethical. It would seem that the answer to such a problem is quite simple — "Don't do it." However, as with so many other topics, matters are not quite that simple. Deception in one form or another is fairly widespread in psychological research. Menges (1973) indicated that only 3 percent of the psychological investigations he examined provided *complete* information to the participating subjects. Furthermore, Diener and Crandall (1978) suggested that "direct lying to subjects" occurred in perhaps 19 to 44 percent of recent psychological research (p. 74), although subjects are routinely debriefed and their questions are answered following their participation.

The issue of deception in research remains very controversial, as it should (for instance, see Baumrind, 1985; Fisher, 1986; Trice, 1986). There are a number of reasons why this is so and why we find such startling figures as those noted above. In many cases, certain psychological research cannot be conducted or would be extremely difficult with *totally* nondeceptive procedures. There are circumstances when we can expect that full information may change our subjects' behavior or performance. For example, if we are studying the amount of influence friends have on opinions concerning drug use, complete information about the purpose of the investigation may alter subjects' susceptibility to such influence. In addition, there are situations where the focus of a particular study actually *requires* deception, or deception is a part of the investigation.

Because these types of studies involve some degree of deception, are they therefore unethical? We cannot answer this question so simply. Deception must be considered in relation to the risk of harm and other issues, as we have seen before.

Ethical matters are of particular concern to researchers working in child behavior disorders. Such subjects are often more "at risk" or more vulnerable to exploitation by thoughtless or uninformed investigators. Beyond this fact, the nature of many of the problems that require study with such a population further complicates our ethical considerations. Research on child behavior disorders thus presents a considerable challenge — one of improving our knowledge base for more effective treatment, while simultaneously providing the necessary protection for a vulnerable group. Is it ethical to single out children with learning disabilities or seizure disorders for study and observation, even treatment in a classroom, and thus to draw more attention to their disorders? When is it justified to try a new, unresearched treatment on a child? How accurate must an assessment technique or diagnostic test prove to be before it should be used routinely? Is it ever better to base our choices of treatments to administer on clinical experience than on controlled research tests? Both design considerations and ethical questions affect our answers to such questions.

SUMMARY

Research is a major source of objective information regarding causes and treatment of child behavior disorders. Because information produced by research is systematically and objectively collected, it tends to be more accurate and reliable than that obtained by casual observation and common-sense reasoning. Research procedures are much more systematic and the requirements of evidence are much more stringent than those used in more informal information seeking. Therefore, some knowledge of research principles is important for those who are consumers of research and are attempting to make decisions about treatment of children with behavior disorders.

Psychological research has often been classified into two general types: experimental and nonexperimental. Nonexperimental research tends to be descriptive, whereas experimental research often examines causal relationships through manipulations of participants' behavior. Each approach is appropriate for different research questions and settings. Likewise, each approach has certain advantages and limitations that must be considered. Even within each general approach, there are a variety of specific designs or methods that may be used, depending on the circumstances of the particular study being planned.

Prior to its initiation, the planning of an investigation is crucial to the soundness of a study and the reliability of results obtained. In the selection of an appropriate experimental design, many procedural matters must receive attention. The design and procedures must minimize threats to the study's validity. When a study has high internal validity, the results can be attributed to the experimental variable rather than to some other source. With high external validity, research findings can be generalized to the larger population from which the research participants were drawn.

These types of validity are essential if research is to be dependable and meaningful.

In addition to being concerned about validity, a researcher must take precautions to avoid ethical violations in the process of conducting a study. Behavioral scientists face some particularly difficult ethical issues when studying child behavior disorders, because children (and their caretakers) may lack the capacity to make informed judgments about the advisability of participating in research projects. In all cases, children as well as adults must be allowed to terminate their research participation at any time they choose.

Students who have found the concepts presented in this chapter fascinating may well become the social scientists of tomorrow. Those who have found it completely uninteresting and unintelligible may find graduate work in research and statistics to be a real trial. There are more important and valid tests of one's career interests, of course, but most graduate research programs in clinical and counseling psychology, nursing, and medicine involve training in research theory and practice.

chapter

12

Classification of Childhood Behavior Disorders

KEY TERMS

Classification.   The ordering of objects or behaviors into groups by using a common set of characteristics.

Diagnosis.   The actual assigning of objects or behaviors to groupings within a classification system.

Reliability.   A determination of how consistently a classification system measures phenomena. For example, a classification system with good reliability consistently places the same types of behaviors into the same grouping.

Validity.   A classification system's ability to measure what it proposes to measure. For example, if the developers of a classification system propose that a system is capable of grouping and classifying childhood behavior disorders, then the system has good validity if it is able to group most childhood behavior disorders encountered by clinicians and researchers.

OVERVIEW OF CLASSIFICATION

Classification is the key to understanding large groups of events. Every day we classify people, objects, events, and situations so that we can understand and relate to them better. Without classification, we would be left in a sea of unrecognizable, unique events. We have all been in situations in which little or nothing is familiar—for example, the first day at a large university where no one is known. However, over time we learn to recognize people and to classify them as friends, colleagues, rivals, students who have shared classes, and interesting people we want to know. In effect, we have classified the environment, understand it, and feel comfortable with it.

All learning requires some type of classification in which we begin to place new objects into familiar groups (Brunner, 1963; Brunner, Goodnow, & Austin, 1956). Classification has proved particularly useful in the diagnosis and treatment of physical disease. After recognizing a disease, physicians can often predict its course, identify its probable origin, and recommend an appropriate course of treatment; in several cases, disease prevention is even possible. For example, German measles (rubella) can be identified readily in adults from laboratory tests and from the appearance of symptoms such as a skin rash. If German measles strikes a woman during the first 3 months of pregnancy, her unborn child can be born deaf or blind, and may be mentally retarded. However, because physicians can accurately classify German measles, it can be treated with improved outcomes for the child. Preferably, women can be vaccinated to prevent the occurrence of the disease. In this instance, proper classification of a physical disease leads to effective treatment and prevention procedures; without classification, German measles would be just another skin rash.

Like physical illnesses, behavior disorders can be identified through classification procedures. However, each child is an individual with a unique set of problems. In addition, the "symptoms" or signs that are associated with behavior disorders are not as discrete and identifiable as the symptoms for German measles. Individuality, uniqueness, and ambiguous symptoms are the enemies of any classification system. These systems require general characteristics that are readily identifiable. However, even with these difficulties, major advances have been made in the classification and diagnosis of behaviorally disordered children. These classification advances have facilitated the understanding, treatment, and possibly the prevention of some of these disorders.

Classification: What Is It?

Classification is more than a description of phenomena. It goes beyond description and involves the grouping or placement of objects or behaviors into distinct classes or sets. Sokal (1974, p. 116) has defined general classification procedures of all sciences as "the ordering or arrangement of objects into groups or sets on basis of their relationships. These relationships can be based on observable or inferred properties." Sokal's definition suggests that there must be some general or common feature that identifies objects and determines their placement within a set of categories. These common features or relationships are specified in a classification rule or *operational definition* (Bridgman, 1927). These good operational definitions include a set of objective criteria or rules that can be used to decide whether a particular case belongs within a specific category (Hempel, 1965). An operational definition serves as a judgment test to determine whether an object or behavior belongs within a certain category.

Satisfactory operational definitions provide clearly stated objective criteria that can be understood and used similarly by various people. Ambiguity and personal interpretation are be held to a minimum by good operational definitions. For example, IQ scores might be used as part of the operational definition to classify mentally retarded children. An IQ score of below 70 on standard intelligence test can be used as one criterion to judge a child as mentally retarded. This operational definition of retardation seems to work well with children at the extreme ranges of the IQ continuum. For instance, a child with an IQ score of 150 is certainly not mentally retarded, and a child with an IQ score of 20 is most probably retarded. Difficulties develop, however, toward the midpoint of this retardation continuum, or at values around 70. If a child has an IQ of 70 and performs poorly at school but is well adjusted and competent in his nonacademic everyday life, then it is unclear whether the child is retarded or not. As the example demonstrates, operational definitions are never perfect, and there often are borderline cases in which they break down.

Good operational definitions for classifications systems share several characteristics. First, they specify many points of comparisons (not just one, as in the IQ test example). Second, the definitions are clear and objective. The characteristics specified in the definition should be measurable and, if possible, observable. Third, the definitions should be used similarly by everyone. In properly classifying mental retardation, for example, psychologists typically specify a range of IQ scores (below an IQ of 70), measures of adaptive behavior (behavior needed to function independently), and a time span within which the condition first occurred (the developmental period of childhood or adolescence) (Grossman, 1977).

Classification and Diagnosis

We have already defined *classification* as the ordering of objects or behaviors into sets or groups using operational definitions. An *identification* or *diagnostic* process is the actual assigning of objects or behaviors to groupings within a classification system (Sokal, 1974). A botanist may identify an unknown plant by matching the plant's observable characteristics with the operational definitions included in the botanical classification system. *Diagnosis* is the psychological equivalent of the botanical identification process.

However, true scientific classification goes beyond simply describing something and leads to diagnosis and understanding. The word *diagnosis* actually combines two ancient Greek words: *dia,* which means "two" or "apart," and *gignoskein,* which means "to know or perceive." Literally, diagnosis means to distinguish or differentiate (R. E. Kendall, 1975), or, as Achenbach (1974, p. 568) has stated, "to reduce uncertainty."

Diagnosing a behavior disorder is, then, the process of using an accepted classification system to match a person's unknown behavior characteristics to a set of operational definitions. In clinical practice with children, this process allows a psychologist to assign a child's behavior to a subcategory of the classification system. The matching and assigning of behavior to a subcategory results in naming or diagnosing the child's behavior disorder. This process differentiates or separates a specific diagnosis from other diagnostic categories within a classification system. The end product is a *differential diagnosis* of the child's condition.

It should be clear from this discussion that a *child* is not diagnosed by the classification process; only the child's *behavior disorder* is diagnosed (Rutter, 1965). All classification systems (as we will discover) are imperfect, have some errors associated with them, and may lead to errors in categorization. They are only imperfect models of a child's behavior, and it is a mistake to believe that a child conforms exactly to the behavioral description of a diagnostic category. Each child is unique, and a diagnostic label is only an approximate description of a child's behavior. Exceptions are the rule.

The Purpose of Classification

Having a commonly understood language is essential to the success of any human enterprise. Nations, races, and organizations share a common language that is collectively understood. Classification systems provide a similar language function for science. In the absence of such a common terminology, scientific communication will be beset with confusion and misunderstanding (Rutter, 1965). With agreement on a common classification language, clinicians in different locales can communicate with each other, information can be shared, and the development of scientific theory can progress (Blashfield & Draguns, 1976b). Without a common classification language, we have a clinical Tower of Babel in which no one speaks the same language.

Ideally, a classification system helps to unify the study of behavior disorders so that terminology is standardized, communication is facilitated, and facts can be established concerning the behavior disorder's *etiology* (origin or cause). Good classification systems can also help predict the course of a behavior disorder, its *prognosis* (probable outcome), and its likely response to different types of treatments. However, these benefits are in the ideal sense and may not totally apply to child psychopathology. The development of classification systems for childhood behavior disorders is of recent origin, and such systems have been criticized for their imperfections (Hallahan & Kauffman, 1986; Hobbs, 1975a). But there is some evidence of benefits when standard classification schemes are used with behaviorally disordered children.

In most cases the causes of childhood behavior disorders are not known, probably because many of these conditions have varied and complex causes (see Chapter 2). Several different causes may produce the same type of behavior disorder, and different behavior disorders may result from the same similar causes. Accurate classification can aid in ferreting out the important contributing causes of behavioral disturbances (Chess & Hassibi, 1978; Rutter, 1965; Zubin, 1967). For example, classifying autistic children by strict diagnostic guidelines has helped pinpoint two probable causes of infantile autism: transmission of a recessive gene, and a fragile-X chromosome break (Levitas et al., 1983; Ritvo, Freeman, Mason-Brothers, Mo, & Ritvo, 1984). Similarly, studies of children classified as having attention deficit disorder have shown that some of these children have neurological abnormalities; this, in turn, suggests that the condition may in part be caused by physical abnormalities (as reviewed by Ross & Ross, 1982; Rutter, 1965). Although these studies are not conclusive, they are important in helping unravel the complex causes of behavior disorders. Without accurate classification, this research would not be possible.

Accurate prognosis is facilitated by accurately classifying children into diagnostic categories. This is important because most parents want to know the likely outcome for their children. Will they live an average adult life style, or will they continue to have difficulty throughout their lives? These prognostic determinations are made by scientific researchers who accurately classify children and then employ longitudinal studies to evaluate the children's adjustment in later years (Patterson, 1983; Robins, 1966, 1979; Walker et al., 1986; Weiss & Hechtman, 1986). For example, if a study follows three children with different diagnoses—an autistic child, a withdrawn child,

and an antisocial-aggressive child—we can fairly successfully predict the likely outcomes for each of these children. If the autistic child is mentally retarded and has no language, the likely outcome in adulthood is poor (DeMyer et al., 1973). The likely outcome for the withdrawn child is relatively good in adulthood, in comparison to the poor outcome of the antisocial-aggressive child (D. P. Morris, Soroker, & Burruss, 1954; H. H. Morris, Escoll, & Wexler, 1956; Robins, 1966, 1979; Walker et al., 1986). All of these predictions can be in error, especially when they are made for individual children. We cannot say for sure that a particular child will have a good or bad outcome even if accurately classified. However, given accurate classification and good longitudinal research, statistically accurate predictions can be made for most children so classified.

Another advantage to accurate classification of a childhood behavior disorder is to predict the child's probable response to a particular treatment. The number of children with attention deficit disorder who respond to stimulant medication, and the effects of this medication over time, can be predicted (Ross & Ross, 1982; Weiss & Hechtman, 1986). Phenylketonuria (PKU) provides another excellent example of the advantages of reliable classification. PKU, discussed in greater detail in Chapter 9, is a condition produced by an inherited enzyme defect which results in improper oxidation of particular protein substances and damage to the nervous system that causes mental retardation. Before PKU was identified through urine and blood tests, it was responsible for 1 percent of people institutionalized because of severe retardation (Liebert, Poulos, & Stauss, 1974). Correct classification of this disorder has led to an effective treatment (placing the child on a special diet) that prevents mental retardation. However, if the condition is not diagnosed in infancy and diet therapy is not provided, the child's prognosis is very poor, and permanent retardation is extremely likely. Thus, in addition to providing a common language for clinicians and scientists, a good classification system may permit reliable predictions regarding a behavior disorder's cause, course, and response to treatment.

Possibly one of the most important reasons for the classification of behavior disorders, but one of the least obvious ones, is to generate finances for the treatment and research of children suffering from behavior disorders. Children must be classified or labeled according to an acceptable system in general use before treatment programs in clinics, hospitals, and schools can be funded (Chess & Hassibi, 1978; Gallagher, Forsythe, Ringelheim, & Weintraub, 1975). Funding makes treatment services possible through insurance payments, school districts, and federal agencies. Similarly, research into the causes and best treatment approaches for behavior disorders is often confined to children specific diagnoses. For instance, various federal and private agencies and foundations have specified by diagnostic categories (such as infantile autism, childhood drug dependency, depression, and stress-related disorders) the types of research projects they are willing to fund.

In summary, the development of classification systems helps to establish a standard scientific language that can be used by clinicians and researchers in their daily work. Classification aids in the identification of causes of behavior disorders, establishment of prognosis, and the development of effective treatment methods. Moreover, classification often determines whether private and government funds are provided for treatment and research on behavior disorders. But classification systems are imperfect humanmade systems that are used with complex, highly individualized, naturally occurring behavior. It is important to understand how to judge the adequacy of classification systems.

Criteria for Behavior Classification Systems

Good classification systems have several features in common. A good system can be used with high reliability or consistency by different diagnosticians. It includes a manageable number of behavior disorders, and it describes, as closely and as concisely as possible, how these disorders exist in nature. A classification system should also be useful to clinicians and researchers so that it is utilized for its practical information and not as a mere mechanism to secure treatment and research funds. In addition, since the nature of psychopathology changes with age, classification systems for use with children should be flexible enough to address issues of growth and development.

Reliability Reliability depends on consistency. Gelfand and Hartman (1984) have clarified the term reliability as follows: A friend or acquaintance, if unreliable, is inconsistent; thus little confidence can be placed in her. In contrast, a reliable friend behaves consistently and can be depended on. The key term here is *consistency.* A behavior classification system is not reliable (inconsistent) if under similar conditions the same behaviors are not classified the same way. For example, during reading times (similar conditions) in Mrs. Jones's classroom, a child's hitting others, moving about the room without permission, and talking out of turn might be equally likely to be diagnosed as unsocialized aggression or hyperactivity. We would call this procedure unreliable. For example, if one clinician observes the same child misbehaving on two separate occasions and arrives at two different diagnoses, we would say that the system's *test-retest reliability* is poor. A different type of reliability involves two clinicians. If two clinicians observe the same behavior simultaneously and arrive at two different diagnoses, we would conclude that the *interrater* reliability of the classification used is questionable.

The possible causes of low reliability have been researched by several investigators (as reviewed by Blashfield, 1984). These causes include poor training of clinicians in the use of the classification system, the inconsistency of the patient's behavior, and inadequacy of the classification system (Helzer, et al., 1977; Ward, Beck, Mendelson, Mock, & Erbaugh, 1962). Few data are available on the reliability of classification systems devised especially for children (Achenbach, 1980; Quay, 1979). The fact that children change and develop rapidly over time presents a particular problem for diagnosticians. What was diagnosed

---

BOX 12-1 • The DSM-III-R Classification Definitions for Oppositional Defiant Disorder and Conduct Disorder; Solitary Type

OPPOSITIONAL DISORDER

Differential diagnosis. Normal oppositional behavior in 18-to-36-month-old children, Conduct Disorder, Schizophrenia, Pervasive Developmental Disorders, Attention Deficit Disorder, Mental Retardation, Chronic Organic Mental Disorders.

DIAGNOSTIC CRITERIA

Note: Consider a criterion met only if the behavior is considerably more frequent than that of most people of the same mental age.

   A. A disturbance of at least six months during which at least five of the following are present:
   (1) often loses temper
   (2) often argues with adults
   (3) often actively defies or refuses adult requests or rules, e.g., refuses to do chores at home
   (4) often deliberately does things that annoy other people, e.g., grabs other children's hats
   (5) often blames others for his or her own mistakes
   (6) is often touchy or easily annoyed by others
   (7) is often angry and resentful
   (8) is often spiteful or vindictive
   (9) often swears or uses obscene language
   Note: The above items are listed in descending order of discriminating power based on data from a national field trial of the DSM-III-R criteria for Disruptive Behavior Disorders.
   B. Does not meet the criteria for Conduct Disorder, and does not occur exclusively during the course of a psychotic disorder, Dysthymia, or a Major Depressive, Hypomanic, or Manic Episode.

Criteria for severity of Oppositional Defiant Disorder:

Mild: Few, if any, symptoms in excess of those required to make the diagnosis **and** only minimal or no impairment in school and social functioning.

Moderate: Symptoms or functional impairment intermediate between "mild" and "severe."

Severe: Many symptoms in excess of those required to make the diagnosis **and** significant and pervasive impairment in functioning at home and school and with other adults and peers.

---

as a problem at one point may be radically changed in 6 months, as we have discussed in Chapter 1. Operational definitions that are unclear and overlap (share common descriptive terms or symptoms with other operational definitions) greatly reduce interrater reliability (Zigler & Phillips, 1960, 1961). For example, if a classification system has separate categories for an op-

Box 12-1 (Continued)

CONDUCT DISORDER

Differential diagnosis. Isolated acts of antisocial behavior (Childhood or Adolescent Antisocial Behavior—V codes), Oppositional Disorder.

CONDUCT DISORDER

A. **A disturbance of conduct lasting at least six months, during which at least three of the following have been present:**
    (1) **has stolen without confrontation of a victim on more than one occasion (including forgery)**
    (2) **has run away from home overnight at least twice while living in parental or parental surrogate home (or once without returning)**
    (3) **often lies (other than to avoid physical or sexual abuse)**
    (4) **has deliberately engaged in fire-setting**
    (5) **is often truant from school (for older person, absent from work)**
    (6) **has broken into someone else's house, building, or car**
    (7) **has deliberately destroyed others' property (other than by fire-setting)**
    (8) **has been physically cruel to animals**
    (9) **has forced someone into sexual activity with him or her**
    (10) **has used a weapon in more than one fight**
    (11) **often initiates physical fights**
    (12) **has stolen with confrontation of a victim (e.g., mugging, purse-snatching, extortion, armed robbery)**
    (13) **has been physically cruel to people**
    Note: The above items are listed in descending order of discriminating power based on data from a national field trial of the DSM-III-R criteria for Disruptive Behavior Disorders.
B. **If 18 or older, does not meet criteria for Antisocial Personality Disorder.**

Criteria for severity of Conduct Disorder:

Mild: Few if any conduct problems in excess of those required to make the diagnosis, **and** conduct problems cause only minor harm to others.

Moderate: Number of conduct problems and effect on others intermediate between "mild" and "severe."

Severe: Many conduct problems in excess of those required to make the diagnosis, **or** conduct problems cause considerable harm to others, e.g., serious physical injury to victims, extensive vandalism or theft, prolonged absence from home.

Source: American Psychiatric Association. (1987). *Diagnostic and statistical manual of mental disorders* (3rd ed.) (Washington, DC: Author), pp. 64–65 and 47–48. Copyright 1987 by the American Psychiatric Association. Reprinted by permission.

positional child and a conduct-disordered child (noncompliant and aggressive) (see Box 12-1), then it may be difficult to reliably select a diagnosis because of the commonalities and shared terms for these two categories (Werry, Methven, Fitzpatrick, & Dixon, 1983).

    The number of categories included in a classification system also affects its reliability. When a system has a few broad categories, such as psychotic and neurotic disorders, then its reliability can be quite good. However, as the similarity and number of categories increase, the reliability of the system decreases, because clinicians are required to make finer and more difficult discriminations between categories (Rutter & Shaffer, 1980; Ward et al., 1962; Zubin, 1967). Child psychiatric classification reliability appears to be only fair. The interrater reliability of the most frequently used classification systems with children has been reported to be approximately 50% (Cantwell, Russell, Mattison, & Will, 1979; Mattison, Cantwell, Russell, & Will, 1979). However, better interrater scores have been reported with older children and certain distinctive categories (Strober, Green, & Carlson, 1981).

Validity   Validity can be defined as a classification system's ability to measure what it proposes to measure. In a sense, validity explains how well a measure describes reality (Howell, Kaplan, & O'Connell, 1979). Validity may be described here as a classification system's accuracy in identifying behavior disorders, as compared to other systems that are known to identify the condition accurately. For example, if a team of experienced clinicians observes and rates a child as depressed, but a classification system's definition does not fit the child's behavior, then the validity of that system would be in doubt. This system of validity is called *concurrent validity,* because a currently accepted standard (the judgments of the team of experienced clinicians) is used to judge the classification system. Concurrent validity is critically important if a new system is going to be accepted and used (Blashfield, 1984; Blashfield & Draguns, 1976a, 1976b; Sundberg, 1977).

Another test for validity is how well a classification system predicts the course and outcome of a behavior disorder. A classification system that accurately identifies infantile autism and has good *predictive validity* might make the following predictions: (1) Autism is a lifelong condition with few changes; (2) the course of the condition is steady, with few improvements or remissions; (3) management of the condition is improved if the child has

some communication skills and near-normal intelligence (is not retarded). Such a classification system provides outcome predictions in addition to identification and labeling.

Reliability and validity often go hand in hand. A system has to have some degree of reliability before it can be either descriptively or predictively valid. Although there is some disagreement in the literature (Carey & Gottesman, 1978), it is generally accepted that a reasonable level or reliability is needed before a system can be tested for validity. In a sense, reliability sets an upper limit on the validity of a system; without good reliability, a system cannot be valid. A system, however, can be highly reliable, but can have low validity (Spitzer & Fleiss, 1974). When this is the case, it generally means that reliable but irrelevant selection criteria, which are in fact unrelated to the conditions, have been used.

Scope and Coverage   The scope of a classification system is the breadth of its coverage (Blashfield, 1984; Blashfield & Draguns, 1976a, 1976b; Cromwell, Blashfield, & Strauss, 1975). *Scope* refers to a classification system's ability to cover either a broad or a narrow spectrum of clinical conditions. If a system has 100 percent or extremely broad coverage, it has a category for every possible problem presented by patients. If a system has only 10 percent coverage (narrow coverage), then it can classify only 10 percent of the cases presented by patients and leaves the rest unclassified. It may seem that classification systems should have the broadest possible coverage, but broad coverage is not always entirely desirable. With broad coverage, there may be many overlapping categories with similar terms, and this reduces reliability (Blashfield, 1984). Excessively broad coverage also produces what are known as "wastebasket" categories. These are broadly defined categories that are designed for idiosyncratic or "exception to the rule" cases that do not fit any other type of category. An example of such a broad category is the category of adjustment disorder in the American Psychiatric Association's (1987) *Diagnostic and Statistical Manual of Mental Disorders,* third edition (DSM-III-R); it is used for troubled youths when other diagnoses do not apply (see Box 12-2).

Overly narrow coverage also creates problems. With narrow coverage, a system's reliability can be quite high, because the operational definitions of the categories are very specific and limiting. The system's validity can also be quite high, but only for a few conditions. If too many conditions remain unclassified because the system is not appropriately flexible, then clinicians and researchers will shun the system. The acceptance and use of a system in making classification decisions are referred to as its *utility* (Hartmann, Roper, & Bradford, 1979). For example, if 50 percent of behavior problems are not covered by the classification scheme, then little is gained by using the system. A classification system must cover enough conditions to make it useful to practitioners.

Parsimonious and Mutually Exclusive Definitions   Good classification systems employ parsimonious and mutually exclusive definitions (Quay, 1979). *Parsimonious* definitions use as few terms as possible to describe behavior disorders. The excessive use of terms tends to confuse users and reduces reliability. Similarly, the reliability of a classification system is increased when definitions are as *mutually exclusive* as possible (that is, when one definition is clearly different from others, with few shared terms). When key terms are shared by two or more definitions of behavior disorders, diagnosticians cannot tell which definition to use. For example, if the word *anxiety* is the key term in a description of phobic reactions and a description of adjustment reactions, then the diagnostician cannot be sure which label to apply.

Classification systems are never perfect. They are always affected by factors such as reli-

---

BOX 12-2 • DSM-III-R Diagnostic Criteria for Adjustment Disorder

A. A reaction to an identifiable psychosocial stressor (or multiple stressors) that occurs within three months of onset of the stressor(s).

B. The maladaptive nature of the reaction is indicated by either of the following:
   (1) impairment in occupational (including school) functioning or in usual social activities or relationships with others
   (2) symptoms that are in excess of a normal and expectable reaction to the stressor(s)

C. The disturbance is not merely one instance of a pattern of overreaction to stress or an exacerbation of one of the mental disorders previously described.

D. The maladaptive reaction has persisted for no longer than six months.

E. The disturbance does not meet the criteria for any specific mental disorder and does not represent Uncomplicated Bereavement.

[Our comment: This category allows the classification of any behavior that affects social or occupational functioning and is assumed to be the results of some "stressor." The diagnostician is left to define what a stressor is, and then "behaviors that are in excess of the normal and expected reaction to the stressor." This is difficult if not impossible task. Clearly, reliability and meaningful validity are sacrificed with such a classification, and what is left is broad coverage and a general label, "adjustment disorder."]

Source: American Psychiatric Association. (1987). *Diagnostic and and statistical manual of mental disorders* (3rd ed., revised) (Washington, DC: Author), p. 300–301. Copyright 1987 by the American Psychiatric Association. Reprinted by permission.

ability, validity, coverage, utility, parsimony, and the mutual exclusiveness of definitions. All of these factors then interface with the level of training and personal preferences of clinicians and researchers using the system. Imperfect systems and the human factor will invariably produce some degree of error. But these systems are necessary in our research, clinical, and educational systems.

CLASSIFICATION SYSTEMS

Accurate classification systems for children's behavior disorders are relatively new phenomena. The first clinically useful system was developed for adult disorders by a German psychiatrist, Emil Kraepelin, in 1899. For the next 50 years, children were not formally included in classification systems. However, during this time a common group of child behavior disorders was recognized. In 1928, Wickman asked 511 elementary teachers and 30 clinicians to assess the serious behavior problems of school children. The teachers reported that conduct problems such as stealing, lying, and inappropriate sexual behaviors were rated as the most serious. In contrast, clinicians rated personality problems such as social withdrawal, depression, and fearfulness as the most serious problems. Other studies (Mutimer & Rosemier, 1967; Schrupp & Gjerde, 1953; Stouffer, 1952) have found similar results: Teachers most frequently identified aggression, disobedience, and destruction of property as serious problems, while clinicians viewed withdrawal, depression, and phobic reactions as the most serious problems. This classification dichotomy of "acting-out" problems and "withdrawal" problems is echoed in all modern classification systems, whether they are statistically, medically, behaviorally, or educationally based.

Statistically Based Classification Systems

A great deal of research has been done on childhood behavior disorders using multivariate statistical methods called *factor analysis* and *cluster analysis*. These sophisticated statistical techniques are used to identify cluster or factors of characteristics that are related or intercorrelated. For example, a factor called *hyperactivity* might include the characteristics of inattention, impulsive behavior, high rates of motor activity, and poor academic success, all of which occur in the same children. Generally, these characteristics are reported by parents or teachers when a child is referred for help, or they may be compiled from behavior checklists that are filled out by teachers.

The availability of computers in the 1960s made possible the extensive use of multivariate statistics in developing classification systems for childhood behavior disorders (Dreger, 1982). Peterson (1961) studied 400 cases referred to a child guidance clinic and derived 58 items that were descriptive of behavior disorders in children. These items were then assembled into a behavior checklist, and 831 elementary-age children were then rated by teachers for behavior problems. Factor analysis demonstrated that the majority of problems of children in schools could be accounted for by two major dimensions—*aggression* (behavior disorders) and *withdrawal* (personality disorders). Minor dimensions were later isolated and included *inadequacy-immaturity* (hyperactivity) (Quay & Quay, 1965), *juvenile delinquency* (Quay, 1964), and *childhood psychosis* (Quay & Peterson, 1975); the last of these was rarely encountered.

Several other studies (Patterson, 1964; Walker, 1970, 1982; Wirt, Lachar, Klinedinst, & Seat, 1977) have found similar factors or clusters of childhood problems. Possibly the most extensive statistical investigation of childhood behavior disorders has been the work of Achenbach and Edelbrock (Achenbach, 1966, 1978, 1982; Achenbach & Edelbrock, 1978, 1979) using the Child Behavior Checklist and Profile (CBCL). This research was conducted on hundreds of children who were observed and rated by their parents and teachers. One group of children had been referred for psychological problems, and the other group (the controls) were nonhandicapped children. Factor analysis of these ratings produced two broad factors: *internalizing* symptoms and *externalizing* symptoms. The internalizing symptoms were emotional difficulties such as anxiety, phobias, overinhibition, fearfulness, worrying, and somatic problems (physical complaints such as headaches and stomachaches). The externalizing problems were directed toward the environment and other people, and included aggression, disobedience, fighting, and to a lesser extent hyperactivity. These researchers also found that problems varied with age and between males and females. This research is discussed further in Chapter 13.

The multivariate classification systems have gained in popularity over the past few years, for several reasons. First, these systems are empirically derived, which means that the problems are first rated by parents and teachers. Then, a rigorous statistical procedure defines which characteristics are interrelated (intercorrelated) and validly form "real" diagnostic clusters. This process is different from other systems (to be discussed shortly), which have used the judgment of a committee of clinicians to decide behavior disorder categories. Second, most multivariate classification systems are developed through the use of standardized behavior checklists, which many clinicians and educators find easy to use. Third, independent investigators have repeatedly found similar clusters of behavior disorders. For instance, most multivariate classification research has found the broad-band behavior disorders or internalizing and externalizing problems with the associated narrow-band problems of aggression, hyperactivity, delinquency, depression, withdrawal, phobias, and others. This type of independently replicated finding adds support to the validity of these systems.

Medical Classification Systems

Some of the most frequently used classification systems are based on a medical model. A pure *disease model* or *medical model* assumes that abnormal behavior is caused by an underlying organic problem, such as a brain lesion, chemical imbalance, genetic abnormality, or infection (Blashfield, 1984; Wing, 1978) (see Chapter 2). The abnormal behavior is assumed to be a symptom produced by some abnormal organic or psy-

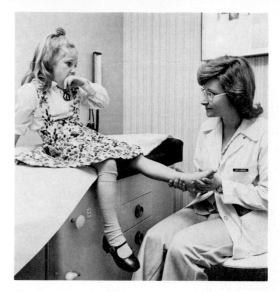

The disease model holds that behavior problems may be traced to underlying physiological causes.

chological condition. Proponents of the disease model assume that treating only the symptom (the abnormal behavior) will not remove the cause of the problem and will result in a continuation of the pathology and probable appearance of a new system (*symptom substitution*).

The disease model involves one additional, optimistic assumption—that observing, describing, and classifying will lead to discovering the biological causes and cures of abnormal behavior patterns (Draguns & Phillips, 1971). This careful strategy of observation and classification has produced dramatic advances in general medicine and some advances in psychiatry. For example, following the accurate diagnosis of syphilis, syphilis spirochetes were discovered to enter the central nervous system and to cause general *paresis* (a pattern of physical and mental breakdown). Also, several progressive neurological diseases such as Huntington's chorea (psychosis accompanied by progressive loss of muscular control) were found to have a genetic basis. However, despite intensive efforts with new biological diagnostic tools such as computerized tomography (image-enhanced brain x-ray scans), researchers have been unable to identify physiological causes for the vast majority of behavior disorders. Most classification systems based on a medical model have lacked substantial biological evidence for their definitions of behavior disorders.

Robert Spitzer, chairman of the Task Force on Nomenclature of the American Psychiatric Association, has had a powerful influence in defining mental disorders. The task force has had the responsibility for developing the official classification systems for the American Psychiatric Association (currently, DSM-III and its proposed revision, DSM-III-R). Spitzer has emphasized the view that mental disorders are medical disorders—that they may have an underlying biological cause, such as mental retardation or organic brain syndrome. However, many disorders that need to be covered in a classification system do not have a demonstrated biological cause, and thus Spitzer has developed a bridging definition of *mental disorder* (see Table 12-1). It is presumed that future advances may include demonstrations of biological causes for at least some mental disorders.

There are several classification systems that are based at least partially on the medical model. There are other medical classification systems,

Table 12-1
Spitzer and Wilson's Definition of Mental Disorder

1. The manifestations of the condition are primarily psychological and involve alterations in behavior. However, it includes conditions manifested by somatic changes, such as psycho-physiological reactions, if an understanding of the cause and course of the condition is largely dependent on the use of psychological concepts, such as personality, motivation, and conflict.

2. The condition in its full blown state is regularly and intrinsically associated with subjective distress, generalized impairment in social effectiveness of functioning, or voluntary behavior that the subject wishes he could stop because it is regularly associated with physical disability or illness.

3. The condition is distinct from other conditions in terms of the clinical picture and, ideally, follow-up, family studies, and response to treatment.

Source: R. L. Spitzer and T. Wilson. (1975). Nosology and the official psychiatric nomenclature. In M. Freeman, H. I. Kaplan, and B. J. Sadlock (Eds.), *Comprehensive textbook of psychiatry* (2nd ed., Vol. 2) (Baltimore: Williams and Wilkins), p. 829. Reprinted by permission.

such as those of the Group for the Advancement of Psychiatry (GAP) (1974), and the ninth edition of the *International Classification of Diseases* (ICD-9; World Health Organization, 1977) (see Box 12-3 for a brief explanation of these systems). But in the United States, the various editions of the *Diagnostic and Statistical Manual of Mental Disorders* (DSM) of the American Psychiatric Association have been the most important.

DSM-I and DSM-II   The various editions of the DSM have been developed by the American Psychiatric Association through its expert task force since 1952. This task force, a committee of experts, decides through a process of discussion and compromise what categories should be included and how they should be defined. The committee process is very different from the development of multivariate classification systems, discussed earlier. It is ironic that the "S" in DSM stands for *Statistical,* which is not a very accurate description of the actual development of these systems.

The first edition of the DSM (DSM-I) was published in 1952 as a unifying, standard classification system for adult and psychiatric disorders. The need for such a system became apparent during World War II, when large numbers of men were mobilized to fight, and over 90 percent of the psychiatric cases referred to military psychiatrists did not fit any existing classification system (Ullmann & Krasner, 1965). However, the DSM-I was inadequate for children because it included only two basic categories: adjustment reaction (infancy, childhood, and adolescence) and schizophrenic reaction, childhood type. Clinicians who worked with children found these classification categories overly general and incomplete.

In 1968, a second edition of the DSM (DSM-II) was introduced. The DSM-II included more categories for children's disorders; however, the operational definitions were still difficult to apply. The clinician was given little direction in deciding whether a child must have all or most of the symptoms described in a particular category in order to receive a particular diagnosis (Fish, 1969; Spitzer, Sheehy, & Endicott, 1977). The diagnostic ambiguity of the categories and the overuse of "waste-basket" categories such as adjustment reaction (Cerreto & Tuma, 1977) made this system unsatisfactory for use with children. A system was needed that added more specific and useful information and went beyond merely categorizing a mental disorder.

DSM-III and DSM-III-R The DSM-III classification system, which was published in 1980, is a radical departure from the DSM-I and DSM-II systems (Spitzer & Endicott, 1978; Spitzer et al., 1977). The earlier systems were categorical systems in which the classification process was intended to lead to one diagnosis or category. The DSM-III system, however, differs from the previous system in several ways. First, the task force that developed the DSM-III set the goal that each disorder should be defined *without* assumptions about the cause of the disorder. This atheoretical approach was used to prevent the classification system from representing one biased theoretical perspective. Second, the DSM-III is greatly expanded and includes many additional categories of childhood behavior disorders, such as attention deficit disorder, conduct disorder, infantile autism, pervasive developmental disorders, and others.

Third, the DSM-III is a *multiaxial* classification system instead of a categorical system. For behavior disorders, the DSM-III provides more than a diagnostic label; it adds a set of dimensions *(axes)* that are coded along with the psychiatric diagnosis. The first axis for a child is the principal psychiatric diagnosis (for example, attention deficit disorder with hyperactivity); the second axis includes any developmental problem the child might have (for example, developmental reading disorder); the third axis includes any physical disorders (such as allergies); the fourth axis includes any psychosocial stressors (for instance, divorce of parents), and the fifth axis is a rating of the highest level of *adaptive functioning* (intellectual and social functioning) for the child. The formal DSM-III diagnosis for our example of a hyperactive child with reading difficulties and severe family problems would look like the following:

Axis I   314.01 Attention deficit disorder with hyperactivity

Attention problems have many possible causes.

Axis II   315.00 Developmental reading disorder

Axis III   Physical condition—allergies

Axis IV   Psychosocial stressor: Divorce of parents in the past year: rated 5—severe

Axis V   Highest level of adaptive functioning: rated 5—poor

Another example, with background information, using the new DSM-III-R, is given in Box 12-4 for a severely anxious child.

The DSM-III is clearly superior to its prede-

BOX 12-3 • Medical Classification Systems

PSYCHOANALYTIC CLASSIFICATION

There are few formal classification systems based on Freudian psychoanalytic theory. It may be debatable whether psychoanalytic theory is medically based. However, a basic premise of psychoanalytic theory is that abnormal behaviors are symptoms of underlying emotional disturbances. These disturbances generally are repressed sexual impulses or developmental crises associated with the psychosexual stages of development outlined by Freud or Erik Erikson. Many of the concepts associated with the psychosexual stages of Freud and the social maturational stages of Erikson are found in other medical and educational classification systems. These stages are set out in Table 12-2.

Table 12-2
Freud's and Erikson's stages of development

FREUD'S PSYCHOSEXUAL STAGES	APPROXIMATE AGE	ERIKSON'S PSYCHOSOCIAL STAGES
Oral	First year	Basic trust vs. mistrust
Anal	Second year	Autonomy vs. shame, doubt
Phallic	Third to fifth years	Initiative vs. guilt
Latency	Sixth year to puberty	Industry vs. inferiority
Genital	Adolescence	Identity vs. role confusion
	Early adulthood	Intimacy vs. isolation
	Middle adulthood	Generativity vs. stagnation
	Old age	Integrity vs. despair

GROUP FOR THE ADVANCEMENT OF PSYCHIATRY (GAP) SYSTEM

The GAP system is a psychoanalytically based classification system developed in 1966. The GAP system is based on nine separate categories, as shown in Table 12-3.

cessors. It has more categories for childhood behavior disorders, and its multiaxial system provides more information for individual cases. However, the system has its critics. The "atheoretical" assumption of the DSM-III has been criticized by several researchers who feel that the system is in fact theoretically based on the medical model (Faust & Miner, 1986; Schacht & Nathan, 1977; Taylor, 1983). Moreover, Harris (1979) has charged that the DSM-III includes many behaviors (such as reading disorder, arithmetic disorder, and underachievement disorder) that are educational

---

Box 12-3 (Continued)

Table 12-3
Child psychiatric conditions from the group for the advancement of psychiatry

1. Healthy response of early childhood—developmental crisis type, acute, mild manifested by separation anxiety and clinging behavior.
2. Reactive disorder of early childhood—acute, moderate, manifested by regressive encopresis, thumb-sucking, and withdrawn behavior.
3. Developmental deviation of later childhood—delayed maturational pattern type, chronic, moderate, manifested by impulsive behavior, low frustration tolerance, continued enuresis, reading disability, and persistence of prelogical thought processes.
4. Psychoneurotic disorder of later childhood—phobic type, acute, severe, manifested by ritualistic behavior, counting compulsions, and obsessive rumination.
6. Psychotic disorder of later childhood—schizophreniform type, chronic, severe, manifested by autistic behavior, associative (thought) disorder, resistance to change, whirling, echolalia, ritualistic behavior, and panic states.

7. a. Psychophysiologic skin disorder of later childhood—chronic, moderate, manifested by neurodermatitis and excoriations.
   b. Personality disorder—overly inhibited type, chronic, severe, manifested by withdrawn behavior, learning inhibition, and hesitant speech.
8. Brain syndrome of early childhood—chronic, moderate, manifested by hyperkinesis, impulsive behavior, distractibility, and difficulties in coordination.
9. a. Mental retardation of adolescence—chronic, mild.
   b. Psychotic disorder—schizophrenic type, chronic, moderate, manifested by autistic behavior, associative (thought) disorder, and continuing enuresis.

Source: Group for the Advancement of Psychiatry. (1974). *Psychopathological disorders in childhood: Theoretical considerations and a proposed classification* (New York: Jason Aronson), p. 216. Copyright 1974 by the Group for the Advancement of Psychiatry. Reprinted by permission.

WORLD HEALTH ORGANIZATION (WHO) CLASSIFICATION

WHO has developed a series of classification systems for diseases, with the intent of standardizing the diagnosis of medical disorders internationally. The basic classification systems have been gathered together in a volume called the *International Classification of Diseases* (ICD). The mental disorder component of the ICD is multiaxial, with four primary axes: (1) clinical psychiatric syndromes, (2) intellectual level, (3) associated biological factors, and (4) psychosocial influences. The most recent of the ICD volumes is the ICD-9, which is very similar to DSM-III. While the ICD-9 has 39 mental disorder categories related to children, the DSM-III has 45 categories.

T a b l e   12-4
DSM-III-R Classification: Axes I and II Categories and Codes

Disorders Usually First Evident in Infancy, Childhood, or Adolescence

---

Disruptive behavior disorders (49)
314.01   Attention-deficit hyperactivity disorder (50)
            Conduct disorder (53)
312.20   group type
312.00   solitary aggressive type
312.90   undifferentiated type
313.81   Oppositional defiant disorder (56)

Anxiety disorders of childhood or adolescence (58)
309.21   Separation anxiety disorder (58)
313.21   Avoidant disorder of childhood or adolescence (61)
313.00   Overanxious disorder (63)

Eating disorders (65)
307.10   Anorexia nervosa (65)
307.51   Bulimia nervosa (67)
307.52   Pica (69)
307.53   Rumination disorder of infancy (70)
307.50   Eating disorder NOS

Gender identity disorders (71)
302.60   Gender identity disorder of childhood (71)
302.50   Transsexualism (74)
            Specify sexual history: asexual, homosexual, heterosexual, unspecified
302.85* Gender identity disorder of adolescence or adulthood, nontranssexual type (76)
            Specify sexual history: asexual, homosexual, heterosexual, unspecified
302.85* Gender identity disorder NOS

Tic disorders (78)
307.23   Tourette's disorder (79)
307.22   Chronic motor or vocal tic disorder (81)
307.21   Transient tic disorder (81)
            Specify: single episode or recurrent
307.20   Tic disorder NOS

Elimination disorders (82)
307.70   Functional encopresis (82)
            Specify: primary or secondary type
307.60   Functional enuresis (84)
            Specify: primary or secondary type
            Specify: nocturnal only, diurnal only, nocturnal and diurnal

Speech disorders not elsewhere classified (85)
307.00* Cluttering (85)
307.00* Stuttering (86)

DEVELOPMENTAL DISORDERS
Note: These are coded on Axis II.

Mental retardation (28)
317.00   Mild mental retardation
318.00   Moderate mental retardation
318.10   Severe mental retardation
318.20   Profound mental retardation
319.00   Unspecified mental retardation

Pervasive developmental disorders (33)
299.00   Autistic disorder (38)
            Specify if childhood onset
299.80   Pervasive developmental disorder NOS

Specific developmental disorders (39)
            Academic skills disorders
315.10   Developmental arithmetic disorder (41)
315.80   Developmental expressive writing disorder (42)
315.00   Developmental reading disorder (43)
            Language and speech disorders
315.39   Developmental articulation disorder (44)
315.31* Developmental expressive language disorder (45)
315.31* Developmental receptive language disorder (47)
            Motor skills disorder
315.40   Developmental coordination disorder (48)
315.90* Specific developmental disorder NOS

Other developmental disorders (49)
315.90* Developmental disorder NOS

Other disorders of infancy, childhood, or adolescence (88)
313.23   Elective mutism (88)
313.82   Identity disorder (89)
313.89   Reactive attachment disorder of infancy or early childhood (91)
307.30   Stereotypy/habit disorder (93)
314.00   Undifferentiated attention-deficit disorder (95)

Source: American Psychiatric Association. (1987). *Diagnostic and statistical manual of mental disorders,* (3rd ed., revised) (Washington, DC: Author), pp. 3–4. Copyright 1987 by the American Psychiatric Association. Reprinted by permission.

BOX 12-4 • Bobby: Example of a Child with an Avoidant Disorder

Bobby is a 10-year-old whose mother has come to see the school counselor. She has been concerned because he has been getting more quiet and shy around everyone. Bobby has always been a shy child and preferred playing alone. Bobby has had some language difficulties, particularly pronouncing certain words. In addition, Bobby's parents have had marital difficulties. She was not worried until recently, when he began telling her he didn't want to go to school because he didn't want to be around all those children. The teacher told his mother that she never saw him play with other children, but felt that he was just shy. However, 6 months ago when the family had a small reunion, Bobby began sobbing and saying that he didn't want to go. Bobby has always been friendly with the family; although shy, he used to like seeing them all. When his mother began asking Bobby what was wrong, he said that he was afraid. Lately, he has also been telling her he feels lonely. When she suggests that he play with some children in the neighborhood, he says he can't and goes to his room, where she often finds him crying. When she talks to him, he says he wants friends but is too afraid.

The multiaxial DSM-III-R diagnosis for Bobby would be as follows:

Axis I   313.21 Avoidant disorder of childhood or adolescence
Axis II   Developmental articulation disorder
Axis III   None
Axis IV   Moderate—parents have marital difficulties
Axis V   Current Global Assessment Functioning (GAF): 60-Moderate
              Past year (GAF): 60-Moderate

Source: Cater. (1987). *School psychologist's perceptions of internalizing and externalizing behaviorally disordered children.* Unpublished doctoral dissertation, University of Utah. Adapted by permission.

---

rather than psychiatric in nature, and that thus might best be left out of the domain of psychiatric disorders. Some of the syndromes included in the DSM-III (such as attention deficit disorder without hyperactivity) have not been detectable by multivariate techniques (Achenbach, 1980), and much of the necessary empirical validation (concurrent or predictive) for many of the new diagnostic disorders has not been provided (Rutter & Shaffer, 1980).

The validity and reliability of the DSM-III axes have also been criticized. For the broad diagnostic categories, the interrater reliability of the DSM-III appears acceptable (Cantwell et al., 1979; Mattison et al., 1979; Werry et al., 1983). However, for the finer discriminations demanded by a multiaxial system, the reliability and validity of the system fall to lower levels (Fernando, Mellsop, Nelson, Peace, & Wilson, 1986; Werry et al., 1983). Possibly one of the most damaging cri-

tiques of the DSM-III was a survey of its utilization and consumer satisfaction by 1000 practicing psychiatrists and residents (psychiatry students in training) (Jampala, Sierles, & Taylor, 1986). In this survey, 35 percent of the psychiatrists and 20 percent of the residents said they would stop using the DSM-III if it were not required. One of the serious faults uncovered in this survey was that 48 percent of the psychiatrists' patients and 36 percent of the residents' patients who received official diagnoses did not fit the minimum criteria of the DSM-III categories. That is, the diagnostic categories failed to accommodate almost half of the patients. A major weakness of the DSM-III, as perceived by the psychiatrists, was that they (48%) "do not believe in the validity of the DSM III criteria" (Jampala et al., 1986, p. 151).

At this time, development efforts have been completed to revise the DSM-III (American Psychiatric Association, 1987). Several categories (such as infantile autism) are being redefined, while other categories are being dropped. For example, attention deficit disorder without hyperactivity will be dropped, and only attention deficit disorder with hyperactivity will be included (see Table 12-4). However, the multiaxial structure of the system will be the same. However, on axis V the clinician is asked to rate the child's behavior on a numbered scale from 1 to 90. This Global Assessment of Functioning Scale (GAF) sets very serious and dangerous symptoms at a rating of 1, moderate difficulty at about 60, and symptoms absent or minimal at a rating of 90. More reliability and validity research is needed on many aspects of the DSM-III-R, but it, like the DSM-III, is being primarily designed by task force committees (25 advisory committees and 230 expert consultants). It is difficult to eliminate clinical bias and clinical politics in such a process, especially when empirical evidence is largely lacking.

Behavioral Classification

Behavioral classification stands in direct contrast to classification based on a medical model, in that it neither emphasizes nor assumes underlying causes of behavior disorders (Goldfried & Kent, 1972; Hartmann et al., 1979; Nelson, 1983; Ullmann & Krasner, 1969). According to the behavioral view, "responses or behaviors were interpreted as samples of what a person does in particular situations, rather than as *signs* of what a person *has*" (Nelson, 1983, p. 196). What is important to the behavioral classification process is how the abnormal behavior is maintained by the environment. Although some disorders (such as autism and some mental retardation) may be caused by an organic dysfunction, the behavioral approach assumes that the problem behaviors can still be managed by environmental manipulation. Very little emphasis in clinical work is placed on how the problem has developed. The emphasis on the behavior rather than on an underlying cause is reflected in the painstaking descriptions of behavioral responses that make up behavioral classifications.

To answer the question of how behaviors are maintained, the behavioral clinician performs a *functional analysis* of the child's behavior (Bijou & Peterson, 1971). A functional analysis attempts to determine the environmental events that produce the deviant behavior. For example, a mother may tell her child that it is time to go to bed (the *antecedent event,* or the one that occurs before the behavior), at which time the child may start to throw a tantrum (undesirable behavior), which is followed by the mother relenting and letting the child stay up longer (a positive consequence for the child). We can see from this example that the antecedents set the occasion for the response and that the consequence acts to increase or decrease the occurrence of the response. This behavioral classification system has been called the *ABC system* (A = antecedent, B = behavior, and C = consequence).

The behavioral classification system puts a high premium on identifying target clinical behaviors, which are then accurately measured (Kanfer, 1985; Kazdin, 1985; Kratochwill, 1985; Mash, 1985). Inferred qualities such as anxiety or emotional trauma, which cannot be directly observed, are de-emphasized by most behaviorists. However, cognitively oriented behavior therapists (P. C. Kendall & Urbain, 1981; Mahoney, 1974; Meichenbaum, 1977) are willing to rely on verbal reports of internal cognitive states (such as the child's reports of fearfulness or impulses to get out of her seat during class time). Behavioral classification emphasizes observation and precise measurement of behavior. This is done by classifying a child's problem as a *response excess* (a response too high in frequency—for example, throwing tantrums), *response deficit* (a response too low in frequency—for example, delayed language skills), or caused by inappropriate *stimulus control* (the right response but emitted in the wrong environment—for example, using a newly learned conversational skill during a test in the classroom) (Bijou & Peterson, 1971; Kanfer & Saslow, 1965). With this conceptual framework for classification, the detailed description of each behavior becomes important, including the behavior *topography* (the physical description of the response), *frequency* (how often it occurs), *duration* (how long the response lasts), and *amplitude* (response intensity) (Tryon, 1976).

With the emphasis on setting events, behavior, and consequences, good behavioral classification systems also take into account other important variables. Kanfer and Saslow (1965) have developed a formal model for behavioral diagnosis, which is given in Table 12-5. This model classifies problems as response excesses and deficits, but also includes an analysis of the child's biological, social, and cultural surroundings, which could be affecting his behavior. The behavioral classification system is more closely tied to a treatment strategy than are alternative classification systems such as the DSM-III-R. Frequent behavioral observations are taken, and if a treatment strategy is

not effective, it is changed until a more effective intervention is found.

Behavioral classification has several distinct advantages. Since behavioral systems emphasize direct measurement of observable behavior, the reliability of these systems is generally good. There are few inferred characteristics or assumptions that might reduce reliability by producing observer disagreement. The validity (reality) of behavioral systems is also high, because the behaviors to be classified and the functional analysis to be performed take place in the context of the child's problem environment. However, direct assessment done in the problem environment can have drawbacks caused by the intrusion of an observer, which can inject artificiality into the situation *(observer reactivity)*. Behavioral classification

T a b l e 12-5
Kanfer and Saslow's Behavioral Guide to a Functional Analysis of Individual Behavior

1. *Initial Analysis of the Problem Situation:* The client's major complaints are categorized into classes of behavioral excesses and deficits. Each behavior is described in terms of frequency, intensity, duration, and appropriateness of form. As an additional indispensable feature, the behavioral assets of the patient are also listed so they can be used in a therapy program.
2. *Clarification of the Problem Situation:* Consideration is given to people and circumstances in the client's environment which tend to maintain the problem behaviors and how these behaviors affect the client and others in the environment. Attention is given also to the consequences of changes in these behaviors that may result from intervention.
3. *Motivational Analysis:* Assessment is made of what types of stimuli reinforce the client and how these reinforcers could be used in an intervention program. Attention is given both to pleasurable stimuli that the client views positively and to aversive stimuli that the client fears or avoids.
4. *Developmental Analysis:* What are the limitations of the client's physical condition

(defective vision, hearing, residual illness, etc.) or sociological environment (urban versus rural, ethnic, socioeconomic status, etc.)? Could these biological and developmental variables relate to the client's current problem?
5. *Analysis of Self-Control:* To what extent and in what situations can the client control his problem behavior? Can the client's self-controlling behavior be used in an intervention program?
6. *Analysis of Social Relationships:* Who are the most significant people in the client's environment? Assess how these relationships influence each other, and how important people in the client's environment can participate in the intervention program.
7. *Analysis of the Social-Cultural-Physical Environment:* The client's behavior is compared to the norms of the client's environment. Such a comparison allows an assessment of how the client's behavior is viewed by others in his environment, how this view will change as the environmental setting changes (e.g., school, home, friends, or work), and what the limitations of the environment are.

Source: F. H. Kanfer and G. Saslow. (1965). Behavioral analysis: An alternative to diagnostic classification. *Archives of General Psychiatry, 12,* 848–853. Adapted by permission.

also places high value on the individual and describes each problem uniquely. This is in direct contrast to classification systems that try to fit individuals into predefined categories.

One study has investigated the reliability of using behavioral classification by experienced clinicians (Wilson & Evans, 1983). This study had 118 members (Ph.D. or Psy.D. level) of the influential Association for Advancement of Behavior Therapy (AABT) assess three written case descriptions of three common childhood disorders: fearfulness, conduct disorder, and social withdrawal. The members were asked (1) to describe their impressions of the major difficulties characterizing each child, (2) to state treatment goals, and (3) to rank-order treatment goals. The overall reliability between clinicians in selecting a first-priority behavior for treatment was only 38 percent. There was considerable variability in selecting behaviors for treatment. Surprisingly, 22 percent of the behavior therapists participating in this study also used loose psychodynamic and intrapsychic terminology (for instance, "internalized hostility," "insecure child," "poor self-concept") in their behavioral classification of the cases. This study demonstrates the strength of traditional concepts of psychopathology and shows that practicing behavior therapists may have some difficulty in reliably using behavioral classification systems.

Others have criticized the behavioral classification approach for failing to deal with human aims and values (Shoben, 1966), which are important but not directly observable behaviors. The emphasis on observation and measurement has been viewed by some clinicians as mechanistic, possibly missing the richness of human thought and emotion that other systems try to take into account. A complete divorce from labels and formal psychiatric diagnosis has also been difficult for most behavioral classification systems. Even major behavioral textbooks (Bellack, Hersen, & Kazdin, 1982; Morris & Kratochwill, 1983; Ullmann & Krasner, 1969; Yates, 1970) divide their subject matter according to a traditional medical orientation (for example, depression, infantile autism, schizophrenia, phobias, and so on) (Draguns & Phillips, 1971).

In many clinical settings where behavioral classification and assessment are used, it is not uncommon to see a formal diagnosis from the DSM-III-R coupled with a behavioral classification. This joint use of the two systems has been encouraged (Taylor, 1983) and is generally unavoidable, because insurance companies, federally funded programs, and school systems usually require a formal psychiatric diagnosis before they will fund treatment efforts. The major advantage of behavioral classification is in its practical treatment applications.

Educational Classification

More behaviorally disordered children are classified with special educational classification systems than with any other type of system. Teachers spend considerable time with children and have significant opportunities to observe many of the children's problems. Problems such as aggression toward peers and teachers, phobic reactions to the school environment (school phobia), and attention problems are common examples of behavior disorders that are exhibited in schools. However, even though they are widely used, educational classification systems are generally poorly constructed and include a mixture of medical, psychoanalytic, and behavioral concepts.

Categorical educational classification systems are designed by state boards of education and are used primarily by local school districts for funding purposes. Funds to schools are tied to the number of children classified as handicapped, resulting in classification systems with extremely broad coverage. Common categories in educational classification systems include mental retardation, learning disabilities, communication disorders, physical handicaps, and behavior disorders. The federal definition of a severe emotional disturbance (behavior disorder) is found in the regulations of the Education for All Handicapped Children Act of 1975 (P.L. 94-142):

(i) The term means a condition exhibiting one or more of the following characteristics over a long period of time and to

marked degree, which adversely affects educational performance:

(a) **An inability to learn which cannot be explained by intellectual, sensory, or health factors;**

(b) **An inability to build or maintain satisfactory interpersonal relationships with peers and teachers;**

(c) **Inappropriate types of behaviors or feelings under normal circumstances;**

(d) **A general pervasive mood of unhappiness or depression;**

(e) **A tendency to develop physical symptoms or fears associated with personal or school problems.**

(ii) **The term includes children who are schizophrenic. The term does not include children who are socially maladjusted, unless it is determined they are seriously emotionally disturbed (Education for All Handicapped Children Act of 1975, Section 121a.5).**

State definitions for the classification of behavior disorders generally are patterned after this federal definition because of funding requirements. If a child fits this definition, then the state educational system becomes eligible for federal funds. The basic components of most state definitions are found in Table 12-6 (Cullinan, Epstein, & McLinden, 1986).

The federal and state definitions of behavior disorders have been severely criticized (as reviewed by the U.S. Department of Education, 1985). First, some educators feel that the federal definition is so vague that it defies reliable use (Kauffman, 1982; Walker, Reavis, Rhode, & Jenson, 1985). Kauffman (1982) has stated that "One is forced to conclude that the federal definition is, if not claptrap, at least dangerously close to nonsense" (p. 4). Second, this definition overrepresents children who have internalizing problems (such as physical symptoms, fears, depression, and unhappiness), and ignores children with externalizing problems (Jenson, 1985). In fact, this definition does not define "socially maladjusted" children, but excludes them from special

Table 12-6
Components of State Definitions

1. *Disorders of emotion/behavior.* The student's emotions or behaviors are generally improper, immature, or show evidence of a specific form of disturbance.
2. *Interpersonal problems.* Limitations in developing and/or maintaining satisfactory social relations with peers or adults.
3. *Learning/achievement problems.* The student is having achievement or learning problems, or further, his or her emotional or behavior disorders are causing such problems.
4. *Deviation from norm.* Emotions or behaviors are unusual, inappropriate, or inferior with respect to some standard.
5. *Chronicity.* The problems are of long standing.
6. *Severity.* The problems are extremely serious or intense, or exhibited across several situations.
7. *Etiology.* The problems are clearly attributed to some causal phenomenon.
8. *Prognosis.* Special education and services are reserved for students who are most likely to improve.
9. *Exclusions.* Conditions that exempt the student from being defined as behaviorally disordered, even though he or she may evidence social, emotional, or learning problems like those previously mentioned.
10. *Special education needed.* The student is not suited for regular education or will be served more appropriately through some type of special services.
11. *Certification.* The student's eligibility for special services is based on approval by some designated individual or group, or is determined through specific assessment procedures.

Source: D. Cullinan, M. H. Epstein, and D. McLinden. (1986). Status and change in state administrative definitions of behavior disorder. *School Psychology Review, 15,* 383–392. Reprinted by permission.

education services. Clearly, this definition ignores the reality (validity) that most of the behaviorally disordered children referred for special education are socially maladjusted. Third, there are no studies on the reliability of educational classification systems. No one knows for sure how reliably these systems are applied, or whether they are applied in a capricious or biased manner.

It is ironic that the most frequently used classification system has poor validity and no known reliability characteristics. Educational classification is actually a politically and financially designed system, with no prescribed educational or treatment procedure. Once a child is educationally classified and placed, then other systems such as behavioral classification are generally used for educational and treatment purposes.

THE EFFECTS OF LABELING THROUGH CLASSIFICATION

Labeling, or diagnosis, is the end product of most classification processes. Such labeling should reduce uncertainty and should permit the beginning of research or treatment for a child. This is the ideal situation; in reality, however, labeling a child's behavior can produce several unanticipated harmful side effects.

The label of mental illness can adversely affect other's perceptions of a child's potential (Hobbs, 1975a; Jones, 1972; Mercer, 1975). An adolescent who has been labeled a delinquent may be distrusted by others and denied employment opportunities. Minority children who are incorrectly labeled as mentally retarded may be segregated into special education classes and denied the opportunities of regularly placed students. A child labeled as autistic or schizophrenic may be given up as hopeless and sent to languish in a large institution. Those labeled as having minimal brain dysfunction may cease trying to improve their own behavior, which they attribute to brain damage. In all of these situations, people react more to the labels than to the characteristics of the children. It is assumed that the labels accurately describes the children. In essence, the

children are depersonalized (Blashfield & Draguns, 1976b), and all of their special qualities and unique personality are ignored.

Opportunity is important to all of us, particularly in education and employment. Rather than opening doors to treatment and return to normalized environments, labeling can restrict or lock a child into dead-end placements. Gallagher (1972) estimates that only 10 percent of all children placed in special education classes and schools in large cities ever return to regular education placements. Nationally, only 45 percent of children labeled as behaviorally disordered are educated in regular or resource classrooms. The majority are placed in restrictive settings, such as self-contained classrooms, special schools, or homebound/hospital placements (U.S. Department of Education, 1985).

In her research on mentally retarded children in California, Jane Mercer found that in the 1970s only 19 percent of the special education students were ever mainstreamed or returned to regular school (cited in Krasner, 1976). A large percentage of children labeled as mentally retarded either dropped out of school without an adequate education (23 percent), were eventually expelled or sent to other restrictive placements such as institutions (46 percent), or were eventually deemed too old to complete the school program (12 percent). If used inappropriately, classification labels can lock many doors that lead back to normal environments.

The *self-fulfilling prophecy* is another important aspect of labeling. In this process, a child's behavior is actually shaped, though unknowingly, to conform to a label. A teacher or a parent may either consciously or unconsciously expect a child to behave in accordance with the diagnosis the child has been given, and the child eventually behaves that way consistently. In effect, the expectations (either correct or incorrect) held by a teacher or parent actually shape the anticipated behaviors of a child. For example, parents may be particularly alert to deviant or antisocial behavior if a child is labeled "predelinquent." Consequently, the parents may lecture and scold the child, and may attend particularly to her undesirable behavior and ignore her positive behavior. As a result, the child may behave even more antisocially than before she was labeled. The self-fulfilling effect of labeling can result from failure to look beyond the label at the child as an individual. Evidence exists that supports the self-fulfilling prophecy concept (Beez, 1968; Rivers, Henderson, Jones, Ladner, & Williams, 1975); Box 12-5 presents a well-known example of such research (Rosenthal & Jacobson, 1968). Although there are replication problems (Rosenthal & Jacobson, 1968) and methodological problems (Barber & Silver, 1968; Thorndike, 1968) with the study in Box 12-5, other research (Foster, Ysseldyke, & Reese, 1975; Ysseldyke & Foster, 1978) has found similar results.

Labels generally emphasize behavioral deficits and negative behaviors; rarely do they highlight positive behavior or accomplishments. This negative focus affects the teacher's expectation of handicapped children's capabilities (Foster et al., 1975; Ysseldyke & Foster, 1978). It also undoubtedly affects the child's view of herself. Some labels such as mental retardation are particularly damaging to the child's self-esteem, since no one is proud of being dull (Guskin, Bartel, & MacMillan, 1975). Children may try to appear normal even when the handicap is obvious, such as blindness or severe retardation (Edgerton, 1967; Goffman, 1963; Guskin et al., 1975; Jones, 1972). Labels may also affect parents, who may want their children to appear less handicapped and so may shop among clinicians to find one who will provide more socially acceptable labels. For example, learning disabilities may be considered more socially acceptable by parents than mental retardation or emotional disturbance.

The labeling process affects the child's parents, the expectations of the child's teachers, schooling opportunities, and the child's self-esteem. Individual information about the child is either lost or ignored through the labeling and classification process. So why label? Labeling is necessary to gain services for handicapped children and funds to support these services. With very few exceptions, funding is dependent on labeling (Gallagher, et al., 1975). Labeling has the

Children must be diagnostically labeled in order to receive special education services. Without labels, many handicapped children would not be served and later would have no recourse for special help.

effect of focusing society's attention on problems, and then interest groups such as those formed by affected families can press for solutions to these problems (Kolstoe, 1972). Without a diagnostic label that is given through an accepted classification process, a child probably will not receive services. As an illustration, let us consider the case of *Doe v. San Francisco Unified School District* (Martin, 1977). In this case, an 18-year-old high school student graduated from school but was functionally illiterate. The boy and his parents brought suit against the school district on grounds of negligence in failing to provide instruction in basic skills. Ultimately, the court could not decide on an acceptable standard of basic education for a normal (unlabeled) student, so the case was dismissed. Doe had never been labeled as educationally handicapped.

The opposite ruling might have occurred in the Doe case if he had been labeled and classified as handicapped. For example, a similar case in New Hampshire is currently being heard in which a National Honor Society student's parents are suing the school district for not providing appropriate special education services. The student, Karen, had difficulty reading and progressed to the ninth grade primarily by cheating: "I did a lot of taking other kids' papers, erasing their names. Just cheating mostly. I really didn't think about it.

BOX 12-5 • Pygmalion in the Classroom

Eliza: . . .You see, really and truly, apart from the things anyone can pick up (the dressing and the proper way of speaking, and so on), the difference between a lady and a flower girl is not how she behaves, but how she's treated. I shall always be a flower girl to Professor Higgins, because he always treats me as a flower girl, and always will; but I know I can be a lady to you, because you always treat me as a lady, and always will.

G. B. Shaw, *Pygmalion*

Eliza Doolittle, as the quote indicates, was a simple flower girl in a George Bernard Shaw play whom Professor Higgins transformed into a lady by training her to dress and speak properly. However, she was destined to be just a flower girl to Professor Higgins because he *expected* her to be so, no matter how ladylike she behaved.

Teachers can have similar expectations about their students, depending on the students' labels, as demonstrated in an experiment by Rosenthal and Jacobson (1968). In this experiment, children in the first through the sixth grades from the Oak School were tested by teachers using a nonverbal IQ test (Test of General Ability, or TOGA) at the beginning of the school year. Half of the children were randomly selected (the experimental group), and the teachers were told that the test scores indicated that these children would show unusual academic gains during the coming school year. The other half of the children who were tested (the control group) started the school year without a prediction of unusual academic gains. Actually, the experimental group did not differ significantly from the control group in IQ test scores; what was being tested was the effect of the teachers' expectations on the children's progress.

At the end of the year all the children were again tested with the TOGA IQ test, and the scores between the experimental and control groups were compared. The results (see Figure 12-1) show that the experimental-group children in the first and second grades made large gains in IQ points (15 more points for the first-graders and 9 more points for the second-graders) than the control group. Since the experimental group had not differed from the control group at the beginning of the school year, the difference in IQ points seemed to be a result of the teachers' expectation that the children in the experimental group would do better academ-

It was a question of survival" (1986). Although Karen was an honors student, student council president, and captain of the soccer team, she was also labeled learning-disabled in the ninth grade. The school authorities, however, "did little more than assure her she wasn't stupid" and provided little remedial work. Karen's parents placed her in a private remedial school, and now she is a college freshman. The important point is that Karen was labeled as handicapped and had grounds to sue for recovery of the special education costs (although the case is still being reviewed). Doe had never been labeled as handicapped, and his case was dismissed.

Labels are necessary, and they are here to stay in the treatment of children with behavior disorders. Clinicians must develop classification procedures to minimize the bad effects of labeling and to maximize accuracy and access to appropriate services. New approaches to classification are being developed for children that go beyond human capabilities and judgment.

ARTIFICIAL INTELLIGENCE AND CLASSIFICATION

Important new developments are being made in classification via artificial intelligence—that is, computer-based classification with *expert systems*. These systems are called "expert" because a

Box 12-5 (Continued)

FIGURE 12-1. Gains in total IQ in six grades.

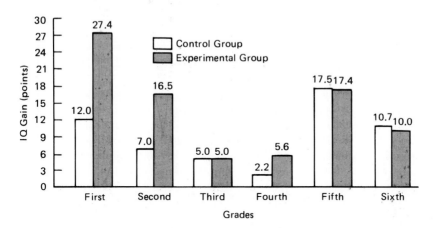

ically. The children in third through sixth grades in the experimental group, however, did not show large gains in IQ points when compared to their control groups. A possible reason why the older children did not differ is that these children had well-established reputations, and the teacher's expectations could not be easily changed.

No one knows exactly why the younger children made such large IQ gains. It might have been that since the teachers expected higher academic performance from this group, they gave these students more attention or encouragement, which resulted in better test scores.

Source: R. L. Rosenthal and L. Jacobson. (1968). *Pygmalion in the classroom: Teacher expectation and pupils' intellectual development* (New York: Holt, Rinehart and Winston). Copyright 1968 by Holt, Rinehart and Winston, Inc. Reprinted by permission of the publisher.

Table 12-7
Evaluation of Classification Systems

System	Reliability	Validity	Coverage	Parsimony	Mutually Exclusive Definitions	Usage
DSM-III-R	Fair	Fair	Moderate	Questionable	Questionable	Frequent
GAP	Fair	Fair	Broad	Questionable	Questionable	Infrequent
ICD-9	Fair	Fair	Moderate	Questionable	Questionable	Frequent (internationally)
Behavioral classification	Good	Good	Moderate	Good	Good	Moderate to infrequent
Educational classification	Questionable	Questionable	Broad	Questionable	Questionable	Frequent

computer is programmed to make decisions like a human expert. For example, A. Hoffmeister and J. Ferraro (personal communication, 1986) have programmed an IBM personal computer, using an artificial intelligence system called the MI-Infer-

ence Engine, to make classification decisions concerning handicapped children. Originally, the MI-Inference Engine system was developed at Stanford University to make difficult medical diagnoses. Hoffmeister and Ferraro (personal com-

---

BOX 12-6 • Marty, a Boy with Multiple Classifications

Marty is an 8-year-old boy who has had a great deal of difficulty during the past year getting along with his family and teachers. Basically, his problem is aggressive behavior—he just does not get along with anyone. When someone makes a request of Marty, he explodes and often breaks things and hurts people. Recently Marty's behavior came to a head when he was caught stealing money from his mother's purse. His mother locked his bicycle up for a week because of the stealing incident. To get even, he opened up a trap door in the bathroom which led to the basement and covered the opening with a rug. He then filled the bathtub full of water, got in, and started to scream to his mother for help. When she ran into the bathroom, she fell through the trap door and broke both her ankles.

Clearly, Marty has a behavior disorder in which aggression and the inability to take directions from adults are key problems. What follows is how a number of classification systems would diagnose his behavior.

GAP: *Personality disorder: tension discharge disorder.* Children in this category exhibit chronic behavioral patterns of emotional expression of aggressive and sexual impulses that conflict with society's norms. They directly act out their feelings or impulses toward people or society in antisocial or destructive fashion, rather than inhibiting or repressing these responses and developing other modes of psychological defense or symptomatology.

DSM-III-R: Conduct disorder, solitary aggressive type. The essential features are a failure to establish a normal degree of affection, empathy, or bonding with others; a pattern of aggressive antisocial behavior; and behavior difficulties at school.

Axis   I: **Clinical psychiatric syndrome: conduct disorder, solitary aggressive type**
Axis II: **Developmental disorder: reading disorder**
Axis:III: **Physical disorder: none**
Axis IV: **Psychosocial stressors: insufficient parental control**
Axis V: **Current global assessment functioning (GAF)—60 moderate**
            Past year (GAS)—50 serious symptoms

Behavioral classification: *High rates of aggressive behavior* (verbal and physical).

Antecedents: **Requests or commands from adults**
Behavior: **Excessive rates of hitting, temper tantrums, destruction of property**
Consequences: **Escape from or avoidance of complying to requests from parents and teachers**

Educational classification (Utah State Board of Education): *Behaviorally handicapped.* A behaviorally handicapped child is distinguished by inability or difficulty in handling problems, or by ineffective methods of adjusting or coping. Behaviorally handicapped children tend to resort to immature, unrealistic, aggressive, acting-out, withdrawal, or avoidance behaviors in trying to find solutions.

munication, 1986) have adapted the system to diagnose learning-disabled and behaviorally handicapped children. They have programmed the system to hold in its memory the state educational systems classification rules, the federal classification rules, and 600 research findings concerning the accurate classification of learning-disabled children. The system repeatedly asks for information about a child, consults the rules and research findings held in its memory, and then gives a probability statement that a child is actually learning-disabled.

The accuracy of a diagnosis using this system is dependent on the quality of the information that is fed into it. However, when compared to human judgment using the same information, the computer was 50 percent more accurate in diagnosing learning disabilities. This process will not replace human clinicians, but it is now being used as a second opinion with difficult cases. In the future, it may also recommend research-based intervention strategies for behaviorally handicapped children.

SUMMARY

Classification systems vary as to their use (funding, placement, treatment, and/or research) and their theoretical foundations (medical, behavioral, or educational); accordingly, the systems differ in soundness and usage. Table 12-7 lists the various classification systems reviewed in this chapter and shows how each system might be evaluated against a criterion. As Table 12-7 indicates, when we expect too much from a classification system and want a category for every possible disorder, we get a system with overly extensive coverage and reduced reliability. This often happens when funding is dependent on labels. When we expect specific treatment decisions from a classification system and recognize that each system is limited, then we get better reliability and validity and a narrowing of coverage. Box 12-6 gives a short history of a child with a behavior disorder and then classifies the child's behavior according to a number of the systems reviewed.

What is important to remember about classification systems and their uses with children is that all classification systems are imperfect models, with the imperfections being dependent on the primary uses of the system and its theoretical foundations. Second, no *child* is classified; only the child's *behavior* is classified. If we classify a child and speak of him only as having the disorder, then we may stigmatize the child and expect and stimulate difficult behaviors. If a child's problem *behavior* alone is classified, we assume that the child may have many strengths aside from the problem and that the problem behavior can be changed with appropriate treatment.

chapter

13

Assessment of Childhood Behavior Disorders

KEY TERMS

Assessment.   An information-gathering process that leads to decisions concerning classification, placement, treatment, and program evaluation.

Behavioral Observation.   An assessment technique in which data are collected by observing a subject and then recording the occurrence of behaviors using an observation code.

Criterion-Referenced Test.   A test that emphasizes a child's absolute mastery of a specific skill area or behavior.

False Positive.   An error in which an assessment process has positively identified a problem when one does not exist.

Norm-Referenced Test.   A test that emphasizes a child's relative standing in comparison to a group of children.

Psychological Test.   An objective and standardized measure of a sample of behavior.

Structured Interview.   An interview in which a subject is asked a set of predetermined questions concerning a problem or situation.

Utility.   The extent to which the assessment information gathered is used to make a cost-effective decision.

OVERVIEW OF ASSESSMENT

What does it take to accurately assess behaviorally disordered children? Are complicated psychological measures needed to identify such children? Or can parents and teachers easily and accurately identify them? What are the advantages and limitations of psychological assessment?

In this chapter, we answer these questions and discuss several assessment methods that are used to make decisions concerning children's behavior problems. We review specific assessment techniques, such as psychological testing, psychiatric interviewing, and behavioral observation. In addition, we discuss criteria for judging the adequacy of assessment procedures and offer recommendations for judging assessment practices.

Assessment: A Definition

Assessment can be like politics or religion. It is difficult to get a consensus from professionals about such basic issues as an accepted definition for assessment. Table 13-1 lists several definitions of assessment from a number of leading textbooks on the subject. The first thing that stands out from this list is the diversity of the characteristics of assessment. However, most of these definitions do

Table 13-2
Types of Information and Collection Procedures Used in Assessment

Tests	Standardized intelligence and achievement tests
	Projective personality tests
	Objective personality tests
	Criterion-referenced tests
Observations	Objective behavior observations by an independent observer
	Self-monitoring
	Behavior ratings by teachers or parents
Interviews	Behavioral interviews
	Social history interviews
	Child psychiatric examinations

emphasize some common features. First, precise *measurement* is stressed in most of these definitions. Second, comprehensive *information gathering* is essential to good assessment practices.

Assessment methods used to gather information can vary from systematic procedures (such as structured behavioral observation) to relatively unstructured procedures (such as informal interviews). Table 13-2 depicts the various types of information that can be gathered and the procedures that can be used to collect this information.

Table 13-1
Common Definitions of Assessment

1. Clinical assessment is the process in which clinicians gain understanding of the patient necessary for making informed decisions. (Korchin, 1976, p. 124)
2. Assessment refers to the procedures and processes employed in collecting information about or evidence of human behavior. (Shertzer & Linden, 1979, p. 13)
3. *Assessment*, a broader term, refers to the entire process involved in collecting information about persons and using it to make important predictions and inferences. (Graham & Lilly, 1984, p. 337)
4. Assessment: A procedure used to evaluate an individual so that he or she can be described in terms of current functioning and also so that predictions can be made concerning future functioning. Tests are used in the assessment process. (Kaplan & Saccuzzo, 1982, p. 521)
5. The technique of gaining information about someone else for use in making a decision— assessment—was undoubtedly part of the earliest social interactions when one cave person made a judgment about another. (Weiner & Stewart, 1983, p. 4)

Sources: J. R. Graham and R. S. Lilly. (1984). *Psychological testing* (Englewood Cliffs, NJ: Prentice-Hall); R. M. Kaplan and D. P. Saccuzzo. (1982). *Psychological testing: Principles, applications, and issues* (Monterey, CA: Brooks/Cole); S. J. Korchin. (1976). *Modern clinical psychology* (New York: Basic Books); B. Shertzer and J. D. Linden. (1979). *Fundamentals of individual appraisal: Assessment techniques for counselors* (Boston: Houghton Mifflin); E. A. Weiner and B. J. Stewart. (1983). *Assessing individuals: Psychological and educational tests and measures* (Boston: Little, Brown).

However, good assessment should go beyond merely collecting information; it involves decisions about classification, diagnosis, placement, and treatment (Cronbach, 1960; P. Cole, personal communication, 1978).

Classification and Diagnostic Decisions Most classification systems (medical, educational, and behavioral) base a diagnosis on some type of assessment information. For example, psychological tests and psychiatric interviews are commonly used to arrive at a diagnosis.

Placement Few children are placed in special education or treatment settings without a decision that is at least partially based on assessment information. For example, before a child can be placed in most special education settings, he must be given a battery of academic, intellectual, and behavioral assessment measures to see whether a legitimate need exists for such a placement.

A battery of tests is needed because courts have seriously questioned the practice of using the sole judgment of a professional or just one test, such as an IQ test, as a criterion for placement (Martin, 1979). Too many abuses have occurred when just one test is used. For example, to reach decisions regarding the placement of retarded children, the American Association for Mental Deficiency suggests administering an IQ test as well as using a behavior checklist (the Adaptive Behavior Scales) that requires behavioral observation.

Treatment and Program Planning Good assessment procedures lead to specific treatment recommendations. For instance, some types of prescriptive checklists pinpoint a child's deficiencies and prescribe treatment programs.

Evaluation Assessment procedures such as psychological tests are frequently used to evaluate both an individual child's progress in a treatment program and the treatment program as a whole (Salvia & Ysseldyke, 1981). For example, academic achievement tests can be used to assess a child's academic achievement gains over a year's time. These tests are generally administered in the fall and then again in the spring to assess individual gains. It is also possible to average the scores from all the children in a special program from the fall and then to compare them to spring scores to determine how effective an academic program is as a whole.

In summary, assessment is a two-part process. First, measurements are taken and information is gathered. Second, decisions are made from the information regarding classification, placement, treatment, and evaluation of a child. The information-gathering phase of assessment substantially affects the appropriateness of the decisions made concerning the child. If the information is in error or inadequate, then the accuracy of decisions will be affected. It is critical to understand how the quality of assessment information is judged.

Standards for Assessment

Any type of assessment method is subject to error; no method is perfect. For instance, if we are trying to measure the motor activity of children in a classroom, and several of these children are ill, then our activity measurements will probably be lower than if the children were in good health. In a sense, the information gathered by an assessment method is only an approximation of the real phenomenon that is being measured, because of error. In our example, the random event that the children are sick results in an underestimate of motor activity. This type of error that happens by chance has been termed *random error* (Althauser & Herberlein, 1970; Carmines & Zeller, 1979; Nunnally, 1962; Wert & Linn, 1970). Another type of error that also affects assessment is *systematic error*. With systematic errors, the assessment procedure or the person using it is *always* off by a certain degree. With our example, a systematic error in measurement may occur because the pedometer (a device that measures activity) malfunctions and always records too low a record of motor activity. Both random and systematic errors are important because they are at the root of difficulties with assessment reliability and validity.

Reliability The *reliability* of an assessment procedure is a measure of the consistency of the procedure (Anastasi, 1982). For example, if a measure is repeatedly given, it is considered reliable if the same or similar scores are yielded each time. Conceptually, we can assume that the information given by an assessment device contains the true score (Swanson & Watson, 1982). However, on each administration of the assessment procedure random error is always present, and this affects the true score. If the assessment procedure is unreliable, then large amounts of random error are present, causing the assessment score to vary greatly. If only a small amount of random error is present, then the scores are similar and cluster around the true score. For example, if an intelligence test is repeatedly given to a child who has a true IQ score of 100, and the test results are 50, 107, 36, and 129, then the measure is unreliable. However, if the test scores are 105, 99, 103, and 101 (which are close to the true score of 100), then the test is reliable. Factors that reduce the degree of consistency of information and result in significant random error include the following:

1. **Ambiguous assessment procedures that leave a great deal of interpretation up to the evaluator.**
2. **Poorly trained evaluators who are not familiar with the assessment procedures.**
3. **Widely changing or varying behavior of the children being evaluated (as in our example of motor activity and ill children).**
4. **Growth and development, which cause differences in children's ability and behavior (common when significant periods of time elapse between assessments).**
5. **Varying assessment conditions, such as a loud or distracting environment.**

There are two basic types of reliability that are important in judging assessment procedures for children. Our example of repeated IQ testing is an example of *test-retest reliability,* which is obtained by using an assessment measure, waiting, and then readministering the procedure. If the results are similar for the occasions on which the assessment procedure is repeated, then the procedure has good test-retest reliability.

Interrater reliability is different from test-retest reliability in that two evaluators use the same assessment procedure at the same time on the same subject. For example, a behavioral observation code may be used by two observers simultaneously watching a child in a classroom. If both observers record similar scores for the child, the coding system is considered to have good reliability.

If the information that is gathered by an assessment measure is not reliable, then a child is at risk. If the measure has poor test-retest reliability, then it becomes difficult to use the measure to judge treatment effectiveness. Is the difference between the assessment measures taken before and after treatment a function of the treatment's effectiveness or an artifact of random error? Similarly, interrater reliability is important in identifying behaviorally disordered children. If one observer judges a child's behavior to be problematic and another judges it to be normal, then the disagreement may result in the child's not getting help.

Validity Although reliability is a measure of random error, it is not a measure of systematic error, which also affects assessment information. Validity is a much better measure of systematic error. As stated in Chapter 12, *validity* is a reality check on how accurately a procedure measures what it purports to measure (Anastasi, 1982). For instance, if a new test purports to diagnose children's behavior disorders accurately, we may compare the results of the new test on several children with the diagnostic judgment of a group of experienced clinical psychologists. If the test's results closely match the results from the psychologists, we assume that it has good validity. However, if the results are not similar, we may question the test's validity. It is important to point out in this example that if the test has poor validity, it will always (or systematically) be in disagreement with the psychologists' judgment. If the test has poor reliability, it will sometimes agree and sometimes disagree (randomly), with the psychologists' results.

It is also important to point out that the criterion (in this example, the psychologists' diagnostic judgment) that is used to judge the new test must be valid to make this procedure useful. If neither assessment procedure (the criterion measure or the new test) has high validity, one cannot be used as a criterion against which to judge the other. This type of validity is called *concurrent validity*, because the new assessment procedure is administered at the same time (concurrently) as the valid criterion (the psychologists' judgment). Good concurrent validity is necessary if a new assessment measure is going to be accepted and used by practitioners in the field.

Similar to concurrent validity is *predictive validity*, in which predictions about the future are made. For predictive validity, the criterion variable that is used in judging an assessment procedure is some type of future outcome. For example, if an autistic child has an intelligence score of 50 or lower and has no language, then the future outcome for the child will probably be poor (institutionalization, unemployment, dependence). In this example, the IQ score and language ability overshadow all other variables in predicting the future. They will have good predictive validity in forecasting the future of autistic children if indeed autistic children have poor outcomes that exhibit these characteristics. Unfortunately, they do (Rutter, 1978).

Other types of validity used to judge the adequacy of assessment procedures include content, construct, and face validity. *Content validity* is the extent to which an assessment device actually contains or represents items found in the content area that it is designed to measure. The sampling of assessment items should be sufficient to give an adequate representation of the area being assessed (Messick, 1980; Swanson & Watson, 1982). For example, a social skills behavior checklist used to assess a child's peer relations should contain enough items to adequately represent the essential skills needed to interact with peers. An example of such a checklist is illustrated in Figure 13-1 (Brown, Black, & Downs, 1984). Academic achievement tests constitute another case in which content validity is important. If an achievement test purports to measure the arithmetic skills of third-graders, then the test should have some arithmetic problems from the third-grade curriculum. Sattler (1982, p. 23) has listed three basic questions that are central in establishing the content validity of an assessment measure:

1. **Are the questions appropriate test questions and does the test measure the domain of interest?**
2. **Does the test contain enough information to cover appropriately what it is supposed to measure?**
3. **What is the level of mastery at which the content is being assessed?**

Construct validity indicates how well an assessment procedure represents a *theoretical construct* such as a trait, ability, or characteristic (Anastasi, 1982). Such theoretical constructs include extroversion and dependency (traits), intelligence and creativity (abilities), and depression, anxiety, and honesty (characteristics). Construct validity is measured in an indirect way, by using test scores to predict some other features of the test taker's behavior. For instance, if a test actually measures anxiety, then children who score high on anxiety should behave differently from children who score low. Anxiety often interferes with performance on demanding tasks, such as solving difficult mathematics problems. If children who score high on the anxiety test also perform more poorly on demanding tasks than do children with low anxiety, then we may conclude that the test has measured the construct of anxiety. Of course, the high- and low-scoring children would have to be matched on other variables such as intelligence and quantitative ability, which could also affect performance on the difficult mathematical problems. Construct validity is very important for personality inventories and behavior checklists that rely upon *factor analysis* (a statistical procedure used to identify behaviors or traits that cluster together or are related to each other) to diagnose behavior disorders.

A test is said to have good *face validity* if the test appears to a test developer to be relevant and valid. Generally, items are first selected by a test developer because she feels they represent a content area. This initial item selection is based on personal judgment and experience of the test developer. It can never be a substitute for the more rigorous forms of validity that have already been discussed. Many items have to be discarded when they are found to be inadequate according to other validity measures.

FIGURE 13-1. **Example of a social skills behavior checklist.**

PEER RELATIONS

Rate each of the following behaviors using the 1–6 scale according to your observations of how frequently the student displays the behavior under appropriate conditions with peers in the classroom and in other areas of the school (hallway, lunchroom, playground, etc.)

PEER RELATIONS TARGET BEHAVIORS

Write the number(s) of the skill(s) that were given a

rating of 2, 3, or 4: _____

1 — No opportunity to observe the behavior
2 — Never uses the skill
3 — Rarely uses the skill
4 — Occasionally uses the skill and/or uses it at incorrect times
5 — Often uses the skill under appropriate conditions
6 — Always uses the skill under appropriate conditions

1	2	3	4	5	6	
☐	☐	☐	☐	☐	☐	13. COMPLIES WITH REASONABLE REQUESTS to help or share with peers.
☐	☐	☐	☐	☐	☐	14. ACCEPTS CRITICISM from peers regarding his/her possible inappropriate behavior.
☐	☐	☐	☐	☐	☐	15. ACCEPTS "NO" FOR AN ANSWER when requests are denied or when not getting his/her way with peers.
☐	☐	☐	☐	☐	☐	16. GREETS when encountering familiar peers.
☐	☐	☐	☐	☐	☐	17. INTRODUCES SELF when encountering unfamiliar peers.
☐	☐	☐	☐	☐	☐	18. MAKES REQUESTS before using peers' belongings or when approaching peers to ask for help, explanations, instructions, etc.
☐	☐	☐	☐	☐	☐	19. GIVES COMPLIMENTS about qualities or accomplishments of peers.
☐	☐	☐	☐	☐	☐	20. ACCEPTS COMPLIMENTS from peers praising or recognizing him/her.
☐	☐	☐	☐	☐	☐	21. MAKES CONVERSATION when in the company of peers in informal situations.
☐	☐	☐	☐	☐	☐	22. PARTICIPATES IN ACTIVITIES with peers in informal situations.
☐	☐	☐	☐	☐	☐	23. DISAGREES APPROPRIATELY when not understanding or disagreeing with peers' criticisms or denials.
☐	☐	☐	☐	☐	☐	24. GIVES NEGATIVE FEEDBACK to peers regarding their possible inappropriate behavior.
☐	☐	☐	☐	☐	☐	25. RESISTS PEER PRESSURE when urged to participate with peers engaging in inappropriate behavior.
☐	☐	☐	☐	☐	☐	26. REPORTS PEER BEHAVIOR to adults when peers are about to or have engaged in serious inappropriate behavior, and ignores minor inappropriate behavior.
☐	☐	☐	☐	☐	☐	27. APOLOGIZES voluntarily to peers after engaging in inappropriate or accidental behavior.
☐	☐	☐	☐	☐	☐	28. VOLUNTEERS to assist peers when it appears they may need assistance.

Source: L. J. Brown, D. D. Black, and J. C. Downs. (1984). *School Social Skills Rating Scale* (East Aurora, NY: Slosson Educational). Reprinted by permission.

Other factors that affect the adequacy of assessment of children include the reactivity of the assessment procedure and the ability of the procedure to handle substantial developmental changes in children. *Reactivity* is the extent to which an assessment procedure itself alters the behavior of the subject who is being assessed (Foster & Cone, 1986; Goldfried & Linehan, 1977; Harris & Lahey, 1982). If an observer goes to a classroom to collect data on a child, and the observer's presence makes the child behave atypically, then we get an invalid estimate of the child's behavior. In this case, the observer may be a stranger who stands out in the class and makes the child feel uncomfortable. Similarly, if giving the child a test booklet causes him to become so anxious that he cannot perform at his best, then the information gathered by the test is an inaccurate estimate of the child's true potential. In these examples, the observer's obtrusive presence or the test booklet's intimidating presentation have altered the actual behavior of the child being assessed.

The child's developmental level can also affect the validity of an assessment measure. If a child is too young or developmentally incapable of responding to the assessment procedure (for instance, a procedure that requires writing), then the procedure is not valid for use with the child. An example in which a child's developmental level can interfere with a test's construct and predictive validity is seen in the use of some intelligence tests with very young children. Intelligence tests given to children younger than age 5 do not correlate well with measures taken when the child is older, such as readministered intelligence tests or academic performance. This issue is discussed more fully when intelligence tests are reviewed.

In summary, validity is a measure of systematic error in assessment that can affect a procedure's usefulness. Factors that can limit the validity of a measure include the following:

1. **The wrong or irrelevant content area is sampled.**
2. **The measure's reactivity affects the behavior of the child being assessed.**
3. **The child's developmental level is inade-**
quate to meet the demands of the procedure.
4. **The measure's reliability is low, thus setting an upper limit on validity.**

Utility   Assessment information is only valuable if it is used to make decisions concerning a behaviorally disordered child's placement and treatment. Without these decisions, the assessment process is only half accomplished. Yet many behaviorally disordered children are expensively assessed with little thought about treatment. The last method used to judge the adequacy of an assessment technique is the utility of the technique in making practical decisions. The *utility* of an assessment procedure is the extent to which the assessment information gathered is used to make a cost-effective decision (Cronbach, 1960; Hartmann, Roper, & Bradford, 1979).

In judging the practical utility of an assessment procedure, three general questions have to be answered (Wiggins, 1973):

1. **What is the percentage of correct and incorrect decisions made using the assessment measure?**
2. **What are the values or costs associated with making a correct or incorrect decision?**
3. **What are the costs involved in getting the assessment information?**

The importance of the first and second questions is fundamental to any assessment technique. No practitioner, teacher, or parent wants to use an assessment technique that can lead to incorrect decisions. However, many assessment techniques lead to dubious decisions if they are used incorrectly or with the wrong population. The cost of an incorrect decision also varies with the type of behavior disorder. For example, making a wrong decision and not identifying an autistic child for treatment may later have dramatic implications for the child. When a condition truly exists and it is missed, this type of error is called a *false negative*. In this example, valuable time is wasted that could have been used for early intervention.

In the opposite type of situation, an assessment technique might incorrectly identify a child as having a behavior disorder. This type of error may not be costly if the behavior disorder is a relatively minor condition, such as an adjustment reaction. However, the costs can be quite high if the behavior disorder is stigmatizing. For example, identifying culturally or racially different children as mentally retarded because they score poorly on an intelligence test can have damaging results. This type of error is called a *false positive*. The word *positive* may be a bit confusing here; it means that the assessment process has positively identified a problem when one does not exist.

The last question concerning utility is important and often overlooked. The cost of collecting the information is important for parents, insurance companies, and taxpayers, who have to pay the bills for assessment. If information is expensively collected and does not address treatment issues, then by definition the assessment procedure has poor utility. Accuracy in decisions and cost-effectiveness are central to good utility. Inexpensive but erroneous information is no bargain. Correct information that is extremely expensive to gather also has limited utility. Good utility is balanced on the correctness of the information, its cost, and the decisions based on the information.

PSYCHOLOGICAL TESTS

Generally, when people think of assessment, they think of psychological tests. These tests are used to assess characteristics ranging from a child's academic abilities to her fantasy life. In general, "a psychological test is essentially an objective and standardized measure of a sample of behavior" (Anastasi, 1982, p. 22). An important aspect of this definition is the term *standardized measure,* because it indicates that explicitly defined procedures are to be employed in administering the test. Intelligence tests, academic achievement tests, and personality tests for children are all standardized so that comparisons can be made between the children now taking the test and the group of children on whom the test was first developed.

The standardization of a test can be viewed as a psychological experiment in which the con-

ditions (procedures) are held constant so that an accurate result can be obtained. Holding the testing conditions *constant* generally means the following:

1. **The same items or test questions are given in the same order to all subjects.**
2. **The same test instructions are given to all subjects in an identical fashion.**
3. **All subjects have the same amount of time to finish the test.**
4. **The testing environment is held relatively constant and free from noise and distraction for all subjects. (Korchin, 1976, pp. 201–203)**

If these conditions are met, then the results obtained from the standardization group define what is normal for other children, and these results are commonly referred to as testing "norms" (see Box 13-1). Groups of children included in the standardization sample should generally resemble those who will be tested later. The sample should reflect the characteristics of the population of children with whom the test will be used routinely. For example, the standardization group should be of the appropriate age, developmental level, ethnic background, socioeconomic level, and geographical distribution (Anastasi, 1982).

What Tests Measure

Our definition of a *psychological test* includes the idea that a person's behavior is sampled. This definition emphasizes the fact that some type of behavior, whether it is academic performance, intellectual ability, or abnormal behavior, is directly sampled or observed in a specific situation. Once the sample has been collected or the observation has been made in a situation, then comparisons to standardized norms can be made to determine the child's abilities and deficiencies.

There are alternative views to this *sample-situation approach,* which propose that psychological tests measure *traits* and *states* (this view is described but not advocated by Mischel, 1968, 1979). The trait view holds that test scores are signs of underlying traits that govern behavior. These traits are assumed to be stable across time and situations. In a sense, a trait is a shorthand

BOX 13-1 • The Normal Curve and Assessment

The *normal curve* is a mathematical concept that allows meaningful comparisons of different assessment scores. An example of the normal or "bell"-shaped curve is given in Figure 13-2. Actually, this curve is a representation of many scores; some are high, some are low, but most of them are average. The *average* or *mean score* is represented on the curve by the ✕. The hump at the average indicates that most scores are average or near-average. As we get to the extreme scores (at the ends of the curve), the curve gets flatter, indicating that there are fewer scores in these ranges. The SDs on the curve are *standard deviation markers.* A standard deviation is a statistical measure of variability on the curve. It is also an indicator of the percentage of scores that fall within the standard deviation markers. For example, approximately 68 percent of all the scores are 1 standard deviation up and 1 standard deviation down from the mean. Also, standard deviations can be measured from the ends of the curve. For example, 97.7 percent of all the scores fall on or below the +2 SD mark on the curve.

FIGURE 13-2. Normal curve with T and Z scores.

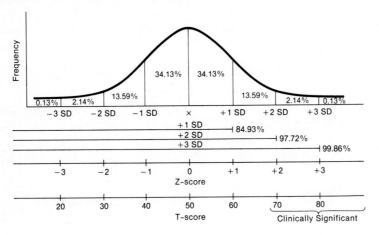

The normal curve is important for assessment because it allows a psychologist to make meaningful judgments about how average or different a particular score might be. If a score is average, we know that approximately 50 percent of all the other scores are above and 50 percent are below the average score. In a sense, the average score is right in the middle of the distribution. Also, if a score is +2 SD from the mean, it is in the range that many psychological tests and checklists describe as "clinically different." For instance, if a score on the hyperactivity factor of the Achenbach Child Behavior Profile is +2 SD from the mean, then the score is considered clinically significant. This is because 98 percent of all the other children in the standardization group fell on or below this mark. Only 2 percent (a very small number) of the children in this group were above the +2 SD mark. This 2 percent would have been the very hyperactive children.

There are also several different types of standard scores that are used in assessment. A T-score has a mean of 50 and a standard deviation of 10. A Z-score has a mean of 0 and a standard deviation of 1. These scores are important because such tests as the Personality Inventory for Children (PIC) and the Achenbach Child Behavior Profile use T-scores in measuring a child's performance on the normal curve. These tests are discussed in detail later in this chapter.

method of describing a child's personality or behavior. Trait words are engrained in our everyday language and are used to describe a child's behavior, irrespective of his immediate surroundings or history. For example, a child might be labeled lazy, outgoing (extroverted), shy (introverted), or dependent.

There is no simple answer to the question of the trait versus sample-situation approach in psychological assessment (Ozer, 1986). Some theorists believe that behavioral stability varies across situations according to the individual assessed (Bem & Allen, 1974). Others feel that if averages from several people are used to determine a trait, then important sources of individual differences are lost (Mischel, 1983). Single test measures of a trait have generally had poor reliability and validity across situations (Mischel, 1968). However, multiple measures of a trait over several situations and times improve the reliability and validity of a trait measure (Epstein, 1979). For example, a single test that reports a child as being an "aggressive type" would probably have poor reliability. However, several confirming measures, including the test score, a teacher interview, and an observation of the child in school, would be far more reliable and valid.

Possibly the best answer to the trait versus sample-situation controversy is the compromise position of the *interactionalists* (Bowers, 1973; Ekenhammer, 1974), who believe that behavior is a product of both the person (traits) and the situation. According to this view, people do have traits that govern their behavior; however, situations are always exerting strong effects that can influence traits. For assessment purposes, the interactionalists value multiple measures of traits and the recognition of the powerful effects of environmental situations on behavior.

Intelligence Tests

When the term "psychological test" is mentioned, many individuals think of intelligence tests with their accompanying complex tasks, questions, and puzzles. These tests were originally designed as a series of complex problems to screen children for academic readiness. In 1905, Alfred Binet was appointed by the French Ministry of Public Instruction to design an intelligence test consisting of 30 subtests containing problems of increasing difficulty, which were designed to measure children's judgment, reasoning, and comprehension (Anastasi, 1982; Sattler, 1982). The original version of Binet's test (Binet & Simon, 1905) was developed by administering the test problems to normal children as well as to mentally retarded children and adults. What made Binet's work unique was the development of norms so that comparison could be made between handicapped and nonhandicapped children (Sattler, 1982).

Shortly after Binet's original work, L. M. Terman (1916) helped refine and standardize the test on American children. Terman and others (Stern, 1914) developed the idea of the IQ or intelligence quotient for use in comparing the relative intelligence of children at different ages. To calculate an IQ, a child's mental age (as determined by how well she does on the test) is divided by her chronological age and multiplied by 100 (IQ = mental age/chronological age $\times$ 100). For example, if the child scores on the test at the 76-month level (mental age) and is 8 years old (chronological age is thus 96 months), then her IQ would be 80 (76/96 $\times$ 100). The average child has a mental age approximately equal to his chronological age, and so has an IQ of approximately 100 (i.e., IQ 100 = 96 months mental age/96 months chronological age $\times$ 100).

Since the Binet intelligence test was first devised, many types of intelligence tests for children have been developed (see Table 13-3). One of the most frequently used children's intelligence tests is the Wechsler Intelligence Scale for Children—Revised (WISC-R). A basic advantage of the WISC-R is that it combines both verbal subscales and performance or motor subscales in assessing a child's intellectual ability (see Table 13-4). The WISC-R thus yields an overall intelligence score, plus separate verbal and performance IQ scores, which can be useful in assessing children who are more proficient in one area than the other.

Both the Stanford-Binet and the WISC-R are popular intelligence tests for children, and both have good reliability characteristics. However,

Standardized materials and procedures are used in IQ testing.

there is a great deal of controversy over the construct validity of intelligence tests—that is, over exactly what intelligence is.

Binet (Binet & Simon, 1905) considered intelligence to be a set of abilities comprising comprehension, reasoning, judgment, and the ability to adapt. Wechsler (1958, p. 7) has similarly defined intelligence to be a set of abilities including the capacity "to act purposefully, to think rationally, and to deal effectively with the environment." All of these definitions rely on an indirect measure of intelligence by sampling selected behaviors under controlled conditions. In essence, intelligence is inferred:

No one, however, has seen a thing called intelligence. Rather, we observe differences in the ways people behave—either difference in everyday behavior in a variety of situations or differences in responses to standard stimuli or sets of stimuli; then we *infer* a construct called *intelligence*. In this sense,

intelligence is an inferred entity, a term or construct we use to explain differences in present behavior and to predict differences in future behavior. (Salvia & Ysseldyke, 1981, p. 244)

The "predicted differences" depend upon what intelligence tests sample and measure, and these tests primarily measure the following: (1) *verbal ability,* which is associated with general information and language acquired at home; and a general factor of (2) *perceptual* and *performance* ability associated with reasoning, problem solving, and comprehension. Other factors that may be measured by intelligence tests include the ability to attend to a task, numerical reasoning, recall, and memory. Since all of these abilities are particularly important in school settings, intelligence tests are good at predicting success in schools (Aiken, 1979; Anastasi, 1982; Hallahan & Kauffman, 1986).

The standardized intelligence tests for school-

Table 13-3

Types of Intelligence Tests for Children

Wechsler Intelligence Scale for Children—Revised (WISC-R). This is one of the best intelligence tests for children through adolescence (6–16 years). It contains both a verbal and a nonverbal performance component and yields a Verbal IQ, a Performance IQ, and a Full Scale IQ. Excellent reliability and validity characteristics.

Wechsler Preschool and Primary Scale of Intelligence (WPPSI). This test is similar to the WISC-R, except that it is used with younger children (4 to 6). It also yields a Verbal IQ, a Performance IQ, and a Full Scale IQ. Excellent reliability and validity characteristics. The WPPSI is currently under revision.

Standord-Binet Intelligence Test. This test is an outgrowth of Binet's early work with intelligence. It has been revised several times, with the newest revision done in 1986. It yields a global measure of intelligence and can be used with children from ages 2 to 12. Excellent reliability and validity.

Slosson Intelligence Test. This test has been modeled after the Stanford-Binet but is much shorter. It can be used with individuals from age 5 to age 27. Its standardization has been criticized, and it should be used not as a complete intelligence test but as a screening test.

Leiter International Performance Scale (LIPS). This is a nonverbal intelligence test that is useful for individuals who cannot talk. The test is a series of puzzles based on small blocks. The test can be used with 2-year-old children up to adults. This test has been criticized because the norms are outdated and the standardization is inadequate. It should be used with children only when other, verbally based intelligence tests cannot be used.

Kaufman Assessment Battery for Children (K-ABC). This intelligence test is designed for children ages 2 to 12. It assesses two types of intellectual processing: simultaneous processing and successive processing. This test has excellent reliability and validity characteristics, but more research is needed to determine whether it adds any useful information that the WISC-R or the Stanford-Binet misses.

age children are not always applicable to younger preschool children. The reason is that assessment of infants and preschoolers differs from the assessment of older children in several ways. Younger children tend to be less motivated, to be more distractible, and to have less sophisticated verbal skills than older children. Most infant and preschool intelligence tests measure motor ability and developing social behavior. The results from intelligence tests for very young children and infants correlate poorly with the children's later intellectual ability at school age (Bayley, 1970; Lewis, 1973; McCall, Hogarty, & Hurlburt, 1972; Thomas, 1970). Infant intelligence tests such as the Cattell Infant Intelligence Scale or the Bayley Infant Scales best predict conditions associated with neurological abnormalities or developmental disorders. Infant and preschool tests are limited, however, in predicting later school performance or behavior disorders.

While intelligence scores are fairly good predictors of school achievement for older children, the exact relationship between intelligence test results and childhood behavior disorders is less clear. There appears to be a direct link between later adjustment (prognosis) and a child's IQ score for the conditions of mental retardation (Ando & Yoshimura, 1978) and infantile autism (DeMyer, Hingtgen, & Jackson, 1981; Rutter, 1978). The lower the IQ score, the poorer the prognosis for these conditions. For children with conduct disorder and attention deficit disorder, the relationship with intelligence is less clear. Kauffman (1985), in his review of behaviorally disordered children, found that these children tended to score in the dull-normal range. Sattler (1982) has reported that on average delinquents have higher scores on the Performance IQ than on the Verbal IQ for the Wechsler Intelligence Tests. However, this difference is not consistent enough to be a diagnostic sign for deliquency (Sattler, 1982). For children with attention deficit disorder, Weiss and Hechtman (1986) have reviewed a series of studies and reported that IQ can be an important variable in predicting academic success and adult outcome for these children, particularly when combined

Table 13-4

The Verbal and Performance Subscales of the Wechsler Intelligence Scale for Children—
Revised (WISC-R)

Verbal Subscales

Information: A series of 30 questions that assess a child's knowledge of the world and his culture.

Comprehension: A series of 17 questions that require answers measuring social judgment, common sense, and the ability of the child to organize information.

Arithmetic: Eighteen timed questions that measure elementary knowledge of arithmetic and the ability of the child to concentrate.

Similarities: Seventeen pairs of words such as "In what way are a wheel and ball alike?" The child must explain the relationship or basis for the similarity.

Vocabulary: Thirty-two words listed in order of increasing difficulty (ranging from "knife" to "dilatory") that the child must define. This subscale is designed to measure a comprehension of words, which is highly correlated with general intelligence.

Digit Span: This optional subscale consists of a series of numbers ranging in length from two digits (2-5) to eight digits (6-9-1-6-3-2-5-8). In the Digits Forward test, the child must repeat the number after the examiner says it. In the Digits Backward test, the child must repeat the numbers backwards after hearing them said forwards. The Digit Span subtest measures a child's ability to attend and concentrate as well as his immediate rote memory.

Performance Subscales

Picture Completion: The child must tell what is missing in a series of pictures. The subscale measures visual alertness, memory, and attention to details.

Picture Arrangement: A series of 12 cartoon drawings on separate cards, which must be arranged in a story-telling sequence. This is a timed subtest that measures the child's ability to identify causal sequences and arrange them in a temporal sequence.

Block Design: A timed test in which a child must reproduce a design printed on a card by arranging a series of blocks. This subtest measures a child's dexterity and ability to visually analyze a design into component parts.

Object Assembly: A timed subtest in which the child is required to put together picture puzzles consisting of a girl, a horse, a car, and a face. This subtest measures visual-motor coordination, thinking, and persistence.

Coding: A timed subtest in which two unrelated symbols must be memorized and written down. For example, the number 3 is paired with a + sign. Each time the child encounters the number 3 on the worksheet he must write a +. This subtest measures writing ability, memory, and attention to detail.

Mazes: A timed optional subtest in which a child is required to solve a series of maze problems with an increasing number of blind alleys. This subtest measures problem-solving skills, visual-motor coordination, and persistence.

Adapted from D. Wechsler. (1958). *The measurement and appraisal of adult intelligence,* 4th ed (Baltimore: Williams & Wilkins).

with other factors such as socioeconomic status, presence of learning disabilities, and family conditions. The links between IQ and other childhood disorders, such as suicide (Pfeffer, 1986) or anxiety disorders (Gittelman, 1986), are less robust.

In summary, standardized intelligence tests have good test-retest reliability and interrater reliability. For construct validity, there are some disagreements; however, for predictive validity, intelligence tests have value in forecasting later academic achievement and adjustment for school-age children. The diagnostic utility of intelligence tests is limited. Clearly, intellectual assessment is important in diagnosing mental retardation and infantile autism, both in defining the severity of the condition and in estimating the child's prognosis and future outcome; for other types of behavior disorders, however, intelligence tests are less useful. For very young children, intelligence tests are best at uncovering developmental delays and have limited predictive validity for school performance or the development of behavior disorders. Intelligence tests have virtually *no* utility by themselves in identifying behaviorally disordered children. Characteristics such as *subtest patterning* (specific patterns of subtest scores) or the difference between Verbal and Performance IQ scores are not reliable or valid in identifying behaviorally disordered children (Mark, 1984; Sattler, 1982).

Projective Tests

Projective techniques are very different from standardized intelligence tests. The latter are based on standardized groups and permit users to make comparisons among children. Most projective tests are not based on rigorous standardization procedures, but stem from the *projective hypothesis* (Anastasi, 1982; Sundberg, 1977) — that is, the assumption that a child is driven by underlying psychological forces such as sexual and aggressive urges. These urges emerge early in a child's development and are affected by family interactions. It is thought that for some children, these underlying forces can be so disturbing that they are blocked from consciousness by repression and denial. To attempt to reveal the unconscious urges, projective techniques employ ambiguous or open-ended stimuli on which the child has to project meaning and structure; thus, in an indirect way, they may reveal unconscious conflicts.

A major distinguishing feature of projective techniques is to be found in their assignment of a relatively *unstructured* task, i.e., a task that permits an almost unlimited variety of responses. In order to allow free play to the individual's fantasy, only brief general instructions are provided. For the same reason, the test stimuli are usually vague or ambiguous. The underlying hypothesis is that the way in which the individual perceives and interprets material, or "structures" the situation, will reflect fundamental aspects of her or his psychological functioning. In other words, it is expected that the test materials will serve as a sort of screen on which respondents "project" their characteristic thought processes, needs, anxieties, and conflicts. (Anastasi, 1982, p. 564)

The projective hypothesis is based primarily on psychoanalytic assumptions regarding children's behavior. Pathological traits and underlying emotional forces are supposedly revealed by deviant responses to the ambiguous projective stimuli. The assessment of direct samples of behavior collected under standardized testing conditions is de-emphasized as revealing only shallow surface symptoms.

Projective techniques can be categorized into five basic groups (Lindzey, 1959, 1961):

1. *Association techniques.* A child is asked to tell what she sees in a set of materials (such as inkblots) or to give the first word that comes into her mind after the therapist says a word *(word association).*
2. *Construction techniques.* In this approach, a child is asked to create a product such as a story after she has seen some test materials (for example, in the Thematic Apperception Test the child makes up a story to accompany a set of pictures).
3. *Completion techniques.* A child is asked to complete a statement or brief story *(sentence completion test).*
4. *Choice-of-ordering technique.* A child is asked to rank a set of materials in order of preference (for example, to indicate which of a set of picture activities would be most enjoyable).
5. *Expressive techniques.* A child is asked to create a product of her own choice (for instance, to play in sand or do a finger painting).

The association and construction techniques are the most frequently used with children — for example, the Rorschach Inkblot Test (Rorschach, 1948) (see Figure 13-3) and the Thematic Apper-

FIGURE 13-3. An inkblot used in the Rorschach Test.

Source: H. Rorschach. (1948). *Psychodiagnostics: A diagnostic test based on perception* (4th ed.) (New York: Grune & Stratton). Reprinted by permission.

Table 13-5

Interpretation of Data from the Rorschach Test for Children and Adults

Response to Cards	Interpretation
Blood content followed by evasion:	Hostile impulses defended against by avoidance, resentful passive compliance or withdrawal
Color naming, cool colors:	Depressive trend which is defended against
Color denial and avoidance:	Withdrawal tendency
Body mutilation:	Casual fantasies or fears
Smoke:	Children, retardates; with average or above average intelligence, apprehension, depression, social maladjustment
Gums and teeth:	Aggressive response to frustrated dependency needs; more common in adolescents and children; resentfulness
Completely unmodified, unqualified terse responses:	Children; organics; people in trouble with the law; persons resistant to social pressure

Source: J. Gilbert. (1978). *Interpreting psychological test data* (New York: Van Nostrand Reinhold). Reprinted by permission of publisher. Copyright © 1975 by Van Nostrand Reinhold.

ception Test (TAT; Murray, 1943). The Rorschach Inkblot Test was first developed in Germany for use primarily with adults, but also has been widely used with children (Halpern, 1953). The test consists of 10 cards with symmetrical inkblots, half of which are black and white and half of which are colored. The cards are shown to the child one at a time in a set order, and the child is asked what each inkblot represents *(free-association stage).* Later, more detailed information is gathered by asking the child to justify his responses and to describe them in more detail *(inquiry stage).* There are several ways to score Rorschach responses (Exner, 1969, 1974), and Table 13-5 lists a number of interpretations based on responses to the cards.

The TAT is second only to the Rorschach both in clinical usage and published studies (Korchin, 1976; O'Leary & Johnson, 1979). The TAT is a constructive projective technique in which 20 to 30 cards (such as the one depicted in Figure 13-4) are shown to a child; each card consists of a drawing or fantasy scene. A card is shown to a child, who is then asked to make up a story about the picture. The child's stories are tape-recorded or written down. After a sufficient number of cards have been shown (the number may vary

FIGURE 13-4. A sample picture from the Thematic Apperception Test.

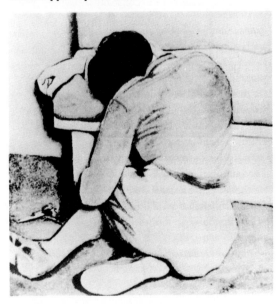

Source: H. A. Murray. (1943). *Thematic Apperception Test manual* (Cambridge, MA: Harvard University Press). Reprinted by permission.

from clinician to clinician), the results are interpreted. The interpretation generally includes major elements of the story, such as the choice of a hero, the needs and qualities of the hero, the basic themes of the story, the emotional tone, and the general outcome of the story. In clinical practice, there is no universally accepted method for scoring the TAT cards.

A similar technique to the TAT is the Children's Apperception Test (CAT; Bellak, 1954). This technique is used with younger children (ages 3 to 10), and is based on pictures of animals instead of adults. The pictures depict scenes designed to elicit responses on sibling rivalry, attitudes toward parents, aggression, feeding problems, toileting behavior, acceptance, and loneliness. It is assumed that young children relate more easily to animals than to adults. A similar story-telling technique, but with a unique set of projective stimuli (a television quiz show), is Gardner's (1971) mutual story-telling technique (see Box 13-2).

Although projective techniques have been extremely popular, their usefulness with behaviorally disordered children has been repeatedly criticized. Because according to the projective hypothesis the stimuli associated with these tests have to be ambiguous, their reliability is generally low. Even the validity of the projective hypothesis itself has been criticized (Anastasi, 1982; Epstein, 1966). Anastasi (1982) regards projective techniques as "clinical tools" and not as psychological tests, because they do not measure up to acceptable psychometric standards of basic reliability and validity. Similarly, research reviews of projective techniques and of their use with behaviorally disordered children have questioned their utility (Gittelman-Klein, 1978, 1980). One leading researcher (Gittelman-Klein, 1978) has stated concerning projective techniques, "[S]ometimes they tell us poorly something we already know" (p. 160).

Child Personality Tests

Personality inventory tests are trait measures consisting of hundreds of questions; several questions correlate or cluster with one another and thus form an indication of a trait. For example, 50 questions from a 600-question personality inventory may statistically interrelate with one another, forming a description of a trait such as hyperactivity. All personality inventories are given under standardized conditions with a normed comparison group. The most frequently used personality tests are the California Psychological Inventory, the Minnesota Multiphasic Personality Inventory (MMPI), the Jessness Personality Inventory, and the Personality Inventory for Children (PIC).

One of the most comprehensive personality inventories for children is the PIC (Lachar, 1982; Wirt, Lachar, Klinedinst, & Seat, 1977). This test consists of 600 "yes" and "no" questions that a parent fills out in relation to the child. The test is then scored, and the individual scores are transposed to a profile sheet. The profile sheet consists of several factors or traits (for example, hyperactivity, social skills, withdrawal; see Table 13-6) and permits comparison to the standardization group of nonhandicapped children. For example, the average score for a nonhandicapped child on

Table 13-6
The Scales of the Personality Inventory for Children

Scale Name	Abbreviation
Validity and screening scales	
Lie	L
F	F
Defensiveness	DEF
Adjustment	ADJ
Clinical scales	
Achievement	ACH
Intellectual Screening	IS
Development	DVL
Somatic Concern	SOM
Depression	D
Family Relations	FAM
Delinquency	DLQ
Withdrawal	WDL
Anxiety	ANX
Psychosis	PSY
Hyperactivity	HPR
Social Skills	SSK

Source: R. D. Wirt, D. Lachar, J. K. Klinedinst, and P. D. Seat. (1977). *Multidimensional description of child personality: Manual for the Personality Inventory for Children* (Los Angeles: Western Psychological Services), p. 9. Reprinted by permission.

BOX 13-2 • Gardner's Description of the Mutual Story-Telling Technique

"Good morning, boys and girls. I'd like to welcome you once again to Dr. Gardner's 'Make-Up-A-Story Television Program.' As you all know, we invite children to our program to see how good they are at making up stories. Naturally, the more adventure or excitement a story has, the more interesting it is to the people who are watching at their television sets. Now it's against the rules to tell stories about things you've read or have seen in the movies or on television, or about things that really happened to you or anyone you know.

"Like all stories, your story should have a beginning, a middle, and an end. After you've made up a story, you'll tell us the moral of the story. We all know that every good story has a moral.

"Then after you've told your story, Dr. Gardner will make up a story too. He'll try to tell one that's interesting and unusual, and then he'll tell the moral of his story.

"And now, without further delay, let me introduce to you a boy (girl) who is with us today for the first time. Can you tell us your name, young man?"

I then ask the child a series of brief questions that can be answered by single words or brief phrases such as his age, address, school grade, and teacher. These simple questions diminish the child's anxiety and tend to make him less tense about the more unstructured themes involved in "making up a story." Further diminution of anxiety is accomplished by letting him hear his own voice at this point by playback, something which most children enjoy. He is then told:

"Now that we've heard a few things about you, we're all interested in hearing the story you have for us today."

At this point most children plunge right into their story, although some may feel the need for "time to think." I may offer this pause; if it is asked for by the child, it is readily granted. There are some children for whom the pause is not enough, but who nevertheless still want to try. In such instances, the child is told:

"Some children, especially when it's their first time on this program, have a little trouble thinking of a story, but with some help from me they're able to do so. Most children don't realize that there are millions of stories in their heads they don't know about. And I know a way to help get out some of them. Would you like me to help you get out one of them?"

---

any factor of the PIC profile sheet is T-50, and a clinically significant score for most factors is T-70 (two standard deviations from the mean—see Box 13-1). This test is also unique in that it gives a series of validity scales describing the informant's (parent's) response characteristics (DEF = defensive, L = lying, F = symptom exaggeration). In addition, there are overall adjustment (ADJ), achievement (ACH), intellectual screening (IS), development (DVL), and family relations (FAM) scales. An example of how a PIC profile was interpreted for a hyperactive boy is given in Box 13-3.

The reliability of subscales within most per-

sonality inventories ranges from adequate for some subscales to poor for others. The reliabilities for the subscales of the PIC are good, with the test-retest reliability scores for the 16 profile scales averaging .86 (Wirt et al., 1977), although some scales (such as the defensiveness scale) had marginal reliabilities. Similarly, concurrent validity for the clinical factors, when compared to independent ratings of parents, teachers, and clinicians, was good. However, trait-based personality assessments of children that rely on a single measure predict poorly across different situations and times. To demonstrate good predictive validity, multiple measurements of a trait (Epstein, 1979)

Box 13-2 (Continued)

Most children assent to this. I then continue:

"Fine, here's how it works. I'll start the story and when I point my finger at you, you say exactly what comes into your mind at that time. You'll then see how easy it is to make up a story. Okay. Let's start. Once upon a time—a long, long time ago—in a distant land—far, far away—there lived a _____."

I then point my finger, and it is a rare child who does not offer some fill-in word at this point. If the word is "dog," for example, I then say, "And that dog _____" and once again point to the patient. I follow the statement provided by the child with "And then _____" or "The next thing that happened was _____." Every statement the child makes is followed by some introductory connective and by pointing to the child to supply the next statement. That and no more—the introduction of specific phrases or words would defeat the therapist's purpose of catalyzing the youngster's production of his own created material and of sustaining, as needed, its continuity.

For most children, this approach is sufficient to get them over whatever hurdles there are for them in telling a story. If this is not enough, however, it is best to drop this activity in a completely casual and non-reproachful manner, such as: "Well, today doesn't seem to be your good day for story-telling. Perhaps we'll try again some other time."

While the child is engaged in telling his story, I jot down notes, which are not only of help in analyzing the child's story, but serve also as a basis for my own. At the end of the child's story and his statement of its moral, I may ask questions about specific items in the story. The purpose here is to obtain additional details, which are often of help in understanding the story. Typical questions might be: "Was the fish in your story a man or a lady?" "Why was the fox so mad at the goat?" "Why did the bear do that?" If the child hesitates to tell the moral of his story or indicates that there is none, I usually reply: "What, a story without a moral? Every good story has some lesson or moral!" The moral that this comment usually does succeed in eliciting from the child is often significantly revealing of the fundamental psychodynamics of the story.

Source: R. A. Gardner. (1971). *Thereputic communication with children. The mutual story-telling technique* (New York: Jason Aronson), pp. 25–26. Reprinted by permission.

should be taken, and the effects of situational variables in the environment should be taken into account (Mischel, 1979). Very few personality inventories for children currently meet these two requirements.

Educational Tests

Most of the prestige and publicity of testing goes to psychological testing; however, most of the actual testing done with children is academic or educational. The importance of educational ability and its relationship to successful treatment of behaviorally disordered children are critical. Researchers have found high correlations be-

tween academic deficiencies and conduct disorders (Rutter & Yule, 1973), and between academic deficiencies and hyperactivity (Lambert & Sandoval, 1980; Weiss & Hechtman, 1986). If academic deficits are ignored and not assessed for behaviorally disordered children, most therapeutic gains will not be maintained in the long term.

The most frequently administered educational tests are standardized achievement tests. Basic achievement tests, such as the Peabody Individual Achievement Test (PIAT), the Stanford Achievement Tests (SAT), the California Achievement Test (CAT), the Metropolitan Achievement Test (MAT), and the Wide Range Achievement

BOX 13-3 • Personality Inventory for Children (PIC) Analysis of a Hyperactive Child

FIGURE 13-5. Profile study: Hyperactivity.

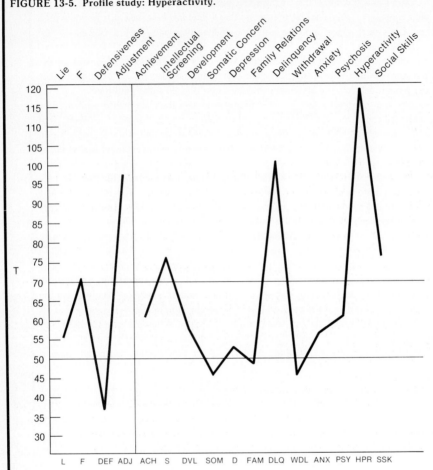

SUPPLEMENTAL SCALE SCORES

	AGM	AGN	ASO	CDY	DP	EGO	EXC	EXT	INT
Raw Score	29	12	21	22	26	30	10	27	9
T-score	79	88	91	41	101	28	69	88	58
	INF	I-E	K	LDP	RDS	SR	SD	SM	
Raw Score	1	35	11	29	8	19	14	9	
T-score	61	72	23	60	69	40	20	51	

Box 13-3 (Continued)

PRESENTING CLINICAL PROBLEM

This 9-year-old boy was referred to the clinic by his pediatrician because he was very overactive and a serious behavior problem at school.

PROFILE ANALYSIS

1. *Profile Interpretability*

The validity scales indicate the profile [see Figure 13-5] to be interpretable, though the very high ADJ suggests the respondent sees the child to be quite disturbed.

2. *Response Styles Tendencies*

The mother is expressing a moderate degree of distress surrounding the clinical problem (F, ADJ) and the somewhat elevated F may indicate that she selectively perceives and reacts to the negative aspect of the child's behavior, thereby supporting its reoccurrence. At the same time, this mother would appear to be open and verbally accessible, suggesting a favorable response to clinical intervention (DEF).

3. *Emotional Disturbances*

The elevated Adjustment Scale (ADJ) clearly indicates the presence of emotional disturbance.

4. *Linear Scanning*

The Achievement Scale (ACH) is elevated above its cutting score and the poor Development Scale (DVL) is borderline, suggesting mild academic problems. However, the profile peaks on the Delinquency (DLQ) and Hyperactivity (HPR) scales, indicating disruptive hyperactivity and conduct problems, both of which stand out clearly in the clinical picture.

There are moderate elevations on Development (DVL) and the Supplemental Scales. Reality Distortion (RDS) and Excitement (EXC), and considerable elevation on Social Skills (SSK) and the Supplemental Scales of Aggression (AGN) and Asocial Behavior (ASO). These data suggest that both further pediatric neurological and neuropsychological studies be conducted.

The boy's mother was involved in a car accident while she was still pregnant. The boy was born three weeks premature. Apparently, the boy was hard to manage since early childhood. Following the death of his mother from cancer when he was five years old, his maternal grandmother cared for him, making little effort to manage him. He was described by the clinic psychologist as having temper tantrums, sleeping problems, and bad dreams, and as showing a very high activity level "even when watching

Box 13-3 (Continued)

Box 13-3 (Continued)

television and doing other favored activities." The PIC was administered at this time.

The pediatrician had been treating the child with Ritalin for five months after the PIC was administered, at which time the staff psychiatrist reported that the medicine had "been helping him to remain calmer and perform better in school." School staff and the psychiatrist thought the medicine had reduced the boy's activity level to within normal limits. He could sit still in a chair for about ten minutes. However, he took money from his parents three times, and chewing gum from a store during the five-month period. The behavior problem had not been reduced. The father had remarried during the past year, and both parents were seen as sincerely desiring to work together with their child on these problems.

5. *Group Profile Comparison*

The profile configuration of this study is similar in topography to that of the group profile for hyperactive boys. The DLQ and HPR scales are much more elevated than in the group profile. The similarity suggests that this boy will appear behaviorally similar to that of boys diagnosed as hyperactive.

6. *Supplemental Scale / Critical Item Inspection*

The supplemental scales do not add to this profile interpretation. The critical items convey the volatile nature of the boy's behavior.
Sample Critical Items:
My child has had to have drugs to relax. (T)
My child seems to enjoy destroying things. (T)
The school says my child needs help in getting along with other children. (T)
At times, my child scratches his (her) face until it bleeds. (T)
My child has been in trouble for attacking others. (T)
My child smashes things when angry. (T)
The child's mother frequently has crying spells. (T)
School teachers complain that my child can't sit still. (T)
My child was a premature or overdue baby. (T)
Neither parent has ever been mentally ill. (F)

Source: R. D. Wirt, D. Lachar, J. K. Klinedinst, and P. D. Seat. (1977). *Multidimensional description of child personality: Manual for the personality inventory for children* (Los Angeles: Western Psychological Services), pp. 56–57. Reprinted by permission.

Test (WRAT), assess basic academic skills such as reading, mathematics, spelling, and general information (see Figure 13-6). Standardized achievement tests, in effect, "sample the products of past formal and informal educational experiences. They measure the extent to which a student has profited from schooling and/or like experiences compared to others of the same age or grade" (Salvia & Ysseldyke, 1978, p. 125). The tests are *norm-referenced,* because they compare an individual child to the standardized comparison norms of a group (Glaser, 1963). Norm-referenced

FIGURE 13-6. The individual record booklet for the Peabody Individual Achievement Test (PIAT), showing the skills assessed and the profile of results.

PIAT Peabody Individual Achievement Test
INDIVIDUAL RECORD BOOKLET
by Lloyd M. Dunn, Ph.D. and Frederick C. Markwardt, Jr., Ph.D.

Name _____ Sex: M F

(last)   (first)   (middle initial)   (circle)

School _____

(or agency or address)

Teacher _____

(or counselor or supervisor)

Examiner _____

Testing Time _____ Grade _____ Code _____

(min.)   (or phone)   (or race or descent)

Age Data

Date of testing _____ (year) (month) (day)

Date of birth _____ (year) (month) (day)

Age at testing _____ (years) (months)

Test Scores

Norms Recorded (Check one) .... ▶ ☐ Age ☐ Grade

▼ Subtests	Raw Scores	Equivalents	Percentile Ranks	Standard Scores
Mathematics ▶				
Reading Recognition ▶				
Reading Comprehension ▶				
Spelling ▶				
General Information ▶				
Total Test ▶				

Circle the equivalent and/or percentile rank scores plotted on the profile.

Intelligence Test Data

▼ Name of Test	Date at testing	I.Q. Score	Adjusted M.A.

Note: See Part 1 of the Manual on calculating adjusted M.A.

Profile

Columns: Adjusted M.A. | Chronological Age | Grade Placement | Mathematics | Reading Recognition | Reading Comprehension | Spelling | General Information | Total Test | Percentile Rank | I.Q. Score

Chronological Age	Grade Placement	Percentile Rank	I.Q. Score
18-2	13.0		
17-8	12.5		
17-2	12.0	99	133
16-8	11.5	98	130
16-2	11.0	96	127
15-8	10.5	94	124
15-2	10.0	92	121
14-8	9.5	88	118
14-2	9.0	84	115
13-8	8.5	79	112
13-2	8.0	73	109
12-8	7.5	66	106
12-2	7.0	58	103
11-8	6.5	50	100
11-2	6.0	42	97
10-8	5.5	34	94
10-2	5.0	27	91
9-8	4.5	21	88
9-2	4.0	16	85
8-8	3.5	12	82
8-2	3.0	8	79
7-8	2.5	6	76
7-2	2.0	4	73
6-8	1.5	2	70
6-2	1.0	1	67
5-8	0.5K		
5-2	0.0K		
4-8	0.5N		
4-2	0.0N		
3-8	Pre-		
3-2	School		

Note: To assess the significance of difference between subject scores consult the reliability section of Part IV of the Manual.

AGS

Published by
American Guidance Service, Inc. • Publishers' Building, Circle Pines, Minn. 55014

Source: L. M. Dunn and F. C. Markwardt. (1970). *Peabody Individual Achievement Test* (Circle Pines, MN: American Guidance Service). Copyright 1970 by American Guidance Service, Inc. Reprinted by permission.

Table 13-7

Social Speech Objectives from the Brigance Inventory of Early Development

OBJECTIVES: By *(date)*, when in the appropriate situation, *(child's name)* will . . . (add as appropriate)

1. point, gesture, or verbalize wants and needs.
2. respond appropriately when asked a simple "yes" or "no" question.
3. call at least ____ persons by name.
4. ask for food by name at the table.
5. verbalize toilet needs.
6. respond appropriately when asked a question involving two or more choices.
7. say "thank you" and "please" appropriately and without being reminded.
8. deliver a simple message.
9. show an interest in the conversation of others.
10. make verbal greeting (e.g., "Hi").
11. acknowledge compliments or thanks.
12. say "Excuse me" when disturbing or interrupting.
13. participate in a conversation without monopolizing it.
14. answer the phone and summon the person requested.
15. deliver a two-part oral message.
16. answer the phone, take a simple message, and deliver the message to the right person.

Source: A. H. Brigance. (1978). *Brigance Diagnostic Inventory of Early Development* (North Billerica, MA: Curriculum Associates), p. 130. Copyright 1978 by Curriculum Associates, Inc. Reprinted by permission.

achievement tests emphasize an individual's relative standing compared to the group on which the test was standardized. For example, a norm-referenced achievement test might indicate that an individual third-grade child is below average (as determined by the standardization group) in reading and spelling but on grade level for mathematics.

A problem with norm-referenced tests is that they indicate global deficiencies, but they tell us little about a child's specific deficiencies. By contrast, *criterion-referenced* tests provide a great deal of information about individual deficiencies. Criterion-referenced tests measure the absolute mastery a child has over a specific skill area or behavior (Glaser, 1963). A child is compared to a specific standard or criterion, not a comparison group. This objectively defined standard is called a *domain;* it consists of subskills that increase in difficulty from simple to complex. Table 13-7 presents the domain of social speech objectives (a set of reference criteria) from the Brigance Diagnostic Inventory of Early Development (Brigance, 1978). In this example, the first step in social language is to point, gesture, or indicate needs verbally. The most complex step to be measured is taking a message from the phone and delivering it to the right person. The child's score is determined by the number of speech skills she can demonstrate.

Both standardized achievement tests and criterion-referenced tests have been praised and criticized for a variety of reasons. The content validity of standardized achievement tests has been criticized because of the poor overlap between the items on the test and what is actually taught in the classroom (Jenkins & Pany, 1978). In addition, standardized achievement tests have been criticized because they yield a composite or average score and do not give information about specific deficiencies that need remediation (Shapiro & Lentz, 1985, 1986). Criterion-referenced tests have been criticized because it is difficult to get agreement from educators about what the essential educational objectives are and which of them are necessary for complete mastery (Ebel, 1971; Lidz, 1979). "They [criterion-referenced tests] require a degree of detail in the specification of objectives or outcomes that is quite unrealistic to expect and impractical to use, except at the most elementary level of education" (Ebel, 1971, p. 284).

However, even with their difficulties, standardized achievement tests and criterion-referenced tests are necessary in assessing most behaviorally disordered children. Again, the combination of multiple academic measures is the best way of compensating for the drawbacks of individual tests. Even using the child's daily performance

Direct observation of a child's behavior is the most straightforward form of assessment. Little interpretation is left to the observer who must use a standard set of behavior codes and a structured data-collection system.

in the classroom curriculum is an excellent assessment process for behaviorally disordered children. This technique, called *curriculum-based assessment,* shows particular promise because the assessment uses the actual curriculum materials in the child's classroom (Shapiro & Lentz, 1986).

BEHAVIORAL OBSERVATION METHODS

Behavioral observation is the most direct form of assessment. A basic assumption of behavioral assessment is that public events, rather than private or assumed underlying traits, are the important target for measurement (Haynes, 1978). Another assumption of behavioral observation is that the environment in which the behavior occurs is critically important to the learning and maintenance of that behavior. Unlike other tests, in which the child comes to the evaluator's office to be assessed, the evaluator who is doing a behavioral observation goes to the child's environment to collect the data. Gathering information in the environment in which the problem behavior naturally occurs may be a more informative method, in that

the events preceding the behavior (antecedents), the behavior itself, and the events following the behavior (consequences) can be directly observed and measured (the ABC method of assessment; see Chapter 12).

There are several methods for collecting observational data (see Box 13-4), each of which has advantages and disadvantages, depending on the type of behavior being observed. Each of these methods, however, requires the precise definition of *target behaviors,* which leaves little guesswork or interpretations to the observer. For example, an adequate definition of in-seat behavior for a hyperactive child may read: "The child must be sitting on the chair with both feet on the floor, both buttocks touching the seat, with his hands on the desk." Target behaviors are generally defined in terms of (1) the duration or time involved in responding, (2) the intensity or amplitude of the response, or (3) the topography of the response. In addition, target behaviors can be classed as discrete responses that have a clear beginning and ending, such as biting or hitting, or nondiscrete responses that do not have clear beginning or end-

---

BOX 13-4 • Observation Methods

FREQUENCY RECORDING

Frequency recording has also been called *tallying* or *event recording.* With this method, an observer simply counts the number of times a behavior occurs within a predetermined amount of time (for example, the number of head bangs in a 10-minute period). A restriction of the frequency method is that it should be used with discrete behaviors—that is, behaviors that have a clear onset or offset, such as head bangs. Behaviors that do not have a clear start or ending, such as a conversation between two people, are difficult to measure with the frequency method. The types of behaviors with which the frequency method has been used include eye contact, self-stimulation, and self-injurious behavior.

INTERVAL RECORDING

Interval recording is the most popular method of recording behavior, because it can be used with both discrete and nondiscrete behaviors. With interval recording, a block of time is divided into small equal units. For example, a 10-minute period of observation time may be broken into ten 1-minute intervals of time. If the target behavior occurs during a 1-minute interval, it is scored. Generally, only one behavior is scored per interval even if more than one behavior occurs. This type of system does not depend on the starting or stopping of a behavior. The only requirement is that the behavior must be scored if it occurs during the 1-minute interval. The types of target behaviors that interval recording has been used with include play activity, aggressive behaviors, and eating and drinking.

DURATION RECORDING

Duration recording must also be used with discrete behaviors that have a clear onset and offset. The duration of a behavior is generally timed from the onset to the offset of the behavior. This type of method is useful when the amount of time a subject engages in a behavior is important. Duration methods have been used to assess time spent doing homework, watching television, engaging in an exercise program, and thumbsucking.

LATENCY RECORDING

With latency recording, the amount of time from some stimulus to the start of a behavior is timed. Again, this requires a discrete response with a clear onset. The latency method is useful when the lapse in time from a stimulus to the starting of a behavior is important. For example, latency recording has been used to measure how long it takes a child to start to comply after a request has been given by an adult.

---

ing, such as a long conversation between two people (see Box 13-4).

A set of explicitly defined target behaviors designed for observation in one environmental set-

ting, such as a classroom, playground, or home, is called an *observational code.* An observational code has the advantage of describing several different behaviors that can occur in one setting, giving a global picture of the child's behavior in that setting. This observational global picture has been likened to a photograph of a behavior (Foster & Cone, 1986; Kent & Foster, 1977). If the camera's settings are incorrectly adjusted or the camera is improperly used, then the picture will be inaccurate and fuzzy. The accuracy of the picture produced by an observation system depends on a precise observational code and proper selection of the observation system.

A good example of an observational code that is used with an interval data collection system is given in Table 13-8. This code includes 29 be-

Table 13-8
Behavioral Observation Code Used with Families

AP	Approval
AT	Attention
CM	Command
CN	Command negative
CO	Compliance
CR	Cry
DI	Disapproval
DP	Dependency
DS	Destructiveness
HR	High rate (occurring at a high frequency and over time so that the behavior is aversive)
HU	Humiliate
IG	Ignore
IN	Indulgence (doing something helpful for another individual who is capable of doing it for himself without being asked)
LA	Laugh
NC	Noncompliance
NE	Negativism
NO	Normative (routine behavior which fits no other code)
NR	No Response
PL	Play
PN	Physical negative
PP	Physical positive
RC	Receive (when a person receives an object from another person and shows no response)
SS	Self-stimulation (a child bounces, rocks body, or sucks thumb)
TA	Talk
TE	Tease
TH	Touch
WH	Whine
WK	Work
YE	Yell

Source: J. B. Reid. (1978). *A social learning approach to family intervention: Vol. 2. Observation in the home setting* (Eugene, OR: Castalia). p. 35. Reprinted by permission of the author and the publisher.

haviors that are used to describe the interactions between a child and his family (Reid, 1978). These behaviors range from positive behaviors such as "approval" and "play" to very negative behaviors such as "humiliate," "tease," and "destructiveness."

Response Discrepancy Observation

One problem with observational techniques is that they do not generally allow comparison to standardized norms. In most instances, children are compared to themselves. For example, a child may be observed prior to and after an intervention, with the comparison of interest being the difference between the pre- and postintervention observations. However, such a comparison does not tell an observer what is average, below-average, or exceptional performance for that particular setting. A variation of standard observational techniques, *response discrepancy observation,* has been developed to allow meaningful normative comparisons (Alessi, 1980; Deno, 1980).

The term *response discrepancy* means that a discrepancy or difference between the observed behavior of a target child (referred child) and an index child (nonreferred child) is assessed. Data are collected simultaneously on the target and index child across several intervals for direct comparison. The major advantage of this system is that it allows normative comparisons across children, and yet it still permits the pre- and postintervention comparisons for individual children.

An example of an application of a response discrepancy system is given in Figure 13-7. The behaviors observed in a classroom with this system included physical contact, noise, off-task behavior, and out-of-place behavior. Three identified children who were referred for assessment (their names are abbreviated as Pe, Pa, and Ma) and their nonreferred classroom peers were observed. When comparisons were made, it could be seen that both Pe and Pa were having difficulty in being out of place as compared to their peers; however, this was not a problem for Ma. Being off task was a problem for both Pa and Ma, but this was not a problem for Pe as compared to classroom peers.

FIGURE 13-7. A comparison of three behaviorally disordered children (referred to as Pa, Ma, and Pe) and their peers using a response discrepancy model of observation.

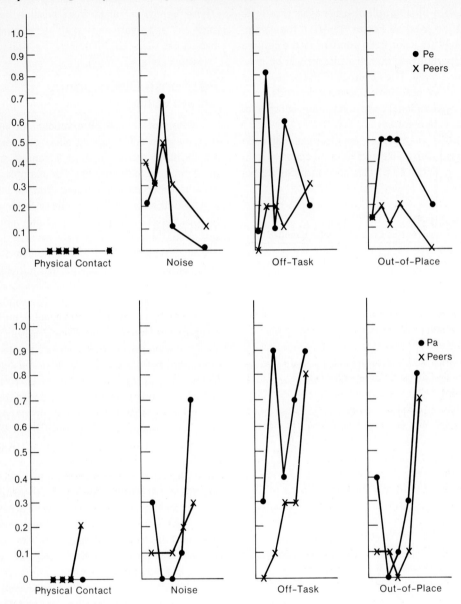

Source: S. L. Deno. (1980). Direct observation approach to measuring classroom behavior. *Exceptional Children, 46,* 396–399. Reprinted by permission.

Being noisy was a problem for Ma, while Pe was actually less noisy than her peers. In fact, the only difference between Pe and her peers was the problem behavior of being out of place.

Both standard and response discrepancy observation techniques present several methodological problems that affect reliability, validity, and cost (Foster & Cone, 1986; Wildman & Erickson,

FIGURE 13-7. (*Continued*)

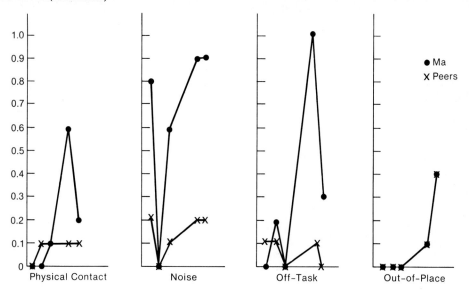

1977). First, behavioral observation requires a considerable time investment in training observers to use the various codes and collect the data. Lack of familiarity with the definitions of target behaviors can significantly reduce the reliability of recorded data. Continual training and recalibration with behavior definitions decreases observer disagreements and increases interrater reliability. Observer *drift* is another factor that affects observer reliability (Johnson & Bolstad, 1973; O'Leary & Kent, 1973). Drift usually occurs when two observers in an observation team agree closely, but both have drifted away from using the original definitions of the target behaviors (Foster & Cone, 1986). In effect, the observers have unintentionally changed the original definitions of the target behaviors by frequently discussing them. Drift can usually be detected if a third, unfamiliar observer randomly checks the observer teams. Closely related to observer drift is observer *bias*, in which the observer has an expectation about the kind of behavior that a child should exhibit (Kass & O'Leary, 1970; Skindrud, 1973). For example, if an observer is told to take activity data on a "hyperactive child," she may score the behavior in the direction of overactivity even when the child's behavior is normal. Also, when observ-

ers know a treatment attempt is under way, they may see improvement in the treated child's behavior when none actually exists. Keeping the observer as naive as possible about the child's background is one way of partially controlling bias. Unfortunately, this solution is generally not practical in most clinical and educational settings.

Observer bias and drift affect the reliability of using observational techniques. *Reactivity* affects the validity of observational techniques. "A reactive measure is one which affects the object it is designed to measure" (Haynes, 1978). In a sense, reactivity is a characteristic of obtrusive as opposed to unobtrusive observational measures (Harris & Lahey, 1982). For instance, an obtrusive observer may stare at a child in a classroom while taking data. Such an observer will probably make the child feel uneasy and thus will affect the natural way the child behaves in the classroom. A less obtrusive observer might observe from a partially hidden vantage point (for instance, from behind a one-way mirror or a partition) and make himself as inconspicuous as possible.

Self-Monitoring

Behavioral observation does not necessarily require independent observers who are trained to

BOX 13-5 • Self-Recording and Study Behavior

An experiment conducted by Broden, Hall, and Mitts (1971) investigated the effects of self-recording behavior on increasing a child's study behavior in the classroom. The subject was an eighth-grade junior high school student named Liza who had been failing her history course. Weekly counseling sessions in which her poor academic performance was discussed had failed to change Liza's study behavior. Observation in the classroom indicated that Liza studied only a small percentage of the time even when she told the counselor that she would "really try" to do better. Her talking about the problem with the counselor and her actually doing something about it in class were not highly related.

Self-recording was implemented by asking Liza to record her study behavior on a slip of paper "when she thought of it." Study and non-study behavior were defined as follows:

> "Study" was defined as attending to the teacher-assigned tasks and meant that when it was appropriate Liza should be facing the teacher, writing down lecture notes, facing a child who was responding to a teacher question, or reciting when called upon by the teacher. "Non-study" behavior meant that Liza was out of her seat without permission, talking out without being recognized by the teacher, facing the window, fingering non-academic objects such as her make-up, comb, or purse, or working on an assignment for another class. (Broden, Hall, & Mitts, 1971, p. 192)

Figure 13-8 presents the results of the self-recording on Liza's study behavior. During the baseline conditions (Baseline₁ and Baseline₂) when no self-recording was occurring. Liza studied only 30 percent of the time. However, when she started to self-record (Self-Recording₁ and Self-Recording₂), her study behavior jumped to approximately 80 percent of the class time. When the teacher was asked to pay attention and praise Liza for study behavior and Liza was self-recording (Self-Recording Plus Praise condition), her studying increased further to 88 percent of the time. At this point Liza was asked not to record her own behavior, and the teacher continued to give her special attention for studying (Praise Only condition); the study behavior stayed at 77 percent. Prior to the experiment, the teacher had not been able to motivate Liza to study. The last condition was a return to baseline (Baseline₃) in which self-recording and teacher praise were stopped. It can be seen in Figure 13-8 that Liza's studying behavior continued. She had begun studying in her history class without special help. In Liza's next report card, she had improved her history grade from a D— to a passing C.

It should be remembered that the main intervention in this experiment was self-recording,

---

collect data on someone else; a child can be taught to collect data on herself. This saves money and training time, and also produces an unexpected benefit: The observed behavior may change simply as a result of the data recording. In a sense, the person may react to collecting data on a target behavior by changing the behavior. For example, Herbert and Baer (1972) found that having mothers self-monitor positive statements they made to their children increased the frequency of such positive statements. Similarly, Jen-

son, Paoletti, and Petersen (1984) reduced chronic throat clearing in a child by simply having him record on a golf counter each time he coughed. Box 13-5 describes another situation in which the studying behavior of an eighth-grade girl was improved by self-monitoring.

Behavioral changes such as these are due to reactivity, which frequently increases appropriate behavior and decreases inappropriate behaviors. However, these effects are generally temporary unless they are specifically rewarded (Bornstein,

Box 13-5 (Continued)

FIGURE 13-8. Liza's study behavior.

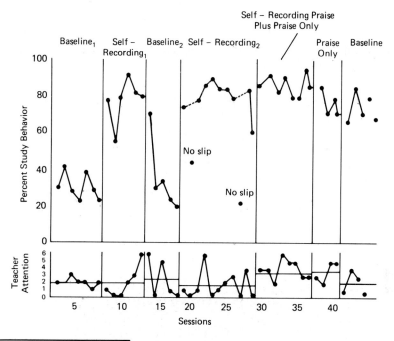

Source: M. Broden, R. V. Hall, and B. Mitts. The effect of self-recording on the classroom behavior of two eighth grade students. *Journal of Applied Behavior Analysis. 4,* 191–200. Copyright 1971 by the Society for Experimental Analysis of Behavior, Inc. Reprinted by permission.

an observation technique. No rewards were promised to Liza, nor is it likely that teacher praise by itself would have changed Liza's study behavior so dramatically. Broden and associates suggested that requiring her to observe and record her studying probably became a cue to start studying, thus increasing the time Liza spent on schoolwork.

Hamilton, & Bornstein, 1986). Rhodes, Morgan, and Young (1981) used a self-monitoring procedure with behaviorally disordered students, who rated their own appropriate behavior in a special education classroom and awarded themselves reward points. The teachers would randomly match their ratings with the students' ratings. If there was a 100% match, a student earned a bonus point; if the match was only 90% correct, the student was allowed to keep his awarded points; if the match was below 90%, the student lost all of his points. The effects of this study were dramatic, with students behaving appropriately and accurately assessing their behaviors. Eventually, the self-monitoring with random matching was used to return the students to regular education classes.

BEHAVIOR CHECKLISTS

When behavior checklists are used, raters who are familiar with a child are asked to score the child's behavior along several predetermined dimensions.

Unlike behavioral observation, which utilizes systematic recording techniques, behavior checklists seldom use tally, duration, or interval scoring methods. Instead, an adult (parent, teacher, or ward attendant) is asked to rate a child's behavior in comparison to a standard or to the behaviors of other children. For example, the checklist shown in Figure 13-9 requires a teacher to assign behavior a rating of 2 ("very true"), 1 ("sometimes true"), or 0 ("not true") if the teacher has observed the child engaging in the behavior in the past 6 months.

Factor analysis is commonly used to identify behavioral dimensions included in checklists (see Chapter 12). Checklists such as the Conners Teacher Rating Scale (Conners, 1969), the Behavior Problem Checklist (Quay, 1977; Quay & Peterson, 1975), the Walker Problem Behavior Identification Checklist—Revised (Walker, 1970, 1983), and the Child Behavior Checklist (Achenbach, 1979) identify *broad-spectrum factors*, such as internalizing behaviors (problems directed inward toward the self) and externalizing behaviors (problems directed toward others and the environ-

FIGURE 13-9. A sampling of questions from the Child Behavior Checklist—Teacher's Report Form.

Below is a list of items that describe pupils. For each item that describes the pupil now or within the past 2 months, please circle the 2 if the item is very true or often true of the pupil. Circle the 1 if the item is somewhat or sometimes true of the pupil. If the item is not true of the pupil, circle the 0.

0 1 2 1. Act too young for his/her age	0 1 2 31. Fears he/she might think or do something bad
0 1 2 2. Hums or makes other odd noises in class	0 1 2 32. Feels he/she has to be perfect
0 1 2 3. Argues a lot	0 1 2 33. Feels or complains that no one loves him/her
0 1 2 4. Fails to finish things he/she starts	0 1 2 34. Feels others are out to get him/her
0 1 2 5. Behaves like opposite sex	0 1 2 35. Feels worthless or inferior
0 1 2 6. Defiant, talks back to staff	0 1 2 36. Gets hurt a lot, accident–prone
0 1 2 7. Bragging, boasting	0 1 2 37. Gets in many fights
0 1 2 8. Can't concentrate, can't pay attention for long	0 1 2 38. Gets teased a lot
0 1 2 9. Can't get his/her mind off certain thoughts; obsessions (describe): _____	0 1 2 39. Hangs around with others who get in trouble
	0 1 2 40. Hears things that aren't there (describe):
0 1 2 10. Can't sit still, restless, or hyperactive	0 1 2 41. Impulsive or acts without thinking
0 1 2 11. Clings to adults or too dependent	0 1 2 42. Likes to be alone
0 1 2 12. Complains of loneliness	0 1 2 43. Lying or cheating
	0 1 2 44. Bites fingernails
0 1 2 13. Confused or seems to be in a fog	0 1 2 45. Nervous, high strung, or tense
0 1 2 14. Cries a lot	0 1 2 46. Nervous movements or twitching (describe)
0 1 2 15. Fidgets	
0 1 2 16. Cruelty, bullying, or meanness to others	0 1 2 47. Overconforms to rules
0 1 2 17. Daydreams or gets lost in his/her thoughts	0 1 2 48. Not liked by other pupils
0 1 2 18. Deliberately harms self or attempts suicide	0 1 2 49. Has difficulty learning
	0 1 2 50. Too fearful or anxious

Source: T. M. Achenbach and C. Edelbrock. (1980). *Child Behavior Checklist-Teacher's Report Form* (Burlington: University of Vermont, Department of Psychiatry), p. 3. Reprinted by permission.

ment). The broad-spectrum factors are then further subdivided into *narrow-band factors,* such as aggression, hyperactivity, depression, and social withdrawal.

Figure 13-10 gives an example of a profile sheet from the Child Behavior Checklist (Achenbach, 1979), which shows the broad and narrow factors. One or both parents fill out the checklist in Figure 13-10, and then the scores are transposed onto a profile sheet. In this example, both the father (dotted line) and the mother (solid line) rated the child's behavior; their individual scores of 0, 1, or 2 for each item from the checklist are listed below the factors on the profile sheet (for example, "Argues" was rated as a 1 by the father and a 2 by the mother under the aggressive factor). The profile sheet also allows a normative comparison to a standardization group. For example, if the scores of the individual factors are above T-70 (dotted line across the profile), then 98% of the standardization population fell on or below this line. The T-70 scores, which are two standard deviations from the mean, are considered clinically significant for most of the factors. In this particular case, the mother rated the aggressive factor as significant (T-75), while the father rated it as nonsignificant (T-62), indicating disagreement between the parents about the severity of the child's aggressive problems.

The advantage of most behavior checklists is that they have good validity, particularly if they are derived using multivariate statistics. In addition, most behavior checklists have good reliability characteristics. For instance, the test-retest reliability for the total score from the Child Behavior Checklist (Achenbach, 1979) is over .90. There are also several disadvantages in using behavior checklists with behaviorally disordered children. First, most behavior checklists do not have validity scales to determine whether the informant filling out the checklist is over- or underreporting problem behaviors. The only way of determining this is to use another validity check, such as a behavioral observation. Second, most checklists are only *descriptive* in assessing a behavior. Once the behavior is identified and described, they tell us little about what to do. However, behavior checklists

can go beyond a description and function in a *prescriptive* manner (Foster, 1974; Popovich, 1977; Walls, Werner, Bacon, & Zane, 1977). For example, Jenson, Preator, Ballou, Reavis, and Freston (1987) and Beck (1986) have developed checklists for children with infantile autism and behaviorally disordered children, respectively; these checklists identify problem behaviors and then prescribe the scientifically based interventions for the problem behaviors.

INTERVIEWING

Interviewing has been called the "clinician's basic technique" (Korchin, 1976) and the "universal method" of data collection (O'Leary & Johnson, 1979). Interviewing with a child and his parents is generally used to start an assessment process that may involve other techniques after basic information has been gathered. Interviewing includes such widely used techniques as a *social history* (a history of a client's social development), an *intake interview* (a method used to decide whether an agency's facilities meet the client's needs), a *child psychiatric interview* (a health and psychiatric history), a *diagnostic interview,* a *behavioral interview,* a *research interview,* and many more.

There are several reasons why interviewing is such a popular assessment technique (Evans & Nelson, 1986). First, interviewing generally utilizes open-ended questions, which allow a child or parent to explain or elaborate answers instead of being forced to choose an answer from a predetermined list. Second, interviewing helps to establish a relationship between a clinician and a client, which facilitates the assessment process. Unlike formal psychological testing, in which the interaction between the evaluator and client is kept to a minimum, interviewing involves a less structured exchange of information. Interviewing both the child and parent together *(conjoint interview)* also gives the clinician a picture of the family's interaction. For example, the following questions can be answered:

1. **Does the parent set rules for the child during the interview and consistently enforce them?**

FIGURE 13-10. Profiles scored from Child Behavior Checklists filled out by the mother and father of an 8-year-old girl.

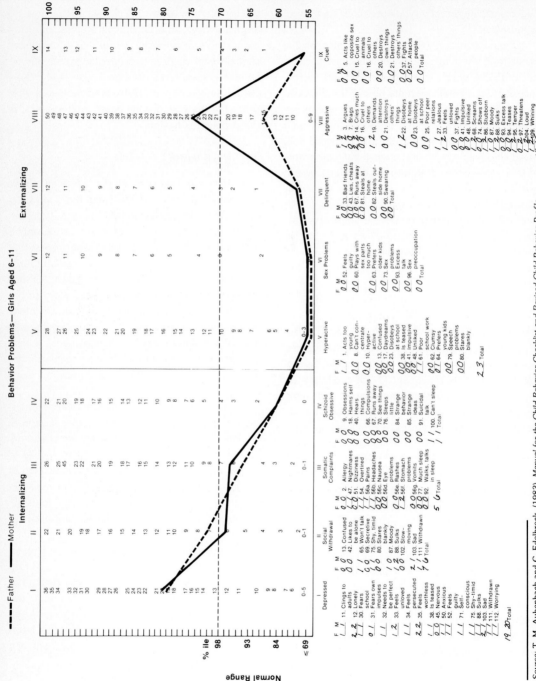

Source: T. M. Auhenbach and C. Edelbrock. (1983). Manual for the Child Behavior Checklist and Revised Child Behavior Profile (Burlington: University of Vermont, Department of Psychiatry), pp. 117–118. Reprinted by permission.

Interviewing is the most popular type of assessment procedure used with children and their parents. The interview format allows a clinician to develop a relationship with the child and explore interesting points that might not be included in other assessment techniques.

2. Are the rules overly harsh, or are they lax and easily broken with no consequences?

3. Is the child highly dependent and does she cling to the parent, or is she independent, exploring the office while the parent talks?

4. Do the parent and child disagree in answering questions that the interviewer asks, and how are these disputes handled?

5. Does the parent have exceptionally high or low expectations for the child that can be observed during the interview?

Several new *diagnostic interviews* have been developed over the past decade; these, as the term indicates, are used primarily to diagnose and classify children (Bierman & Schwartz, 1986). Most of these interviews contain open-ended questions that a child or adolescent answers, such as the Diagnostic Interview for Children and Adolescents (Herjanic & Reich, 1982). Other interviews,

such as the Child Assessment Schedule (CAS), contain a series of questions that parallel the major childhood disorders listed in the DSM-III (Hodges, Kline, Stern, Cytryn, & McKnew, 1982). By answering a set of questions, the child provides the information that is essential in making a formal DSM-III diagnosis. For example, Table 13-9 contains a series of questions from the CAS that is used in making the DSM-III diagnosis of a simple child phobia. The CAS also provides information about the child's school adjustment and friends, as well as observational judgments about the child.

Related to the diagnostic interview is the *child psychiatric interview.* The psychiatric interview is performed by a medical doctor with the intent of providing a diagnostic formulation and recommendations for treatment. Generally, the psychiatric interview consists of a mental status exam and a basic content section. The mental status exam has

Table 13-9

Questions and Observations from the Child
   Assessment Schedule (CAS) That Are Used in
   Diagnosing a Simple Phobia

Questions Asked Child
   Are you afraid of being embarrassed?
   Do you feel fearful of going to school?
   Are you afraid of animals?
   Are you afraid of heights, or being on the top of buildings
      or hills?
   Does being in a closed space, like a small area, closet, or
      room make you fearful?

Source: K. Hodges, J. Kline, D. Kashani, L. Cytryn, L. Stern, and D.
McKnew. (1982). *Child Assessment Schedule* (Unpublished manuscript, University of Missouri). Reprinted by permission of the authors.

been defined as "a description of the child's appearance and behavior during two or three hours
of psychiatric interviewing" (Simmons, 1974, p.
35). The content section includes the child's direct
answers to the psychiatrist's questions, such as "If
you could have three wishes, what would they
be?" Of particular interest to most child psychiatrists is the genetic and developmental history of
the child. Many child psychiatric evaluations also
include projective techniques, a brief neurological
screening, and an observation of the child at play.
A good example of a child psychiatric evaluation
is that of Kestenbaum and Bird (1978), which is
outlined in Table 13-10. This basic outline covers
all aspects of mental status, from physical appearance through language and thinking. The interviewer's questions cover the child's feelings,
dreams, moral judgments, and ability to deal with
anxiety. Only a topic outline is provided, and the
psychiatrist is free to phrase questions as she
chooses.

The *behavioral interview* is fundamentally different from the diagnostic and psychiatric interviews, primarily because the emphasis is not
placed on a diagnostic classification. Instead, in a
behavioral interview stress is placed on assessing
the child's environment, and particularly on a
functional analysis of that environment (Gelfand &
Hartmann, 1984; Haynes & Jensen, 1978; Holland, 1970; Morganstern, 1976; Turkat, 1986). A
functional analysis involves pinpointing target behaviors and assessing antecedents (events that

precede a behavior) and consequences (events
that follow a behavior). Antecedents and consequences are important because they can maintain
or reinforce the occurrence of a problem
behavior.

An outline for a behavioral interview of parents, suggested by Gelfand and Hartmann (1984),
is given in Table 13-11. The interviewer first attempts to specify problem target behaviors that
can be measured. The rate of frequency (last incident, rate, changes in rate) is determined to see
whether the behavior is unusually high or low in
frequency. The setting (antecedent and consequences) is also assessed to determine how the environment maintains the problem behaviors. This
method also allows the interviewer to inquire
about attempts that parents may have made in
the past (usually unsuccessful ones) to modify the
problem behavior.

It is difficult to judge the soundness of most
interviewing techniques, because of the lack of objective research and the diversity of interviewing
techniques. However, some general guidelines
exist. Parents are likely to report data that are
distorted to conform with cultural stereotypes
(McCord & McCord, 1961); they may report exceptionally fast development (precocity) for their
children (Hetherington & Martin, 1979); and they
are least reliable about events with high emotional
content (Wenar & Coulter, 1962). The reliability
of interview information varies with the child's
age, with younger children tending to be less reliable reporters (Edelbrock, Costello, Dulcan,
Kalas, & Conover, 1985). Most diagnostic interviews are reliable for broad diagnostic categories,
but they are far less reliable in providing specific
information about syndromes or behavior (Edelbrock, Costello, Dulcan, Kalas, & Conover, 1985).

SUMMARY

Assessment methods are information-gathering
procedures that should lead to sound decisions
concerning the diagnosis and treatment of behaviorally disordered children. The individual assessment procedures differ in their methods of information collection and in their theoretical

Table 13-10

Outline of the Mental Health Assessment Form for School-Aged Children

Part I—Mental Status

    I. Physical Appearance
       A. General attractiveness
       B. Physical characteristics
       C. Physical maturation
       D. Observable deviations in physical characteristics
       E. Grooming and dress
       F. Gender differential (clearly looks male or female)

    II. Motoric Behavior and Speech
       A. Motor activity
       B. Motor coordination
       C. Presence of unusual motoric patterns, habit patterns, and mannerisms
       D. Speech

    III. Relatedness during Interview
       A. Quality of relatedness as judged by nonverbal behavior
       B. Quality of relatedness as judged by verbal behavior

    IV. A. Inappropriate affect
       B. Constriction of affect
       C. Elated affect
       D. Depressive affect
       E. Labile (changing, unstable) affect
       F. Over-anxious affect
       G. Angry affect
       H. Histrionic (exaggerated mannerisms, theatrical) affect

    V. Language and Thinking
       A. Overall intelligence
       B. Cognitive functions (e.g., memory, ability to reason, use of vocabulary)
       C. External reality testing (e.g., absence of hallucinations, illusions, and perceptual distortions)
       D. Use of language

       E. Thought processes
       F. Attention span

Part II—Content of the Interview

    VI. Feeling States
       A. Depression
       B. Elation
       C. Mixed disturbances (other)
       D. Anger
       E. Anxiety

    VII. Interpersonal Relations
       A. The child's relationship to his family
       B. The child's relationship with other adult authority figures
       C. Relations with peers
       D. Relationships to pets
       E. Modes of interaction with others
       F. Aggressive behavior
       G. Sexual behavior

    VIII. Symbols Representation (Dreams and Fantasies)
       A. Fantasy
       B. Dreams

    IX. Self-Concept
       A. Dissatisfaction with self
       B. Comparison of self to peers
       C. Comparison between self and ideal self

    X. Conscience—Moral Judgment
       A. Deficit in development of conscience
       B. Antisocial behavior

    XI. General Level of Adaption
       A. Personality characteristics
       B. Defense mechanisms
       C. Maladaptive solutions in dealing with anxiety

Source: C. J. Kestenbaum and H. R. A. Bird. (1978). A reliability study of the Mental Health Assessment Form for School-Aged Children. *Journal of the American Academy of Child Psychiatry, 17,* 338–347. Reprinted by permission of the authors and Yale University Press.

assumptions about what they are measuring. Some assessment procedures use extremely structured and standardized collection methods, such as intelligence tests, and others use relatively unstructured collection methods, such as projective techniques and interviews. The theoretical assumptions about the types of information gathering also differ widely. Observations, checklists, and criterion-referenced tests generally sample behavior directly. Personality inventories, projective tests, and some intelligence tests are assumed to measure the underlying traits or constructs that control behavior across different situations and time. The direct sample techniques value observable behavior, and the trait techniques value underlying traits and consider observable behavior to be only a reflection of these underlying traits.

Without exception, no assessment procedure

Table 13-11
Initial Caretaker Interview

These are the basic questions to ask caretakers concerning the child's problem behavior:
1. Specific description
   "Can you tell me what (child's name)'s problem seems to be?" (If caretaker responds in generalities such as, "He is always grouchy," or that the child is rebellious, uncooperative, or overly shy, ask him to describe the behavior more explicitly.)
   "What, exactly, does (he or she) do when (he or she) is acting this way? What kinds of things will (he or she) say?"
2. Last incident
   "Could you tell me just what happened the last time you saw (the child) acting like this? What did you do?"
3. Rate
   "How often does this behavior occur? About how many times a day (or hour or week) does it occur?"
4. Changes in rate
   "Would you say this behavior is starting to happen more often, less often, or staying about the same?"
5. Setting
   "In what situations does it occur? At home? At school? In public places or when (the child) is alone?" (If in public places) "Who is usually with him? How do they respond?"
   "At what times of day does this happen?"
   "What else is (the child) likely to be doing at the time?"
6. Antecedents
   "What usually has happened right before (he or she) does this? Does anything in particular seem to start this behavior?"
7. Consequent events
   "What usually happens right afterwards?"
8. Modification attempts
   "What things have you tried to stop (him or her) from behaving this way?"
   "How long did you try that?"
   "How well did it work?"
   "Have you ever tried anything else?"

Source: D. M. Gelfand and D. P. Hartmann. (1984). *Child behavior analysis and therapy* (2nd ed.) (New York: Pergamon Press), pp. 230–232. Reprinted by permission.

is perfect, and all procedures are subject to measurement error. Each procedure can be judged by its ability to meet a basic set of reliability and validity criteria. Assessment procedures that are not reliable are not consistent in their information-gathering capabilities. An unreliable procedure cannot have good validity; reliability sets an upper limit on validity.

Because any single assessment procedure is subject to error, and because none has perfect reliability or validity, it is good clinical practice to use multiple measures in assessing a child. If one procedure is weak in an area, then a second or third procedure may cover this area. For example, an IQ test can be used in diagnosing mental retardation; however, an IQ test used by itself is subject to significant error. Other measures, such as checklists to assess how well a child adapts at home and school, behavioral observation of the child, interviewing of parents and caretakers, and academic testing, are needed to make an adequate diagnosis of mental retardation. It should be remembered, however, that using assessment, even multiple-measure assessment, merely to label a child is an expensive mistake. To be useful, assessment should aid the clinician in both the classification and treatment of the child.

chapter

14

Treatment of Children's Adjustment Problems

KEY TERMS

Antipsychotic Drugs. Also called Neuroleptic Drugs. Drugs that reduce psychotic thinking and behavior in adults and that may control aggressive, disoriented, severely overactive, or highly disturbed children.

Insight. In psychotherapy, the client's coming to recognize and accept the reasons for her own behavior as interpreted by the psychotherapist.

Nondirective Counseling. A counseling technique developed by Carl Rogers in which the client determines the pace and direction of each session and of the helping process in general.

Psychoactive Drugs. Pharmacological agents that affect psychological functioning, including alertness, attention, mood, motivation, and impulse control.

Unconditional Positive Regard. A technique in nondirective or client-centered counseling in which the counselor expresses unqualified acceptance for whatever the client says or does, within the limits of safety.

INTRODUCTION

There are as many unanswered questions about how to help troubled children as there are about why they require help. Many different treatment approaches have been developed since the first professional treatment interventions for children emerged during the early 20th century. Some therapists treat the child alone; others focus attention on the problems of the parents; and still others require the participation of the whole family. Some forms of psychotherapy aim to reduce the child's internal psychological conflict and to produce self-understanding, which is expected to result in positive behavior change. Alternative approaches focus on behavior change, expecting that improved self-esteem and reduced tension will follow the child's behavioral improvements. Although most therapists agree on healthy, conflict-free functioning as the goal of treatment, there are many disagreements on how to achieve this result.

This chapter reviews the major individual and group approaches to the treatment of children's abnormal behavior. Individual children's needs and characteristics determine which type of treatment will be most helpful for them. We point out the necessity of matching treatment type to the child's age or developmental level and to the type, etiology, duration, and intensity of the disorder. The effectiveness of psychotherapy and of drug therapy is evaluated, as are the risks and benefits associated with particular therapy techniques and drugs.

DEVELOPMENTAL CONSIDERATIONS

Children historically have not been the major focus of attention in psychiatry or psychology, so child therapy draws heavily upon philosophies and techniques first developed for use with adults. Largely as an afterthought, adult therapeutic techniques were handed down and altered to suit children. As a result, some therapy practices do not really suit children very well. How much modification of adult techniques is required depends largely upon the age and developmental level of the child client. A full appreciation of this point requires some familiarity with the principles of cognitive and social development presented in developmental psychology textbooks such as those by Hetherington and Parke (1986) and Helms and Turner (1986). As developmental theory and research reveal, there may be wider differences in the thinking and problem solving of infants and toddlers versus adults than in the cognitions of adults from highly dissimilar cultures (such as members of nomadic tribes versus American suburban professionals). Clearly, one must be very cautious about applying adult-based theories of psychopathology, assessment, and treatment to the developing child (Bierman, 1983).

Very young child clients generally require the most modification of adult treatment approaches. Clinicians who work with children must have appropriate training, experience, and great skill. Those who typically work with adult clients may be awkward and ineffective in dealing with the young, since rather different techniques for information gathering and communication are required by the two groups. One of the greatest obstacles to therapeutic progress is children's seeming lack of motivation to make any change in themselves (Chess & Hassibi, 1978). Psychotherapy's effectiveness is largely determined by the client's eagerness to improve and willingness to engage in joint problem solving with the therapist. It is formidably difficult to transform one's outlook and behavior; to do so requires continuing effort and dedication. This type of arduous and tedious effort over an extended time period generally fails to appeal to children. In fact, children themselves only rarely seek psychological treatment; they are usually referred by their parents and teachers. Children may not be sufficiently cognitively and socially mature to perceive that they have an adjustment problem, or may feel that others are solely to blame for their difficulties. Thus, the child may blame classmates, a teacher, siblings, or a stepparent, and may assume no personal responsibility for deviant behavior, mood problems, or other difficulties.

At the beginning of treatment, the child may

be an unwilling participant delivered for treatment by angry or despairing parents. The child's understandable suspicion of the psychotherapist and his reluctance to enter into a treatment program create obstacles of a type that may be minimal among self-referred adult psychotherapy clients. Anna Freud (1945) wisely observed that the first great challenge for any child psychotherapist is to win the child's trust. Some child treatment techniques, such as play therapy and the therapist's use of acceptance, warmth, and positive reinforcement, are used partly to build the child's trust and cooperation as necessary prerequisites for producing change.

The child's age and cognitive development help to determine the appropriate treatment type. The characteristics typical of children of different ages are a major consideration in the choice of treatment, as Table 14-1 indicates. Younger and less cognitively and socially skilled children may require *skill-building* interventions, as do children of any age who have very serious developmental delays, psychosis, or mental retardation. These children's major problems are in acquiring social and intellectual skills, rather than in combating psychological constraints blocking existing abilities. In contrast, the *insight-oriented*, conversational approaches are better suited to older, more sophisticated, and more affluent youngsters

suffering from anxiety, depression, fears, or other types of emotional distress. Thus both age and problem type must be considered in treatment choice. Let us hold the discussion of problem type in abeyance for a moment, and consider how a child's age limits treatment selection.

Infants and Toddlers

Until they are 3 or 4 years old, children are unskilled in language; their understanding of others' speech is primitive, and their own productive speech skills are even more limited. Consequently, it is impossible to treat very young children's adjustment problems through the interview methods characteristic of adult psychotherapy. It is even difficult to detect any except the most gross physical and intellectual problems in the early years. The most common causes for referral at this age are gross developmental delays in motor skills, delays in social skills such as regulating social interactions, and lags in language development. Young children who are very slow in achieving developmental milestones such as sitting alone, walking, and talking may be diagnosed and offered special help. Such developmentally delayed infants are usually treated by enriching their environments and giving them extra practice. In *environmental enrichment*, the infant is provided with a rich variety of experiences to

Table 14-1
Children's Ages, Characteristics, and Psychotherapy Treatment Methods

Age	Typical Characteristics	Common Treatment Methods
Infants and toddlers	Nonverbal or limited language skills; limited cognitive, motor, and social abilities	Provision of social, sensory, and motor stimulation in play
Preschool children	Highly active; limited productive language ability; immature understanding of social interactions; limited insight	Operant training through reward and punishment; play therapy; parent training; preschool programs
Elementary school children	Highly active; limited conversational ability; lack motivation and insight	Operant training and behavior therapy; play therapy; parent training
Preadolescent and adolescent youth	Rebellious; suspicious of adults; blame others; lack motivation to change	Group psychotherapy; family therapy; individual psychotherapy

stimulate his visual, auditory, and tactile senses. Adult caretakers play with and talk to the infant to promote development, and the baby receives special exercises and dietary supplements if necessary. Parents may be trained to carry out these procedures with their infants at home. A similar skill-building approach is used with older children and adults who are severely retarded or psychotic.

Preschool Children

Many preschool children are sociable and highly active, but not yet proficient in language and problem solving. Special preschool programs are available for preschoolers who are language-delayed, show problems in motor or social development, or exhibit bizarre psychotic behavior. Other problems for which preschoolers may receive psychological attention include extreme shyness, selective mutism, uncontrollable aggression, and fearfulness. Many children this age are very responsive to rewards such as adult attention and praise, treats, and activities, and such reinforcers are used to induce them to improve their behavior in many preschool treatment programs. However, young children's understanding of social situations is limited (Shantz, 1975), and they sometimes offer strange and highly idiosyncratic explanations of the reasons for their own and other people's behavior (Karniol, 1978). As Bierman (1983) has observed, young children lack the abstract reasoning skills that enable adults to puzzle out cause-and-effect behavioral sequences; to anticipate others' feelings, thoughts, and courses of action; and to evaluate their own fears and anxieties. These cognitive limitations make the achievement of insight difficult at best. As a result, therapy with preschoolers often takes the form of play or instruction in practical skills, which is more natural and less intimidating than adult-style serious conversation. However, the type of treatment delivered might be determined more by the theoretical orientation of the therapist than by the child's age and abilities.

Elementary School Children

When children enter elementary school, they may begin to develop problems in school achieve-ment and adjustment, and the boys in particular may have trouble in controlling their levels of activity and aggression (see Chapter 1). Their growing language, cognitive, and social skills enable older children to benefit from verbal treatment methods, although their immaturity continues to present cognitive constraints. For example, younger elementary school children may have great difficulty in understanding that people (including themselves) are neither all good nor all bad, but represent some mixture of the two (Bierman, 1983; Harter, 1977). However, even the older school children may find play a more comfortable and familiar form of self-expression than conversation. Accordingly, many of the therapies for 6- to 10-year-old children incorporate elements of fantasy and play. During middle childhood, retarded and autistic children continue to require intensive skill training and are seldom given conventional play therapy. Children with less severe cognitive and emotional problems may also need to learn specific skills, but in addition they might benefit from play or group therapy.

Preadolescents and Adolescents

Folklore maintains that adolescence is a time of rebellion against adult authority and of intense striving for individuality and independence. Although many adolescents escape the turmoil that is supposed to occur at this time, others experience problems with parents and teachers, drug and alcohol misuse, crimes against property, and sexual behavior (Jessor & Jessor, 1977). It is not surprising, then, that adolescents are frequently reported to be suspicious of therapists and other adults, defiant, and resistant to others' attempts to help or control them. Adolescents rarely volunteer to become therapy clients, but are referred by schools or juvenile court authorities or are treated at their parents' insistence. Such unwilling clients often blame others for their own problems and lack the motivation to change their own behavior. Group treatment methods are often used with adolescents in order to create a less threatening, more inviting atmosphere and to attempt to enlist peer support for positive behavior changes. Some adolescents flatly refuse to engage in individual therapy, which they fear will place the onus for their plight on them, but will consent to join a teen or family therapy group (Schomer, 1978). Teenagers who are fearful, withdrawn, anxious, or depressed are more often given individual verbal psychotherapy, perhaps in conjunction with the administration of psychoactive drugs. In general, the older the child is, the more applicable the adult forms of psychotherapy are.

MAJOR APPROACHES TO TREATMENT

Children require individualized treatment programs. Weekly outpatient therapy sessions over a period of weeks or months may suffice to treat minor adjustment problems of children from strong and stable families, but devastating disorders such as autism, major brain damage, or profound mental retardation may require institutionalization. There are many different types of treatment to choose among, as will be described.

Children under the age of 10 years are most likely to receive some type of *play therapy,* in which the child expresses her needs, feelings, and conflicts in unstructured play sessions. Some approaches to play therapy attempt to help the child achieve insight into her feelings as she expresses them in play, while others stress the importance of sheer emotional release. The *behavior therapies* have a contrasting philosophy, focusing on behavioral improvement and direct modification of the child's maladaptive behavior. Both play therapy and behavior therapy can be conducted with individuals or as *group therapy.* A therapy group consists of a therapist and a small number of children whose interactions with each other and with the therapist serve a therapeutic function. Finally, *drug therapy* is used to provide relief from symptoms (such as inattentiveness, restlessness, and irritability) that interfere with the child's functioning.

The use of one type of intervention does not preclude using another simultaneously or at some other time. Most therapists use combinations of methods (called an *eclectic* approach) in their attempts to help troubled children (Koocher & Pedulla, 1977). Thus, a child diagnosed as having

attention deficit disorder with hyperactivity might receive special education services at school for his academic deficits, and nondirective play therapy or behavior therapy for his inattentiveness and inability to concentrate on schoolwork. Alternatively, behavior therapy might be combined with psychostimulant drugs. Even though the different interventions are discussed separately, they are often used concurrently. Unfortunately for researchers, exposure to multiple interventions may benefit children, but it makes it difficult to impossible to discern which specific treatments are effective and which are not. In addition to choosing among individual, play, group, and family treatments, parents must select a therapist according to her theoretical orientation to treatment. The different theories of psychotherapy are discussed next.

Insight-Oriented Therapies

To have *insight* into a problem is to grasp its nature and origins. Such understanding may lead to acceptance of oneself or a situation, and to a reduction in feelings of anger or anxiety. The goals of *insight-oriented therapy* are to resolve internal conflict and to help the child master developmental crises (such as school entry, the birth of a sibling, or parental divorce) or to pass through one of Erikson's or Freud's psychosocial stages (Freedheim & Russ, 1983). The insight-oriented therapies discussed in this section include *psychoanalytic (psychodynamic) therapy* and *client-centered* or *nondirective counseling.* These approaches assume that inner emotional turmoil lies at the heart of the child's problem. The child's disturbed behavior presumably results from underlying emotional conflict, much as a high fever is caused by infection, according to medical explanations of pathology (see Chapter 2). As examples, in the client-centered explanation, the problem can be traced to parental and societal demands that the child behave perfectly, while the psychoanalytic view attributes psychopathology to abnormalities occurring at one of the early psychosexual stages. Resulting negative emotions or symptoms persist until treatment intervenes.

The psychodynamically oriented psychotherapist attempts to reduce the child's unconscious emotional disturbance in the belief that the best way to relieve the behavioral symptoms is to remove their cause. This type of therapy is termed *insight-oriented* because enlightenment about one's feelings is expected to remove the need to repress or deny them, so the psychopathology should disappear. As in other forms of play therapy, the psychodynamic therapist attempts to create a warm and accepting atmosphere in which the sad, angry, or unloved child feels accepted and completely free to express herself. Simply experiencing the freedom to communicate anger or anxiety is presumed to have some beneficial effect. Beyond that, the insight-oriented psychotherapist may interpret the meaning of the child's communications to help the child explore her own true wishes and emotions and come to terms with them. To achieve this goal, the therapist may comment on or reflect the child's fear, anxiety, or rage. In addition, some psychoanalytic therapists interpret the meaning of the child's dreams, play themes, and fantasies.

Insight-oriented therapists concentrate on work with individual children or groups, rather than on environmental manipulation as the behavioral therapists do. Children are helped to deal with their world as it presently exists and with their families, teachers, and peers as they are. Although a child's therapist may recommend therapy for the parents also, separate therapists usually treat child and parents. Most insight-oriented therapists believe that sharing a therapist might lead to rivalry within the family and to real or perceived disloyalty on the part of the therapist. The primary goal of the insight-oriented interventions is to help the child accept herself and others. We review two approaches here—the psychodynamic and the client-centered—both of which aim to help children to clarify their understanding of their problems.

Child Psychoanalysis and Analytic Play Therapy

Schools of thought in child psychoanalysis. Child psychoanalysis was the first insight-oriented treatment for children. Sigmund Freud's psychoanalytic methods were devised for adults,

but later were modified for children by his daughter, Anna Freud, by Melanie Klein, and others. Anna Freud (1946, 1965) and her associates represent the dominant viewpoint among child analysts in the United States. She held that the chief goal of psychoanalytically oriented therapy is to liberate the child's developmental processes, which have been partly or totally blocked by remnants of past emotional upsets or by overgratification (A. Freud, 1965; Lesser, 1972). Continuing threats to the child's psychosocial development are presented by emotions of which the child is unaware, such as jealousy of the same-sex parent or of a new sibling. Alternatively, failure to progress normally can result from the child's finding extreme satisfaction in infantile modes of pleasure such as sucking, biting, urinating, and soiling, and their presumed psychological derivatives of dependency, insistence on cleanliness and order, consuming possessiveness, and hostility and aggression (see Chapter 2). Psychoanalysis is not begun, however, when the child's actual circumstances are disturbing, as in the death of a parent, a crippling accident, or serious illness of some family member.

As in work with adults, the analyst subtly attempts to draw the child's attention to his own unconscious thoughts in order to deal with them constructively. The vehicle for communication is the child's free play with a few simple toys, such as modeling clay, finger paints, toy vehicles, and doll families and doll houses. The analyst studies the child's play for evidence of inhibitions or fears of expressing certain ideas, and for repetitive themes that might indicate unresolved emotional conflicts. After building the child's trust, the analyst begins to interpret the child's play behavior. In Anna Freud's approach, interpretations initially focus on the child's emotions. For example, the child might be helped to recognize his feelings of rage at his father for leaving the family or for retaining the major allegiance and sexual partnership of the child's mother. To achieve this end, the analyst might comment on how angry the child seems in his attacks on the play materials. Later in the analysis, when the child is able to accept the interpretation, the therapist may suggest that a certain toy represents the child or the father. Interpretations of dreams may also help the child achieve insight. The emotional relationship between the child and analyst is particularly important, although different from that in adult analysis. Anna Freud believed that unlike adults, children do not develop a true transference neurosis in which the analysand unrealistically directs his feelings about his parents toward the analyst. This age difference in reaction is believed to occur because, unlike most adults, children in analysis continue to interact with their parents on a daily basis.

British child analysts are largely influenced by Melanie Klein (1932/1949), who developed an approach to child analysis that focuses on the assumed psychosexual significance of the child's play. Klein's followers offer the child symbolic translations of the meaning of the child's play behavior. To illustrate, the analyst might suggest that a child's interest in manipulating oranges or balls represents a desire to feed from his mother's breast, or that another child's causing toy cars to collide is an enactment of sexual intercourse between the child's parents. The child's play is thus interpreted in a manner similar to interpretations of an adult's free associations.

Although Klein maintained that even infants can profit from analytic intervention, most analysts do not treat children younger than 4 or 5 years of age, nor do they work with adolescents. Adolescents are believed to be in a transitional state—not yet ready for adult-style free association on the analytic couch, but too old for analytic play therapy. Anna Freud believed that few adolescents are appropriate candidates for psychoanalytic treatment, although there has been a recent increase in work with teenagers (Scharfman, 1978). The adolescent problems most commonly treated include obsessions (unwelcome recurring thoughts and preoccupations), phobias, and physical complaints with a completely psychological basis (such as biologically inexplicable fainting spells, vision impairment, lassitude, and headaches). Thus psychoanalysis and psychoanalytic therapy see relatively little usage in most clinical settings, because they are recommended for use with only a limited range of ages and types of problems.

Effectiveness and cost of psychoanalytic treatment. Most analytic work with children takes the form of less intensive and less demanding analytic play therapy rather than true analysis. Analytic play therapy is less intense, sessions are less frequent, and goals fall far short of the personality reorganization sought in true psychoanalysis. Whereas child psychoanalysis requires 3 to 5 years with four or five treatment sessions per week, analytic play therapy essentially halves that time and aims for symptom relief, such as the reduction of mild anxiety, depression, or hostility (Chess & Hassibi, 1978). True child psychoanalysis is seldom used because there are very few child psychoanalysts (Finch & Cain, 1968). Analytic training usually involves earning the M.D., completing a residency in psychiatry, and then receiving further training in child psychoanalysis accompanied by a personal analysis. As a result, it is prohibitively expensive, because treatment of even a single patient requires much of a highly trained analyst's time. Moreover, analysis is not useful in treating most forms of child disturbance, since serious psychological disturbances and mental retardation are ruled out (A. Freud, 1965; Johnson, Rasbury, & Siegel, 1986). Most child analysands are the mildly disturbed children of highly educated, upper-income parents who have been analyzed themselves (A. Freud, 1945; Scharfman, 1978). Although traditional child psychoanalysis is a rare treatment technique, many psychotherapists incorporate some elements of analytic theory and technique into their work with children (Koocher & Pedulla, 1977). Child psychoanalysts claim that their therapy can prevent children from developing psychological disturbances (A. Freud, 1945; Klein, 1932/1949), but there is no objective research evidence to support such a conclusion. One study (Heinicke, 1969) found that 9-year-old boys with adjustment problems improved more when given four treatment sessions per week than when given just one session. However, rater bias could have produced the results favoring the more intensive treatment schedule, because the raters may have known which boys were treated more intensively. Most therapists are firm believers in their own work, so unverified case reports and even clients' testimonials must be viewed with some skepticism. Thus far, there is no controlled research verification of the analysts' claims of therapeutic effectiveness.

Melanie Klein believed even more strongly in the psychological sophistication of very young children than did the Freudians. Objective psychological research findings, however, suggest that young children have great difficulty in understanding adult interpretations of social interactions (Livesley & Bromley, 1973). Before about 8 years of age, most children have only a primitive understanding of intentions, motives, and feelings (Piaget, 1932/1965; Shantz, 1975). Young children also may fail to appreciate the other person's point of view and do not understand how others perceive them (Selman, 1976). Emotionally disturbed children may reason even less effectively about interpersonal relations than do their normal age-mates. In studies of the reasoning skills of boys institutionalized for psychological disorders, it was found that they performed less maturely than age-mates specifically on problems concerning social relations, although their reasoning about purely physical problems was unimpaired (Selman, 1980; Selman & Jacquette, 1977). Because of these cognitive limitations, it appears unlikely that children can truly understand complex psychodynamic explanations of their thoughts and feelings. The benefits children may derive from analytic treatment possibly result more from the warm and accepting therapeutic relationship than from the interpretations of the analyst. In summary, there is little to convince the skeptic that child psychoanalytic treatments are effective. However, this statement will become a familiar theme as we examine the other treatment approaches. Perhaps the most consistent finding is that the quality of the therapist-child relationship is especially important to the child's progress.

Nondirective Play Therapy
Elements of client-centered treatment.
Like psychoanalytic therapy, client-centered or nondirective treatment was first developed for use with adults. Carl Rogers (1951) maintains that each person possesses a persistent tendency toward psychological growth and self-actualization. People strive to overcome anxiety, depression, and other negative emotions, and to fulfill their own talents and abilities. These healthy tendencies can be blocked by harmful experiences such as rejection, which can cause decreased self-esteem. Client-centered therapy aims to combat the effects of such threatening experiences by helping the client develop more realistic expectations and move toward self-acceptance. The method of doing so gives the initiative to the client to control the direction and rate of the therapeutic process. The client chooses the conversation's theme, while the therapist maintains a nonjudgmental, accepting atmosphere to help the client comprehend and accept her own feelings. The therapist refrains from interpretation, but encourages disclosure, occasionally making clarifying statements to reflect and focus on the client's views. This helps the client to move beyond self-blame to acceptance of herself and others.

Clearly, this conversational technique is not appropriate for young children, who have difficulty in expressing themselves and conceptualizing social relations. Therefore, Virginia Axline (1947, 1976) and others have adapted Rogers's approach for use in play therapy with children. The therapy remains nondirective in that the child, rather than the therapist, directs the activities. The therapist sets only a few limits in the interests of safety: The child is not allowed to harm himself or others, and no property destruction is permitted. Within these broad limits, the child is free to do as he pleases, play with whatever toys he wants, and talk or not as he chooses. The therapist's words, expressions, and actions are directed to conveying *unconditional positive regard* for the child. That is, the child is valued and accepted no matter what he does or says. It is presumed that the child's behavior problems are caused by a profound lack of self-acceptance, which has perhaps been acquired through the disapproval of parents or others. The therapist attempts to increase the child's positive self-regard by indicating that the child's actions and attitudes

When children are allowed to play with toys in an unstructured way, they may act out symbolically many of their psychological problems.

are completely acceptable. Box 14-1 presents an illustrative excerpt from the unusual case of a delinquent boy in nondirective therapy. This type of therapy is not often used with highly aggressive children such as this one.

Filial therapy. A variation of client-centered therapy called *filial therapy* trains parents to act as nondirective therapists for their own disturbed children (Guerney, 1964). Small groups of parents meet with a trainer and learn to listen to, accept, and reflect or rephrase the emotional content of their children's behavior. To illustrate, if a child complains that a sibling won't share her toys, the parent/therapist might comment on how sad or angry the child must feel about such a selfish action. The parent must refrain from criticizing the child or instructing her in how to behave. During special therapeutic sessions at home, the parent acts as a nondirective therapist for the child. This is an unfamiliar and difficult role for parents to assume, and extensive training and supervision are required. There is some evidence that trained parents become more accepting and understanding toward their children, and the children more

freely express negative as well as positive feelings toward their parents (Stover, Guerney, & O'Connell, 1971). However, it is unlikely that hostile or rejecting parents could be persuaded to try this highly permissive, understanding approach.

Effectiveness of nondirective therapy. Nondirective therapy can be used with children of many ages. Compared with analytic treatment, the client-centered approach is brief and inexpensive. Therapists from varying educational backgrounds can be trained in the basic technique in a short time, but experience is required to master its nuances. Nondirective therapy is not generally used with psychotic children or those with brain damage or mental retardation. Such children need more than increased self-acceptance, because they lack basic cognitive and social skills. Nondirective techniques have been used with children who have various nonsevere emotional and academic problems. Although this form of treatment is often considered to be effective, the successful outcomes reported may be due in part to the mild, relatively benign nature of the children's problems. Follow-up data indicate that these types of

---

BOX 14-1 • Nondirective Play Therapy with a Delinquent Boy

Virginia Axline, one of the developers of nondirective play therapy, has published several accounts of this treatment approach, including the book entitled *Dibs: In Search of Self* (Axline, 1964), which provides an excellent and detailed description of child therapy. In the following passage, Axline describes a dramatic therapeutic encounter with a 12-year-old boy who had an extensive history of delinquent behavior.

In the excerpt, note that the boy initiates the conversation. The therapist rephrases and reflects the boy's statements, but does not introduce new topics for discussion. Nevertheless, the child indicates that the treatment is changing him or, rather, allowing him to change.

"Strangest thing that ever happened to me," he commented slowly. "Dragged through one court lecture after another. End up coming here because I'm a no-good kid. What happens? Nothin'. Nothin', but time for me to spend as I want to spend it. Any way seems all right in here. So I'm used to squandering time, see? The faster it's over, the better I like it, see? Now all of a sudden I'm confused. I turn into a miser about my time. I want this to last, see? I can't understand it at all. I ask myself who is crazy here — you or me? How come, all of a sudden, no lectures? Has everybody finished all the yellin' and cussin' they had for me? Don't you know who you got in here? Don't you know I'm a no-good kid that'll probably end up killing somebody? . . . "

"It is baffling and difficult for you to understand how you do feel about all this," said the therapist.

"It don't really seem to matter what it is that's happening. You stay the same. I ain't suspicious of you any more. I think maybe you're crazy, see. Maybe you don't know about what people are really like — mean — and I hate their guts. Maybe I'm crazy! Maybe in here we're both of us crazy, see?" He quickly went over to the table and with a sweep of his arm flung all the toys off the table onto the floor. He turned and looked defiantly at the therapist. "Well?" he demanded. "So what?"

"You say what," the therapist replied quietly.

The boy dug his hands through his hair, uttered a sound like a groan.

"I'm a tough kid, see?" he said with a trace of desperation in his voice. "I can't suddenly get soft spots deep inside of me. I can't get so — so slowed down I — I feel all my feelings!"

Source: Axline, V. M. (1955). Therapeutic play procedures and results. *American Journal of Orthopsychiatry, 124*, 618–619. Reprinted by permission.

---

problems tend to dissipate with time, whether or not professional treatment is obtained (Levitt, 1971). Also, some of the therapy outcome studies are seriously flawed: Children were selectively assigned to treated and untreated groups, and ratings were made by teachers, parents, and therapists who were aware of which children received the treatment (Barrett, Hampe, & Miller, 1978; Hartmann, Roper, & Gelfand, 1977). Nevertheless, when only the well-conducted evaluation studies are considered, children receiving some form of psychotherapy show more improvement than untreated children. This positive effect has been observed for all forms of psychotherapy (Casey & Berman, 1985).

Group Psychotherapy

Treating children in groups saves professional time and provides special therapeutic experience resulting from interactions with age-mates (Abramowitz, 1976). Nearly every theoretical approach to individual psychotherapy has its group therapy counterpart. Nondirective play therapy groups and behavior therapy groups are used with younger children, and adult-style discussion group therapy is used with adolescents (Rosenbaum, 1972). Techniques such as Moreno's *psychodrama* (1975), in which dramatic scenes are enacted by the group, and Slavson's *activity group therapy* (Slavson & Schiffer, 1975) have been especially popular. In activity group therapy, small groups containing a mix of aggressive and withdrawn boys meet with a therapist for weekly play sessions. The children work at art or construction projects, play games, have refreshments, and go on outings. The therapist serves as a model of maturity, rationality, and self-control, teaching by example rather than admonition. Thus when the children make a mess of the room, the therapist says nothing, but begins to put things in order. There is typically much defiance, rough-housing, and destructive play in the earlier sessions, but the therapist's example has an eventual impact, and the group's activity becomes more constructive and controlled. Slavson and Schiffer (1975) maintain that the shy boys become more outgoing and confident, and the wild, aggressive ones become more controlled as a result of the therapist's infuence and the increasingly constructive group interaction. This type of treatment requires superhuman forbearance if highly aggressive children are included, since their antisocial activities may outlast most therapists. As the following sections indicate, delinquent and seriously aggressive children may profit more from behavior therapy.

Earlier reviewers were guarded about the benefits of group psychotherapy with children (Abramowitz, 1976). However, a recent comprehensive review found play, group, and individual treatments to be equally effective, or more effective than no treatment (Casey & Berman, 1985). The group behavioral methods, which are discussed next, appear to be highly effective for certain types of disorders. In particular, the work of Clement and his associates (Clement & Milne, 1967) showed that shy, withdrawn boys profited more from behavioral play group therapy in which they received rewards for assertive behavior than from conventional group therapy.

Behavior Therapy

Many behavioral interventions directly modify the child's maladaptive behavior, rather than attempting to change the child's attitudes first and hoping for later behavioral improvement, as is typical of conventional psychotherapy. Fearful children are taught to relax or to approach the feared situation in small and successful steps. Children with specific learning disabilities are given carefully devised instructional materials emphasizing skill building and may receive privileges or other reinforcement for their efforts. Shy, withdrawn children are given instruction, practice, performance feedback, and rewards for their attempts to approach and interact with other children. All of these programs teach children specific skills and motivate them to practice until their abilities have noticeably improved. Behavior therapists believe that most child behavior problems result from faulty or inadequate learning experiences, rather than from internal psychological conflict. Whatever the etiology, behaviorists presume that current environmental factors maintain the maladaptive behavior and can be manipulated to produce improvements. Often family members and teachers are instructed in new methods of child management designed to eliminate persistent problems, and sometimes the therapist has little direct contact with the child, since the environment is thought to be of primary causal importance. In the behavioral view, environmentally produced child behavioral improvements will also improve the youngster's attitudes and self-concept, because success builds self-esteem. In contrast, the insight-oriented therapies assume that emotional change must precede any significant, enduring behavioral improvement.

Types of Behavior Therapy   Behavioral treatment methods originated in the laboratory research and theories of American experimental psychologists. B. F. Skinner (Skinner & Ferster, 1957) illustrated the power of positive reinforcement in producing behavioral change in humans and other species (see Chapter 2). Skinner's work inspired a large group of psychologists to apply operant learning principles to a variety of human ills, ranging from the treatment of autistic behaviors in children to environmental problems such as wastage of electrical power, trash disposal, and vandalism control. Above all, the behavior analysts have insisted on precise definitions of clients' problems. Thus, for instance, the exact aggressive behaviors of a child are the treatment target, and not some vague concept of "hostility" or "antisocial attitude." To give another example, observations are conducted to discriminate the peer-directed behaviors of popular and unpopular children, and then the rejected ones are trained in those behaviors, such as greeting others and inviting them to join in on some activity (Gottman, Gonso, & Rasmussen, 1975). Those behaviorists influenced by Skinner focus on highly controlled research evaluations of intervention procedures, an approach termed the *experimental analysis of behavior*. In contrast to the applied behavior analysts' insistence on dealing only with publicly observable actions, the *cognitive-behavior therapy* approach attends to clients' private cognitions about self and others, as well as to overt behavior (Craighead, Meyers, Wilcoxon-Craighead, & McHale, 1983). Bandura (1969, 1977) demonstrated the utility of *observational learning* or *modeling* as a therapy technique and illustrated the importance of cognitive variables such as self-perceived efficacy in the behavior change process. The cognitive-behavior therapy approach emphasizes the acquisition of self-regulation routines, which is discussed as a new direction for the field of child psychopathology in Chapter 15. The behavioral approach differs from others in its background in experimental psychology; in its insistence on precise behavioral definitions; and in its emphasis on the collection of reliable data on the client's behavior before, during, and following treatment (Krasner, 1971; Ullmann & Krasner, 1965). Ideally, the outcome of behavioral treatment can be objectively and reliably measured (Mahoney, Kazdin, & Lesswing, 1974).

Observation   The first stage of behavior therapy consists of careful observation of the child's behavior, most often in the natural school or home setting. Together with the adults concerned, the behavior therapist determines precisely which of the child's behaviors should be altered and in what manner. A possible list of target behaviors for an aggressive child might include taunting and hitting other children, issuing rude commands, and defying adults' instructions. After target behavior identification, baseline rates of occurrence are recorded to provide a standard against which to measure the effects of treatment. Often both desirable and undesirable actions are recorded, because the treatment aims to increase the first and decrease the latter. These observations also may provide clues concerning environmental controls over the child's activities. The use of extensive observational data in the formulation of treatment programs is a distinctive feature of the behavioral approach.

Increasing Rates of Desirable Behavior Behavioral techniques for promoting desirable child behavior include modeling, verbal instructions, and shaping or reinforcing closer and closer approximations to the desired behavior. In teaching a new behavior, the therapist might first model or demonstrate the action, and then use verbal or physical *prompts* to assist the child in performing the response. For example, the therapist may wish to teach a new speech sound to a developmentally delayed little girl. First the therapist demonstrates the required sound ("Mmm"), and then instructs the child to imitate it ("Mary, say 'mmm' "). At first, any sound the child makes is reinforced in order to encourage her vocalization. A hug, praise, or even a bit of food may be given to reinforce the girl's vocal attempts. To help the child approximate the correct sound more closely, the therapist may use a prompt to direct the child's attention to important information—for example, holding a bit of food beside his own mouth while uttering the sound. As a further aid, the therapist may gently squeeze the child's lips together as the child makes a sound. This physical prompt increases the chances that the girl will give a reinforceable approximation to the "mmm" sound. The therapist's physical assistance is removed or *faded* as soon as possible, lest the child's performance become dependent on it. A skillful therapist soon teaches the child to make the required speech sound upon request, and then moves on to teach her other sounds and words. As the child progresses, more ambitious efforts are required for a reward, perhaps several words or an entire sentence.

The therapist's goal is to achieve spontaneous speech, so the artificial reinforcement for speech is gradually decreased and finally entirely removed. This *operant learning* approach to speech training with developmentally delayed children is described in detail by Murdock and Hartmann (1975) and Sloane and MacAulay (1968), and similar approaches have been used to teach normal and deviant children a wide variety of developmentally appropriate skills.

Reducing Rates of Undesirable Behavior

Behavior therapy treats children's behavior problems first by promoting positive actions, and, if that does not suffice, by directly reducing the rate and intensity of negative acts. Most attempts to reduce inappropriate behavior do not occur in isolation, but are accompanied by programs to encourage desirable behavior and teach new skills. The ultimate goal is to teach the child new and more adaptive modes of responding. The techniques most commonly employed to control deviant behavior include *extinction,* which is accompanied by reinforcement of alternative, desired responses; *time out from positive reinforcement; response cost; token reinforcement programs;* and *overcorrection.* Some of these techniques are used with many types of child problems, while others, such as overcorrection, are confined to use with only the most seriously disturbed and delayed children. These techniques are described in the following passages. Each method has its advantages and problems, and is appropriate for use under particular circumstances, as will be pointed out. A careful analysis of the child's behavior, the effects of previous treatment efforts, and in some cases a thorough scrutiny of the treatment plan by

a review board are required in order to select the safest, least restrictive, and most effective treatment course.

Extinction. In an *extinction* procedure, reinforcement previously given for a particular behavior is discontinued. The child is neither threatened nor prevented from performing the response, but reinforcement is withheld when she does so. The rewarding consequence's absence eventually results in a reduction of the previously reinforced behavior. In one case (Williams, 1959), the exhausted parents of a 2-year-old boy who adamantly refused to go to sleep at night were instructed to put their son to bed at bedtime pleasantly but firmly, and then to leave the room. Previously, they had returned time after time over many hours to attempt to comfort the screaming, rampaging little boy. At first, he cried even louder and longer than before, but the parents persisted in their program to withdraw their reinforcing attention from his inappropriate behavior. Within a week he was going to bed happily and without complaint, as were his relieved parents. In other settings, withdrawal of adult attention has also decreased young children's inappropriate behavior. Nursery school teachers have reduced shy children's clinging and exclusive interaction with adults by ignoring it and instead praising them when they approach other children (Allen, Hart, Buell, Harris, & Wolf, 1964). Kindergarten children's quarreling and fighting have also diminished when the classroom teacher has placed such behavior on an extinction schedule by ignoring it (Brown & Elliott, 1965)—a procedure unlikely to succeed with the more seriously aggressive actions of older students.

Therapists must correctly identify and be able to control children's reinforcers in order to use extinction procedures effectively. These conditions are often difficult to achieve in the complex, varied world of children. Control is imperfect when there are too many different sources of reinforcement from too many people, ranging from classmates to parents. Consequently, extinction is used most often with closely supervised young children or in tightly controlled educational and treatment programs. Most older children are less dependent on adults, more influenced by peers, and better able to leave unreinforcing situations, thus defeating adults' attempts to place their misbehavior on extinction.

Time out from positive reinforcement. A useful alternative to extinction is *time out from positive reinforcement,* which is withholding reinforcing events briefly when the child has misbehaved. Often this technique involves briefly isolating the child in an unoccupied room or other uninteresting location. Each time-out period is short, ranging from a minute or less for very young or highly disturbed children to a maximum of about 10 minutes of continuous appropriate behavior for older ones (Gelfand & Hartmann, 1984). When the specified time period has elapsed and the child is behaving calmly and appropriately, the time-out period is terminated. However, screaming, kicking, throwing, or destroying things all extend the time-out period until the child regains self-control. In addition, the child must clean up any mess she has made before the incident is over. In most cases, the child's angry, destructive behavior ceases after the first or second time-out occasion because it draws no reinforcement.

Isolation is not necessary, since any brief withdrawal of reinforcement can produce time out. Time-out procedures can consist of pinning a brightly colored ribbon on a child to indicate that he is receiving time out and temporarily should not be responded to (Foxx & Shapiro, 1978), or of having the child briefly go to a desk removed from the classroom group (LeBlanc, Busby, & Thomson, 1974; Scarboro & Forehand, 1975). There are many ways to achieve the temporary removal of reinforcing events, which is the essence of time out.

When correctly and consistently administered, time out is an effective and humane way of controlling young children's moderately severely disruptive, antisocial, or aggressive actions (Hall & Hall, 1980). The technique requires that there be some level of ongoing reinforcement to withhold, so it will be ineffective in highly punitive social environments. In consequence, the time-out method is nearly always used in combination with a program of reinforcement for the child's desirable behavior, which teaches appropriate conduct and ensures that there is reinforcement to withhold if necessary.

Response cost. *Response cost* is a punishment procedure that results in the loss of previously earned rewards. This technique is commonly used in homes and treatment programs, and it essentially fines children for misbehavior. Many educational and therapeutic programs for children are run on *points systems* or *token economies,* which utilize points or tokens as reinforcers and fines for breaking the rules. When employed correctly and fairly, response cost is a mild and useful deterrent to proscribed behavior, especially if it is combined with positive reinforcement for appropriate conduct, a system described next.

Token reinforcement programs. Some children's problems are so severe that informal or limited intervention tactics fail to bring about improvement. The *token economy* or *token reinforcement* program consists of a set of rules specifying the manner in which children may earn points or tokens toward desired activities. Most token programs also include fines for certain types of misbehavior (response cost). These programs encourage children to behave as well as possible in order to earn various types of privileges. A sample token reinforcement program for an individual child is described in Box 14-2.

Token economy programs were first developed for use with severely disturbed adult mental hospital patients (Ayllon & Azrin, 1968), but quickly became popular for use with disturbed school children (O'Leary & O'Leary, 1972), in residential treatment programs with delinquents (Phillips, Phillips, Fixsen, & Wolf, 1971), and in helping parents deal with their own disturbed children (Kazdin, 1977; Patterson, Reid, Jones, & Conger, 1975). The Achievement Place project (also described in Chapter 5) is an excellent residential treatment program for antisocial and delinquent boys. This token economy program is carried out by trained teaching parents who supervise *every* aspect of the boys' lives, administering points for appropriate behavior and fines

In overcorrection, the teacher guides the child in practicing more appropriate behavior.

for problem behaviors. Achievement Place homes have been notably successful in reducing the boys' antisocial behavior and promoting appropriate academic behavior, at least while they remain in the program (Phillips et al., 1971). Graduates of Achievement Place community group homes are less often charged with new offenses than are those who receive alternative forms of treatment. However, the Achievement Place graduates claim to commit only slightly fewer new, undetected offenses than do comparison groups (Braukmann, Kirigin, & Wolf, 1976). The answer to the question of how to help delinquent youths still eludes us (see Chapter 5). In general, the more structured token economy programs are somewhat more effective in reducing antisocial, delinquent behavior than are the insight- and relationship-oriented approaches, perhaps because the structured programs teach youngsters specific academic and social skills (Cavior & Schmidt, 1978; Craft, Stephenson, & Granger, 1964; Quay, 1979).

Overcorrection. The unusual technique of overcorrection is used with severely retarded or psychotic children who do not respond to other corrective measures. Some of these children engage in repetitive, self-stimulatory activities, which preoccupy them for long periods of time and prevent them from learning more appropriate behaviors. They may repeatedly clap or flap their hands, stamp their feet, weave their heads from side to side, or mouth their bodies or other objects. Their bizarre routines have resisted treatment and lead others to avoid them and effectively exclude them from instructional activities. Foxx and Azrin (1973) developed the technique of overcorrection, which has proved to be remarkably effective in reducing self-stimulation. Immediately after the occurrence of self-stimulation, the therapist (1) firmly tells the child "No," and restrains the child if necessary to stop the inappropriate movements; (2) tells the child to perform a simple exercise for a required, brief time period, usually about 15 seconds; (3) physically guides the child in the exercise; and (4) instructs the child to engage in several different exercises for 2 to 5 minutes. (This

BOX 14-2 • The Case of Malevolent Maude

To illustrate the use of a token reward program with an individual child in a home setting, let us consider the case of a girl whom Patterson and his colleagues have chosen to call Malevolent Maude. Although only 10 years old and four feet tall, Maude was truly formidable. Her talent for lying, stealing, physically attacking, and generally infuriating others made her disliked by adults and children alike. Those who quarreled with her received impudent and insulting notes or found their favorite possessions smashed, destroyed, or missing. Through this type of behavior, Maude "could reduce most adults half again her size to smoldering impotence" (Patterson et al., 1975, p. 31).

The social learning program used by Patterson and his colleagues at the Oregon Social Learning Center first required Maude's parents to read a brief manual on the use of behavior principles with children. Then Maude and her parents met with a therapist for *contingency contracting*. In the contracting process, her parents were helped to identify specific behaviors they wished Maude to engage in or to avoid. Then parents and child agreed on a contract under which Maude earned points for not lying, for doing the dishes, for not swearing or stealing, and for complying with her parents' requests. She lost points for failing to behave appropriately, as indicated in Table 14-2. Her total points were tallied every day to determine her bedtime and other privileges. If she earned 10 points during the day, Maude went to bed at 8:30, had a special dessert, and had her mother read to her for half an hour. Less points earned Maude fewer rewards. In order to stay up until 8:30 and watch television, she needed 6 points; for earning only 4 points, she lost the opportunity to watch television; 0 points meant that she had to go to bed earlier at 7:30; and behaving so badly that she lost 5 points moved her bedtime forward to 6:30. A similar contract was worked out with Maude's teacher to improve Maude's school performance.

Observations conducted in homes and schools show that this type of intervention produces a 60 percent to 75 percent reduction in the treated child's rates of deviant behavior (Patterson, Cobb, & Ray, 1973). In contrast, comparable untreated children show no reduction in deviant behavior over a similar time span (Wiltz & Patterson, 1974). After treatment, fathers assume

punishment technique seems to indicate that disturbed children dislike exercise as much as many adults do.) When the inappropriate behavior results in physical damage, *restitutional overcorrection* is used to restore the environment to a state even better than it was prior to the damage. For example, a child who smears food or feces on a wall might be required to wash the entire wall, producing (in theory) a wall even cleaner than the one the child despoiled. In contrast, *positive practice overcorrection* may be used even when there is no damage to the environment. The child simply practices carrying out exercises—for example, alternately sitting down and standing up, copying designs, or completing simple hand exercises. Overcorrection procedures have successfully in-

creased autistic and retarded children's visual attention to teachers (Foxx, 1977), and reduced their inappropriate foot tapping (Epstein, Doke, Sajwaj, Sorrell, & Rimmer, 1974).

Limitations of overcorrection are that it is new and little understood; it is fairly restrictive and time-consuming to administer; and it interrupts other instructional programs for extended periods. There is no clear conceptual basis for overcorrection, which may be why it sometimes fails (Barnard, Christopherson, Altman, & Wolf, 1974). One comparative study (Foxx & Azrin, 1973) found overcorrection to be more effective than several other procedures, including reinforcement for appropriate behavior, and painting an ill-tasting solution on a child's hand

---

Box 14-2 (Continued)

Table 14-2

The token economy system used with Malevolent Maude

TARGET BEHAVIOR	POINTS EARNED FOR GOOD BEHAVIOR	POINTS LOST FOR BAD BEHAVIOR	OTHER NEGATIVE CONSEQUENCES
Stealing	1 for not stealing	5 for stealing	2 hours of housework
Swearing	3 for not swearing	1 for swearing	None
Noncompliance	2 for complying	1 for not complying	Time out in her room
Cleaning room	2 for cleaning	None	None
Washing dishes	1 for washing dishes	None	None
Lying	1 for not lying	None	None

Source: G. R. Patterson, J. B. Reid, R. R. Jones, and R. E. Conger. (1975). *A social learning approach to family intervention: Vol. 1. Families with aggressive children* (Eugene, OR: Castalia), p. 15. Reprinted by permission of the authors and the Castalia Publishing Company.

a greater role as disciplinarians and family members treat each other more positively. Moreover, the beneficial effects of treatment persist for a year or longer (Patterson & Fleischman, 1979).

Sources: G. R. Patterson, J. B. Reid, R. R. Jones, and R. E. Conger. (1975). *A social learning approach to family intervention: Vol. 1. Families with aggressive children* (Eugene, OR: Castalia); G. R. Patterson, J. A. Cobb, and R. S. Ray. (1973). A social engineering technology for retraining the families of aggressive boys. In H. E. Adams and I. Unikel (Eds.), *Issues and trends in behavior therapy* (Springfield, IL: Charles C Thomas); G. R. Patterson and M. J. Fleischman. (1979). Maintenance of treatment effects: Some considerations concerning family systems and follow-up data. *Behavior Therapy, 10,* 168–185; N. A. Wiltz and G. R. Patterson. (1974). An evaluation of parent training procedures designed to alter inappropriate aggressive behavior of boys. *Behavior Therapy, 5,* 215–221.

to prevent him from mouthing it incessantly. Typically, overcorrection is used sparingly and only in combination with positive reinforcement programs.

Physical punishment. Physical punishment is very rarely used in treatment because it is painful, it is coercive, and it sets a bad example for children. Punishment is a last resort when all available alternatives have been exhausted. Some severely disturbed children tear out their own hair, knock out their teeth, repeatedly fling themselves from high places, or beat their heads against walls so that they detach their retinas and become blind. When highly disturbed psychotic, brain-damaged, or retarded children threaten to do damage to themselves, something must be done.

Present alternatives are straitjacket restraints 24 hours a day to prevent self-injury; heavy sedation, which clouds perception and thinking; or some form of physical punishment. Since restraint and sedation are coercive and deprive children of learning opportunities, physical punishment is sometimes employed. Lovaas and Simmons (1969) reported striking success in suppressing self-directed physical attacks through harmless but painful electric shocks. Usually only 3 to 12 shocks are required in all, so the child's discomfort is as minimal as possible. After their self-injurious behavior has been eliminated, disturbed children appear happier, more attentive, and easier to teach. Nevertheless, review boards and treatment centers seldom approve the use of physical punishment with children, whatever their problems or prospects.

If a distasteful treatment is to be used, it should be more effective than any alternatives. Punishment is not always effective, and Romanczyk and Goren (1975) have found that in some cases shock may not completely suppress children's self-injurious behavior. Moreover, the less coercive overcorrection treatment has virtually eliminated self-injurious behavior in some children (Harris & Romanczyk, 1976; Kelly & Drabman, 1977), as has immobilization, in which for 15 seconds an adult seated behind the child grasps the child's forearms and gently holds the child's hands at her sides to prevent self-stimulatory behavior (Bitgood, Crowe, Suarez, & Peters, 1980). Other alternatives to painful shock are described by Gelfand and Hartmann (1984). Shock punishment is little used today, and is only employed after the failure of less restrictive methods, such as overcorrection and time out (Repp & Dietz, 1974).

Desensitization and Relaxation Techniques
As noted in Chapter 4, children who are immobilized by fear and anxiety may be treated by *desensitization* and *relaxation training*. In desensitization, the child is helped to imagine or encounter closer and closer approximations to the aversive situation while maintaining a state of relaxation. Another approach used by Cautela and Groden (1978) simply teaches the child muscle relaxation techniques to use whenever she encounters a difficult and stressful situation. The evidence for the effectiveness of desensitization and relaxation training comes chiefly from therapists' reports and so is inconclusive (Hatzenbuehler & Schroeder, 1978; Richards & Siegel, 1979). One well-conducted study did not find either systematic (imaginal) desensitization or traditional child psychotherapy to be more helpful than no therapy in the treatment of children with phobias (Miller, Barrett, Hampe, & Noble, 1972). As indicated later, modeling and supported encounters with the feared situation hold more promise than desensitization or relaxation.

Social Learning Approaches
  Modeling and guided participation.
Carefully conducted comparison studies have shown social learning procedures to be effective in reducing children's fearful and avoidant behavior (Kirkland & Thelen, 1977; Rosenthal & Bandura, 1978). *Modeling* demonstrations of appropriate actions are used to teach clients new skills, such as how to deal with exposure to heights, stressful social situations, or feared animals such as dogs. The model's demonstration also shows the client that engaging in the feared behavior has no adverse consequences, and may even have some positive ones (as when the person begins to enjoy meeting and talking with new acquaintances). Modeling approaches to the treatment of fears are reviewed more fully in Chapter 4.

Bandura's (1977) self-efficacy theory suggests that treatment should be based on procedures that convince children of their capacity to cope with frightening situations. The self-confidence born of success should encourage initially fearful children to meet future challenges confidently and master them. Consequently, one would expect that procedures such as witnessing others acting bravely should help convince the phobic child that he can do the same. In addition, actually entering the avoided situation and coping with it successfully *(guided participation treatment)* often constitute the most potent intervention (Rosenthal & Bandura, 1978). In the guided participation procedure, fearful clients first observe models coping successful with the feared situation. Next they gradually participate more actively, at first being physically guided by the model and relying on protective equipment such as gloves to touch snakes or dogs and restraining harnesses when encountering heights. Finally, after meeting success at each preceding step, they attempt to cope independently with the feared situation. Box 14-3 describes a guided participation modeling procedure for use with young children with snake phobia.

  Effectiveness of modeling and guided participation. Modeling procedures have proved

---

BOX 14-3 • Posie the Therapist: The Treatment of Children's Snake Phobia through Guided Participation

---

Many children fear snakes, but some are so fearful that they become terrified at the very thought of a snake. Brunehilde Ritter (1968) developed modeling procedures to treat such snake phobic children who were between 5 and 11 years of age. The most successful treatment involved having a small group of children watch the adult therapist playing with Posie, a harmless, 4-foot-long corn snake. The therapist petted Posie, talked to her and to the children, and picked Posie up and placed her inside a cage. Then in a guided participation procedure, each child put his hand on the therapist's arm as she stroked Posie gently. In gradual steps, the children were helped to pet Posie themselves, to pick her up, and hold her, and to take turns playing with the snake and instructing the other children to do so. Another group of children simply observed the modeling sequence while models engaged in progressively bolder interactions with Posie (a no-participation modeling procedure). In comparison with control group children who received no treatment, both the modeling-only and the modeling-and-guided-participation groups improved. The children reported they experienced less fear of snakes and after treatment they could actually pick up and play with snakes, whereas the untreated children could not. The guided participation treatment was more effective than was modeling alone. At the conclusion of treatment a behavioral avoidance test was conducted that required the children to handle snakes. All of the behavior test items were successfully performed by 80 percent of the guided participation group; 53 percent of the modeling-only group performed all test items, but none (0 percent) of the control group could do so. To prevent the now-fearless treated children from approaching poisonous snakes, they were told to be cautious because some snakes are actually dangerous, and were instructed to try their new snake-handling skills only under adult supervision.

Source: B. Ritter. (1968). The group desensitization of children's snake phobias using vicarious and contact desensitization procedures. *Behaviour Research and Therapy, 6,* 1–6.

---

helpful for clients of all ages and for a range of problems, including nursery school children's social withdrawal (O'Connor, 1972), students' examination anxiety (Jaffe & Carlson, 1972; Mann & Rosenthal, 1969), children's fear of swimming (Lewis, 1974), small-animal phobias (Bandura, Blanchard, & Ritter, 1969), and fear of surgical and dental procedures (Melamed & Siegel, 1975; Taylor, Ferguson, & Wermuth, 1977). Fearful adults sometimes profit from *covert modeling* (Kazdin, 1973), in which the client imagines an appropriate modeling episode—for example, visualizing people confidently entering the dentist's office. Young children may be unable to generate and control imaginal modeling scenes and consequently may require in-person or filmed models (Rosenthal & Bandura, 1978).

In addition to their effectiveness, modeling techniques are efficient and inexpensive, requiring only six to eight sessions to solve the problem on the average (Gelfand, 1978; Gelfand & Hartmann, 1984). A limitation is that thus far only a very narrow range of children's problems have proven amenable to modeling procedures, mostly disorders of anxiety and specific fears (Ollendick, 1979). Consequently, the clinical utility of modeling therapy is limited at present. However, modeling processes are a prominent though unacknowledged part of most other forms of therapy, such as *behavioral language training,* which involves reinforcing the child for imitating the therapist's speech, as well as activity group therapy and client-centered approaches in which the therapist presents a model of maturity, compassion, and self-control. New self-regulation procedures, which are discussed in Chapter 15, explicitly use modeled demonstrations of coping skills. Like reinforcement processes, modeling influences are included in virtually all forms of psychotherapy.

Marital and Family Therapy

Each year thousands of Americans enter marital counseling and family therapy in an attempt to save troubled marriages, reduce friction among family members, and alleviate children's psychological problems. The treatment approaches discussed previously typically treat individual psychopathology, while the systems-oriented family therapy approach portrays the entire family unit as malfunctioning and causing its members to engage in maladaptive behavior. Family therapists point out that families target particular members as deviant when, in fact, the entire family interactional system is at fault. For instance, Patterson (1975) found that children referred by their parents for treatment for aggression were no more aggressive than their supposedly normal siblings. Thus the entire family becomes the focus of assessment and treatment, rather than individual members. "This concept of the family as a unit, a dynamic system and not just a group of individuals, is the central unifying concept in family therapy today" (Buckley, 1977, p. 26). Treating the couple or family conjointly is a reasonable and effective method for improving the marital relationship and easing tensions (Gurman & Kniskern, 1978).

Types of Family Therapy   Types of conjoint family therapy range from the psychoanalytic to various systems analyses and behavioral interventions. Ackerman (1966), one of the first family therapy practitioners, integrated concepts from psychoanalysis and role therapy to explain family processes. Ackerman used confrontational tactics and blunt accusations to disrupt customary but maladaptive family interaction patterns and to force family members to recognize existing problems. For example, the therapist might point out how one person persistently refuses to recognize

another's needs and how the other acquiesces but also sabotages.

The *systems approach* to conjoint family therapy (Haley, 1963; Jackson & Weakland, 1961; Satir, 1967) emphasizes the need to understand the roles played by every family member. Systems analysis views the identified patient's problem as attributable to the family's atypical interactions. In fact, a child's deviant behavior may serve some function for the family, perhaps by distracting attention from an unhappy marriage; thus the others may unknowingly encourage and maintain the child's problem behavior. Thus the family maintains its balance or homeostasis and manages to remain together to fulfill at least some of its members' needs for security, affection, and support. To maintain the shaky balance, the family tends to resist any form of change, including improvements (Haley, 1963; Jackson, 1965). In this analysis, it is imperative that the treatment include the entire family.

Therapists with a systems or communications orientation analyze the verbal and nonverbal messages exchanged in family interactions. Satir (1967) has stressed the importance of covert *family rules* governing each member's responding. The therapist strives to uncover these rules and to allow the family to change them. A possible family rule may allow the younger daughter to foment quarrels among the others while seeming to be good beyond reproach. Or the covert rule may allow the mother to dominate the others through physical complaints about headaches, insomnia, and fatigue. The therapist clarifies these rules and so provides the family with an opportunity to make positive changes. Other tactics used by communications therapists include relabeling individuals' behaviors in more positive terms. For example, the therapist may refer to a child's behavior as "grown-up" and "independent," when the others have termed it "stubborn" or "selfish." Alternatively, the therapist may "prescribe the symptom" and direct family members to exaggerate their customary behavior (such as being overly critical or negative), which may help them recognize their problems.

Family therapy can help to modify faulty interaction patterns of victimization, passive aggression, and other forms of deviant behavior. As the text explains, the prognosis is more favorable when fathers agree to participate than when they do not.

A charismatic psychotherapist named Salvador Minuchin (1974) has developed a form of intervention termed *structural family therapy* for use with families of children and adolescents who are delinquent, are addicted to drugs, or have physical problems such as asthma, diabetes, or anorexia nervosa, the mysterious self-starvation disorder (see Chapter 7). Minuchin conceptualizes sets or inadequate problem-solving strategies as central to family problems. In families under stress, the same unsuccessful sets are used time after time, even in inappropriate circumstances. A mother may continue to restrict and confine her teenage son, who appropriately has begun to strive for independence. The father may take the side of the son, and the other children may be divided. The same dysfunctional pattern may recur many times, separating parents from children and perpetuating family turmoil. This pattern is typical of an *enmeshed family,* in which the members continuously intrude into each other's affairs. The structural family therapist attempts to strengthen the alliance between the parents and to encourage parents and children to interact with others of their age, both within and outside the family. In *disengaged families,* the isolated members have very little impact on each other, so the therapist attempts to facilitate contact, to improve communication, and to define each person's role in family functioning.

Minuchin advocates a very active role for the therapist, temporarily joining the family in a position of leadership in order to disclose and evaluate the family structure. The therapist then forms coalitions with the different factions in turn, challenging family members' perceptions of social reality and assigning them homework tasks to complete between therapy sessions. These procedures are designed to create circumstances to transform maladaptive family structures.

Behavioral family therapy moves interaction patterns away from reliance on coercion and toward more adaptive exchanges of positive reinforcement (Patterson et al., 1975). *Contingency contracting* is frequently used to ensure that the child's desirable behaviors are noted and reinforced by his parents and that the child understands exactly what behaviors are required of him. *Modeling* and *role playing* are used to teach family members how to respond to each other more positively. Therapy sessions may be held in the family's home, so that the therapist can observe their behavior and implement treatment programs in a natural setting.

Some combined approaches to family therapy employ techniques adapted from various theoretical orientations. Alexander's *functional family therapy* (Alexander & Malouf, 1983) employs a systems perspective on the family, but also uses behavioral methods such as modeling and contingency contracting to modify specific problem behaviors. In Alexander's approach, families of adolescent delinquents are trained to communicate with each other more clearly and accurately, to increase reciprocity in their exchanges as opposed to one person's dominance, and to encourage the consideration of alternative solutions for problems. These interaction modes resemble those of well-functioning families. The treatment effects seem to be long-lasting, and the siblings benefit as well as the delinquent youths themselves (Klein, Alexander, & Parsons, 1977).

Effectiveness of Marital and Family Therapies   After an extensive literature review, DeWitt (1978) concluded that conjoint family treatment is equal or superior to other methods. A number of comparative studies either have reported no differences in effectiveness between conjoint and other methods, or have found differences favoring the conjoint approach. Rates of improvement of children treated with conjoint therapy are reported to be 71 or 72 percent (DeWitt, 1978; Gurman & Kniskern, 1978); this is comparable to improvement rates for individual psychotherapy (Bergin, 1971). Some outcome studies have reported that behaviorally oriented family therapy for children's antisocial aggression is extremely effective and that its effects are long-lived (Patterson & Fleischman, 1979). Alexander and Parsons (1973) reported that their functional family therapy was dramatically effective in reducing teenagers' delinquent behavior when compared

with client-centered and psychoanalytically oriented family counseling. Other studies (Bernal, Klinnert, & Schultz, 1980; Bernal & Margolin, 1976) found few differences between client-centered and behavioral methods in the treatment of antisocial conduct by young children of welfare mothers. However, the mothers felt more competent and judged their children as better behaved following the behavioral treatment. A recent review by Todd and Stanton (1983) reported family therapy to be as successful as other therapy types, but not more so, with the different types of family therapy being equivalent in effectiveness across the entire range of child and family problems. Treatment outcomes often are better when fathers participate, regardless of whether the parents are together or separated (Love, Kaswan, & Bugental, 1972; Shapiro & Budman, 1973; Todd & Stanton, 1983). When both partners agree to participate in counseling, there is some chance of improving dyadic and parent-child relationships, but if either parent refuses to take part, the outlook worsens. This finding may reflect a generally worse prognosis for children of embattled parents than for those of parents in intact or reconciled marriages.

Residential Treatment

Long-term residential treatment is used in the most serious cases of pervasive developmental delay, mental retardation, and psychosis. Residential treatment removes children from their homes and communities and confines them in the most restrictive setting, so it is not used unless absolutely necessary. And yet approximately 450,000 American children currently require inpatient care (Irwin, 1982). Those who must be institutionalized meet some or all of the following criteria (Hersov & Bentovim, 1977): (1) They are dangerous to themselves or others; (2) their behavior is so bizarre or deviant that outpatient care is inappropriate; (3) their problems are complex and require intensive observation, assessment, and treatment not possible elsewhere; or (4) the family is unsupportive, absent, or highly pathological. Otherwise, the less restrictive outpatient treatment modalities are preferable.

In addition to ethical reasons for preferring outpatient treatment whenever possible, long-term institutionalization is seldom used because it is prohibitively expensive. In 1980, a 1-year stay for a child in a public residential treatment center cost as much as $40,000 (Romanczyk, Kistner, & Crimmins, 1980), and the price is undoubtedly much higher today. Consequently, residential care is limited to children who are unmanageable; who require 24-hour-a-day supervision or special medical care; or who pose some type of danger. There are few treatment alternatives for such seriously disturbed youngsters who simply must be institutionalized, so comparative treatment outcome research is rare. Such research requires assigning children randomly to inpatient and outpatient interventions in order to evaluate the relative effectiveness of the different treatments, and in many cases outpatient care is out of the question (Quay, 1979). One residential program has been carefully evaluated, however: Project Re-Ed, a residential treatment program for highly aggressive or withdrawn 6- to 12-year-old boys. In this program, specially trained teachers work intensively with small groups of children for many hours each day. The children receive both counseling and special education services, and a liaison teacher works with the parents and families to increase their acceptance of the disturbed children and to teach the adults appropriate child management skills. The goal is to increase the correspondence between the child's behavior and others' expectations of him so that both will be more satisfied. The boys spend an average of 8 months in the Project Re-Ed center, returning home over weekends and vacations to maintain contact with their families and communities.

Project Re-Ed has been successful in many respects (Hobbs, 1966; Quay, 1979; Weinstein, 1969, 1974). Treatment substantially improved the boys' behavior as rated by their parents, counselors, and referring agencies such as schools. As compared to a matched but untreated group, boys who participated in Project Re-Ed showed improved self-esteem, decreased impulsivity, and fewer academic problems. This comparison indicates that Project Re-Ed is better than no treatment, but it does not compare the program with a good outpatient intervention. Furthermore, it is not known which elements of the program are responsible for its success; however, the special education services did reduce the children's academic difficulties and helped the children maintain their behavior improvements during an 18-month follow-up period. In contrast, boys with continuing academic difficulties tended to deteriorate behaviorally (Weinstein, 1974).

Drug Treatments

Psychoactive drugs (those that affect mood, activity level, or thinking) can provide relief from some of the troublesome behaviors associated with children's psychological disturbances. The types of problems most often treated with drugs include the attention deficits and impulsivity that accompany attention deficit disorder with hyperactivity (ADD-H); psychotic children's agitation, disorganization, or apathy; and toileting problems such as enuresis (involuntary urination, particularly bedwetting). In addition, the past decade has witnessed an increased interest in the pharmacological treatment of children's depressed affect and mood instability (Rancurello, 1986). There have been some controlled experiments on the use of drugs to combat yet other types of childhood disorders, but for the most part only uncontrolled clinical trials have been reported. In general, these three uses—with ADD-H, psychotic or pervasively developmentally delayed, or incontinent children—remain the most proven and accepted (Rancurello, 1986; Wiener, 1984). Pharmacological treatment of children aims to reduce disruptive, disorganized, and inappropriate behavior patterns and to allow children to become more responsive to educational and psychotherapeutic interventions. Thus, drugs do not cure children's psychopathology at present, although this is a future possibility. In most cases medication is used to eliminate or control the deviant behaviors that interfere with children's social and intellectual development.

The clinical or therapeutic classification of drugs for juveniles is based on effects on adults, for whom the drugs were originally developed

Table 14-3

Drugs Commonly Used to Treat Children for Behavior Disorders

Clinical Classification	Generic Name	Trade Name	Primary Use
Stimulants	Dextroamphetamine Methylphenidate	Dexedrine Ritalin	To control impulsivity and inattentiveness in hyperactive children
Antidepressants (tricyclics)	Imipramine Amitriptyline Desipramine	Tofranil Elavil Pertofrane Norpranin	To relieve enuresis (involuntary urination); to treat affective disorders
Antipsychotics or major tranquilizers	Chlorpromazine	Thorazine Largactil Navane	To reduce excitability and aggression in retarded, brain-injured, and psychotic children

(Wiener & Jaffe, 1977). Drugs such as dextroamphetamine (Dexedrine) and methylphenidate (Ritalin) are called *stimulants* because of their alerting, antifatiguing functions with mature people. Another group of drugs are termed *antidepressants* because they combat adult depression, elevate mood, increase enjoyment in life, and stabilize mood states. These include agents such as the tricyclic amines, imipramine (Tofranil) and amitriptyline (Elavil); the monoamine (MAO) inhibitors; and lithium carbonate for use in manic-depressive disorders. In addition, the *antipsychotic* or *neuroleptic drugs* developed for the control of agitated and irrational behavior in adult schizophrenic patients are sometimes administered to otherwise uncontrollable retarded or psychotic youngsters. Table 14-3 shows the clinical classification, the generic and trade names, and the primary uses of some psychoactive medications given to children and adolescents.

Children's physiological functioning differs from that of adults in some important respects, and research results with adults do not always predict children's responses to the same chemical agents. Some drugs prescribed for adults affect children differently and have different uses in child treatment. Sometimes the child's developing body reacts to drugs in a unique and unexpected manner, as is particularly likely to be true for infants and very young children, who lack the enzymes required to metabolize stimulants and some

other drugs (Coffey, Shader, & Greenblatt, 1983). Some drugs are eliminated from children's bodies more rapidly, and optimum dosage levels per unit of body weight may differ markedly for children and adults (Yaffe & Danish, 1977). Simply administering a child the adult dosage per kilogram of body weight can result in an overdose or can prove insufficient. The child is an immature organism, not simply a miniature adult, and must be treated accordingly. Furthermore, adolescents' drug reactions may differ from those of both children and adults. One group of reviewers flatly stated that on the basis of the drug treatment literature, It should not be assumed that adolescents respond in the same manner as adults (Rifkin, Wortman, Reardon, & Siris, 1986). Clearly, much more research is required in order to develop appropriate pharmacological treatments for children and adolescents.

Another complicating factor for the physician is that child psychological disorders may differ significantly from those of adults. Some childhood problems such as ADD-H are virtually unknown among adults, and five of the major DSM-III diagnostic categories are confined exclusively to infants, children, and adolescents (Gelfand & Peterson, 1985). Moreover, children are much less adequate reporters of their moods and other internal psychological states than are adults, and this fact makes evaluation of psychoactive drugs difficult. The preceding considerations clearly warn against an uncritical application of adult-based drug treatments to child populations.

Stimulant Drugs   As early as the 1930s, stimulant drugs were known to increase hyperactive children's attentiveness and to improve their classroom demeanor, but only during the past 20 years have these drugs come into widespread medical use (Wiener & Jaffe, 1977). ADD-H is probably the disorder most often treated with any form of psychoactive drugs, and stimulants are the drugs most often prescribed for this and other childhood psychiatric disorders (McDaniel, 1986a). ADD-H is described in Chapters 5 and 8, and can be briefly characterized as a disturbance in impulse control, attention, planful problem solving, and rule-governed behavior. Stimulants act on ADD-H children in the same manner as they affect normal children and adults: they aid performance on long, dull, effortful tasks on which motivation wanes and attention tends to wander (Sroufe, 1975; Whalen & Henker, 1976). Psychostimulant medication typically aids performance on these types of tasks in classroom settings (Conners & Taylor, 1980; Loney, 1986). Some researchers have reported that appropriate dosages of the stimulant methylphenidate (Ritalin) improve children's classroom assignment completion rates and their accuracy, as well as increasing their on-task behavior (Rapport, DuPaul, Stoner, & Jones, 1986). In most cases, although children attend to their school work better, their class standing does not improve. Stimulant-produced attentional gains do not automatically translate into better academic grades or higher standardized achievement test scores (McDaniel, 1986b). Concomitant psychosocial treatments such as behavior therapy and special education classes are necessary in order to raise ADD-H children's academic achievement (Conners & Werry, 1979; Ross & Ross, 1982).

There is general agreement that stimulant drugs such as methylphenidate can improve ADD-H children's task-related behavior in 60 to 90 percent of the cases (Whalen & Henker, 1976). Nevertheless, there is substantial disagreement on the advisability of long-term administration of psychostimulants to children. Symptoms are wors-ened or there are negative side effects in as many as 10 percent of the cases (Cantwell, 1977). Unpleasant side effects are usually worst at the inception of treatment and include insomnia, irritability, nausea and gastric upset, sadness, crying, and elevated systolic blood pressure. The most serious side effect is a profound loss of appetite, which can lead to the suppression of a child's natural growth in height and weight (Wiener, 1984). It is not known whether growth stunting is completely avoidable (Mates & Gittelman, 1983; Wiener, 1984), although some experts indicate that periodic drug withdrawal intervals or "holidays" permit adequate catch-up growth (Conners & Werry, 1979). When administered therapeutically, stimulants are not addictive, and there are no apparent negative behavioral side effects of long-term use (Beck, Langford, MacKay, & Sum, 1975; Weiss, 1975).

Antipsychotic Drugs   The antipsychotic or neuroleptic drugs include phenothiazines, thioxanthenes, and haloperidol. The drugs were originally developed for use with psychotic adults and are used with children chiefly to control the violent and overexcited behavior of profoundly retarded, brain-injured, or psychotic patients. Specifically, antipsychotic drugs have proved useful in reducing mentally retarded children's assaultiveness, destructiveness, self-injury, and extreme restlessness. Unfortunately, these medications also act as sedatives, reducing the children's alertness substantially and impairing their thinking and problem-solving abilities (Wiener, 1984; Winsberg & Yepes, 1978). Troublesome to very serious side effects include muscle rigidity and *dyskinesia* (involuntary tongue protrusion, grimacing, drooling, tremor, and stereotyped movements of the head, extremities, and trunk). These undesirable effects can be controlled by other medication, but they make antipsychotic medication a less appealing form of treatment for seriously disturbed children. It is actually misleading to label these drugs as *antipsychotic,* because although they make highly disturbed children more manageable, they do not reduce other psychotic behaviors such as thought and language disturbances. Rather, the antipsychotic drugs reduce withdrawal, severe overactivity, and destructiveness in some children who are psychotic, retarded, or have pervasive developmental disorders (Gittelman-Klein, Spitzer, & Cantwell, 1978). However, serious experimental design limitations make research findings about the antipsychotic drugs' effectiveness only tentative at best (Campbell, 1985).

Antidepressant Drugs

Antidepressants to treat enuresis. Tricyclic antidepressant drugs are useful in the relief of depression in adults, but are also used with children for a very different purpose. Antidepressants are used to control involuntary daytime wetting or night bedwetting (enuresis) in children over the age of 6 years. The most commonly prescribed antidepressant, imipramine (Tofranil), effectively reduces wetting in 60 to 80 percent of the cases while the child continues to take the drug. A major drawback is that relapse generally follows drug withdrawal (Blackwell & Currah, 1973). Moreover, imipramine only reduces but does not eliminate enuresis, and high dosages can produce dangerous cardiovascular side effects and seizures. Even low dosages may produce trembling, sweating, irritability, and wakefulness (Greenberg & Stephans, 1977). It seems unnecessary to resort to pharmacological treatment of enuresis, because behavioral treatment methods employing simple buzzer alarm devices to signal urination are relatively effective and produce no unwanted side effects (Azrin, Bugle, & O'Brien, 1971). The device consists of a buzzer that sounds when the child urinates outside the toilet. The alarm alerts the child and his parents and allows him to complete urination in the toilet rather than in bed or in his pants. After several such occurrences, and when he receives reinforcement for appropriate use of the toilet, even a severely mentally retarded child can become toilet-trained.

Antidepressants for children's mood disorders. As Chapter 4 indicates, it has only recently been discovered that children can suffer from true depression and other affective disorders. It would seem reasonable to test the effects on children of the antidepressant medications,

particularly the safer tricyclics, which have proven so successful in the treatment of adult affective disorders. A complicating factor is that childhood depression is so newly recognized as a clinical syndrome that there is much disagreement regarding its diagnosis. This makes treatment evaluation research difficult to perform adequately. Now, however, the standard psychiatric diagnostic manual, DSM-III, provides the same general criteria for use in judging depression in people of all ages, and new tests and observational procedures have been developed for use with children. Despite these advances, the research evidence is mixed. One respected group of psychiatric researchers reported antidepressant medication to be effective in reducing depressive symptoms in children (Puig-Antich, 1982; Puig-Antich et al., 1979). Other authorities cautiously suggest that antidepressants may be helpful in some precisely diagnosed groups (Johnson et al., 1986). Still a third view is that there is no better intervention: "Despite limitations such as side effects, the high probability of being left with residual symptoms even after 'remission' and the way in which the use of medication may convey unwarranted optimism and certainty about recovery, there are no competing nondrug treatments that have been proven as effective" (Rancurello, 1986, p. 388). This diversity of views suggests that there is much to be discovered regarding treatment of juvenile affective disorders.

Guidelines for Drug Therapy

Any drug that is potent enough to affect psychological functioning is likely to have moderate to severe negative side effects. Therefore, the administration of drugs is a moderately restrictive, potentially dangerous treatment that should be undertaken with caution. Wiener (1977) has offered the following suggestions regarding the appropriately conservative use of drug therapy:

1. **Drug therapy should almost always be an additional intervention and not the sole or chief treatment.**
2. **In most cases, psychological and educational treatments should be attempted before medication is prescribed.**

3. A thorough physical and psychosocial evaluation of the child should precede any administration of drugs.
4. Drug therapy should be part of a formal treatment plan, with specific and well-defined goals, monitoring for side effects, and periodic follow-up evaluations.
5. Therapy should begin with the minimum therapeutic dose of a well-tested drug. The dose should be increased until either improvement is noted or unwanted side effects occur.
6. Drug holidays or drug-free periods should be included to establish the earliest time at which the drug therapy can be discontinued.

Authorities in child psychopharmacology are very cautious about prescribing drugs for children. Safer methods such as psychotherapy should be tried first, and medication should never be relied on as the sole answer to the child's problems. The child must be protected from the unwise and indiscriminate use of drugs, and should receive the smallest dosage possible and for the briefest period necessary. Chemotherapy has a demonstrated place in the treatment of child psychopathology, but only when used wisely and conservatively.

SUMMARY

Table 14-4 summarizes the therapeutic approaches presented in this chapter. Children's characteristics, such as their age, type of disorder, and family circumstances, determine the type of treatment they receive. Younger, less socially and cognitively skilled children are more likely to receive structured, skill-building interventions, whereas older, less disturbed ones may receive insight-oriented individual and conjoint family therapy in addition to learning new skills. Insight-oriented psychoanalytic or nondirective therapy aims to help the child understand her own emotions and desires, thereby reducing the emotional conflict that is presumed to underlie the problem. Behavioral and educational approaches attempt to remedy the child's skill deficits. Behavioral

Table 14-4
Range and Focus of Therapeutic Approaches

Recipients	Treatment Type
The child alone	Psychoanalytic play therapy, nondirective play therapy, individual behavior therapy, drug therapy
The classroom or play group	Classroom token reinforcement programs, group play therapy, discussion group therapy
The parents and target child	Filial therapy, parent-child behavior therapy, Project Re-Ed
The parents alone	Group therapy for parents, parent training, self-help manuals
All family members	Conjoint family therapy

techniques such as modeling and shaping are used to teach the child new routines. Desirable behavior is reinforced and undesirable behavior is reduced by various procedures, such as extinction, time out from reinforcement, response cost, overcorrection, or (rarely) physical punishment. Conjoint family therapy is used when the child's problems stem from faulty family communications and maladaptive interactions. Children who do not profit from these outpatient treatments and who are dangerously unmanageable may be institutionalized. Behavioral therapists have demonstrated repeated success in improving children's specific behaviors, and the available research evidence indicates that there is a genuine, though modest, positive effect from all major types of child psychotherapy.

Drugs may reduce the occurrence of disruptive behaviors; they are usually not used alone, but accompany psychosocial treatments. Stimulant drugs are moderately successful in treating children with attention deficits, particularly in combination with behavior therapy. Tricyclic antidepressant medication helps children with enuresis, at least temporarily, and may be useful in the treatment of childhood depression and other affective disorders. Antipsychotic drugs are typically used only with psychotic, retarded, or pervasively developmentally delayed children who are severely disorganized or violent.

The few available comparative treatment studies have shown that modeling and guided participation are particularly useful in treating phobias. As compared to other approaches, structured educational and behavioral methods are somewhat more successful overall in the treatment of antisocial and delinquent youngsters, as well as severely psychotic or retarded ones. Family therapy is as effective as individual or group psychotherapy, and all are superior to no treatment. Both stimulant drugs and behavior therapy help ADD-H children, although behavior therapy is safer and may be longer-lasting. A combination of psychotherapy and drug treatment, where possible, is effective in the treatment of ADD-H, psychotic conditions, and possibly affective disorders.

chapter

15

New
Directions

KEY TERMS

Due Process.   Constitutional guarantee to legal procedures designed to protect individuals' rights and liberties—For example, the right to confront one's accuser.

Self-Instruction.   A self-regulation training technique in which the person gives himself verbal instructions on how to proceed, first aloud and then covertly.

Self-Regulation.   A form of therapy in which the client is taught first to recognize a problem in self-control, and then how to manage herself and to reward herself for successful accomplishment.

Status Offenders.   Children who engage in activities that are criminal only for juveniles, such as drinking alcohol, smoking, and truancy.

OVERVIEW OF NEW DEVELOPMENTS IN CHILD PSYCHOPATHOLOGY

All fields of study change and develop over time. This final chapter is devoted to the identification and discussion of some emerging trends in the diagnosis, prevention, and treatment of childhood psychological disorders. Innovation occurs in many different areas, so this chapter discusses

439

new trends in some highly diverse aspects of this field of study.

Throughout the discussion, it is clear that children's rights and status in society are in the process of change. New developments in the field of child law are considered, as well as the evolving definitions of children's needs and their legal and human rights. The legal questions to be considered include the following: Are children legally considered to be persons, or are their rights and prerogatives more restricted than those of adults? Can children legally control the type and severity of discipline their parents can impose on them? When their parents separate, do children have the right to live with the parent they prefer, or are parental rights dominant? Must parents obtain treatment for their disturbed children? Can they institutionalize their children against their wills? Under what circumstances do children have due process rights and other rights guaranteed to adults under the U.S. Constitution? These are searching questions that strike at the heart of our beliefs about the capacities of children and the nature of childhood. The quest for answers takes us into many different areas of study, including law, ethics, social science, and government; this illustrates the interdisciplinary nature of the field of childhood psychopathology.

We also discuss new assessment techniques that are geared to children's cognitive developmental levels, as well as to the growing appreciation of the child's role in adult-child relationships. In the treatment realm, we consider how even young children can learn some measure of self-control. *Prevention* of psychological disturbance has long been a professional goal; however, recent prevention programs have been more numerous and generally more effective than in the past, and we discuss some of these. Finally, we discuss the rise in alternative child care patterns in the United States, and we describe some barriers to effective child care and prevention services.

QUESTIONS REGARDING CHILDREN'S RIGHTS

Do children have a right to be loved? We know that loving care is good for children and that its lack is keenly felt. Yet no such right exists in law. It is important to distinguish between legal rights and human or moral rights. *Human rights* are the conditions necessary for children to become healthy, well-adjusted, competent, and productive citizens. The right to be loved and wanted is a human right to a condition that is highly desirable but not mandated by law. In contrast, a *legal right* is "an enforceable claim to the possession of property or authority or to the enjoyment of privileges or immunities" (Rodham, 1979, p. 21). Legal rights are guaranteed by the U.S. Constitution or by statute, and are enforced by the police and the courts. Some but not all human rights are guaranteed by law, but all are widely recognized as serving the child's needs and interests.

Human Rights for Children

All of the world's countries and communities attempt to guard children's welfare as each society interprets it. Reflecting this concern, the United Nations General Assembly (1973) has adopted a declaration listing the human rights due to children. All children are supposed to be accorded these rights, regardless of age, sex, nationality, social status, religion, or physical or mental condition. The United Nations has specified that the best interests of the *child,* not of parents, teachers, or others, should be the most important consideration in formulating legislation. The laws should protect children and provide them the opportunity to develop in a healthy fashion. All children should have adequate prenatal and postnatal care; adequate nutrition and housing; free, compulsory education; and recreation opportunities. This is an ambitious agenda for a world that sees millions of children go hungry, ill-housed, medically untreated, and deprived of the ordinary comforts of life, each year.

In the psychological and social spheres, the United Nations has declared that children should be raised in an atmosphere of affection and emotional security. Ideally, they should be cared for by their parents. Children who are separated from their parents, especially their mothers, should receive special societal protection. Children should be spared all forms of cruelty, neglect, and exploitation for commercial gain. They should be among the first to receive relief in times of natural disaster, famine, or war. To ensure peaceful relations among the peoples of the world, the United Nations has urged that children be protected from discrimination and prejudice, whether racial, religious, political, or any other type. Any day's news accounts demonstrate just how far we are from achieving these humane goals.

Foster (1974; Foster & Freed, 1972) has offered a "Bill of Rights" for children, which extends the U.N. declaration to include treatment issues (see Table 15-1). Economic hardship in much of the world confines these suggested rights only to children in the wealthiest societies, but ideally all children should receive these protections. Adults should be sensitive to children's concerns and grant them some rights under the law. If they are to protect themselves, children should be able to act independently in certain respects. For example, they should be able to seek medical or other care they need, regardless of their parents' unwillingness or inability to do so. It would be helpful for readers to refer to the human rights listed in Table 15-1 while considering the legal ones described in the following section. Ultimately, the two rosters of rights—the human and the legal—should correspond completely in order to promote child development.

Children's Legal Rights

In too many nations, a high proportion of the children as well as the adults lack adequate food, housing, and basic medical care (see descriptions in Chapter 3). Wealthier countries can realistically require parents to provide adequate physical care for their dependent children, but in subsistence societies such mandates would be meaningless. In fact, economically favored nations provide legal penalties for the physical neglect or abuse of children, as described in Chapter 3. However, parents in industrialized nations are legally required only to feed, protect, and educate their offspring, but not to provide for their psychological needs for love and esteem. Nevertheless, as Chapter 3 describes, adults are legally prohibited from abusing children physically or sexually.

This section reviews some of the legal rights of children, many of which have been only recently enacted into law. Both children and adults now enjoy a broader range of civil rights than was true over 50 years ago. During most historical eras, children were regarded as their parents' property much as livestock and equipment were, and were largely subjected to their parents' wishes regardless of the nature of these wishes (as described in Chapter 1). More recently, govern-

---

Table 15-1
A "Bill of Rights" for Children

A child has a *moral right* and should have a *legal right:*

1. To be regarded as a *person* within the family, at school, and before the law.
2. To receive parental love and affection, discipline and guidance, and to grow to maturity in a home environment which enables him to develop into a mature and responsible adult.
3. To be supported, maintained, and educated to the best of parental ability, in return for which he has the *moral* duty to honor his father and mother.
4. To receive fair treatment from all in authority and to be heard and listened to.
5. To earn and keep his own earnings, and to be *emancipated* from the parent-child relationship when that relationship has broken down and he has left home due to abuse, neglect, serious family conflict, or other sufficient cause, and when his best interests would be served by the temination of parental authority.
6. To be free of legal disabilities or incapacities save where such are convincingly shown to be necessary and protective of his actual best interests.
7. To seek and obtain medical care and treatment counseling.
8. To receive special care, consideration, and protection in the administration of law and justice so that his best interests always are a paramount factor.

Source: H. H. Foster, Jr. (1974). *A "Bill of Rights" for children* (Springfield, IL: Charles C Thomas), p. xv. Reprinted by permission of the author and the publisher.

ments have taken steps to care for children whose parents cannot or will not do so. During the last century, laws were enacted to protect children from unscrupulous employers; to make free public education compulsory; to prohibit neglect of and cruelty toward children; and to provide care for orphaned, abandoned, and wayward juveniles. Today's governments intervene to protect children who lack adequate parental supervision. These attempts to ensure children's safety do not grant them the legal status of adults, however. Recent lawsuits have produced judicial decisions that children possess certain constitutional rights. In defined circumstances, children must be given legal representation independent of their parents (Keniston, 1977)—a decision that recognizes the fact that parents' and children's interests do not always coincide (Weithorn, 1985). This legal development is exemplified in the U.S. Supreme Court decision discussed next.

Rights of Juveniles Threatened with Institutionalization   The 1967 Supreme Court decision *In re Gault* held that minors who might be deprived of their freedom and sent to correctional institutions have prescribed rights. Under the due process clause of the Fourteenth Amendment to the Constitution, they must be given notice that a hearing will be held; they have a right to be represented by counsel and they have a privilege against being forced to give self-incriminating testimony. Minors (through their attorneys) may also confront their accusers and cross-examine witnesses as adults do. The Court later ruled that juveniles cannot be sent to correctional institutions on mere suspicion of guilt, but have to be proven guilty by the same exacting standard as that used with adults (that is, "beyond a reasonable doubt"). In contrast to adults, children have no right to a jury trial (Rodham, 1979). Still, children do possess some legal rights and can no longer simply be sent to a correctional facility because some adult wants it so.

The legal protection for a *status offender* is somewhat less clear than for those accused of delinquency. Children sometimes defy their parents, run away from home, choose friends their parents

abhor, and generally prove impossible to manage. It is frequently unclear just how much of the fault in such a case can be attributed to the child or adolescent and how much to the parents. Some parents ultimately ask the juvenile court to declare their recalcitrant children to be incorrigible "persons in need of supervision." Such children may be sent to detention facilities, training schools, or other correctional facilities, sometimes for long periods, because their parents want to be relieved of them. One survey conducted in New York State found that 43 percent of the juveniles held in adult jails were *status offenders*—youths imprisoned for acts that are illegal only for minors and not for older persons, such as persistent truancy, disobedience of parents, use of alcohol, sexual activity, and associating with undesirable companions ("The Detention and Jailing of Juveniles," Hearings before the Subcommittee to Investigate Juvenile Delinquency of the Senate Committee on the Judiciary. Ninety-Third Congress, First Session, March, 8, 1973; cited in Keniston, 1977). Imprisonment places adolescents at great psychological and physical risk by grouping them with more serious juvenile and adult offenders whose influence can prove harmful. The status offenders present particular problems, which have led the Carnegie Council on Children (cited in Keniston, 1977) to advocate legal emancipation from parents for adolescents at war with their parents, and who are capable of living independently or with limited supervision. Several states have enacted laws to permit such teenagers to be declared legally independent of their parents and to be considered adults for most legal purposes. Their parents must consent to or at least fail to oppose their teenagers' emancipation so that the young people can live away from home. However, they must find jobs and support themselves, because their parents no longer do so. This seems a sad but constructive solution when family feuds are severe and adolescents are capable of making their own way in life.

Bases for Restriction of Children's Liberty   Box 15-1 presents a philosopher's argument for according children the same legal rights as adults.

BOX 15-1 • **Equal Rights for Children**

Philosopher Howard Cohen (1985) has said that "Children, in my view, should be entitled to all of the rights adults are entitled to in law and in custom" (p. 150). This view contrasts sharply with the prevalent law and opinion that children should be protected above all, even when such protection deprives them of their liberty. For example, children's custody may be awarded to the parent they dislike; they may be unwillingly removed from the home of legally defined "unfit" parents or caretakers; they are legally compelled to attend school; and their lives may be otherwise controlled to further their ultimate welfare. In Cohen's view, one should treat people equally unless and until there is a justification for unequal treatment (Feinberg, 1973). This implies that the burden of proof is on those who would treat adults and children differently. If the argument is offered that children lack adult mental capacities, then this must be scientifically demonstrated. In fact, it is sometimes difficult to establish group differences in such abilities between adults and children. Both adults and children can be enticed into supporting unscrupulous politicians who treat them and others unjustly while appearing to be respectable and fair. Both age groups can act impulsively and contrary to their own long-term financial and occupational interests, and can otherwise reason and behave irrationally. And because individual children develop their full reasoning capacities at different ages (and some older people may lose their mental acuity), it is impossible to maintain fairly that 21 years or some other arbitrarily selected age represents the age of reason.

　　Even proponents of equal legal rights for children recognize the existence of gross age differences in capacity, however, and would choose not to extend all liberties to inexperienced and cognitively limited preschoolers or to children with mental retardation or other cognitive handicaps (Cohen, 1985). To make wise decisions, children may require educational and financial advisors, but then so do most adults. With such assistance, children would not harm themselves nor be harmed by others; they would be free to live with whom they choose, seek the type of medical treatment they might prefer, and manage their own financial affairs with the assistance of objective adult counselors. Cohen (1980, 1985) acknowledges that this goal would be difficult to attain because of numerous practical and theoretical difficulties. However, he believes that under the present system, children are systematically and unjustly being denied their legitimate rights.

Sources: H. Cohen. (1980). *Equal rights for children* (Totowa, NJ: Littlefield, Adams); H. Cohen. (1985). Ending the double standard: Equal rights for children. In A. Cafagna, R. T. Peterson, and C. Staudenbaur (Eds.), *Child nurturance: Philosophy, children, and the family* (Vol. 1) (New York: Plenum); J. Feinberg. (1973). *Social philosophy* (Englewood Cliffs, NJ: Prentice-Hall).

Few people agree with such an extreme view, and most believe that some restriction of children's rights is good for them. Teitelbaum and Ellis (1978) have offered three principal reasons for legal restrictions on children's liberty:

1. *Vulnerability to harm.* Children require greater protection because they are more vulnerable than adults. They are prohibited from harmful activities such as smoking, drinking alcohol, using drugs, and engaging in dangerous and taxing work in order to protect their health.

2. *Immature judgment.* Children cannot make informed decisions about important matters because they are uninformed and unable to foresee the long-range consequences of their decisions.

3. *Maintenance of family strength.* The family is the best and most appropriate agent for the socialization and protection of the child. The child is legally prohibited from

leaving the family and from defying the parents' wishes. These prohibitions aim to maintain family strength, cohesion, and discipline. They are presumed to meet children's psychological needs for stability in parental care (Goldstein, Freud, & Solnit, 1979).

These three rationales have historically been used in the framing of British and American legislation and judicial decisions regarding children's rights and welfare. These views have been particularly influential in the context of institutionalization, other treatment decisions, and in child custody cases, as will be explained in the following passages. Such decisions pit the child's personal liberty and due process considerations against the authority of the state and the parents (Cohen, 1985; Koocher, 1983). As a reform measure, the Carnegie Council on Children (cited in Keniston, 1977) endorsed legislative and judicial changes that would do the following:

Children do not have the same observational or memory capacities as adults, yet they can state their preferences in child custody cases and in trials of alleged child abusers. The central question is, Under what circumstances can their testimony be believed?

1. Ensure a full due process hearing on any placement of a child in a treatment institution for more than a few weeks.
2. Ensure that institutionalized children's cases are given periodic judicial reviews, so that they are not forgotten and can be speedily returned to normal home living.
3. Insist that the child receive the least restrictive type of specialized care needed for functioning in the regular community.

The last two of the Carnegie Council's recommendations have, in fact, been required by the U.S. Supreme Court.

Judicial decisions in the past 20 years have increasingly recognized minors' constitutional rights. However, there are significant limitations. As noted previously, in the case of *Parham v. J. R.* (1979), the Supreme Court ruled that parents may institutionalize their children for treatment, and that the children have no right to independent legal counsel or a due process hearing but must obey their parents' wishes in the matter. The Court held that children's liberty interests are adequately safeguarded by their parents' concern for them and by the competence and impartiality of the admitting physician. (Note, however, that private for-profit hospitals may have a financial interest in admitting as many patients as possible.) The justices viewed treatment institutions as neither coercive nor punitive in nature, and assumed that children lack the information and insight necessary to make wise treatment decisions. Thus, due process rights are more limited for children than for adults when institutionalization is at issue. This limitation is reasonable when children actually need institutionalization and are given care of adequate quality. To prevent abuses of the system, the Court also required that public institutions meet high professional standards and that children initially be admitted only as outpatients. Decisions regarding institutionalization must be made by an interdisciplinary team, and periodic reviews are mandated to determine whether the child is ready to return home. Unfortunately, relatively few of our uniformly poorly funded public institutions can meet the Court's high standards (Plotkin, 1979). In fact, the questionable quality of care in institutions is a matter of considerable public and professional concern.

Child Custody Decisions   When parents separate or divorce, one of them usually gains sole custody of the children and the other receives visitation privileges. Parents knowingly or unwittingly may encourage their children to take sides in their marital disputes, and children develop strong preferences regarding whether they live with their mother or father. These child custody debates often become the focus of acrimonious family arguments. Some states require consideration of children's wishes in custody decisions if the children are at least 12 or 14 years old (Siegel & Hurley, 1977). Children's desires are given greater weight if they are strongly held, and lesser weight if (1) the court decides that the child has insufficient mental capacity to make a wise choice; (2) undue influence has been exerted on the child by a parent; or (3) the child's preference is based on a desire to escape from reasonable and desirable but firm discipline (Siegel & Hurley, 1977). Whatever the circumstances, the judge may require the child to publicly state a preference for a custodial parent, which is also an upsetting public rejection of the other parent (Emery, Hetherington, & DiLalla, 1984). Judges attempt to base custody decisions on the best interests of the child (*Finlay* v. *Finlay*, 1925, p. 626), but it is extremely difficult to decide just what those best interests may be (see Emery et al., 1984, for an excellent discussion of the topic). If children are very young, it is usually presumed that it is best that they be in their mother's custody. While older children may be placed with either parent, the vast majority reside with their mothers (Emery et al., 1984).

Children's Rights in the Schools   If one were to rank the most time-consuming of children's activities, the hours spent in sleep would be first, followed by television viewing, play, and school attendance. Schooling provides students with essential skills such as verbal and mathematical literacy, and teachers and schoolmates are important child socialization agents. In the past, most parents simply assumed that schools would act in

It is difficult for a child and a parent to say goodbye, especially in cases of divorce that require that the child leave one parent to join the other. The faces of this girl and her mother reveal their sorrow and apprehension. In many cases the issue is resolved by the father's disappearance.

the best interests of the children, and there were very few parental challenges to the authority and wisdom of teachers and principals. To maintain discipline, disobedient and troublesome pupils were simply expelled from school. A survey taken in 1972 revealed that of 24 million children surveyed, 1 million had been suspended from school at some time during that year. In addition, many were physically punished for defiant or aggressive behavior, and the severely emotionally or physically handicapped children were mostly excluded from public schools altogether (Children's Defense Fund, 1974). Despite compulsory education laws, schooling was generally considered more a privilege for the normal and well-behaved then a right for all. But in the early 1970s the situation began to change, and federal courts decreed that, like normal children, the handicapped had a right to free public education, preferably in regular classrooms (*Mills* v. *Board of Education,* 1972; *Pennsylvania Association for Retarded Children* v. *Commonwealth of Pennsylvania,* 1971).

The ground-breaking federal Education for All Handicapped Children Act of 1975 (P.L. 94-142; see Box 15-2) specified that public schools must adequately serve emotionally, mentally, and physically handicapped children and their families. Whereas previously families had to bear

---

BOX 15-2 • Excerpts from Regulations under Public Law 94-142

121a.5 Handicapped children

(a) As used in this part, the term "handicapped children" means those children evaluated in accordance with 121a.530–121a.534 as being mentally retarded, hard of hearing, deaf, speech impaired, visually handicapped, seriously emotionally disturbed, orthopedically impaired, other health impaired, deaf-blind, multi-handicapped, or as having specific learning disabilities, who because of those impairments need special education and related services.

121a.302 Residential placement

If placement in a public or private residential program is necessary to provide special education and related services to a handicapped child, the program, including non-medical care and room and board, must be at no cost to the parents of the child.

INDIVIDUALIZED EDUCATION PROGRAMS

121a.340 Definition

As used in this part, the term "individualized education program" means a written statement for a handicapped child that is developed and implemented in accordance with 121a.341–121a.349.

121a.343 Meetings

(a) *General.* Each public agency is responsible for initiating and conducting meetings for the purpose of developing, reviewing, and revising a handicapped child's individualized education program. . . .
(d) *Review.* Each public agency shall initiate and conduct meetings to periodically review each child's individualized education program and if appropriate revise its provisions. A meeting must be held for this purpose at least once a year.

121a.344 Participants in meetings

(a) *General.* The public agency shall insure that each meeting includes the following participants:

(1) A representative of the public agency, other than the child's teacher, who is qualified to provide, or supervise the provision of, special education.
(2) The child's teacher.
(3) One or both of the child's parents, subject to 121a.345.
(4) The child, where appropriate.
(5) Other individuals at the discretion of the parent or agency.

nearly the entire financial and personal burden of training or educating their handicapped youngsters, henceforth the public schools were required to do so. Unfortunately, no additional money was appropriated for this praiseworthy endeavor, so school districts were compelled to assume sizable additional costs without federal assistance. P.L. 94-142 is costly because it requires free and appropriate individualized education for every child. Schools are prohibited from excluding handicapped children simply because they are difficult or expensive to educate. Teachers are not always

---

Box 15-2 (Continued)

(b) *Evaluation personnel.* For a handicapped child who has been evaluated for the first time, the public agency shall insure:

(1) **That a member of the evaluation team participates in the meeting; or**
(2) **That the representative of the public agency, the child's teacher, or some other person is present at the meeting who is knowledgeable about the evaluation procedures used with the child and is familiar with the results of the evaluation.**

121a.345 Parent participation

(a) Each public agency shall take steps to insure that one or both of the parents of the handicapped child are present at each meeting or are afforded the opportunity to participate including:

(1) **Notifying parents of the meeting early enough to insure that they will have an opportunity to attend; and**
(2) **Scheduling the meeting at a mutually agreed on time and place.**

(b) The notice under paragraph (a) (1) of this section must indicate the purpose, time, and location of the meeting, and who will be in attendance.
(c) If neither parent can attend, the public agency shall use other methods to insure parent participation, including individual or conference telephone calls.
(d) A meeting may be conducted without a parent in attendance if the public agency is unable to convince the parents that they should attend. In this case the public agency must have a record of its attempts to arrange a mutually agreed on time and place such as:

(1) **Detailed records of telephone calls made or attempted and the results of those calls.**
(2) **Copies of correspondence sent to the parents and any responses received, and**
(3) **Detailed records of visits made to the parents' home or place of employment and the results of those visits.**

(e) The public agency shall take whatever action is necessary to insure that the parent understands the proceedings at a meeting, including arranging for an interpreter for parents who are deaf or whose native language is other than English.
(f) The public agency shall give the parent, on request, a copy of the individualized education program.

121a.346 Content of individualized education program

The individualized education program for each child must include:
(a) A statement of the child's present levels of educational performance;

Box 15-2 (Continued)

assumed to be in the right in disputes with children who are difficult to manage, and these children cannot be expelled from school without a fair hearing. A more restrictive, special education classroom placement can be used only if a student has found it impossible to adjust to the regular classroom situation (Martin, 1979). The emphasis is on "mainstreaming" or integrating atypical students with their normal classmates as much as possible.

Judges and legislators have assumed that contact with normal classmates is highly advanta-

---

Box 15-2 (Continued)

(b) A statement of annual goals, including short term instructional objectives;

(c) A statement of the specific special education and related services to be provided to the child, and the extent to which the child will be able to participate in regular educational programs;

(d) The projected dates for initiation of services and the anticipated duration of the services; and

(e) Appropriate objective criteria and evaluation procedures and schedules for determining, on at least an annual basis, whether the short term instructional objectives are being achieved.

121a.347 Private school placements

(a) *Developing individualized education programs.* (1) Before a public agency places a handicapped child in, or refers a child to, a private school or facility, the agency shall initiate and conduct a meeting to develop an individualized education program for the child in accordance with 121a.343.

COMPREHENSIVE SYSTEM OF PERSONNEL DEVELOPMENT

121a.380 Scope of system

Each annual program plan must include a description of programs and procedures for the development and implementation of a comprehensive system of personnel development which includes:

(a) The inservice training of general and special educational instructional, related services, and support personnel;

(b) Procedures to insure that all personnel necessary to carry out the purposes of the Act are qualified and that activities sufficient to carry out this personnel development plan are scheduled; and

(c) Effective procedures for acquiring and disseminating to teachers and administrators of programs for handicapped children significant information derived from educational research, demonstration, and similar projects, and for adopting, where appropriate, promising educational practices and materials developed through those projects.

121a.503 Independent educational evaluation

(a) *General.*

(1) The parents of a handicapped child have the right under this part to obtain an independent educational evaluation of the child . . .

(2) Each public agency shall provide to parents, on request, information about where an independent educational evaluation may be obtained.

geous for normal socialization of handicapped children, but there may be risks as well (Zigler & Muenchow, 1980). Normal children can be cruel to those who are different in any way and can make their school life miserable. Mentally retarded and other handicapped children often are excluded by their peers, and visitors to public schools observe that they are always in one another's company because they are shunned by the other students. Research studies of the effects of mainstreaming as compared with special placement are badly needed in order to identify the

---

Box 15-2 (Continued)

(3) For the purposes of this part:
   (i) "Independent educational evaluation" means an evaluation conducted by a qualified examiner who is not employed by the public agency responsible for the education of the child in question.
   (ii) "Public expense" means that the public agency either pays for the full cost of the evaluation or insures that the evaluation is otherwise provided at no cost to the parent . . .

121a.504 Prior notice; parent consent

(a) *Notice.* Written notice which meets the requirements under 121a.505 must be given to the parents of a handicapped child a reasonable time before the public agency:

(1) Proposes to initiate or change the identification, evaluation, or educational placement of the child or the provision of a free appropriate public education to the child, or
(2) Refuses to initiate or change the identification, evaluation, or educational placement of the child or the provision of a free appropriate public education to the child.

(b) Consent.

(1) Parental consent must be obtained before:
   (i) Conducting a preplacement evaluation; and
   (ii) Initial placement of a handicapped child in a program providing special education and related services.

(2) Except for preplacement evaluation and initial placement, consent may not be required as a condition of any benefit to the parent or child.

121a.506 Impartial due process hearing

(a) A parent or a public educational agency may initiate a hearing on any of the matters described in 121a.504 (a) (1) and (2).
(b) The hearing must be conducted by the State educational agency or the public agency directly responsible for the education of the child, as determined under State statute, State regulation, or a written policy of the State educational agency.
(c) The public agency shall inform the parent of any free or low-cost legal and other relevant services available in the area if:

(1) The parent requests the information; or
(2) The parent or the agency initiates a hearing under this section.

Box 15-2 (Continued)

types of academic environments that most benefit special students' intellectual and social development. At present, there is no convincing evidence that students can learn better when mainstreamed than when segregated (Quinn, 1985). Unless special efforts are made, they are the victims of *de facto* segregation in the public schools they attend. Parents also enjoy expanded rights regarding their child's education under P.L. 94-142. They must be consulted on their child's classroom placement and special services, which they need not pay for privately. If properly implemented,

---

Box 15-2 (Continued)

PROTECTION IN EVALUATION PROCEDURES

121a.530 General.
(a) Each State educational agency shall insure that each public agency establishes and implements procedures which meet the requirements of 121a.530–121a.534.
(b) Testing and evaluation materials and procedures used for the purposes of evaluation and placement of handicapped children must be selected and administered so as not to be racially or culturally discriminatory.

LEAST RESTRICTIVE ENVIRONMENT

121a.550 General
(a) Each State educational agency shall insure that each public agency establishes and implements procedures which meet the requirements of 121a.550–121a.556.
(b) Each public agency shall insure:

(1) That to the maximum extent appropriate, handicapped children, including children in public or private institutions or other care facilities, are educated with children who are not handicapped, and

(2) That special classes, separate schooling, or other removal of handicapped children from the regular educational environment occurs only when the nature or severity of the handicap is such that education in regular classes with the use of supplementary aids and services cannot be achieved satisfactorily.

121a.551 Continuum of alternative placements
(a) Each public agency shall insure that a continuum of alternative placements is available to meet the needs of handicapped children for special education and related services.
(b) The continuum required under paragraph (a) of this section must:

(1) Include the alternative placements listed in the definition of special education under 121a.13 of Subpart A (instruction in regular classes, special classes, special schools, home instruction, and instruction in hospitals and institutions), and

(2) Make provision for supplementary services (such as resource room or itinerant instruction) to be provided in conjunction with regular class placement.

Source: Education for All Handicapped Children Act of 1975 (P.L. 94-142), 42 Fed. Reg. 42474–42514 (1977).

the legislation aimed to help handicapped students actually will do so.

Children's Needs and Rights Regarding Treatment   The law does not require that child psychotherapy clients' needs and interests be completely protected. In treatment as in other realms, children are granted less autonomy than adults. It is widely assumed that the parents know best regarding psychological and medical treatment decisions. Yet the child's interests may differ from those of the parents, and "it is the child who will suffer if the gamble is lost" (Keniston, 1977, p. 202). Thus practitioners have a special obligation to protect children's moral or human rights in treatment decisions. Table 15-2 describes some of the human rights that should be accorded to children in treatment.

The question of children's rights becomes acute when the use of unpleasant, confining, or coercive treatment methods is considered. In addition to reinforcement for appropriate behavior, a child's treatment plan may include some form of punishment, such as verbal criticism or brief periods of time out from ongoing positive reinforcement (see the discussion of aversive therapies in Chapter 14). Many treatment agencies and schools now require a mandatory independent evaluation of each proposed treatment plan, to be conducted by people who are not personally involved in the child's treatment. Keniston (1977) has advocated that any extreme therapy such as electric shock, psychosurgery, or aversive methods should be reviewed by a peer review board or ethics committee acting independently of the therapist and the child's parents. Such autonomy is important because therapists could prove to be uncritical proponents of aversive methods and could unduly influence anxious and insecure parents to agree, so an unbiased independent evaluation is necessary.

Children's Rights and Restrictive Treatments   Children's wishes should be considered in choosing their treatments, especially if the more intrusive and restrictive treatments are employed. Most intellectually normal adolescents are capable of making competent treatment decisions (Weithorn, 1985), and children as young as 9 years or even less may be capable of some participation in such choices (Lewis, Lewis, & Lefkwunigue, 1978). Treatments can be ranked according to how innocuous or radical they are. Most forms of psychotherapy closely resemble the child's everyday activities and require no special safeguards, whereas the more restrictive treatments may deprive children of their freedom in some way. For example, sedative medication de-

T a b l e 15-2
A "Bill of Rights" for Children in Psychotherapy

1. *The Right to Be Told the Truth.* Children should be informed of events that affect them and should never be lied to by the therapist. As Ross (1980) has stated, "When children are old enough to be talked to, they are old enough to be told the truth" (p. 68).
2. *The Right to Be Treated as a Person.* This implies that the child's right to privacy and confidentiality should be respected and the therapist should not divulge information shared by the child in treatment sessions nor should sessions be recorded or observed without the child's knowledge or permission.
3. *The Right to Be Taken Seriously.* The therapist, in particular, should listen carefully to the child and neither dismiss nor make light of the child's observations, opinions, or feelings.
4. *The Right to Participate in Decision Making.* Like adults, children should be allowed to express their opinions in matters involving their lives, and their opinions should carry some weight. Too often adults make the important decisions involving children and only later inform the children. Therapists surely should not behave in this cavalier fashion toward children.

Sources: G. P. Koocher. (1976). A bill of rights for children in psychotherapy. In G. Koocher (Ed.), *Children's rights and the mental health professions* (New York: Wiley). Also, A. O. Ross. (1980). *Psychological disorders of children,* (2nd ed.) (New York: McGraw-Hill).

creases children's alertness and ability to learn, and other restrictive treatments may confine them to institutions or physically restrain them. For these reasons, the use of restrictive treatment is legally constrained.

Drug treatment (described in Chapter 14) may be considered intrusive because it denies the child his customary control over his own behavior and may cause temporary or permanent undesirable side effects. Medication is a less desirable form of intervention than are most psychological therapies, for the following reasons:

1. The child has more choice to act as a free agent when psychotherapy is used because psychotherapy can be resisted or rejected by unwilling clients but drugs cannot (Shapiro, 1974).

2. Drugs may make children more manageable, but do not require them or their parents to learn new and better ways to cope with problems (Grinspoon & Singer, 1973).

3. Most drugs that are strong enough to affect mood and behavior produce unwanted side effects, some of which can prove dangerous immediately or in the future.

4. Drugs can be misused by the child or family members (Weithorn, 1979). They also can be used punitively. In the case of *Morales* v. *Turman* (1974), the U.S. District Court in Texas ruled that juveniles held in correctional institutions must be protected from "indiscriminate, unsupervised, unnecessary, or excessive psychotropic medication" when used as an alternative to psychotherapy. In this case, institutional staff members punished boys by administering intramuscular injections of tranquilizers. In another case (*Nelson* v. *Hyne*, 1974), the court ruled that such injections represented cruel and unusual punishment when given by inadequately trained and medically unqualified personnel. Even in outpatient settings, drugs may be given too readily because parents and teachers complain about a child's behavior. Chapter 14 offers rigorous guidelines concerning the use of psychoactive drugs with children.

Most ethical and legal codes now insist that the *least restrictive treatment* criterion be applied when choosing a course of treatment. That is, children should be given the safest, least confining treatment that could be expected to prove effective. Only when the milder techniques prove unhelpful are more radical solutions considered. Treatment plans are implemented only with parent's informed approval and with the consent of children who are old enough to participate.

CLINICAL PROCEDURES BASED ON DEVELOPMENTAL PSYCHOLOGY

Increasing numbers of clinicians who work with children are using information drawn from developmental psychology in their practices. As previous chapters indicate, traditional child clinical approaches were based on techniques used with adults, and subsequently adapted for children with less than total success in many instances. In the past several decades, developmental psychologists have amassed a wealth of knowledge concerning the ways in which children of different ages perceive events, reason about them, and then act. For too long, this information failed to reach the child clinicians who actually worked with troubled children. In fact, most clinicians and developmentalists appeared to be supremely uninterested in each other's work. This mutual isolation had many causes, including contrasting research philosophies and interests, and the dominance of adult over child psychiatry (Gelfand & Peterson, 1985). Today, however, these barriers are falling as growing numbers of developmental psychologists study the clinical problems associated with child abuse, divorce, inadequate parenting, mental retardation, and a host of other conditions. For their part, clinicians are becoming aware of the developmental research findings relevant to their work. And increasing numbers of professionals are seeking joint training in developmental and clinical psychology (Gelfand & Peterson, 1985; Routh, 1985). We now describe some of the fruits of this collaboration.

Language proficiency is one of the many behavioral areas in which age differences are readily apparent. The clinical interview is perhaps the most important single diagnostic tool for assessing and treating adults, but it is difficult to use with young children. A diagnostician who attempts to give an adult-style, open-ended diagnostic interview to a 5-year-old faces nearly certain defeat. The child may fail to comprehend the interviewer's questions and eventually may simply fall into puzzled silence. The interviewer will find it helpful to know that according to developmental psychology research, many children this age think about themselves and others in ways that are very *concrete* ("All pretty children are nice"), *undifferentiated* (they are unable to distinguish between related emotions such as anger, fear, and sadness), and *polarized* in their emotions (they believe that a person is either nice or bad, but cannot be a little of both) (Bierman, 1983; Bierman & Schwartz, 1986). Lacking relevant information about the cognitive development of very young children, an inadequately prepared diagnostician may mistakenly conclude that a typical 5-year-old is upset, confused, or intellectually dull. Yet if interviewed competently, children can provide unique information not otherwise available about their perceptions, emotions, and self-evaluations. The preceding example illustrates the importance of sensitivity to a child client's developmental level as a prerequisite for any effective clinical interaction.

Some clinicians are now using research information about children's cognitive capacities in their applied work. Karen Bierman and her associates (Bierman, 1983; Bierman & Schwarts, 1986) have drawn on the research literature and their own clinical experience to devise useful methods for interviewing youngsters. They see children in familiar settings, such as a playroom for preschool children and a schoolroom with school materials and tasks for older ones. Interviewing techniques are adapted to match the child's verbal and conceptual skills and her expectations regarding her own and the interviewer's roles. Clinical experience and training alone may help clinicians develop specialized techniques for use with children, but knowledge of developmental principles simplifies the task.

A second domain in which developmental research contributes to clinical practice lies in an appreciation of the two-way interaction between children and adults. Most clinical theories are one-directional, stressing the impact of adults on children. Yet developmentalists now favor *bidirectional* or *transactional* views, in which all participants in social interactions are seen as continuously affecting each other. Thus it is just as likely that having a difficult, hyperactive child makes parents irritable as it is that irritable parents make the child difficult and overly active. It is distinctly possible that parents and children engage in repeated cycles of mutual antagonism, making it impossible to identify a culprit and a victim (Gurman & Kniskern, 1980). In fact, all children actively contribute to their own development by (usually unknowingly) controlling their parents' behavior (Belsky & Tolan, 1981; Maccoby & Martin, 1983). Unfortunately, few clinicians except the systems-oriented family therapists have incorporated the concept of reciprocal parent-child influence into their work (see Chapter 14). There is suggestive evidence of reciprocal parent-child influence in some cases of hyperactivity and child abuse (Houts, Shutty, & Emery, 1985). This preliminary work suggests that clinicians should be alert to the possibility of faulty parent-child interactions; it also illustrates the potential value of developmental research to practitioners. Overall, the work on developmental psychopathology suggests that students planning a career in child and family practice should also study developmental psychology.

A NEW THERAPY: SELF-REGULATION TRAINING

Many forms of treatment are discussed in Chapter 14, but one seems so new in concept that it deserves special attention in this chapter on innovations. *Self-regulation training* is new in that, from the beginning of the treatment, the aim is to provide the client with the tools for self-control. And the idea that such self-directed techniques can be taught to children is truly revolutionary. Some disturbed children are particularly poor at controlling themselves, so therapists have devised special routines for teaching them self-regulation (Meichenbaum, 1979). Children are systematically taught to observe, evaluate, and provide appro priate consequences for their own behavior. That is, they bring their behavior under the control of consequences that they administer themselves with only minimal external guidance. There are two major types of self-regulation training: (1) the *operant* method developed by Karoly and Kanfer (1982), and (2) the more cognitive *self-instructional* technique of Meichenbaum (1979) and Kendall and his colleagues (Kendall & Finch, 1979; Kendall & Hollon, 1979). The operant method consists of four steps: (1) deciding to modify a certain behavior; (2) selecting a behavorial goal; (3) monitoring and evaluating one's own behavior compared to the goal; and (4) selecting and delivering the specified reward or other consequences, depending upon the merit of one's behavior. The operant approach stresses the management of self-reinforcement contingencies as the major factor in treatment.

In contrast, the self-instructional procedure emphasizes the control exerted by self-directed speech. Training in self-instruction was first used with children who were impulsive, careless in their work, and likely to abandon difficult projects prematurely. Meichenbaum (1977, 1979) developed self-instructional procedures to train impulsive children to monitor and control their own problem-solving activities. Meichenbaum's cognitive self-instruction training begins with the therapist demonstrating appropriate problem-solving procedures to the child. The child imitates the therapist's behavior, giving instructions to herself first aloud and then silently. Meichenbaum and Goodman (1971) described the transfer of control from therapist to client as follows:

1. **The adult performs the task while giving himself instructions aloud (modeling).**
2. **The adult gives the child instructions on how to perform the task (external guidance).**
3. **The child performs the task while instructing herself aloud (overt self-instruction).**
4. **The child whispers instructions to herself while performing the task (gradual removal of overt self-guidance).**
5. **The child rehearses the instructions to herself silently while performing the task (covert self-guidance).**

This cognitive self-instruction procedure trains the child to pause in order to understand the problem and to consider several possible solutions rather than plunging ahead impulsively with a doomed plan (see Table 15-3). Moreover, the child is shown how to detect and correct errors in a mature and controlled fashion, as opposed to throwing a temper tantrum or crying. In the final step, the child evaluates the adequacy of her efforts: If she has succeeded, she rewards herself; if not, she begins again.

Self-regulation training has been offered to treat children with a number of different problems that are resistant to more traditional treatment efforts. Self-regulation instruction has been at least partially successful in treating such difficult problems as verbal or physical aggression, delinquency, fears and phobias, social withdrawal, impulsivity and inattention to school assignments, and other learning problems (see recent reviews by Craighead, Meyers, Wilcoxon-Craighead, & McHale, 1983; Gelfand & Hartmann, 1984; Karoly & Kanfer, 1982; Kazdin, 1982; Shure & Spivack, 1982). Self-instructional training is flexible and can be tailored to children's individual needs and developmental levels (Craighead et al., 1983; Furman, 1980; Higa, Tharp, & Calkins, 1978; O'Leary & Dubey, 1979). Children who possess the necessary social or problem-solving skills may require training only in self-observation and self-reward, but not in self-instruction techniques. For example, instructing elementary school students only in accurate self-observation has greatly increased the students' attention to the teacher and to their work (Drabman, Spitalnik, & O'Leary, 1973). Acquaintance with the research on developmental changes in children's cognitive capacities is invaluable for the child cognitive therapist.

As yet, however, self-regulation training is no panacea. Treatment is not always successful (Gelfand & Hartmann, 1984), and even the positive outcomes may result more from the precisely defined behavioral measures used in treatment and evaluation than from some inherent advantage of self-regulation methods (Casey & Berman, 1985). That is, the greatest therapy-produced positive change is typically found for measures of fear, anxiety, and cognitive indexes of the control of hy-

Table 15-3

Components of Cognitive Self-Instruction

Step in Self-Instruction	Examples of Self-Instruction
1. Pausing to define the problem	"What does the teacher want me to do?" "I must stop and think before I begin."
2. Considering several alternative solutions	"What plans could I try?" "How well would that work?" "What else might work?"
3. Giving self-instructions on how to perform the task	"I have to go slowly and carefully." "Okay, draw the line down, down, good; then to the right . . . Remember, go slowly."
4. Checking one's work and correcting errors calmly	"Have I got it right so far? That's a mistake. I'll just erase it." "That's o.k. . . . Even if I make an error, I can go on slowly and carefully."
5. Reinforcing oneself for a correct solution	"Good, I'm doing fine." "I've done a pretty good job." "Good for me!"

Sources: D. Meichenbaum and J. Goodman. (1971). Training impulsive children to talk to themselves: A means of developing self-control. *Journal of Abnormal Psychology, 77,* 115-126; V. Douglas, P. Parry, P. Marton, and C. Garson. (1976). Assessment of a cognitive training program for hyperactive children. *Journal of Abnormal Child Psychology, 4,* 389-410.

Overt self-instruction can help children perform difficult academic tasks. This little girl finds that fingers come in handy for solving arithmetic problems. Later, as she becomes more skilled, she will drop the aid of counting audibly while she works. Cognitive behavior therapists train children to give instructions to themselves during the early stages of skill acquisition.

peractivity. These measures are typically used in behavioral and cognitive-behavioral therapy studies, and closely resemble therapeutic activities included in the treatments themselves. In effect, therapy trains the children to improve on the very scales and observations used to evaluate therapy effects. Consequently, results indicating that behavioral and cognitive interventions are particularly successful relative to other approaches may simply reflect the use of specific, therapy-related outcome measures, rather than the more traditional indexes of improvements in self-concept, personality, or school achievement (Casey & Berman, 1985). It may be inherently more difficult to enhance a child's self-esteem or to change her personality than it is to teach her a specific skill, such as to approach a feared situation or to control her hyperactivity and impulsivity in particular settings. Consequently, the cognitive-behavioral therapists may appear to be more successful than the client-centered therapists simply because they treat less resistant conditions and choose more achievable goals.

A second problem with cognitive-behavior therapy is that children's improved behavior may not generalize beyond the original training task (Craighead et al., 1983; Gresham, 1985). That is, a child who has received self-instructional training to become less impulsive in copying designs accurately in the clinic or school may fail to use the same self-instructional techniques when completing his math assignments at home. The limited generalization of therapy effects is a serious problem for nearly all forms of treatment, and self-regulation training is no exception (Gresham, 1985). Cognitive-behavior therapists are attempting to remedy this weakness by teaching children two different types of procedures: one intervention to acquire skills necessary to perform a particular task, and another to solve various other types of problems. Children first learn very specific self-control instructions, which aid them in the task at hand, and then later are taught more general self-direct problem-solving tactics and when to use them (Schleser, Meyers, & Cohen, 1981). Ironically, children who have learned how to monitor, evaluate, and reward their own appropriate behavior

may not know exactly *when* to do so. According to Friedling and O'Leary (1979), "Teaching children why and when to use self-instruction, and ensuring that they do, may be as important as teaching them how to self-instruct" (p. 218).

The most important point about this new move to teach self-regulation skills is that therapy clients, even very young ones, are being helped to assume more responsibility and autonomy as they face life's inevitable problems. Today, children are less often seen as objects to be manipulated by adults than as independent agents operating in a complex and interdependent social world. This conclusion holds true whether minors' legal rights are considered or whether they are offered self-regulation training: Children are gaining in the degree to which they are viewed as having rights and interests separate from those of their families, their schools, or their therapists.

THE PREVENTION OF PSYCHOPATHOLOGY

Prevention is preferable to remediation. It seems insensitive, wasteful, and negligent to permit children to develop emotional and behavioral disorders that could be prevented. Effective prevention programs would not only eliminate needless suffering of great numbers of children and families, but would also save millions of dollars required to treat or imprison them. Treatment of disturbed people is extremely expensive, especially when they must be institutionalized or if they become antisocial and engage in assault, theft, or the destruction of property. Perhaps some portion of the cases of psychosis, severe retardation, or criminal activity could be avoided through the development of effective prevention programs.

Prevention efforts have been most strikingly successful in medicine, where many more lives have been saved through preventive public health measures than through better-publicized, more glamorous technological achievements, such as refined surgical techniques or the invention of artificial organs. The lives of countless millions of people have been saved by public health advances, including improved sanitation; safe drinking water; and immunization against diseases that were previously often fatal, such as smallpox, diphtheria, polio, and measles. In contrast, few if any psychological disorders can be traced to a single, controllable disease agent, so prevention of psychopathology is inherently more complicated than is purifying drinking water or immunizing people against diseases. Yet it is quite possible to devise measures to prevent the development of many different behavioral and emotional disturbances, as this section discloses. Clues to the development of effective preventive and early intervention techniques have been provided by recent research identifying groups at risk for the development of particular problems. Prevention efforts also have profited from research developments in the understanding of the nature and natural course of disorders, and from advances in treatment. Here, we first describe some groups of children at heightened risk for psychopathology because of such factors as their genetic makeup, deficits in their rearing, or hazards in their physical and social environments. Then we outline the present and potential means for preventing these high-risk children from developing psychological disorders. In line with the book's social science emphasis, we describe psychological and educational interventions rather than the purely biological or medical ones. Many medical prevention measures are discussed in previous chapters, especially those aimed at major contributors to children's problems (Chapter 3), at learning disabilities (Chapter 8), and at mental retardation (Chapter 9).

Research on prevention requires a large and highly trained professional staff, together with considerable amounts of time, money, and other resources, so it is uncommon compared with less ambitious investigations of diagnosis and treatment. Moreover, to determine whether prevention has succeeded, it is necessary to assign participants randomly to experimental groups and then much later to compare the prevalence of psychopathology for the prevention group with the disorder rates for one or more different control groups (see Chapter 11 for information about research designs). Since some forms of psychopathology may require years to develop, the treated and control groups may have to be observed for as long as 10 or 20 years in order to determine whether the preventive intervention has been effective. Another, less expensive possibility is to compare a prevention treatment group's rate of disorder with that of some previously studied group. But as Chapter 1 indicates, longitudinal studies are only now beginning to document the long-term prognosis for children with various types of cognitive, social, and academic problems. Children who have many or serious adjustment problems, or who have significant problems in the control of antisocial behavior, are likely to continue to display disordered behavior for many years. Nevertheless, it is often difficult to specify which children are at heightened risk of developing later adjustment difficulties. One research tactic is to assess the adjustment of children who may be vulnerable because their parents suffer from alcoholism, affective disorder, schizophrenia, or some other debilitating condition. Study of the problems of such presumably high-risk children can provide clues about their expected long-term adjustment status. If the presumably high-risk groups' problems do exceed those of children of otherwise comparable but psychologically normal parents, then these particular parental conditions may endanger the children's psychological development. Furthermore, if children of parents with a *particular type* of psychopathology show certain cognitive, social, or school-related deficits, then it would be worthwhile to study this group more closely and to develop prevention programs for them.

Research has revealed that the children of parents with some forms of psychopathology do develop excessively high rates of problems (Gelfand, Ficula, and Zarbatany, 1986; Watt, 1979, 1985). Some children are at risk for developing the specific disorder their parents have (Billings & Moos, 1983). They may also suffer from other types of disturbances more typical of children of their age and developmental level, such as academic achievement problems, enuresis, social withdrawal, poor peer relations, and truancy (for instance, see Orvaschel, 1983; Weintraub, Prinz,

& Neale, 1978; Welner, Welner, McCrary, & Leonard, 1977). Researchers have found that the children of parents with certain types of psychopathology are especially likely to develop serious problems themselves. These parental disorders include depression (Orvaschel, 1983) and schizophrenia (Masten & Garmezy, 1985). Furthermore, neglected, abused, and unwanted children may fail to develop normally, as may the children of alcoholics, drug addicts, and violent criminals (Gelfand et al., 1986; Kirkegaard-Sørenson & Mednick, 1975). There is a possible connection between juvenile antisocial aggression and a constellation of predisposing factors, including having a lower-socioeconomic-status family with a father who displays criminal, violent behavior (Glueck & Glueck, 1968), especially if combined with alcohol abuse (Cadoret & Cain, 1980; Jones, 1968). Children exposed to family violence often are themselves inappropriately aggressive (George & Main, 1979), and tend to have behavior problems and serious social deficits (Wolfe, Jaffe, Wilson, & Zak, 1985). Research data indicate that children with seriously psychologically disturbed or violent parents are particularly vulnerable to psychopathology.

Preventing Disturbance in Children of Schizophrenic or Depressed Parents

Schizophrenic Parents   Children whose parents are schizophrenic are at significant risk for developing the same or some other serious disorder. Having one schizophrenic parent increases a child's risk for later developing schizophrenia from 1 percent to approximately 10 percent (Masten & Garmezy, 1985). If *both* parents are schizophrenic, their children's risk for later developing the disorder rises to a remarkable 35 percent or more (Ledingham, Schwartzman, & Serbin, 1984). Even allowing for researchers' possible bias toward confirming their expectations by inadvertently misdiagnosing known relatives of schizophrenics as deviant, the risk of psychopathology is high for the offspring of affected parents. The family resemblance in schizophrenia may be ge-

netically based (see Chapters 2 and 10 for details) or may be traced to deviant rearing practices, or both heredity and environment may play a role. Whatever the etiology, schizophrenic parents in the acute phases of the disorder are highly inadequate social models for their children, and most do not interact with their children in a warm, consistent fashion. Because schizophrenic parents must work hard to maintain their own precarious adjustment, it seems unlikely that they could be easily trained in appropriate child-rearing practices.

Some efforts to help the children of schizophrenics have aimed to make them more independent of their periodically incapacitated parents. Anthony (1972) has devised a program for school-age children of psychotic parents, to give them both the support of professional helpers and instruction in self-help to assist them during times of family crisis. In Anthony's program, mental health workers provide crisis counseling for these children and may prescribe tranquilizing drugs for them when their parents become seriously upset. Group and individual nondirective therapy is given to help the youngsters interpret their parents' frightening psychotic behavior. Like many other such interventions, this one has not yet been rigorously evaluated. At present, much more is known about risk factors in the development of schizophrenia than about how to intervene to prevent the occurrence of the disorder. Other interventions include both affected parents and their children. Goodman (1984) has initiated a program for families headed by schizophrenic or depressed low-income parents, featuring home-based social support, training in parenting, day care for the children, and assistance in utilizing community services. Skills taught include social problem solving, reality recognition, improved parent-child relationships, and effective use of community services. Predictably, the children of better-functioning parents with more stable marriages seem to profit most from this program (Watt, 1986).

School-based programs also have been developed for the young children of schizophrenic patients (Garmezy, 1974). On the island of Mauritius, situated in the Indian Ocean, a research team headed by Mednick (Mednick, 1974; Mednick, Venables, Schulsigner, & Cudeck, 1982) conducted a large longitudinal study of the physical and psychological development of high-risk children, including some with psychotic parents. A portion of the high-risk youngsters were given an enriched nursery school experience in hopes of optimizing their development. After 3 years, observations indicated that the children from the high-risk sample who had received the nursery school intervention were doing well socially, but the results of more rigorously controlled evaluations have not been reported. A somewhat similar nursery school program for children at risk for psychological disorders has been instituted at the University of Vermont (Rolf, Fischer, & Hasazi, 1982). Children identified as being at risk for psychopathology were enrolled in a special day care program, were given individualized play therapy or behavior therapy and peer modeling interventions, and were provided with coaching in needed

language and development skills. Their families also received parent training and other help as needed. The children were reported to benefit from this program in several ways: They performed better on tests of developmental competence (such as IQ tests), their visual perception and language skills improved, and they were less aggressive and better controlled in their everyday social interactions (Rolf et al., 1982). Future years will reveal whether such programs do provide enduring help for the children of psychotic parents and other troubled children.

Parents with Affective Disorder Research results indicate that having a parent with a serious affective dysfunction, such as severe bipolar (manic-depressive) affective disorder or major depression, presents significant psychological risk to a child. Surprisingly, parental affective disorder may prove even more disturbing to children than parental schizophrenia (Seifer, Sameroff, &

BOX 15-3 • **Life with a Depressed Mother**

As she slipped deeper and deeper into depression, 32-year-old Kathy began to consider herself more a slave to her children than a loving mother. When her children were born, she quit her job willingly in order to be a full-time, devoted homemaker, and was once an exemplary wife and mother. Then the descent of a major depressive episode left her too confused, shaky, and preoccupied to complete simple tasks such as preparing meals, and too tearful and inattentive to care for her children well. Kathy's depression seems to have adversely affected her three children. Kendra, her 6-year-old, has become a bad-tempered tyrant, ordering her indecisive mother about, calling her stupid, and throwing wild tantrums. Even John, the placid 4-year-old, has lost his customary good humor, because his mother is too tired and irritable to want to play with him any more. At 6 months, the baby, Laurie, appears withdrawn, sour, and peevish. Her despondent mother doesn't hold or play with her often, and feeding has become an unpleasant chore, because Laurie spits up much of the food that Kathy tries to force on her.

   It is almost certainly true that their family life will improve when Kathy's depression lifts, either naturally over time or as a result of treatment. To bring about faster improvement in Kathy's mothering, a home visitor program might be introduced. The visitor could be a pediatric or public health nurse, a social worker, or a psychologist who is trained to assist depressed mothers to become more responsive to their children. The intervention could prompt Kathy to resume her old positive and instructive interchanges with her children, and to be firmer and more consistent with her troubled oldest child as well. Early intervention programs of this type hold considerable promise in preventing psychopathology in children of psychiatrically disturbed patients.

Jones, 1981). Parents with severe affective disorders may become insensitive to the needs of their children; may monitor the children poorly and so fail to protect them from common hazards; and may present sad, angry, helpless, and joyless models for their children's emulation (Orvaschel, 1983). Box 15-3 presents the case of a depressed mother and her interactions with her three small children. In turn, the offspring of incapacitated depressed parents tend to develop more than their share of problems of many types. As infants and preschoolers, these youngsters may have problems in forming secure attachments to their parents; they may also display difficulties in regulating their expression of emotions, in controlling aggressive impulses, and in sharing and cooperating with others (Zahn-Waxler-Cummings, McKnew, and Radke-Yarrow, 1984). Later, they are likely to develop problems in controlling their behavior at school, and to have learning and achievement difficulties (Neale, Winters, & Weintraub, 1984). There are also very high rates of depression among the children of affectively disordered parents (Cytryn, McKnew, Bartko, Lamour, Hamovit, et al., 1982; Orvaschel, 1983). Research is needed in the development of effective preventive interventions for emotionally disturbed parents and families.

School-Based Programs for High-Risk Children

There have been many different efforts to shape school curriculums so as to aid high-risk children. Perhaps the most ambitious and best-known of such programs is that developed by Cowen and his associates to provide early detection of elevated risk status and prevention of school maladjustment (Cowen, Gesten, & Wilson, 1979). The Primary Mental Health Project has many appealing features and has been used in over 300 schools in the United States. Elementary school children are screened for academic and social problems, and those who either have or seem likely to develop such problems are identified. These children are assigned to trained nonprofessional aides, who work with them individually under the supervision of mental health professionals. The aides are selected for their warmth and interest in children; they tutor the students in academic and social skills, and offer many types of informal help. Studies indicate that the teachers, the aides, and the school mental health workers all consider the program to be effective in improving the children's adjustment and their social and academic competency (Cowen, 1977; Cowen et al., 1979). However, formal evaluations have been less positive, with some reports of little or no tangible benefits for children who have participated (Cowen et al., 1975). When positive effects on child adjustment have been found, they have been small compared to the effects typically produced by psychotherapy (Stein & Polyson, 1984). In addition, some of the child evaluations were performed by teachers and project staff who believed strongly in the program's effectiveness, so the project's value has not yet been convincingly established. In similar work with younger preschool children, Rickel and Smith (1979) demonstrated that Cowen's Primary Mental Health Project intervention did improve children's scores significantly on a measure of development that predicts future school success (the Caldwell Preschool Inventory). The results with the nursery school children suggest that Cowen's approach has real promise, at least for younger children, and that it merits further development and evaluation.

The preceding studies indicate that with sufficient effort and adequate funding, social scientists may be able to devise interventions to prevent or reduce the human suffering associated with mental illness and behavior disorders. As pointed out in Chapter 3 on social conditions, it is already known that much physical illness, retardation, and behavioral dysfunction can be eliminated by the provision of very simple, often inexpensive measures, such as adequate nutrition, sanitation, the control of environmental poisons, and prenatal medical care. Many public health measures have been taken by the wealthy, industrialized nations, but few countries are moving forcefully to protect children from the blight of avoidable psychopathology.

ALTERNATIVE CHILD CARE PATTERNS

Another social movement affecting children is the trend toward the provision of daily child care by adults other than parents. The community has a vital interest in the quality of care given its children, and local community support for child care in the form of day care centers or informal arrangements is associated with low rates of child abuse and neglect (Bronfenbrenner, Moen, & Garbarino, 1984; Garbarino & Sherman, 1980). Economic pressures increasingly demand that both parents be employed, and the women's movement has produced both greater acceptance of maternal employment and a greater range of occupational opportunities for women. Moreover, high divorce rates (and the accompanying prevalence of maternal custody and sole financial responsibility for the children) have forced many women to find jobs who otherwise might not choose to do so. The effects on children of parental marital discord and divorce are discussed in Chapter 3, so the present section addresses mainly the impact of maternal employment and day care on children. In the United States, more than 56 percent of all women with children under the age of 6 years are employed, as are 70 percent of those with children between the ages of 6 and 18, although many work part-time rather than full-time (U.S. Bureau of the Census, 1982). That is, a clear and growing majority of women with children are employed outside the home. As a result, child care patterns are changing rapidly and will probably continue to do so for a number of years (Hoffman, 1979). How will these changes affect children?

During the past century, middle-class mothers were their children's primary caregivers; this role, however, is now increasingly played by relatives, babysitters, day care workers, and some fathers (Lamb, Chase-Lansdale, & Owen, 1979). Maternal employment in itself does not seem to harm children. According to some studies, it actually decreases the mothers' overprotectiveness, increases mothers' self-esteem, and positively affects daughters by building their self-esteem and

their academic and occupational competence (Eccles & Hoffman, 1984; Hoffman, 1979). A cautionary note is indicated by a few studies that have found that some sons of middle-class employed mothers develop academic achievement problems (Gold & Andres, 1978a). It may be that busy employed mothers and fathers have neither the time nor the energy to oversee their sons' homework. Also, in working-class families, the mother's holding a job may stem from financial hardship rather than intrinsic interest in the work. This public testimony to the family's financial needs may make the father appear occupationally unsuccessful, undermine his role in the family, and consequently strain the father-son relationship (Eccles & Hoffman, 1984; Gold & Andres, 1978b). Nevertheless, most research has found maternal employment to have either no ill effects on the family or positive ones. This is fortunate, considering the rapidly growing numbers of employed mothers.

One of the major concerns of working parents is the guidance, supervision, and care their children receive while the parents are at work (Yankelovich, Skelly, White, Inc., 1981). Most preschool children of working mothers are cared for at home by babysitters or in the homes of relatives, neighbors, or others (U.S. Department of Health, Education and Welfare, 1978). However, increasing numbers of infants and children are being enrolled in day care centers. As more and more women take regular jobs, the dwindling supply of individual day care providers will expand the enrollment in day care centers even further (Hofferth, 1979).

Initially, many people feared that organized day care experiences would not be good for children. In fact, most studies have shown remarkably few ill effects of adequate-quality day care services. In a review of the effects of day care, Belsky and Steinberg (1978) reported that day care often *promoted* the cognitive development of low-income children and had no adverse effects on the cognitive development of middle-class ones. A more recent review by the same authors produced a similar conclusion: Day care makes little difference in child development, except for help-

Increasing numbers of children attend day care centers for many hours each week. Good day care centers have been found to promote children's development, but state and federal funding is needed.

ing children from severely disadvantaged backgrounds (Belsky, Steinberg, & Walker, 1982). However, most recently Belsky has concluded that entry into day care in the first year of life could create adjustment problems (Belsky, 1986). Socially, attending a day care center seems to increase children's rates of both positive and negative interactions with peers; that is, they become both more friendly and more aggressive (Schwarz, Strickland, & Krolick, 1974). It is noteworthy that in other nations day care does not appear to heighten children's aggression as it does in the United States, so cultural differences may be responsible for the day care children's increased aggressiveness in this country (Hoffman, 1979). It is apparent that much more research is needed on the complex effects of group child care.

In the United States, some large employers provide day care services for their workers, but most day care is offered by private centers on a for-profit basis. Since most working mothers' salaries are modest, they must find the most economical means of caring for their youngsters while they are on the job. These financial limitations too often result in inadequate care of the children, who must stay at physically unappealing centers staffed by temporary, ill-trained, and low-paid workers with little commitment to their work. This is not a recipe for high-quality care. A national study of day care (*Final Report of the National Day Care Study*, 1979) revealed that the quality of day care was primarily related to two factors: (1) the size of the child groups in the center, and (2) the preparation of the caregivers. The youngest children require the most attention, so the report recommended there be no more than 4 infants per caregiver and that, regardless of the number of helpers, groups not exceed 8 younger or 12 older infants. Under these conditions, the low-income urban children studied seemed to thrive in day care centers. Caregiver qualifications were less important for the infants and toddlers, but teachers' background and training became much more vital for older preschool children. Caregivers with education or training relevant to the care of young children, such as formal courses or in-service education, influenced children more positively than did those without such preparation.

Rapid staff turnover, which is typical of many centers, seems to be bad for children, who show a decided preference for caregivers they have been with for longer periods (Cummings, 1980). Group size is important, in that the social and cognitive development of 3- to 5-year-olds is improved in groups smaller than 18 children. Larger groups are associated with poorer-quality care, child apathy, and smaller gains on developmental tests. Surprisingly, the number of children per caregiver is less important than the number of children in the group. It is possible that in larger groups, caregivers prefer to interact with each other rather than to attend to the children. This review of day care research indicates that good group care can benefit some children, and seems not to be harmful. However, the best care is likely to be the most expensive, since it entails small groups and more skilled and probably better-paid staff members. Without the financial contributions of governments and employers, many parents cannot affort the type of care they want for their children.

When budgets are cut, children's services, including day care, are endangered. Public displays of concern, such as this one, bring families' needs to public attention and help create political support for day care services.

BARRIERS TO EFFECTIVE CHILD CARE AND PREVENTION SERVICES

Children are less able to speak for themselves and assert their rights than are adults. Too often they receive substandard services because they lack the means to promote their own welfare. While another underserved group, the elderly, is gaining political strength and receiving expanded government services, children living in poverty are losing ground. Services to poor mothers and their dependent children are cut and then cut again, so their situation worsens. This apparent age-based discrimination may result from children's dependence on adults to protect their rights, while the elderly can act for themselves directly (Rodham, 1979). Children are politically disenfranchised: they can neither lobby nor vote, and they have few powerful political advocates. They do not control their own money and are dependent on their parents in all aspects of their lives. Moreover, children are inexperienced and trusting, so they are easily abused and exploited by adults (Vardin & Brody, 1979). Children need concerned and knowledgeable adult advocates.

Some adult advocates organize groups to further children's welfare. Examples include the Children's Defense Fund, an active Washington, D.C., lobbying organization; the Carnegie Council on Children, which compiles and issues influential reports; PTA organizations at schools; and special advocacy committees formed by professional organizations, such as the Committee on Children, Youth, and Families of the American Psychological Association. These groups attempt to influence their parent organizations, other influential private groups, the public, and Congress so as to protect children and promote their welfare. Child advocacy groups bring suits to ensure that children are receiving appropriate educational and treatment services, and they monitor legislative proceedings to increase budgets for important services and to uphold children's rights (Knitzer, 1976; Zigler & Finn, 1984). Many more such advocacy organizations are needed to help the nation's children.

Public attitudes and national economic problems pose further obstacles to efforts to improve child care and prevent psychopathology. A staggering federal deficit, resulting high inflation rates, and economic stagnation combine to reduce public nonmilitary spending. Adequate child care is expensive and requires public and corporate funding much beyond what parents alone can afford. Public unwillingness to support federal funding for child care, for education, and for mental health programs wastes human potential and produces avoidable adjustment problems and crime, especially among the least affluent sectors of the economy. Although providing federal funding may not cure problems, inadequate resources aggravate them.

Even were there adequate financing, we would lack the professional people to staff human services adequately. Here, again, state and federal funding could improve the situation by providing financial support for professional training. Today most professionals want to treat rather than to prevent (Gelfand & Hartmann, 1977). Psychologists, social workers, nurses, and psychiatrists are trained to diagnose and treat people with adjustment problems, but are ill prepared to prevent disorders. New training programs in prevention are needed for students and practicing professionals. As stated earlier, preventive interventions are difficult to evaluate because their effects are delayed and may be subtle and complex. Sometimes the benefits are apparent in partici-

pants' improved functioning only many years after the intervention has taken place. Preventionists must have extraordinary reserves of patience and commitment to their work.

There is much to be done, and far too little time, public interest, or financing; yet it is important to overcome these barriers to effective programming. Without early intervention many serious problems will persist and worsen, particularly among youngsters with the most persistent conditions, such as conduct disorders, developmental disabilities, or psychotic reactions. Being born into unfortunate families with inadequate parents should not doom children for life. Instead, they should share the opportunities available to their more fortunate age-mates. Prevention programs are developing, although they remain inadequately financed and few in number. They bear the seeds of an improved quality of life for future generations.

SUMMARY

Concerned individuals and international child protection organizations have suggested that children's human and legal rights be greatly expanded to guarantee all children health, safety, education, and freedom. Actually, children's legal rights are limited. In the United States, many constitutionally guaranteed rights of adults have been extended in limited form to children as well. For example, children arrested for criminal offenses must be given a due process hearing, including representation by a lawyer, and cannot be convinced unless they are shown to be guilty beyond a reasonable doubt. However, minors cannot have jury trials, and they may be compelled to participate in treatment if their parents so desire. Children's liberty is restricted in order to protect them because they lack mature judgment and are more vulnerable to harm than are adults. Restrictions are also imposed to maintain family strength and discipline.

By law, physcially, emotionally, and mentally handicapped children are entitled to appropriate individualized education at public expense. They must be educated and treated in the least coercive and least restrictive fashion possible. Lack of adequate funding prevents many schools from achieving this high standard, however, and a lack of evaluative research prevents us from knowing what types of educational placements benefit handicapped children the most. A small but active number of voluntary and professional groups serve as public advocates for children's welfare.

New developments in clinical services for children include the integration of knowledge from developmental psychology in their assessment and treatment. In line with the expansion of minors' legal rights, developmental psychologists now view children as more active determiners of caretakers' perceptions of and reactions to them than was formerly realized. Adults do not simply shape children, but are often equally affected by them. Viewing children as capable of some degree of self-determination, psychologists are devising self-regulation training programs for children who are impulsive, hyperactive, aggressive, or withdrawn. These efforts assume that children can learn effective self-regulation skills that they can later use in problematic situations. Thus far the research indicates that children can learn specific self-control practices in training situations, but that it is difficult to teach them general skills for use in other tasks and settings.

Another trend is toward the development of new preventive services for children and families. Some projects identify and treat children who are at risk of developing psychopathology because their parents suffer from psychological disorders such as alcohol or drug addiction, serious affective disorders, and schizophrenia. Then these high-risk children and their families are given such services as enrollment of the younger children in special nursery schools, counseling and therapy for parents and older children, instruction for the parents in child rearing, and self-care training for the children. Other projects identify school children who are at risk of developing adjustment problems and then provide them with psychological services in the schools. It would be premature to evaluate the success of such preventive efforts now, but they hold considerable promise.

Striking increases in the rate of maternal employment have changed child care patterns in our society. More infants and children now are cared for by babysitters, relatives, and day care center staffs. By itself, maternal employment seems to have few if any detectable ill effects on the children. However, the quality of alternative care is a major concern for parents and can affect children's development. The best care is expensive, requiring trained caretakers, small groups of children, and low staff turnover rates. Many parents find such desirable day care difficult to afford.

There are economic, political, and attitudinal obstacles to providing good alternative care for the nation's children and to developing effective problem prevention programs. Yet the laissez-faire alternative of putting most of the burden on the parents is stressful for them and serves children poorly. A few professional and private organizations, and some federal agencies, are dedicated to advocating children's interests. To a large extent, the quality of a nation is revealed in its commitment to caring for its members who are powerless, ill, vulnerable, and incapable of protecting their own interests. Thus, our commitment to helping troubled children, to preventing suffering in future generations, and to pursuing solutions for major social ills is a reflection of our own best qualities and a guarantee of the welfare of the children of tomorrow.

References

CHAPTER 1

Achenbach, T. M., & Edelbrock, C. S. (1978). The classification of child psychopathology: A review and analysis of empirical effects. **Psychological Bulletin, 78,** 1275–1301.

Agras, W. S., Chaplin, H. N., & Oliveau, D. C. (1972). The natural history of phobia. **Archives of General Psychiatry, 26,** 315–317.

Al-Issa, I. (1982a). Gender and adult psychopathology. In I. Al-Issa (Ed.), **Gender and psychopathology.** New York: Academic Press.

Al-Issa, I. (1982b). Gender and child psychopathology. In I. Al-Issa (Ed.), **Gender and psychopathology.** New York: Academic Press.

American Psychiatric Association. (1980). **Diagnostic and statistical manual of mental disorders** (3rd ed.). Washington, DC: Author.

Ariès, P. (1962). **Centuries of childhood: A social history of family life** (R. Baldick, Trans.). London: Gape.

Asians in college. (1986, August 5). **New York Times,** p. 26y.

Bachman, J. G. (1970). **Youth in transition: The impact of family background and intelligence on tenth-grade boys** (Vol. 2). Ann Arbor: Institute for Social Research, University of Michigan.

Bartak, L., & Rutter, M. L. (1975). A three-and-one-half- to four-year follow-up study of special educational treatment of autistic children. In R. Wirt, G. Winokur, & M. Roff (Eds.), **Life history research in psychopathology** (Vol. 4). Minneapolis: University of Minnesota Press.

Beckman, D. (1977). **The mechanical baby: A popular history of the theory and practice of child raising.** Westport, CT: Lawrence Hill.

Bell, R. Q., Weller, G. M., & Waldrop, M. F. (1971). Newborn and preschooler: Organization of behavior and relations between periods. **Monographs of the Society for Research in Child Development, 36** (0 to 2, Serial No. 142).

Berg, I. (1970). A follow-up study of school phobic adolescents admitted to an inpatient unit. **Journal of Child Psychology and Psychiatry and Allied Disciplines, 11,** 37–47.

Borstelmann, L. J. (1983). Children before psychology: Ideas about children from antiquity to the late 1800s. In W. Kessen (Ed.), **Handbook of child psychology** (4th ed., vol. 1). New York: Wiley.

Bremner, R. H. (Ed.). (1971). **Children and youth in America: A documentary history. Vol. 2. 1866–1932.** Cambridge, MA: Harvard University Press.

Bronfenbrenner, U. (1979). **The ecology of human development.** Cambridge, MA: Harvard University Press.

Bruch, H. (1982). Anorexia nervosa: Therapy and theory. **American Journal of Psychiatry, 139,** 1531–1538.

Brumberg, J. J. (1986). "Fasting girls": Reflections on writing the history of anorexia nervosa. In A. B. Smuts & J. W. Hagen (Eds.), History and research in child development. **Monographs of the Society for Research in Child Development, 50** (4–5, Serial No. 211).

Bukowski, W. M., & Newcomb, A. F. (1984). Stability and determinants of sociometric status and friendship choice: A longitudinal perspective. **Developmental Psychology, 20,** 941–952.

Clifford, A. (1923). **The diary of the Lady Anne Clifford** (V. Sackville-West, Ed.). London: Heinemann.

Coie, J. D., & Dodge, K. A. (1983). Continuities and change in children's social status: A five-year longitudinal study. **Merrill-Palmer Quarterly, 29,** 261–281.

Coleman, J. C., Butcher, J. N., & Carson, R. C. (1980). **Abnormal psychology and modern life** (6th ed). Glenview, IL: Scott, Foresman.

Crisp, A. H. (1976). How common is anorexia nervosa? A prevalence study. **British Journal of Psychiatry, 128,** 349–354.

Crowther, J., Bond, L., & Rolf, J. (1981). The incidence, prevalence, and severity of internalizing and externalizing behavior problems among preschool children in day care. **Journal of Abnormal Child Psychology, 9,** 23–42.

deMause, L. (1974). The evolution of childhood. In L. deMause (Ed.), **The history of childhood.** New York: Psychohistory Press.

Donovan, J. E., & Jessor, R. (1985). Structure of problem behavior in adolescence and young adulthood. **Journal of Consulting and Clinical Psychology, 53,** 890–904.

Douvan, E., & Adelson, J. (1966). **The adolescent experience.** New York: Wiley.

Dunn, J., Kendrick, C., & MacNamee, R. (1981). The reaction of first-born children to the birth of a sibling: Mothers' reports. **Journal of Child Psychology and Psychiatry, 22,** 1–18.

Eaton, M. E., Sletten, I. W., Kitchen, A. D., & Smith, R. J. (1971). The Missouri automated psychiatric history: Symptom frequencies, sex differences, use of weapons and other findings. **Comprehensive Psychiatry, 12,** 264–267.

Erikson, E. H. (1956). The problems of ego identity. **Journal of the American Psychoanalytic Association, 4,** 56–121.

Fagot, B. I. (1977). Consequences of moderate cross-gender behavior in preschool children. **Child Development, 48,** 902–907.

Gandevia, B. (1977). A comparison of the heights of boys transported to Australia from England, Scotland and Ireland c. 1840, with later British and Australian developments. **Australian Paediatric Journal, 13,** 91–97.

Gelfand, D. M., & Peterson, L. (1985). **Child development and psychopathology.** Beverly Hills, CA: Sage.

Goodenough, F. L. (1931). **Anger in young children.** Minneapolis: University of Minnesota Press.

Gordon, M. (1978). **The American family in social-historical perspective** (2nd ed). New York: St. Martin's Press.

Granell de Aldaz, E., Vivas, E., Gelfand, D. M., & Feldman, L. (1984). Estimating the prevalence of school refusal and school related fears in Venezuelan children. **Journal of Nervous and Mental Disease, 172,** 722–729.

Greenfeld, J. (1978). **A place for Noah.** New York: Holt, Rinehart & Winston.

Greenfeld, J. (1986). **A client called Noah: A family journey continued.** New York: Henry Holt.

Huston, A. C. (1983). Sex-typing. In P. H. Mussen (General Ed.), **Handbook of child psychology** (4th ed.): **Vol. 4. Socialization, personality, and social development** (E. M. Hetherington, Vol. Ed.). New York: Wiley.

Jessor, R., & Jessor, S. L. (1977). **Problem behavior and psychosocial development: A longitudinal study of youth.** New York: Academic Press.

Jordan, C., & Tharp, R. G. (1979). Culture and education. In A. Marsella, R. Tharp, & T. Ciborowski (Eds.), **Perspectives on cross-cultural psychology.** New York: Academic Press.

Jordan, T. E. (1985). Transported to Van Diemen's Land: The boys of the **Frances Charlotte** (1832) and **Lord Goderich** (1841). **Child Development, 56,** 1092–1099.

Kagan, J. (1978). The child in the family. In A. Rossi, J. Kagan, & T. Hareven (Eds.), **The family.** New York: Norton.

Kelly, T. J., Bullock, L. M., & Dykes, M. K. (1978).

Behavioral disorders: Teachers' perceptions. **Exceptional Children, 43,** 316–318.

Kessen, W. (1965). **The child.** New York: Wiley.

Kohlberg, L., LaCrosse, J., & Ricks, D. (1972). The predictability of adult mental health from childhood behavior. In B. Wolman (Ed.), **Manual of child psychopathology.** New York: McGraw-Hill.

Kramer, M. (1977). **Psychiatric services and the changing institutional scene, 1950–1985** (DHEW Publication No. ADM 77-77-433). Washington, DC: U.S. Government Printing Office.

Lamb, M. E., & Roopnarine, J. F. (1979). Peer influences on sex-role development in preschoolers. **Child Development, 50,** 1219–1222.

Levine, M., & Levine, A. (1970). **A social history of helping services.** New York: Appleton-Century-Crofts.

Lewinsohn, P. M., & Amenson, C. S. (1981). An investigation into the observed sex difference in prevalence of unipolar depression. **Journal of Abnormal Psychology, 90,** 1–13.

Lewis, W. W. (1965). Continuity and intervention in emotional disturbance: A review. **Exceptional Children, 31,** 465–475.

Loeber, R. (1982). The stability of antisocial and delinquent child behavior: A review. **Child Development, 53,** 1431–1446.

Macfarlane, J. W. (1963). From infancy to adulthood. **Childhood Education, 39,** 336–342.

Macfarlane, J. W. (1964). Perspectives on personality consistency and change from The Guidance Study. **Vita Humana, 7,** 115–126.

Macfarlane, J. W., Allen, L., & Honzik, M. (1954). **A developmental study of the behavior problems of normal children between twenty-one months and fourteen years.** Berkeley: University of California Press.

Marsella, A. J. (1979). Cross-cultural studies of mental disorders. In A. Marsella, R. Tharp, & T. Ciborowski (Eds.), **Perspectives on cross-cultural psychology.** New York: Academic Press.

Maziade, M., Capéraà, M., Laplante, B., Boudreault, B., Thivierge, J., Cote, R., & Boutin, P. (1985). The value of difficult temperament among 7-year-olds in the general population for predicting psychiatric diagnosis at age 12. **American Journal of Pediatrics, 142,** 943–946.

McCall, R. B., Appelbaum, M. I., & Hogarty, P. S. (1973). Developmental changes in mental performance. **Monographs of the Society for Research in Child Development, 38** (Serial No. 150).

Meissner, W. W. (1965). Parental interaction of the adolescent boy. **Journal of Genetic Psychology, 107,** 225–233.

Moore, T. (1976). Stress in normal childhood. In L.

Levi (Ed.), **Society, stress and disease: Childhood and adolescence** (Vol. 2). London: Oxford University Press.

Murphy, J. M. (1976). Psychiatric labeling in cross-cultural perspective. **Science, 191,** 1019–1028.

Nash, S. E., & Feldman, S. S. (1981). Sex role and sex-related attributions: Constancy and change across the family life cycle. In M. E. Lamb & A. L. Brown (Eds.), **Advances in developmental psychology** (Vol. 1). Hillsdale, NJ: Erlbaum.

Offer, D., & Offer, J. B. (1975). **From teenage to young manhood: A psychological study.** New York: Basic Books.

O'Leary, K. D., Vivian, D., & Nisi, A. (1985). Hyperactivity in Italy. **Journal of Abnormal Child Psychology, 13,** 485–500.

Pollock, L. A. (1983). **Forgotten children: Parent-child relations from 1500 to 1900.** Cambridge, England: Cambridge University Press.

Quay, H. D. (1979). Residential treatment. In H. D. Quay & J. S. Werry (Eds.), **Psychopathological disorders of childhood** (Vol. 2). New York: Wiley.

Rekers, G. A. (1977). Assessment and treatment of childhood gender problems. In B. B. Lahey & A. E. Kazdin (Eds.), **Advances in clinical child psychology** (Vol. 1). New York: Plenum.

Rie, H. E. (1971). Historical perspectives on concepts of child psychopathology. In H. Rie (Ed.), **Perspectives in child psychopathology.** Chicago: Aldine-Atherton.

Robins, L. N. (1966). **A sociological and psychiatric study of sociopathic personality.** Baltimore: Williams & Wilkins.

Rolf, J., Hakola, J., Klemchuk, H., & Hasazi, J. (1976). **The incidence, prevalence and severity of behavior disorders among preschool aged children.** Paper presented at the meeting of the Eastern Psychological Association, New York.

Rosenfeld, G. (1971). **"Shut those thick lips!" A study of slum school failure.** New York: Holt, Rinehart & Winston.

Rubin, R. A., & Balow, B. (1971). Learning and behavior disorders: A longitudinal study. **Exceptional Children, 38,** 293–299.

Rubin, R. A., & Balow, B. (1978). Prevalence of teacher identified behavior problems: A longitudinal study. **Exceptional Children, 45,** 102–111.

Rutter, M., & Garmegy, N. (1983). Developmental psychopathology. In P. H. Mussen (General Ed.), **Handbook of child psychology** (4th ed.): Vol. 4, **Socialization, personality, and social development** (E. M. Hetherington, Vol. Ed.). New York: Wiley.

Shepherd, M., Oppenheim, B., & Mitchell, S. (Eds.).

(1971). **Childhood behaviour and mental health.** London: University of London Press.

Shorter, E. (1975). **The making of the modern family.** New York: Basic Books.

Snapper, K. J., & Ohms, J. S. (1977). **The status of children 1977.** Washington, DC: U.S. Government Printing Office.

Sparks, J. L., & Younie, W. J. (1969). Adult adjustment of the mentally retarded: Implications for teacher education. **Exceptional Children, 36,** 13–18.

Spitzka, E. C. (1890). Insanity. In J. Keating (Ed.), **Cyclopaedia of the diseases of children, medical and surgical.** Philadelphia: J. B. Lippincott.

Stewart, L. J. (1962). Social and emotional adjustment during adolescence as related to the development of psychosomatic illness in adulthood. **Genetic Psychology Monographs, No. 65,** 175–215.

Strauss, J. S. (1979). Social and cultural influences on psychopathology. **Annual Review of Psychology, 30,** 397–415.

Tuchman, B. (1978). **A distant mirror: The calamitous 14th century.** New York: Knopf.

U.S. Office of Education, Bureau of Education for the Handicapped. (1975, May 16). **State education agency estimates unserved by type of handicap.** Washington, DC: Author, Aid to State Branch.

Watson-Gegeo, K. A., & Boggs, S. T. (1977). From verbal play to talk-story: The role of routines in speech events among Hawaiian children. In S. Ervin-Tripp & C. Mitchell-Kernan (Eds.), **Child discourse.** New York: Academic Press.

Watt, N. F. (1986). Prevention of schizophrenic disorders. In B. Edelstein & L. Michelson (Eds.), **Handbook of prevention.** New York: Plenum.

Weiner, I. B. (1982). **Child and adolescent psychopathology.** New York: Wiley.

Werner, E. E., Bierman, J. M., & French, F. E. (1971). **The children of Kauai.** Honolulu: University of Hawaii Press.

Werner, E. E., & Smith, R. S. (1977). **Kauai's children come of age.** Honolulu: University of Hawaii Press.

Winn, M. (1983, May 8). The loss of childhood. **New York Times Magazine,** pp. 18, 21–23, 26, 28, 30.

Zax, M., & Cowen, E. L. (1967). Early identification and prevention of emotional disturbance in a public school. In E. L. Cowen, E. Gardner, & M. Zax (Eds.), **Emergent approaches to mental health problems.** New York: Appleton-Century-Crofts.

Zigler, E., & Phillips, L. (1960). Social effectiveness and symptomatic behaviors. **Journal of Abnormal and Social Psychology, 61,** 231–238.

CHAPTER 2

Audi, R. (1976). B. F. Skinner on freedom, dignity, and the explanation of behavior. **Behaviorism, 4,** 163–186.

Awards for distinguished scientific contributions: 1980. (1981). **American Psychologist, 36,** 27–34.

Bandura, A. (1968). A social learning interpretation of psychological dysfunctions. In P. London & D. Rosenhan (Eds.), **Foundations of abnormal psychology.** New York: Holt, Rinehart & Winston.

Bandura, A. (1969). **Principles of behavior modification.** New York: Holt, Rinehart & Winston.

Bandura, A. (1977). **Social learning theory.** Englewood Cliffs, NJ: Prentice-Hall.

Bandura, A. (1981). Self-referent thought: The development of self-efficacy. In J. Flavell & L. Ross (Eds.), **Social cognitive development.** New York: Cambridge University Press.

Bandura, A., & Walters, R. J. (1963). **Social and personality development.** New York: Holt, Rinehart & Winston.

Biglan, A., & Kass, D. J. (1977). The empirical nature of behavior therapies. **Behaviorism, 5,** 1–15.

Bregman, E. (1934). An attempt to modidfy the emotional attitude of infants by the conditioned response technique. **Journal of Genetic Psychology, 45,** 169–198.

Buhler, C. D., & Allen, C. (1972). **Introduction to humanistic psychology.** Monterey, CA; Brooks/Cole.

Cairns, R. B., & Valsiner, J. (1984). Child psychology. **Annual Review of Psychology, 35,** 553–578.

Chaplin, J.P., & Krawiec, T.S. (1979). **Systems and theories of psychology** (4th ed.). New York: Holt, Rinehart & Winston.

Chomsky, N. (1959). Review of **Verbal Behavior** by B. F. Skinner. **Language, 35,** 26–58.

Cicchetti, D. (1984). The emergence of develpmental psychopathology. **Child Development, 55,** 1–7.

Elkind, D. (1976). **Child development and education.** New York: Norton.

English, H. B. (1929). Three cases of the "conditioned fear response." **Journal of Abnormal and Social Psychology, 34,** 221–225.

Epstein, S. (1973). The self-concept revisited: Or a theory of a theory. **American Psychologist, 28,** 404–416.

Erikson, E. H. (1963). **Childhood and society** (2nd ed.). New York Norton.

Erikson, E. H. (1968). **Identity: Youth and crisis.** New York: Norton.

Ferster, D. B., & Skinner B. F. (1957). **Schedules of reinforcement.** New York: Appleton.

Flavell, J. H. (1963). **The developmental psychology of Jean Piaget.** New York: Van Nostrand Reinhold.

Freud, A. (1946). **The ego and the mechanisms of defence.** New York: International Universities Press.

Freud, S. (1965). **New introductory lectures on psychoanalysis** (J. Strachey, Trans.). New York: Norton. (Original work published 1933).

Gelfand, D. M., & Peterson, L. (1985). **Child develpment and psychopathology.** Beverly Hills, CA: Sage.

Gelman, R., & Baillargeon, R. (1983). A review of some Piagetian concepts. In P. H. Mussen (General Ed.) **Handbook of child psychology** (4th ed.): **Vol. 3. Cognitive development** (J. H. Flavell & E. M. Markman, Vol. Eds.). New York: Wiley.

Hall, C. S. (1954). **A primer of Freudian psychology.** Cleveland, OH: World.

Hall, C. S., & Lindzey, G. (1978). **Theories of personality** (3rd ed.). New York Wiley.

Harris, B. (1979) Whatever happened to Little Albert? **American Psychologist, 34,** 151–160.

Hartmann, H., Kris, E., & Loewenstein, R. M. (1947). Comments on the formation of psychic structures. In A. Freud, H. Hartman, & E. Kris (Eds.), **The psychoanalytic study of the child** (Vol. 2). New York: International Universities Press.

Hilgard, E. R., & Bower, G. H. (1975). **Theories of learning** (4th ed.). Englewood Cliffs, NJ: Prentice-Hall.

Jones, E. (1953–1957). **The life and work of Sigmund Freud** (3 vols.). New York: Basic Books.

Kessler, S. (1975). Psychiatric genetics. In D. Hamburg & S. Brodie (Eds.), **American handbook of psychiatry: Vol. 6. New psychiatric frontiers.** New York: Basic Books.

Kohlberg, L. (1969). **Stages in the development of moral thought and action.** New York: Holt, Rinehart & Winston.

Kohlberg, L. (1981a). **Philosophy of moral development.** New York: Harper & Row.

Kohlberg, L. (1981b). Moral education in the schools: A developmental view. In M. Kaplan & R. Yablans-Magid (Eds.), **Life-span develpmental psychology: Personality and socialization.** New York: Academic Press.

Kringlen, E. (1976). Twins—still our best method. **Schizophrenia Bulletin, 2,** 429–433.

Kuhn, T. S. (1970). **The structure of scientific revolutions** (2nd ed.). Chicago: University of Chicago Press.

Marx, M. H., & Hillix, W. A. (1979). **Systems of the-**

ories in psychology (3rd ed.). New York: Mc-Graw-Hill.

Maslow, A. H. (1970). **Motivation and personality** (2nd ed.). New York: Harper & Row.

Mendlewicz, J., Linkowski, P., Guroff, J. J., & van Praag, H. M. (1979). Color blindness linkage to bipolar manic-depressive illness: New evidence. **Archives of General Psychiatry, 36,** 1442–1447.

Miller, N. E., & Dollard, J. (1941). **Social learning and imitation.** New Haven, CT: Yale University Press.

Mischel, W. (1968). **Personality and assessment.** New York: Wiley.

Mischel, W. (1973). Toward a cognitve social learing re-conceptualization of personality. **Psychological Review, 80,** 252–283.

Mischel, W. (1976). **Introduction to personality** (2nd ed.). New York: Holt, Rinehart & Winston.

Munroe, R. (1955). **Schools of psychoanalytic thought.** New York: Holt, Rinehart & Winston.

Pauling, L. (October 31–November 3, 1962). Biological treatment of mental illness. In M. Kinkel (Ed.), **Proceedings of the second international conference of the Manfred Sakel Foundation.** New York: New York Academy of Medicine.

Pavlov, I. P. (1972). **Conditioned reflexes.** London: Oxford University Press.

Phillips, J. L. (1975). **The origins of intellect: Piaget's theory.** San Francisco: W. H. Freeman.

Rapoport, D. (1951). The autonomy of the ego. **Bulletin of the Menninger Clinic, 15,** 113–f123.

Reed, E. (1975). Genetic anomalies in development. In F. Horowitz (Ed.), **Review of child development research** (Vol 4). Chicago: University of Chicago Press.

Reese, H. W., & Overton, W. F. (1970). Models and theories of development. In L. R. Goulet & P. B. Baltes (Eds.), **Life-span developmental psychology: Research and theory.** New York: Academic Press.

Rogers, C. R. (1961). **On becoming a person.** Boston: Houghton Mifflin.

Rogers, C. R. (1967). Carl Rogers. In E. G. Boring & G. Lindzey (Eds.), **A history of psychology in autobiography** (Vol. 5). New York: Appleton-Century-Crofts.

Rotter, J. B. (1954). **Social learning and clinical psychology,** Englewood Cliffs, NJ: Prentice-Hall.

Scarr, S., & Kidd, K. K. (1983). Developmental behavior genetics. In P. H. Mussen (General Ed.), **Handbook of child psychology** (4th ed.): **Vol. 2. Infancy and developmental psychology** (M. M. Haith & J. J. Campos, Vol. Eds.). New York: Wiley.

Scherzer, A. L., & Ilson, J. B. (1969). Normal intelligence in the Lesch-Nyhan syndrome. **Pediatrics, 44,** 116–119.

Selye, H. (1980). The stess concept today. In I. L. Kutash, L. B. Schesinger, & Associates (Eds.), **Handbook on stess and anxiety.** San Francisco: Jossey-Bass.

Selye, H. (1982). History and present status of the stress concept. In L. Goldberger & S. Breznitz (Eds.,), **Handbook of stress: Theoretical and clinical aspects.** New York: Free Press.

Skinner, B. F. (1953). **Science and human behavior.** New York: Macmillan.

Skinner, B. F. (1967). B. F. Skinner. In E. G. Boring & G. Lindzey (Eds.), **A history of psychology in autobiography** (Vol. 5). New York: Appleton-Century-Crofts.

Sroufe, L. A., & Rutter, M. (1984). The domain of developmental psychopathology. **Child Development, 55,** 17–29.

Stevenson, H. (1983). How children learn—the quest for a theory. In P. H. Mussen (General Ed.), **Handbook of child psychology** (4th ed.): **Vol. 1. History, theory, and methods** (W. Kessen, Vol, Ed.). New York: Wiley.

Thomas, R. M. (1979). **Comparing theories of child development.** Belmont, CA Wadsworth.

Watson, J. B., & Rayner, R. Z. (1920). Conditioned emotional reactions. **Journal of Experimental Psychology, 3,** 1–4.

Werry, J. S. (1979). Organic factors. In H. D. Quay & J. S. Werry (Eds.), **Psychopathological disorders of childhood** (2nd ed.). New York: Wiley.

Widtschi, E. (1971). Overripeness of the egg as a possible cause in mental and physical disorders. In I. Gottesman & L. Erlenmeyer-Kimmling (Eds.), Differential reproduction in individuals with mental and physical disorder. **Social Biology Supplement, 18,** S9–S15.

Yablonsky, L. (1962). **The violent gang.** New York: Crowell-Collier and Macmillan.

CHAPTER 3

Allen, L. R., & Britt, D. W. (1983). Social class, mental health, and mental illness: The impact of resources and feedback. In R. D. Felner, L. A. Jason, J. N. Moritsugu, & S. S. Farber (Eds). **Preventive psychology.** New York: Pergamon Press.

Annest, J. L., Mahaffey, K., Cox, D. H., & Roberts, M.

S. (1982). **Blood lead levels for persons 7 months–74 years of age: United States 1976–1980** (DHHS Publication No. PHS 82-1250). Washington, DC: U.S. Government Printing Office.

Bane, M. J. (1979). Marital disruption and the lives of children. In G. Levinger & O. C. Moles (Eds.), **Divorce and separation: Context, causes, and consequences.** New York: Basic Books.

Barrett, D. E. (1984). Malnutrition and child behavior: Conceptualization, assessment and an empirical study of social-emotional functioning. In J. Brozek & B. Schurch (Eds.), **Malnutrition and behavior: Critical assessment of key issues.** Lausanne, Switzerland: Nestle Foundation.

Barrett, R. P., & Zigmond, N. K. (1979, September). **Subclinical lead poisoning: A new dimension to learning problems?** Paper presented at the meeting of the American Psychological Association, New York.

Beaton, G. H., & Ghassemy, H. (1982). Supplementary feeding programs for young children in developing countries. **American Journal of Clinical Nutrition, 35,** 864–917.

Bee, H. (1978). The effects of poverty. In H. Bee (Ed.), **Social issues in developmental psychology** (2nd ed.). New York: Harper & Row.

Bernard, J. M., & Nesbitt, S. (1981). Divorce: An unreliable predictor of children's emotional predispositions. **Journal of Divorce,** 4, 31–42.

Birch, H. G., & Gussow, J. D. (1970). **Disadvantaged children: Health, nutrition, and school failure.** New York: Harcourt Brace Jovanovich.

Block, J. H., Block, J., & Gjerde, P. F. (1986). The personality of children prior to divorce: A prospective study. **Child Development, 57,** 827–840.

Bradley, R., & Caldwell, B. (1976). The relation of infants' home environments to mental test performance at fifty-four months: A follow-up study. **Child Development, 47,** 1172–1174.

Bradley, R. H., & Caldwell, B. M. (1978). Screening the environment. **American Journal of Orthopsychiatry, 48,** 114–130.

Brenner, M. H. (1973). **Mental illness and the economy.** Cambridge, MA: Harvard University Press.

Broad, W. J. (1981). Sir Isaac Newton: Mad as a hatter. **Science, 213,** 1341–1344.

Brooks-Gunn, J., & Furstenberg, F. F. (1986). The children of adolescent mothers: Physical, academic, and psychological outcomes. **Developmental Review, 6,** 224–251.

Browne, A., & Finkelhor, D. (1986). Impact of child sexual abuse: A review of the research. **Psychological Bulletin, 99,** 66–77.

Bryson, J. E., & Bentley, C. P. (1980). **Ability grouping of public school students: Legal aspects of classification and tracking methods.** Charlottesville, VA: Michie.

Burgess, R. L. (1978). Child abuse: A social-interactional analysis. In B. B. Lahey & A. E. Kazdin (Eds.), **Advances in clinical child psychology** (Vol. 2). New York: Plenum.

Carew, J. V. (1977). Social class, experience and intelligence in young children. In H. McGurk (Ed.), **Ecological factors in human development.** Amsterdam: North-Holland.

Child abuse incidence and reporting by hospital: Significance of severity, class, and race. (1985). **American Journal of Public Health, 75,** 56–60.

Child Abuse Prevention and Treatment Act of 1973, §5102, 42 U.S.C. (1982).

Christiansen, N. (1984). Social effects of a family food supplementation and a home stimulation program. In J. Brozek & B. Schurch (Eds.), **Malnutrition and behavior: Critical assessment of key issues.** Lausanne, Switzerland: Nestle Foundation.

Cicchetti, D., Taraldson, B. J., & Egeland, B. (1978). Perspectives in the treatment and understanding of child abuse. In A. P. Goldstein (Ed.), **Prescriptions for child mental health and education.** New York: Pergamon Press.

Cohen, D. J., Johnson, W. T., & Caparulo, B. K. (1976). Pica and elevated blood lead level in autistic and atypical children. **American Journal of Diseases of Children, 130,** 47–48.

Collins, G. (1982, May 13). Studies find sexual abuse of children is widespread. **New York Times,** pp. C1, C10.

Collins, R. C. (1983, Summer). Head Start: An update on program effects. **Newsletter of the Society for Research in Child Development,** pp. 1–2.

Daly, M., & Wilson, M. I. (1980). Abuse and neglect of children in evolutionary perspective. In R. D. Alexander & D. W. Tinkle (Eds.), **Natural selection and social behavior.** New York: Chiron.

David, O., Hoffman, S. P., Sverd, J., & Clark, J. (1977). Lead and hyperactivity: Lead levels among hyperactive children. **Journal of Abnormal Child Psychology, 5,** 405–416.

DeFrancis, V. (1969). **Protecting the child victim of sex crimes committed by adults.** Denver, CO: American Humane Association.

Delicardie, E. R., & Cravioto, J. (1974). Behavioral responsiveness of survivors of clinically severe malnutrition to cogitive demands. In J. Cravioto (Ed.), **Early malnutrition and mental development.** Uppsala, Sweden: Almquist & Wiksell.

Education for All Handicapped Children Act of 1975, P.L. No. 94-142.

Epstein, J. L. (1980). **After the bus arrives: Resegregation in desegregated schools.** Paper presented at the meetings of the American Educational Research Association, Boston.

Egeland, B., & Jacobvitz, D. (1984). **Intergenerational continuity of parental abuse: Causes** and consequences. Paper presented at the Conference on Biosocial Perspectives in Abuse and Neglect, York, ME.

Feshbach, N. D. (1973). Cross-cultural studies of teaching styles in four-year-olds and their mothers. In A. Pick (Ed.), **Minnesota Symposia in Child Psychology** (Vol. 7). Minneapolis: University of Minnesota Press.

Field, T. (1980). Interactions of preterm and term infants with their lower and middle class teenage and adult mothers. In T. Field, S. Goldberg, D. Stern, & A. Sostek (Eds.), **High-risk infants and children: Adult and peer interactions.** New York: Academic Press.

Field, T. (1983). Social interactions between high-risk infants and their mothers, fathers, and grandmothers. In B. B. Lahey & A. E. Kazdin (Eds.), **Advances in clinical child psychology** (Vol. 6). New York: Plenum.

Field, T., Widmayer, S., Stringer, S., & Ignatoff, E. (1980). Teenage, lower class black mothers and their preterm infants: An intervention and developmental follow-up. **Child Development, 51,** 426–436.

Finn, J. D. (1982). Patterns in special education placement as revealed by the OCR surveys. In National Research Council (Ed.), **Placing children in special education: A strategy for equity.** Washington, DC: National Academy Press.

Folb, E. A. (1980). **Runnin' down some lines: The language and culture of black teenagers.** Cambridge, MA: Harvard University Press.

Forehand, G., Ragosta, J., & Rock, D. (1976). **Conditions and processes of effective school desegregation** (Final Report, U.S. Office of Education, Department of Health, Education & Welfare). Princeton, NJ: Educational Testing Service.

Friedrich, W. N., & Boriskin, J. A. (1976). The role of the child in abuse: A review of the literature. **American Journal of Orthopsychiatry, 49,** 692–697.

Garbarino, J. (1977). The human ecology of child maltreatment: A conceptual model for research. **Journal of Marriage and the Family, 39,** 721–735.

Garbarino, J., & Ebata, A. (1981, June). **Ethnic and cultural differences in child maltreatment.** Paper presented at the Conference on Research Issues in Prevention, sponsored by the National Committee for the Prevention of Child Abuse and the Johnson Foundation, Racine, WI.

Garbarino, J., Guttmann, E., & Seeley, J. W. (1986). **The psychologically battered child.** San Francisco: Jossey-Bass.

Garbarino, J., & Sherman, D. (1980). High-risk neighborhoods and high-risk families: The human ecology of child maltreatment. **Child Development, 51,** 188–198.

Garmezy, N., & Streitman, S. (1974). Children at risk: The search for the antecedents of schizophrenia. Part I: Conceptual model for research models. **Schizophrenia Bulletin, 8,** 14–90.

Gelles, R. J. (1979). **Family violence.** Beverly Hills, CA: Sage.

George, C., & Main, M. (1979). Social interactions of young abused children: Approach, avoidance, and aggression. **Child Development, 50,** 306–318.

Gerard, H. B., & Miller, N. (1975). **School desegregation: A long-term study.** New York: Plenum.

Gil, D. G. (1970). **Violence against children: Physical child abuse in the United States.** Cambridge, MA: Harvard University Press.

Ginsburg, H. (1972). **The myth of the deprived child.** Englewood Cliffs, NJ: Prentice-Hall.

Glick, P. C. (1979). Children of divorced parents in demographic perspective. **Journal of Social Issues, 35,** 112–125.

Grantham-McGregor, S. (1984). Rehabilitation following clinical malnutrition. In J. Brozek & B. Schurch (Eds.), **Malnutrition and behavior: Critical assessment of key issues.** Lausanne, Switzerland: Nestle Foundation.

Grantham-McGregor, S., Stewart, M., Powell, C., & Schofield, W. N. (1979, February). Effect of stimulation on mental development of the malnourished child. **Lancet,** 200–201.

Grossman, M., Coote, D., Edwards, L. N., Shakotko, R. A., & Chermichovsky, D. (1980). **Determinants of children's health.** New York: National Bureau of Economic Research.

Guidubaldi, J., Perry, J. D., & Cleminshaw, H. K. (1984). The legacy of parental divorce: A nationwide study of family status and selected mediating variables on children's academic and social competencies. In B. B. Lahey & A. E. Kazdin (Eds.), **Advances in clinical child psychology** (Vol. 7). New York: Plenum.

Hess, R., & Shipman, V. C. (1967). Cognitive elements in maternal behavior. In J. Hill (Ed.), **Minnesota Symposia in Child Psychology** (Vol. 1). Minneapolis: University of Minnesota Press.

Hetherington, E. M., Cox, M., & Cox, R. (1978). The aftermath of divorce. In J. H. Stevens, Jr. & M. Matthews (Eds.), **Mother-child and father-child relations.** Washington, DC: National Association for the Education of Young Children.

Hetherington, E. M., Cox, M., & Cox, R. (1979). Play and social interaction in children following divorce. **Journal of Social Issues, 4,** 26–49.

Hetherington, E. M., Cox, M., & Cox, R. (1982). Effects of divorce on parents and children. In M. Lamb (Ed.), **Nontraditional families.** Hillsdale, NJ: Erlbaum.

Hetherington, E. M., Featherman, D. L., & Camara, K. A. (1981). **Intellectual functioning and** achievement of children in one-parent households. Unpublished manuscript, National Institute of Education.

Hetherington, E. M., & Parke, R. D. (1979). **Child psychology: A contemporary viewpoint** (2nd ed.). New York: McGraw-Hill.

Hunter, R. S., & Kilstrom, N. (1979). Breaking the cycle in abusive families. **American Journal of Psychiatry, 136,** 1320-1322.

Jensen, A. R. (1969). How much can we boost IQ and scholastic achievement? **Harvard Educational Review, 39,** 1-123.

Jensen, A. R. (1977). Cumulative deficit in IQ of blacks in the rural South. **Developmental Psychology, 13,** 184-191.

Joos, S. K., & Pollitt, E. (1984). Effects of supplementation on behavioral development in children up to the age of two years: A comparison of four studies. In J. Brozek & B. Schurch (Eds.), **Malnutrition and behavior: Critical assessment of key issues.** Lausanne, Switzerland: Nestle Foundation.

Kamin, L. J. (1974). **The science and politics of IQ.** New York: Wiley.

Kaplan, S. J., Pelcovitz, D., Salzinger, S., & Ganeles, D. (1983). Psychopathology of parents of abused and neglected children and adolescents. **Journal of the American Academy of Child Psychiatry, 22,** 238-244.

Kaufman, J., & Zigler, E. (1986). **Do abused children become abusive parents?** Unpublished manuscript, Yale University.

Keniston, K. (1977). **All our children: The American family under pressure.** New York: Harcourt Brace Jovanovich.

Klaus, M. H., & Kennell, J. H. (1976). **Maternal-infant bonding.** St. Louis: C. V. Mosby.

Kulka, R. A., & Weingarten, H. (1979). The long-term effects of parental divorce in childhood on adult adjustment. **Journal of Social Issues, 4,** 50-78.

Kurdek, L. A., & Berg, B. (1983). Correlates of children's adjustment to their parents' divorce. In L. A. Kurdek (Ed.), **Children and divorce.** San Francisco: Jossey-Bass.

Kurdek, L. A., & Siesky, A. E. (1980). An interview study of parents' perceptions of their children's reactions and adjustment to divorce. **Journal of Divorce, 3,** 5-18.

Labov, W. (1970). The logic of nonstandard English. In F. Williams (Ed.), **Language and poverty.** Chicago: Markham.

Laosa, L. M. (1984). Social policies toward children of diverse ethnic, racial, and language groups in the United States. In H. W. Stevenson & A. E. Siegel (Eds.), **Child development research and social policy.** Chicago: University of Chicago Press.

Larry, P. v. Riles, Civil No. C-71-2270. 343 F Supp. 1306 (N.D. Calif. 1972).

Lazar, I., & Darlington, R. (1982). Lasting effects of early education: A report from the Consortium for Longitudinal Studies. **Monographs of the Society for Research in Child Development, 47** (2-3, Serial No. 195).

Lechtig, A., Delgado, H., Lasky, R., Yarbrough, C., Klein, R., Habicht, J. P., & Behar, M. (1975). Maternal nutrition and fetal growth in developing societies. **American Journal of Diseases of Children, 129,** 434-437.

Levin, H. M. (1977). A decade of policy developments in improving education and training for low-income populations. In R. Haveman (Ed.), **A decade of federal antipoverty programs: Achievements, failures, and lessons.** New York: Academic Press.

Lewis, M., & Freedle, R. (1977). The mother and infant communication system: The effects of poverty. In H. McGurk (Ed.), **Ecological factors in human development.** Amsterdam: North-Holland.

Lynn, L. E., Jr. (1977). A decade of policy developments in the income-maintenance system. In R. Haveman (Ed.), **A decade of federal antipoverty programs: Achievement, failures, and lessons.** New York: Academic Press.

Magidson, J. (1977). Towards a causal model approach for adjusting for pre-existing differences in the nonequivalent control group situation: A general alternative to ANCOVA. **Evaluation Quarterly, 1,** 399-420.

Magnuson, E. (1983, September 5). Child abuse: The ultimate betrayal. **Time,** 16-18.

Magrab, P. R., Sostek, A. M., & Powell, B. A. (1984). Prevention in the prenatal period. In M. C. Roberts & L. Peterson (Eds.), **Prevention of problems in childhood: Psychological research and applications.** New York: Wiley-Interscience.

Mann, J., Harrell, A. V., & Hurt, M., Jr. (1978). A review of Head Start research since 1969. In B. Brown (Ed.), **Found: Long-term gains from early intervention.** Boulder, CO: Westview Press.

Minuchin, P. P., & Shapiro, E. K. (1983). The school as a context for social development. In P. H. Mussen (General Ed.), **Handbook of child psychology** (4th ed.): **Vol. 4. Socialization, personality, and social development** (E. M. Hetherington, Vol. 4). New York: Wiley.

Money, J., & Annecillo, C. (1976). IQ changes following change of domicile in the syndrome of reversible hyposomatotropinism (psychosocial dwarfism). **Psychoneuroendocrinology, 1,** 427-429.

Naeye, R. L., Diener, M. M., & Dellinger, W. S. (1969). Urban poverty: Effects of prenatal nutrition. **Science, 166,** 1206.

National Center on Child Abuse and Neglect. (1979).

Child sexual abuse: Incest, assault, and sexual exploitation (DHEW Publication No. OHDS 79-30166). Washington, D.C.: U.S. Government Printing Office.

National Center on Child Abuse and Neglect. (1981). **Executive summary: National study of the incidence and severity of child abuse and neglect** (DHHS Publication No. OHDS 81-30329). Washington, DC: U.S. Government Printing Office.

National Center for Health Statistics. (1982, May 12). **Vital and health statistics.** (Advance Data No. 79, Supplemental Exhibit 4). Washington, DC: U.S. Government Printing Office.

Needleman, H. L., & Bellinger, D. (1984). The developmental consequences of childhood exposure to lead: Recent studies and methodological issues. In B. B. Lahey & A. E. Kazdin (Eds.), **Advances in clinical child psychology** (Vol. 7). New York: Plenum.

Needleman, H. L., Gunnoe, C., Leviton, A., Reed, R. R., Peresie, H., Maher, C., & Barrett, P. (1979). Deficits in psychologic and classroom performance in children with elevated dentine lead levels. **New England Journal of Medicine, 300,** 689-695.

Okun, A. M. (1972). **The battle against unemployment.** New York: Norton.

Parke, R. D. (1978). Children's home environments: Social and cognitive effects. In I. Altman & J. F. Wohlwill (Eds.), **Children and the environment.** New York: Plenum Press.

Parke, R. D., & Collmer, C. W. (1975). Child abuse: An interdisciplinary analysis. In E. M. Hetherington (Ed.), **Review of child development research** (Vol. 5). Chicago: University of Chicago Press.

Peters, M. F., & McAdoo, H. (1983). The present and future of alternative ethnic lifestyles in ethnic American culture. In E. Macklin & D. Rubin (Eds.), **Contemporary families and alternative lifestyles.** Beverly Hills, CA: Sage.

Reid, J. B. (1984). Social-interactional patterns in families of abused and nonabused children. In C. Zahn-Waxler, M. Cummings, & M. Radke-Yarrow (Eds.), **Social and biological origins of altruism and aggression.** Cambridge, England: Cambridge University Press.

Reinhard, D. W. (1977). The reaction of adolescent boys and girls to the divorce of their parents. **Journal of Clinical Child Psychology, 2,** 21-23.

Reveron, D. (1982, May). Racism: Mental illness rates reflect that burden on blacks in America. **APA Monitor,** pp. 7, 24.

Ricciuti, H. (1977a). Adverse social and biological influences on early development. In H. McGurk (Ed.), **Ecological factors in human development.** Amsterdam: North-Holland.

Ricciuti, H. N. (1977b). Malnutrition and psychological development. In E. M. Hetherington & R. Parke

(Eds.), **Contemporary readings in child psychology.** New York: McGraw-Hill.

Rogeness, G. A., Suchakorn, A., Amrung, M. D., Macedo, C. A., Harris, W. R., & Fisher, C. (1986). Psychopathology in abused or neglected children. **Journal of the American Academy of Child Psychiatry, 25,** 659-665.

Rohrlich, J. A., Ranier, R., Berg-Cross, L., & Berg-Cross, G. (1977). The effects of divorce: A research review with a developmental perspective. **Journal of Clinical Child Psychology, 6,** 51-54.

Russell, D. E. (1986). **The secret trauma: Incest in the lives of girls and women.** New York: Basic Books.

Rutter, M. (1978). Family, area and school influences in the genesis of conduct disorders. In L. Hersov, M. Berger, & D. Shaffer (Eds.), **Aggression and anti-social behavior in childhood and adolescence.** Oxford: Pergamon Press.

Rutter, M., Yule, B., Quinton, D., Rowlands, O., Yule, W., & Berger, M. (1975). Attainment and adjustment in two geographical areas: III: Some factors accounting for area differences. **British Journal of Psychiatry, 126,** 520-533.

Sameroff, A. J., & Chandler, M. J. (1975). Reproductive risk and the continuum of caretaking casualty. In F. Horowitz (Ed.), **Review of child development research** (Vol. 4). Chicago: University of Chicago Press.

Scarr, S. (1981). **Race, social class, and individual differences.** Hillsdale, NJ: Erlbaum.

Schneider, K. (1986, September 9). Scientific advances lead to era of food surplus around world. **New York Times,** pp. Y19-Y20.

Scott, R. B., & Winston, M. R. (1976). The health and welfare of the black family in the United States. **American Journal of Diseases of Children, 130,** 704-707.

Seitz, V., Apfel, N. H., & Efron, C. (1978). Long-term effects of early intervention: The New Haven Project. In B. Brown (Ed.), **Found: Long-term gains from early intervention.** Boulder, CO: Westview Press.

Select Committee on Children, Youth, and Families, U.S. House of Representatives. (1983). **U.S. children and their families: Current conditions and recent trends.** Washington, DC: U.S. Government Printing Office.

Shinn, M. (1978). Father absence and children's cognitive development. **Psychological Bulletin, 85,** 295-324.

Silverstein, B., & Krate, R. (1975). **Children of the dark ghetto.** New York: Praeger University Series.

Smith, B. (1979). It ain't what you say, it's the way you say it: Exercises for teaching mainstream American English to Ebonics-speaking children. **Journal of Black Studies, 9,** 491–493.

Smith, S. M., & Hanson, R. (1974). 134 battered children: A medical and psychological study. **British Medical Journal, iii,** 666–670.

St. John, N. H. Y. (1975). **School desegregation: Outcomes for children.** New York: Wiley.

Stark, R., & McEvoy, J., III. (1970). Middle-class violence. **Psychology Today,** pp. 107–112.

Starr, R. H. (1982). A research-based approach to the prediction of child abuse. In R. H. Starr (Ed.), **Child abuse prediction: Policy implications.** Cambridge, MA: Ballinger.

Stein, Z. A., & Susser, M. W. (1976). Prenatal nutrition and mental competence. In J. D. Lloyed-Still (Ed.), **Malnutrition and intellectual development.** Littleton, MA: Publishing Sciences Group.

Stein, Z. A., Susser, M. W., Saenger, G., & Marolla, F. (1975). **Famine and human development: The Dutch hunger winter of 1944–1945.** New York: Oxford Press.

Stephan, W. G. (1978). School desegregation: An evaluation of predictions made in **Brown v. Board of Education. Psychological Bulletin, 85,** 217–238.

Straus, M. A., Gelles, R. J., & Steinmetz, S. K. (1980). **Behind closed doors: Violence in the American family.** Garden City, NY: Doubleday/Anchor.

Streissguth, A. P., & Bee, H. L. (1972). Mother-child interactions and cognitive development in children. In W. W. Hartup (Ed.), **The young child: Reviews of research.** Washington, DC: National Association for the Education of Young Children.

Suarez, J. M., Weston, N. L., & Hartstein, N. B. (1978). Mental health interventions in divorce proceedings. **American Journal of Orthopsychiatry, 48,** 273–283.

Subcommittee on Public Assistance and Unemployment Compensation, Committee on Ways and Means, U.S. House of Representatives. (1985). **Children in poverty** (Serial No. 99-18). Washington, DC: U.S. Government Printing Office.

Svejda, M., Campos, J., & Emde, R. (1979, February). **Mother-infant bonding reconsidered: Some recent results.** Paper presented at the meeting of the Western Psychological Association, San Diego.

Thurstone, D. L., Middlecamp, J. N., & Mason, E. (1955). The late effects of lead poisoning. **Journal of Pediatrics, 47,** 413–423.

Tufts' New England Medical Center, Division of Child Psychiatry (1984). **Sexually exploited children: Service and research project.** Final report for the Office of Juvenile Justice and Delinquency Prevention. Washington, DC: U.S. Department of Justice.

U.S. Bureau of the Census. (1977). Persons of Spanish origin in the United States, March 1977. In **Current population reports,** (Series P-20, No. 317). Washington, DC: U.S. Government Printing Office.

U.S. Bureau of the Census. (1978). Marital status and living arrangements. In **Current population reports** (Series P-20, No. 338). Washington, DC: U.S. Government Printing Office.

U.S. Bureau of the Census. (1982). Characteristics of the population below the poverty level: 1980. In **Current population reports** (Series P-60, No. 133). Washington, DC: U.S. Government Printing Office.

U.S. Bureau of the Census. (1985). **Current population reports** (Series P-60, No. 149). Washington, DC: U.S. Government Printing Office.

U.S. Bureau of the Census. (1987a). **Current population reports** (Series P-20). Washington, DC: U.S. Government Printing Office.

U.S. Bureau of the Census (1987b). **National data book and guide to sources. Statistical abstract of the United States** (107th ed.). U.S. Department of Commerce Bureau of the Census. Washington, DC: U.S. Government Printing Office.

U.S. Department of Health and Human Services. Public Health Service (1985). **Health status of minorities and low income groups.** (DHHS Publication No. HRS-P-DV85-D). Washington, DC: U.S. Government Printing Office.

U.S. Department of Labor. (1979). **Employment and training report of the president, 1979** (No. 029-000-00359-9). Washington, DC: U.S. Government Printing Office.

Wagner, H. (1972). Attitudes toward and of disadvantaged students. **Adolescence, 7,** 435–446.

Wallerstein, J. S., & Kelly, J. B. (1974). The effects of parental divorce: The adolescent experience. In E. J. Anthony & C. Koupernik (Eds.), **The child in his family: Vol. 3. Children at psychiatric risk.** New York: Wiley.

Wallerstein, J. S., & Kelly, J. B. (1975). The effects of parental divorce: Experiences of the preschool child. **Journal of the American Academy of Child Psychiatry, 14,** 600–616.

Wallerstein, J. S. & Kelly, J. B. (1980). **Surviving the breakup: How children and parents cope with divorce.** New York: Basic Books.

Werner, E. E., Bierman, J. M., & French, F. E. (1971). **The children of Kauai.** Honolulu: University of Hawaii Press.

White, J. (1984). **The psychology of blacks: An Afro-American perspective.** Englewood Cliffs, NJ: Prentice-Hall.

Williams, G. J. R. (1983). Child abuse. In C. E. Walker & M. C. Roberts (Eds.), **Handbook of clinical child psychology.** New York: Wiley.

Wolfe, D. A. (1985). Child-abusive parents: An empirical review and analysis. **Psychological Bulletin, 97,** 462-482.

Zajonc, R. B. (1976). Family configuration and intelligence. **Science, 192,** 227-236.

Zajonc, R. B. (1986). The decline and rise of scholastic aptitude scores: A prediction derived from the confluence model. **American Psychologist, 41,** 862-867.

Zigler, E., & Butterfield, E. C. (1968). Motivational aspects of changes in IQ test performance of culturally deprived nursery school children. **Child Development, 49,** 1155-1162.

Zigler, E., Abelson, W. D., & Seitz, V. (1973). Motivational factors in the performance of economically disadvantaged children on the Peabody Picture Vocabulary Test. **Child Development, 39,** 1-14.

Zill, N. (1983). **Happy, healthy and insecure.** Garden City, NY: Doubleday/Anchor.

CHAPTER 4

Abraham, K. (1966). Notes on the psycho-analytical investigation and treatment of manic-depressive insanity and allied conditions. In B. Lewis (Ed.), **On character and libido development.** New York: Norton.

Abramson, L. Y., Seligman, M. E. P., & Teasdale, J. D. (1978). Learned helplessness in humans: Critique and reformulation. **Journal of Abnormal Psychology, 87,** 49-73.

Achenbach, T. M., & Edelbrock, C. S. (1978). The classification of child psychopathology: A review and analysis of empirical efforts. **Psychological Bulletin, 85,** 1275-1301.

Adams, P. L. (1973). **Obsessive children.** Baltimore: Penguin.

Alexander, A. B. (1977). Behavioral methods in the clinical management of chronic asthma. In R. Williams & W. D. Gentry (Eds.), **Behavioral approaches to medical practice.** Cambridge, MA: Ballinger.

Alexander, A. B., Miklich, D. R., & Hershkoff, H. (1972). The immediate effects of systematic relaxation training on peak expiratory flow rates in asthmatic children. **Psychosomatic Medicine, 34,** 388-394.

American Psychiatric Association. (1980). **Diagnostic and statistical manual of mental disorders** (3rd ed.) Washington, DC: Author.

Anderson, B. J., Miller, J. P., Auslander, W. F., & Santiago, J. V. (1981). Family characteristics of diabetic adolescents: Relationship to metabolic control. **Diabetes Care, 4,** 586-594.

Bandura, A. (1969). **Principles of behavior modification.** New York: Holt, Rinehart & Winston.

Bandura, A., Blanchard, E. B., & Ritter, B. (1969). Relative efficacy of desensitization and modeling approaches for inducing behavioral, affective, and attitudinal changes. **Journal of Personality and Social Psychology, 13,** 173-199.

Bandura, A., & Menlove, F. L. (1968). Factors determining vicarious extinction of avoidance behavior through symbolic modeling. **Journal of Personality and Social Psychology, 8,** 99-108.

Baron, M., Klotz, J., Mendlewica, J., & Rainer, J. (1981). Multiple-threshold transmission of affective disorders. **Archives of General Psychiatry, 38,** 79-84.

Bauer, D. H. (1976). An exploratory study of developmental changes in children's fears. **Journal of Child Psychology and Psychiatry, 17,** 69-74.

Bauer, D. H. (1980). Childhood fears in developmental perspective. In L. A. Hersov & I. Berg (Eds.), **Out of school: Modern perspectives in truancy and school refusal.** Chichester, England: Wiley.

Beck, A. T. (1974). The development of depression: A cognitive model. In R. Friedman & M. Katz (Eds.), **The psychology of depression: Contemporary theory and research.** Washington, DC: V. H. Winston.

Berg, I. (1970). A follow-up study of school phobic adolescents admitted to an in-patient unit. **Journal of Child Psychology and Psychiatry, 11,** 37-47.

Berg, I. (1981). When truants and school refusers grow up. **British Journal of Psychiatry, 141,** 208-210.

Berg, I., Butler, A., & Hall, G. (1976). The outcome of adolescent school phobia. **British Journal of Psychiatry, 128,** 80-85.

Berlin, I. N. (1986). Psychopathology and its antecedents among American Indian adolescents. In B. B. Lahey & A. E. Kazdin (Eds.), **Advances in clinical child psychology** (Vol. 9). New York: Plenum.

Bibring, E. (1953). The mechanism in depression. In P. Greenacre (Ed.), **Affective disorders.** New York: International Universities Press.

Bregman, E. (1934). An attempt to modify the emotional attitudes of infants by the conditioned response technique. **Journal of Genetic Psychology, 45,** 169-196.

Breuer, J., & Freud, S. (1955). Studies on hysteria. (J. Strachey, Ed. and Trans.) **Standard edition of the complete psychological works of Sigmund Freud** (Vol. 2). London: Hogarth Press. (Original work published 1895)

Cadoret, R. J. (1978). Evidence for genetic inheritance of primary affective disorder. **American Journal of Psychiatry, 135,** 463–466.

Campos, J. J., Campos, R., & Stenberg, C. (1981). Perception, appraisal, and emotion: The onset of social referencing. In M. Lamb & L. Sherrod (Eds.), **Infant social cognition.** Hillsdale, NJ: Erlbaum.

Carlson, G. A. (1984). Classification issues of bipolar disorders in childhood. **Psychiatric Developments, 2,** 273–285.

Carlson, G. A., & Cantwell, D. P. (1980). Unmasking masked depression in children and adolescents. **American Journal of Psychiatry, 137,** 361–368.

Carney, R. M., Schechter, D., & Davis, T. (1983). Improving adherence to blood glucose testing in insulin-dependent diabetic children. **Behavior Therapy, 14,** 247–254.

Childers, P., & Wimmer, M. (1971). The concept of death in early childhood. **Child Development, 42,** 1299–1301.

Cicchetti, D., & Schneider-Rosen, K. (Eds.). (1984). **Childhood depression.** San Francisco: Jossey-Bass.

Coleman, J., Wolkind, S. M., & Ashley, L. (1977). Symptoms of behaviour disturbance and adjustment to school. **Journal of Child Psychology and Psychiatry, 18,** 201–210.

Crook, T., & Eliot, J. (1980). Parental death during childhood and adult depression: A critical review of the literature. **Psychological Bulletin, 87,** 252–259.

Cytryn, L., & McKnew, D. H. (1974). Factors influencing the changing clinical expression of the depressive process in children. **American Journal of Psychiatry, 131,** 879–881.

Delamater, A. M. (1986). Psychological aspects of diabetes mellitus in children. In B. B. Lahey & A. E. Kazdin (Eds.), **Advances in clinical child psychology** (Vol. 9). New York: Plenum.

Diggory, J. C. (1976). Some trends in U.S. suicide rates: 1933–1968. In E. Schneidman (Ed.), **Suicidology: Contemporary developments.** New York: Grune & Stratton.

Dizmang, L. H., Watson, J., May, P. A., & Bopp, J. (1974). Adolescent suicide at an Indian reservation. **American Journal of Orthopsychiatry, 44,** 43–49.

Dohrenwend, B. S., & Dohrenwend, B. P. (1974). **Stressful life events: Their nature and effects.** New York: Wiley.

Dweck, C. S. (1977). Learned helplessness: A developmental approach. In J. Schulterbrandt & A. Raskin (Eds.), **Depression in childhood: Diagnosis, treatment, and conceptual models.** New York: Raven Press.

English, H. H. (1929). Three cases of the "conditioned fear response." **Journal of Abnormal Psychology, 24,** 221–225.

Felner, R. D. (1984). Vulnerability in childhood: A preventive framework for understanding children's efforts to cope with life stress and transitions. In M. C. Roberts & L. Peterson (Eds.), **Prevention of problems in childhood.** New York: Wiley.

Felner, R. D., Primavera, J., & Cauce, A. M. (1981). The impact of school transitions: A focus for preventive efforts. **American Journal of Community Psychology, 9,** 449–459.

Ferster, C. B. (1974). Behavioral approaches to depression. In R. Friedman & M. Katz (Eds.), **The psychology of depression: Contemporary theory and research.** New York: Wiley.

Ficula, T., Gelfand, D. M., Richards, G., & Ulloa, A. (1983, August). **Factors associated with school refusal in adolescents.** Paper presented at the meeting of the American Psychological Association, Anaheim, CA.

Foa, E. B., Steketee, G., & Milby, J. B. (1980). Differential effects of exposure and response prevention in obsessive-compulsive washers. **Journal of Consulting and Clinical Psychology, 48,** 71–79.

Frederick, C. J. (1976). Trends in mental health: Self-destructive behavior among younger age groups. **Keynote, 4,** 3–5.

Freud, A. (1977). Fears, anxieties, and phobic phenomena. **Psychoanalytic Study of the Child, 32,** 85–90.

Freud, S. (1950). Analysis of a phobia in a five-year-old boy. In J. Riviere (Ed. and Trans.), **Collected papers** (Vol. 3). London: Hogarth Press. (Original work published 1909)

Freud, S. (1965). Mourning and melancholia. In J. Strachey (Ed. and Trans.), **Standard edition of the complete psychological works of Sigmund Freud** (Vol. 1). London: Hogarth Press. (Original work published 1917)

Galloway, D. (1983). Size of school, socio-economic hardship, suspension rates and persistant unjustified absence from school. **British Journal of Educational Psychology, 46,** 40–47.

Gehlen, F. (1977). Toward a revised theory of hysterical contagion. **Journal of Health and Social Behavior, 18,** 27–35.

Gelfand, D. M. (1978). Social withdrawal and negative emotional states: Behavioral treatment. In B. B. Wolman, J. Egan, & A. O. Ross (Eds.), **Handbook of treatment of mental disorders in childhood and adolescence.** Englewood Cliffs, NJ: Prentice-Hall.

Gelfand, D. M., & Peterson, L. (1985). **Child development and psychopathology.** Beverly Hills, CA: Sage.

Gershon, E. S., Bunney, W. E., Jr., Leckman, J. F., Van Eerdewegh, M., & De Bauche, B. A. (1976). The inheritance of affective disorders: A review of data and of hypotheses. **Behavior Genetics, 6,** 227–261.

Gittelman, R. (1985). Anxiety disorders in children. In B. B. Lahey & A. E. Kazdin (Eds.), **Advances in clinical child psychology** (Vol. 8). New York: Plenum.

Gittelman-Klein, R. (1977). Definitional and methodological issues concerning depressive illness in children. In J. Schulterbrandt & A. Raskin (Eds.), **Depression in childhood: Diagnosis, treatment, and conceptual models.** New York: Raven Press.

Gordon, D. A., & Young, R. D. (1976). School phobia: A discussion of aetiology, treatment and evaluation. **Psychological Reports, 39,** 783–804.

Granell de Aldaz, E., Vivas, E., Gelfand, D., & Feldman, L. (1984). Estimating the prevalence of school refusal and school-related fears: A Venezuelan sample. **Journal of Nervous and Mental Disease, 172,** 722–729.

Granell de Aldaz, E., Feldman, L., Vivas, E., & Gelfand, D. M. (1987). Characteristics of Venezuelan school refusers: Toward the development of a high risk profile. **Journal of Nervous and Mental Disease, 175,** 402–407.

Graziano, A. M., DeGiovanni, I. S., & Garcia, K. A. (1979). Behavioral treatment of children's fears: A review. **Psychological Bulletin, 86,** 804–830.

Harris, B. (1979). Whatever happened to little Albert? **American Psychologist, 34,** 151–160.

Herzog, D. B., & Rathbun, J. M. (1982). Childhood depression: Developmental considerations. **American Journal of Diseases of Children, 136,** 115–120.

Hersov, L. (1960). Persistent non-attendance at school. **Journal of Child Psychology and Psychiatry, 1,** 130–136.

Holland, J. V., Kaplan, D. M., & Davis, S. D. (1974). Interschool transfers: A mental health challenge. **Journal of School Health, 44,** 74–79.

Iga, M. (1967). Japanese adolescent suicide and social structure. In E. S. Shneidman (Ed.), **Essays in self-destruction.** New York: Science House.

Jakimow-Venulet, B. (1981). Hereditary factors in the pathogenesis of affective illness. **British Journal of Psychiatry, 139,** 450–456.

Jersild, A. T., & Holmes, F. B. (1935). **Children's fears** (Child Development Monograph No. 20). New York: Teachers College, Columbia University.

Johnson, A. M., Falstein, E. J., Szurek, S. A., & Svendsen, M. (1941). School phobia. **American Journal of Orthopsychiatry, 11,** 702–711.

Johnson, G. F. S., & Leeman, M. M. (1977). Analysis of familial factors in bipolar affective illness. **Archives of General Psychiatry, 34,** 1074–1083.

Kashani, J. H., Ray, J. S., & Carlson, G. A. (1984). Depression and depression-like states in preschool-age children in a child development unit. **American Journal of Psychiatry, 141,** 1397–1402.

Kennedy, W. A. (1965). School phobia: Rapid treatment of fifty cases. **Journal of Abnormal Behavior, 70,** 285–289.

Koski, M. L., & Kumento, A. (1977). The interrelationship between diabetic control and family life. **Pediatric and Adolescent Endocrinology, 3,** 41–45.

Kovacs, M., & Beck, A. T. (1977). An empirical-clinical approach toward a definition of childhood depression. In J. Schulterbrandt & A. Raskin (Eds.), **Depression in childhood: Diagnosis, treatment, and conceptual models.** New York: Raven Press.

Kovacs, M., Feinberg, T. L., & Crouse-Novak, M. (1984). Depressive disorders in childhood: II. A longitudinal study of the risk for a subsequent major depression. **Archives of General Psychiatry, 41,** 643–649.

Kramer, A. D., & Feiguine, R. J. (1981). Clinical effects of amitriptyline in adolescent depression: A pilot study. **Journal of the American Academy of Child Psychiatry, 20,** 636–644.

Lachenmeyer, J. R. & Gibbs, M. S. (Eds.). (1982). **Psychopathology in childhood.** New York: Gardner Press.

Lapouse, R., & Monk, M. A. (1959). Fears and worries in a representative sample of children. **American Journal of Orthopsychiatry, 29,** 803–813.

Lefkowitz, M. M., & Burton, N. (1978). Childhood depression: A critique of the concept. **Psychological Bulletin, 85,** 716–726.

Leon, G. R. (1977). **Case histories in deviant behavior: An interactional perspective** (2nd ed.). Boston: Holbrook Press.

Lester, D. (1979). Sex differences in suicidal behavior. In E. S. Gomberg & V. Franks (Eds.), **Gender and disordered behavior.** New York: Brunner/Mazel.

Lewinsohn, P. M. (1974). A behavioral approach to depression. In R. Friedman & M. Katz (Eds.), **The psychology of depression: Contemporary theory and research.** Washington, DC: V. H. Winston.

Lewinsohn, P. M., & Amenson, C. S. (1981). An investigation into the observed sex difference in prevalence of unipolar depression. **Journal of Abnormal Psychology, 90,** 1–13.

Lowe, K., & Lutzker, J. R. (1979). Increasing compliance to a medical regime with a juvenile diabetic. **Behavior Therapy, 10,** 57–64.

Lumsden, W. W. (1980). Intentional self-injury in school age children. **Journal of Adolescence, 3,** 217–228.

Macfarlane, J. W., Allen, L., & Honzik, M. P. (1954). **A developmental study of the behavior problems of normal children between 21 months and 14 years.** Berkeley: University of California Press.

Mahler, M. (1952). On child psychosis and schizophrenia: Autistic and symbiotic infantile psychosis. In A. Freud, H. Hartmann, E. Kris (Eds.), **Psychoanalytic study of the child** (Vol. 7). New York: International Universities Press.

Malmquist, C. P. (1977). Childhood depression: A clinical and behavioral perspective. In J. Schulterbrandt & A. Raskin (Eds.), **Depression in childhood: Diagnosis, treatment, and conceptual models.** Rockville, MD: U. S. Department of Health, Education and Welfare.

Marine, E. (1968). School refusal: Who should intervene? **Journal of School Psychology, 7,** 63-70.

McDonald, E., & Sheperd, G. (1976). School phobia: An overview. **Journal of School Psychology, 14,** 291-306.

McKnew, D. H., Jr., & Cytryn, L. (1973). Historical background in children with affective disorder. **American Journal of Psychiatry, 130,** 1278-1280.

McNeal, E. T., & Cimbolic, P. (1986). Antidepressants and biochemical theories of depression. **Psychological Bulletin, 99,** 361-374.

Miller, I. W., III, & Norman, W. H. (1979). Learned helplessness in humans: A review and attribution theory model. **Psychological Bulletin, 86,** 93-118.

Miller, L. C., Barrett, C. L., Hampe, E., & Noble, H. (1972). Factor structure of children's fears. **Journal of Consulting and Clinical Psychology, 39,** 264-268.

Mills, H. L., Agras, W. S., Barlow, D. H., & Mills, J. R. (1975). Compulsive rituals treated by response prevention. **Archives of General Psychiatry, 32,** 933-936.

Minuchin, S., Baker, L., Rosman, B., Liebman, R., Millman, L., & Todd, T. (1975). A conceptual model of psychosomatic illness in children. **Archives of General Psychiatry, 32,** 1031-1038.

Morris, R. J., & Kratochwill, T. R. (1983). **Treating children's fears and phobias.** New York: Pergamon Press.

Mosse, H. L. (1974). The psychotherapeutic management of children with masked depression. In S. Lesse (Ed.), **Masked depression.** New York: Jason Aronson.

National Institute of Mental Health. (1973). **Utilization of mental health facilities—1971** (DHEW Publication No. NIH-74-657). Washington, DC: U.S. Government Printing Office.

Opie, I., & Opie, P. (1959). **Lore and language of school children.** Oxford: Oxford University Press.

Orvaschel, H., (1983). Maternal depression and child dysfunction. In B. B. Lahey & A. E. Kazdin (Eds.), **Advances in clinical child psychology** (Vol. 6). New York: Plenum.

Orvaschel, H., & Weissman, M. M. (1985). Epidemiology of anxiety disorders in children: A review. In R. Gittelman (Ed.), **Anxiety disorders of children.** New York: Guilford Press.

Petit, J. M., & Biggs, J. T. (1977). Tricyclic antidepressant overdoses in adolescent patients. **Pediatrics, 59,** 283-287.

Petti, T. A., & Conners, C. K. (1983). Changes in behavioral ratings of depressed children treated with imipramine. **Journal of the American Academy of Child Psychiatry, 22,** 355-360.

Pfeffer, C. R. (1981). Suicidal behavior of children: A review with implications for research and practice. **American Journal of Psychiatry, 138,** 154-159.

Pfeffer, C. R., Conte, H. R., & Plutchik, R. (1979). Suicidal behavior in latency age children: An empirical study. **Journal of the American Academy of Child Psychiatry, 18,** 674-692.

Posnanski, E., Mokros, H., Grossman, J., & Freeman, L. (1985). Diagnostic criteria in childhood depression. **American Journal of Psychiatry, 142,** 1168-1173.

Puig-Antich, J., & Gittelman, R. (1982). Depression in childhood and adolescence. In E. S. Paykel (Ed.), **Handbook of affective disorders.** Edinburgh: Churchill Livingstone.

Purcell, K. (1975). Childhood asthma, the role of family relationships, personality, and emotions. In A. Davids (Ed.), **Child personality and psychopathology: Current topics** (Vol. 2). New York: Wiley.

Purcell, K., Brady, D., Chai, H., Muser, J., Molk, L., Gordon, N., & Means, J. (1969). The effect on asthma in children of experimental separation from the family. **Psychosomatic Medicine, 31,** 144-164.

Rachman, D. (1977). The conditioning theory of fear acquisition: A critical examination. **Behaviour Research and Therapy, 15,** 375-389.

Rachman, S., & Hodgson, R. (1980). **Obsessions and compulsion.** Englewood Cliffs, NJ: Prentice-Hall.

Reuters News Agency. (1977). Children's suicides show increase in Japan. **The Salt Lake Tribune,** November 11, p. 4D.

Richter, N. C. (1984). The efficacy of relaxation training with children. **Journal of Abnormal Child Psychology, 12,** 319-344.

Rincover, A., Newsom, D. C., & Carr, E. G. (1979). Using sensory extinction procedures in the treatment of compulsivelike behavior of developmentally disabled children. **Journal of Consulting and Clinical Psychology, 47,** 695–701.

Ritter, B. (1968). The group desensitization of children's snake phobias using vicarious and contact desensitization procedures. **Behaviour Research and Therapy, 6,** 1–6.

Roberts, M. C., & Peterson, L. (Eds.). (1984). **Prevention of problems in childhood.** New York: Wiley.

Rodriguez, A., Rodriguez, M., & Eisenberg, L. (1959). The outcome of school phobia: A follow-up study based on 41 cases. **American Journal of Psychiatry, 116,** 540–544.

Rosenthal, T. L., & Bandura, A. (1978). Psychological modeling; Theory and practice. In S. L. Garfield & A. E. Bergin (Eds.), **Handbook of psychotherapy and behavior change** (Vol. 2). New York: Wiley.

Rouché, B. (1978, August 21). Annals of medicine: Sandy. **The New Yorker,** pp. 63–70.

Rutter, M., & Garmezy, N. (1983). Developmental psychopathology. In P. H. Mussen (General Ed.), **Handbook of child psychology** (4th ed.): **Vol. 4. Socialization, personality, and social development** (E. M. Hetherington, Vol. Ed.). New York: Wiley.

Rutter, M., Tizard, J., & Whitmore, K. (Eds.). (1981). **Education, health and behaviour.** Huntington, NY: Krieger. (Originally published, 1970)

Samuelson, F. J. B. (1980). Watson's little Albert, Cyril Burt's twins, and the need for a critical science. **American Psychologist, 35,** 619–625.

Santiago, J. V. (1984). Effect of treatment on the long-term complications of IDDM. **Behavioral Medicine Update, 6,** 26–31.

Schafer, R. (1960). The loving and beloved superego in Freud's structural theory. **Psychoanalytic Study of the Child, 15,** 163–188.

Schoonover, S. C. (1983). Depression. In E. L. Bassuk, S. C. Schoonover, & A. J. Gelenberg (Eds.), **The practitioner's guide to psychoactive drugs.** New York: Plenum.

Seligman, M. E. P. (1975). **Helplessness: On depression, development, and death.** San Francisco: W. H. Freeman.

Shaffer, D. (1974). Suicide in childhood and early adolescence. **Journal of Child Psychology and Psychiatry, 15,** 275–291.

Shaffer, D., & Fisher, P. (1981). The epidemiology of suicide in children and young adolescents. **Journal of the American Academy of Child Psychiatry, 20,** 545–565.

Shafi, M., Carrigan, S., Wittinghill, J. R., & Derrick, A. (1985). Characteristics of suicidal children and adolescents. **American Journal of Psychiatry, 142,** 1061–1064.

Shore, J. H., Bopp, J. H., Waller, T. R., & Dawes, J. W. (1972). A suicide prevention center on an Indian reservation. **American Journal of Psychiatry, 128,** 1086–1091.

Stahl, S. M., & Lebedun, M. (1974). Mystery gas: An analysis of mass hysteria. **Journal of Health and Social Behavior, 15,** 44–50.

Sterba, E. (1959). Child analysis. In M. Levitt (Ed.), **Readings in psychoanalytic psychology.** New York: Appleton.

Swift, C. F., Seidman, F., & Stein, H. (1967). Adjustment problems in juvenile diabetics. **Psychosomatic Medicine, 29,** 555–571.

Toolan, J. M. (1968). Suicide in childhood and adolescence. In H. Resnik (Ed.), **Suicidal behaviors: Diagnosis and management.** Boston: Little, Brown.

U.S. Bureau of the Census. (1985). **Statistical abstracts of the U.S., 1986: National data book and guide to sources (106th ed.).** Washington, DC: U.S. Government Printing Office.

U.S. Department of Health, Education and Welfare. (1975). **Dropout prevention.** Washington, DC: Educational Resources Information Center. (ERIC Document Reproduction Service No. ED 105–354)

Van Winkel, N. (1981). **Native American suicide in New Mexico: A comparative study, 1957–1979.** Unpublished master's thesis, University of New Mexico.

Waldron, S. (1976). The significance of childhood neurosis for adult mental health. **American Journal of Psychiatry, 133,** 532–538.

Waller, D., & Eisenberg, L. (1980). School refusal in childhood: A psychiatric-paediatric perspective. In L. Hersov & I. Berg (Eds.), **Out of school.** Chichester, England: John Wiley.

Walton, D., & Mather, M. D. (1963). The application of learning principles to the treatment of obsessive-compulsive states in the acute and chronic phases of illness. **Behaviour Research and Therapy, 1,** 163–174.

Watson, J. B., & Rayner, R. (1920). Conditioned emotional reactions. **Journal of Experimental Psychology, 3,** 1–14.

Weissman, M. M., Meyers, J. K., & Harding, P. S. (1978). Psychiatric disorders in a U.S. urban community: 1975–1976. **American Journal of Psychiatry, 135,** 459–462.

Welner, A., Welner, Z., & Fishman, R. (1979). Psychiatric adolescent inpatients: Eight- to ten-years follow-up. **Archives of General Psychiatry, 36,** 698–700.

Werry, J. S., & Quay, H.C. (1971). The prevalence of behavior symptoms in younger elementary school children. **American Journal of Orthopsychiatry, 41** 136–143.

Wolfenstein, M. (1966). How is mourning possible? **Psychoanalytic Study of the Child, 21,** 93–123.

Wolpe, J. (1958). **Psychotherapy by reciprocal inhibition.** Stanford, CA: Stanford University Press.

CHAPTER 5

Abikoff, H., & Gittelman, R. (1985). The normalizing effects of methylphenidate on the classroom behavior of ADDH children. **Journal of Abnormal Child Psychology, 13,** 33–44.

Achenbach, T. M. (1982). **Developmental psychopathology** (2nd ed.). New York: Wiley.

Aichhorn, A. (1964). **Delinquency and child guidance: Selected papers.** (O. Fleischman, P. Kramer, & H. Ross, eds.). New York: International Universities Press.

American Psychiatric Association (1980). **Diagnostic and statistical manual of mental disorders** (3rd ed.). Washington, DC: Author.

American Psychiatric Association, Work Group to Revise DSM-III. (1985). **Diagnostic and statistical manual of mental disorders** (3rd ed., revised, draft). Washington, DC: American Psychiatric Association.

Ayllon, T., & Rosenbaum, M. S. (1977). The behavioral treatment of disruption and hyperactivity in school settings. In B. B. Lahey & A. E. Kazdin (Eds.), **Advances in clinical child psychology** (Vol. 1). New York: Plenum.

Bandura, A. (1973). **Aggression: A social learning analysis.** Englewood Cliffs, NJ: Prentice-Hall.

Bandura, A., Ross, D., & Ross, S. A. (1963). Imitation of filmed mediated aggressive models. **Journal of Abnormal and Social Psychology, 66,** 3–11.

Bandura, A., & Walters, R. H. (1959). **Adolescent aggression.** New York: Ronald Press.

Barkley, R. A. (1977). A review of stimulant drug research with hyperactive children. **Journal of Child Psychology and Psychiatry, 18,** 137–165.

Barkley, R. A. (1985). Attention deficit disorders. In P. H. Bornstein & A. E. Kazdin (Eds.), **Handbook of clinical behavior therapy with children.** Homewood, IL: Dorsey Press.

Barkley, R. A., & Cunningham, C. E. (1978). Do stimulant drugs improve the academic performance of hyperkinetic children? **Clinical Pediatrics, 17,** 85–92.

Barkley, R. A., & Cunningham, C. E. (1979). The effects of methylphenidate on the mother-child interactions of hyperactive children. **Archives of General Psychiatry, 36,** 201–208.

Barkley, R. A., & Jackson, T. (1976). **The effects of** methylphenidate on autonomic arousal and its relationship to improvement in activity and attention in hyperactive children. Unpublished manuscript, Bowling Green State University.

Barkley, R. A., Karlsson, J., & Pollard, S. (1985). Effects of age on the mother-child interactions of ADD-H and normal boys. **Journal of Abnormal Child Psychology, 13,** 631–637.

Barkley, R. A., & Ullman, D. G. (1975). A comparison of objective measures of activity and distractibility in hyperactive and nonhyperactive children. **Journal of Abnormal Child Psychology, 3,** 231–244.

Baron, R. A. (1977). **Human aggression.** New York: Plenum.

Bartollos, C., Miller, S. J., & Dinitz, S. (1976). **Juvenile victimization: The institutional paradox.** New York: Wiley.

Battle, E. S., & Lacey, B. (1972). A context for hyperactivity in children, over time. **Child Development, 43,** 757–773.

Bernal, M. E. (1969). Behavioral feedback in the modification of the brat behaviors. **Journal of Nervous and Mental Disease, 148,** 375–385.

Bernal, M. E., Duryee, J. S., Pruett, H. L., & Burns, B. J. (1968). Behavior modification and the brat syndrome. **Journal of Consulting and Clinical Psychology, 32,** 447–455.

Bradley, C. (1937). The behavior of children receiving benzedrine. **American Journal of Psychiatry, 94,** 577–585.

Bugental, D. B., Whalen, C. K., & Henker, B. (1977). Causal attributions of hyperactive children and motivational assumptions of two behavior-change approaches: Evidence for an interactionist position. **Child Development, 48,** 874–884.

Cadoret, R. J. (1978). Psychopathology in adopted-away offspring of biological parents with antisocial children. **Archives of General Psychiatry, 35,** 176–184.

Campbell, S. B., Breaux, A. M., Ewing, L. J., & Szumowski, E. K. (1986). Correlates and predictors of hyperactivity and aggression: A longitudinal study of parent-referred problem preschoolers. **Journal of Abnormal Child Psychology, 14,** 217–234.

Campbell, S. B., & Paulauskas, S. (1979). Peer relations in hyperactive children. **Journal of Child Psychology and Psychiatry, 20,** 233–246.

Cantwell, D. P. (1975). Epidemiology, clinical picture and classification of the hyperactive child syndrome. In D. P. Cantwell (Ed.), **The hyperactive child.** New York: Spectrum.

Carter, K. (1987). **School psychologist's perceptions of childhood psychopathology.** Unpublished doctoral dissertation, University of Utah.

Charles, L., & Schain, R. (1981). A four-year follow-up study of the effects of methylphenidate on the behavior of academic achievement of hyperactive children. **Journal of Abnormal Child Psychology, 9,** 495–505.

Chase, S. N., & Clement, P. W. (1985). Effects of self-reinforcement and stimulants on academic performance in children with attention deficit disorder. **Journal of Clinical Child Psychology, 14,** 323–333.

Chess, S., & Thomas, A. (1983). **Origins and evolution of behavior disorders: From infancy to early adult life.** New York: Brunner/Mazel.

Christiansen, K. O. (1974). Seriousness of criminality and concordance among Danish twins. In R. Hood (ed.), **Crime, criminology, and public policy.** London: Heinemann.

Clements, S. D. (1966). **Minimal brain dysfunction—terminology and identification** (U.S. Public Health Service Publication No. 1415). Washington, DC: U.S. Government Printing Office.

Cline, V. B., Croft, R. G., & Courrier, S. (1973). Desensitization of children to television violence. **Journal of Personality and Social Psychology, 27,** 360–365.

Cloninger, C. R., Reich, T., & Guze, S. B. (1978). Genetic-environmental interactions and antisocial behaviour. In R. D. Hare & D. Schalling (Eds.), **Psychopathic behaviour: Approaches to research.** Chichester, England: Wiley.

Comstock, G. A., & Rubinstein, E. A. (1972). (Eds.). **Television and social behavior.** Washington, DC: U.S. Government Printing Office.

Conners, C. K. (1969). A teacher rating scale for use in drug studies with children. **American Journal of Psychiatry, 126,** 884–888.

Conners, C. K. (1980). Artificial colors and the diet of disruptive behavior: Current status of research. In R. M. Knights & D. J. Bakker (Eds.), **Treatment of hyperactive and learning disabled children.** Baltimore: University Park Press.

Conners, C. K. (1986). [Medical grand rounds, University of Utah Medical School, Salt Lake City].

Crowe, R. (1974). An adoption study of antisocial personality. **Archives of General Psychiatry, 31,** 785–791.

Cruickshank, W. M., Bentzen, F. A., Ratzeburg, F. H.,

& Tannhauser, M. T. (1961). **A teaching method for brain injured and hyperactive children.** Syracuse, NY: Syracuse University Press.

Cunningham, C. E., & Barkley, R. A. (1978). The effects of methylphenidate on the mother-child interactions of hyperactive identical twins. **Developmental Medicine and Child Neurology, 20,** 634–642.

Cunningham, C. E., & Barkley, R. A. (1979). The role of academic failure in hyperactive behavior. **Journal of Learning Disabilities, 11,** 15–21.

Cunningham, C. E., Siegel, L., & Offord, D. (1980). **Peer relations among hyperactive children.** Paper presented at the meeting of the American Psychological Association, Montréal.

David, O. J., Clark, J., & Voeller, K. (1972). Lead and hyperactivity. **Lancet, ii,** 900–903.

deHass, P. A., & Young, D. R. (1984). Attention styles of hyperactive and normal girls. **Journal of Abnormal Child Psychology, 12,** 531–546.

Dishion, T. J., Loeber, R., Stouthamer-Loeber, M., & Patterson, G. R. (1984). Skills deficits and male adolescent delinquency. **Journal of Abnormal Child Psychology, 12,** 37–54.

Douglas, V. I. (1972). Stop, look, and listen: The problem of sustained attention and impulse control in hyperactive and normal children. **Canadian Journal of Behavioural Science, 4,** 259–282.

Douglas, V. I. (1974). Are drugs enough? To treat or to train the hyperactive child. In C. K. Conners (Ed.), **Clinical use of stimulant drugs in children.** New York: Excerpta Medica.

Dubey, D. R., O'Leary, S. G., & Kaufman, K. F. (1983). Training parents of hyperactive children in child management: A comparative outcome study. **Journal of Abnormal Child Psychology, 11,** 229–246.

Ebaugh, L. D. (1923). Neuropsychiatric sequelae of acute epidemic encephalitis in children. **American Journal of Diseases of Children, 67,** 89–97.

Eron, L. D. (1963). Relationship of TV viewing habits and aggressive behavior in children. **Journal of Abnormal and Social Psychology, 67,** 193–196.

Eron, L. D., & Huesmann, L. R. (1984). The control of aggressive behavior by changes in attitudes, values, and the conditions of learning. In R. J. Blanchard & D. C. Blanchard (Eds.), **Advances in the study of aggression** (Vol. 1), New York: Academic Press.

Fagan, J. A., & Hartstone, E. (1984). Strategic planning in juvenile justice—defining the toughest kids. In R. A. Mathias, P. DeMuro, & R. S. Albinson (Eds.), **Violent juvenile offenders.** San Francisco: National Council on Crime and Delinquency.

Farrington, D. P. (1978). The family backgrounds of aggressive youths. In L. A. Hersov & D. Shaffer (Eds.), **Aggression and anti-social behavior in childhood and adolescence.** New York: Pergamon Press.

Federal Bureau of Investigation (1984). **Uniform crime reports in the United States (1970–1984).** Washington, DC: U.S. Government Printing Office.

Feingold, B. F. (1975a). Hyperkinesis and learning disabilities linked to artificial food flavors and colors. **American Journal of Nursing, 75,** 797–803.

Feingold, B. F. (1975b). **Why is your child hyperactive?** New York: Random House.

Feshbach, S. (1956). The catharsis hypothesis and some consequences of interaction with aggressive and neutral play objects. **Journal of Personality, 24,** 449–462.

Fleischman, M. J. (1981). A replication of Patterson's "Intervention for boys with conduct problems." **Journal of Consulting and Clinical Psychology, 49,** 342–351.

Forehand, R. (1977) Child noncompliance to parental requests: Behavior analysis and treatment. In H. Hersen, R. M. Eisler, & P. M. Miller (Eds.), **Progress in behavior modification** (Vol. 5). New York: Academic Press.

Forehand, R., King, H. E., Peeds, S., & Yoder, P. (1975). Mother-child interactions: Comparison of a noncompliant clinic group and a non-clinic group. **Behaviour Research and Therapy, 113,** 79–84.

Forehand, R., & McMahon, R. J. (1981). **Helping the noncompliant child: A clinician's guide to parent training.** New York: Guilford Press.

Freeman, E. (1962). **Effects of aggressive expression after frustration on performance: A test of the catharsis hypothesis.** Unpublished doctoral dissertation, Stanford University.

Freud, S. (1933). **Introductory lectures on psychoanalysis** (J. Strachey, Trans.). New York: Norton.

Gensheimer, L. K., Mayer, J. P., Gottschalk, R., & Davidson, W. S. (1986). Diverting youth from the juvenile justice system: A meta-analysis of intervention efficacy. In S. J. Apter & A. P. Goldstein (Eds.), **Youth violence: Programs and prospects.** New York: Pergamon Press.

Gerbner, G., Gross, L., Morgan, D., & Signorielli, N. (1980). The "mainstreaming" of America: Violence Profile No. 11. **Journal of Communication, 30,** 10–29.

Gittelman-Klein, R., Klein, D. F., Abikoff, S., Katz, A., Gloisten, C., & Kates, W. (1976). Relative efficacy of methylphenidate and behavior modification in hyperkinetic children: An interim report. **Journal of Abnormal Child Psychology, 4,** 361–379.

Glueck, S., & Glueck, E. (1940). **Juvenile delinquents grown up.** New York: Commonwealth Fund.

Glueck, S., & Glueck, E. (1950). **Unraveling juvenile delinquency.** New York: Commonwealth Fund.

Glueck, S., & Glueck, E. (1959). **Predicting delinquency and crime.** Cambridge, MA: Harvard University Press.

Glueck, S., & Glueck, E. (1970). **Toward a typology of juvenile offenders: Implications for therapy and prevention.** New York: Grune & Stratton.

Goldstein, A. P., Glick, B., Reiner, S., Zimmerman, D., & Coultry, T. M. (1987). **Aggression replacement training: A comprehensive intervention for aggressive youth.** Champaign, IL: Research Press.

Goldstein, A. P., Sprafkin, R. P., Gershaw, N. J., & Klein, P. (1980). **Skillstreaming the adolescent: A structured learning approach to teaching prosocial skills.** Champaign, IL: Research Press.

Goldstein, K. (1942). **After-effects of brain injury in war.** New York: Grune & Stratton.

Gordon, M. (1979) The assessment of impulsivity and mediating behaviors in hyperactive and nonhyperactive boys. **Journal of Abnormal Child Psychology, 7,** 317–326.

Graham, P., Rutter, M., & George, S. (1973). Temperamental characteristics as predictors of behavior disorders in children. **Journal of Orthopsychiatry, 43,** 328–339.

Griest, D. L., & Wells, K. C. (1983). Behavior family therapy with conduct disorders in children. **Behavior Therapy, 14,** 37–53.

Griffin, B. S., & Griffin, C. T. (1978). **Juvenile delinquency in perspective.** New York: Harper & Row.

Halperin, J. M., Gittelman, R., Klein, D., & Rudel, R. (1984). Reading-disabled hyperactive children: A distinct subgroup of attention deficit disordered with hyperactivity. **Journal of Abnormal Child Psychology, 12,** 1–14.

Harley, J. P., & Matthews, C. G. (1980). Food additives and hyperactive children: Experimental investigations. In R. M. Kinghts & D. J. Bakker (Eds.), **Treatment of hyperactive and learning disabled children.** Baltimore: University Park Press.

Haskell, M. R., & Yablonsky, L. (1970). **Crime and delinquency.** Chicago: Rand McNally.

Hechtman, L., Weiss, G., Perlman, T., & Amsel, R. (1984). Hyperactives as young adults: Initial predictors of adult outcome. **Journal of the American Academy of Child Psychiatry, 23,** 250–260.

Hechtman, L., Weiss, G., Perlman, T., & Tuck, D. (1981). Hyperactives as young adults: Various clinical outcomes. In S. C. Feinstein, J. G. Looney, A. Z. Schwartzberg, & A. D. Sorosky (Eds.), **Annals of the American Society for Adolescent Psy-**

chiatry (Vol. 9). Chicago: University of Chicago Press.

Hefferon, W. A., Martin, C. A., & Welsh, R. J. (1984). Attention deficit disorder in three pairs of monozygotic twins: A case report. **Journal of the American Academy of Child Psychiatry, 23,** 299–301.

Hendersen, H. S., Jenson, W. R., & Erken, N. (1986). Focus article: Variable interval reinforcement for increasing on task behavior in classrooms. **Education and Treatment of Children, 9,** 250–263.

Herbert, M. (1978). **Conduct disorders of childhood and adolescence: A behavioral approach to assessment and treatment.** New York: Wiley.

Hetherington, E. M. (1979). Divorce: A child's perspective. **American Psychologist, 34,** 851–858.

Hetherington, E. M., Cox, M., & Cox, R. (1977a). The aftermath of divorce. In J. H. Stevens, Jr., & M. Mattews (Eds.), **Mother-child, father-child behaviors.** Washington, DC: N.A.F.Y.C.

Hetherington, E. M., Cox, M., & Cox, R. (1977b). **The development of children in mother-headed families.** Paper presented at the Conference on Families in Contemporary America, George Washington University, Washington, DC.

Hetherington, E. M., & Martin, B. (1979). Family interaction. In H. C. Quay & J. S. Werry (Eds.), **Psychopathological disorders of childhood** (3rd ed.) New York: Wiley.

Hodges, W. F. (1986). **Interventions for children of divorce: Custody, access, and psychotherapy.** New York: Wiley.

Hohman, L. B. (1922). Post-encephalitic behavior disorders in children. **Johns Hopkins Hospital Bulletin, 33,** 372–375.

Hollander, H. E., & Turner, F. D. (1985). Characteristics of incarcerated delinquents: Relationship between developmental disorders, environmental and family factors, and patterns of offense and recidivism. **Journal of the American Academy of Child Psychiatry, 24,** 221–226.

Jacob, R. G., O'Leary, K. D., & Rosenbald, C. (1978). Formal and informal classroom settings: Effects on hyperactivity. **Journal of Abnormal Child Psychology, 6,** 47–60.

Jenkins, R. L. (1973). **Behavior disorders of childhood and adolescence.** Springfield, IL: Charles C Thomas.

Jenkins, R. L., & Boyer, A. (1968). Types of delinquent behavior and background factors. **International Journal of Social Psychiatry, 14,** 65–76.

Jenkins, R. L., & Hewitt, L. (1944). Types of personality structure encountered in child guidance clinics. **American Journal of Orthopsychiatry, 14,** 84–94.

Jenson, W. R. (1978). Behavior modification in second-ary schools: A review. **Journal of Research and Development in Education. 11,** 53–63.

Jenson, W. R., Reavis, K., & Rhodes, G. (1987). A conceptual analysis of childhood behavior disorders: A practical educational approach. In B. Scott & J. Gilliam (Eds.), **Topics in behavior disorders,** Austin, TX: Behavioral Learning Center.

Jones, R. R., Weinrott, M. R., & Howard, J. R. (1981). **The national evaluation of the teaching family model.** Rockville, MD: National Institute of Mental Health, Center for Studies in Crime and Delinquency.

Jurkovic, G. J., & Prentice, N. M. (1977). Relation of moral and cognitive development to dimensions of juvenile delinquency. **Journal of Abnormal Psychology, 86,** 414–420.

Kagan, J. (1966). Reflection-impulsivity: The generality and dynamics of conceptual tempo. **Journal of Abnormal Psychology, 71,** 17–24.

Kazdin, A. E. (1985). **Treatment of antisocial behavior in children and adolescents.** Homewood, IL: Dorsey Press.

Kenny, D. J. (1952). **An experimental test of the catharsis theory of aggression.** Unpublished doctoral dissertation, University of Washington.

Kesler, J. (1987). **Corrective reading: A method for changing the learning rate of behavior disordered children.** Unpublished master's thesis, University of Utah.

Kessler, J. W. (1980). History of minimal brain damage. In H. E. Rie & E. D. Rie (Eds.), **Handbook of minimal brain dysfunction: A critical review.** New York: Wiley.

Kirigin, K., Braukmann, C. J., Atwater, J. D., & Wolf, M. M. (1982). An evaluation of teaching-family (Achievement Place) group homes for juvenile offenders. **Journal of Applied Behavior Analysis, 15,** 1–16.

Kirigin, K. A., Wolf, M. M., Braukmann, C. J., Fixsen, D. L., & Phillips, E. L. (1979). Achievement Place: A preliminary outcome evaluation. In J. S. Stumphauzer (Ed.), **Progress in behavior therapy with delinquents.** Springfield, IL: Charles C Thomas.

Kirkland, K. D., & Thelen, M. H. (1977). Uses of modeling in child treatment. In B. B. Lahey & A. E. Kazdin (Eds.), **Advances in clinical child psychology** (Vol. 1). New York Plenum.

Klein, D. F., & Gittelman-Klein, R. (1975). **Problems in the diagnosis of minimal brain dysfunction and hyperkinetic syndrome.** Unpublished manuscript.

Kohlberg, L. (1969). Stage and sequence: The cognitive-development approach to socialization. In D. A. Goslin (Ed.), **Handbook of socialization theory and research.** Chicago: Rand McNally.

Kohlberg, L. (1973). **Collected papers on moral development and moral education.** Cambridge, MA: Center for Moral Education, Harvard University.

Kohn, M. (1977). **Social competence, symptoms, and underachievement in childhood: A longitudinal perspective.** Washington, DC: V. H. Winston.

Koles, M., & Jenson, W. R. (1985). A comprehensive treatment approach for chronic firesetting in a boy. **Journal of Behavior Therapy and Experimental Psychiatry, 16,** 81–86.

Lahey, B., Hobbs, S. A., Kupfer, D. L., & Delamater, A. (1979). Current perspectives on hyperactivity and learning disabilities. In B. Lahey (Ed.), **Behavior therapy with hyperactive and learning disabled children.** New York: Oxford University Press.

Lahey, B., Stempniak, M., Robinson, E. J., & Tyroler, M. J. (1978). Hyperactivity and learning disabilities as independent dimensions of child behavior problems. **Journal of Abnormal Psychology, 87,** 333–340.

Lambert, N. M., & Sandoval, J. (1980). The prevalence of learning disabilities in a sample of children considered hyperactive. **Journal of Abnormal Child Psychology, 8,** 33–50.

Langhorne, J. E., Loney, J., Paternite, C. E., & Bechtoldt, H. P. (1976). Childhood hyperkinesis: A return to the source. **Journal of Abnormal Psychology, 85,** 201–209.

Lewis, D. O., & Balla, D. A. (1976). **Delinquency and psychopathology.** New York: Grune & Stratton.

Leyens, J. P., Camino, R., Parke, D., & Berkowitz, L. (1975). Effects of movie violence on aggression in a field setting. **Journal of Personality and Social Psychology, 32,** 346–360.

Liebert, R. M., & Baron, R. A. (1972). Some immediate effects of televised violence on children's behavior. **Developmental Psychology, 6,** 469–475.

Liebert, R. M., Sprafkin, J. N., & Davidson, E. S. (1982). **The early window: Effects of television on children and youth.** New York: Pergamon Press.

Loeber, R., & Patterson, G. R. (1981). The aggressive child: A concomitant of a coercive system. **Advances in Family Intervention, Assessment and Theory, 2,** 47–87.

Loeber, R., & Schmaling, K. B. (1985a). Empirical evidence for overt and covert patterns of antisocial conduct problems: A metaanalysis. **Journal of Abnormal Child Psychology, 13,** 337–352.

Loeber, R., & Schmaling, K. B. (1985b). The utility of differentiating between mixed and pure forms of antisocial child behavior. **Journal of Abnormal Child Psychology, 13,** 315–336.

Loeber, R., Weissman, W., & Reid, J. B. (1983). Family interactions of assaultive adolescents, stealers, and nondelinquents. **Journal of Abnormal Child Psychology, 11,** 1–14.

Loney, J., Whaley-Klahn, M. A., Kosier, T., & Conboy, J. (1981). **Hyperactive boys and their brothers at 21: Predictors of aggression and antisocial outcomes.** Paper presented at a meeting of the Society for Life History Research, Monterey, CA.

Lyle, J., & Hoffman, H. R. (1972). Children's use of television and other media. In E. A. Rubinstein, G. A. Comstock, & J. P. Murray (Eds.), **Television in day-to-day life: Patterns of use.** Washington, DC: U.S. Government Printing Office.

Mallick, S. K., & McCandless, B. R. (1966). A study of catharsis of aggression. **Journal of Personality and Social Psychology, 4,** 591–596.

Marlowe, M. Cossairt, A., Moon, C., Errera, J., MacNeel, A., Peak, R., Ray, J., & Schroeder, C. (1985). Main and interaction effect of metallic toxins on classroom behavior. **Journal of Abnormal Child Psychology, 13,** 185–198.

Mash, E. J., & Dalby, J. T. (1979). Behavioral interventions for hyperactivity. In R. L. Trites (Ed.), **Hyperactivity in children: Etiology, measurement, and treatment implications.** Baltimore: University Park Press.

Mash, E. J., & Johnston, C. (1983). Parental perceptions of child behavior problems, parenting self-esteem, and mothers' reported stress in younger and older hyperactive and normal children. **Journal of Consulting and Clinical Psychology, 51,** 86–99.

McCord, W., McCord, J., & Zola, I. K. (1959). **Origins of crime.** New York: Columbia University Press.

McGee, R., Williams, S., & Silva, P. A. (1984). Behavioral and developmental characteristics of aggressive, hyperactive and aggressive-hyperactive boys. **Journal of the American Academy of Child Psychiatry, 23,** 270–279.

Mednick, S. A., & Hutchings, B. (1978). Genetic and physiological factors in antisocial behavior. **Journal of the American Academy of Child Psychiatry, 17,** 209–223.

Mendelson, W., Johnson, N., & Stewart, M. A. (1971). Hyperactive children as teenagers: A follow-up study. **Journal of Nervous and Mental Disease, 153,** 273–279.

Menkes, M. M., Rowe, J. S., & Menkes, J. H. (1967). A twenty year follow-up study on the hyperkinetic child with minimal brain dysfunction. **Pediatrics, 39,** 393–399.

Messer, S. B. (1976). Reflection-impulsivity: A review. **Psychological Bulletin, 83,** 1026–1052.

Morgan, D., & Jenson, W. R. (in press). **Teaching behaviorally disordered children: **Preferred practices.** Columbus, OH: Charles E. Merrill.

Morris, H. H., Escoll, P. J., & Wexler, R. (1956). Aggressive behavior disorders of childhood: A follow-up study. **American Journal of Psychiatry, 112,** 991-997.

Morrison, J. R. (1980). Adult psychiatric disorders in parents of hyperactive children. **American Journal of Psychiatry, 137,** 955-958.

Morrison, J. R., & Stewart, M. A. (1971). A family study of the hyperactive child syndrome. **Biological Psychiatry, 3,** 189-195.

Nelsen, E. A. (1969). Social reinforcement for expression vs. suppression of aggression. **Merrill-Palmer Quarterly, 15,** 259-278.

Offord, D. R., Allen, N., & Abrams, N. (1978). Parental psychiatric illness, broken homes, and delinquency. **Journal of the American Academy of Child Psychiatry, 17,** 224-238.

O'Leary, D. K. (1980). Pills or skills for hyperactive children. **Journal of Applied Behavior Analysis, 13,** 191-204.

O'Leary, D. K., Pelham, W. E., Rosenbaum, A., & Price, G. H. (1976). Behavioral treatment of hyperkinetic children. **Clinical Pediatrics, 15,** 510-515.

O'Leary, S. G., & O'Leary, D. K. (1980). Behavioral treatment for hyperactive children. In R. M. Knights & D. J. Bakker (Eds.), **Treatment of hyperactive and learning disordered children.** Baltimore: University Park Press.

Orris, J. B. (1969). Visual monitoring performance in three subgroups of male delinquents. **Journal of Abnormal Psychology, 74,** 227-229.

Olweus, D. (1979). Stability of aggressive reaction patterns in males: A review. **Psychological Bulletin, 86,** 852-875.

Olweus, D. (1984). Development of stable aggression reaction patterns in males. In R. J. Blanchard & D. C. Blanchard (Eds.), **Advances in the study of aggression** (Vol. 1). New York: Academic Press.

Parke, R. D., & Slaby, R. G. (1983). The development of aggression. In P. H. Mussen (General Ed.), **Handbook of child psychology** (4th ed.): **Vol. 4. Socialization, personality, and social development** (E. M. Hetherington, Vol. Ed.). New York: Wiley.

Patterson, G. R. (1964). An application of conditioning techniques to the control of a hyperactive child. In L. P. Ullman & L. Krasner (Eds.), **Case studies in behavior modification.** New York: Holt, Rinehart & Winston.

Patterson, G. R. (1974). Interventions for boys with conduct problems: Multiple settings, treatments, and criteria. **Journal of Consulting and Clinical Psychology, 42,** 471-481.

Patterson, G. R. (1976a). The aggressive child: Victim and architect of a coercive system. In E. J. Mash, L. A. Hamerlynck, & L. C. Handy (Eds.), **Behavior modification and families.** New York: Brunner/Mazel.

Patterson, G. R. (1976b). Follow-up analysis of behavioral treatment program for boys with conduct problems: A reply to Kent. **Journal of Consulting and Clinical Psychology, 44,** 299-301.

Patterson, G. R. (1982). **Coercive family process.** Eugene, OR: Castalia.

Patterson, G. R. (1984). Siblings: Fellow travelers in the coercive process. In R. J. Blanchard & D. C. Blanchard (Eds.), **Advances in the study of aggression** (Vol. 1). New York: Academic Press.

Patterson, G. R. (1986). Performance models for antisocial boys. **American Psychologist, 41,** 432-444.

Patterson, G. R., & Fleischman, M. J. (1979). Maintenance of treatment effects: Some considerations concerning family systems and follow-up data. **Behavior Therapy, 10,** 168-185.

Patterson, G. R., Jones, R., Whittier, J., & Wright, M. A. (1965). A behaviour modification technique for the hyperactive child. **Behaviour Research and Therapy, 2,** 217-226.

Patterson, G. R., Ray, R. S., Shaw, D. A., & Cobb, J. A. (1969). **Manual for coding of family interactions** (Document #01234, Microfiche, 440 Park Avenue, New York, NY 10016).

Patterson, G. R., & Reid, J. B. (1970). Reciprocity and coercion: Two facets of social systems. In C. Neuringer & J. D. Michael (Eds.), **Behavior modification in clinical psychology.** New York: Appleton-Century-Crofts.

Patterson, G. R., Reid, J. B., Jones, J., & Conger, R. E. (1975). **A social learning approach to family intervention: Vol. 1. Families with aggressive children.** Eugene, OR: Castalia.

Pelham, W. E., Bender, M. E., Caddell, J., Booth, S., & Moorer, S. H. (1985). Methylphenidate and children with attention deficit disorder. **Archives of General Psychiatry, 42,** 948-952.

Peterson, D. R., Quay, H. C., & Tiffany, T. L. (1961). Personality factors related to juvenile delinquency. **Child Development, 32,** 355-372.

Phillips, E. L. (1968). Achievement Place: Token reinforcement procedure in a home style rehabilitation setting for predelinquent boys. **Journal of Applied Behavior Analysis, 1,** 213-223.

President's Commission on Law Enforcement and Administrative Justice. (1967). **The challenge of crime in a free society.** Washington, DC: U.S. Government Printing Office.

Prinz, R. J., Connors, P. A., & Wilson, C. C. (1981). Hyperactive and aggressive behaviors in childhood: Intertwined dimensions. **Journal of Abnormal Psychology, 9,** 191–202.

Prinz, R. J., Roberts, W. A., & Hantman, E. (1980). Dietary correlates of hyperactive behavior in children. **Journal of Consulting and Clinical Psychology, 48,** 760–769.

Quay, H. C. (1964). Dimensions of personality in delinquent boys as inferred from the factor analysis of case history data. **Child Development, 35,** 479–484.

Quay, H. C. (1965). Psychopathic personality as pathological stimulation seeking. **American Journal of Psychiatry, 122,** 180–183.

Quay, H. C. (1969). Dimensions of personality in delinquent boys as inferred from the factor analysis of case history data. **Child Development, 35,** 479–484.

Quay, H. C. (1972). Patterns of aggression, withdrawal, and immaturity. In H. C. Quay & J. S. Werry (Eds.), **Psychopathological disorders of childhood.** New York: Wiley.

Quay, H. C. (1977). Psychopathic behavior: Reflections on the nature, origins, and temperament. In F. Weizman & I. Uzgiris (Eds.), **Structuring of experience.** New York: Plenum.

Rie, E. D., & Rie, H. E., (1977). Recall, retention and Ritalin. **Journal of Clinical and Consulting Psychology, 45,** 967–972.

Rie, H. E. (1980). Definitional problems. In H. E. Rie & E. D. Rie (Eds.), **Handbook of minimal brain dysfunction: A critical review.** New York: Wiley.

Rie, H. E., & Rie, E. D. (1980). **Handbook of minimal brain dysfunctions: a critical review,** New York: Wiley.

Rie, H. E., Rie, E. D., Stewart, S., & Ambuel, J. P. (1976a). Effects of methylphenidate on underachieving. **Journal of Consulting and Clinical Psychology, 44,** 250–269.

Rie, H. E., Rie, E. D., Stewart, S., & Ambuel, J. P. (1976b). Effects of Ritalin on underachieving children: A replication. **American Journal of Orthopsychiatry, 46,** 313–322.

Robins, L. N. (1966). **Deviant children grown up.** Baltimore: Williams & Wilkins.

Robins, L. N. (1974). **Deviant children grown up.** Huntington, NY: Krieger.

Robins, L. N. (1979). Follow-up studies. In H. C. Quay & J. S. Werry (Eds.), **Psychopathological disorders of childhood** (3rd ed.). New York: Wiley.

Roff, J. D., & Wirt, R. D. (1984). Childhood aggression and social adjustment as antecedents of delinquency. **Journal of Abnormal Child Psychology, 12,** 111–126.

Rosen, L. A., O'Leary, S. G., & Conway, G. (1985). The withdrawal of stimulant medication for hyperactivity: Overcoming detrimental attributions. **Behavior Therapy, 16,** 538–544.

Rosen, L. A., O'Leary, S. G., Joyce, S. A., Conway, G., & Pfiffner, L. J. (1984). The importance of prudent negative consequences for maintaining the appropriate behavior of hyperactive students. **Journal of Abnormal Child Psychology, 12,** 581–604.

Rosenthal, R. H., & Allen, T. W. (1978). An examination of attention, arousal, and learning dysfunctions of hyperactive children. **Psychological Bulletin, 85,** 689–715.

Ross, D. M., & Ross, S. A. (1976). **Hyperactivity: Research, theory, and action.** New York: Wiley.

Ross, D. M., & Ross, S. A. (1982). **Hyperactivity: Current issues, research, and theory.** New York: Wiley.

Routh, D. K. (1980). Developmental and social aspects of hyperactivity. In C. K. Whalen & B. Henker (Eds.), **Hyperactive children: The social ecology of identification and treatment.** New York: Academic Press.

Routh, D. K., & Schroeder, C. S. (1976). Standardized playroom measures as indices of hyperactivity. **Journal of Abnormal Child Psychology, 4,** 199–207.

Russo, D. C., Cataldo, M. F., & Cushing, P. J. (1981). Compliance training and behavioral covariation in the treatment of multiple behavior problems. **Journal of Applied Behavior Analysis, 14,** 209–222.

Rutter, M. (1977). Brain damage syndromes in childhood: Concepts and findings. **Journal of Child Psychology and Psychiatry, 18,** 1–21.

Rutter, M. (1979). Maternal deprivation, 1972–1978: New findings, new concepts, new approaches. **Child Development, 50,** 283–305.

Rutter, M. (1982). Syndromes attributed to minimal brain dysfunction in childhood. **American Journal of Psychiatry, 139,** 21–33.

Rutter, M. (1983). Stress, coping, and development. In N. Garmezy & M. Rutter (Eds.), **Stress, coping, and development in children.** New York: McGraw-Hill.

Rutter, M., Tizard, J., & Whitmore, K. (Eds.). (1970). **Education, health, and behaviour.** London: Longmans.

Rutter, M., Tizard, J., Yule, W., Graham, P., & Whitmore, K. (1976). Research report: Isle of Wight Studies (1964–1974). **Psychological Medicine, 6,** 313–332.

Rutter, M., & Yule, W. (1973). Specific reading retardation. In L. Mann and D. Sabatino (Eds.), **The first review of special education.** Philadelphia: Buttonwood Farms.

Rutter, M., & Yule, W. (1978). Reading difficulties. In

M. Rutter & L. Hersov (Eds.), **Child psychiatry: Modern perspectives.** Oxford: Blackwell Scientific Publications.

Safer, D. J., & Allen, R. P. (1976). **Hyperactive children: Diagnosis and management.** Baltimore: University Park Press.

Safer, D. J., Allen, R. P., & Barr, E. (1972). Depression of growth in hyperactive children on stimulants. **New England Journal of Medicine, 287,** 217-220.

Sarason, S. B. (1949). **Psychological problems in mental deficiency.** New York: Harper.

Satterfield, J. H., Cantwell, D. P., & Satterfield, B. T. (1979). Multimodal treatment: A one year follow-up of 87 hyperactive boys. **Archives of General Psychiatry, 36,** 965-974.

Schneider, M. (1974). Turtle technique in the classroom. **Teaching Exceptional Children, 7,** 22-24.

Schneider, M., & Robin, A. L. (1973). **The turtle manual.** Technical publication, Point of Woods Laboratory School, State University of New York at Stony Brook.

Schwarz, J. C. (1979). Childhood origins of psychopathology. **American Psychologist, 34,** 879-885.

Seeberg, E. (1943). Analysis of aggression in a five-year-old girl. **American Journal of Orthopsychiatry, 13,** 53-62.

Semier, I., Eron, J., Myerson, L. D., & Williams, J. (1967). Relationship of aggression in third grade children to certain pupil characteristics. **Psychology in the Schools, 4,** 85-88.

Signorielli, N., Gross, L., & Morgan, M. (1982). Violence in television programs: Ten years later. In **Television and behavior: Ten years of scientific progress and implications for the 80's.** Washington, DC: U.S. Government Printing Office.

Skinner, B. F. (1954). **Science and human behavior.** New York: Macmillan.

Stewart, M. A., & Olds, S. W. (1973). **Raising a hyperactive child.** New York: Harper & Row.

Stewart, M. A., Thach, B. T., & Freidin, M. R. (1970). Accidental poisoning and the hyperactive child syndrome. **Diseases of the Nervous System, 31,** 403-407.

Strasburg, P. A. (1984). Recent national trends in serious juvenile crime. In R. A. Mathais, P. DeMuro, & R. S. Allensen (Eds.), **Violent juvenile offenders.** San Francisco: National Council on Crime and Delinquency.

Strauss, A. A., & Kephart, N. C. (1955). **Psychopathology and education of the brain-injured child: Vol. 2. Progress in theory and clinic.** New York: Grune & Stratton.

Strauss, A. A., & Lehtinen, L. E. (1947). **Psychopathology and education of the brain-injured child.** New York: Grune & Stratton.

Strecker, E. (1929). Behavior problems in encephalitis. **Archives of Neurology and Psychiatry, 21,** 137-144.

Strecker, E., & Ebaugh, F. (1924). Neuropsychiatric sequelae of cerebral trauma in children. **Archives of Neurology and Psychiatry, 12,** 443-453.

Stumphauzer, J. S. (Ed.). (1979). **Progress in behavior therapy with delinquents.** Springfield, IL: Charles C Thomas.

Swanson, J. M., & Kinsbourne, M. (1980). Artificial color and hyperactive behavior. In R. M. Knights & D. J. Bakker (Eds.), **Treatment of hyperactive and learning disabled children.** Baltimore: University Park Press.

Taylor, H. G., & Fletcher, J. M. (1983). Biological foundations of "specific developmental disorders": Methods, findings, and future directions. **Journal of Clinical Child Psychology, 12,** 46-65.

Thomas, A., & Chess, S. (1977). **Temperament and development.** New York: Brunner/Mazel.

Thomas, A., Chess, S., & Birch, H. G. (1969). **Temperament and behavior disorders in children.** New York: New York University Press.

Thomas, M. H., Horton, R. W., Lippincott, E. C., & Drabman, S. (1977). Desensitization to portrayals of real-life aggression as a function of exposure to television violence. **Journal of Personality and Social Psychology, 23.**

Torgerson, A. M. (1976). **Temperamental differences in infants: Their cause as shown through twin studies.** Unpublished doctoral dissertation, University of Oslo, Norway.

Tredgold, C. H. (1908). **Mental deficiency (amentia).** New York: Wood.

Trites, R. L., Tryphonas, H., & Ferguson, H. B. (1980). Diet treatment for hyperactive children with food additives. In R. M. Knights & D. J. Bakker (Eds.), **Treatment of hyperactive and learning disabled children.** Baltimore: University Park Press.

Tryphonas, H. (1979). Factors possibly implicated in hyperactivity: Feingold's hypothesis and hypersensitivity reactions. In R. L. Trites (Ed.), **Hyperactivity in children: Etiology, measurement, and treatment implications.** Baltimore: University Park Press.

Varley, C. K. (1984). Diet and the behavior of children with attention deficit disorder. **Journal of the American Academy of Child Psychiatry, 23,** 182-185.

Vedder, C. B. (1979). **Juvenile offenders.** Springfield, IL: Charles C Thomas.

Wahl, G., Johnson, S. M., Johansson, S., & Martin, S. (1974). An operant analysis of child-family interaction. **Behavior Therapy, 5,** 64-78.

Walker, H. M., O'Neill, R., Shinn, M., Ramsey, B., Patterson, G. R., Reid, J., & Capaldi, D. (1986). **Lon-**

gitudinal assessment and long term follow-up of antisocial behavior in fourth grade boys: **Rationale, methodology, measures, and results.** Unpublished manuscript, University of Oregon.

Wallander, J. L., & Hubert, N. C. (1985). Long-term prognosis for children with attention deficit disorder with hyperactivity (ADD/H). In B. B. Lahey & A. E. Kazdin (Eds.), **Advances in clinical child psychology** (Vol. 8). New York: Plenum.

Webster's ninth new collegiate dictionary. (1983). Springfield, MA: Merriam.

Webster-Stratton, C. (1983, May). Intervention approaches to conduct disorders in young children. **Nurse Practitioner,** pp. 23–34.

Weiss, G., & Hechtman, L. T. (1986). **Hyperactive children grown up: Empirical findings and theoretical considerations.** New York: Guilford Press.

Weiss, G., Minde, K., Werry, J. S., Douglas, V. I., & Nemeth, E. (1971). Studies on the hyperactive child: VII. Five year follow-up. **Archives of General Psychiatry, 24,** 409–414.

Wells, K. C., & Forehand, R. (1981). Childhood behavior problems in the home. In S. M. Turner, K. S. Calhoun, & H. E. Adams (Eds.), **Handbook of clinical behavior therapy.** New York: Wiley.

Wells, K. C., & Forehand, R. (1985). Conduct and oppositional disorders. In P. H. Bornstein & A. E. Kazdin (Eds.), **Handbook of clinical behavior therapy with children.** Homewood, IL: Dorsey Press.

Wender, P. J. (1971). **Minimal brain dysfunction in children.** New York: Wiley.

Wender, P. J. (1972). The minimal brain dysfunction syndrome in children. **Journal of Nervous and Mental Disease, 155,** 55–71.

Whalen, C. K., & Henker, B. (1976). Psychostimulants and children: A review and analysis. **Psychological Bulletin, 83,** 1113–1130.

Whalen, C. K., Henker, B., Collins, B. E., Fink, D., & Dotemoto, S. (1979). A social ecology of hyperactive boys: Medication effects in systematically structured classroom environments. **Journal of Applied Behavior Analysis, 12,** 65–81.

Whalen, C. K., Henker, B., & Hinshaw, S. P. (1985). Cognitive-behavioral therapies for hyperactive children: Premises, problems, and prospects. **Journal of Abnormal Child Psychology, 13,** 391–410.

Willerman, L. (1973). Activity level and hyperactivity in twins. **Child Development, 44,** 288–293.

Wiltz, N. A., & Patterson, G. R. (1974). An evolution of parent training procedures designed to alter inappropriate aggressive behavior in boys. **Behavior Therapy, 5,** 215–221.

Witkin, H. A., Mednick, S. A., Schulsinger, F., Bakkestrom, E., Christiansen, K. O., Goodenough, D. R., Hirschhorn, K., Lundsteen, C., Owen, D. R., Philip, J., Rubin, D. B., & Stocking, M. (1976). Criminality in XYY and XXY men. **Science, 196,** 547–555.

Wolf, S. (1971). Dimensions and clusters of symptoms in disturbed children. **British Journal of Psychiatry, 118,** 421.

Wolraich, M., Drummond, T., Salomon, M. K., O'Brian, M. L., Sivage, C. (1978). Effects of methylphenidate alone and in combination with behavior modification procedures on the behavior and academic performance of hyperactive children. **Journal of Abnormal Child Psychology, 6,** 149–161.

CHAPTER 6

Albino, J. E. (1984). Prevention by acquiring health-enhancing habits. In M. C. Roberts & L. Peterson (Eds.), **Prevention of problems in childhood.** New York: Wiley.

Austin, G. A. (1978). **Perspectives on the history of psychoactive substance use.** Rockville, MD: National Institute on Drug Abuse.

Bandura, A. (1977). **Social learning theory.** Englewood Cliffs, NJ: Prentice-Hall.

Barry, H., III. (1977). Alcohol. In S. Pradhan & S. Dutta (Eds.), **Drug abuse: Clinical and basic aspects.** St. Louis: C. V. Mosby.

Bass, M. (1970). Sudden sniffing death. **Journal of the American Medical Association, 212,** 2075.

Biase, D. V. (1973). Some approaches to the treatment of adolescent drug addicts and abusers. In E. Harms (Ed.), **Drugs and youth: The challenge of today.** New York: Pergamon Press.

Blum, R. H., & Associates. (1972). **Horatio Alger's children.** San Francisco: Jossey-Bass.

Botvin, G. J. (1982). Broadening the focus of smoking prevention strategies. In T. Coates, A. Peterson, & C. Perry (Eds.), **Promoting adolescent health: A dialogue on research and practice.** New York: Academic Press.

Brecher, E. M., & the Editors of **Consumer Reports** (Eds.). (1972). **Licit and illicit drugs.** Boston: Little, Brown.

Brook, J. S., Whiteman, M., Gordon, A. S., & Cohen, P. (1986). Some models and mechanisms for explaining the impact of maternal and adolescent characteristics on adolescent stage of drug use. **Developmental Psychology, 22,** 460–467.

Cohen, S. (1977). Abuse of inhalants. In S. Pradhan & S. Dutta (Eds.), **Drug abuse: Clinical and basic aspects.** St. Louis: C. V. Mosby.

Comstock, E. G., & Comstock, B. S. (1977). Medical evaluation of inhalant abusers. In C. Sharp & M. Brehm (Eds.), **Review of inhalants: Euphoria to dysfunction** (NIDA Research Monograph No. 15). Washington, DC: U.S. Government Printing Office.

Cooper, J. R. (Ed.). (1977). **Sedative-hypnotic drugs: Risks and benefits** (NIDA Research Monograph No. ADM 792). Washington, DC: U.S. Government Printing Office.

Demone, H. W., Jr., & Wechsler, H. (1976). Changing drinking patterns of adolescents since the 1960s. In M. Greenblatt & M. Schuckit (Eds.), **Alcoholism problems in women and children.** New York: Grune & Stratton.

Dole, V. P., Nyswander, M. E., & Warner, A. (1968). Successful treatment of 750 criminal addicts. **Journal of the American Medical Association, 206,** 2710–2711.

Evans, R. I., Rozelle, R. M., Mittelmark, M. B., Hansen, W. B., Bane, A. L., & Havis, J. (1978). Deterring the onset of smoking in children: Knowledge of immediate physiological effects and coping with peer pressure, media pressure, and parent modeling. **Journal of Applied Social Psychology, 8,** 126–135.

Flaxman, J. (1976). Quitting smoking. In W. Craighead, A. Kazdin, & M. Mahoney (Eds.), **Behavior modification: Principles, issues, and applications.** Boston: Houghton Mifflin.

Flay, B. R., D'Avernas, J. R., Best, J. A., Kersell, M. W., & Ryan, K. B. (1982). Cigarette smoking: Why young people do it and ways of preventing it. In P. McGrath & P. Firestone (Eds.), **Pediatric and adolescent behavioral medicine.** New York: Springer-Verlag.

Flay, B. R., Johnson, C. A., & Hansen, W. B. (1984). Evaluation of a mass media enhanced smoking prevention and cessation program. In J. P. Baggaley & J. Sharpe (Eds.), **Experimental research in TV instruction** (Vol. 5). Montréal: Concordia University.

Frazier, T. M., Davis, G. H., Goldstein, H., & Goldberg, I. D. (1961). Cigarette smoking and prematurity: A prospective study. **American Journal of Obstetrics and Gynecology, 81,** 988–996.

Freud, S. (1884). **The cocaine papers.** Trans. S. Edminster. Vienna: Dunquin, 1963.

Glantz, M. D. (Ed.). (1984). **Correlates and consequences of marijuana use** (NIDA Research Monograph No. ADM 84-1276). Washington, DC: U.S. Government Printing Office.

Goodstadt, M. S., Sheppard, M. A., & Chan, G. C. (1982). An evaluation of two school-based alcohol education programs. **Journal of Studies on Alcohol, 43,** 352–369.

Greene, E. (1985). Cocaine, glamorous status symbol of the "Jet Set," is fast becoming many students' drug of choice. **Chronicle of Higher Education, 32,** 1, 34–35.

Greenspan, S. I. (1977). Substance abuse: An understanding from psychoanalytic, developmental, and learning perspectives. In J. Blaine & D. Julius (Eds.), **Psychodynamics of drug dependence** (NIDA Research Monograph No. 12). Washington, DC: U.S. Government Printing Office.

Hamilton-Russell, M. A. (1971). Cigarette smoking: Natural history of a dependence disorder. **British Journal of Medical Psychology, 44,** 1–15.

Horan, J. J., & Harrison, R. P. (1981). Drug use by children and adolescents. In B. B. Lahey & A. E. Kazdin (Eds.), **Advances in clinical child psychology** (Vol. 4). New York: Plenum.

Huba, G. J., Wingard, J. A., & Bentler, P. M. (1979). Beginning adolescent drug use and peer and adult interaction patterns. **Journal of Consulting and Clinical Psychology, 47,** 265–276.

Jarvik, M. E., Cullen, J. W., Gritz, E. R., Vogt, T. M., & West, L. J. (Eds.). (1977). **Research on smoking behavior** (NIDA Research Monograph No. 17). Washington, DC: U.S. Government Printing Office.

Jessor, R., & Jessor, S. L. (1977). **Problem behavior and psychosocial development.** New York: Academic Press.

Jessor, R., & Jessor, S. L. (1978). Theory testing in longitudinal research on marijuana use. In D. Kandel (Ed.), **Longitudinal research on drug use.** Washington, DC: Hemisphere.

Johnston, L. D., O'Malley, P. M., & Bachman, J. G. (1985). **Use of licit and illicit drugs by America's high school students, 1975–1984** (NIDA Research Monograph No. ADM 85-1394). Washington, DC: U.S. Government Printing Office.

Julius, D., & Renault, P. (1976). **Narcotic antagonists: Naltrexone** (NIDA Research Monograph No. 9). Washington, DC: U.S. Government Printing Office.

Kandel, D. B. (1973). Adolescent marijuana use: Role of parents and peers. **Science, 181,** 1067–1081.

Kandel, D. B. (1978). Similarity in real-life adolescent pairs. **Journal of Personality and Social Psychology, 36,** 306–312.

Kandel, D. B., & Faust, R. (1975). Sequence and stages in patterns of adolescent drug use. **Archives of General Psychiatry, 4,** 281–292.

Kandel, D. B., Kessler, R. C., & Margulies, R. Z. (1978). Antecedents of adolescent initiation into stages of drug use: A developmental analysis. In

D. B. Kandel (Ed.), **Longitudinal research on drug use: Empirical findings and methodological issues.** Washington, D.C.: Hemisphere.

Kandel, D. B., Murphy, D., & Karus, D. (1985). Cocaine use in young adulthood: Patterns of use and psychosocial correlates. In N. J. Kozel & E. H. Adams (Eds.), **Cocaine use in America: Epidemiologic and clinical perspectives** (NIDA Research Monograph No. 61). Washington, DC: U. S. Government Printing Office.

Lander, B. (1973). Attitudes toward methadone maintenance. In E. Harms (Ed.), **Drugs and youth: The challenge of today.** New York: Pergamon Press.

Lichtenstein, E. (1982). The smoking problem: A behavioral perspective. **Journal of Consulting and Clinical Psychology, 50,** 804–819.

Louria, D. (1977). The epidemiology of drug abuse rehabilitation. In M. Glatt (Ed.), **Drug dependence: Current problems and issues.** Baltimore: University Park Press.

Lukoff, I. F. (1977). Consequences of use: Heroin and other narcotics. In J. Rittenhouse (Ed.), **The epidemiology of heroin and other narcotics** (NIDA Research Monograph No. ADM 78-750). Washington, DC: U.S. Government Printing Office.

Marijuana as medicine. (1978, July 17). **New York Times,** p. A16.

McAlister, A. L., Perry, C., Killen, J., Slinkard, L. A., & Maccoby, N. (1980). A pilot study of smoking, alcohol, and drug abuse prevention. **American Journal of Public Health, 70,** 719–721.

Meredith, H. V. (1975). Somatic changes during prenatal life. **Child Development, 46,** 603–610.

Milgram, G. G., & Nathan, P. (1986). Efforts to prevent alcohol abuse. In B. Edelstein & L. Michelson (Eds.), **Handbook of prevention.** New York: Plenum.

Miller, J. D., & Cisin, I. (1983). **Highlights from the national survey on drug abuse: 1982** (NIDA Research Monograph No. ADM 83-1277). Washington, DC: U.S. Government Printing Office.

Miller, W. R. (1985). Motivation for treatment: A review with special emphasis on alcoholism. **Psychological Bulletin, 98,** 84–107.

Nathan, P. (1983). Failures in prevention: Why can't we prevent the devastating effect of alcoholism and drug abuse. **American Psychologist, 38,** 459–467.

National Clearinghouse for Drug Abuse Information. (1975, April). **Treatment of drug abuse: An overview** (Series 34, no. 1). Washington, DC: U.S. Government Printing Office.

National Commission of Marijuana and Drug Abuse. (1972). **Marijuana: A signal of misunderstanding.** Washington, DC: U.S. Government Printing Office.

Newcomb, M., Hula, G., & Bentler, P. (1983). Mothers' influence on the drug use of their children: Confirmatory tests of direct modeling and mediational theories. **Developmental Psychology, 19,** 714–726.

NIDA. (1985). Community Epidemiology Work Group Proceedings. Patterns and trends in drug abuse: A national and international perspective (Division of Epidemiology and Statistical Analysis, NIMH). Washington, DC: U.S. Government Printing Office.

O'Malley, P. M., Johnston, L. D., & Bachman, J. G. (1985). Cocaine use among American adolescents and young adults. In N. J. Kozel & E. H. Adams (Eds.), **Cocaine use in America: Epidemiologic and clinical perspectives** (NIDA Research Monograph No. 61.) Washington, DC: U.S. Government Printing Office.

Peterson, R. C. (1984). Marijuana overview. In M. D. Glantz (Ed.), **Correlates and consequences of marijuana use** (NIDA Research Monograph No. ADM 84-1276). Washington, DC: U.S. Government Printing Office.

Platt, J. J., & Labate, C. (1976). **Heroin addiction: Theory, research, and treatment.** New York: Wiley.

Resnick, R. B. & Resnick, E. B. (1984). Cocaine abuse and its treatment. **Psychiatric Clinics of North America, 7,** 713–728.

Salmon, R., & Salmon, S. (1977). The causes of heroin addiction—A review of the literature. Part I. **International Journal of the Addictions, 12,** 679–696.

Schinke, S. P., & Gilchrist, L. D. (1985). Preventing substance abuse with children and adolescents. **Journal of Consulting and Clinical Psychology, 53,** 596–602.

Schonberg, S. K., & Schnoll, S. H. (1986). Drugs and their effects on adolescent users. In G. Beschner & A. S. Friedman (Eds.), **Teen drug use.** Lexington, MA: D. C. Heath.

Secretary of Health, Education and Welfare. (1980). **Marijuana and health: Eighth Annual Report to the U.S. Congress from the Secretary of Health, Education and Welfare, 1980** (DHEW Publication No. ADM 80-945). Washington, DC: U.S. Government Printing Office.

Sells, S. B., & Simpson, D. D. (1977). Evaluation of treatment for youth in the Drug Abuse Report Program (DARP) (IBR Report 77-9). Fort Worth: Texas Christian University, Institute of Behavioral Research.

Sells, S. B. (1979). Treatment effectiveness. In R. Dupont, A. Goldstein, & J. O'Donnell (Eds.), **Handbook on drug abuse.** National Institute on Drug Abuse. Washington, DC: U.S. Government Printing Office.

Severson, H. H., & Ary, D. V. (1983). Sampling bias

due to consent procedures with adolescents. **Addictive Behaviors, 8,** 433–437.

Silberberg, N. E., & Silberberg, M. C., (1974). Glue sniffing in children: A position paper. **Journal of Drug Education, 4,** 301–307.

Simpson, D. D., Savage, L. J., Lloyd, M. R., & Sells, S. B. (1978). Evaluation of drug abuse treatment based on first year followup. In **National followup study of admissions to drug abuse treatments in the DARP during 1969–1972** (NIDA Research Monograph No. ADM 77-496). Washington, DC: U.S. Government Printing Office.

Smart, R. G. (1977). Social policy and the prevention of drug abuse: Perspectives on the unimodal approach. In M. Glatt (Ed.), **Drug dependence: Current problems and issues.** Baltimore: University Park Press.

Stein, J. A., Swisher, J. D., Hu, T., & McDonnall, N. (1984). Cost-effectiveness evaluation of a Channel One program. **Journal of Drug Education, 14,** 251–269.

Streissguth, A. P. (1976). Maternal alcoholism and the outcome of pregnancy: A review of the fetal alcohol syndrome. In M. Greenblatt & M. Schuckit (Eds.), **Alcoholism problems in women and children.** New York: Grune & Stratton.

Streissguth, A. P., Landesman-Dwyer, S., Martin, J. P., & Smith, D. W. (1980). Teratogenic effects of alcohol in humans and laboratory animals. **Science, 209,** 353–361.

Streissguth, A. P., Martin, D. C., Martin, J. C., & Barr, H. M. (1981). The Seattle longitudinal prospective study on alcohol and pregnancy. **Neurobehav-**

ioral Toxicology and Teratology, 3, 223–233.

Stuart, R. B. (1974). Teaching facts about drugs: Pushing or preventing? **Journal of Educational Psychology, 66,** 189–201.

Tinklenberg, J. R. (1977). Abuse of marijuana. In S. Pradhan & S. Dutta (Eds.), **Drug abuse: Clinical and basic aspects.** St. Louis: C. V. Mosby.

Ulleland, C. N. (1972). The offspring of alcoholic mothers. **Annals of the New York Academy of Sciences, 197,** 167–169.

U.S. Department of Health, Education and Welfare (DHEW). (1977). **The smoking digest.** Washington, DC: U.S. Government Printing Office.

U.S. Department of Health, Education and Welfare (DHEW). (1979). **Smoking and health: A report of the Surgeon General** (DHEW Publication No. PHS 79-50066). Washington, DC: U.S. Government Printing Office.

U.S. Public Health Service. (1976). **Adult use of tobacco: 1975.** Atlanta, GA: Centers for Disease Control.

Wagenaar, A. C. (1983). **Alcohol, young drivers, and traffic accidents.** Lexington, MA: Heath.

Wald, P., & Hutt, P. (1972). The drug abuse survey project. In Ford Foundation Drug Abuse Survey Project (Ed.) **Dealing with drug abuse: A report to the Ford Foundation.** New York: Praeger.

Zucker, R. A. (1976). Parental influences on the drinking patterns of their children. In M. Greenblatt & M. Schuckit (Eds.), **Alcoholism problems in women and children.** New York: Grune & Stratton.

CHAPTER 7

Abraham, S. F., & Beumont, P. J. V. (1982). How patients describe bulimia or binge eating. **Psychological Medicine, 12,** 625–635.

Abraham, S., Collins, G., & Nordsieck, M. (1971). Relationship of childhood weight status to morbidity in adults. **HSMHA Health Reports, 86,** 273–284.

Acredolo, L. P., & Goodwyn, S. W. (1985). Symbolic gesturing in language development. **Human Development, 28,** 50–56.

Agras, W. S., Barlow, T. H., Chapin, H. N., Abel, G. G. & Leitenberg, H. (1974). Behavior modification of anorexia nervosa. **Archives of General Psychiatry, 30,** 343–352.

American Speech-Language-Hearing Association (ASHA). (1979, October 31). **Fact sheet on communicative disorders.**

Asher, P. (1966). Fat babies and fat children: The prog-

nosis of obesity in the very young. **Archives of Diseases in Childhood, 41,** 672.

Avari, D. N., & Bloodstein, O. (1974). Adjacency and prediction in school-age stutterers. **Journal of Speech and Hearing Research, 17,** 33–40.

Azrin, N. H., & Nunn, R. G. (1974). A rapid method of eliminating stuttering by a regulated breathing approach. **Behavior Research and Therapy, 12,** 279–286.

Azrin, N. H., & Nunn, R. G. (1977). **Habit control in a day.** New York: Pocket Books.

Bakwin, H., & Bakwin, R. M. (1972). **Behavior disorders in children** (4th ed.). Philadelphia: W. B. Saunders.

Barrios, B. A., & Pennebaker, J. W. (1983). A note on the early detection of bulimia nervosa. **Behavior Therapist, 6** (2), 18–19.

Bauermeister, J. J., & Jemail, J. A. (1975). Modification of "elective mutism" in the classroom setting: A case study. **Behavior Therapy, 6,** 246–250.

Bauta, H. B. (1974). Evaluation of a new anorexic agent in adolescence. **Connecticut Medicine, 38,** 460.

Berg, I. (1981). Child psychiatry and enuresis. **British Journal of Psychiatry, 139,** 247–248.

Berg, I., Forsythe, I., Holt, P., & Watts, J. (1983). A controlled trial of "Senokot" in faecal soiling treated by behavioural methods. **Journal of Child Psychology and Psychiatry and Allied Disciplines, 24,** 543–549.

Blackwell, B., & Currah, J. (1973). The psychopharmacology of nocturnal enuresis. In I. Kolvin, R. C. MacKeith & S. R. Meadow (Eds.), **Bladder control and enuresis.** Philadelphia: J. B. Lippincott.

Blegvad, B., & Hvidegaard, T. (1983). Hereditary dysfunction of the brain stem auditory pathways as the major cause of speech retardation. **Scandinavian Audiology, 12,** 179–187.

Blood, G. W. (1985). Laterality differences in child stutterers: Heredity, severity levels, and statistical treatments. **Journal of Speech and Hearing Disorders, 50,** 66–72.

Bloodstein, O., Alper, J., & Zisk, P. (1965). Stuttering as an outgrowth of normal disfluency. In D. A. Barbara (Ed.), **New directions in stuttering: Theory and practice.** Springfield, IL: Charles C Thomas.

Boberg, E., Yeudall, L. T., Schopflocher, D., & Bo-Lassen, P. (1983). The effect of an intensive behavioral program on the distribution of EEG alpha power in stutterers during the processing of verbal and visuospatial information. **Journal of Fluency Disorders, 8,** 245–263.

Boller, F. (1976). Treatment of nightmares. **Medical Journal of Australia, 2,** 548.

Boskind-Lodahl, M., (1976). Cinderella's stepsisters: A feminist perspective on anorexia nervosa and bulimia. **Signs: Journal of Women in Culture and Society, 2,** 342–356.

Boskind-Lodahl, M., & White, W. C. (1978). The definition and treatment of bulimarexia in college women—a pilot study. **Journal of American College Health Association, 27,** 84–97.

Bourdon, K. H., & Silber, D. E. (1970). Perceived parental behavior among stutterers and nonstutterers. **Journal of Abnormal Psychology, 75,** 93–97.

Brady, J. P., & Berson, J. (1975). Stuttering, dichotic listening, and cerebral dominance. **Archives of General Psychiatry, 32,** 1449–1452.

Bricker, W. A., & Bricker, D. D. (1974). An early language training strategy. In R. L. Schiefelbusch & L. L. Lloyd (Eds.), **Language perspectives—acquisition, retardation, and intervention.** Baltimore: University Park Press.

Brody, J. E. (1980, February 5). Tending to obesity,

inbred tribe aids diabetes study. **New York Times,** pp. C1, C5.

Brook, G. C., Lloyd, J. K., & Wolff, O. H. (1974). Rapid weight loss in children. **British Medical Journal, iii,** 44.

Brooker, A. E. (1982). Behavioral treatment of obsessive-compulsive disorders: Current status. **Psychological Reports, 50,** 1035–1044.

Bruch, H. (1957). **The importance of overweight.** New York: Norton.

Bruch, H. (1978). **The golden cage: The enigma of anorexia nervosa.** Cambridge, MA: Harvard University Press.

Brutten, G. J., & Trotter, A. C. (1985). Hemispheric interference: A dual-task investigation of youngsters who stutter. **Journal of Fluency Disorders, 10,** 77–85.

Bullen, B. A., Monello, L. F., Cohen, H., & Mayer, J. (1963). Attitudes toward physical activity, food and family in obese and nonobese adolescent girls. **American Journal of Clinical Nutrition, 12,** 1–11.

Bullen, B. A., Reed, R. R., & Mayer, J. (1964). Physical activity of obese and non-obese adolescent girls appraised by motion picture sampling. **American Journal of Clinical Nutrition, 14,** 211–223.

Caille, P., Abrahamsen, P., Girolami, C., & Sorbye, B. (1977). Theory approach to a case of anorexia nervosa. **Family Process, 16,** 455–465.

Calhoun, J., & Koenig, K. P. (1973). Classroom modification of elective mutism. **Behavior Therapy, 4,** 700–702.

Casper, R. C., Eckert, E. D., Halmi, K. A., Goldberg, S. C., & Davis, J. M. (1980). Bulimia: Its incidence and clinical importance in patients with anorexia nervosa. **Archives of General Psychiatry, 37,** 1030–1035.

Chess, S., & Hassibi, M. (1978). **Principles and practices of child psychiatry.** New York: Plenum.

Clutter, M. H., & Freeman, F. (1984). Stuttering: The six blind men revisited. **Journal of Fluency Disorders, 9,** 89–92.

Coates, T. J., & Thoresen, C. E. (1978). Treating obesity in children and adolescents: A review. **American Journal of Public Health, 68,** 143–151.

Cohen, E. A., Gelfand, D. M., Dodd, D. K., Jensen, J., & Turner, C. (1980). Self-control practices associated with weight loss maintenance in children and adolescents. **Behavior Therapy, 11,** 26–37.

Cohen, M. S., & Hanson, M. L. (1975). Intersensory processing efficiency of fluent speakers and stutterers. **British Journal of Disorders of Communication, 10,** 111–122.

Colligan, R. C., Ferdinande, R. J., Lucas, A. R., & Duncan, J. W. (1983). A one-year followup study of adolescent patients hospitalized with anorexia nervosa. **Journal of Developmental and Behavioral Pediatrics, 4,** 278-279.

Colligan, R. W., Colligan, R. C., & Dillard, M. K. (1977). Contingency management in the classroom treatment of long-term mutism: A case report. **Journal of School Psychology, 15,** 9-17.

Collipp, P. (1971). Childhood obesity—to treat or not to treat. **Medical Times, 99,** 155.

Committee on Nutrition, American Academy of Pediatrics. (1967). Obesity in childhood. **Pediatrics, 40,** 455-467.

Conture, E. G., Schwartz, H. D., & Brewer, D. W. (1985). Laryngeal behavior during stuttering: A further study. **Journal of Speech and Hearing Research, 28,** 233-240.

Cooper, E. B., & Cooper, C. S. (1985). Clinician attitudes toward stuttering: A decade of change (1973-1983). **Journal of Fluency Disorders, 10,** 19-33.

Costello, J., & Bosler, S. (1976). Generalization and articulation instruction. **Journal of Speech and Hearing Disorders, 41,** 359-373.

Court, J. M. (1972). A trial of fenfluramine in children with obesity associated with reduced muscle activity. **South African Medical Journal, 46,** 132.

Crick, F., & Mitchison, G. (1983). The function of dream sleep. **Nature, 304,** 111-114.

Crisp, A. H. (1982). Anorexia nervosa at normal body weight: The abnormal-normal weight control syndrome. **International Journal of Psychiatry in Medicine, 11,** 203-233.

Crisp, A. H., Palmer, R. L., & Kalucy, R. S. (1976). How common is anorexia nervosa? A prevalence study. **British Journal of Psychiatry, 128,** 549-554.

Cromer, R. F. (1981). Reconceptualizing language acquisition and cognitive development. In R. L. Schiefelbusch & D. D. Bricker (Eds.), **Early language acquisition and intervention.** Baltimore: University Park Press.

Crosby, N. D. (1950). Essential treatment: Successful treatment based on physiological concepts. **Medical Journal of Australia, 2,** 533-543.

Diedrich, W. M., & Carr, D. B. (1984). Identification of speech disorders. **Journal of Developmental and Behavioral Pediatrics, 5,** 38-41.

Dippe, S. E. (1978). Anorexia nervosa: A self-imposed disease. **Arizona Medicine, 35,** 171-172.

Dische, S., Yule, W., Corbett, J., & Hand, D. (1983). Childhood nocturnal enuresis: Factors associated with outcome of treatment with an enuresis alarm. **Developmental Medicine and Child Neurology, 25,** 67-80.

D'Odorico, L., & Franco, F. (1985). The determinants of baby talk: Relationship to context. **Journal of Child Language, 12,** 567-586.

Doleys, D. M. (1977). Behavioral treatments for nocturnal enuresis in children: A review of the recent literature. **Psychological Bulletin, 84,** 30-54.

Doleys, D. M. (1979a). Assessment and treatment of childhood encopresis. In A. J. Finch, Jr., & P. C. Kendall (Eds.), **Clinical treatment and research in child psychopathology.** New York: Spectrum.

Doleys, D. M. (1979b). Assessment and treatment of childhood enuresis. In A. J. Finch, Jr., & P. C. Kendall (Eds.), **Clinical treatment and research in child psychopathology.** New York: Spectrum.

Doleys, D. M. (1983). Enuresis and encopresis. In T. H. Ollendick & M. Hersen (Eds.) **Handbook of child psychopathology.** New York: Plenum.

Doleys, D. M., McWhorter, A. Q., Williams, S. C., & Gentry, W. R. (1977). Encopresis: Its treatment and relation to nocturnal enuresis. **Behavior Therapy, 8,** 77-82.

Doleys, D. M., & Wells, K. C. (1975). Changes in functional bladder capacity and bed-wetting during and after retention control training. **Behavior Therapy, 6,** 685-688.

Dollard, J., & Miller, N. (1950). **Personality and psychotherapy: An analysis in terms of learning, thinking, and culture.** New York: McGraw-Hill.

Dornbusch, S. M., Carlsmith, J. M., Duncan, P. D., Gross, R. T., Martin, J. A., Ritter, P. L., & Siegel-Gorelick, B. (1984). Sexual maturation, social class, and the desire to be thin among adolescent females. **Journal of Developmental and Behavioral Pediatrics, 5,** 308-314.

Dunn, J., & Kendrick, C. (1982). The speech of two- and three-year-olds to infant siblings: "Baby talk" and the context of communication. **Journal of Child Language, 9,** 579-595.

Dworkin, J. P., & Culatta, R. A. (1985). Oral structural and neuromuscular characteristics in children with normal and disordered articulation. **Journal of Speech and Hearing Disorders, 50,** 150-156.

Education for All Handicapped Children Act of 1975, P.L. 94-142.

Emerick, L. L., & Hatten, J. T. (1979). **Diagnosis and evaluation in speech pathology** (2nd ed.). Englewood Cliffs, NJ: Prentice-Hall.

Evans, C. (1984). **Landscapes of the night: How and why we dream.** New York: Viking Press.

Evans, M. (1985). Self-initiated speech repairs: A reflection of communicative monitoring in young children. **Developmental Psychology, 21,** 365-371.

Evesham, M., & Fay, F. (1985). Stuttering relapse: The effect of a combined speech and psychological reconstruction program. **British Journal of Disorders of Communication, 20,** 237-248.

Fairburn, C. G. (1980). Self-induced vomiting. **Journal of Psychosomatic Research, 24,** 193-197.

Fairburn, C. G. (1981). A cognitive behavioral approach to the treatment of bulimia. **Psychological Medicine, 11,** 707–711.

Fairburn, C. G., & Cooper, P. J. (1982). Self-induced vomiting and bulimia nervosa. **British Medical Journal, 284,** 1153–1155.

Fay, W. H. (1984). Yes/no answers and the verbally delayed child. **Topics in Early Childhood Special Education, 4,** 73–81.

Ferguson, J. M. (1975). **Learning to eat: Behavior modification for weight control.** Palo Alto, CA: Bull.

Fernald, A. (1985). Four-month-old infants prefer to listen to motherese. **Infant Behavior and Development, 8,** 181–195.

Finley, W. W. (1971). An EEG study of sleep of enuretics at three age levels. **Clinical Electroencephalography, 1,** 35–39.

Finley, W. W., Besserman, R. L., Bennett, L. F., Clapp, R. K., & Finley, P. M. (1973). The effect of continuous, intermittent, and "placebo" reinforcement on the effectiveness of the conditioning treatment for enuresis nocturna. **Behaviour Research and Therapy, 11,** 289–297.

Finley, W. W., & Wansley, R. A. (1976). Use of intermittent reinforcement in a clinical-research program for the treatment of enuresis nocturna. **Journal of Pediatric Psychology, 4,** 24–27.

Fisher, C., Kahn, E., Edwards, A., & Davis, D. (1973). A psychophysiological study of nightmares and night terrors: The suppression of stage 4 night terrors with diazepam. **Archives of General Psychiatry, 28,** 252–259.

Forsythe, W. I., & Merrett, J. D. (1969). A controlled trial of imipramine ("Tofranil") and nortriptyline ("Allegron") in the treatment of enuresis. **British Journal of Clinical Practice, 23,** 210–215.

Friedman, R., & Kargan, N. (1973). Characteristics and management of elective mutism in children. **Psychology in the Schools, 10,** 249–252.

Garces, L., Kenny, F., & Drash, A. (1968). Cortisol secretion rate during fasting of obese adolescent subjects. **Journal of Clinical Endocrinology and Metabolism, 28,** 18–43.

Garfinkel, P. E., & Garner, D. M. (1982). **Anorexia nervosa: A multidimensional perspective.** New York: Brunner/Mazel.

Garfinkel, P. E., Moldofsky, H., & Garner, D. M. (1980). The heterogeneity of anorexia nervosa. **Archives of General Psychiatry, 37,** 1036–1040.

Garn, S. M., Clark, D. C., & Guire, K. E. (1975). Growth, body composition, and development of obese and lean children. In M. Winick (Ed.), **Childhood obesity.** New York: Wiley.

Gilbert, E. H., & DeBlassie, R. R. (1984). Anorexia nervosa: Adolescent starvation by choice. **Adolescence, 19,** 817–826.

Gold, M. S., Pottash, A. L., Sweeny, A. R., Martin, D. M., & Davies, R. V. (1980). Further evidence of hypothalamic-pituitary dysfunction in anorexia nervosa. **American Journal of Psychiatry, 137,** 101–102.

Gray, B. B. (1968). **Some effects of anxiety deconditioning upon stuttering behavior.** Monterey, CA: Monterey Institute for Speech and Hearing.

Green, R. S., & Rau, J. H. (1974). Treatment of compulsive eating disturbances with anticonvulsant medication. **American Journal of Psychiatry, 131,** 428–432.

Green, R. S., & Rau, J. H. (1976). Diphenylhydantoin treatment of bulimia. **American Journal of Psychiatry, 133,** 1093.

Greiner, J. R., Fitzgerald, H. E., & Cooke, P. A. (1986). Speech fluency and hand performance on a sequential tapping task in left- and right-handed stutterers and nonstutterers. **Journal of Fluency Disorders, 11,** 55–69.

Griffith, E. E., Schnelle, J. F., McNees, M. P., Bissinger, C., & Huff, T. M. (1975). Elective mutism in a first grader: The remediation of a complex behavioral problem. **Journal of Abnormal Child Psychology, 3,** 127–134.

Grinker, J., Price, J. M., & Greenwood, M. R. C. (1976). Studies of taste in childhood obesity. In D. Novin, W. Wyrwicka, & G. A. Bray (Eds.), **Hunger: Basic mechanisms and clinical implications.** New York: Raven Press.

Gruber, L., & Powell, R. L. (1974). Responses of stuttering and nonstuttering children to a dichotic listening task. **Perceptual and Motor Skills, 38,** 263–264.

Guilleminault, C., Carskadon, M., & Dement, W. C. (1974). On the treatment of rapid eye movement narcolepsy. **Archives of Neurology, 30,** 90–93.

Halmi, K. A. (1974). Anorexia nervosa: Demographic and clinical features of 94 cases. **Psychosomatic Medicine, 36,** 18–25.

Halmi, K. A. (1978). Anorexia nervosa: Recent investigations. **Annual Review of Medicine, 29,** 137–148.

Halmi, K. A. (1985). The diagnosis and treatment of anorexia nervosa. In D. Shaffer, A. A. Erhardt, & L. Greenhill (Eds.), **The clinical guide to child psychiatry.** New York: Free Press.

Halmi, K. A., Falk, J. R., & Schwartz, E. (1981). Binge-eating and vomiting: A survey of a college population. **Psychological Medicine, 11,** 697–706.

Halmi, K. A., & Larson, L. (1977). Behavior therapy in anorexia nervosa. In S. Feinstrin (Ed.), **Adolescent psychiatry: Developmental and clinical studies.** New York: Jason Aronson.

Hammar, S. L., Campbell, M. M., Campbell, V. A., Moores, N. L., Sareen, C., Gareis, F. J., & Lucas,

B. (1972). An interdisciplinary study of adolescent obesity. **Journal of Pediatrics, 80,** 373–383.

Hammar, S. L., Campbell, V., & Woolley, J. (1971). Treating adolescent obesity: Long-range evaluation of previous therapy. **Clinical Pediatrics, 10,** 46–52.

Hardman, M. L., Drew, C. J., & Egan, M. W. (1987). **Human exceptionality: Society, school, and family** (2nd ed.). Boston: Allyn & Bacon.

Hawkins, R. C., & Clement, P. F. (1980). Development and construct validation of a self-report measure of binge eating tendencies. **Addictive Behaviors, 5,** 219–226.

Heald, F. P., & Hollander, R. J. (1965). The relationship between obesity in adolescence and early growth. **Journal of Pediatrics, 67,** 35–38.

Healey, E. C. (1984). Fundamental frequency contours of stutterers' vowels following fluent stop consonant productions. **Folia Phoniatrica, 36,** 145–151.

Helm, N., Butler, R. B., & Benson, D. F. (1977). Acquired stuttering. **Neurology, 27,** 349–350.

Herzog, D. B. (1982). Bulimia: The secretive syndrome. **Psychosomatics, 23,** 481–483, 487.

Hirsch, J. (1975). Cell number and size as a determinant of subsequent obesity. In M. Winick (Ed.), **Childhood obesity.** New York: Wiley.

Homzie, M. J., & Lindsay, J. S. (1984). Language and the young stutterer: A new look at old theories and findings. **Brain and Language, 22,** 232–252.

Hornby, G., & Jensen-Procter, G. (1984). Parental speech to language delayed children: A home intervention study. **British Journal of Disorders of Communication, 19,** 97–103.

Houts, A. C., Liebert, R. M., & Padawer, W. (1983). A delivery system for primary enuresis. **Journal of Abnormal Child Psychology, 11,** 513–519.

Hutchinson, B. B., Hanson, M. L., & Mecham, M. J. (1979). **Diagnostic handbook of speech pathology.** Baltimore: Williams & Wilkins.

Ingram, D. (1976). Current issues in child phonology. In D. M. Morehead & A. E. Morehead (Eds.), **Normal and deficient child language.** Baltimore: University Park Press.

James, J. E. (1983). Parameters of the influences of self-initiated time-out from speaking on stuttering. **Journal of Communication Disorders, 16,** 123–132.

Jehu, D., Morgan, R. T. T., Turner, A., & Jones, A. (1977). A controlled trial of the treatment of nocturnal enuresis in residential homes for children. **Behaviour Research and Therapy, 15,** 1–16.

Johnson, W., Brown, S. F., Curtis, J. F., Edney, C. W., & Keaster, J. (1948). **Speech handicapped school children.** New York: Harper & Row.

Johnston, J. M., & Johnston, G. T. (1972). Modification of consonant speech-sound articulation in young children. **Journal of Applied Behavior Analysis, 5,** 233–246.

Jordan, H. A., & Levitz, L. S. (1975). Behavior modification in the treatment of childhood obesity. In M. Winick (Ed.), **Childhood obesity.** New York: Wiley.

Kales, A., & Kales, J. D. (1974). Sleep disorders. **New England Journal of Medicine, 290,** 487–499.

Kales, J., Jacobson, A. & Kales, A. (1968). Sleep disorders in children. In L. Abt & B. F. Riess (Eds.), **Progress in clinical psychology** (Vol. 8). New York: Grune & Stratton.

Keilbach, H. (1976). Treatment of an 8-year-old boy with encopresis acquisita as main symptom. **Praxis der Kinderpsychologie und Kinderpsychiatrie, 25,** 81–91.

Keith, P. R. (1975). Night terrors: A review of the psychology, neurophysiology, and therapy. **Journal of the American Academy of Child Psychiatry, 14,** 477–489.

Kiester, E., Jr. (1976). Doctor, I keep falling asleep. What's wrong with me? **Today's Health, 54**(1), 40–43, 45.

Knittle, J. L. (1972). Obesity in childhood: A problem in adipose tissue cellular development. **Journal of Pediatrics, 81,** 1048–1059.

Knittle, J. L. (1975). Basic concepts in the control of childhood obesity. In M. Winick (Ed.), **Childhood obesity.** New York: Wiley.

Knopf, I. J. (1979). **Childhood psychopathology: A developmental approach.** Englewood Cliffs, NJ: Prentice-Hall.

Kolb, L. C. (1977). **Modern clinical psychiatry.** Philadelphia: W. B. Saunders.

Kurtz, H., & Davidson, S. (1974). Psychic trauma in an Israeli child: Relationship to environmental security. **American Journal of Psychotherapy, 28,** 438–444.

LaGrone, D. M. (1979). Primary anorexia nervosa in an adolescent male. **Southern Medical Journal, 72,** 501–502.

Landman, G. B., & Rappaport, L. (1985). Pediatric management of severe treatment-resistant encopresis. **Journal of Developmental and Behavioral Pediatrics, 6,** 349–351.

Lawrence, B. M. (1984). Conversation and cooperation: Child linguistic maturity, parental speech, and helping behavior of young children. **Child Development, 55,** 1926–1935.

Leon, G., & Dinklage, D. (1983). Childhood obesity and anorexia nervosa. In T. H. Ollendick & M. Hersen (Eds.) **Handbook of child psychopathology.** New York: Plenum.

Leon, G. R., Lucas, A. R., Colligan, R. C., Ferdinande, R. J., & Kamp, J. (1985). Sexual, body-image, and personality attitudes in anorexia nervosa. **Journal of Abnormal Child Psychology, 13,** 245–257.

Leon, G. R., & Roth, L. (1977). Obesity: Psychological causes, correlations, and speculations. **Psychological Bulletin, 84,** 117–139.

Levine, M. D. (1975). Children with encopresis: A descriptive analysis. **Pediatrics, 56,** 412–416.

Liebman, R., Minuchin, S., Baker, L, & Rosman, B. L. (1975). The treatment of anorexia nervosa. **Current Psychiatric Therapies, 15,** 51–57.

Linden, W. (1980). Multi-component behavior therapy in a case of compulsive binge-eating followed by vomiting. **Journal of Behavior Therapy and Experimental Psychiatry, 11,** 297–300.

Lloyd, J. K., Wolff, O. H., & Whelan, W. (1961). Childhood obesity: A long-term study of height and weight. **British Medical Journal, ii,** 145–147.

Lorber, J. A. (1966). A controlled trial of anorectic drugs. **Archives of Diseases in Childhood, 41,** 309.

Lorber, J., & Rendleshort, J. (1961). Obesity in childhood: A controlled trial of phenmetrazine, amphetamine resinate, and diet. **Quarterly Review of Pediatrics, 16,** 93.

Loro, Jr., A. D., Fisher, E. B., Jr., & Levenkron, J. C. (1979). Comparison of established and innovative weight-reduction treatment procedures. **Journal of Applied Behavior Analysis, 12,** 141–155.

Lovibond, S. H., & Coote, M. A. (1970). Enuresis. In C. G. Costello (Ed.), **Symptoms of psychopathology.** New York: Wiley.

Madsen, C. H., Jr., Hoffman, M., Thomas, D. R., Koropsak, E., & Madsen, C. K. (1975). Comparisons of toilet training techniques. In D. M. Gelfand (Ed.), **Social learning in childhood: Readings in theory and application** (2nd ed.). Monterey, CA: Brooks/Cole.

Mahoney, M. J., & Mahoney, K. (1976a). **Permanent weight control: A total solution to the dieter's dilemma.** New York: Norton.

Mahoney, M. J., & Mahoney, K. (1976b). Treatment of obesity: A clinical exploration. In B. J. Williams, S. Martin, & J. P. Foreyt (Eds.), **Obesity: Behavioral approaches to dietary management.** New York: Brunner/Mazel.

Maloney, M., & Klykylo, W. M. (1983). An overview of anorexia nervosa, bulimia, and obesity in children and adolescents. **Journal of the American Academy of Child Psychology, 22,** 99–107.

Manning, W. H., Trutna, P. A., & Shaw, C. K. (1976). Verbal versus tangible reward for children who stutter. **Journal of Speech and Hearing Disorders, 41,** 52–62.

Marston, M. (1970). Compliance with medical regi-

mens: A review. **Nursing Research, 19,** 312–323.

Mather, P. L., & Black, K. N. (1984). Heredity and environmental influences on preschool twins' language skills. **Developmental Psychology, 20,** 303–308.

Mayer, J. (1975). Obesity during childhood. In M. Winick (Ed.), **Childhood obesity.** New York: Wiley.

McConaghy, N. (1969). A controlled trial of imipramine, amphetamine, pad-and-bell conditioning and random wakening in the treatment of nocturnal enuresis. **Medical Journal of Australia, 2,** 237–239.

Mendelson, W. B., Gillin, J. C., & Wyatt, R. J. (1977). **Human sleep and its disorders.** New York: Plenum Press.

Milisen, R. (1971). The incidence of speech disorders. In L. E. Travis (Ed.), **Handbook of speech pathology and audiology.** New York: Appleton-Century-Crofts.

Monello, L. F., & Mayer, J. (1963). Obese adolescent girls: An unrecognized "minority" group? **The American Journal of Clinical Nutrition, 13,** 35–39.

Moore, W. H., Jr., & Lang, M. K. (1977). Alpha symmetry over the right and left hemispheres of stutterers and control subjects preceding massed oral readings: A preliminary investigation. **Perceptual and Motor Skills, 44,** 223–230.

Mowrer, D. E., Baker, R. L., & Schutz, R. E. (1968). Operant procedures in the control of speech articulation. In H. N. Sloane, Jr., & B. D. MacAuley (Eds.), **Operant procedures and remedial speech and language training.** Boston: Houghton Mifflin.

Mowrer, O. H., & Mowrer, W. M. (1938). Enuresis: A method for its study and treatment. **American Journal of Orthopsychiatry, 8,** 436–459.

Mullins, A. G. (1958). The prognosis in juvenile obesity. **Archives of Diseases in Childhood, 33,** 307–314.

Muuss, R. E. (1985). Adolescent eating disorder: Anorexia nervosa. **Adolescence, 20,** 525–536.

Nathan, S., & Pisula, D. (1970). Psychological observations of obese adolescents during starvation treatment. **Journal of the American Academy of Child Psychiatry, 9,** 722–740.

Nettelbeck, T., & Langeluddecke, P. (1979). Dry-bed training without an enuresis machine. **Behaviour Research and Therapy, 17,** 403–404.

Nigram, R. (1983). Role of classroom teacher in helping a child with misarticulation. **Hearing Aid Journal, 4,** 15–17.

Olswang, L. B., & Bain, B. A. (1985). The natural occurrence of generalization during articulation treatment. **Journal of Communication Disorders, 18,** 109-129.

Parkes, J. D., & Fenton, G. W. (1973). Levo (−) amphetamine and dextro (+) amphetamine in the treatment of narcolepsy. **Journal of Neurology, Neurosurgery and Psychiatry, 36,** 1076-1081.

Peake, T., & Borduin, C. (1977). Combining systems, behavioral and analytical approaches to the treatment of anorexia nervosa: A case study. **Family Therapy, 4,** 49-56.

Perkins, W. H. (1977). **Speech pathology: An applied behavioral science** (2nd ed.), St. Louis: C. V. Mosby.

Perkins, W. H., Rudas, J., Johnson, L., & Bell, J. (1976). Stuttering: Discoordination of phonation with articulation and respiration. **Journal of Speech and Hearing Research, 19,** 509-522.

Powers, M. H. (1971). Functional disorders of articulation—symptomatology and etiology. In L. E. Travis (Ed.), **Handbook of speech pathology and audiology.** New York: Appleton-Century-Crofts.

Pyle, R. L., Mitchell, J. E., & Eckert, E. D. (1981). Bulimia: A report of 34 cases. **Journal of Clinical Psychiatry, 42,** 60-64.

Quay, H. C., & Werry, J. S. (Eds.). (1979). **Psychopathological disorders of childhood** (2nd ed.). New York: Wiley.

Rau, J. H., & Green, R. S. (1975). Compulsive eating: A neuropsychologic approach to certain eating disorders. **Comprehensive Psychiatry, 3,** 223-231.

Richardson, S. O. (1983). Differential diagnosis in delayed speech and language development. **Folia Phoniatrica, 35,** 66-80.

Rimm, I. J., & Rimm, A. A. (1976). Association between juvenile onset obesity and severe adult obesity in 73,532 women. **American Journal of Public Health, 6,** 479-481.

Rivlin, R. S. (1975). The use of hormones in the treatment of obesity. In M. Winick (Ed.), **Childhood obesity.** New York: Wiley.

Rohner, J. J., & Sanford, E. J. (1975). Imipramine toxicity. **Journal of Urology, 114,** 402-403.

Rosen, J. C., & Leitenberg, H. (1982). Bulimia nervosa: Treatment with exposure and response prevention. **Behavior Therapy, 13,** 117-124.

Russell, G. (1979). Bulimia nervosa: An ominous variant of anorexia nervosa. **Psychological Medicine, 9,** 429-448.

Ryan, B. P. (1971a). Operant procedures applied to stuttering therapy for children. **Journal of Speech and Hearing Disorders, 36,** 264-280.

Ryan, B. P. (1971b). A study of the effectiveness of the S-Pack program in the elimination of frontal lisping

behavior in third-grade children. **Journal of Speech and Hearing Disorders, 36,** 390-396.

Schaefer, C. E., & Millman, H. L. (1977). **Therapies for children: A handbook of effective treatments for problem behaviors.** San Francisco: Jossey-Bass.

Schaffer, H. R., Hepburn, A., & Collis, G. M. (1983). Verbal and nonverbal aspects of mothers' directives. **Journal of Child Language, 10,** 337-355.

Schiefelbusch, R. L. (Ed.). (1978). **Bases of language intervention.** Baltimore: University Park Press.

Schilson, E. A., & Van Valkenburg, M. (1984). Childhood obesity: A family systems perspective. **Family Therapy, 11,** 105-113.

Schlesier-Stropp, B. (1984). Bulimia: A review of the literature. **Psychological Bulletin, 95,** 247-257.

Scott, H. W., Dean, R. H., Shull, H. J., & Gluck, F. W. (1976). Metabolic complications of jejunoileal bypass operations for morbid obesity. **Annual Review of Medicine, 27,** 397-405.

Sheehan, J. G., & Costly, M. S. (1977). A reexamination of the role of heredity in stuttering. **Journal of Speech and Hearing Disorders, 42,** 47-49.

Shenker, R. C., & Finn, P. (1985). An evaluation of the effects of supplemental "fluency" training during maintenance. **Journal of Fluency Disorders, 10,** 257-267.

Shipley, E. F., Kuhn, I. F., & Madden, E. C. (1983). Mothers' use of superordinate category terms. **Journal of Child Language, 10,** 571-588.

Silverman, F. H. (1976). Communicative success: A reinforcer of stuttering? **Perceptual and Motor Skills, 43,** 398.

Slorach, N., & Noehr, B. (1973). Dichotic listening in stuttering and dyslalic children. **Cortex, 9,** 295-300.

Smolak, L., & Weinraub, M. (1983). Maternal speech: Strategy or response? **Journal of Child Language, 10,** 369-380.

Sommers, R. K., Brady, W. A., & Moore, W. H., Jr. (1975). Dichotic ear preferences of stuttering children and adults. **Perceptual and Motor Skills, 41,** 931-938.

Stangler, R. S., & Printz, A. M. (1980). DSM-III: Psychiatric diagnosis in a university population. **American Journal of Psychiatry, 137,** 937-940.

Starfield, B., & Mellits, E. D. (1968). Increase in functional bladder capacity and improvements in enuresis. **Journal of Pediatrics, 72,** 483-487.

Straughn, J. H., Potter, W. K., Jr., & Hamilton, S. H., Jr. (1965). The behavioral treatment of an elective mute. **Journal of Child Psychology and Psychiatry and Allied Disciplines, 6,** 125-130.

Strober, M. (1981). The significance of bulimia in juvenile anorexia nervosa: An exploration of possible etiologic factors. **International Journal of Eating Disorders, 1,** 28-43.

Strober, M. (1984). Stressful life events associated with bulimia in anorexia nervosa. **International Journal of Eating Disorders, 3,** 1-13.

Stuart, R. B. (1967). Behavioural control of overeating. **Behaviour Research and Therapy, 5,** 357-365.

Stunkard, A. J. (1979). Behavioral medicine and beyond: The example of obesity. In O. F. Pomerleau & J. P. Brady (Eds.), **Behavioral medicine: Theory and practice.** Baltimore: Williams & Wilkins.

Stunkard, A. J., & Burt, V. (1967). Obesity and the body image: II. Age at onset of disturbances in the body image. **American Journal of Psychiatry, 123,** 1443-1447.

Stunkard, A. J., & Pestka, J. (1962). The physical activity of obese girls. **American Journal of Diseases of Children, 103,** 812-817.

Swift, W. J. (1985). Assessment of the bulimic patient. **American Journal of Orthopsychiatry, 55,** 384-396.

Tiegerman, E. (1985). The social bases of language acquisition. In D. K. Bernstein & E. Tiegerman (Eds.), **Language and communication disorders in children.** Columbus, OH: Charles E. Merrill.

Tolstrup, K. (1975). The treatment of anorexia nervosa in childhood and adolescence. **Journal of Child Psychology and Psychiatry and Allied Disciplines, 16,** 75-78.

Tramer, M. (1934). Elektiver mutismus bei kindern. **Zeitschrift für Kinderpsychiatrie, 1,** 30-35.

Turner, R. K. (1973). Conditioning treatment of nocturnal enuresis. In I. Kolvin, R. C. MacKeith, & S. R. Meadow (Eds.), **Bladder control and enuresis.** Philadelphia: J. B. Lippincott.

Turner, S. M., Hersen, M., Bellack, A. S., & Wells, K. C. (1979). Behavioural treatment of obsessive-compulsive neurosis. **Behavioural Research and Therapy, 17,** 95-106.

U.S. Department of Education. (1985). **To assure the free appropriate public education of all handicapped children: Seventh annual report to Congress on the implementation of the Education of the Handicapped Act.** Washington, DC: U.S. Government Printing Office.

Van Buskirk, S. S. (1977). A two-phase perspective on the treatment of anorexia nervosa. **Psychological Bulletin, 84,** 529-538.

Van Der Kooy, D., & Webster, C. D. (1975). A rapidly effective behavior modification program for an electively mute child. **Journal of Behavior Therapy and Experimental Psychiatry, 6,** 149-152.

Van Riper, C., & Emerick, L. (1984). **Speech correction: An introduction to speech pathology and audiology.** Englewood Cliffs, NJ: Prentice-Hall.

Van Tassel, E. B. (1985). The relative influence of child and environmental characteristics on sleep disturbances in the first and second years of life. **Journal of Developmental and Behavioral Pediatrics, 6,** 81-85.

VanThorre, M. D., & Vogel, F. X. (1985). The presence of bulimia in high school females. **Adolescence, 20,** 45-51.

Varni, J. W., & Banis, H. T. (1985). Behavior therapy techniques applied to eating, exercise, and diet modification in childhood obesity. **Journal of Developmental and Behavioral Pediatrics, 6,** 367-372.

Verhulst, F. C., Van Der Lee, J. H., Akkerhuis, G. W., Sanders-Woudstra, J. A. R., Timmer, F. C., & Donkhorst, I. D. (1985). The prevalence of nocturnal enuresis: Do DSM-III criteria need to be changed? A brief research report. **Journal of Child Psychology and Psychiatry and Allied Disciplines, 26,** 989-993.

Wadden, T. A., Stunkard, A. J., & Brownell, K. D. (1983). Very low calorie diets: Their efficacy, safety, and future. **Annals of Internal Medicine, 99,** 675-684.

Wadden, T. A., Stunkard, A. J., Brownell, K. D., & Day, S. C. (1984). Treatment of obesity by behavior therapy and very low calorie diet: A pilot investigation. **Journal of Consulting and Clinical Psychology, 52,** 692-694.

Wagner, W. G., & Matthews, R. (1985). The treatment of nocturnal enuresis: A controlled comparison of two models of urine alarm. **Journal of Developmental and Behavioral Pediatrics, 6,** 22-26.

Wahler, R. G., Sperling, K. A., Thomas, M. R., & Teeter, W. C. (1970). The modification of childhood stuttering: Some response-response relationships. **Journal of Experimental Child Psychology, 9,** 411-428.

Weil, W. B., Jr. (1977). Current controversies in childhood obesity. **Journal of Pediatrics, 91,** 175-187.

Weiss, C. D., & Lillywhite, H. S. (1976). **A handbook for prevention and early intervention: Communicative disorders.** St. Louis: C. V. Mosby.

Wermuth, B. M., Davis, K. L., Hollister, L. E., & Stunkard, A. J. (1977). Phenytoin treatment of the binge-eating syndrome. **American Journal of Psychiatry, 134,** 1249-1253.

Werry, J. S., & Bull, D. (1975). Anorexia nervosa: A case study using behavior therapy. **Journal of the American Academy of Child Psychiatry, 14,** 646-651.

White, J. J., Cheek, D., & Haller, J. A. (1974). Small

bowel bypass is applicable for adolescents with morbid obesity. **American Surgeon, 40,** 704–708.

White, W. C., & Boskind-White, M. (1981). An experiential-behavioral approach to the treatment of bulimiarexia. **Psychotherapy: Theory, Research, and Practice, 18,** 501–507.

Williamson, D. A., Sanders, S. H., Sewell, W. R., Haney, J. N., & White D. (1977). The behavioral treatment of elective mutism: Two case studies. **Journal of Behavior Therapy and Experimental Psychiatry, 8,** 143–149.

Williamson, D. A., Sewell, W. R., Sanders, S. H., Haney, J. N., & White D. (1977). The treatment of reluctant speech using contingency management procedures. **Journal of Behavior Therapy and Experimental Psychiatry, 8,** 151–156.

Winick, M. (Ed.). (1975). **Childhood obesity.** New York: Wiley.

Wohl, M. T. (1968). The electric metronome—an evaluative study. **British Journal of Disorders of Communication, 3,** 89–98.

Wolfe, V. I., & Irwin, R. B. (1975). Feedback modification in instrumental conditioning of articulation. **Perceptual and Motor Skills, 40,** 770.

Wooley, S. C., Wooley, O. W., & Dyrenforth, S. R. (1979). Theoretical, practical, and social issues in behavioral treatments of obesity. **Journal of Applied Behavior Analysis, 12,** 3–25.

Wright, L. (1980). The standardization of compliance procedures, or the mass production of ugly ducklings. **American Psychologist, 35,** 119–122.

Wulbert, M., Nyman, B. A., Snow, D., & Owen, Y. (1973). The efficacy of stimulus fading and contingency management in the treatment of elective mutism: A case study. **Journal of Applied Behavior Analysis, 6,** 435–441.

Yates, A. J. (1970). **Behavior therapy.** New York: Wiley.

CHAPTER 8

Abrams, A. L. (1968). Delayed and irregular maturation versus minimal brain injury: Recommendations for a change in current nomenclature. **Clinical Pediatrics, 7,** 344–349.

Adelman, H. S. (1979). Diagnostic classification of LD: Research and ethical perspectives as related to practice. **Learning Disability Quarterly, 2**(3), 5–16.

Ahn, H., Prichep, L., John, E. R., Baird, H., Trepetin, M., & Kaye, H. (1980). Developmental equations reflect brain dysfunctions. **Science, 210,** 1259–1262.

Ausubel, D. P., Sullivan, E. V., & Ives, S. W. (1980). **Theory and problems of child development** (3rd ed.). New York: Grune & Stratton.

Ayres, A. J. (1975). Sensorimotor foundations of academic ability. In W. M. Cruickshank & D. P. Hallahan (Eds.), **Perceptual and learning disabilities in children: Research and theory** (Vol. 2). Syracuse, NY: Syracuse University Press.

Bauer, R. H. (1977). Memory processes in children with learning disabilities: Evidence for deficient rehearsal. **Journal of Experimental Child Psychology, 24,** 415–430.

Baxley, G., & LeBlanc, J. M. (1976). The hyperactive child: Characteristics, treatment, and evaluation of research design. In H. Reese (Ed.), **Advances in child development and behavior** (Vol. 11). New York: Academic Press.

Benton, A. L., & Pearl, D. (Eds.). (1978). **Dyslexia:** **An appraisal of current knowledge.** New York: Oxford University Press.

Bryan, T. H. (1974). Learning disabilities: A new stereotype. **Journal of Learning Disabilities, 7,** 304–309.

Bryan, T. H., & Bryan, J. H. (1982). **Understanding learning disabilities.** (3rd ed.). Palo Alto, CA: Mayfield.

Chinn, P. L. (1979). **Child health maintenance: Concepts in family-centered care** (2nd ed.). St. Louis: C.V. Mosby.

Cott, A. (1972). Megavitamins: The orthomolecular approach to behavioral disorders and learning disabilities. **Academic Therapy, 7,** 245–257.

Cruickshank, W. M. (1972). Some issues facing the field of learning disability. **Journal of Learning Disabilities, 5,** 380–388.

Cruickshank, W. M. (1977). Myths and realities in learning disabilities. **Journal of Learning Disabilities, 10,** 51–58.

Deloach, T. F., Earl, J. M., Brown, B. S., Poplin, M. S., & Warner, M. M. (1981). LD teachers' perceptions of severely learning disabled students. **Learning Disability Quarterly, 4**(4), 343–358.

Denckla, M. B. (1979). Childhood learning disabilities. In K. M. Heilman & E. Valenstein (Eds.). **Clinical neuropsychology.** New York: Oxford University Press.

Deshler, D. D., Schumaker, J. B., Lenz, B. K., & Ellis, E. (1984). Academic and cognitive interventions for LD adolescents: Part II. **Journal of Learning Disabilities, 17,** 170-179.

Divorky, D. (1974). Education's latest victim: The "LD" kid. **Learning, 3,** 20-25.

Drew, C. J., & Altman, R. (1970). Effects of input organization and material difficulty on free recall. **Psychological Reports, 27,** 335-337.

Dumaresq, M. (1976). **The relationship of stimulus organization, response cuing, and practice to the free recall performance of learning disabled children.** Unpublished doctoral dissertation, University of Oregon.

Dykman, R. A., Ackerman, P. T., Clements, S. D., & Peters, J. E. (1971). Specific learning disabilities: An attentional deficit syndrome. In H. R. Myklebust (Ed.), **Progress in learning disabilities** (Vol. 2). New York: Grune & Stratton.

Education for Handicapped Children Act of 1975 (P.L. 94-142).

Feingold, B. F. (1976). Hyperkinesis and learning disabilities linked to the ingestion of artificial food colors and flavors. **Journal of Learning Disabilities, 9,** 551-559.

Finch, A. J., Jr., & Spirito, A. (1980). Use of cognitive training to change cognitive processes. **Exceptional Education Quarterly, 1,** 31-39.

Frank, J., & Levinson, H. (1973). Dysmetic dyslexia and dyspraxia. **Journal of the American Academy of Child Psychiatry, 12,** 690-701.

Freibergs, V., & Douglas, V. I. (1969). Concept learning in hyperactive and normal children. **Journal of Abnormal Psychology, 74,** 388-395.

Freston, C. W., & Drew, C. J. (1974). Verbal performance of learning disabled children as a function of input organization. **Journal of Learning Disabilities, 7,** 34-38.

Gaddes, W. H. (1980). **Learning disabilities and brain function: A neuropsychological approach.** New York: Springer-Verlag.

Gibson, E. J., Gibson, J. J., Pick, A. D., & Osser, H. (1962). A developmental study of the discrimination of letter-like forms. **Journal of Comparative and Physiological Psychology, 55,** 897-906.

Goldstein, D., & Myers, B. (1980). Cognitive lag and group differences in intelligence. **Child Study Journal, 10**(2), 119-132.

Goldstein, K. (1936). The modifications of behavior consequent to cerebral lesions. **Psychiatric Quarterly, 10,** 586-610.

Goldstein, K. (1939). **The organism.** New York: American Book.

Hall, R. J. (1980). Cognitive behavior modification and information-processing skills of exceptional children. **Exceptional Education Quarterly, 1,** 9-15.

Hallahan, D. P., & Cruickshank, W. M. (1973). **Psy-cho-educational foundations of learning disabilities.** Englewood Cliffs, NJ: Prentice-Hall.

Hallahan, D. P., Kauffman, J. M., & Ball, D. W. (1973). Selective attention and cognitive tempo of low achieving and high achieving sixth grade males. **Perceptual and Motor Skills, 36,** 579-583.

Hallahan, D. P., Kauffman, J. M., & Lloyd, J. W. (1985). **Introduction to learning disabilities** (2nd ed.). Englewood Cliffs, NJ: Prentice-Hall.

Hallgren, B. (1950). Specific dyslexia ("congenital word blindness"): A clinical and genetic study. **Acta Psychiatrica et Neurologica, 65,** 1-279.

Hammill, D. D., Leigh, J. E., McNutt, G., & Larsen, S. C. (1981). A new definition of learning disabilities. **Learning Disability Quarterly, 4**(4), 336-342.

Harber, J. R. (1981). Learning disability research: How far have we progressed? **Learning Disability Quarterly, 4,**(4), 372-381.

Hardman, M. L., Drew, C. J., & Egan, M. W. (1987). **Human exceptionality: Society, school, and family** (2nd ed.). Boston: Allyn & Bacon.

Hasazi, J. E., & Hasazi, S. E. (1972). Effects of teacher attention on digit-reversal behavior in an elementary school child. **Journal of Applied Behavior Analysis, 5,** 157-162.

Healey, J. M. (1984). Developmental deep dyslexia: Implications for the "right-hemisphere" hypothesis. **Journal of Educational Neuropsychology, 3**(1), 27-44.

Henker, B., & Whalen, C. K. (1980). The changing faces of hyperactivity: Retrospect and prospect. In C. K. Whalen & B. Henker (Eds.), **Hyperactive children: The social ecology of identification and treatment.** New York: Academic Press.

Hermann, K. (1959). **Reading disability: A medical study of word-blindness and related handicaps.** Springfield, IL: Charles C Thomas.

Home wrecker: Tyke leaves trail of terror. (1982, July 29). **The Daily Progress,** pp. A1, A8.

Houck, C. K. (1984). **Learning disabilities: Understanding concepts, characteristics, and issues.** Englewood Cliffs, NJ: Prentice-Hall.

Hynd, C. R., & Hynd, G. W. (1984). Recent neuropsychological research: Do practical implications exist? **Journal of Educational Neuropsychology, 3**(1), 1-18.

Hynd, G. W., & Cohen, M. (1983). **Dyslexia: Neuropsychological theory, research, and clinical differentiation.** New York: Grune & Stratton.

Idol-Maestas, L., Lloyd, S., & Lilly, S. (1981). A noncategorical approach to direct service and teacher education. **Exceptional Children, 48,** 213-220.

John, E. R., Ahn, H., Prichep, L., Trepetin, M., Brown, D., & Kaye, H. (1980). Developmental equations for the electroencephalogram. **Science, 210,** 1255-1258.

Kagan, J. (1983). Retrieval difficulty in reading disability. **Topics in Learning and Learning Disabilities, 3**(1), 75-83.

Kass, C. E. (1969). Introduction to learning disabilities. **Seminars in Psychiatry, 1,** 240-244.

Kavale, K., & Nye, C. (1981). Identification criteria for learning disabilities: A survey of the research literature. **Learning Disability Quarterly, 4**(4), 383-388.

Kinsbourne, M., & Caplan, P. (1979). **Children's learning and attention problems.** Boston: Little, Brown.

Kirk, S. A. (1963). Behavioral diagnosis and remediation of learning disabilities. In **Proceedings, Conference on Exploration into the Problems of the Perceptually Handicapped Child, First Annual Meeting** (Vol. 1), Chicago.

Lerner, J. S. (1981). **Children with learning disabilities** (3rd ed.). Boston: Houghton Mifflin.

Licht, B. G. (1984). Cognitive-motivational factors that contribute to the achievement of learning-disabled children. In J. K. Torgesen & G. M. Senf (Eds.), **Annual review of learning disabilities** (Vol. 2). **Published by Journal of Learning Disabilities.**

Licht, B. G., & Kistner, J. A. (1986). Motivational problems of learning-disabled children: Individual differences and their implications for treatment. In J. K. Torgesen & B. Y. L. Wong (Eds.), **Psychological and educational perspectives on learning disabilities.** New York: Academic Press.

Lloyd, J. (1980). Academic instruction and cognitive behavior modification: The need for attack strategy training. **Exception Education Quarterly, 1,** 53-65.

Lynn, R., Gluckin, N. D., & Kripke, B. (1979). **Learning disabilities: An overview of theories, approaches, and politics.** New York: Free Press.

Lockey, S. D., Sr. (1977). Hypersensitivity to tartrazine (FD & C yellow No. 5) and other dyes and additives present in foods and pharmaceutical products. **Annals of Allergy, 38,** 206-210.

McKinney, J. D., & Haskins, R. (1980). Cognitive training and the development of problem-solving strategies. **Exceptional Education Quarterly, 1,** 41-51.

Mercer, C. D. (1983). **Students with learning disabilities** (3rd ed.). Columbus, OH: Charles E. Merrill.

Myklebust, H., & Boshes, B. (1969). **Final report: Minimal brain damage in children** (U.S. Public Health Service Contract No. 108-65-142). Evanston, IL: Northwestern University.

Page-El, E., & Grossman, H. (1973). Neurologic ap-

praisal in learning disorders. **Pediatric Clinics of North America, 20,** 599-605.

Parker, T. B., Freston, C. W., & Drew, C. J. (1975). Comparison of verbal performance of normal and learning disabled children as a function of input organization. **Journal of Learning Disabilities, 8,** 386-393.

Pelham, W. E. (1983). The effects of psychostimulants on academic achievement in hyperactive and learning disabled children. **Thalamus, 3**(1), 2-48.

Pelham, W. E., & Ross, A. O. (1977). Selective attention in children with reading problems: A development study of incidental learning. **Journal of Abnormal Child Psychology, 5,** 1-8.

Ramirez, P. M. (1982). Brain-behavior relationships relevant to the neuroeducational assessment of learning disorders. **Journal of Educational Neuropsychology, 2**(1), 1-23.

Raskin, L. M. (1968). A developmental study of long-term memory in the perception of apparent movement. **Psychonomic Science, 10,** 397-398.

Raskin, L. M. (1971). Long-term perceptual memory in children with learning disabilities. **Journal of Learning Disabilities, 4,** 182-185.

Rie, H. E., Rie, E. D., Stewart, S., & Ambuel, J. P. (1976a). Effects of methylphenidate on underachieving children. **Journal of Consulting and Clinical Psychology, 44,** 250-260.

Rie, H. E., Rie, E. D., Stewart, S., & Ambuel, J. P. (1976b). Effects of Ritalin on underachieving children: A replication. **American Journal of Orthopsychiatry, 46,** 313-322.

Rosenthal, R. H., & Allen, T. W. (1978). An examination of attention, arousal, and learning dysfunctions of hyperkinetic children. **Psychological Bulletin, 85,** 689-715.

Rourke, B. P. (1976). Reading retardation in children: Developmental lag or deficit. In R. M. Knights & D. J. Bakker (Eds.), **The neuropsychology of learning disorders: Theoretical approaches.** Baltimore: University Park Press.

Simpson, R. L., King, J. D., & Drew, C. J. (1970). Free recall by retarded and nonretarded subjects as a function of input organization. **Psychonomic Science, 19,** 334.

Smith, C. R. (1983). **Learning disabilities: The interaction of learner, task, and setting.** Boston: Little, Brown.

Spring, C., & Sandoval, J. (1976). Food additives and hyperkinesis: A critical evaluation of the evidence. **Journal of Learning Disabilities, 9,** 560-569.

Strawser, S., & Weller, C. (1985). Use of adaptive behavior and discrepancy criteria to determine learning disabilities severity subtypes. **Journal of Learning Disabilities, 18**(4), 205-212.

Suiter, M. L., & Potter, R. E. (1978). The effects of

paradigmatic organization on verbal recall. **Journal of Learning Disabilities, 11,** 247–250.

Swanson, H. L. (1979). Developmental recall lag in learning-disabled children: Perceptual deficit or verbal mediation deficiency? **Journal of Abnormal Child Psychology, 7,** 199–210.

Swanson, J. M., & Kinsbourne, M. (1980). Food dyes impair performance of hyperactive children on a laboratory learning test. **Science, 207,** 1485–1487.

Sykes, D. H., Douglas, V. I., & Morgenstern, G. (1973). Sustained attention in hyperactive children. **Journal of Child Psychology and Psychiatry, 14,** 213–220.

Tarver, S. G., Hallahan, D. P., Kauffman, J. M., & Ball, D. W. (1976). Verbal rehearsal and selective attention in children with learning disabilities: A developmental lag. **Journal of Experimental Child Psychology, 22,** 375–385.

Torgesen, J. K. (1982). The learning disabled child as an inactive learner: Educational implications. **Topics in Learning and Learning Disabilities, 2,** 45–52.

Torgesen, J., & Dice, C. (1980). Characteristics of research on learning disabilities. **Journal of Learning Disabilities, 13,** 531–535.

Torgesen, J. K., & Licht, B. G. (1983). The learning disabled child as an inactive learner: Retrospect and prospects. In J. D. McKinney & L. Feagans (Eds.), **Current topics in learning disabilities** (Vol. 1). Norwood, NJ: Ablex.

U.S. Department of Education. (1985). **To assure the free appropriate public education of all handicapped children: Seventh annual report to Congress on the implementation of the Education of the Handicapped Act.** Washington, DC: U.S. Government Printing Office.

Vaughn, R. W., & Hodges, L. (1973). A statistical survey into a definition of learning disabilities: A search for acceptance. **Journal of Learning Disabilities, 6,** 658–664.

Wallace, G., & McLoughlin, J. A. (1979). **Learning disabilities: Concepts and characteristics** (2nd ed.). Columbus, OH: Charles E. Merrill.

Walmsley, S. A. (1984). Helping the learning disabled child overcome writing disabilities in the classroom. **Topics in Learning and Learning Disabilities, 3**(4), 81–90.

Wedell, K. L. (1973). **Learning and perceptuomotor disabilities in children.** New York: Wiley.

Weller, C. (1980). Discrepancy and severity in the learning disabled: A consolidated perspective. **Learning Disability Quarterly, 3,** 84–89.

Weller, C. Strawser, S., & Buchanan, M. (1985). Adaptive behavior: Designator of a continuum of severity of learning disabled individuals. **Journal of Learning Disabilities, 18**(4), 201–204.

Wender, P. H. (1973). **The hyperactive child: A handbook for parents.** New York: Crown.

Werner, H., & Strauss, A. A. (1939). Types of visuomotor activity in their relation to low and high performance ages. **Proceedings of the American Association on Mental Deficiency, 44,** 163–168.

Werner, H., & Strauss, A. A. (1941). Pathology of figure-background relation in the child. **Journal of Abnormal and Social Psychology, 36,** 236–248.

Whalen, C. K., & Henker, B. (1976). Psychostimulants and children: A review and analysis. **Psychological Bulletin, 83,** 1113–1130.

Wunderlich, R. C. (1973). Treatment of the hyperactive child. **Academic Therapy, 8,** 375–390.

Yearbook of special education (1st ed.). (1975–1976). Chicago: Marquis Who's Who.

Ysseldyke, J., & Algozzine, B. (1979). Perspectives on assessment of learning disabled students. **Learning Disability Quarterly, 4,** 3–13.

CHAPTER 9

Abel, E. L. (1984). **Fetal alcohol syndrome and fetal alcohol effects.** New York: Plenum.

Abramson, H. (Ed.). (1973). **Symposium on the functional physiopathology of the fetus and neonate** (3rd ed.). St. Louis: C. V. Mosby.

Alpern, B. P., & Boll, T. J. (1972). **The developmental profile.** Aspen, CO: Psychological Development Publications.

American Psychiatric Association. (1980). **Diagnostic and statistical manual of mental disorders** (3rd ed.). Washington, DC:) Author.

Arey, L. B. (1974). **Developmental anatomy: A textbook and laboratory manual of embryology.** (7th rev. ed.). Philadelphia: W. B. Saunders.

Babson, S. G., Pernoll, M. L., Benda, G. L., & Simpson, K. (1980). **Diagnosis and management of the fetus and neonate at risk** (4th ed.). St. Louis: C. V. Mosby.

Baer, D. M., & Guess, D. (1971). Receptive training of adjectival inflections in mental retardates. **Journal of Applied Behavior Analysis, 4,** 129–139.

Baer, D. M., Peterson, R. F., & Sherman, J. A.

(1967). The development of imitation by reinforcing behavioral similarity to a model. **Journal of the Experimental Analysis of Behavior, 10,** 405–416.

Baird, P. A., & Sandovnick, A. D. (1985). Mental retardation in over half-a-million consecutive live-births: An epidemiological study. **American Journal of Mental Deficiency, 89,** 323–330.

Baird, P. A., & Sandovnick, A. D. (1986). Reply to Richardson, Koller, and Katz. **American Journal of Mental Deficiency, 90,** 451–452.

Balinsky, B. I. (1981). **An introduction to embryology** (5th ed.). Philadelphia: W. B. Saunders.

Bank-Mikkelsen, N. E. (1969). A metropolitan area in Denmark, Copenhagen. In R. B. Kugel & W. Wolfensberger (Eds.), **Changing patterns in residential services for the mentally retarded.** Washington, DC: President's Committee on Mental Retardation.

Baumeister, A. A., & Hamlett, C. L. (1986). A national survey of state-sponsored programs to prevent fetal alcohol syndrome. **Mental Retardation, 24,** 169–173.

Berman, J. L., & Ford, R. (1970). Intelligence quotients and intelligence loss in patients with phenylketonuria and some variant states. **Journal of Pediatrics, 77,** 764–770.

Binet, A., & Simon, T. (1905). Méthodes nouvelles pour le diagnostic du niveau intellectual des anormaux. **L'Anneé psychologique, 11,** 191–244.

Birch, H. G., Richardson, S. A., Baird, D., Horobin, G., & Illsley, R. (1970). **Mental subnormality in the community: A clinical and epidemiological study.** Baltimore: Williams & Wilkins.

Birenbaum, A., & Re, M. A. (1979). Resettling mentally retarded adults in the community—almost 4 years later. **American Journal of Mental Deficiency, 83,** 323–329.

Blatt, B., & Kaplan, F. (1966). **Christmas in purgatory.** Boston: Allyn & Bacon.

Burt, R. A. (1976). Authorizing death for anomalous newborns. In A. Milunsky & G. J. Annas (Eds.), **Genetics and the law.** New York: Plenum.

Carr, E., Schreibman, L., & Lovaas, O. I. (1975). Control of echolalic speech in psychotic children. **Journal of Abnormal Child Psychology, 3,** 331–351.

Carter, C. H. (1978). **Medical aspects of mental retardation** (2nd ed.). Springfield, IL: Charles C Thomas.

Carter, C. H. (1979). **Handbook of mental retardation syndromes** (3rd rev. ed.) Springfield, IL: Charles C Thomas.

Cegelka, W. J., & Tyler, J. L. (1970). The efficacy of special class placement for the mentally retarded in proper perspective. **Training School Bulletin, 67,** 33–68.

Centers for Disease Control. (1984). Fetal alcohol syndrome: Public Awareness Week. **Morbidity and Mortality Weekly Report, 33,** 1–2.

Cheseldine, S., & McConkey, R. (1979). Parental speech to young Down's syndrome children: An intervention study. **American Journal of Mental Deficiency, 83,** 612–620.

Chess, S., Korn, S. J., & Fernandez, P. B. (1971). **Psychiatric disorders of children with congenital rubella.** New York: Brunner/Mazel.

Chinn, P. C., Drew, C. J., & Logan, D. R. (1979). **Mental retardation: A life cycle approach** (2nd ed.). St. Louis: C. V. Mosby.

Cooper, L. Z., & Krugman, S. (1966). Diagnosis and management: Congenital rubella. **Pediatrics, 37,** 335–338.

Cooper, T., Wilton, K., & Glynn, T. (1985). Prevalence, school progress and referral of mildly retarded children in regular classes. **Exceptional Children, 52,** 5–11.

Cox, D. R., & Epstein, C. J. (1985). Comparative gene mapping of human chromosome 21 and mouse chromosome 16. **Annals of the New York Academy of Sciences, 450,** 169–177.

Deno, E. (1970). Special education as developmental capital. **Exceptional Children, 37,** 229–237.

Doll, E. A. (1953). **The measurement of social competence: A manual for the Vineland Social Maturity Scale.** Minneapolis: Educational Testing Bureau.

Dorland's illustrated medical dictionary (25th ed.). (1974). Philadelphia: W. B. Saunders.

Drew, C. J., & Buchanan, M. L. (1979). Research on teacher education: Status and need. **Teacher Education and Special Education, 2**(2), 50–55.

Drew, C. J., Logan, D. R., & Hardman, M. L. (1984). **Mental retardation: A life cycle approach.** St. Louis: C. V. Mosby.

Duff, R., & Campbell, A. (1973). Moral and ethical dilemmas in the special-care nursery. **New England Journal of Medicine, 289,** 890–894.

Edgerton, R. B. (1967). **The cloak of competence.** Berkeley: University of California Press.

Edgerton, R. B. (1984). **Lives in process.** Washington, DC: American Association on Mental Deficiency.

Edgerton, R. B., & Bercovici, S. M. (1976). The cloak of competency: Years later. **American Journal of Mental Deficiency, 80,** 485–497.

Education for All Handicapped Children Act of 1975 (P.L. 94-142).

Epstein, C. J., Cox, D. R., & Epstein, L. B. (1985). Mouse trisomy 16: An animal model of human trisomy 21 (Down syndrome). **Annals of the New York Academy of Sciences, 450,** 157–168.

Garber, H., & Heber, R. F. (1977). The Milwaukee Project: Indications of the effectiveness of early intervention in preventing mental retardation. In P.

Mittler (Ed.), **Research to practice in mental retardation: Care and intervention** (Vol. 1). Baltimore: University Park Press.

Garcia, E., Guess, D., & Byrnes, J. (1973). Development of syntax in a retarded girl using procedures of imitation, reinforcement, and modelling. **Journal of Applied Behavior Analysis, 6,** 299–310.

Goldstein, H., Moss, J. W., & Jordan, L. J. (1965). **The efficacy of special class training on the development of mentally retarded children.** (U.S. Office of Education, Cooperative Research Program, Project No. 619). Urbana: University of Illinois, Institute for Research on Exceptional Children.

Grossman, H. J. (Ed.). (1977). **Manual on terminology and classification in mental retardation.** Washington, DC: American Association on Mental Deficiency.

Grossman, H. J. (1983). **Classification in mental retardation.** Washington, DC: American Association on Mental Deficiency.

Hardman, M. L. (1980). The role of congress in decisions related to the withholding of medical treatment from seriously ill newborns. **Journal of the Association for Persons with Severe Handicaps, 9**(1), 3–7.

Hardman, M. L., & Drew, C. J. (1978). Life management practices with the profoundly retarded: Issues of euthanasia and withholding treatment. **Mental Retardation, 16,** 390–396.

Hardman, M. L., & Drew, C. J. (1980). Parent consent and the practice of withholding treatment from the severely defective newborn. **Mental Retardation, 18,** 165–169.

Hardy, J. B., McCracken, G. B., Jr., Gilkeson, M. R., & Sever, J. L. (1969). Adverse fetal outcome following maternal rubella after the first trimester of pregnancy. **Journal of the American Medical Association, 207,** 2414–2420.

Hayden, A. H., & McGinness, G. D. (1977). Bases for early intervention. In E. Sontag (Ed.), **Educational programming for the severely and profoundly handicapped.** Reston, VA: Council for Exceptional Children.

Heber, R. F. (1959). A manual on terminology and classification in mental retardation. **American Journal of Mental Deficiency, 64** (Monograph Supplement).

Heber, R. F., Dever, R. B., & Conry, J. (1968). The influence of environmental and genetic variables on intellectual development. In H. J. Prehm, L. A. Hamerlynck, & J. E. Crosson (Eds.), **Behavioral research in mental retardation.** Eugene: University of Oregon Press.

Heber, R. F., & Garber, H. (1971). An experiment in the prevention of cultural-familial mental retardation. In D. A. Primrose (Ed.), **Proceedings of the Second Congress of the International Associ-**

ation for the Scientific Study of Mental Deficiency. Warsaw: Polish Medical Publishers.

Hellman, L. M., & Pritchard, J. A. (1971). **Williams obstetrics** (14th ed.). New York: Appleton-Century-Crofts.

Jackson v. Indiana. (1972). 406 U.S. 715.

Kindred, M., Cohen, J., Penrod, D., & Shaffer, T. (Eds.). (1976). **The mentally retarded citizen and the law.** New York: Free Press.

Knox, W. E. (1972). Phenylketonuria. In J. B. Stanbury, D. S. Wyngaarden, & D. S. Frederickson (Eds.), **The metabolic basis of inherited disease** (3rd ed.). New York: McGraw-Hill.

Koch, J. (1979). **International summit on prevention of mental retardation from biomedical causes** (Document No. HE 23.102:D62). Washington, DC: U.S. Government Printing Office.

Koops, B. L., Morgan, L. J., & Battaglia, F. C. (1982). Neonatal mortality risk in relation to birth weight and gestational age: Update. **Journal of Pediatrics, 101,** 972.

Lemkau, P. V., & Imre, P. D. (1969). Results of a field epidemiologic study. **American Journal of Mental Deficiency, 73,** 858–863.

Lindsjö, A. (1974). Down's syndrome in Sweden: An epidemiological study of a three-year material. **Acta Paediatrica Scandinavica, 63,** 571–576.

Lovaas, O. I. (1976). A program for the establishment of speech in psychotic children. In L. Wing (Ed.), **Early childhood autism.** Oxford: Pergamon Press.

MacMillan, D. L. (1982). **Mental retardation in school and society** (2nd ed.). Boston: Little, Brown.

MacMillian, D. L., & Semmel, M. I. (1977). Evaluation of mainstreaming programs. **Focus on Exceptional Children, 6**(4), 8–14.

Menkes, J. H., Hurst, P. L., & Craig, J. M. (1954). A new syndrome: Progressive familial infantile cerebral dysfunction associated with an unusual urinary substance. **Pediatrics, 14,** 462–467.

Mercer, J. R. (1973). **Labelling the mentally retarded.** Berkeley: University of California Press.

Miller, W. A., & Erbe, R. W. (1978). Prenatal diagnosis of genetic disorders. **Southern Medical Journal, 71,** 201–207.

Mikkelsen, M., & Stene, J. (1970). Genetic counseling in Down's syndrome. **Human Heredity, 20,** 457–464.

Murdock, J. Y., Garcia, E. E., & Hardman, M. L. (1977). Generalizing articulation training with trainable mentally retarded subjects. **Journal of Applied Behavior Analysis, 10,** 717–733.

Nirje, B. (1969). The normalization principle and its human management implications. In R. B. Kugel & W. Wolfensberger (Eds.), **Changing patterns in residential services for the mentally retarded.**

Washington, DC: President's Committee on Mental Retardation.

Ohwaki, S., & Stayton, S. E. (1978). The relation of length of institutionalization to the intellectual functioning of the profoundly retarded. **Child Development, 49,** 105-109.

Orelove, F. P., & Hanley, C. D. (1977). **School accessibility survey.** Unpublished manuscript, University of Illinois.

Palyo, W. J., Cooke, T. P., Schuler, A. L., & Apolloni, T. (1979). Modifying echolalic speech in preschool children: Training and generalization. **American Journal of Mental Deficiency, 83,** 480-489.

Penrose, L. S. (1967). The effects of change in maternal age distribution upon the incidence of mongolism. **Journal of Mental Deficiency Research, 11**(1), 54-57.

Polloway, E. A. (1984). The integration of mildly retarded students in the schools: A historical overview. **Remedial and Special Education, 5**(4), 18-24.

President's Committee on Mental Retardation. (1977). **Mental retardation: Past and present.** Washington, DC: U.S. Government Printing Office.

Ramey, C. T., & Campbell, F. A. (1977). Prevention of developmental retardation in high risk children. In P. Mittler (Ed.), **Research to practice in mental retardation: Care and intervention** (Vol. 1). Baltimore: University Park Press.

Ramey, C. T., & Campbell, F. A. (1979a). Compensatory education for disadvantaged children. **School Review, 87,** 171-189.

Ramey, C. T., & Campbell, F. A. (1979b). Early childhood education for disadvantaged children: Effects on psychological processes. **American Journal of Mental Deficiency, 81,** 318-324.

Richards, B. W. (1967). The effect of trends in age at childbirth on incidence and chromosomal type. **Journal of Mental Subnormality, 13,** 3-13.

Richardson, S. A., Koller, H., & Katz, M. (1986). Comments on Baird and Sandovnick's "Mental retardation in over half-a-million consecutive livebirths: An epidemiological study." **American Journal of Mental Deficiency, 90,** 449-450.

Risley, T. R., & Wolf, M. M. (1967). Establishing functional speech in echolalic children. **Behaviour Research and Therapy, 5,** 73-88.

Robinson, N. M., & Robinson, H. B. (1976). **The mentally retarded child: A psychological approach** (2nd ed.). New York: McGraw-Hill.

Scheerenberger, R. C. (1983). **A history of mental retardation.** Baltimore: Paul H. Brookes.

Schumaker, J., & Sherman, J. A. (1970). Training generative verb usage by imitation and reinforcement procedures. **Journal of Applied Behavior Analysis, 3,** 273-287.

Sever, J. L. (1970). Infectious agents and fetal disease. In H. A. Waisman, & G. R. Kerr (Eds.), **Fetal growth and development.** New York: McGraw-Hill.

Silberberg, D. H. (1969). Maple syrup urine disease metabolites studied in cerebellum cultures. **Journal of Neurochemistry, 16,** 1141-1146.

Snyderman, S. E., Norton, P. M., Roitman, E., & Holt, L. E., Jr. (1964). Maple syrup urine disease with particular reference to dietotherapy. **Pediatrics, 34,** 454-472.

Stainback, S., & Stainback, W. (1985). **Integration of students with severe handicaps into regular schools.** Reston, VA: Council for Exceptional Children.

Strickland, S. P. (1971). Can slum children learn? **American Education, 7**(6), 3-7.

Tarjan, G., Wright, S. W., Eyman, R. K., & Keeran, C. V. (1973). Natural history of mental retardation: Some aspects of epidemiology. **American Journal of Mental Deficiency, 77,** 369-379.

U.S. Department of Education. (1985). **To assure the free appropriate public education of all handicapped children: Seventh Annual Report to Congress on the implementation of the Education of the Handicapped Act.** Washington, DC: U.S. Government Printing Office.

Vacc, N. A. (1972). Long term effects of special class intervention for emotionally disturbed children. **Exceptional Children, 39,** 15-22.

Wehman, P., & Hill, J. (1982). Preparing severely handicapped youth for less restrictive environments. **Journal of the Association for the Severely Handicapped, 7**(1), 33-39.

Westall, R. G., Dancis, J., & Miller, S. (1957). Maple sugar urine disease. **American Journal of Diseases of Children, 94,** 571-572.

Wilcox, B., & Bellamy, T. (1982). **Design of high school programs for severely handicapped students.** Baltimore: Paul H. Brookes.

World Health Organization. (1978). **International classification of diseases** (9th rev. ed., Vol. 1). Geneva: Author.

Wright, L. (1971). The theoretical and research base for a program of early stimulation care and training of premature infants. In J. Hellmuth (Ed.), **Exceptional infant** (Vol. 2). New York: Brunner/Mazel.

Wright, S. W., & Tarjan, G. (1957). Phenylketonuria. **American Journal of Diseases of Children, 93,** 405-419.

CHAPTER 10

Abraham, K. (1955). **Selected papers on psychoanalysis.** New York: Basic Books.

Ajuriaguerra, J. (1971). **Manuel de psychiatrie de l'enfant.** Paris: Masson et Cie.

American Psychiatric Association. (1980). **Diagnostic and statistical manual of mental disorders** (3rd ed.). Washington, DC: Author.

August, J., Stewart, M. A., & Tsai, L. (1981). The incidence of cognitive disabilities in the siblings of autistic children. **British Journal of Psychiatry, 138,** 416-422.

Babigian, H. M. (1980). Schizophrenia: Epidemiology. In H. I. Kaplan, A. M. Freedman, B. J. Sadock (Eds.), **Comprehensive Textbook of Psychiatry.** Baltimore: Williams & Wilkins.

Barrera, R. D., Lobato-Barrera, D., & Sulzer-Azaroff, B. (1980). A simultaneous treatment comparison of three expressive language training programs with a mute autistic child. **Journal of Autism and Developmental Disorders, 10,** 21-37.

Bartak, L., Rutter, M., & Cox, A. (1975). A comparative study of infantile autism and specific developmental receptive language disorder: 1. The children. **British Journal of Psychiatry, 126,** 127-145.

Bender, L. (1953). Childhood schizophrenia. **Psychiatric Quarterly, 27,** 663-681.

Bender, L., Corbrinik, L., Faretra, G., & Sankar, D. (1966). The treatment of childhood schizophrenia with LSD and VML. In M. Rinkel (Ed.), **Biological treatment of mental illness.** New York: L. C. Page.

Bettelheim, B. (1967). **The empty fortress.** New York: Free Press.

Bleuler, E. (1950). **Dementia praecox or the group of schizophrenias** (J. Zinkin, Trans.). New York: International Universities Press. (Original work published 1911).

Boatman, M. J., & Szurek, S. (1960). **A clinical study of childhood schizophrenia.** In D. D. Jackson (Ed.), **The etiology of schizophrenia.** New York: Basic Books.

Broen, W. E. (1973). Limiting the flood of stimulation: A protective deficit in chronic schizophrenics. In R. L. Solso (Ed.), **Contemporary issues in cognitive psychology:** *The Loyola Symposium.* Washington, DC: V. H. Winston.

Brown, J. L. (1978). Long term follow-up of 100 "atypical" children of normal intelligence. In M. Rutter & E. Schopler (Eds.), **Autism: A reappraisal of concepts and treatment.** New York: Plenum.

Campbell, M., Anderson, L. T., Deutsch, S. I., & Green, W. H. (1984). Psychopharmacological treatment of children with the syndrome of autism. **Pediatric Annals, 13,** 309-316.

Campbell, M., Hardesty, A. S., Burdock, E. I. (1978). Demographic and perinatal profile of 105 autistic children: A preliminary report. **Psychopharmacology Bulletin, 14,** 36-39.

Cantwell, D. P., Baker, L., & Rutter, M. (1978). Family factors. In M. Rutter & E. Schopler (Eds.), **Autism: A reappraisal of concepts and treatment.** New York: Plenum.

Carr, E. G. (1977). The motivation of self-injurious behavior: A review of some hypotheses. **Psychological Bulletin, 84,** 800-816.

Carr, E. G. (1979). Teaching autistic children to use sign language: Some research issues. **Journal of Autism and Developmental Disabilities, 9,** 345-360.

Carr, E. G., Newsom, C. D., & Binkoff, J. A. (1976). Stimulus control of self-destructive behavior in a psychotic child. **Journal of Abnormal Child Psychology, 4,** 139-153.

Carr, E. G., Schreibman, L., & Lovaas, O. I. (1975). Control of echolalic speech in psychotic chldren. **Journal of Abnormal Child Psychology, 3,** 331-351.

Chess, S. (1977). Follow-up report on autism in congenital rubella. **Journal of Autism and Childhood Schizophrenia, 7,** 69-81.

Chess, S., Korn, S. J., & Fernandez, P. B. (1971). **Psychiatric disorders of children with congenital rubella.** New York: Brunner/Mazel.

Churchill, D. W. (1971). Effects of success and failure in psychotic children. **Archives of General Psychiatry, 25,** 208-214.

Cohen, D. J., Volkmar, F. R., & Paul, R. (1986). Issues in the diagnoses and phenomenology of pervasive developmental disorders. **Journal of the American Academy of Child Psychiatry, 25,** 158-161.

Coleman, M., & Gillberg, C. (1985). **The biology of autistic syndromes.** New York: Praeger.

Cox, A., Rutter, M., Newman, S., & Bartak, L. (1975). A comparative study of infantile autism and specific developmental receptive language disorder: II. Parental characteristics. **British Journal of Psychiatry, 126,** 146-159.

Creak, M. (1961). Schizophrenic syndrome in childhood. Progess report of the the the working party. **British Medical Journal, 2,** 889-890.

Creak, M. (1963). Childhood psychosis: A review of 100 cases. **British Journal of Psychiatry, 109,** 84-89.

Dawson, G., & Galpert, L. (1984). A developmental model for facilitating the social behavior of autistic children. In E. Schopler & G. B. Mesibov (Eds.), **Social behavior in autism.** New York: Plenum.

DeMyer, M. K., Barton, S., DeMyer, W. E., Norton, J.

A., Allen, J., & Steele, R. (1973). Prognosis in autism: A follow-up study. **Journal of Autism and Childhood Schizophrenia,** 199–246.

DeMyer, M. K., Barton, S., Alpern, G. D., Kimberlin, C., Allen, J., Yang, E., & Steele, R. (1974). The measured intelligence of autistic children. **Journal of Autism and Childhood Schizophrenia, 4,** 42–60.

DeMyer, M. K., Hingtgen, J. N., & Jackson, R. K. (1981). Infantile autism reviewed: A decade of research. **Schizophrenia Bulletin, 7,** 388–451.

Devany, J., & Rincover, A. (1982). Self-stimulatory behavior and sensory reinforcement. In R. L. Koegel, A. Rincover, & A. L. Egel (Eds.), **Educating and understanding autistic children.** San Diego: College-Hill Press.

Deykin, E. Y., & MacMahon, G. (1979). Viral exposure and autism. **American Journal of Epidemiology, 109,** 628–638.

Drotar, D. A. (1978). A critique of the double-bind theory of infantile autism. **Journal of the American Academy of Child Psychiatry, 17,** 46–48.

Durand, V. M. (1982). A behavioral/pharmacological intervention for the treatment of severe self-injurious behavior. **Journal of Autism and Developmental Disorders, 12,** 243–251.

Edelson, S. M., Taubman, M. T., & Lovaas, I. O. (1983). Some social contexts of self-destructive behavior. **Journal of Abnormal Child Psychology, 11,** 299–312.

Eggers, C. (1978). Course and prognosis of childhood schizophrenia. **Journal of Autism and Childhood Schizophrenia, 8,** 21–26.

Eisenberg, L. (1957). The course of childhood schizophrenia. **Archives of Neurology and Psychiatry,** 1957, *78,* 69–83.

Eisenberg, L., & Kanner, L. (1956). Early infantile autism, 1943–1955. **American Journal of Orthopsychiatry, 26,** 556–566.

Favell, J. E., McGimsey, J. F., & Jones, M. L. (1978). The use of physical restraint in the treatment of self-injury and as a positive reinforcer. **Journal of Applied Behavior Analysis, 11,** 225–241.

Fay, W. H., & Schuler, A. L. (1980). **Emerging language in autistic children,** Baltimore: University Park Press.

Ferster, C. B. (1961). Positive reinforcement and behavioral deficits of autistic children. **Child Development, 32,** 437–456.

Ferster, C. B., & DeMyer, M. K. (1962). A method for the experimental analysis of the behavior of autistic children. **American Journal of Orthopsychiatry, 32,** 89–98.

Fish, B. (1976). Pharmacotherapy for autistic and schizophrenic children. In E. Ritvo, B. J. Freeman, & P. Tanguary (Eds.), **Autism: Diagnosis, current research and management.** New York: Spectrum.

Folstein, S., & Rutter, M. A. (1978). A twin study of individuals with infantile autism. In M. Rutter & E. Schopler (Eds.), **Autism: A reappraisal of concepts and treatment.** New York: Plenum.

Fowle, A. (1968). Atypical leukocyte pattern of schizophrenic children. **Archives of General Psychiatry, 18,** 666–679.

Foxx, R. M. (1979). **Harry: Behavioral treatment of self-abuse** [Film]. Champaign, IL: Research Press.

Foxx, R. M., & Dufrense, D. (1984). "Harry": The use of physical restraint as a reinforcer, timeout from restraint, and fading restraint in treating a self-injurious man. **Analysis and Intervention in Developmental Disabilities, 4,** 1–13.

Freeman, B. J., & Ritvo, E. R. (1984). The syndrome of autism: Establishing the diagnosis and principles of management. **Pediatric Annals, 13,** 284–296.

Freeman, B. J., Ritvo, E. R., Needleman, R., & Yokota, A. (1985). The stability of cognitive and linguistic parameters in autism: A five-year prospective study. **Journal of the American Academy of Child Psychiatry, 24,** 459–464.

Fulwiler, R. L., & Fouts, R. S. (1976). Acquisition of American Sign Language by a non-communicating autistic child. **Journal of Autism and Childhood Schizophrenia, 6,** 43–51.

Gillberg, C. (1986). Brief report: Onset at age 14 of a typical autistic syndrome. A case report of a girl with herpes simplex encephalitis. **Journal of Autism and Developmental Disorders.** 16, 369–375.

Gillberg, C., Schaumann, H. (1982). Social class and autism. *Journal of Autism and Developmental Disorders.* 12, 223–241.

Goldberg, B., & Soper, H. H. (1963). Childhood psychosis or mental retardation: A diagnostic dilemma. 1. Psychiatric and psychological aspects **Canadian Medical Association Journal, 89,** 1015–1019.

Goldfarb, W. (1964). Childhood schizophrenia. *Archives of General Psychiatry, 11,* 621–634.

Green, W. H., Campbell, M., Hardesty, A. S., Grega, D. M., Padron-Gayol, M., Shell, J., & Erlenmeyer-Kimling, L. (1984). A comparison of schizophrenic and autistic children. **Journal of the American Academy of Child Psychiatry, 23,** 399–409.

Hanson, D. R., & Gottesman, I. I. (1976). The genetics, if any, of infantile autism and childhood schizophrenia. **Journal of Autism and Childhood Schizophrenia, 6,** 209–234.

Hermelin, B., & O'Conner, N. (1970). **Psychological experiments with autistic children.** Oxford: Pergamon Press.

Horner, R. D., & Barton, E. S. (1980. Operant techniques in the analysis and modificaton of self-injurious behavior: A review. **Behavioral Research of Severe Developmental Disabilities, 1,** 61–91.

Howlin, P. (1984). An overview of social behavior in autism. In E. Schopler & G. B. Mesibov (Eds.), **Social behavior in autism.** New York: Plenum.

Howlin, P., Marchant, R., Rutter, M., Berger, M., Hersov, L., & Yule, W. (1973). A home-based approach to the treatment of autistic children. **Journal of Autism and Childhood Schizophrenia, 3,** 303–336.

Hung, D. W. (1978). Using self-stimulation as reinforcement for autistic children. **Journal of Autism and Childhood Schizophrenia, 8,** 355–366.

Hung, D. W., Rotman, Z., Cosentino, A., & McMillan, M. (1983). Cost and effectiveness of an educational program for autistic children using a systems approach. **Education and Treatment of Children, 6,** 47–68.

Hutt, C., & Ounsted, C. (1966). The biological significance of gaze aversion with particular reference to the syndrome of infantile autism. **Behavior Science, 11,** 346–356.

Hutt, S. J., & Hutt, C. (1970). **Behavior studies in psychiatry.** Oxford: Pergamon Press.

Itard, J. M. G. (1962). **The wild boy of Aveyron.** New York: Appleton-Century-Crofts. (Original work published 1799).

Jenson, W. R., Preator, K., Ballou, C., Reavis, K., & Freston, C. (1987). **Autism prescriptive checklist and interventions manual.** Portland, OR: A.S.I.E.P.

Jenson, W. R., Young, R., Clare, S., & West, R. (1986). **Effective education of autistic children: The "core behavior management approach,"** Austin: Texas Council for Children with Behavior Disorders.

Kallman, F. J., & Roth, B. (1956). Genetic aspects of preadolescent schizophrenia. **American Journal of Psychiatry, 112,** 599–606.

Kanner, L. (1943). Autistic disturbances of affective contact. **Nervous Child, 2,** 217–250.

Kanner, L. (1971a). Childhood psychosis: A historical overview. **Journal of Autism and Childhood Schizophrenia, 1,** 14–19.

Kanner, L. (1971b). Follow-up study of 11 autistic children originally reported in 1943. **Journal of Autism and Childhood Schizophrenia, 1,** 119–145.

King, P. D. (1975). Early infantile autism: Relation to schizophrenia. **Journal of the American Academy of Child Psychiatry,** 1975, *14,* 666–682.

Koegel, R. L., & Covert, A. (1972). The relationship of self-stimulation to learning in autistic children.

Journal of Applied Behavior Analysis, 5, 381–387.

Koegel, R. L., Firestone, P.B., Kramme, K. W., & Dunlap, G. (1974). Increasing spontaneous play by suppressing self-stimulation in autistic children. **Journal of Applied Behavior Analysis, 7,** 521–528.

Koegel, R. L., & Schriebman, L. (1977). Teaching autistic children to respond to simultaneous multiple cues. **Journal of Experimental Child Psychology, 24,** 299–311.

Koegel, R. L., Schreibman, L., Britten, K. R., Burke, J. C., & O'Neill, R. E. (1982). A comparison of parent training to direct child treatment. In R. L. Koegel, A. Rincover & A. L. Egel (Eds.), **Educating and understanding autistic children.** San Diego: College-Hill Press.

Kolvin, I. (1971). Psychoses in childhood—A comparative study. In M. Rutter (Ed), **Infantile autism: Concepts, characteristics and treatment.** London: Churchill Livingstone.

Kolvin, I., Garside, R., & Kidd, J. (1971). Studies in the childhood psychoses: IV. Parental personality and attitude and childhood psychoses. **British Journal of Psychiatry, 118,** 403–406.

Kolvin, I., Ounsted, C., Richardson, L., & Garside, R. (1971). Studies in the childhood psychoses. III. The family and social background in childhood psychoses. **British Journal of Psychiatry, 118,** 396–402.

Kraepelin, E. (1896). *Psychiatrie.* Leipzig: Meiner.

Lockyer, L., & Rutter, M. (1969). A five to fifteen-year follow-up study of infantile psychosis: 3. Psychological aspects. **British Journal of Psychiatry, 115,** 865–882.

Lockyer, L., & Rutter, M. (1970). Five to fifteen-year follow-up study of infantile psychosis: 4. Patterns of cognitive ability. **British Journal of Social and Clinical Psychology, 9.** 152–163.

Lord, C., & Hopkins, J. M. (1986). The social behavior of autistic children with younger and same-age non-handicapped peers. **Journal of Autism and Developmental Disorders, 16,** 249–262.

Lotter, V. (1966). Epidemiology of autistic conditions in young children: 1. Prevalence. **Social Psychiatry, 1,** 124–137.

Lotter, V. (1974). Factors related to outcome in autistic children. **Journal of Autism and Childhood Schizophrenia, 4,** 263–277.

Lotter, V. (1978). follow-up studies. In M. Rutter & E. Schopler (Eds.), **Autism: A reappraisal of concepts and treatment.** New York: Plenum.

Lovaas, I. I., Berberich, J. P., Perloff, B., & Schaeffer, B. (1966). Acquisition of imitative speech by schizophrenic children. **Science, 151,** 705–707.

Lovaas, O. I., Koegel, R. L., & Schreibman, L. (1979).

Stimulus overselectivity in autism: A review of the research. **Psychological Bulletin, 86,** 1236–1254.

Lovaas, O. I., Koegel, R. L., Simmons, J. O. & Long, J. (1973). Some generalization and follow-up measures on autistic children in behavior therapy. **Journal of Applied Behavior Analysis, 6,** 131–165.

Lovaas, O. I., & Schreibman, L. (1971). Stimulus overselectivity of autistic children in a two stimulus situation. **Behaviour Research and Therapy, 9,** 305–310.

Lovaas, O. I., Schreibman, L. & Koegel, R. L. (1974). A behavior modification approach to the treatment of autistic children. **Journal of Autism and Childhood Schizophrenia, 4,** 111–129.

Lowe, L. (1966). Families of children with early childhood schizophrenia. **Archives of General Psychiatry, 14,** 26–30.

Lubs, H. A. (1969). A marker X-chromosome. **American Journal of Human Genetics, 2,** 231–244.

Mahler, M. (1952). On child psychosis and schizophrenia: Autistic and symbiotic infantile psychosis. **Psychoanalytic Study of the Child, 7,** 286–305.

Makita, K. (1966). The age of onset of childhood schizophrenia. **Folia Psychiatrica et Neurologia Japonica, 20,** 111–121.

Margolies, P. J. (1977). Behavioral approaches to the treatment of early infantile autism: **A review. Psychological Bulletin, 84,** 249–264.

Markowitz, P. I. (1983). Autism in a child with congenital cytomegalovirus infection. **Journal of Autism and Developmental Disorders, 13,** 249–253.

Meiselman, K. C. (1971). Training chronic nonparanoid schizophrenics in dual modality attention (Doctoral dissertation, University of California). **Dissertation Abstracts International, 32,** 6654B.

Mirenda, P., Donnellan, A., & Yoder, D. (1983). Gaze behavior: A new look at an old problem. **Journal of Autism and Developmental Disorders, 13,** 397–409.

Mirsky, A. F., & Duncan, C. C. (1986). Etiology and expression of schizophrenia: Neurobiological and psychosocial factors. **Annual Review of Psychology, 37,** 291–320.

Ney, P. G., Palvesky, A. E. & Markley, J. (1971). Relative effectiveness of operant conditioning and play therapy in childhood schizophrenia. **Journal of Autism and Childhood Schizophrenia, 1,** 337–349.

Ollendick, T. H., & Hersen, M. (1983). A historical overview of child psychopathology. In T. H. Ollendick & M. Hersen (Eds.), **Handbook of child psychopathology,** New York: Plenum.

Paluszny, M. (1979). **Autism: A practical guide for parents and professionals.** Syracuse, NY: Syracuse University Press.

Park, C. C. (1982). **The siege: The first eight years of an autistic child.** Boston: Little, Brown.

Petty, L. K., Ornitz, E. M., Michelman, J. D., & Zimmerman, E. G. (1984). Autistic children who become schizophrenic. **Archives of General Psychiatry, 41,** 129–135.

Pickering, D., & Morgan, S. B. (1985). Parental ratings of treatments of self-injurious behavior. **Journal of Autism and Developmental Disorders, 15,** 303–310.

Pingree, C. B. (1984). Parents versus autism: Our pediatrician, the coach. **Pediatric Annals, 13,** 330–338.

Pollack, M. (1960). Comparison of childhood, adolescent, and adult schizophrenics. **Archives of General Psychiatry, 2,** 652–660.

Potter, H. (1933). Schizophrenia in children. **American Journal of Psychiatry, 12,** 1253–1268.

Rank, B. (1949). Adaption of psychoanalytic technique for the treatment of young children with atypical development. **American Journal of Orthopsychiatry, 19,** 130–139.

Rapoport, J. L., Rumsey, J., Duavas, R., Schwartz, R., Kessler, N., Culten, N., & Rapoport, S. I., (1983). Cerebral metabolic rate for glucose in adult autism as measured by positron emission tomography. **Journal of Blood Flow Metabolism, 1,** 264–265.

Reider, R. O., Mann, L. S., Weinberger, D., van Kammen, D. P., & Post, R. M. (1983). Computer tomographic scans in patients with schizophrenia, schizoaffective, and bipolar affective disorder. **Archives of General Psychiatry, 40,** 735–739.

Reiser, D., & Brown, J. (1964). Patterns of later development of children with infantile psychosis. **Journal of the American Academy of Child Psychiatry, 3,** 650–667.

Rett, A. (1966). **Über ein Zerebral-Atrophisches Syndrome bei Hyperammonamie.** Vienna: Bruder Hollinek.

Richer, J. M. (1978). The partial noncommunication of culture to autistic children—an application of human ethology. In M. Rutter & E. Schopler (Eds.), **Autism: A reappraisal of concepts and treatment.** New York: Plenum.

Ricks, D. M. (1972). **The beginnings of vocal communication in infants and autistic children.** Unpublished M. D. thesis, University of London.

Rimland, B. (1964). **Infantile autism.** New York: Appleton-Century-Crofts.

Rimland, B. (1973). High-dosage levels of certain vitamins in the treatment of children with severe mental disorders. In D. Hawkins & L. Pauling (Eds.), **Orthomolecular psychiatry.** San Francisco: W. H. Freeman.

Rimland, B. (1978, August). Inside the mind of an autistic savant. **Psychology Today.** pp. 68–80.

Rincover, A., Peoples, A., & Packard, D. (1976). **Sensory excitation and sensory reinforcement in psychotic children.** Paper presented at the annual meeting of the American Psychiatric Association, Washington, DC.

Rincover, A. (1978). Sensory extinction: A procedure for eliminating self-stimulatory behavior in autistic children. **Journal of Abnormal Child Psychology, 6,** 299–310.

Ritvo, E. R., Freeman, B. J., Mason-Brothers, A., Mo, A., & Ritvo, A. (1985). Concordance for the syndrome of autism in 40 pairs of afflicted twins, **American Journal of Psychiatry, 142,** 74–77.

Ritvo, E. R., Freeman, B. J., Geller, E., & Yuwiler, E. (1983). Effects of fenfluramine on 14 autistic outpatients. **Journal of the American Academy of Child Psychiatry, 22,** 549–558.

Ritvo, E. R., Mason-Brothers, A., Jenson, W. R., Freeman, B. J., Mo, M., Pingree, C. B., Petersen, P. B., & McMahon, W. M. (1986). **A report of one family with four autistic siblings and four families with three autistic siblings.** Unpublished manuscript, Neuropsychiatric Institute, UCLA School of Medicine.

Ritvo, E. R., Spence, M. A., Freeman, B. J., Mason-Brothers, A., Mo, A., & Marazita, M. L. (1985). **Evidence of autosomal recessive inheritance of autism in 46 multiple incidence families.** Unpublished manuscript, Neuropsychiatric Institute, UCLA School of Medicine.

Rosenthal, D. (1972). Three adoption studies of heredity in the schizophrenic disorders. **International Journal of Mental Health, 1,** 63–75.

Rosenthal, D., Wender, P. H., Kety, S. S., Welner, J. & Schulsinger, F. (1971). The adoptive way offspring of schizophrenics. **American Journal of Psychiatry, 128,** 307–311.

Rumsey, J. M., Rapoport, J. L., & Sceery, W. R. (1985). Autistic children as adults: Psychiatric, social, and behavioral outcomes. **Journal of the American Academy of Child Psychiatry, 24,** 465–473.

Runco, M. A., Charlop, M. H., & Schreibman, L. (1986). The occurrence of autistic children's self-stimulation as a function of familiar versus unfamiliar stimulus conditions. **Journal of Autism and Developmental Disorders, 16,** 31–44.

Rutter, M. (1970). Autistic children: Infancy to adulthood. **Seminars in Psychiatry, 12,** 435–450.

Rutter, M. (1974). The development of infantile autism. **Psychological Medicine, 4,** 147–163.

Rutter, M. (1977). Infantile autism and other psychoses. In M. Rutter & L. Hersov (Eds.), **Child psychiatry: Modern approaches.** Oxford: Blackwell.

Rutter, M. (1978a). Developmental issues and prognosis. In M. Rutter & E. Schopler (Eds.), **Autism: A reappraisal of concepts and treatment.** New York: Plenum.

Rutter, M. (1978b). Language disorder and infantile autism. In M. Rutter & E. Schopler (Eds.), **Autism: A reappraisal of concepts and treatment.** New York: Plenum.

Rutter, M., Greenfield, D., & Lockyer, L. A. (1967). A five to fifteen year follow-up study of infantile psychosis: II. Social and behavioral outcome. **British Journal of Psychiatry, 113,** 1183–1199.

Rutter, M., & Lockyer, L. A. (1967). A five to fifteen year follow-up study of infantile psychosis: I. Description of sample. **British Journal of Psychiatry, 113,** 1169–1182.

Schain, R. J., & Yannet, H. (1960). Infantile autism: An analysis of 50 cases and a consideration of certain neurophysiological concepts. **Journal of Pediatrics, 57,** 560–567.

Schopler, E. (1969). **Parents of psychotic children as scapegoats.** Paper presented at the meeting of the American Psychological Association, Washington, DC.

Schopler, E., & Dalldorf, J. (1980). Autism: Definition, diagnosis, and management. **Hospital Practice, 15,** 64–73.

Schopler, E., & Mesibov, G. B. (1984). Introduction to social behavior in autism. In E. Schopler & G. B. Mesibov (Eds.), **Social behavior in autism.** New York: Plenum.

Schopler, E., Mesibov, G., & Baker, A. (1982). Evaluation of treatment for autistic children and their parents. **Journal of the American Academy of Child Psychiatry, 21,** 262–267.

Schopler, E., & Olley, J. G., (1980). Public school programming for autistic children. **Exceptional Children, 46,** 461–463.

Schreibman, L., & Lovaas, O. I. (1973). Overselective response to social stimuli by autistic children. **Journal of Abnormal Child Psychology, 1,** 152–168.

Schreibman, L., & Mills, J. I. (1983). Infantile autism. In T. H. Ollendick & M. Hersen (Eds.), **Handbook of child psychopathology.** New York: Plenum.

Schroeder, S. R., Schroeder, C. S., Smith, B., & Dalldorf, J. (1978). Prevalence of self-injurious behaviors in a large state facility for the retarded: A three year follow-up study. **Journal of Autism and Childhood Schizophrenia, 8,** 261–269.

Selfe, L. (1977). **Nadia: A case of extraordinary drawing ability in an autistic child.** New York: Harcourt Brace Jovanovich/Harvest.

Singh, N. N., & Millichamp, J. C. (1985). Pharmacological treatment of self-injurious behavior in mentally retarded persons. **Journal of Autism and Developmental Disorders, 15,** 257–267.

Soper, S. (1987). **Factors influencing the institutional placement of mentally retarded and au-**

tistic persons. Unpublished bachelor's honors thesis, University of Utah.

Stubbs, E. C., Ash, E., & Williams, C. P. S. (1984). Autism and congenital cytomegalovirus. **Journal of Autism and Developmental Disorders, 14,** 183–189.

Stubbs, G. E., Crawford, M. L., Burger, D. R., & Vandenbark, A. A. (1977). Depressed lymphocyte responsiveness in autistic children. **Journal of Autism and Childhood Schizophrenia, 7,** 49–56.

Szurek, S. A. (1956). Psychotic episodes and psychotic maldevelopment. **American Journal of Orthopsychiatry, 26,** 519–543.

Taft, L. T., & Goldfarb, W. (1964). Prenatal and perinatal factors in childhood schizophrenia. **Developmental Medicine and Child Neurology, 6,** 32–43.

Tinbergen, N. (1974). Ethology and stress diseases. **Science, 185,** 20–26.

Tsai, L., Stewart, M. A., Faust, M., & Shook, S. (1982). Social class distribution of fathers of children enrolled in the Iowa autism program. **Journal of Autism and Developmental Disorders, 12,** 211–221.

Torrey, E. F., & Peterson, M. R. (1976). The viral hypothesis of schizophrenia. **Schizophrenia Bulletin, 2,** 136–146.

Townes, P. L. (1982). Fragile-X syndrome: A jigsaw with picture emerging. **American Journal of Diseases of Children, 136,** 389–391.

Ullmann, L., & Krasner, L. (1969). **A psychological approach to abnormal behavior.** Englewood Cliffs, NJ: Prentice-Hall.

Vaillant, G. E. (1964). Prospective prediction of schizophrenic remission. **Archives of General Psychiatry, 11,** 509–518.

Van Wagenen, L., Jenson, W. R., Worsham, N. & Petersen, P. B. (1985). The use of hand signs to teach a color discrimination to a developmentally disabled boy. **Australian Journal of Human Communication Disorders, 13,** 143–152.

Varni, J., Lovaas, O. I., Koegel, R. L., & Everett, N. L. (1979). An analysis of observational learning in autistic and normal children. **Journal of Abnormal Child Psychology, 7,** 31–43.

Walker, G. R., Hinerman, P. S., Jenson, W. R., & Petersen, P. B. (1982). Sign language as a prompt to teach a verbal "yes" and "no" discrimination to an autistic boy. *Child Behavior Therapy, 3,* 77–86.

Warren, R. P., Margaretten, C., Pace, N. C., & Foster, A. (1986). Immune abnormalities in patients with autism. **Journal of Autism and Developmental Disorders, 16,** 189–197.

Watson, M. S., Leckman, J. K., Annex, B., Breg, W. R., Boles, D., Volkmar, F. R., & Cohen, D. J. (1984). Fragile-X in a survey of 74 autistic males. *New England Journal of Medicine.*

Watt, N. F. (1974). **Patterns of childhood social development in adult schizophrenics.** Unpublished manuscript.

Watt, N. F., & Lubensky, A. W. (1976). Childhood roots of schizophrenia. **Journal of Consulting and Clinical Psychology, 44,** 363–375.

Wilhelm, H., & Lovaas, O. I. (1976). Stimulus overselectivity: A common feature in autism and mental retardation. **American Journal of Mental Deficiency, 81,** 227–241.

Wilson, S. A. (1912). Progressive lenticular degeneration: A familial nervous disease associated with cirrhosis of the liver. **Brain, 34,** 295.

Wing, J. (1968). [Review of B. Bettelheim, *The empty fortress*]. **British Journal of Psychiatry, 114,** 788–791.

Worsham, N., Jenson, W. R., & Drew, C. (1984). **Using simultaneous communication to teach counting behavior to an autistic boy.** Unpublished manuscript, Department of Special Education, University of Utah.

CHAPTER 11

Achenbach, T. M. (1978). **Research in developmental psychology: Concepts, strategies, methods.** New York: Free Press.

American Psychological Association, (1981). Ethical principles of psychologists. *American Psychologist, 36,* 633–685.

Bailey, K. D. (1982). **Methods of social research** (2nd ed.) New York: Free Press.

Barlow, D. H., & Hersen, M. (1984). **Single case experimental designs: Strategies for studying behavior change** (2nd ed.). New York: Pergamon Press.

Baumrind, D. (1985). Research on using intentional deception: Ethical issues revisited. **American Psychologist, 40,** 165–174.

Blanco, R. F., & Rosenfeld, J. G. (1978). **Case studies in clinical and school psychology.** Springfield, IL: Charles C Thomas.

Campbell, D. T. (1957). Factors relevant to the validity of experiments in social settings. **Psychological Bulletin, 54,** 297–312.

Campbell, D. T., & Stanley, J. C. (1963). Experimental and quasi-experimental designs for research on teaching. In N. L. Gage (Ed.), **Handbook** of research on teaching. Chicago: Rand McNally.

Cochran, W. G. (1977). **Sampling techniques** (3rd ed.). New York: Wiley.

Cook, T. D., & Campbell, D. T. (1979). **Quasi-experimentation: Design and analysis issues for field settings.** Chicago: Rand McNally.

Diener, E., & Crandall, R. (1978). **Ethics in social and behavioral research.** Chicago: University of Chicago Press.

Drew, C. J., & Hardman, M. L. (1985). **Designing and conducting behavioral research.** New York: Pergamon Press.

Drew, C. J., Logan, D. R., & Hardman, M. L. (1984). **Mental retardation: A life cycle approach** (3rd ed.). St. Louis: C. V. Mosby.

Fisher, K. (1986). Ethics in research: Having respect for the subject. **The APA Monitor, 17,**1, 34–35.

Gelfand, D. M., & Hartmann, D. P. (1984). **Child behavior analysis and therapy** (2nd ed.). New York: Pergamon Press.

Goldstein, H. (1979). **The design and analysis of longitudinal studies: Their role in the measurement of change.** New York: Academic Press.

Hartmann, D. P. (Ed.). (1982). **Using observers to study behavior: New directions for methodology of social and behavioral science.** San Francisco: Jossey-Bass.

Kazdin, A. E. (1980). **Research design in clinical psychology.** New York: Harper & Row.

Kazdin, A. E. (1982). **Single-case research designs: Methods for clinical and applied settings.** New York: Oxford University Press.

Keith-Spiegel, P. (1976). Children's rights as participants in research. In G. P. Koocher (Ed.), **Children's rights and the mental health profession.** New York: Wiley.

Kerlinger, F. N. (1973). **Foundations of behavioral research** (2nd ed.). New York: Holt, Rinehart & Winston.

Kratochwill, T. R. (ed.). (1978). **Single subject research: Strategies for evaluating change.** New York: Academic Press.

Masling, J., & Stern, G. (1969). Effect of the observer in the classroom. **Journal of Educational Psychology, 60,** 351–354.

Menges, R. J. (1973). Openness and honesty versus coercion and deception in psychological research. **American Psychologist, 28,** 1030–1034.

Mercatoris, M., & Craighead, W. E. (1974). Effects of nonparticipant observation on teacher and pupil classroom behavior. **Journal of Educational Psychology, 66,** 512–519.

Mischel, W. (1968). **Personality and assessment.** New York: Wiley.

Morrow, L. W., Burke, J. G., & Buell, B. J. (1985). Effects of a self-recording procedure on the attending to task behavior and academic productivity of adolescents with multiple handicaps. **Mental Retardation, 23,** 137–141.

Nesselroade, J. R., & Baltes, P. B. (eds.). (1979). **Longitudinal research in the study of behavior and development.** New York: Academic Press.

Parker, T. B., Freston, C. W., & Drew, C. J. (1975). Comparison of verbal performance of normal and learning disabled children as a function of input organization. **Journal of Learning Disabilities, 8,** 386–393.

Siegel, P. S., & Ellis, N. R. (1985). Note on the recruitment of subjects for mental retardation research. **American Journal of Mental Deficiency, 89,** 431–433.

Sudman, S. (1976). **Applied sampling.** New York: Academic Press.

Tawney, J. W., & Gast, D. L. (1984). **Single subject research in special education.** Columbus, OH: Charles E. Merrill.

Trice, A. D. (1986). Ethical variables? **American Psychologist, 41,** 482–483.

Turnbull, H. R., III. (ed.). (1977). **Consent handbook.** Washington, DC: American Association on Mental Deficiency.

Welch, R. F., & Drew, C. J. (1972). Effects of reward anticipation and performance expectancy on the learning rate of EMR adolescents. **American Journal of Mental Deficiency, 77,** 291–295.

Wermuth, B. M., Davis, K. L., Hollister, L. E., & Stunkard, A. J. (1977). Phenytoin treatment of the binge-eating syndrome. **American Journal of Psychiatry, 134,** 1249–1253.

White, G. D. (1977). the effects of observer presence on the activity level of families. **Journal of Applied Behavior Analysis, 10,** 734.

Wolf, S. (1959). The pharmacology of placebos. **Pharmacological Review, 11,** 689–704.

CHAPTER 12

Achenbach, T. M. (1966). The classification of children's psychiatric symptoms: A factor analytic study. **Psychological Monographs: General and Applied, 615,** 1–37.

Achenbach, T. M. (1974). **Developmental psycho-pathology.** New York: Ronald Press.

Achenbach, T. M. (1978). The Child Behavior Profile: I. Boys aged 6-11. **Journal of Clinical and Consulting Psychology, 46,** 478-488.

Achenbach, T. M. (1980). The DSM III classification of psychiatric disorders in infancy, childhood, and adolescence. **Journal of the American Academy of Child Psychiatry, 19,** 395-412.

Achenbach, T. M. (1982). **Developmental psycho-pathology** (2nd ed.). New York: Wiley.

Achenbach, T. M., & Edelbrock, C. S. (1978). The classification of child psychopathology: A review and analysis of empirical efforts. **Journal of Consulting and Clinical Psychology, 78,** 1275-1301.

Achenbach, T. M., & Edelbrock, C. S. (1979). The Child Behavior Profile: II. Boys aged 12-16 and girls 6-11 and 12-16. **Journal of Consulting and Clinical Psychology, 47,** 223-233.

American Psychiatric Association. (1952). **Diagnostic and statistical manual of mental disorders.** Washington, DC: Author.

American Psychiatric Association. (1968). **Diagnostic and statistical manual of mental disorders** (2nd ed.). Washington, DC: Author.

American Psychiatric Association. (1980). **Diagnostic and statistical manual of mental disorders** (3rd ed.). Washington, DC: Author.

American Psychiatric Association. (1987). **Diagnostic and statistical manual of mental disorders** (3rd ed., revised, draft). Washington, DC: American Psychiatric Association.

Barber, T. X., & Silver, M. J.(1968). Pitfalls in data analysis and interpretation: A reply to Rosenthal. **Psychological Bulletin Monograph, 70,** 48-62.

Beez, W. V. (1968). Influence of biased psychological reports on teacher behavior and pupil performance. **Proceedings of the 76th Annual Convention of the American Psychological Association, 3,** 605-606.

Bellack, A. S., Hersen, M., & Kazdin, A. E. (1982). **International handbook of behavior modification and therapy.** New York: Plenum.

Bijou, S. W,. & Peterson, R. F. (1971). Functional analysis in the assessment of children. In P. McReynolds (Ed.), **Advances in psychological assessment.** Palo Alto, CA: Science and Behavior Books.

Blashfield, R. K. (1984). **The classification of psychopathology: Neo-Kraepelinian and quantitative approaches.** New York: Plenum.

Blashfield, R. K., & Draguns, J. G. (1976a). Evaluation criteria for psychiatric classification. **Journal of Abnormal Psychology, 85,** 1940-1950.

Blashfield, R. K., & Draguns, J. G. (1976b). Toward a taxonomy of psychopathology: The purpose of psychiatric classification. **British Journal of Psychiatry, 129,** 1574-1583.

Bridgman, P. W. (1927). **The logic of modern physics.** New York: Macmillan.

Brunner, J. S. (1963). **On knowing: Essays for the left hand.** Cambridge, MA: Harvard University Press.

Brunner, J. S., Goodnow, J. J., & Austin, G. A. (1956). **Study of thinking.** New York: Wiley.

Cantwell, D. P., Russell, A. T., Mattison, R., & Will, L. (1979). A comparison of the DSM-II and DSM-III in the diagnosis of childhood psychiatric diagnosis. I. Agreement with expected diagnosis. **Archives of General Psychiatry, 36,** 1208-1213.

Carey, G., & Gottesman, I. I. (1978). Reliability and validity in binary ratings. **Archives of General Psychiatry, 35,** 1454-1459.

Cater, C. (1987). **School psychologist's perceptions of internalizing and externalizing behaviorally disordered children.** Unpublished doctoral dissertation, University of Utah.

Cerreto, M. C., & Tuma, J. M. (1977). Distribution of DSM II diagnosis in a child psychiatric setting. **Journal of Abnormal Child Psychology, 5,** 147-155.

Chess, S., & Hassibi, K. (1978). **Principles of child psychiatry.** New York: Plenum.

Cromwell, R. L., Blashfield, R. K., & Strauss, J. S. (1975). Criteria for classification systems. In N. Hobbs (Ed.), **Issues in the classification of children** (Vol. 1). San Francisco: Jossey-Bass.

Cullinan, D., Epstein, M. H., & McLinden, D. (1986). Status and change in state administrative definitions of behavior disorder. **School Psychology Review, 15,** 383-392.

DeMyer, M. K., Barton, S., DeMyer, W. E., Norton, J. A., Allen, J., & Steele, R. (1973). Prognosis in autism: A follow-up study. **Journal of Autism and Childhood Schizophrenia, 3,** 199-246.

Draguns, J. G., & Phillips, L. (1971). **Psychiatric classification and diagnosis: An overview and critique.** Morristown, NJ: General Learning Press.

Dreger, R. M. (1982). The classification of children and their emotional problems.**Clinical Psychology Review, 2,** 349-385.

Edgerton, R. B. (1967). **The cloak of competence: Stigma in the lives of the mentally retarded.** Berkeley: University of California Press.

Education for All Handicapped Children Act of 1975 (P. L. 94-142).

Faust, D., & Miner, R. A. (1986). The empiricist and his new clothes: DSM-III in perspective. **American Journal of Psychiatry, 143,** 962-967.

Fernando, T., Mellsop, G., Nelson, K., Peace, K., & Wilson, J. (1986). The reliability of Axis V of the

DSM-III. **American Journal of Psychiatry, 143,** 752–755.

Fish, B. (1969). Limitation of the new nomenclature for children's disorders. **International Journal of Psychiatry, 7,** 393–398.

Foster, G. G., Ysseldyke, J. E., & Reese, J. (1975). I never would have seen it if I hadn't believed it. **Exceptional Children, 41,** 469–474.

Gallagher, J. J. (1972). The special education contract for mildly handicapped children. **Exceptional Children, 38,** 527–535.

Gallagher, J. J., Forsythe, P,. Ringelheim, D., & Weintraub, F. J. (1975). Funding patterns and labeling. In N. Hobbs (Ed.), **Issues in the classification of children** (Vol. 1). San Francisco: Jossey-Bass.

Gelfand, D. M., & Hartmann, D. P. (1984). **Child behavior analysis and therapy** (2nd ed.). New York: Pergamon Press.

Goffman, E. (1963). **Stigma: Notes on the management of spoiled identity.** Englewood Cliffs, NJ: Prentice-Hall.

Goldfried, M. R., & Kent, R. N. (1972). Traditional versus behavioral assessment: A comparison of methodological and theoretical assumption. **Psychological Bulletin, 77,** 409–420.

Group for the Advancement of Psychiatry (GAP). (1974). **Psychopathological disorders in childhood: Theoretical considerations and a proposed classification.** New York: Jason Aronson.

Guskin, S. L., Bartel, N. R., & MacMillan, D. L. (1975). Perspectives of the labeled child. In N. Hobbs (Ed.), **Issues in the classification of children** (Vol. 1). San Francisco: Jossey-Bass.

Hallahan, D. P., & Kauffman, J. M. (1986). **Exceptional children** (3rd ed.). Englewood Cliffs, NJ: Prentice-Hall.

Harris, S. L. (1979). DSM-III—Its implication for children. **Child Behavior Therapy, 1,** 37–48.

Hartmann, D. P., Roper, B. L., & Bradford, D. C. (1979). Some relationships between behavioral and traditional assessment. **Journal of Behavioral Assessment, 1,** 3–21.

Helzer, J. E., Robins, L. N., Taibleson, M., Woodruff, R. A., Reich, T., & Wish, E. D. (1977). Reliability of psychiatric diagnosis. **Archives of General Psychiatry, 34,** 129–132.

Hempel, C. G. (1965). **Aspects of scientific explanation and other essays in the philosophy of science.** New York: Free Press.

Hobbs, N. (1975a). **The future of children.** San Francisco: Jossey-Bass.

Hobbs, N. (Ed.). (1975b). **Issues in the classification of children** (Vols. 1 and 2). San Francisco: Jossey-Bass.

Howell, K. W., Kaplan, J. S., & O'Connell, Y. O. (1979). **Evaluating exceptional children: A task analysis approach.** Columbus, OH: Charles E. Merrill.

Jampala, V. C., Sierles, F. S., & Taylor, M. A. (1986). Consumers' views of DSM-III: Attitudes and practices of U.S. psychiatrists and 1984 graduating residents. **American Journal of Psychiatry, 143,** 148–153.

Jenson, W. R. (1985). **Severely emotionally disturbed vs. behavior disorders: Consideration of a label change** (Field Report #2, University of Utah Graduate School of Education Report Series). Salt Lake City: University of Utah.

Jones, R. L. (1972). Labels and the stigma in special education. **Exceptional Children, 38,** 553–564.

Kanfer, F. H. (1985). Target selection for clinical change programs. **Behavioral Assessment, 7,** 7–20.

Kanfer, F. H., & Saslow, G. (1965). Behavioral analysis: An alternative to diagnostic classification. **Archives of General Psychiatry, 12,** 848–853.

Kauffman, J. M. (1982). Social policy issues in special education and related services for emotionally disturbed children and youth. In M. M. Noel & N. G. Haring (Eds.), **Issues in educating the emotionally disturbed: Identification and program planning** (Vol. 1). Seattle: University of Washington Press.

Kazdin, A. E. (1985). Selection of target behaviors: The relationship of the treatment focus to clinical dysfunction. **Behavioral Assessment, 7,** 33–47.

Kendall, P. C., & Urbain, E. S. (1981). Cognitive-behavioral intervention witha hyperactive girl: Evaluation via behavioral observation and cognitive performance. **Behavioral Assessment, 3,** 345–357.

Kendall, R. E. (1975). **The role of diagnosis in psychiatry.** Oxford: Blackwell.

Kraeplin, E. (1899). **Psychiatrie.** Leipzig: Barth.

Kolstoe, O. (1972). Programs for the retarded: A replay to the critics. **Exceptional Children, 39,** 51–56.

Krasner, W. (1976). **Labeling the children.** Washington, DC: U.S. Department of Health, Education and Welfare.

Kratochwill, T. R. (1985). Selection of target behaviors in behavioral consultation. **Behavioral Assessment, 7,** 49–61.

Liebert, R. M., Poulos, R. W., & Strauss, G. D. (1974). **Developmental psychology.** Englewood Cliffs, NJ: Prentice-Hall.

Levitas, A., Haggerman, R. J., Braden, M., Rimland, B., McBogg, P., & Matus, I. (1983). Autism and the fragile X syndrome. **Journal of Developmental and Behavioral Pediatrics, 4,** 151–158.

Mahoney, M. (1974). **Cognition and behavior modification.** Cambridge, MA: Ballinger.

Martin, R. (1977). Minimum level of education. **Law and Behavior, 2,** 2.

Mash, E. J. (1985). Some comments on target selection in behavior therapy. **Behavioral Assessment, 7,** 63–78.

Mattison, R., Cantwell, D. P., Russell, A. T., & Will, L. A. (1979). A comparison of DSM-II and DSM-III in the diagnosis of childhood psychiatric disorders: II. Interrater agreement. **Archives of General Psychiatry, 36,** 1217–1222.

Meichenbaum, D. (1977). **Cognitive-behavior modification: An integrated approach.** New York: Plenum.

Mercer, J. R. (1975). Psychological assessment and the rights of children. In N. Hobbs (Ed.), **Issues in the classification of children** (Vol. 1). San Francisco: Jossey-Bass.

Mischel, W. (1968). **Personality and assessment.** New York: Wiley.

Morris, D. P., Soroker, E., & Burruss, G. (1954). Follow-up studies of shy, withdrawn children. **American Journal of Orthopsychiatry, 24,** 743–754.

Morris, H. H., Escoll, P. J., & Wexler, R. (1956). Aggressive behavior disorders of childhood: A follow-up study. **American Journal of Psychiatry, 112,** 991–997.

Morris, R. J., & Kratochwill, R. T. (1983). **The practice of child therapy.** New York: Pergamon Press.

Mutimer, D., & Rosemier, R. A. (1967). Behavior problems of children viewed by teachers and children themselves. **Journal of Consulting Psychology, 31,** 583–587.

Nelson, R. O. (1983). Behavior assessment: Past, present, and future. **Behavioral Assessment, 5,** 195–206.

Patterson, G. R. (1964). An empirical approach to the classification of disturbed children. **Journal of Clinical Psychology, 20,** 326–337.

Patterson, G. R. (1983). **Longitudinal assessment of fourth grade boys.** (National Institute of Mental Health Research Grant). Eugene: Oregon Social Learning Center.

Peterson, D. R. (1961). Behavior problems of middle childhood. **Journal of Consulting Psychology, 25,** 205–209.

Quay, H. C. (1964). Dimensions of personality in delinquent boys as inferred from the factor analysis of case history data. **Child Development, 35,** 477–484.

Quay, H. C. (1979). Classification. In H. C. Quay & J. S. Werry (Eds.), **Psychopathological disorders of childhood** (2nd ed.). New York: Wiley.

Quay, H. C., & Peterson, D. R. (1975). **Manual for the problem behavior checklist.** Unpublished manuscript.

Quay, H. C., & Quay, L. C. (1965). Behavior problems in early adolescence. **Child Development, 36,** 215–220.

Ritvo, E. R., Freeman, B. J., Mason-Brothers, A., Mo, A., & Ritvo, A. (1985). Concordance for the syndrome of autism in 40 pairs of afflicted twins. **American Journal of Psychiatry, 142,** 74–77.

Rivers, L. W., Henderson, D. M., Jones, R. L., Ladner, J. A., & Williams, R. L. (1975). Mosaic of labels for black children. In N. Hobbs (Ed.), **Issues in the classification of children** (Vol. 1). San Francisco: Jossey-Bass.

Robins. L. N. (1966). **Deviant children grown up.** Baltimore: Williams & Wilkins.

Robins, L. N. (1979). Follow-up studies. In H. C. Quay & J. S. Werry (Eds.), **Psychopathological disorders of childhood** (2nd ed.). New York: Wiley.

Rosenthal, R. L., & Jacobson, L. (1968). **Pygmalion in the classroom: Teacher expectation and pupils' intellectual development.** New York: Holt, Rinehart & Winston.

Ross, D. M., & Ross, S. A. (1982). **Hyperactivity: Current issues, research, and theory.** New York: Wiley.

Rutter, M. (1965). Classification and categorization in child psychiatry. **Journal of Child Psychology and Psychiatry, 6,** 71–83.

Rutter, M., & Shaffer, D. (1980). DSM III: A step forward or back in terms of the classification of child psychiatric disorders. **Journal of the American Academy of Child Psychiatry, 19,** 371–394.

Schacht, T., & Nathan, P. E. (1977). But is it good for psychologists? Appraisal and status of the DSM III. **American Psychologist, 32,** 1017–1025.

Schrupp, M. H., & Gjerde, C. M. (1953). Teacher growth in attitudes towards behavior problems children. **Journal of Education Psychology, 44,** 203–214

Shoben, E. J. (1966). Personal worth in educational counseling. In J. D. Krumboltz (Ed.), **Revolutions in counseling.** Boston: Houghton Mifflin.

Sokal, R. R. (1974). Classification: Purposes, principles, progress, prospects. **Science, 185,** 1115–1123.

Spitzer, R. L., & Endicott, J. (1978). Medical and mental disorders: Proposed definition and criteria. In R. L. Spitzer & D. F. Klein (Eds.), **Critical issues in psychiatric diagnosis.** New York: Raven Press.

Spitzer, R. L., & Fleiss, J. L. (1974). A re-analysis of the reliability of psychiatric diagnosis. **British Journal of Psychiatry, 125,** 341–347.

Spitzer, R. L., Sheehy, M., & Endicott, J. (1977). DSM III: Guided principles. In V. Rakoff, H. Stancer, & H. B. Kewards (Eds.), **Psychiatric diagnosis.** New York: Brunner/Mazel.

Spitzer, R. L., & Wilson, P. T. (1975). Nosology and the official psychiatric nomenclature. In M. Freeman, H. I. Kaplan, & B. J. Sadlock (Eds.) **Com-**

prehensive textbook of psychiatry (2nd ed., Vol. 2). Baltimore: Williams & Wilkins.

Stouffer, G. A. (1952). Behavior problems of children as viewed by teachers and mental hygienists. Mental Hygiene, 36, 271–285.

Strober, M., Green, J., & Carlson, G. (1981). The reliability of psychiatric diagnosis in hospitalized adolescents: Interrater agreement using the DSM III. Archives of General Psychiatry, 38, 141–145.

Sundberg, N. D. (1977). Assessment of persons. Englewood Cliffs, NJ: Prentice-Hall.

Taylor, C. B. (1983). DSM-III and behavioral assessment. Behavioral Assessment, 5, 5–14.

Thorndike, R. L. (1968). [Review of R. Rosenthal & L. Jacobson, Pygmalion in the classroom]. American Educational Research Journal, 5, 708–711.

Tryon, W. (1976). A system of behavioral diagnosis. Professional Psychology, 4, 495–506.

Ullman, L. P., & Krasner, L. (1965). Case studies in behavior modification. New York: Holt, Rinehart & Winston.

Ullmann, L. P., & Krasner, L. (1969). A psychological approach to abnormal behavior. Englewood Cliffs, NJ: Prentice-Hall.

U.S. Department of Education. (1985). Special study on terminology: Comprehensive review and evaluation report. Washington, DC: U.S. Government Printing Office.

U.S. Department of Health, Education and Welfare (1968). Report of the National Citizen Advisory Committee on Vocational Rehabilitation. Washington, DC: U.S. Government Printing Office.

Walker, H. M. (1970). Walker Problem Behavior Identification Checklist. Los Angeles: Western Psychological Services.

Walker, H. M. (1982). Walker Problem Behavior Identification Checklist—revised. Los Angeles: Western Psychological Services.

Walker, H. M., O'Neill, R., Shinn, M., Ramsey, B., Patterson, G. R., Reid, J., & Capaldi, D. (1986). Longitudinal assessment and long term follow up of antisocial behavior in fourth grade boys: Rationale, methodology, measures, and results. Unpublished manuscript, Oregon Social Learning Center, Eugene.

Walker, H. M., Reavis, H. K., Rhode, G., & Jenson, W. R. (1985). A conceptual model for delivery of behavioral services to behavior disordered children in a continuum of educational settings. In A. Kazdin & P. Bornstein (Eds.), Handbook of clinical behavior therapy with children. Homewood, IL: Dorsey Press.

Ward, C. H., Beck, A. T., Mendelson, M., Mock, J. E., & Erbaugh, J. K. (1962). The psychiatric nomenclature. Archives of General Psychiatry, 7, 198–205.

Weiss, G., & Hechtman, L. T. (1986). Hyperactive children grown up: Empirical findings and theoretical considerations. New York: Guilford Press.

Werry, J. S., Methven, R. J., Fitzpatrick, J., & Dixon, H. (1983). The interrater reliability of DSM III in children. Journal of Abnormal and Child Psychology, 11, 341–354.

Wickman, E. K. (1928). Children's behavior and teacher's attitudes. New York: Commonwealth Fund.

Wilson, F. E., & Evans, I. M. (1983). The reliability of target-behavior selection in behavioral assessment. Behavioral Assessment, 5, 15–32.

Wing, J. K. (1978). Reasoning about madness. London: Oxford University Press.

Wirt, R. D., Lachar, D., Klinedinst, J. K., & Seat, P. D. (1977). Multidimensional description of child personality: A manual for the Personality Inventory for Children. Los Angeles: Western Psychological Services.

World Health Organization. (1977). International classification of diseases (9th ed.). Geneva: Author.

Yates, A. J. (1970). Behavior therapy. New York: Wiley.

Ysseldyke, J. E., & Foster, G. C. (1978). Bias in teacher's observation of emotionally disturbed and learning disabled children. Exceptional Children, 44, 613–615.

Zigler, E., & Phillips, L. (1960). Social effectiveness and symptomatic behaviors. Journal of Abnormal and Social Psychology, 62, 231–238.

Zigler, E., & Phillips, L. (1961). Psychiatric diagnosis: A critique. Journal of Abnormal and Social Psychology, 63, 607–618.

Zubin, J. (1967). Classification of the behavior disorders. Annual Review of Psychology, 18, 373–406.

CHAPTER 13

Achenbach, T. M. (1979). The Child Behavior Profile: An empirically based system for assessing children's behavioral problems and competencies. International Journal of Mental Health, 7, 24–42.

Achenbach, T. M., & Edelbrock, C. (1980). Child Behavior Checklist—Teacher's Report Form. Burlington: University of Vermont, Department of Psychiatry.

Achenbach, T. M., & Edelbrock, C. (1983). **Manual for the Child Behavior Checklist and Revised Child Behavior Profile.** Burlington: University of Vermont, Department of Psychiatry.

Aiken, L. R. (1979). **Psychological testing and assessment.** Boston: Allyn & Bacon.

Alessi, G. F. (1980). Behavioral observation for the school psychologist: Response-discrepancy model. **School Psychology Review, 9,** 31–45.

Althauser, R. P., & Herberlein, T. A. (1970). Validity and the multitrait multimethod matrix. In E. F. Borgatta & G. W. Bohrnstedt (Eds.), **Sociological methodology.** San Francisco: Jossey-Bass.

Anastasi, A. (1982). **Psychological testing** (5th ed.). New York: Macmillan.

Ando, H., & Yoshimura, I. (1978). Prevalence of maladaptive behavior in retarded children as a function of IQ and age. **Journal of Abnormal Child Psychology, 6,** 345–350.

Bayley, N. (1970). Development of mental abilities. In P. H. Mussen (General Ed.), **Carmichael's manual of child psychology** (3rd ed.). Vol. I. New York: Wiley.

Beck, R. (1986). **RIDES Project.** Great Falls, MT: Great Falls School District.

Bellak, L. (1954). **The Thematic Apperception Test and the Children's Apperception Test in clinical use.** New York: Grune & Stratton.

Bem, D. J., & Allen, A. (1974). On predicting some of the people some of the time: The search for cross-situational consistencies in behavior. **Psychological Review, 81,** 506–520.

Bierman, K. L., & Schwartz, L. A. (1986). Clinical child interviews: Approaches and developmental considerations. **Journal of Child and Adolescent Psychotherapy, 3,** 267–278.

Binet, A., & Simon, T. (1905). Méthodes nouvelles pour le diagnostic du niveau intellectuel des anormaux. **L'Année Psychologique, 11,** 191–244.

Bornstein, P. H., Hamilton, S. C., & Bornstein, M. T. (1986). Self-monitoring procedures. In A. R. Ciminero, K. S. Calhoun, & H. E. Adams (Eds.), **Handbook of behavioral assessment** (2nd ed.). New York: Wiley.

Bowers, K. S. (1973). Situationalism in psychology: An analysis and a critique. **Psychological Review, 80,** 307–336.

Brigance, A. H. (1978). **Brigance Diagnostic Inventory of Early Development.** North Billerica, MA: Curriculum Associates.

Broden, M., Hall, R. V., & Mitts, B. (1971). The effect of self-recording on the classroom behavior of two eighth grade students. **Journal of Applied Behavior Analysis, 4,** 191–200.

Brown, L. J., Black, D. D., & Downs, J. C. (1984). **School Social Skills Rating Scale.** East Aurora, NY: Slosson Educational.

Carmines, E. G., & Zeller, R. A. (1979). Reliability and validity assessment. In J. L. Sullivan (Ed.), **Series: Quantitative applications in social sciences,** Beverly Hills, CA: Sage.

Conners, C. K. (1969). A teacher rating scale for use in drug studies with children. **American Journal of Psychiatry, 126,** 884–888.

Cronbach, L. J. (1960). **Essentials of psychological testing.** New York: Harper & Row.

DeMyer, M. K., Hingtgen, J. N., & Jackson, R. K. (1981). Infantile autism reviewed: A decade of research. **Schizophrenia Bulletin, 7,** 388–451.

Deno, S. L. (1980). Direct observation approach to measuring classroom behavior. **Exceptional Children, 46,** 396–399.

Dunn, L. M., & Markwardt, F. C. (1970). **Peabody Individual Achievement Test.** Circle Pines, MN: American Guidance Service.

Ebel, R. L. (1971). Criterion-referenced measurements: Limitations. **School Review, 79,** 282–288.

Edelbrock, C., Costello, A. J., Dulcan, M. K., Kalas, R., & Conover, N. C. (1985). Age differences in the reliability of the psychiatric interview of the child. **Child Development, 56,** 265–275.

Ekenhammer, B. (1974). Interactionism in personality from a historical perspective. **Psychological Bulletin, 81,** 1026–1048.

Epstein, S. (1966). Some theoretical considerations on the nature of ambiguity and the use of stimulus dimensions in projective techniques. **Journal of Consulting Psychology, 30,** 183–192.

Epstein, S. (1979). The stability of behavior: I. On predicting most of the people much of the time. **Journal of Personality and Social Psychology, 37,** 1097–1126.

Evans, I. M., & Nelson, R. O. (1986). Assessment of children. In A. R. Ciminero, K. S. Calhoun, & H. E. Adams (Eds.), **Handbook of behavioral assessment** (2nd ed.). New York: Wiley.

Exner, J. E., Jr. (1969). **The Rorschach systems.** New York: Grune & Stratton.

Exner, J. E., Jr. (1974). **The Rorschach: A comprehensive system.** New York: Wiley.

Foster, R. W. (1974). Camelot Behavioral Checklist. Lawrence, Kan.: Camelot Behavioral Systems.

Foster, S. L., & Cone, J. D. (1986). Design and use of direct observation. In A. R. Ciminero, K. S. Calhoun, & H. E. Adams (Eds.), **Handbook of behavioral assessment** (2nd ed.). New York: Wiley.

Gardner, R. A. (1971). **Therapeutic communication with children: The mutual story-telling technique.** New York: Jason Aronson.

Gelfand, D. M., & Hartmann, D. P. (1984). **Child behavior analysis and therapy** (2nd ed.). New York: Pergamon Press.

Gilbert, J. (1978). **Interpreting psychological test data.** New York: Van Nostrand Reinhold.

Gittelman-Klein, R. (1978). Validity of projective tests for psychodiagnosis for children. In R. L. Spitzer & D. F. Klein (Eds.), **Critical issues in psychiatric diagnosis.** New York: Raven Press.

Gittelman-Klein, R. (1980). The role of tests for differential diagnosis in child psychiatry. **Journal of the American Academy of Child Psychiatry, 19,** 413–438.

Gittelman, R. (Ed.). (1986). **Anxiety disorders of childhood.** New York: Guilford Press.

Glaser, R. (1963). Instructional technology and the measurement of learning outcome: Some questions. **American Psychologist, 18,** 519–522.

Goldfried, M. R., & Linehan, M. M. (1977). Basic issues in behavioral assessment. In A. R. Ciminero, K. S. Calhoun, & H. E. Adams (Eds.), **Handbook of behavioral assessment.** New York: Wiley.

Graham, J. R., & Lilly, R. S. (1984). **Psychological testing.** Engelwood Cliffs, NJ: Prentice-Hall.

Hallahan, D. P., & Kauffman, J. M. (1986). **Exceptional children** (3rd ed.). Englewood Cliffs, NJ: Prentice-Hall.

Halpern, F. (1953). **A clinical approach to children's Rorschachs.** New York: Grune & Stratton.

Harris, F. C., & Lahey, B. B. (1982). Subject reactivity in direct observation assessment: A review and critical analysis. **Clinical Psychology Review, 2,** 523–538.

Hartmann, D. P., Roper, B. L., & Bradford, D. C. (1979). Some relationships between behavioral and traditional assessment. **Journal of Behavioral Assessment, 1,** 3–21.

Haynes, S. N. (1978). **Principles of behavioral assessment.** New York: Gardner Press.

Haynes, S. N., & Jensen, B. J. (1979). The interview as a behavioral assessment instrument. **Behavioral Assessment, 1,** 97–106.

Herbert, E. W., & Baer, D. M. (1972). Training parents as behavior modifiers: Self-recording of contingent attention. **Journal of Applied Behavior Analysis, 5,** 139–149.

Herjanic, B., and Reich, W. (1982). Development of a structural psychiatric interview for children. Agreement between child and parent on individual symptoms. **Journal of Abnormal Child Psychology, 10,** 307–324.

Hetherington, E. M., & Martin, B. (1979). Family inter-

action. In H. C. Quay & J. S. Werry (Eds.), **Psychopathological disorders of childhood** (2nd ed.). New York: Wiley.

Hodges, K., Kline, J., Kashani, D., Cytryn, L., Stern, L., & McKnew, D. (1982). **Child Assessment Schedule.** Unpublished manuscript, University of Missouri.

Hodges, K., Kline, J., Stern, L., Cytryn, L., & McKnew, D. (1982). The development of a child assessment interview for research and clinical use. **Journal of Abnormal Child Psychology, 10,** 173–189.

Holland, C. J. (1970). An interview guide for behavioral counseling with parents. **Behavior Therapy, 1,** 70–79.

Jenkins, R. J., & Pany, D. (1978). Standardized achievement tests: How useful for special education? **Exceptional Children, 44,** 448–453.

Jenson, W. R., Paoletti, P., & Petersen, P. B. (1984). Self-monitoring plus a contingency to reduce a chronic throat clearing tic in a child. **The Behavior Therapist, 7,** 192.

Jenson, W. R., Preator, K., Ballou, C., Reavis, K., & Freston, C. (1987). **Autism prescriptive checklist and interventions manual.** Portland, OR: A.S.I.E.P.

Johnson, S. M., & Bolstad, O. D. (1973). Methodological issues in naturalistic observation: Some problems and solutions for field research. In L. A. Hamerlynck, L. C. Handy, & E. J. Mash (Eds.), **Behavioral change: Methodology, concepts, and practice.** Champaign, IL: Research Press, 1973.

Kaplan, R. M., & Saccuzzo, D. P. (1982). **Psychological testing: Principles, applications, and issues.** Monterey, CA: Brooks/Cole.

Kass, R. E., & O'Leary, K. D. (1970). **The effects of observer bias in field-experimental settings.** Paper presented at the Behavior Analysis in Education Symposium, University of Kansas.

Kauffman, J. M. (1985). **Characteristics of children's behavior disorders** (3rd ed.). Columbus, OH: Charles E. Merrill.

Kent, R. A., & Foster, S. L. (1977). Direct observation procedures: Methodological issues in applied settings. In A. R. Ciminero, K. S. Calhoun, & H. E. Adams (Eds.), **Handbook of behavioral assessment.** New York: Wiley.

Kestenbaum, C. J., & Bird, H. R. A. (1978). A reliability study of the Mental Health Assessment Form for School-Aged Children. **Journal of the American Academy of Child Psychiatry, 17,** 338–347.

Korchin, S. J. (1976). **Modern clinical psychology.** New York: Basic Books.

Lachar, D. (1982). **Personality Inventory for Children (PIC), revised format: Manual supple-**

ment. Los Angeles: Western Psychological Services.

Lambert, N. M., & Sandoval, J. (1980). The prevalence of learning disabilities in a sample of children considered hyperactive. **Journal of Abnormal Child Psychology, 8,** 33–50.

Lewis, M. (1973). Infant intelligence tests: Their use and misuse. **Human Development, 16,** 108–118.

Lidz, C. S. (1979). Criterion referenced assessment: The new bandwagon? **Exceptional Children, 46,** 131–132.

Lindzey, G. (1959). On the classification of projective techniques. **Psychological Bulletin, 56,** 158–168.

Lindzey, G. (1961). **Projective techniques and cross cultural research.** New York: Appleton.

Mark, S. J. (1984). **An investigation of the freedom from distractability factor with attention deficit disorder children and conduct disordered children.** Unpublished master's thesis, University of Utah.

Martin, R. (1979). **Educating handicapped children: The legal mandate.** Champaign, IL: Research Press.

McCall, R. B., Hogarty, P. S., & Hurlburt, N. (1972). Transitions in infant sensorimotor development and the prediction of childhood IQ. **American Psychologist, 27,** 728–748.

McCord, J., & McCord, W. (1961). Cultural stereotypes and the validity of interviews for research in child development. **Child Development, 32,** 171–185.

Messick, S. (1980). Test validity and the ethics of assessment. **American Psychologist, 35,** 1012–1027.

Mischel, W. (1968). **Personality assessment.** New York: Wiley.

Mischel, W. (1979). On the interface of cognition and personality: Beyond the person-situation debate. **American Psychologist, 34,** 740–754.

Mischel, W. (1983). Alternatives in the pursuit of the predictability and consistency of persons: Stable data that yield unstable predictions. **Journal of Personality, 51,** 578–604.

Morganstern, K. P. (1976). Behavioral interviewing: The initial stages of assessment. In M. Hersen & A. S. Bellack (Eds.). **Behavioral assessment: A practical handbook.** New York: Pergamon Press.

Murray, H. A. (1943). **Thematic Apperception Test manual.** Cambridge, MA: Harvard University Press.

Nunnally, J. (1962). **Psychometric theory.** New York: McGraw-Hill.

O'Leary, K. D., & Johnson, S. B. (1979). Psychological assessment. In H. C. Quay & J. S. Werry (Eds.),

Psychopathological disorders of children (2nd ed.). New York: Wiley.

O'Leary, K. D., & Kent, R. (1973). Behavior modification for social action: Research tactics and problems. In L. A. Hamerlynck, L. C. Handy, & E. J. Mash (Eds.), **Behavior change: Methodology, concepts, and practice.** Champaign, IL: Research Press.

Ozer, D. J. (1986). **Consistency in personality: A methodological framework.** Berlin: Springer-Verlag.

Popovich, D. (1977). **Prescriptive behavioral checklist for the profoundly retarded.** Baltimore: University Park Press.

Pfeffer, C. R. (1986). **The suicidal child.** New York: Guilford Press.

Quay, H. C. (1977). Measuring dimensions of deviant behavior: The Behavior Problem Checklist. **Journal of Abnormal Child Psychology, 5,** 277–289.

Quay, H. C., & Peterson, D. R. (1975). **Manual for the Behavior Problem Checklist.** Unpublished manuscript.

Reid, J. B. (1978). **A social learning approach to family intervention: Vol. 2. Observation in the home setting.** Eugene, OR: Castalia.

Rhodes, G., Morgan, D. P., & Young, K. R. (1981). Generalization and maintenance of treatment gains of behaviorally handicapped students from resource rooms to regular classrooms using self-evaluation procedures. **Journal of Applied Behavior Analysis, 16,** 171–188.

Rorschach, H. (1948). **Psychodiagnostics: A diagnostic test based on perception** (4th ed.). New York: Grune & Stratton.

Rutter, M. (1978). Developmental issues and prognosis. In M. Rutter & E. Schopler (Eds.), **Autism: A reappraisal of concepts and treatment.** New York: Plenum.

Rutter, M., & Yule, W. (1973). Specific reading retardation. In L. Mann & D. Sabatino (Eds.), **The first review of special education.** Philadelphia: Buttonwood Farms.

Salvia, J., & Ysseldyke, J. E. (1978). **Assessment in special education and remedial education.** Boston: Houghton Mifflin.

Salvia, J., & Ysseldyke, J. E. (1981). **Assessment in special education and remedial education** (2nd ed.). Boston: Houghton Mifflin.

Sattler, J. M. (1982). **Assessment of children's intelligence and special abilities** (2nd ed.). Boston: Allyn & Bacon.

Shapiro, E. S., & Lentz, F. E. (1985). Assessing academic behavior: A behavioral approach. **School Psychology Review, 14,** 325–338.

Shapiro, E. S., & Lentz, F. E. (1986). Behavioral assessment of academic skills. In T. R. Kratochwill

(Ed.), **Advances in school psychology** (Vol. 5). Hillsdale, NJ: Erlbaum.

Shertzer, B., & Linden, J. D. (1979). **Fundamentals of individual appraisal: Assessment techniques for counselors.** Boston: Houghton Mifflin.

Simmons, J. E. (1974). **Psychiatric examination of children.** Philadelphia: Lea & Febiger.

Skindrud, K. (1973). Field evaluation of observer bias under overt and covert monitoring. In L. A. Hammerlynck, L. S. Handy, & E. J. Mash (Eds.), **Behavior change: Methodology, concepts and practice.** Champaign, IL: Research Press.

Stern, W. (1914). **The psychological methods of testing intelligence.** Baltimore: Warwick & York.

Sundberg, N. D. (1977). **Assessment of persons.** Englewood Cliffs, NJ: Prentice-Hall.

Swanson, H. L., & Watson, B. L. (1982). **Educational and psychological assessment of exceptional children: Theories, strategies, and applications.** St. Louis: C. V. Mosby.

Terman, L. M. (1916). **The measurement of intelligence.** Boston: Houghton Mifflin.

Thomas, H. (1970). Psychological assessment instruments for use with human infants. **Merrill-Palmer Quarterly, 16,** 179–223.

Turkat, I. D. (1986). The behavioral interview. In A. R. Ciminero, K. S. Calhoun, & H. E. Adams (Eds.), **Handbook of behavioral assessment** (2nd ed.). New York: Wiley.

Walker, H. M. (1970). **Walker Problem Behavior Identification Checklist.** Los Angeles: Western Psychological Services.

Walker, H. M. (1983). **Walker Problem Behavior Identification Checklist—revised.** Los Angeles: Western Psychological Services.

Walls, R. T., Werner, T. J., Bacon, A., & Zane, T. (1977). Behavior checklists. In J. D. Cone & R. P. Hawkins (Eds.), **Behavior assessment: New directions in clinical psychology.** New York: Brunner/Mazel.

Wechsler, D. (1958). **The measurement and appraisal of adult intelligence** (4th ed.). Baltimore: Williams & Wilkins.

Weiner, E. A., & Stewart, B. J. (1983). **Assessing individuals: Psychological and educational tests and measurements.** Boston: Little, Brown.

Weiss, G., & Hechtman, L. T. (1986). **Hyperactive children grown up: Empirical findings and theoretical considerations.** New York: Guilford Press.

Wenar, C., & Coulter, J. B. (1962). A reliability study of developmental histories. **Child Development, 33,** 453–462.

Wert, C. E., & Linn, R. N. (1970). Cautions in applying various procedures for determining the reliability and validity of multiple item scales. **American Sociological Review, 35,** 757–759.

Wiggins, J. S. (1973). **Personality and prediction: Principles of personality assessment.** Reading, MA: Addison-Wesley.

Wildman, B. G., & Erickson, M. T. (1977). Methodological problems in behavioral observation. In J. D. Cone & R. P. Hawkins (Eds.), **Behavioral assessment: New directions in clinical psychology.** New York: Brunner/Mazel.

Wirt, R. D., Lachar, D., Klinedinst, J. K., & Seat, P. D. (1977). **Multidimensional description of child personality: A manual for the Personality Inventory for Children.** Los Angeles: Western Psychological Services.

CHAPTER 14

Abramowitz, C. V. (1976). The effectiveness of group psychotherapy with children. **Archives of General Psychiatry, 33,** 320–326.

Ackerman, N. (1966). **Treating the troubled family.** New York: Basic Books.

Alexander, J. F., & Malouf, R. E. (1983). Intervention with children experiencing problems in personality and social development. In P. H. Mussen (General Ed.), **Handbook of child psychology** (4th ed.): **Vol. 4. Socialization, personality, and social development** (E. M. Hetherington, Vol. Ed.). New York: Wiley.

Alexander, J. F., & Parsons, B. V. (1973). Short-term behavioral intervention with delinquent families: Impact on family process and recidivism. **Journal of Abnormal Psychology, 81,** 219–225.

Allen, K. E., Hart, B., Buell, J. S., Harris, F. R., & Wolf, M. M. (1964). Effects of social reinforcement on isolate behavior of a nursery school child. **Child Development, 35,** 511–518.

Axline, V. M. (1974). **Play therapy.** Boston: Houghton Mifflin.

Axline, V. M. (1955). Therapeutic play procedures and results. **American Journal of Orthopsychiatry, 124,** 612–621.

Axline, V. M. (1976). Play therapy procedures and results. In C. Schaefer (Ed.), **The therapeutic use of child's play.** New York: Jason Aronson.

Ayllon, T., & Azrin, N. H. (1968). **The token economy: Motivational system for therapy and rehabilitation.** New York: Appleton-Century-Crofts.

Azrin, N. H., Bugle, C., & O'Brien, F. (1971). Behavioral engineering: Two apparatuses for toilet training retarded children. **Journal of Applied Behavior Analysis, 4,** 249–253.

Bandura, A. (1969). **Principles of behavior modification.** New York: Holt, Rinehart & Winston.

Bandura, A. (1977). **Social learning theory.** Englewood Cliffs, NJ: Prentice-Hall.

Barnard, J. B., Christopherson, E. R., Altman, K., & Wolf, M. M. (1974, September). **Parent mediated treatment of self-injurious behavior using over-correction.** Paper presented at the meeting of the American Psychological Association, New Orleans.

Bandura, A., Blanchard, E. B., & Ritter, B. (1969). Relative efficacy of desensitization and modeling approaches for inducing behavioral, affective, and attitudinal changes. **Journal of Personality and Social Psychology, 13,** 173–199.

Barrett, C. L., Hampe, I. E., & Miller, L. (1978). Research on psychotherapy with children. In S. Garfield & A. E. Bergin (Eds.), **Handbook of psychotherapy and behavior change: An empirical analysis** (2nd ed.). New York: Wiley.

Beck, L., Langford, W. S., MacKay, M., & Sum, G. (1975). Childhood chemotherapy and later drug abuse and growth curve: A follow-up study of 30 adolescents. **American Journal of Psychiatry, 132,** 436–438.

Bergin, A. E. (1971). The evaluation of therapeutic outcomes. In A. E. Bergin & S. Garfield (Eds.), **Handbook of psychotherapy and behavior change.** New York: Wiley.

Bernal, M. E., Klinnert, M. D., & Schultz, L. A. (1980). An evaluation of the effectiveness of training parents of conduct problem children. **Journal of Applied Behavior Analysis, 13,** 677–691.

Bernal, M. E., & Margolin, G. (1976, December). **Outcome of intervention strategies for discipline problem children.** Paper presented at the meeting of the Association for Advancement of Behavior Therapy, New York.

Bierman, K. L. (1983). Cognitive development and clinical interviews with children. In B. B. Lahey & A. E. Kazdin (Eds.), **Advances in clinical child psychology** (Vol. 6). New York: Plenum.

Bitgood, S. C., Crowe, M. J., Suarez, Y., & Peters, R. D. (1980). Immobilization: Effects and side effects on stereotyped behavior in children. **Behavior Modification, 4,** 187–208.

Blackwell, B., & Currah, J. (1973) The psychopharmacology of nocturnal enuresis. In I. Kolvin, R. McKeith, & S. Meadow (Eds.), **Bladder control and enuresis** (Clinics in Developmental Medicine Nos. 48/49). London: Heinemann.

Braukmann, C. J., Kirigin, K. A., & Wolf, M. M. (1976, September). **Achievement Place: The researcher's perspective.** Paper presented at the meeting of the American Psychological Association, Washington, DC.

Brown, P., & Elliott, J. R. (1965). Control of aggression in a nursery school class. **Journal of Experimental Child Psychology, 2,** 103–107.

Buckley, J. J. (1977). Commonalities and differences in theories and techniques of family therapy. In T. Buckley, J. McCarthy, E. Norman, & M. Quaranta (Eds.), **New directions in family therapy.** Oceanside, NY: Dabor Science.

Campbell, M. (1985). Schizophrenic disorders and pervasive developmental disorders/infantile autism. In J. M. Wiener (Ed.), **Diagnosis and psychopharmacology of childhood and adolescent disorders.** New York: Wiley.

Cantwell, D. (1977). Psychopharmacologic treatment of the minimal brain dysfunction syndrome. In J. M. Wiener (Ed.), **Psychopharmacology in childhood and adolescence.** New York: Basic Books.

Casey, R. J., & Berman, J. S. (1985). The outcome of psychotherapy with children. **Psychological Bulletin, 98,** 388–408.

Cautela, J. R., & Groden, J. (1978). **Relaxation: A comprehensive manual for adults, children, and children with special needs.** Champaign, IL: Research Press.

Cavior, H. E., & Schmidt, A. A. (1978). Test of the effectiveness of a differential treatment strategy at the Robert F. Kennedy Center. **Criminal Justice and Behavior, 5,** 131–139.

Chess, S., & Hassibi, M. (1978). **Principles and practice of child psychiatry.** New York: Plenum.

Clement, P. W., & Milne, D. C. (1967). Group play therapy and tangible reinforcers used to modify the behaviour of 8-year-old boys. **Behaviour Research and Therapy, 5,** 301–312.

Coffey, B., Shader, R., & Greenblatt, D. (1983). Pharmacokinetics of benzodiazepines and psychostimulants in children. **Journal of Clinical Psychopharmacology, 3,** 217–225.

Conners, C. K., & Taylor, E. (1980). Pemoline, methylphenidate and placebos in children with MBD. **Archives of General Psychiatry, 37,** 922–930.

Conners, C. K., & Werry, J. S. (1979). Pharmacotherapy. In H. C. Quay & J. S. Werry (Eds.), **Psychopathological disorders of childhood** (2nd ed.). New York: Wiley.

Craft, M., Stephenson, G., & Granger, C. (1964). A controlled trial of authoritarian and self-governing regimens with adolescent psychopaths. **American Journal of Orthopsychiatry, 34,** 543–554.

Craighead, W. E., Meyers, A. W., Wilcoxon-Craighead, L., & McHale, S. M. (1983). Issues in cognitive-behavior therapy with children. In M. Rosenbaum,

C. M. Franks, & Y. Jaffe (Eds.), **Perspective on behavior therapy in the eighties** (Vol. 9). New York: Springer-Verlag.

DeWitt, K. N. (1978). The effectiveness of family therapy: A review of outcome research **Archives of General Psychiatry, 35,** 549–561.

Epstein, L. H., Doke, L. A., Sajwaj, T. E., Sorrell, S., & Rimmer, B. (1974). Generality and side effects of overcorrection. **Journal of Applied Behavior Analysis, 10,** 489–499.

Finch, S. M., & Cain, A. C. (1968). Psychoanalysis of children: Problems of etiology and treatment. In J. Marmon (Ed.), **Modern psychoanalysis.** New York: Basic Books.

Foxx, R. M. (1977). Attention training: The use of overcorrection avoidance training to increase the eye contact of autistic and retarded children. **Journal of Applied Behavior Analysis, 10,** 489–499.

Foxx, R. M., & Azrin, N. H. (1973). The elimination of autistic self-stimulatory behavior by overcorrection. **Journal of Applied Behavior Analysis, 6,** 1–14.

Foxx, R. M., & Shapiro, S. T. (1978). The timeout ribbon: A nonexclusionary timeout procedure. **Journal of Applied Behavior Analysis, 6,** 1–14.

Freedheim, D. K., & Russ, S. R. (1983). Psychotherapy with children. In C. E. Walker & M. C. Roberts (Eds.), **Handbook of clinical child psychology.** New York: Wiley.

Freud, A. (1945). **The psychoanalytic study of the child: Vol. 1. Indications for child analysis.** New York: International Universities Press.

Freud, A. (1965). **Normality and pathology in childhood: Assessments of development.** New York: International Universities Press.

Gelfand, D. M. (1978). Social withdrawal and negative emotional states: Behavioral treatment. In B. B. Wolman, J. Egan, & A. O. Ross (Eds.), **Handbook of mental disorders in childhood and adolescence.** Englewood Cliffs, NJ: Prentice-Hall.

Gelfand, D. M., & Hartmann, D. P. (1984). **Child behavior analysis and therapy** (2nd ed.). New York: Pergamon Press.

Gelfand, D. M., & Peterson, L. (1985). **Child development and psychopathology.** Beverly Hills, CA: Sage.

Gittelman-Klein, R., Spitzer, R., & Cantwell, D. (1978). Diagnostic classifications and psychopharmacological indications. In J. S. Werry (Ed.), **Pediatric psychopharmacology.** New York: Brunner/Mazel.

Gottman, J. M., Gonso, J., & Rasmussen, B. (1975). Social interaction, social competence, and friendship in children. **Child Development, 46,** 709–718.

Greenburg, L. M., & Stephans, J. H. (1977). Use of drugs in special syndromes: Enuresis, tics, school refusal, and anorexia nervosa. In J. M. Wiener (Ed.), **Psychopharmacology in childhood and adolescence.** New York; Basic Books.

Guerney, B., Jr. (1964). Filial therapy: Description and rationale. **Journal of Consulting Psychology, 28,** 304–310.

Gurman, A. A., & Kniskern, D. P. (1978). Research on marital and family therapy: Progress, perspective, and prospect. In S. Garfield & A. E. Bergin (Eds.), **Handbook of psychotherapy and behavior change: An empirical analysis** (2nd ed.). New York, Wiley.

Haley, J. (1963). Marriage therapy. **Archives of General Psychiatry, 8,** 213–224.

Hall, R. V., & Hall, M. C. (1980). **How to use time out.** Lawrence, KS: H & H Enterprises.

Harris, S. L., & Romancyzk, R. G. (1976). Treating self-injurious behavior of a retarded child by overcorrection. **Behavior Therapy, 7,** 235–239.

Harter, S. (1977). A cognitive-developmental approach to children's expression of conflicting feelings and a technique to facilitate such expression in play therapy. **Journal of Consulting and Clinical Psychology, 45,** 417–432.

Hartmann, D. P., Roper, B. L., & Gelfand, D. M. (1977). An evaluation of alternative modes of child psychotherapy. In B. B. Lahey & A. Kazdin (Eds.), **Advances in clinical child psychology** (Vol. 1). New York: Plenum.

Hatzenbuehler, L. C., & Schroeder, H. E. (1978). Desensitization procedures in the treatment of childhood disorders. **Psychological Bulletin, 85,** 831–844.

Heinicke, C. M. (1969). Frequency of psychotherapeutic sessions as a factor affecting outcome: Analysis of clinical ratings and test results. **Journal of Abnormal Psychology, 74,** 533–560.

Helms, D. B., & Turner, J. S. (1986). **Exploring child behavior** (3rd ed.). Monterey, CA: Brooks/Cole.

Hersov, L., & Bentovim, A. (1977). Inpatient units and day-hospitals. In M. Rutter & L. Hersov (Eds.), **Child psychiatry: Modern approaches.** Oxford: Blackwell Scientific Publications.

Hetherington, E. M., & Parke, R. D. (1986). **Child psychology: A contemporary approach** (3rd ed.). New York: McGraw-Hill.

Hobbs, N. (1966). Helping disturbed children: Psychological and ecological strategies. **American Psychologist, 21,** 1105–1115.

Irwin, M. (1982). Literature review. In J. L. Schulman & M. Irwin (Eds.), **Psychiatric hospitalization of children.** Springfield, IL: Charles C Thomas.

Jackson, D. D. (1965). Family rules: The marital quid pro quo. **Archives of General Psychiatry, 12,** 589–595.

Jackson, D. D., & Weakland, J. H. (1961). Conjoint family therapy: Some considerations on theory, technique and results. **Psychiatry, 24,** 30–45.

Jaffe, P. G., & Carlson, P. M. (1972). Modeling therapy for test anxiety: The role of model affect and consequences. **Behaviour Research and Therapy, 10,** 329–339.

Jessor, R., & Jessor, S. L. (1977). **Problem behavior and psychosocial development: A longitudinal study of youth.** New York: Academic Press.

Johnson, J. H., Rasbury, W. C., & Siegel, L. J. (1986). **Approaches to child treatment.** New York: Pergamon Press.

Karniol, R. (1978). Children's use of intention cues in evaluating behavior. **Psychological Bulletin, 85,** 76–85.

Kazdin, A. E. (1973). Covert modeling and the reduction of avoidance behavior. **Journal of Abnormal Psychology, 81,** 87–95.

Kazdin, A. E. (1977). *The token economy.* New York: Plenum.

Kelly, J. A., & Drabman, R. S. (1977). Generalizing response suppression of self-injurious behavior through an overcorrection punishment procedure: A case study. **Behavior Therapy, 8,** 468–472.

Kirkland, K. D., & Thelen, M. H. (1977). Uses of modeling in child treatment. In B. B. Lahey & A. Kazdin (Eds.), **Advances in clinical child psychology** (Vol. 1). New York: Plenum.

Klein, M. (1949). **The psychoanalysis of children.** London: Hogarth Press. (Original work published 1932)

Klein, N. C., Alexander, J. F., & Parsons, B. V. (1977). Impact of family systems intervention on recidivism and sibling delinquency: A model of primary prevention and program evaluation. **Journal of Consulting and Clinical Psychology, 45,** 469–474.

Koocher, G. P., & Pedulla, B. M. (1977). Current practices in child psychotherapy. **Professional Psychology, 8,** 275–287.

Krasner, L. (1971). Behavior therapy. **Annual Review of Psychology, 22,** 483–532.

LeBlanc, J. M., Busby,, K. H., & Thomson, C. L. (1974). The functions of timeout for changing the aggressive behaviors of a preschool child: A multiple baseline analysis. In R. Ulrich, T. Stachnik, & J. Mabry (Eds.), **Control of human behavior** (Vol. 3). Glenview, IL: Scott, Foresman.

Lesser, S. R. (1972). Psychoanalysis with children. In B. Wolman (Ed.), **Manual of child psychopathology.** New York: McGraw-Hill.

Levitt, E. E. (1971). Research on psychotherapy with children. In A. E. Bergin & S. Garfield (Eds.), **Handbook of psychotherapy and behavior change.** New York: Wiley.

Lewis, S. (1974). A comparison of behavior therapy techniques in the reduction of fearful avoidance behavior. **Behavior Therapy, 5,** 648–655.

Livesley, W. J., & Bromley, D. B. (1973). **Person perception in childhood and adolescence.** Chichester, England: Wiley.

Loney, J. (1986). Predicting stimulant drug response among hyperactive children. **Psychiatric Annals, 16,** 16–19.

Lovaas, O. I., & Simmons, J. G. (1969). Manipulation of self-destruction in three retarded children. **Journal of Applied Behavior Analysis, 2,** 143–157.

Love, L. R., Kaswan, J. & Bugental, D. E. (1972). Differential effectiveness of three clinical interventions for different socioeconomic groupings. **Journal of Consulting and Clinical Psychology, 39,** 347–360.

Mahoney, M. J., Kazdin, A. E., & Lesswing, N. J. (1974). Behavior modification: Delusion or deliverance? In C. Franks & G. T. Wilson (Eds.), **Annual review of behavior therapy: Theory and practice.** New York: Brunner/Mazel.

Mann, J., & Rosenthal, T. L. (1969). Vicarious and direct counterconditioning of test anxiety through individual and group desensitization. **Behaviour Research and Therapy, 7,** 359–367.

Mates, J. A.,, & Gittelman, R. (1983). Growth of hyperactive children on maintenance regimen of children. **Schizophrenia Bulletin, 8,** 320–332.

McDaniel, K. D. (1986a). Pharmacologic treatment of psychiatric and neurodevelopmental disorders in children and adolescents (Part 1). **Clinical Pediatrics, 25,** 65–71.

McDaniel, K. D. (1986b). Pharmacologic treatment of psychiatric and neurodevelopmental disorders in children and adolescents (Part 3). **Clinical Pediatrics, 25,** 198–204.

Melamed, B. G., & Siegel, L. J. (1975). Reduction of anxiety in children facing hospitalization and surgery by use of filmed modeling. **Journal of Consulting and Clinical Psychology, 43,** 511–521.

Miller, L. C., Barrett, C. L., Hampe, E., & Noble, H. (1972). Comparison of reciprocal inhibition, psychotherapy, and waiting list control for phobic children. **Journal of Abnormal Psychology, 79,** 269–279.

Minuchin, S. (1974). **Families and family therapy.** Cambridge, MA: Harvard University Press.

Moreno, J. L. (1975). **Psychodrama** (vol. 7). New York: Beacon.

Murdock, J. Y., & Hartmann, B. (1975). **A language development program: Imitative gestures to basic syntactic structures.** Salt Lake City, UT: Word Making Productions.

O'Connor, R. D. (1972). Relative efficacy of modeling, shaping, and the combined procedures for modification of social withdrawal. **Journal of Abnormal Psychology, 79,** 327–334.

O'Leary, K. D., & O'Leary, S. G. (1972). **Classroom management: The successful use of behavior modification.** New York: Pergamon Press.

Ollendick, T. H. (1979). Fear reduction techniques with children. In M. Hersen, R. M. Eisler, & P. M. Miller (Eds.), **Progress in behavior modification** (Vol. 8). New York: Academic Press.

Patterson, G. R. (1975). The aggressive child: Victim or architect of a coercive system. In L. A. Hamerlynck, L. C. Handy, & E. J. Mash (Eds.), **Behavior modification and families: Vol. 1. Theory and research.** New York: Brunner/Mazel.

Patterson, G. R., Cobb, J. A., & Ray, R. S. (1973). A social engineering technology for retraining the families of aggressive boys. In H. E. Adams & I. Unikel (Eds.), **Issues and trends in behavior therapy.** Springfield, IL: Charles C Thomas.

Patterson, G. R., & Fleischman, M. J. (1979). Maintenance of treatment effects: Some considerations concerning family systems and follow-up data. **Behavior Therapy, 10,** 168–185.

Patterson, G. R., Reid, J. B., Jones, R. R., & Conger, R. E. (1975). **A social learning approach to family intervention: Vol. 1. Families with aggressive children.** Eugene, OR: Castalia.

Phillips, E. L., Phillips, E. A., Fixsen, D. L., & Wolf, M. M. (1971). Achievement Place: Modification of the behaviors of the pre-delinquent boys within a token economy. **Journal of Applied Behavior Analysis, 4,** 45–59.

Piaget, J. (1965). **The moral judgement of the child** (M. Gabain, Trans.). New York: Free Press. (Original work published 1932)

Puig-Antich, J. (1982). Major depression and conduct disorder in prepuberty. **Journal of the American Academy of Child Psychiatry, 21,** 118–128.

Puig-Antich, J., Perel, J., Lupatkin, W., Chambers, W. U., Tabrizi, M. A., & Stiller, R. (1979). Plasma levels of imipramine and dimethyl imipramine and clinical response in prepubertal major depressive disorder: A preliminary report. **Journal of the American Academy of Child Psychiatry, 18,** 616–627.

Quay, H. C. (1979). Residential treatment. In H. C. Quay & S. Werry (Eds.,) **Psychopathological disorders of childhood** (2nd ed.). New York: Wiley.

Rancurello, M. (1986). Antidepressants in children: Indications, benefits, and limitations. **American Journal of Psychotherapy, 40,** 377–392.

Rapport, M. D., DuPaul, G. J., Stoner, G., & Jones, J. T. (1986). Comparing classroom and clinic measures of attention deficit disorder: Differential, idiosyncratic, and dose-response effects of methyl-phenidate. **Journal of Consulting and Clinical Psychology, 54,** 334–341.

Repp, A. C., & Dietz, S. M. (1974). Reducing aggressive and self-injurious behavior of institutionalized retarded children through reinforcement of other behaviors. **Journal of Applied Behavior Analysis, 7,** 313–325.

Richards, C. S., & Siegel, L. H. (1979). Behavioral treatment of anxiety states and avoidance behaviors in children. In D. Marholin II (Ed.), **Child behavior therapy** (2nd ed.). New York: Halstead Press.

Rifkin, A., Wortman, R., Reardon, G., & Siris, S. G. (1986). Psychotropic medication in adolescents: A review. **Journal of Clinical Psychiatry, 47,** 400–408.

Ritter, B. (1968). The group desensitization of children's snake phobias using vicarious and contact desensitization procedures. **Behaviour Research and Therapy, 6,** 1–6.

Rogers, C. R. (1951). **Client-centered therapy: Its current practice, implications, and theory.** Boston: Houghton Mifflin.

Romancyzk, R. G., & Goren, E. (1975). Severe self-injurious behavior: The problem of clinical control. **Journal of Consulting and Clinical Psychology, 43,** 730–739.

Romanczyk, R. G., Kistner, J. A., & Crimmins, D. B. (1980). Institutional treatment of severely disturbed children: Fact, possibility, or nonsequitur. In B. B. Lahey & A. E. Kazdin (Eds.), **Advances in clinical child psychology** (Vol. 3). New York: Plenum.

Rosenbaum, M. (1972). Group therapy with adolescents. In B. Wolman (Ed.), **Manual of child psychopathology.** New York: McGraw-Hill.

Rosenthal, T. L., & Bandura, A. (1978). Psychological modeling: Theory and practice. In S. Garfield & A. E. Bergin (Eds.), **Handbook of psychotherapy and behavior change: An empirical analysis** (2nd ed.). New York: Wiley.

Ross, D. M., & Ross, S. A. (1982). **Hyperactivity: Research, theory, and action.** New York: Wiley.

Satir, V. (1967). **Conjoint family therapy: A guide.** Palo Alto, CA: Science and Behavior Books.

Scarboro, M. E., & Forehand, R. (1975). Effects of two types of response contingent time-out on compliance and oppositional behavior of children. **Journal of Experimental Child Psychology, 19,** 252–264.

Scharfman, M. A. (1978). Psychoanalytic treatment. In B. Wolman, J. Egan, & A. Ross (Eds.), **Handbook of treatment of mental disorders in childhood and adolescence.** Englewood Cliffs, NJ: Prentice-Hall.

Schomer, J. (1978). Family therapy. In B. Wolman, J.

Egan, & A. Ross (Eds.), **Handbook of treatment of mental disorders in childhood and adolescence.** Englewood Cliffs, NJ: Prentice-Hall.

Selman, R. L. (1980). **The growth of interpersonal understanding: Developmental and clinical analyses.** New York: Academic Press.

Selman, R. L., & Jacquette, D. (1977). Stability and oscillation in interpersonal awareness: A clinical-developmental analysis. In C. B. Keasy (Ed.), **Nebraska Symposium on Motivation** (Vol. 25). Lincoln: University of Nebraska Press.

Shantz, C. U. (1975). The development of social cognition. In E. M. Hetherington (Ed.), **Review of child development research** (Vol. 5). Chicago: University of Chicago Press.

Shapiro, R., & Budman, S. (1973). Defection, termination, and continuation in family and individual therapy. **Family Process, 12,** 55–67.

Skinner, B. F., & Ferster, C. B. (1957). **Schedules of reinforcement.** New York: Appleton-Century-Crofts.

Slavson, S. R., & Schiffer, M. (1975). **Group psychotherapies for children: A textbook.** New York: International Universities Press.

Sloane, H., & MacAulay, B. (Eds.). (1968). **Operant procedures in remedial speech and language training.** Boston: Houghton Mifflin.

Sroufe, A. L. (1975). Drug treatment of children with behavior problems. In F. Horowitz (Ed.), **Review of child development research** (Vol. 4). Chicago: University of Chicago Press.

Stover, L., Guerney, B. G., Jr., & O'Connell, M. (1971). Measurements of acceptance allowing self-direction, involvement and empathy in adult-child interaction. **Journal of Psychology, 77,** 261–269.

Taylor, C. B., Ferguson, J. M., & Wermuth, B. M. (1977). Simple techniques to treat medical phobias. **Postgraduate Medical Journal, 53,** 28–32.

Todd, T. C., & Stanton, M. D. (1983). Research on marital and family therapy: Answers, issues and recommendations for the future. In B. B. Wolman & G. Stricker (Eds.), **Handbook of family and marital therapy.** New York: Plenum.

Ullmann, L. P., & Krasner, L. (Eds.) (1965). **Case studies in behavior modification.** New York: Holt, Rinehart & Winston.

Weinstein, L. (1969). The Project Re-Ed Schools for emotionally disturbed children: Effectiveness as viewed by referring agencies, parents and teachers. **Exceptional Children, 35,** 703–711.

Weinstein, L. (1974, December). **Evaluation of a program for re-educating disturbed children: A follow-up comparison with untreated children** (Final Report to the Bureau for the Education of the Handicapped, Project Nos. 6-2974 and 55023). Washington, DC: Office of Education, U.S. Department of Health, Education and Welfare.

Weiss, G. (1975). The natural history of hyperactivity in childhood and treatment with stimulant medication at different ages: A summary of research findings. **International Journal of Mental Health, 4,** 213–226.

Whalen, C. K., & Henker, B. (1976). Psychostimulants and children: A review and analysis. **Psychological Bulletin, 83,** 1113–1130.

Wiener, J. M. (1977). Summary. In J. M. Wiener (Ed.), **Psychopharmacology in childhood and adolescence.** New York: Basic Books.

Wiener, J. M. (1984). Psychopharmacology in childhood disorders. In C. R. Lake (Ed.), **Psychiatric clinics of North America** (Vol. 7). Philadelphia: W. B. Saunders.

Wiener, J. M., & Jaffe, S. (1977). History of drug therapy in childhood and adolescent psychiatric disorders. In J. M. Wiener (Ed.), **Psychopharmacology in childhood and adolescence.** New York: Basic Books.

Williams, C. D. (1959). The elimination of tantrum behavior by extinction procedures. **Journal of Abnormal and Social Psychology, 59,** 269.

Wiltz, N. A., & Patterson, G. R. (1974). An evaluation of parent training procedures designed to alter inappropriate aggressive behavior of boys. **Behavior Therapy, 5,** 215–221.

Winsberg, B. G., & Yepes, L. E. (1978). Antipsychotics (major tranquilizers, neuroleptics). In J. S. Werry (Ed.), **Pediatric psychopharmacology.** New York: Brunner/Mazel.

Yaffe, S. J., & Danish, M. (1977). The classification and pharmacology of psychoactive drugs in childhood and adolescence. In J. M. Wiener (Ed.), **Psychopharmacology in childhood and adolescence.** New York: Basic Books.

CHAPTER 15

Anthony, E. J. (1972). Primary prevention with school children. In H. Barten & L. Bellak (Eds.), **Progress in community mental health** (Vol. 2). New York: Grune & Stratton.

Belsky, J. (1986). Infant day care: A cause for concern? **Zero to Three, 6**, 1-6.

Belsky, J., & Steinberg, L. D. (1978). The effects of day care: A critical review. **Child Development, 49**, 920-949.

Belsky, J. Steinberg, L. D. & Walker, A. (1982). The ecology of day care. In M. E. Lamb (Ed.), **Child rearing in nontraditional familes**. Hillsdale, NJ: Erlbaum.

Belsky, J., & Tolan, W. J. (1981). Infants as producers of their own development: An ecological analysis. In R. M. Lerner & N.A. Busch-Rossnagel (Eds.), **Individuals as producers of their own development: A life-span perspective**. New York: Academic Press.

Bierman, K. L. (1983). Cognitive development and clinical interviews with children. In B. B. Lahey & A. E. Kazdin (Eds.), **Advances in clinical child psychology** (Vol. 6) New York: Plenum.

Bierman, K. L. & Schwartz, L. A. (1986). Clinical child interviews: Approaches and developmental considerations. **Journal of Child and Adolescent Psychotherapy. 3**, 267-278.

Billings, A. G., & Moos, R. H. (1983, August). **Comparisons of children of depressed and nondepressed parents: A social-environmental perspective**. Paper presented at the meeting of the American Psychological Association, Anaheim, CA.

Bronfenbrenner, U., Moen, P., & Garbarino, J. (1984). Child, family and community. In R. D. Parke (Ed.), **Review of child development research** (Vol. 7). Chicago: University of Chicago Press.

Cadoret, R. & Cain, C. (1980). Sex differences in predictors of antisocial behavior in adoptees. **Archives of General Psychiatry, 37**, 1171-1175.

Casey, R. J., & Berman, J. S. (1985). The outcome of psychotherapy with children. *Psychological Bulletin*, 98, 388-400.

Children's Defense Fund. (1974). **Children out of school in America**. Cambridge, MA: Author.

Cohen, H. (1980). **Equal rights for children**. Totowa, NJ: Littlefield, Adams.

Cohen, H. (1985). Ending the double standard: Equal rights for children. In A. Cafagna, R. T. Peterson, & C. Staudenbaur (Eds.), **Child nurturance: Philosophy, children, and the family** (Vol. 1). New York: Plenum.

Cowen, E. L. (1977). Baby-steps toward primary prevention. **American Journal of Community Psychology, 5**, 1-22.

Cowen, E. L., Gesten, E. L., & Wilson, A. B. (1979). The Primary Mental Health Project (PMHP): Evaluation of current program effectiveness. **American Journal of Community Psychology, 7**, 293-303.

Cowen, E. L., Trost, M. A., Lorion, R. P., Dorr, R. P., Izzo, L. D., & Isaacson, R. (1975). **New ways in school mental health: Early detection and prevention of school maladaptation**. New York: Behavioral Publications.

Craighead, W. E., Meyers, A., Wilcoxon-Craighead, L., & McHale, S. M. (1983). Issues in cognitive-behavior therapy with children. In M. Rosenbaum, C. M. Franks, & Y. Jaffe (Eds.), **Perspectives on behavior therapy in the eighties**. New York: Springer-Verlag.

Cummings, E. M. (1980). Caregiver stability and day care. **Developmental Psychology, 16**, 31-37.

Cytryn, L., McKnew, D. H., Bartko, J. J., Lamour, M., & Hamovit, J. (1982). Offspring of patients with affective disorders: II. **Journal of the American Academy of Child Psychiatry, 21**, 389-391.

Douglas, V., Parry, P., Marton, P., & Garson, C. (1976). Assessment of a cognitive training program for hyperactive children. **Journal of Abnormal Child Psychology, 4**, 389-410.

Drabman, R., Spitalnik, R., & O'Leary, K. D. (1973). Teaching self-control to disruptive children. **Journal of Abnormal Psychology, 82**, 10-16.

Eccles, J. S., & Hoffman, L. W. (1984). Sex roles, socialization, and occupational behavior. In H. W. Stevenson & A. E. Siegel (Eds.), **Child development research and social policy** (Vol. 1). Chicago: University of Chicago Press.

Education for All Handicapped Children Act of 1975 (P. L. 94-142), 42 Fed. Reg. 42474-42514 (1977).

Emery, R. E., Hetherington, E. M., & DiLalla, L. F. (1984). Divorce, children, and social policy. In H. W. Stevenson & A. E. Siegel (Eds.), **Child development research and social policy** (Vol. 1). Chicago: University of Chicago Press.

Feinberg, J. (1973). **Social philosophy**. Englewood Cliffs, NJ: Prentice-Hall.

Final report of the National Day Care Study. (1979). **Executive summary: Children at the center**. Cambridge, MA: Abt Associates.

Finlay v. Finlay, 148 N. E. 624 (N.Y) 1925).

Foster, H. H., Jr. (1974). **A "Bill of Rights" for children**. Springfield, IL: Charles C Thomas.

Foster, H. H., Jr., & Freed, D. J. (1972). A Bill of Rights for children. **Family Law Quarterly, 6**, 343-375.

Friedling, C., & O'Leary, S. G. (1979). Effects of self-instructional training on second- and third-grade hyperactive children: A failure to replicate. **Journal of Applied Behavior Analysis, 12**, 211-219.

Furman, W. (1980). Promoting social development: Developmental implications for treatment. In B. B. Lahey & A. E. Kazdin (Eds.), **Advances in clini-**

cal child psychology (Vol. 3). New York: Plenum.

Garbarino, J., & Sherman, D. (1980). High-risk neighborhoods and high-risk families: The human ecology of child maltreatment. **Child Development, 51**, 188-198.

Garmezy, N. (1974). Children at risk: The search for the antecedents of schizophrenia. Part II: Ongoing research programs, issues, and intervention. **Schizophrenia Bulletin, 9**, 55-125.

Gelfand, D. M., Ficula, T., & Zarbatany, L. (1986). Prevention of childhood behavior disorders. In B. Edelstein & L. Michelson (Eds.), **Handbook of prevention**. New York: Plenum.

Gelfand, D. M., & Hartmann, D. P. (1977). The prevention of childhood behavior disorders. In B. B. Lahey & A. E. Kazdin (Eds.), **Advances in clinical child psychology** (Vol. 1). New York: Plenum.

Gelfand, D. M., & Hartmann, D. P. (1984). **Child behavior analysis and therapy** (2nd ed.). New York: Pergamon Press.

Gelfand, D. M. & Peterson, L. (1985). **Child development and psychopathology**. Beverly Hills, CA: Sage.

George, C., & Main, M. (1979). Social interactions of young abused children: Approach, avoidance, and aggression. **Child Development, 50**, 306-318.

Glueck, S., & Glueck, E. (1968). **Delinquents and nondelinquents in perspective.** Cambridge, MA: Harvard University Press.

Gold, D., & Andres, D. (1978a). Developmental comparisons between adolescent children with employed and non-employed mothers. **Merrill-Palmer Quarterly, 24**, 243-254.

Gold, D., & Andres, D. (1978b). Developmental comparisons between 10-year-old children with employed and non-employed mothers. **Child Development, 49**, 75-84.

Goldstein, J., Freud, A., & Solnit, A. J. (1979). **Before the best interests of the child**. New York: Free Press.

Goodman, S. H. (1984). Children of disturbed parents: The interface between research and intervention. **American Journal of Community Psychology, 12**, 663-687.

Gresham, F. M. (1985). Utility of cognitive-behavioral procedures for social skills training with children: A critical review. **Journal of Abnormal Child Psychology, 13**, 411-424.

Grinspoon, L., & Singer, S. B. (1973). Amphetamines in the treatment of hyperkinetic children. **Harvard Educational Review, 43**, 515-555.

Gurman, A. S., & Kniskern, D. P. (Eds.). (1980). **Handbook of family therapy**. New York: Brunner/Mazel.

Higa, W. R., Tharp, R. G., & Calkins, R. P. (1978). Developmental verbal control of behavior: Implications for self-instructional training. **Journal of Experimental Child Psychology, 26**, 489-497.

Hofferth, S. L. (1979). Day care in the next decade: 1980-1990. **Journal of Marriage and the Family, 41**, 649-658.

Hoffman, L. W. (1979). Maternal employment: 1979. **American Psychologist, 34**, 859-865.

Houts, A. C., Shutty, M. S. & Emery, R. E. (1985). The impact of children on adults. In B. B. Lahey & A. E. Kazdin (Eds.), **Advances in clinical child psychology** (Vol. 8). New York: Plenum.

In re Gault; 387 U.S. 1, 61 (1967).

Jones, M. C. (1968). Personality correlates and antecedents of drinking patterns in males. **Journal of Consulting and Clinical Psychology, 32**, 2-12.

Karoly, P., & Kanfer, F. H. (1982). **Self-management and behavior change: From theory to practice**. New York: Pergamon Press.

Kazdin, A. E. (1982). Current developments and research issues in cognitive-behavioral interventions: A commentary. **School Psychology Review, 11**, 75-82.

Kendall, P. C., & Finch, A. J. (1979). Developing non-impulsive behavior in children's cognitive-behavioral strategies on self-control. In P. C. Kendall & S. Hollon (Eds.). **Cognitive-behavioral interventions: Theory, research, and procedures**. New York: Academic Press.

Kendall, P. C. & Hollon, D. S. (1979). **Cognitive-behavioral interventions: Theory, research, and procedures**. New York: Academic Press.

Keniston, K. (1977). **All our children: The American family under pressure**. New York: Harcourt Brace Jovanovich.

Kirkegaard-Sørenson, L., & Mednick, S. A. (1975). Registered criminality in families with children at high risk for schizophrenia. **Journal of Abnormal Psychology, 84**, 197-204.

Knitzer, J. E. (1976). Child advocacy: A perspective. **American Journal of Orthopsychiatry, 46**, 200-216.

Koocher, G. P. (1976). A Bill of Rights for children in psychotherapy. In G. P. Koocher (Ed.), **Children's rights and the mental health profession**. New York: Wiley.

Koocher, G. P. (1983). Competence to consent: Psychotherapy. In G. B. Melton, G. P. Koocher, & M. J. Saks (Eds.), **Children's competence to consent**. New York: Plenum.

Lamb, M. E., Chase-Lansdale, L., & Owen, M. T. (1979). The changing American family and its implications for infant social development: The sample case of maternal employment. In M. Lewis &

L. Rosenblum (Eds.), **The child and its family**. New York: Plenum.

Ledingham, J. E. Schwartzman, A. E., & Serbin, L. A. (1984). Current adjustment and family functioning of children behaviorally at risk for adult schizophrenia. In A. Doyle, D. Gold, & D. Moskowitz (Eds.), **Children in families under stress**. San Francisco: Jossey-Bass.

Lewis, C. E. Lewis, M. A. & Lefkwunigue, M. (1978). Informed consent by children and participation in an influenza vaccine trial. **American Journal of Public Health, 68**, 1079–1082.

Maccoby, E. E. & Martin, J. A. (1983). Socialization in the context of the family: Parent-child interaction. In P. M. Mussen (General Ed.), **Handbook of child psychology** (4th ed.): **Vol. 4. Socialization, personality, and social development** (E. M. Hetherington, Vol. Ed.).

Martin, R. (1979). **Educating handicapped children: The legal mandate**. Champaign, IL: Research Press.

Masten, A. S. & Garmezy, N. (1985). Risk, vulnerability, and protective factors in developmental psychology. In B. B. Lahey & A. E. Kazdin (Eds.), **Advances in clinical child psychology** (Vol. 8). New York: Plenum.

Mednick, S. A. (1974). Electrodermal recovery and psychopathology. In S. A. Mednick, F. Schulsinger, J. Higgins, & B. Bell (Eds.), **Genetics, environment and psychopathology**. Amsterdam: Elsevier/North-Holland.

Mednick, S. A., Venables, P. H., Schulsinger, F., & Cudeck, R. (1982). The Mauritius Project: An experiment in primary prevention. In M. J. Goldstein (Ed.), **Preventive intervention in schizophrenia: Are we ready?** (DHHS Publication No. ADM 82-1111). Washington, D.C.: U.S. Government Printing Office.

Meichenbaum, D. (1977). **Cognitive-behavior modification: An integrative approach**. New York: Plenum.

Meichenbaum, D. (1979). Teaching children self-control. In B. B. Lahey & A. E. Kazdin (Eds.), **Advances in clinical child psychology** (Vol. 2). New York: Plenum.

Meichenbaum, D., & Goodman, J. (1971). Training impulsive children to talk to themselves: A means of developing self-control. **Journal of Abnormal Psychology, 77**, 115–126.

Mills v. Board of Education, 348 F. Supp. 866 (D.D.C. 1972).

Morales v. Turman, 383 F. Supp. 52 (E.D. Tex. 1974).

Neale, J. M., Winters, K. C. & Weintraub, S. (1984). Information processing deficits in children at high risk for schizophrenia. In N. Watt, E. J. Anthony, L. C. Wynne, & J. E. Rolf (Eds.), **Children at risk**

for schizophrenia: **A longitudinal perspective**. New York: Cambridge University Press.

O'Leary, S. G., & Dubey, D. R. (1979). Applications of self-control procedures by children: A review. **Journal of Applied Behavior Analysis, 12**, 449–465.

Orvaschel, H. (1983). Maternal depression and child dysfunction: Children at risk. In B. B. Lahey & A. E. Kazdin (Eds.), **Advances in clinical child psychology** (Vol. 6). New York: Plenum.

Parham v. J.R., 442 U.S. 584, 603 (1979).

Pennnsylvania Association for Retarded Children v. Commonwealth of Pennsylvania, 334 F. Supp. 1257 (E. D. Pa. 1971).

Plotkin, R. (1979). In the balance: **Parham v. J. R. APA Monitor, 10**, (9–10), 27.

Quinn, K. M. (1985). Legal issues and the schools. In D. Schetky & E. Benedek (Eds.), **Emerging issues in child psychiatry and the law**. New York: Brunner/Mazel.

Rickel, A. U., & Smith, R. L. (1979). Maladapting preschool children: Identification, diagnosis, and remediation. **American Journal of Community Psychology, 7**, 197–208.

Rodham, H. (1979). Children's rights: A legal perspective. In P. Vardin & I. Brody (Eds.), **Children's rights: Contemporary perspectives**. New York: Teachers College Press.

Rolf, J. E., Fischer, M., & Hasazi, J. (1982). Assessing preventive interventions for multirisk preschoolers. In M. J. Goldstein (Ed.), **Preventive intervention in schizophrenia: Are we ready?** (DHHS Publication No. ADM 82-1111). Washington, DC: U.S. Government Printing Office.

Ross, A. O. (1980). **Psychological disorders of children** (2nd ed.). New York: McGraw-Hill.

Routh, D. K. (1985). Training clinical child psychologists. In B. B. Lahey & A. E. Kazdin (Eds.), **Advances in clinical child psychology** (Vol. 8). New York: Plenum.

Schleser, R., Meyers, A. W., & Cohen, R. (1981). Generalization of self-instructions: Effects of general versus specific content, active rehearsal, and cognitive level. **Child development, 52**, 335–340.

Schwarz, J. C., Strickland, R. G., & Krolick, G. (1974). Infant day care: Behavioral effects at preschool age. **Developmental Psychology, 10**, 502–506.

Seifer, R. Sameroff, A. J., & Jones, F. (1981). Adaptive behavior in young children of emotionally disturbed women. **Developmental Psychology, 1**, 251–276.

Shapiro, M. H. (1974). Legislating the control of behavior control: Autonomy and the coercive use of organic therapies. **Southern California Law Review**, 47, 327–356.

Shure, M. B., & Spivack, G. (1982). Interpersonal problem-solving in young children: A cognitive approach to prevention. **American Journal of Community Psychology 10**, 341–356.

Siegel, D. M., & Hurley, S. (1977). The role of the child's preference in custody proceedings. **Family Law Quarterly, 11**, 1–58.

Stein, D. M., & Polyson, J. (1984). The Primary Mental Health Project reconsidered. **Journal of Consulting and Clinical Psychology, 52**, 940–945.

Teitelbaum, L. E., & Ellis, J. W. (1978). The liberty interest of children: Due process rights and their application. **Family Law Quarterly, 12**, 153–202.

United Nations General Assembly. (1973). United Nations Declaration of the Rights of Children. In A. Wilkerson (Ed.), **The rights of children: Emergent concepts in law and society**. Philadelphia: Temple University Press.

U.S. Bureau of the Census. (1982). **Statistical Abstracts of the U.S. 1982–83** (103rd ed.). Washington, DC: U.S. Government Printing Office.

U.S. Department of Health, Education and Welfare. (1978). **The appropriateness of the federal interagency day care requirements (FIDCR)**. Washington, DC: U.S. Government Printing Office.

Vardin, P., & Brody, I. (1979). Introduction. In P. Vardin & I. Brody (Eds.), **Children's rights: Contemporary perspectives**. New York: Teachers College Press.

Watt, N. F. (1979). The longitudinal research base for early intervention. **Journal of Community Psychology, 7**, 158–168.

Watt, N. F. (1986). Prevention of schizophrenic disorders. In B. Edelstein & L. Michelson (Eds.), **Handbook of prevention**. New York: Plenum.

Weintraub, S., Prinz, R. J., & Neale, J. M. (1978). Peer evaluations of the competence of children vulnerable to psychopathology. **Journal of Abnormal Child Psychology, 6**, 461–473.

Weithorn, L. A. (1979). Drug therapy—children's rights. In M. J. Cohen (Ed.), **Drugs and the special child**. New York: Gardner Press.

Weithorn, L. A. (1985). Children's capacities for participation in treatment decision-making. In D. Schetky & E. P. Benedek (Eds.), **Emerging issues in child psychiatry and the law**. New York: Brunner/Mazel.

Welner, Z., Welner, A., McCrary, M. D., & Leonard, M. (1977). Psychopathology in children of inpatients with depression: A controlled study. **Journal of Nervous and Mental Disease, 164**, 408–413.

Wolfe, D. A., Jaffe, P., Wilson, S. K., & Zak L. (1985). Children of battered women: The relation of child behavior to family violence and maternal stress. **Journal of Consulting and Clinical Psychology, 53**, 657–665.

Yankelovich, Skelly, White, Inc. (1981). **The General Mills American Family Report 1980–81**. Minneapolis: General Mills.

Zahn-Waxler, C., Cummings, E. M., McKnew, D. H., & Radke-Yarrow, M. (1984). Affective arousal and social interactions in young children of manic-depressive parents. **Child Development, 55**, 112–122.

Zigler, E. F., & Finn, M. (1984). Applied developmental psychology. In M. H. Bornstein & M. E. Lamb (Eds.), **Developmental psychology: An advanced textbook**. Hillsdale, NJ: Erlbaum.

Zigler, E. F. & Muenchow, S. (1980). Mainstreaming: The proof is in the implementation. **American Psychologist, 34**, 993–996.

NAME INDEX

SUBJECT INDEX

Photo Credits